# The Numismatic Chronicle

*Editorial Committee*

R. A. G. CARSON, *Editor*     C. E. BLUNT

HELEN W. BROWN     PHILIP GRIERSON     G. K. JENKINS

J. P. C. KENT     D. W. MACDOWALL     J. G. POLLARD


SEVENTH SERIES

*Volume XII*


LONDON

THE ROYAL NUMISMATIC SOCIETY

1972

PRINTED IN GREAT BRITAIN
AT THE UNIVERSITY PRESS, OXFORD
BY VIVIAN RIDLER
PRINTER TO THE UNIVERSITY

ILLUSTRATIONS PRINTED BY THE
COTSWOLD COLLOTYPE CO. LTD.

# CONTENTS

# The Damareteion Reconsidered[1]

### R. T. WILLIAMS

[SEE PLATE 1]

1. BOEHRINGER[2] in his monumental work on early Syracusan coinage classified and dated the issues as follows:

| | | | |
|---|---|---|---|
| B. Group | 1 | 530–510 B.C. | Archaic issues. Kraay, pl. iii, 2. |
| | 2 | 510–485 | First dolphins. Kraay, pl. iii, 5. |
| | 3 | 485–479 | Massive issues. Sections 6–11, 12a–e (12e = Damareteion issues). Kraay, pl. iii, 4–5 and 1. |
| | | 479–474 | No coinage. |
| | 4 | 474–450 | Sea-serpent issues. Kraay, pl. iv, 1. |
| | 5–6 | 450–435 | Olive symbol, etc. |
| | | 435–425 | No coinage. |
| Tudeer[3] | I | 425–412 | Signed engravers. |

2. However, it seemed to many numismatists that there were still problems, in particular the two coinless intervals which Boehringer created between 479 and 474 and between 435 and 425. The latter was due, to some extent, to the duality of research at this juncture where Tudeer had begun and Boehringer finished: the reason for the former interval was because, on the one hand, Boehringer believed that his section 12e of group 3, which contained the early decadrachms, was the last section of the massive issues, and that the decadrachm was the Damareteion, struck immediately after Himera in 480,[4] and, on the other hand, he associated the appearance of the sea-serpent in the exergue of group 4 issues with the naval battle between Hiero and the Etruscans off Cumae in 474. These were the corner-stones of his chronology and a very substantial one seemed at least the equation of the

---

[1] A form of this article was given as a paper at the Joint Conference of the Greek and Roman Societies at Cambridge, July 1971. The paper aimed at refuting in particular Kraay's downdating of the Damareteion in his *Greek Coins and History* (here abbreviated to Kraay). I am grateful to the B.M. for providing photographs of their coins in Pl. 1b–c, to the owner for the photograph of his coin, Pl. 1d, to Mrs. S. Hurter for Pl. 1e; to Dr. H. A. Cahn for allowing me to reproduce in Pl. 1f the coin no. 105 from the MMAG Niggeler Catalogue of 1965.

[2] E. Boehringer, *Die Münzen von Syrakus* (1929.) B = Boehringer.

[3] *Die Tetradrachmenprägung von Syrakus in der Periode signierenden Künstler* (1913).

[4] Diodorus xi, 26, 3.

early decadrachm with the Damareteion,[1] secured both by historical reference and style. However, as there are neither historical nor stylistic reasons for these intervals, certainly not for the 479–474 interval when many postulate a glut of coinage resulting from the coining of the Carthaginian indemnity, on any reconstruction of the issues these gaps must be closed.

3. The later gap between 435 and 425 may be closed summarily by extending the end of the sea-serpent group from 450 to 440 and running groups 5–6 from 440 to 425.[2] But it will be the earlier break of 479–474 that will be of more immediate relevance to the present topic. Several numismatists have suggested adjustments to the end of group 3 to bring that down to 474 without destroying the connection between the decadrachms and the Damareteion and Himera. Of these the most recent known to me and the most cogent is that of G. K. Jenkins in his monograph on the coinage of Gela.[3] He extends the end of group 3 right down to 474, but extracts the Damareteion section, 12e, and throws it back to the period immediately after Himera: for this section is not die-linked to the other sections and is quite alien to them in style, except for one Artemis head, R. 276, which is die-linked to the Damareteion section and comes late in that section, but whose nearest stylistic relations belong earlier: R. 201 of 12a [Pl. 1b] and R. 244 of 12d [Pl. 1c] clearly come from the same hand as R. 276 [Pl. 1a]. There is no reason, therefore why the Damareteion section should be placed right at the end of section 12 and the massive issues, but it could be inserted at the end of section 11.

4. However, in the meantime C. M. Kraay and C. Boehringer[4] have rejected the connection both of the early decadrachm with the Damareteion and also of group 4 and its sea-serpent with the battle of Cumae. Kraay's main objection, as I understand it, to E. Boehringer's chronology is that there is far too much coinage, over 140 obverse dies, for the short period of 485–479 (group 3) at a time when in his opinion there was little need for it; and hoard evidence, he maintains, shows that these massive issues with the decadrachm come later. The hoards he adduces are the following:

*Gela 1956*[5]

5. The latest datable coin (Jenkins, *Gela*, pl. 36, 1) which provides a *terminus post quem*, is the Zankle-Messana piece with the initial A in front of the prow, dated probably c. 493;[6] as it was in good condition, a date of c. 490–485 for the hoard seems reasonable at the moment. The latest Syracusan is B. 46, which on Boehringer's dating is c. 490. Kraay dates the burial

---

[1] But of course he was not the first to suggest it; see Schwabacher, *Das Demareteion* (1958). That the sea-serpent commemorates Cumae is not so secure.

[2] Jenkins, *Gela* 66 f., closes the interval less summarily.                                    [3] 23 f.

[4] Kraay, *Greek Coins and History*, ch. 2, 'The Demareteion and Sicilian Chronology'. Christof Boehringer, *JNG* 1968, 67 ff.

[5] Jenkins 20 ff.; Kraay 27 f.                                    [6] Robinson, *JHS* 1946, 14.

of the hoard to 484. Although this date may well not be wrong, the arguments which he used to substantiate it may be criticized. They are based on the coinage of Leontini, of which there was not one coin in the hoard. That is not strictly true, as Kraay points out: only about 80 per cent of the original hoard was recovered, but the authorities were so energetic that they managed to extract a coin of Leontini from someone or other, which Jenkins asserts could hardly have been in the hoard.[1] However, Leontini fell to Gela in the 490s: Gelon of Gela took over Syracuse, according to the traditional chronology, in 485. Kraay's premise is that the coinage of Leontini was inspired by Syracuse and that a Syracusan-inspired coinage at Leontini is only intelligible *after* 485. With this in mind he sets about bringing together as closely as possible the latest Syracusan coins in the Gela hoard with the initial coinage of Leontini.

6. He starts (p. 27) 'the group of Syracusan coins immediately following those which are in the hoard (B. 46) made use of an obverse die borrowed from Leontini'. Borrowing there certainly was,[2] but hardly immediately after. The Syracusan reverse die which was coupled with the Leontini obverse was Boehringer's R. 42. This was used with Syracusan obverses at B. 63, which could be said to be immediately after B. 46, also at B. 117 and B. 118. It developed a flaw during its life and Boehringer showed[3] that the flaw was worst at 118, but worst of all when coupled with the Leontini die and in this final phase the legend was recut. How long after B. 118 R. 42 was brought back into use is uncertain, but one could hardly say that it was immediately after B. 46. However, Kraay concludes that the mint of Leontini was already at work immediately after the date of the burial of the Gela hoard.

7. He then takes a step further—'since Leontini's coinage was modelled on that type of Syracusan coinage, of which there are only three dies in the hoard, it cannot have started much earlier than the burial of the hoard. In fact we must conclude that the coinage of Leontini started at about the time that the Gela hoard was buried'. Now if one recalls Kraay's premise that it is only after 485 that a coinage inspired by Syracuse is intelligible at Leontini, one may find difficulty in disagreeing when he says that the highest date for the hoard is 485 or more probably 484. But there seems to be another flaw in his argument. Everything is based on the assumption that the latest Syracusan coin in the hoard must be as late as the burial date of the hoard. In point of fact the odds are against the Syracusan coins being as late, because the hoard was laid down, and probably saved, at Gela, which in the crucial years of 490–485, on the traditional chronology, was not in the same sphere of influence as Syracuse. One cannot postulate that a hoarder at Gela must have in his hoard Syracusan coins from the latest dies.

---

[1] Kraay 27 n. 3; Jenkins, 151, footnote.
[2] See Kraay, pl. iv, 2–3; *SNG* v, 1913 and 1776.      [3] Catalogue 117.

8. But Kraay's reason for squeezing us into 484 is clear; he is now able to assert (p. 28) 'the really massive issues are not yet under way', which for him should be appearing if Boehringer's chronology is right. Yet even if this hoard is to be dated as late as 485 or 484, it must be emphasized that it does not follow automatically that the latest Syracusan coins must also be of this date.

## Passo di Piazza[1]

9. In this hoard, again found a few miles from Gela, the latest datable coin is a Messenian didrachm with the mule-car obverse (Kraay, pl. iv, 4), which is thought to commemorate the Olympian victory of Anaxilas of Rhegium in the mule-car event, struck either after 484 or 480. The latter seems more likely since these coins were struck on the Attic-Syracusan standard instead of the previous Chalcidian standard and the change seems more likely, as Robinson pointed out,[2] on the occasion of the *rapprochement* between Anaxilas and the Syracusans immediately after Himera than in 484 when he was ranged on the Carthaginian side. The latest Syracusan coin is B. 85, on Boehringer's dating struck soon after 485. Kraay dates the hoard to 484 or 480. The date of 484 of course presents no problems for Syracusan chronology: if it is to be dated c. 480 or later, a discrepancy of only four years is insufficient to warrant the assumption that the Syracusan coins are dated too early. Again one cannot postulate that because a hoard was laid down near Gela in 480 the latest Syracusan coins in the hoard must have been struck in the same year. Nor is it necessary to invoke the defence that the Messenian didrachm, which provides the date for the hoard, is one of those interlopers extracted by an over-energetic gendarmerie.

## Mazzarino[3]

10. This hoard buried north of Gela has for its latest datable coins the didrachms of Himera with the usual cock on the obverse, but a crab on the reverse (Kraay, pl. iv, 5–6), which must have been struck within the decade 482–472, when Theron of Acragas, whose type the crab was, had Himera under his control. The latest Syracusan is B. 333; on Boehringer's chronology, coming up to 480. Kraay dates the hoard to 475 and again notes the discrepancy between his date of the hoard and the latest Syracusan. But if the adjustment which was outline at the beginning is made to Boehringer's chronology, the extension of section 12, to which B. 333 belongs, down to 474, then on this occasion the date of the hoard does coincide exactly with the latest Syracusan.

---

[1] Jenkins 21 f.; Kraay 28.
[2] Op. cit. 17.
[3] Jenkins 22 ff.; Kraay 31; Noe 667 and 188. For the site see Jenkins 154.

*Villabate*[1]

11. Here the latest coin is that of Rhegium (lion/seated oecist) dated by Herzfelder to c. 450.[2] The latest Syracusan is B. 535 in the sea-serpent group; on Boehringer's dating, c. 459. An apparent discrepancy here, but when allowance is made for the closing of the ten-year interval, 435–425, this Syracusan coin may be brought down to the late 450s, where it coincides with the date of the Rhegium coin and allows a date in the 440s for the burial of the hoard—buried in north Sicily, again some considerable distance from Syracuse.

*Seltmann hoard*[3]

12. Kraay adduces as evidence a hoard of coins shown to E. J. Seltmann in north Sicily in 1890: some of these coins Seltman bought and of these he illustrated some. He was, as Kraay says, a practised numismatist, but he was shown the hoard a generation before the publication of Boehringer's monograph and such a person might well in the field have failed to recognize an early tetradrachm of the sea-serpent group if the sea-serpent happened to be off the flan, as frequently it is. The latest coins which Seltmann mentioned are the Himera tetradrachms which may be dated to the 460s: the Syracusan coins in the hoard he says were all Gelonian (485–478). Kraay argues that a hoard of this date (465) would be expected to show at least some examples of the sea-serpent group, and that it does not indicates that the preceding group of Syracusan coins, the massive issues of group 3, must come down to the late 460s (p. 34). Now if all the relevant hoards showed a similar discrepancy to the Seltmann hoard, then the Seltmann hoard might be used as confirmatory evidence; but they do not, so that the Seltmann hoard, unsatisfactorily published as it was, should not be used to bring down the date of the end of group 3 from 474 to the late 460s.

13. Jenkins has asked an interesting question, which he has kindly allowed me to repeat, may the Seltmann hoard have been part of the Villabate hoard? Time and place are close. In this case, the Seltmann hoard would cease to be a problem.

14. A more formidable piece of ammunition Kraay uses is an overstrike; a Syracusan coin, B. 517, was overstruck upon an Apollo tetradrachm of Catana (his pl. v; here **Pl. 1a**). Of the two Catana groups of coins, the bull/nike series and the Apollo series, Kraay believes that the former began in 461, lasted about five years at least, and was then followed by the Apollo issues from c. 456, which must be the *terminus post quem* for the overstrike,

---

[1] Noe 1161; Jenkins 66 ff.; Kraay 35; Evans, *NC* 1894, 291 ff.
[2] *Les Monnaies d'argent de Rhegion* 51, pl. 1, 5.
[3] *ZfN* 1895, 165 ff.; Jenkins 159; Kraay 32.

for this Apollo is about the first in this issue [Pl. 1f].[1] But Boehringer's date for the Syracusan B. 517 would be c. 460. There seems to be a discrepancy here, but, as in the Villabate hoard, when the readjustment is made to allow for the closing of the ten-year interval between 435 and 425, the Syracusan coin can be brought down to the late 450s, which is on the right side of Kraay's *terminus post quem*. Kraay's date of the 40s for the overstrike seems far too late, because both pairs of dies, the Syracusan and the Catanaean, are very close in style, and if the Catana coin was struck c. 456, the Syracusan must follow very soon after [cf. Pl. 1e and f].

15. Kraay's dating of the two Catana series, bull/nike and Apollo, has been accepted above, but there are other arrangements of the coinage. Cahn[2] believes that the bull/Nike series belongs to before 476, that is before the original Catanaeans were ejected by Hiero, and that the Apollo series was instituted on their return in the late 460s, which would then be the *terminus post quem* for the overstrike. The same terminus would be given by the arrangement of Herzfelder[3] who believed that both series ran concurrently from the late 460s. Both these theories would give more elbow-room for the overstrike.

16. Kraay's interpretation of the hoard and overstrike evidence led him to redate the Syracusan issues as follows. He downdates the archaic issues (group 1) to 520–500. Then come a coinless gap of fifteen years—surprising in view of the good condition of the archaic issues in the Gela hoard. The earliest dolphins he allots to 485–480. Then a gold Damareteion, which has not survived, is postulated. The massive issues of group 3 are spread over eighteen years from 479 to 461. The decadrachms belong to c. 461. The sea-serpent issues he places after 461. Now to test some of the repercussions of these new dates on the burial dates of the hoards.

17. Gela, 1956, which Kraay dated to 484, contained Syracusan coins in excellent condition down to late in the group of the earliest dolphins, for which his date is near 480. Thus the hoard will have to be downdated to 480 at least: Syracuse will be the latest in the hoard: there will be no coins in Gela until Gelon has left for Syracuse.[4]

18. For the Passo di Piazza Kraay's lower date is 480. The latest Syracusan, B. 85, well down in the massive issues, on his dating will be c. 475. Again the hoard will have to be downdated and again Syracuse will be the latest in the hoard.

---

[1] I am grateful to Mrs. S. Hurter for this information.

[2] *Knidos* 161.

[3] Quoted by Ashmole, 'Late Archaic and Early Classical Greek Sculpture in Sicily and South Italy', *Proceedings of the British Academy 1934*, p. 24 n. 2.

[4] Jenkins (p. 21) allows about five years to Geloan coinage before the burial of the Gela 1956 hoard.

19. The real crunch comes in the Mazzarino hoard, which Kraay had dated to 475. The latest Syracusan coins in this are associated with the decadrachm, which he dates to 461. The date of the hoard will have to be brought down to the late sixties: Jenkins's Gela Group II will have to be downdated a decade: and the latest Syracusan will be a decade or more later than the latest dated coins in the hoard, the Himera crabs, 482–472.

20. *Complete* hoards will produce important information, but it may be doubted whether even they should of themselves be used to make fine chronological adjustments. Such hoard evidence as has been adduced by Kraay does not seem to me to upset the traditional date for the early decadrachm provided a reconstruction such as Jenkins's is accepted to eliminate the very unlikely coinless gaps.

21. Another argument which both Kraay and C. Boehringer use to undermine the theory that the decadrachm is the Damareteion is epigraphical. The archaic letter koppa is employed in the ethnic of Syracusan coins until B. 49, which on Boehringer's dating is approximately 490/489; thereafter kappa takes its place. However, on the limestone base[1] for the golden tripod and nike which Gelon dedicated at Delphi in commemoration of Himera in 480 koppa was used on the inscription. Therefore, they argue, the coinage from B. 49, on which the last koppa was used, ought to be brought down to c. 480 at least, and consequently the decadrachm will be later than 480 and cannot be the Damareteion.

22. But there are counter arguments. Jeffery in her *Local Scripts of Archaic Greece* is quite specific on the relation between letters on coins and vases, on the one hand, and those on monumental stone inscriptions, on the other. 'Letter forms used by the vase-painter will almost certainly be considerably more developed than those cut by a contemporary mason' (p. 63). Again on coins—'But apart from these instances' (she refers to the special retention by Corinth of the koppa) 'coin legends in general reflect the script in use at the time when the die was cut, the informal script, probably rather than the monumental, for a die-cutter, like a vase-painter, might well prefer to use simple forms for his tiny letters' (p. 65). Thus the discrepancy of date between the koppa on the monument and the first kappa on the coin—separated as they are by about ten years, is not unexpected. Again it seemed to me extremely unlikely that this stone base of limestone would have been quarried in Syracuse and then transported all the way to Delphi. Therefore, the Delphian Amandry was consulted,[2] who replied that the base was a black limestone

---

[1] Tod, *Greek Historical Inscriptions*[2] 17: for a photograph see Woodhead, *Greeks in the West*, fig. 37.

[2] I am grateful to Professor Amandry for the information and to Dr. Peter Warren who obtained it for me.

(calcaire noire) and *almost certainly local Delphian*. The stone then is probably Delphian; the sculptor certainly a Milesian; the mason of the lower part of the inscription an Ionian (Jeffery), perhaps the sculptor himself; is it likely that a mason was sent from Syracuse just to carve the six words of script at the top? Wherever this leaves the issue, we seem to be still further away from the engravers of the coins.

23. Christof Boehringer in his recent article mentioned above (p. 2 n. 4) presents four reasons why, for him, the early decadrachm is not the Damareteion. Two of these have already been dealt with, the hoard evidence, which he deals with only briefly, and the epigraphical, the apparent discrepancy between kappa and koppa; the third is the historical probability that the massive issues postdate 480—this will be discussed below; and finally, the evidence of his new Aetna tetradrachm (his pl. 7, 1; here **Pl. 1f**; 8A; 8E; 9: *Obv.* Athena driving chariot; in exergue, plant. *Rev.* Seated Zeus, AIT-NAION).

24. The new Aetna tetradrachm he decides, rightly, is earlier than the superb, once unique, Brussels tetradrachm. He dates the latter to c. 470 and the new one to 476, the year of the foundation of the state under its new name of Aetna. But now he thinks that this new tetradrachm is contemporary in style with section 11 of the Syracuse group 3 issues, which E. Boehringer had placed before 480: if section 11 were to be brought down to 476 to accommodate the Aitna coin, then the Syracusan decadrachms of section 12e would be that much later again and could not be the Damareteia. Such is his argument and he places the decadrachms in the latter part of Hiero's reign, 470–468.

25. The obverse dies of Syracuse with which he compares the Aetnaean obverse are Boehringer's V. 87, 95, and 116 (his pl. 8): these, apart from the nikai, he says are very close to the Athena die of the Aetna coin—e.g. the proportions of the rump and legs of the first horse, the fanning out of the hind legs, and the grouping of the forelegs; V. 106 and 119 show similar nikai to the Aetnaean with their wings outspread, but their horses are different. There is not a Syracusan coin which combines all these features. This mixture of features taken from Syracusan chariots of the previous few years, which still constituted the bulk of the available coinage, is what one would expect in a local engraver of no great individuality cutting a chariot for the first issues of the Hieronian Aetna: however, if those features which on the Aetna chariot clearly differ from those on section 11 chariots are taken into account, then it will be clear that the Aetna tetradrachm is also influenced by section 12d and the Damareteion section together with associated issues at Leontini, and should, therefore, be later than or at least contemporary with the Damareteion section.

26. Firstly, the low-slung chariot rail, continuing horizontally along and to the front of the car on the Aetna obverse is found elsewhere only in section 12*d* (V. 170 ff.) and on certain Leontini issues contemporary with the Damareteion section (Kraay and Hirmer, *Greek Coins*, pl. 16, 18; *PCG* pl. 15, 44); in the Damareteion section the rail is continuous to the front but not horizontal. Then the pole rising diagonally from the car is rare[1] on Syracusan coins, but is depicted on the decadrachms and two of the associated tetradrachms. The space in front of the Aetna car and behind the horse's tails is more reminiscent of the decadrachms with their less cramped composition. Finally, and more important, the presence of a symbol in the exergue of the Aetna coin occurs only on the majority of the Damareteion section dies and again on the contemporary Leontini issues (lion), and of course on the later Syracusan sea-serpent issues. The symbol on the Aetna coin, whatever plant it represents, clearly sets it apart from section 11 of Syracuse.

27. It might be argued that the Athena who is driving the chariot on the Aetna obverse is rather awkwardly posed with frontal chest (as on the charioteers of some earlier Syracusan chariots) and not in pure profile (as, for example, on the Damareteion); but this position is not a sign necessarily of greater archaism, for this was the only way the engraver could show on her chest the aegis, her essential distinguishing symbol.

28. C. Boehringer's main contribution to the Damareteion controversy that the Aetna coin, dated not before 476, must bring down the Syracusan chronology because in his view its chariot resembles pre-Damareteion chariots, does not seem to me to be formidable: on the contrary, the fact that the influence of the Damareteion and associated issues can be seen on the Aetna coin of 476 should indicate that the Damareteion issues precede 476 or at least should not be later than 476.

29. The objection to E. Boehringer's chronology on the part of Kraay and C. Boehringer that the massive issues should come after 480 and not before is met by Jenkins's rearrangement of the issues which brings them down to 474. But it would be wrong to assume that substantial coinage was not required before 480. For between 485 (if the traditional chronology is accepted)[2] and 480 Gelon had to finance numerous expensive projects in

---

[1] It can be seen on V. 51, 69, 106–7, 142–3.

[2] The traditional chronology is based on Aristotle (*Pol.* 1315ᵇ 34) and Diodorus (xi, 38, 7). Diodorus said that Gelon died in 478: both Diodorus and Aristotle say that he reigned for seven years (in Aristotle this is seven years at Syracuse; in Diodorus it is not clear). Hence 485 for the seizure of power at Syracuse. At the conference I suggested that the chronology of Pausanias (vi, 9, 4–5) and Plutarch (*Vit. Cor.* 16) might be considered. Both believed that Gelon took over Syracuse in 490. If they are right, it is possible that the source of Diodorus and Aristotle was mistaken and confused the length of reign of Hippocrates and Cleander, the predecessors of Gelon in the tyranny, with that of Gelon himself, for Herodotus vii,

Syracuse—Damarete's palace and presumably his own court, housing for the total population of Camarina now removed to Syracuse, also for half the population of Gela and for the well-to-do of the Megarians and the Euboeans, accommodation and pay for his large mercenary force, the execution of the campaign against the Carthaginians to avenge Dorieus (but this may belong before 485), the preparations such as the building of the 200 triremes to meet the inevitable counter attack of the Carthaginians which led up to the battle of Himera.[1] Admittedly, after Himera there might be the Carthaginian indemnity of 2,000 talents to be coined, but the coining of the previous five years must have been far from negligible and greater, for example, than that of Athens before 480 where there were no large-scale building operations involved.

30. There are of course other problems connected with the Damareteion apart from its date. Diodorus' reason why it was called after Damarete, her intercession on behalf of the Carthaginians and the presentation of the crown, has always seemed to me hard to credit. Nor does the statement of Pollux that she went round with a hat collecting jewellery for the war effort appeal to me any more. I think that Holloway[2] was on the right lines when he said that all these smack of the ill-informed conjectures of the man in the street. My own conjecture is that the man in the Syracusan street corrupted the name of an issue of coins into Damareteion from Damatreion; and that later men in the street and historians had to think up reasons why the coin was called apparently after Damarete, and as a result several versions appeared. It must have been a decadrachm, a pentakontalitron, for this could hardly have been invented and for the corruption to have been made to Damareteion the coin ought to have been struck in Damarete's lifetime in Syracuse (after Gelon's death she married Polyzalus of Gela).[3] ΔΑΜΑΡΕΤΕΙΟΝ and ΔΑΜΑΤΡΕΙΟΝ are certainly both aurally and palaeographically very close, but what would be the significance of Damatreion? ΔΑΜΑΤΡΕΙΟΣ or ΔΑΜΑΤΡΙΟΣ[4] means pertaining to Demeter. Δαματρεῖον is her shrine. Gelon had a special relationship with the worship of Demeter; he and his family held the priesthood of Demeter and Kore. From the spoils of Himera Diodorus records that Gelon built fine temples in Syracuse to Demeter and Kore.[5] To explain the signi-

154–5 says that both Cleander and Hippocrates reigned seven years. But it is probable that the authorities on both sides could be right: Gelon got control of Syracuse in 490 and held it from Gela until 485, and only then moved his court to Syracuse, and thus could be said to have ruled in Syracuse only for seven years. Such a chronology would give more room for all Gelon's activities before 480, which seem rather excessive for the five years on the traditional chronology and would also allow more elbow room for the coinage. However, I have no wish to press it, as it may be thought that acceptance of it is a prerequisite for the rejection of Kraay's downdating of the Damareteion.

[1] Herodotus vii, 155 ff.; Diodorus xi, 38, 4.　　　　　　　　[2] *ANS MN* 1964, 2.
[3] Schol. Pindar, 15 (29) b.　　　　　[4] For obvious reasons I have taken Δαμάτρειος.
[5] Herodotus vii, 153, 2; Diodorus xi, 26, 7.

ficance of Damatreion it might be conjectured that after Himera a special issue of coins was struck (the wreath around the head of the goddess on this issue may indicate victory, and this wreath on the coins may be the basis for the gold wreath of Diodorus' version); perhaps this issue was struck in the precinct of Demeter, whereas the regular coinage was struck elsewhere; perhaps the issue was struck from the metal paid into the temple of Demeter by the Carthaginians (Demeter seems a more likely recipient of the Carthaginian gold crown than Damarete):[1] perhaps it was a special issue on the occasion of the dedication of Demeter's temple by Gelon to commemorate Himera. Soon this Damatreion issue (Δαμάτρειον νόμισμα) was corrupted to Damareteion after Gelon's queen Damarete, who it would be nice to think was Demeter's priestess, as her husband was priest.

31. From the numismatic point of view this conjecture has the advantage of releasing the Damareteion issue from its close connection with Himera and of allowing it to float a little further into the 470s, but Damareteion or Damatreion, there seems to me no valid reason yet for downdating it to the end of the 460s.

[1] For gold crowns dedicated to goddesses see Tod, *Greek Historical Inscriptions*[2] 69–70.

# The Demareteion Reconsidered: A Reply

## COLIN M. KRAAY

ON pp. 1–11 R. T. Williams has tried to re-establish the traditional date of the Syracusan Demareteion/decadrachm by countering the arguments which I had adduced in *Greek Coins and History*, ch. ii, in favour of revising Syracusan numismatic chronology and in particular of reducing the date of the decadrachm and its associated issues to the later 460s. In the last few years the debate has continued in both public and private, and, so far as my original arguments are concerned, there has become room for both repentance and reinforcement. But on the central issue, the date of the decadrachm, I remain convinced that not only the traditional date of 480/79, but also the lower date of c. 470, proposed by C. Boehringer, are both too early. The situation has changed in other ways, and in particular through the publication of G. K. Jenkins's exhaustive work on the coinage of Gela. R. T. Williams, too, has made many useful observations, and has sharpened—or blunted—many of the arguments used; in particular I am attracted by his suggestion (para. 30) that the literary tradition has correctly described the Demareteion as a decadrachm, while the occasion of 480/79 may be the result of sheer speculation, based on the name itself (perhaps already corrupt). I had proposed the more complicated thesis that the occasion was correct, but since I believed that the decadrachm was later in date, I had to postulate the existence of a gold Demareteion of which no specimens have survived. These, however, are speculative matters, and the main purpose of the following paragraphs must be once again to set out and evaluate in the light of developments since my original publication in 1969 what hard evidence there is for abandoning the traditional date 480/79 for the minting of the decadrachm.

## The gap in the coinage 479–474 (para. 3)

The intermission in coining which Boehringer postulated between 479 and 474 is historically improbable at a time when the Carthaginian indemnity provided an exceptional supply of silver; Williams approved of Jenkins's rearrangement of Boehringer's Reihe XIIa–e to fill this gap. This problem really has little relevance to the date of the decadrachm for it assumes that the traditional date of 480/79 is correct, and then tries to make more probable the historical picture which derives from that assumption. Nevertheless, since the sequence of issues in Reihe XII*a–e* would retain some interest even in the context of a later date, it is worth examining the validity of Jenkins's proposed rearrangement, which is welcomed by Williams.

The two arrangements can be tabulated as follows:

| Tetradrachms | Boehringer | | Jenkins | |
|---|---|---|---|---|
| 9 obv. | XII*a* | | XII*e* (Demareteion) | 480/79 |
| 14 obv. | XII*b* | | XII*a* | |
| 8 obv. | XII*c* | 480/79 | XII*b* | |
| 7 obv. | XII*d* | | XII*c* | |
| 6 obv. | XII*e* (Demareteion) | | XII*d* | 474 |
| No coinage | | 479–474 | | |
| 44 obv. | | | | |

For Boehringer, Reihe XII as a whole must be concentrated within at most the two years 480/79 because it comes at the end of a long series of issues which has to be fitted in between 485 and 479; Jenkins spreads the same issues over six or seven years. But all are agreed that this is a homogeneous body of coinage showing little internal variation.

When listed and numbered these Reihe look like solid entities following each other in established succession, but in most cases this is far from true; they are (except XII*d* and *e*) stylistic groups of dies which show common features, but between which there are few physical connections. They are made up as follows:

> XII*a* (9 obv.): 139, 140–1, 142, 143 (links to *isolated* 150 in XII*b*), 144–5, 146–7 (links to *isolated* 156 in XII*b*).
> XII*b* (14 obv.): 148, 149, 150 (see 143 in XII*a*), 151–2, 153–5, 156 (see 146–7 in XII*a*), 157, 158, 159, 160–1.
> XII*c* (8 obv.): 162–3 (one rev. die from Reihe XI), 164, 165–6, 167, 168–9.
> XII*d* (7 obv.): 170–6.
> XII*e* (6 obv., 4 drs. only): 194, 195–8, 198E.

In these circumstances, and given the short period involved, there is simply no means of determining the temporal or chronological relations of these coins, except within Reihe XII*d*, where there is the evidence of continuous die-linking, and in *e*, where there are in addition the special features of the Demareteion group. Since we have no means of determining the inter-relationships of the coins in Reihe XII*a–d*, which in a period of intensive production may have been contemporary rather than successive, it is wholly arbitrary to say that Reihe *e* (Demareteion) was contemporary with Reihe *d*, or with Reihe *a*, or even preceded the whole of Reihe *a–d*. Jenkins can find stylistic similarities between *e* and *d*; Williams can find them also between *e* and *a*. In so short a period the artists were the same, and none of this is surprising, or conclusive for the sequence of issues.

Jenkins (p. 23) has another equally insecure argument in favour of his rearrangement. It is based on the deterioration of reverse dies in XII*e*. The evidence can be tabulated as follows:

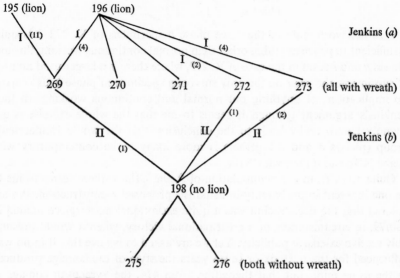

195 (lion)     196 (lion)

I (11)     I
   (4)          I (4)
                  I (2)

269      270      271      272      273   (all with wreath)

                              (1)      (2)

II                    II      II           Jenkins (*b*)
   (1)

198 (no lion)

275                276   (both without wreath)

I, II = states of wear
(11) etc. = no. of specimens recorded in Boehringer

Jenkins *a*

Jenkins points out, what is incontestable, that reverses 269, 272, and 273 exhibit more wear when combined with obverse 198 than with 195–6, and he calls these two phases *a* (Demareteion) and *b* (post-Demareteion). His argument then runs as follows:

1. Phase *b* contains R276 which has a close stylistic relationship to reverses XII*d*, and is therefore contemporary with it. (This may be accepted, though Williams finds a similar relationship with a reverse of XII*a*.)

2. Phase *a* is therefore earlier than both XII*d* and phase *b*.

3. But since 'Reihe *a–d* is homogeneous', phase *a* (Demareteion) should be *earlier* than Reihe *a–d*.

There appears to be a lapse in logic in the last step of the argument, because the 'homogeneity' of Reihe *a–d* does not exclude the alternative that, if phase *b* was contemporary with Reihe XII*d*, then phase *a* could have been contemporary with Reihe XII*c*. Jenkins gets round this by saying that we cannot 'determine how much time elapsed before the dies in question [i.e. R. 269, 272, 273] *were brought back into use*' (my italics), thus implying a definite interval between phases *a* and *b*. But though there could have been such an interval there is absolutely no positive evidence for it. The surviving examples of the three dies are as follows:

|          | 269 | 272 | 273 |
|----------|-----|-----|-----|
| Phase *a* | 15  | 2   | 4   |
| Phase *b* | 1   | 1   | 2   |

The rather worn state of the three phase *b* specimens of R. 272–3 is quite insufficient to prove anything other than normal continuous working through phases *a* and *b*; and in the case of R. 269, where there is a larger total number of specimens, the wear on the only surviving specimen of phase *b* also carries no implications of anything but normal and continuous working. In fact, Jenkins's argument (though it seems to me that the whole exercise is unsoundly based) really leads to the conclusion that the whole Demareteion group (phases *a* and *b* together) is more likely to be contemporary with Reihe XII*c* and *d* than with XII*a*.

Quite apart from the manipulation of Reihe XII*a–e*, there seems to me to be one inherent improbability in Jenkins's proposed reconstruction. We are assured that the decadrachm was a quite exceptional masterpiece minted in 480/79, in circumstances of a great national victory, when it would presumably receive extensive publicity. Yet we are asked to believe that it in no way influenced for the next six or seven years the style of the coinage produced in the same mint, but that thereafter, from 474, the Syracusan coinage in Reihe XIII and XIV suddenly exhibited that influence very clearly.

*The Gela hoard* (paras. 5–8)

The burial of this hoard has now been dated by Jenkins (p. 22) to 485; I am inclined to suggest a year or so later, simply on the grounds that the minting of coinage may not always be the first priority, and that the commission and acceptance of a new design can take up some time. But the difference is not material, and the date itself is not contested by Williams; moreover, the hoard is relevant to the date of the decadrachm only in so far as it bears on the date of the beginning of that huge volume of coinage of which the decadrachm issue constitutes a late phase.

Williams, however, goes on to criticize the arguments by which the date 484 was substantiated. So far as my argument from the coinage of Leontini is concerned I accept entirely his criticisms (paras. 5–6); it now seems to me that the coinage of Leontini (not represented in the Gela hoard) cannot have started before the mid seventies, and therefore can have no immediate bearing on the date of the Gela hoard. Another interesting point raised by Williams (para. 9) is whether in a hoard buried away from Syracuse the date of the latest Syracusan coins included may not be significantly earlier than the date of burial (or the date of the latest local coins). In the present case, if the latest Syracusan coins in the Gela hoard are to be dated 485/4, then the hoard may have been buried a year or two later; or, if the hoard was buried 485/4, then the latest Syracusan coins may be a year or two earlier. Once again this has little direct bearing on the date of the decadrachm, though it does involve a problem of some historical interest—whether the impressive new Syracusan issues with dolphins on reverse were initiated by Gelon after he had made Syracuse his capital in 485 B.C., or were they already in production under the preceding democracy. The question is at present incapable of proof, but to me, at least, the proposition that they were Gelon's is attractive, if only because later they provided the models for the first tetradrachm issues at the subsidiary Deinomenid mints of Gela and Leontini. Since only five obverse dies of this series were dated by Boehringer before 485, the displacement suggested is not large.

*Passo di Piazza hoard* (paras. 9 and 18)

My suggested lower date of c. 480 for this hoard has since received support from Jenkins on the basis of the coins of Gela which it contains (*Gela*, p. 22, 480/478 B.C.). These cover almost the whole range of the didrachms, which were in all probability superseded by tetradrachms on the accession of Polyzalus in 478. Yet in para. 18 Williams says 'the latest Syracusan, Boehringer 85 (obv. V41), *well down in the massive issues* [my italics], will be c. 475'. I find it difficult to see how any version of my chronology could lead to this result. V. 41 is, in fact, listed by Boehringer as the fifteenth obverse die out of a total series of 147, and unless Boehringer's sequence is in need of total revision (which Williams does not suggest) this can hardly be described as 'well down in the massive issues'; it is really right at the beginning, which would be dated 485/4 on the traditional chronology, or 480/79 on mine (and presumably on Jenkins's). Nor does the possibility that Syracusan coins were delayed in reaching Gela offer much scope for manœuvre, for at both these dates Gela and Syracuse were included in the same political unit, within which the interchange of currency appears to have been both swift and easy.

*Mazzarino hoard* (paras. 10 and 19)

With this hoard we at last reach the area of the decadrachm, for whereas Passo di Piazza belongs to the first phase of the massive Syracusan issues, Mazzarino belongs to the last; the latest Syracusan coin is Boehringer 333 from Reihe XIIc, more or less contemporary with the decadrachm and its associated tetradrachms. When I originally dealt with this hoard, it contained nothing, as I then knew it, which could justify a date of burial later than 475 —except, of course, the Syracusan issues, the date of which I was trying to prove—and at 475 it could just be accommodated within the traditional chronology, which postulated an interruption in Syracusan coinage between 479 and 474. Williams, of course, notices (para. 19) that my final conclusion

that the decadrachm is to be dated in the late sixties logically requires that
the burial of the Mazzarino hoard be brought down at least as late, and this
is precisely what I would now do.

Williams's further conclusion, however, that 'Jenkins's Gela Group II will
have to be down-dated a decade', does not follow, though some slighter
adjustment to Jenkins's dates may be required. The Mazzarino hoard is the
earliest to include tetradrachms of Gela, and, though there are only seven
of them, these span almost the whole of Group II, loosely dated by Jenkins
480/475–475/470. Within the first bracket the obvious occasion for the introduction of the tetradrachm is the division on Gelon's death in 478 of his
kingdom into two allied kingdoms of Gela and Syracuse, ruled respectively
by the brothers Polyzalus and Hieron; hitherto the Syracusan tetradrachm
had been the standard coin of Gelon's kingdom, but from 478 Polyzalus, for
reasons of prestige, required his own coinage, analogous but distinct. At the
same time the similar coinage of Leontini may have been started by a third
member of the family (Ainesidemos?), when he acquired a separate realm.
If Group II at Gela represents the coinage of Polyzalus, it may be presumed
to have continued until his death at an uncertain date, but probably before
466. This does not, indeed, bring us to the late sixties, but what Williams
has overlooked is that Jenkins postulates a gap at Gela of between five
and ten years between the end of Group II and the beginning of III, a gap
which on my chronology would coincide with the collapse of Deinomenid
rule at Gela. Our new knowledge of the coinage of Gela now makes it
unlikely that almost the whole of Group II could have been in circulation
by 475, unless indeed most of the reign of Polyzalus is to be denuded of
coinage.

Much the same conclusion can be drawn from the five crab didrachms of
Himera in the hoard. These were issued between c. 483 and 472 and have
recently also been the subject of careful analysis by Jenkins (*Annali* 16–17,
*Supplemento* 21 ff.). Three of the five didrachms were struck from Jenkins's
obverse O13 which is almost at the end of a continuously linked sequence
of obverse dies (O6–O15). The die sequence (*Annali*, p. 27) suggests that only
one pair of dies was normally in use at the same time, so that striking was
not bunched at the beginning of the period. This makes it unlikely that O13
was in use before 475 or that coins struck from it could have been buried on
the other side of Sicily at Mazzarino as early as 475. My conclusion is that
Jenkins's date for the Mazzarino hoard (475/470) is about a decade too early,
and that, as Williams observes (para. 19), 'the latest Syracusan will be a
decade or more later than the latest dated coins in the hoard, the Himera
crabs, 482–472'. This is perfectly acceptable and, indeed, to be expected. Down
to 472 Himera was ruled by Theron, and its mint was, in effect, a branch
mint of Acragas; its didrachms circulated with those of Acragas itself into
east Sicily. In 472 Himera became independent and intiated a small series

of tetradrachms. These had a much more restricted circulation than the didrachms had had, and though they reached Selinus (Noe 109, 949), no specimen can yet be documented from an east Sicilian hoard before the very end of the century (Schiso, N. 931).

## Villabate hoard (para. 11

With an agreed date in the forties this hoard is too late to provide direct evidence on the date of the decadrachm. I only draw attention to my refutation below of the idea that it can have anything to do with Seltmann's hoard (Williams, para. 13).

## Seltmann's hoard

For my case this is the crucial document, for at last it provides a chrono-logical correlation between the coinage of Syracuse and another series with a reliable date; my opponents are, therefore, entitled to minimize its importance, but not to dismiss it altogether. Jenkins (*Gela* 159) says 'details of this hoard are not preserved, except for the Himera pieces', and while this is true for the coins of Gela, it overlooks the eight coins from mints other than Himera which are illustrated, as well as the implications of the eighteen pages which Seltmann devoted to a discussion of the chronology and style of the hoard's contents. Williams has another line in depreciation to explain the absence of certain coins, which is inexplicable on the traditional chronology: Seltmann 'might well *in the field* [my italics] have failed to recognize an early tetradrachm of the sea-serpent group, if the sea-serpent happened to be off the flan, as frequently it is'. Those three words, 'in the field', conjure up the picture of a hurried perusal of coins (perhaps uncleaned?) in the dim light of a peasant's hut. This is not what Seltmann records. He first saw half the hoard in the possession of an 'antiquario', with whom he enjoyed such good relations that when 'some weeks later' the second half of the hoard was acquired, it was sent to Seltmann for his examination, and the two halves were found to cover the same period and the same mints. This was no casual survey, but a considered and leisurely examination of the coins.

Nor need we suppose with Williams that Seltmann, lacking the advantage of Boehringer's work, would have been unable, in the absence of the sea-serpent, to distinguish between issues minted before and after the decadrachm. The distinction is clear in Head's *History of the Coinage of Syracuse*, published sixteen years before, and mentioned by Seltmann in his article. There is no reason at all to doubt Seltmann's assertion that all the Syracusan coins were those attributed to the period of Gelon, 485–478. Indeed, had any later issues been present, there would have been no point to his article; for its purpose was to draw attention to the combination (since wholly neglected), in the same hoard, of issues of Syracuse (in the finest condition) then and since dated 485–478 with issues of Himera, which Seltmann thought might be as late as the fifties, but which in any case cannot well be earlier than 465. Given the predominance of Syracusan coinage in hoards all over Sicily, such a discrepancy cannot be due merely to a time-lag before more recent Syracusan issues reached Himera.

Williams (para. 12) protests that we should use Seltmann's hoard as confirmatory evidence only if 'all the relevant hoards showed a similar discrepancy'. But this is asking too much of ancient evidence; if 'all the relevant hoards' showed the discrepancy, we would not need Seltmann's hoard at all; as it is, his hoard (probably found near Himera) alone preserves this unique chronological correlation. But it is unique only in this. In other respects it is exactly similar to Mazzarino, except that Mazzarino was buried in a quarter of Sicily to which tetradrachms of Himera did not usually pene-⁕trate. As shown above, the Mazzarino hoard cannot be comfortably accommodated within the traditional chronology, for its didrachms of Himera push its burial date down to at least 475 and the Geloan content to a later date still. Another comparable hoard is that from Casulla, near Leontini (Jenkins, *Annali* 16–17, *Supplemento* 31): Syracuse down to Boehringer 324 in Reihe XIIc; Himera didrachms (with crab) from obverses O10, O13, O14, and O15, giving a terminus slightly later than that of Mazzarino. Three hoards are thus known, all of which terminate in Syracuse, Reihe XII, in the neighbourhood of the decadrachm. In all three hoards the didrachms of Himera (which in Seltmann's hoard were only *mittelmässig erhaltene*) suggest a date of burial pushing hard up against, if not beyond, the latest possible date (475) for the associated coins of Syracuse on the traditional chronology. At Mazzarino the end of the Geloan series indicates a date at least some years later than 475, and finally Seltmann's hoard provides a correlation between Reihe XII at Syracuse and tetradrachms of Himera at a date not earlier than c. 465.

One more attempt to make the inconvenient Seltmann hoard vanish must be countered. Williams (para. 13) repeats an 'interesting question' raised by Jenkins as to whether Seltmann's hoard may not be a part of the Villabate (nr. Palermo) hoard. Dates of discovery were close, Seltmann's in 1890, Villabate in 1893; the presence of tetradrachms of Himera in both suggests a common source in north Sicily, since these, as we have seen, did not normally circulate in the east of the island; both were sizeable hoards of 200 or more coins drawn from the usual range of Sicilian mints. But here the resemblance ends, and if the following major differences are considered, it will become evident that two entirely separate hoards must be involved.

1. Composition: Seltmann's hoard contained didrachms certainly from Himera, Leontini, Segesta, Syracuse, and almost certainly from Acragas and Gela as well. Villabate consisted exclusively of tetradrachms.

2. Himera (tetradrachms): Seltmann's included Gutmann and Schwabacher 4 (1 ex.), 7 (6), 12 (1); Villabate, G. and S. 1 (1), 2 (2), 4 (4),

6 (2). This almost complete lack of correspondence would be remarkable if a single hoard had been divided.

3. Syracuse: Seltmann's ends with Reihe XII; Villabate continues to Boehringer 535 (Reihe XV) well within the series signed with a sea-serpent.

There appears to be nothing to recommend the conflation of these two groups, except the consequent disappearance of the disconcerting evidence provided by Seltmann's hoard. In describing the findspot of the Villabate hoard (*NC* 1894, 201) Evans remarks that 'this is the third hoard of similar composition that has been found on this spot during recent years'. Seltmann's hoard was presumably one of the others, and Noe 785 (tetradrachms of Himera only, found in 1894) might be the third.

The evidence provided by the hoards constitutes the solid foundation for the down-dating of the decadrachm, and for the more plausible historical context for the Syracusan and other Sicilian coinages of the period which this allows. Williams (para. 20) insists that '*complete* hoards will produce important information', but a rigorous application of this standard will leave but a handful of usable hoards in the whole Greek world. We have to use the evidence that is available, defective as it may be, in the confidence that the coins that are missing from any hoard will have been removed from motives other than those of proving or disproving a chronological thesis. Finally, it may be queried whether a down-dating of at least fifteen years can really be described as 'a fine chronological adjustment' (para. 20); a discrepancy of such size should be detectable in the hoards, especially within a closed area of circulation like Sicily, where coinage circulated intensively from city to city. But Williams's refutation does not stop at the hoards, and there are still other aspects to be considered.

*The epigraphical argument* (paras. 21–2)

Only after I had already reached my general conclusion that historical considerations and the contents of hoards pointed to a down-dating of the Syracusan coinage, did I observe that on this revised chronology the use of *koppa* on the coins now coincided with the *koppa* on the base of Gelon's dedication at Delphi; this coincidence seemed to me to offer 'some support' for the revised chronology, but according to Williams I had reckoned without the principle that the letter forms on coins tend to be in advance of the monumental script. His evidence for this is a very general statement by L. H. Jeffery in her *Local Scripts of Archaic Greece*, p. 65, which has no specific reference to Syracuse.

Williams makes heavy weather of this whole question, proving that the stone itself is local Delphian and not Syracusan, and that 'it is unlikely that a mason was sent from Syracuse just to carve the six words of the script'. It *is* indeed unlikely. Is it not much more probable that the text of the inscription was transmitted from Syracuse to Delphi on a bronze tablet, or a sheet of papyrus, or even an ostrakon, and that Gelon would no more have wished his inscription to appear in non-Syracusan letters than to be couched in an alien dialect? There is no general principle here that can require the lettering of his coinage to be out of step with that of his inscription. In fact, from Jeffery, p. 265, where she discusses briefly the epigraphy of early Syracusan coinage, it is apparent that the idea (derived from Boehringer) that die-sinkers were quicker than monumental masons to abandon archaic letter forms rests on his early dates for Syracusan coinage; Williams now uses the abandonment of early letters by die-sinkers to justify the early dates. The argument is circular. It is not too much to say that far from supporting the early dates for the coinage the epigraphists have found them an embarrassment.

### *The Aetna tetradrachms* (paras. 23–8)

My case for down-dating the Syracusan coinage was elaborated and published before the new tetradrachm of Aetna became known. I will leave to C. Boehringer the defence of his own thesis that the new tetradrachm of Aetna belongs to a stylistic phase earlier than that of the decadrachm, and that, if this is so, then the decadrachm must be later than 476, the year in which Aetna was founded. Williams, on the other hand, argues plausibly that many details of the Aetna tetradrachm are derived from the common mass of Syracusan coins in circulation, but that some also are taken from the decadrachm, in which case the tetradrachm must be later than the decadrachm. If Williams is right, it will follow on my chronology that the new tetradrachm belongs to the later rather than the earlier years of Hieronian Aetna. And it should not be forgotten that the inhabitants and name of Aetna were transferred to Inessa in 461 (Diod. xi, 76, 3), and it is possibly to this later foundation that the Brussels tetradrachm should be attributed.

### *Historical considerations* (para. 29)

If I am right that the decadrachm is to be dated in the late sixties, this revision of the hitherto accepted chronology will inevitably draw the larger part of the massive issues down after 479, but I have no wish in principle to denude the years between 485 and 480 of all Syracusan coinage; as Williams shows (para. 29), a tyrant's life was an expensive one. For this particular point our only evidence is the Passo di Piazza (near Gela) hoard, but it is a small one of forty-five coins of which only nineteen are Syracusan. On Jenkins's chronology for Gela (with which I am in agreement at this point) its terminal date can hardly be earlier than 480, yet only the first fifteen of the

Syracusan dies are represented. This may possibly be a case of Williams's time-lag whereby the latest issues of Syracuse in the years before 480 are not represented. But even if it could be shown conclusively that there was only a trickle of tetradrachms from Syracuse between 485 and 480, Gelon still had a very abundant coinage of didrachms from the mint of Gela with which to defray the expenses of his reign.

Finally, after the arguments have been presented, all that is left is the historical context. Historical plausibility can never of itself constitute a proof of the validity of a particular reconstruction; the improbable happens, and what looks plausible to us now might appear very different if we knew all the factors in a given situation. Nevertheless, coinage through its very nature is much affected by political circumstances; this relationship between coinage and contemporary history is something which numismatists wrapped up in the minutiae of their subject, have sometimes been slow to explore.

Gelon was already a power in east Sicily before he moved his capital to Syracuse in 485. It may well be that, as Williams suggests (p. 9, n. 2), he had already been controlling Syracuse from Gela for a number of years. But it seems to me unlikely that he initiated the very handsome (and distinctively Syracusan) dolphin coinage of Syracuse, before he had moved his capital there in 485; thereafter until 480 the Syracusan coinage was probably not extensive, for Gelon seems to have retained Gela as his principal mint (coining didrachms) throughout his reign.

After 480 the output of Syracusan coinage increased enormously; bullion was available from the Carthaginian booty, from ransoms for prisoners, and from the 2,000-talent war indemnity. It is clear from Diodorus that the victors of Himera gained a great boost in prosperity, of which the surviving Sicilian temples are impressive testimony. The situation was radically changed by the death of Gelon in 478, for his kingdom was then divided between his brothers Hieron and Polyzalus.

Under Hieron the Syracusan coinage continued to be struck in great and uninterrupted volume; at Gela Polyzalus initiated a new coinage of tetra-drachms, for the obverse of which he adopted the distinctively Syracusan quadriga, thus declaring himself an equal and an ally of Hieron; this coinage appears to have lasted throughout the reign of Polyzalus. We do not know in what circumstances the Deinomenid tyranny came to an end at Gela, but the date of its collapse there was probably not far from 466, when it collapsed at Syracuse; it is at this point between Groups II (Polyzalus) and III that Jenkins postulates an interruption in the coinage of Gela, which on my chronology may have been due to disturbances following the fall of the tyranny.

At Leontini, too, a coinage of tetradrachms, closely modelled on that of Syracuse, was started in the mid-seventies, probably by another member of the Deinomenid family, who managed to carve a fief for himself out of Gelon's kingdom. Coinage continued there parallel to those of Syracuse and Gela, down to the middle or late sixties, when there was a similar change of regime at Leontini. This is marked by the abandonment of the Syracusan quadriga as a coin type, and its replacement from c. 460 by the head of the local god Apollo.

Throughout the period Syracuse remained the major mint, producing a huge series of tetradrachms which culminated c. 465/460 in the decadrachm/ Demareteion issue. We do not know the occasion of this special issue but there are several possibilities in the very last years of the tyranny, or in the following years of civil war from 466 to 461. It is possible that at Syracuse, too, coinage was interrupted at this time, before it was resumed with the long series of issues now signed with the ketos, and minted by the democracy which succeeded the tyranny.

In this whole argument on the date of the Syracusan decadrachm, the traditional chronology rests on the account in Diodorus, which not even Williams is prepared to accept as a whole; few other positive arguments have been adduced in its favour, apart from a number of minor adjustments to make it more plausible. The lower chronology is based essentially on the evidence of the hoards, which does not seem to me to have been successfully impugned; no doubt further finds will in time either confirm or disprove the lower chronology.

# The Gold Coinage of King Pharnaces of the Bosporus

K. V. GOLENKO AND P. J. KARYSZKOWSKI

[SEE PLATES 2-3]

THE gold coins of King Pharnaces II, the son of Mithradates Eupator, a great antagonist of the Romans, are considered to be rarest numismatic remains from the antique Black Sea coasts. In spite of the fact that King Pharnaces ruled in the kingdom of the Cimmerian Bosporus almost seventeen years (63–47 B.C.), no more than a few coins with his name have been known ever since. H. Köhler published some of such coins from different collections; later in the middle of the nineteenth century that summary was somewhat expanded by some other numismatists.[1] Works now a century old have remained the only special essays on the gold coins of King Pharnaces up to the present, not to mention some small publications and the list of weights of the specimens registered at the beginning of the current century.[2] It should be noted that historical literature reflecting events that took place under King Pharnaces' rule is not abundant either.[3]

At the time of writing we have at our disposal data on thirteen or fourteen authentic gold coins of Pharnaces,[4] kept in Paris, Berlin, Munich,

---

[1] H. K. E. Köhler, *Gesammelte Schriften*. ii (SPbg, 1850), 218–22 (a corresponding article was first published in 1823: Médailles grecques, par M. Köhler (SPbg, *s.a*), 506 ff.); J. Sabatier, *Souvenirs de Kertsch et Chronologie du royaume de Bosphore* (SPbg, 1849), 48–9; B. de Koehne, *Musée de feu le prince B. Kotschoubey et Recherches sur l'histoire et la numismatique des colonies grecques en Russie, etc.* ii (SPbg, 1857), 136–40; cf. Prince A. Sibirsky, *Catalogue de médailles de Bosphore Cimmérien* i, 1 (SPbg, 1859), pl. ix, 46–9.

[2] J. P. Meynaerts, 'Notice sur une monnaie d'or de Pharnace II', *RBN* vi (1950), 209–12; Chr. Giel, *Kleine Beiträge zur antiken Numismatik Südrußlands* (Moscow, 1886), S. 10; Ch. Ch. Giel, 'New Acquisitions of my Collection' (Russ.), *ZRAO*, N.S., v (1892), 353; cf. A. L. Berthier de la Garde, 'Materials for Weight Research on the Monetary Systems of Sarmatia and Tauric Chersonese' (Russ.), *N.S.* ii (1913), 104.

[3] As to latest publications, see V. D. Blavatsky, *Panticapaeum* (Russ.) (Moscow, 1964), 129 f.; D. Magie, *Roman Rule in Asia Minor* i (Princeton, 1950), 363 f., 407 f.; V. F. Gaidukevich, *The Kingdom of Bosporus* (Russ.) (Moscow–Leningrad, 1949), 309 f.; cf. also E. Diehl, *Pharnaces (2)*, *RE* xix (1938), col. 1851; D. P. Kallistov, 'Essays on the History of Bosporus at the Roman Period' (Russ.), *VDI* v (1938), no. 4, pp. 174 f.; E. H. Minns, *Scythians and Greeks* (Cambridge, 1913), 588 f.

[4] Information on those coins and bibliography of each specimen are given *infra* in the Appendix, pp. 34 ff.: cf. **Pl. 2** and Figs. 1–2.

Vienna, and New York;[1] there are no coins of his in the museums of the United Kingdom or Soviet Union (the traces of the majority of these coins from Russian private collections of the beginning of the twentieth century have unfortunately been lost). All the above coins are dated by the years of the Pontic era. The year of 243 (55/54 B.C.)[2] is dated on the earliest coin [Pl. 2. 1]; the second coin, minted from the same obverse die as the previous coin [Pl. 2. 2] dated from the year of 244; four coins, two of which are minted with the help of the same obverse die and different reverse dies, date from the following year [Pl. 2. 3–4], and the other two are the result of coining by means of a special pair of dies [Pl. 2. 5–6]; the monogram ✕ first appears on the reverse of the latter. Another four coins, two of which at least are struck from the same obverse die which began its work in the year of 243 of the Pontic era, and from different reverse dies, date from the year 246. A new monogram 𝕏 can be seen on three of them [Pl. 2. 7–8 and Fig. 1],[3] and a symbol in the form of an ivy leaf on the fourth [Pl. 2. 10]. The latter coin was minted by means of a new (third in turn) obverse die; all the coins dated from the year of 247 of the Pontic era (51/50 B.C.) were also minted by means of that new obverse die. The difference in the form of an ivy leaf is preserved on the three specimens dated from the year of 247 but they are minted with the help of two reverse dies [Pl. 2. 11–13].

Coins of Pharnaces which seem to be staters of the Attic standard but of slightly reduced weights[4] have been described by many numismatists, but not always correctly; the reading of the dates, especially, caused great misunderstanding. On the obverse side one can see a head with luxuriant curly locks and crowned with a regal diadem. On the reverse side is a half naked Apollo with a laurel branch in his outstretched right hand, sitting on a throne decorated with lion paws, with a tripod in front of him, his bent left

[1] Here we have pleasure in expressing our thanks to Mr. J. Babelon and Mr. G. Le Rider (Paris), Professor A. Suhle and Dr. E. Erxleben (Berlin), Professor C. Küthmann (Munich), Professor E. Holzmair and Dr. G. Bruck (Vienna), Miss M. Thompson and Dr. G. C. Miles (New York) for their having kindly sent us casts of coins of King Pharnaces; we are also very much obliged to Dr. J. Walker and Dr. D. W. McDowall (London), Dr. F. Fulep (Budapest), Professor B. Mitrea (Bucharest) and Dr. E. Pozzi (Naples) for data on the above coins.

[2] The beginning of the Pontic era is believed to date from October 297 B.C.; see G. Perl, 'The Eras of the Bithynian, Pontic and Bosporan Kingdoms' (Russ.), *VDI* cix (1969), no. 3, pp. 40 f., 58 f.

[3] The third coin of the year of 246 of the Pontic era with the same monogram, having been kept at the Budapest National Museum still at the beginning of the current century, has been lost and nowadays it is known only from a not quite accurate engraving in one of the old numismatic publications: *Musei Hedervarii in Hungaria numos antiquos Graecos et Latinos descripsit anecdotos vel parum cognitos etiam cupreis tabulis incidi curavit Comes M. a Wiczay, etc.* i (Vindobonae, 1814), pl. xix, 425; in the print and in the text (p. 185, note to no. 4435) one finds the year ΓΜϚ of the Pontic Era instead of ϹΜϚ. The weight of the coin is included in the summary of Berthier de la Garde with reference to the year of 246 according to J. Hampel, Keeper of the Budapest Collection before the First World War.

[4] Average weight 8·15 gm., i.e. far less than the average weight of the gold staters of Mithradates Eupator (8·35 gm).

arm leaning upon the lyre; above and below there is placed the following four-line legend: ΒΑΣΙΛΕΩΣ ΒΑΣΙΛΕΩΝ ΜΕΓΑΛΟΥ ΦΑΡΝΑΚΟΥ. In addition, there is one of the above dates behind the back of Apollo, and sometimes a monogram or symbol [Pl. 2]. It should be pointed out that the head on the obverse, as well as the Apollo on the reverse are engraved in a consistent style and correspond in all substantial details [see Pl. 3. 1, 3, 5, 7], and if we ignore the dates and other details, the differences are merely those inherent in any group of ancient coins of the same type produced by different dies over a span of years, as well as distinctions which are not of appreciable significance.

The image on the obverse side of the Pharnaces' staters has been taken as a portrait by all investigators and there are obviously no grounds for doubting the correctness of this view. The individual features of the king crowned with a diadem—a short forehead, hardly noticeable eyebrows, large slightly aquiline nose, fleshy lips, a strongly protruding chin—are emphasized on all the known dies [Pl. 3. 1, 5, 7]. The features of Pharnaces resemble those of his father Mithradates Eupator and his elder brother Ariarathes, King of Cappadocia [Pl. 3. 2, 4, 6].[1] Additionally a suggestion of resemblance to Alexander the Great was imparted to the Pharnaces portrait by the engraver of the second obverse die [Pl. 3. 5]. The same feature occurs on the later tetradrachms of Mithradates Eupator [Pl. 3. 4] whereas the earlier issues (before 89/88 B.C.) of that king [Pl. 3. 2], as well as the coins of his predecessors on the Pontic throne, give portraits in which the individual features are emphasized in an almost naturalistic way.[2] Pharnaces' portrait, generally speaking, is executed in the style of the best traditions of Hellenistic coin-engraving and corresponds to his characterization as given in the writings of ancient authors; they emphasize such traits as his craving for power, his haughtiness and treachery.[3]

As to the Apollo figure, chosen for the reverse side of coins of Pharnaces, it may be explained firstly as imitating the usual reverse type on the coins of the Syrian kings of the house of Seleucus. According to later Hellenistic concepts, a relationship to the Seleucids (Mithradates' mother, Laodice, was

[1] J. Babelon, *Le Portrait dans l'antiquité* (Paris, 1950), 151–2; comp. G. Kleiner, 'Bildnis und Gestalt des Mithridates,' *JDAI* lxviii (1953), 1954, S. 78 ff., 91 ff.; E. T. Newell, *Royal Greek Portrait Coins* (New York, 1937) 47 ff.; Th. Reinach, *Trois Royaumes d'Asie Mineure* (Paris, 1888), 187 ff.; see also B. Simonetta, 'Notes on the Coinage of the Cappadocian Kings', *NC* (1961), 18 ff.

[2] J. Babelon, op. cit. 73 f.; cf. G. Kleiner, 'Das Bildnis Alexanders des Großen', *JDAI* 65/66 (1950/1), 1952, S. 220 ff.; A. N. Zograph, 'The Antique Coins' (Russ.), *MIA*, no. 16 (Moscow–Leningrad, 1951), 71; O. Ya. Neverov, 'Gold Ring with a Portrait of a Hellenistic King' (Russ.), *VDI* cvii (1969), no. 1, pp. 173 ff. At the last time it is supposed that the Mithradatic portrait type on his coins from 89/88 B.C. may be the representation of the king in his role as Dionysus, liberator of Asia (M. Jessop Price, 'Mithradates VI Eupator, Dionysus, and the Coinages of the Black Sea' *NC* 1968, 4).

[3] Vell. Pat. ii, 40; Lucan, *Phars.* x, 475; Suet., *Caes.* 35; Flor. ii, 13, 62; App., *Bell. civ.* ii, 91; Dio xxxvii, 14, 2.

perhaps a daughter of Antiochus IV Epiphanes) allowed the Pontic kings to pretend to a descent from Alexander.[1] On the other hand, it should be taken into account that on the majority of the silver and copper coins of Panticapaeum dating from the reigns of the last Spartocids, Apollo's head or his attributes were represented.[2] Finally, when considering the stylistic features of the type, attention is attracted to the dryish and detailed style of execution, and the way in which the coin specimen is filled simultaneously by many attributes of Apollo—the tripod, the lyre, and the laurel branch, not to mention the laurel wreath on the deity's head [Pl. 3. 1, 3, 5, 7]. Such features occur not only in coin art but also in later Hellenistic art generally.[3]

The gold staters date from a small period of Pharnaces' ruling (55/54–51/50 B.C.). We cannot refer to any circumstances in the internal history of the Bosporan kingdom which could be connected with the sudden appearance and then the unexpected cessation of the gold coins.[4] Certain features of this coinage are of particular interest. For instance, the indication of dates on the coins shows that there was a conscious effort to lay stress on the regularity of issue of these staters; it should be noted that that was the first case of the use of the Pontic regal era in Bosporus. Yet the usage of one and the same obverse die during four years[5] is remarkable, and indicative of a very modest range of coinage. The coins, therefore, seem to have been a mere political gesture rather than a thought-out economic enterprise. In this connection the singularity of the monetary legend must also be noted: in contrast to his predecessors on both the Bosporan and Pontic thrones, Pharnaces is styled in the legend on his staters not merely 'King', but 'Great King of Kings'; the same title of Pharnaces may be encountered in the epigraphic documents dating back to the time of his reign.[6] It should be stressed that that magnificent style hardly conforms to the actual situation of the Bosporus ruler, who had

[1] Just. xxxviii, 7, 1; cf. Th. Reinach, *Trois Royaumes* 179.

[2] A. N. Zograph, op. cit., pl. xli, 16–19, 21–2; xlii, 1–11 (cf. *BMC Thrace*, etc. 6 ff., nos. 12–14, 35–8, 42–7). Apollo's head is also represented on the bronze coins of Panticapaeum minted under Pharnaces (Zograph, pl. xliii, 20–1); see C. V. Golenko, 'From the History of the Coinage in the Bosporus in the First Century B.C.' (Russ.), *NE* ii (1960), 36 ff.

[3] K. Regling, *Die antike Münze als Kunstwerk* (Berlin, 1924), S. 106 f.

[4] In addition to the above works (p. 25 n. 3) see also V. V. Latyshev, *Pontica* (Russ.) (SPbg, 1909), 96 (cf. *IOSPE* ii, pp. xxxiv f.); G. A. Tsvetayeva, 'The Campaign of Pharnaces against Phanagoria in the Light of the Latest Archaeological Discoveries' (Russ.), *MIA*, no. 130 (Moscow, 1965), 234 ff.

[5] Firstly a crack emerges in this die by the bridge of the nose [Pl. 2. 3–4; cf. 1–2], then it was closed up and a new split appears under the edge of the king's neck [Pl. 2. 7–8].

[6] Such in the following dedication found in 1949: [βασιλ]εὺς βασ[ιλέων μέ]γας Φαρνάκ[ης Ἀρ]τέμιδι συμ[βούλωι], *CIRB*, no. 28 (another inscription which is supposed to date from the time of Pharnaces' reign is very much damaged, see ibid., no. 29). It is quite evident that Asander, the successor of Pharnaces, also styled himself 'Great King of Kings' (the corresponding inscription, however, is broken; ibid., no. 30). Later only Rhescuporis II (A.D. 68/69–91/92) and his son Sauromates I (A.D. 92/93–123/24) styled themselves 'Great King of Kings' or 'King of Kings' (ibid., nos. 980, 1048, 1118; see also no. 45) whereas the title 'Great King' had remained in the usage at least by the middle of the third century A.D.

obtained from the hands of the Romans only a part of the domains of his father. Pharnaces, as is known, had betrayed his father; for that betrayal he was rewarded by the Romans: they entered him (for the first time in the history of Bosporus) in the list *amicorum et socium populi Romani.* Thus, in fact the king of Cimmerian Bosporus had to be an obedient executor of Roman designs.[1]

If thus the emission of the gold staters with the pretentious style 'Great King of Kings' cannot be explained through the local or dynastic traditions of Bosporan and Pontic kingdoms[2] and is hardly congruent with the legal status of Pharnaces as a Roman client, to give a correct estimate of that fact it is necessary to dwell upon the significance of the above title at the relevant period of time. The style βασιλεὺς βασιλέων or βασιλεὺς βασιλέων μέγας was systematically used by the Achaemenid sovereigns of Iran; the Parthian kings began to use this title from the last quarter of the second century B.C.[3] Thus on the coins of Mithridates II (123–88/87 B.C.) the following two styles are indicated: 'Great King of Kings' and simply 'King of Kings';[4] the last of them has also been testified by a Greek inscription (c. 110 B.C.)[5] and cuneiform documents (c. 93 B.C.).[6] However, the successors of the King Mithridates II of Parthia—Gotarzes (91–81/80 B.C.), Orodes I (80–76/75 B.C.), Sinatruces (76/75–70/69 B.C.), and Phraates III (70/69–58/57 B.C.)—are content with the more modest title 'Great King'.[7] This fact may be interpreted only by taking into account the whole international situation of the states in the Near East during the first half of the first century B.C.: the creator of one

---

[1] Appian, *Mithr.* 110–11, 113; Dio xxxviii, 11–14. On Pharnaces as a henchman of Rome see V. F. Gaidukewich, op. cit. 311; on the meaning of the terms φίλος καὶ σύμμαχος in respect to the rulers of Hellenistic kingdoms see H. Dessau, *Geschichte der römischen Kaiserzeit* i (Berlin, 1924), SS. 298 f.

[2] Mithradates Eupator, the father of Pharnaces, never bore this title; but in an inscription which is supposed to date from the time of the reign of Dynamis, Mithradates is called posthumous 'Great King of Kings' though his son, the father of Dynamis, bears only the title 'Great King' (*CIRB*, no. 979 = *IOSPE* ii, no. 356). After Pharnaces' death this last style is brought into use in Bosporus (see *CIRB*, nos. 31–2, 34, 39–40, 44, 53, 55, 59, 953, 1049, 1122, 1134–5, 1230, 1242–3, 1245–8, 1254, 1256, 1284); see also p. 28 n. 6.

[3] At the end of the nineteenth century the style was considered to have been brought into use by the Parthian kings since the middle of the second century B.C. (E. Drouin, 'Sur l'origine du titre royal ΒΑΣΙΛΕΥΣ ΒΑΣΙΛΕΩΝ', *La Gazette numismatique*, novembre 1899, no. 2, pp. 27 ff.). Wroth convincingly proved that the first coins with such a title belong to Mithridates II (W. Wroth, 'Re-arrangement of Parthian Coinage', *NC* 1900, 198 ff.; cf. R. Ghirshman, *Iran* (London, 1951), 250–1; G. Le Rider, 'Monnaies à légende grecque et monnaies des rois d'Élymaïde', *Mémoires de la Mission archéologique en Iran* xxxvii (1960), 5 ff.). The below mentioned dates of the ruling of the Parthian Arsacids are given after N. C. Debevoise, *A Political History of Parthia* (Chicago, 1938), 272; cf. also A. G. Bokshchanin, *Parthia and Rome* (Russ.), ii (Moscow, 1966), 301.

[4] *BMC Parthia* 30 ff., no. 66 ff., pls. vii, 6–viii, 9.                    [5] *OGIS* i, no. 430.

[6] R. Campbell-Thompson, *A Catalogue of the Late Babylonian Tablets in the Bodleian Library* (London, 1927), 20.

[7] *BMC Parthia*, pp. xxv ff., 38 ff. Cf. A. Simonetta, 'Notes on the Parthian and Indo-Parthian Issues of the 1st century B.C.', *Actes du Congrès international de Numismatique 1953* (Paris, 1957), 177 ff.

of the greatest powers in the Orient of that period, the Armenian king Tigranes the Great (95–55 B.C.) after the death of Mithridates II also styled himself 'King of Kings'. The reason of taking this style by Armenian Artaxiad was not merely that that he 'conquered many peoples and subdued the power of Parthians',[1] but because according to Appianus 'Tigranes, a son of Tigranes, conquered many neighbouring tribes, which had dynasts of their own, and therefore began to style himself "King of Kings" '. Plutarchus adds that at the time of the king's greatest power 'there were many kings' at Tigranes' court 'with the status of servants and four of them he constantly had at hand as his guides and body-guards'.[2] In the 70s of the first century B.C. Tigranes the Great minted (most likely in Antiochia ad Orontem, Damascus, and probably also in Artaxata) silver and bronze coins with the legend ΒΑΣΙΛΕΩΣ ΒΑΣΙΛΕΩΝ ΤΙΓΡΑΝΟΥ.[3]

The later fate of the royal style 'King of Kings' shows how great its significance was, not only in the eyes of the eastern monarchs but also in the opinion of the Romans. In 70 B.C., on the eve of coming out against Tigranes, Lucullus addressed the latter in a message, in which he styles the ruler of Armenia merely 'King' (whereas several years before, when laying siege to Amisus, the Roman proconsul hoping for the neutrality of the Armenian power styled Tigranes 'King of Kings'). Tigranes took offence and in the reply to the above message of Lucullus did not style the latter 'imperator'.[4] After the downfall of Tigranocerta and Nisibis Pompeius, who had replaced Lucullus, was no less intractable. In spite of being recognized king and included in the number of Roman 'friends and allies' Tigranes, after his capitulation in 66 B.C., had only Armenia in his possession. Sophene and Gordyene were to be passed into the hands of Tigranes Junior; Cappadocia, Galatia, Cilicia, Phoenicia, and Syria had been ceded to Rome.[5] At that period Pompeius recognized Phraates III of Parthia as 'King of Kings'; Phraates had just ascended the throne and, having helped Tigranes Junior, he rendered a great support to the Roman legions.[6] However, as far back

[1] Plut., *Luc.* 21: cf. Strabo xi, 532; Just. xl, 1, 3–4. Cf. Ya. A. Manandyan, *Tigranes II and Rome* (Yerevan, 1943), 28 ff., 48 f., 56 ff.; see also F. Geyer, Tigranes (2)', *RE* vi–A (1936), cols. 971 f.; Th. Reinach, *Mithradates Eupator, König von Pontos* (Leipzig, 1895), S. 96 ff., 306 ff.

[2] App., *Syr.* 48; Plut., *Luc.* 21. Cf. G. A. Tiratsyan, *The Achaemenid Traditions in Ancient Armenia* (Moscow, 1960), 3 f.

[3] *BMC Seleucid Kings* 104, nos. 13–18, pl. xxvii, 8, 11; E. Babelon, *Les Rois de Syrie, d'Arménie et de Commagène* (Paris, 1890), 214, nos. 23–4, pl. xxix, 15; cf. H. Seyrig, 'Trésor monétaire de Nisibe, '*RN* 1955, 85 ff.; E. T. Newell, 'Late Seleucid Mints at Ake-Ptolemais and Damascus,' *NNM* lxxxiv, (1939), 95 ff.; G. Macdonald, 'The Coinage of Tigranes I', *NC* 1902, 196 ff.    [4] Memn. 48; cf. Plut., *Luc.* 14 and 21.

[5] About the terms of the peace treaty see Ya. A. Manandyan, op. cit., 187 ff.; D. Magie, op. cit. i, 357 ff. According to Plutarchus (Pomp. 33) Tigranes was very glad to get that condition, and he promised the Roman legionaries much money in addition to the required indemnity (see also Appian, *Mithr.* 104).

[6] Dio xxxvii, 6, 1–2; a coin of Phraates with the title 'King of Kings' dating back to 64 B.C. is mentioned in literature (see N. C. Debevoise, op. cit. 63).

as in 64 B.C. the Parthians, being indignant at the Romans' non-observance of some preceding promises, invaded Armenia. In response to that Pompeius conceded to a certain expansion of the possessions of Tigranes the Great, who was no longer dangerous for Rome. Now Pompeius returned the style 'King of Kings' to Tigranes; as to Phraates, he was deprived of this title.[1]

In the light of the above we can hardly consider it a mere coincidence that the beginning of the gold coinage of Pharnaces falls in the supposed year of the death of the aged Tigranes. According to Cicero, the latter was still alive in the spring of 56 B.C.; on the other hand, during the Parthian war of Crassus, i.e. in 54–53 B.C., Artavasdes, the son of Tigranes, was the king of Armenia (he was dethroned by Antonius 34 B.C.).[2] Artavasdes, as his coins prove, also adopted the style 'King of Kings',[3] taking advantage of the struggle that was flaring up for the Parthian throne. Phraates III was killed by his sons (the end of 58 or the beginning of 57 B.C.), and his successor, Mithridates III, was soon driven away by his brother Orodes II; Mithridates fled to the Roman province of Syria. Here Mithridates did not win military support from Gabinius, the Roman governor of Syria, and so invaded Mesopotamia. But Mithridates III was besieged at Babylon; at the beginning of 54 B.C., on the eve of Crassus' intrusion into the Parthian possessions, Babylon fell and the unlucky aspirant to the throne was executed.[4] It should be noted that Orodes II (57–37/36 B.C.), having defeated his brother, systematically inserted the style 'King of Kings' or 'Great King of Kings' on the coins, whereas Mithridates III even at the period of his greatest successes contented himself with the simple title 'Great King'.[5]

Numismatic data permit us to define the year of the decease of Tigranes the Great; the data confirm that Pharnaces began to mint his gold staters with the style 'Great King of Kings' immediately after the title had become vacant on the death of its universally recognized holder. Among the coins of Tigranes the Great one can see tetradrachms with the following dates: 241, 242, and 243 of the Pontic era.[6] It is the latter of the above dates on which the coinage of the first of the staters of Pharnaces falls [see **Pl. 2. 1**]. The year 243 falls between October 55 and September 54 B.C.; and, hence, at the end of

---

[1] Dio xxxvii, 6, 2; Plut., *Pomp.* 38. Cf. Ya. A. Manandyan, op. cit. 211; N. C. Debevoise, op. cit. 74.

[2] Cic., *pro Sest.* 59; cf. also Dio xl, 16, 2 and xlix, 39–40; Plut. *Crass.* 19 and *Ant.* 50; Oros. vi, 19, 3. Cf. Ya. A. Manandyan, op. cit. 212.

[3] *BMC Galatia*, 101, no. 1, pl. xiv, 2; E. Babelon, *Les Rois de Syrie* 215, no. 25, pl. xxix, 16 (cf. p. cciv, fig. 43).

[4] N.C. Debevoise, op. cit. 75 ff.; M. M. Dyakonov, *Essays on the History of Ancient Iran* (Russ.) (Moscow, 1961), 209 f.; G. A. Koshelenko, 'The Inland Political Struggle in Parthia' (Russ.), *VDI* lxxxv (1963), no. 3, pp. 57 ff.; A. G. Bokshchanin, op. cit. 40 ff.

[5] *BMC, Parthia* 68 ff., pls. xiv–xviii; cf. A. Simonetta, *Notes on the Parthian and Indo-Parthian Issues* 118 ff.

[6] *BMC, Seleucid Kings* 103, no. 1, pl. xxvii, 5; E. Babelon, *Les Rois de Syrie* 214, nos. 16–17, pl. xxix, 11.

55 B.C., Tigranes was still alive. Pharnaces' adoption of the style 'Great King of Kings' in the same year of 243 of Pontic era, meant that the ruler of Bosporus had come out as a claimant to the political succession of the great Armenian king. Pharnaces was a relative of the latter: the wife of Tigranes, Cleopatra, was a daughter of Mithradates Eupator and sister of Pharnaces.[1] Thus Pharnaces had inherited the ancient Achaemenidian style though not from his father, and the common opinion that the political and military actions of the Bosporan king were merely determined by his desire to restore the great empire of Mithradates Eupator[2] seems to be untrue and oversimplified. On the other hand, Pharnaces' assumption of the title 'Great King of Kings' directly after the death of Tigranes could be considered as a foretoken of the future breaking off with Rome.

To our regret we have not at our disposal any detailed information on the position of Bosporus under Pharnaces. Strictly speaking, only the following four points are reflected in the preserved historical tradition: (1) the seizure of power after the suicide of Mithradates Eupator, (2) the invasion of Asia Minor—through Colchis—at the period of the war between Pompeius and Caesar, (3) the crushing of the Pontic–Bosporan troops by the latter in the battle of Zela, and, finally, (4) the death of Pharnaces in the struggle against the rebellious Asander in Bosporus.[3] However, it is obvious from the casual mentions of Strabo, Appianus, and Cassius Dio that the successor of the great Mithradates possessed the lands stretching from Chersonesus in the south-west to Tanais in the north-east. He fought a war with the tribe of Dandarians, the inhabitants of the Kuban lowland; shortly before his unsuccessful war with Rome Pharnaces subdued Phanagoria, which had been excluded as a part of his possessions by Pompeius.[4] It is also known from the same original sources, that Pharnaces' troops included contingents of many thousands provided by the kings of the tribes of Siracians and Aorsians,[5] and this serves in fact to provide an illustration of a real content for the style βασιλεὺς βασιλέων μέγας as applied to the ruler of Bosporus.

All the above confirms the supposition that the coining of gold staters in the 55/54 to 51/50 B.C. does not seem to have been sufficiently warranted as an internal economic measure of Pharnaces as the king of Bosporus. It was rather a peculiar political demonstration by means of which the son of Mithradates Eupator (who thought himself to be a descendant from Darius Hystaspes in the sixteenth generation)[6] claimed to be the heir not only of his

[1] Appian, *Mithr.* 104; Just. xxxviii, 3, 2.

[2] Cf., e.g., V. D. Blavatsky, op. cit. 130; M. I. Maximova, *The Antique Cities on the South-east Black Sea Coasts* (Russ.) (Moscow–Leningrad, 1956), 294, 296.

[3] For a review and analysis of the sources see D. Magie, op. cit. ii, 1229 ff., 1262 ff.; account of events—ibid. i, 363 f., 407 ff. In addition to the above works (see pp. 25 n. 3, 28 n. 4, 34 n. 1) see also T. R. Holmes, *The Roman Republic and the Founder of the Empire* iii (Oxford, 1923), 508 ff.; M. Rostovtzeff, *The Social and Economic History of the Hellenistic World* ii (Oxford, 1941), 978 ff.          [4] Strabo vii, 309 and ix, 465; Appian, *Mithr.* 113, 120.

[5] Strabo xi, 506.          [6] Appian, *Mithr.* 112; cf. Tac., *Ann.* xii, 18: Just. xxxviii, 7, 1.

alleged or real Achaemenid forefathers but also of the latest great monarchs of the Hellenistic world—Tigranes of Armenia and Mithradates of Pontus. It seems to be even more evident because the issue of gold coins in Bosporus under the last Spartocid kings was to all appearance very limited;[1] on the other hand, the gold staters of Mithradates Eupator are not known among the coin finds in the Crimea and in the Kuban lowland.[2] And finally, the gold coinage in Bosporus in the last years of Mithradates' reign can be explained not by the conditions of local monetary circulation but by the fact that his possessions in that period were confined to Bosporus.[3]

With such understanding of the goal and character of the issue of gold coins by Pharnaces, it becomes quite clear why the staters with the title 'Great King of Kings' were not minted either during the first years of the reign or later, at the moment of the open rising against Rome (48–47 B.C.), at the time when Colchis, Armenia Minor, Pontus, Cappadocia, and Bithynia found themselves under Pharnaces' power in addition to Bosporus:[4] by that time the style 'Great King of Kings' had become the unquestionable property of Orodes II, who immediately after the crushing of Crassus was distracted by internal affairs and only in 52 B.C. was trying to transfer military operations to the territory of the Roman province of Syria. However, that campaign brought no luck to the Parthian arms, and in the summer of the next year a new incursion into Syria occurred. At the same time Artavasdes, who had acknowledged the supreme power of Orodes long before, broke into Cappadocia. It is true that this time the Parthians did not achieve an absolute victory, but the Romans took the menace of a great war in all seriousness. The spring of 50 B.C. brought the resumption of military operations; only the mutiny of Orondopates, the satrap of Mesopotamia, prevented Parthia from establishing a frontier along the Mediterranean coast. The suppression of the above revolt, the reconciliation of the king with his son Pacorus, and the latter's participation in joint rule strengthened the internal situation of the Arsacid state; under those conditions the common political interests of the Parthian and Bosporan rulers in the impending struggle against Rome were evident.[5] It was the facts mentioned that forced Pharnaces to abandon his claims to

[1] D. B. Shelov, *The Coinage of Bosporus in the 6th to 2nd Centuries B.C.* (Russ.) (Moscow, 1956), 184 f., 193 f.; cf. A. N. Zograph, op. cit. 183 f.

[2] One stater of Pharnaces [Pl. 2. 10] and one stater of the archon Asander were found at the same time 'in der Nähe von Kertsch' (Chr. Giel, *Kleine Beiträge*, S. 10).

[3] G. Kleiner, 'Pontische Reichsmünzen', *Istanbuler Mitteilungen* vi (1955), pl. i, 6. M. Jessop Price placed this stater among the Pontic issues of the last decade of the second century B.C. (op. cit. 2 n. 5); but A. G. Zaginailo has demonstrated the coin belongs to the number of Bosporan emissions of the mid 60s ('A Gold Bosporan Coin of Mithradates Eupator' (Russ.), *KS OAM* for 1961 (Odessa, 1963), 113 ff.)

[4] See works indicated at p. 32 n. 3, p. 34 n. 1.

[5] N. C. Debevoise, op. cit. 91 f.; T. R. Holmes, op. cit. 523 f; I. D. Golovko, 'The Struggle between Rome and Parthia at the time from the First to the Second Triumvirate' (Ukr.), *Materials from the History of the North Black Sea Coasts*, iii (Odessa, 1960), 113 f.; A. G. Bokshchanin, op. cit. 59 f.

the title 'Great King of Kings'; at the same time he gave up coining gold staters, which was indissolubly connected with the affectation of that style. Reviewing subsequent historical events does not enter into our task.[1] However, one can see from all the above that the gold coins of the Bosporan king, minted in 55/54–51/50 B.C., are to be considered one of the significant sources for the obscure and intricate history of the peoples of the Near East at the period when it was being taken over by Rome.

## APPENDIX

### LIST OF THE GOLD COINS OF KING PHARNACES OF BOSPORUS[2]

Year 243 of the Pontic era (55/54 B.C.)

1.   **Pl. 2. 1 (Pl. 3. 1—enlarged). Dies: αA (Cast). Weight 8·25 gm.**

Paris. Bibliothèque nationale, Cabinet des médailles (De Luynes coll.) Unknown to Berthier de la Garde, 'Materials for Weight Research on the Monetary Systems of Sarmatia and Tauric Chersonese' (Russ.), NS ii (1913), 104, nos. 8–111, cf. note 31 on p. 131).

J. Babelon, *Catalogue de la Collection de Luynes, Monnaies grecques. III. Asie Mineure et Phénicie.* (Paris, 1930), 3, no. 2396, pl. xc.

Year 244 of the Pontic era (54/53 B.C.)

2.   **Pl. 2. 2. Dies: αB (direct photo). Weight 8·18 gm.**

Location unknown (Grand Duke Alexander Michailovitch coll., 1913; R. Jameson coll. 1924). Mentioned by Berthier de la Garde (p. 104, no. 8/2).

*Collection Robert Jameson. III. Suite des monnaies grecques et impériales romaines.* (Paris, 1924), 96, no. 2146, pl. cxv.

Year 245 of the Pontic era (53/52 B.C.)

3.   **Pl. 2. 3. Dies: αΓ (Cast). Weight 8·07 gm.**

Berlin. Staatliche Museen zu Berlin, Münzkabinett. Mentioned by Berthier de la Garde (p. 104, no. 9/6; weight 8·08 gm.).

J. Friedländer und A. von Sallet, *Das Königliche Münzkabinett* (Berlin, 1877), 136, no. 467.

---

[1] On the campaign of Pharnaces in Asia Minor and his death see (in addition to the works mentioned on p. 25 n. 3, p. 28 n. 4, p. 32 nn. 2–3) G. A. Melikishvili, *From the History of Ancient Georgia* (Russ.) (Tbilisi, 1959), 331 f.; cf. Ye. S. Golubtsova, *The North Black Sea Coasts and Rome at the Beginning of Our Era* (Russ.) (Moscow, 1951), 58 ff. In our opinion the interpretation of the events during the last years of Pharnaces' life by many modern authors is rather doubtful; we intend to dwell on this question in an article about Asander's gold coins.

[2] Editio princeps: C. Suetonii Tranquilli Opera quae extant, Carolus Patinus notis et numismatibus illustravit etc. Basileae, MDCLXXV, p. 25 (engraving); cf. Specimen universae rei nummariae antiquae, etc. auctore Andr. Morellio, Parisiis, MDCLXXXIII, p. 232, tab. XXIV, 1; Achaemenidarum imperium sive regum Ponti, Bosphori et Bithyniae historia ad fidem numismatum accomodata, per J. Foy-Vaillant (Parisiis, 1725), 204 ff.

3–*a*. **Fig. 1.** Dies: αΓ¹ (Cast). Weight 8·17 gm.

Vienna. Bundessammlung von Medaillen, Münzen und Geldzeichen. Mentioned by Berthier de la Garde (p. 104, no. 9/2). Unpublished.

Fig. 1.

4. **Pl. 2. 4.** Dies: αΔ (Cast). Weight 8·12 gm.

Paris. Bibliothèque nationale, Cabinet des médailles (ex Wiczay coll., 1814–28). Mentioned by Berthier de la Garde (p. 104, no. 9/4).

*Wiczay Catalogue* (see above, p. 26, n. 3), p. 185, no. 4435.

D. Sestini, *Descrizione delle medaglie antiche greche del museo Hedervariano dal Bosforo Cimmerio fino al Armenia*, II (Firenze, 1828), 19, no. 1.

Ch. Lenormant, *Trésor de numismatique et de glyptique, etc. Numismatique des rois grecs.* (Paris, 1849), 51, no. 10, pl. xxiv.

Koehne, *Description du Musée Kotschoubey* (see above, p. 25 n. 1), ii, 138, fig.

Sibirsky, *Catalogue des médailles du Bosphore Cimmerien* (see p. 25 n. 1), i, 1 pl. ix, 47.

5. **Pl. 2. 5.** Dies: βE (direct photo). Weight 8·10 gm.

Location unknown (Count Ouvaroff coll., 1887). Mentioned by Berthier de la Garde (p. 104, no. 9/5).

A. V. Oreshnikov, *Catalogue of the Count A. S. Ouvaroff Collection of Antiquities* vii (Russ.) (Moscow, 1887), 60, no. 437, pl. ii.

6. **Pl. 2. 6 (Pl. 3. 5**—enlarged). Dies: βE (Cast). Weight 7·40 gm. (cut).

Paris. Bibliothèque nationale, Cabinet des médailles (Royal coll.). Mentioned by Berthier de la Garde (p. 104, no. 9/7).

T. E. Mionnet, *Description de médailles antiques, etc.* ii (Paris, 1807), 362, no. 22.

E. Q. Visconti, *Iconographie ancienne ou Recueil des portraits authéntiques des empereurs, rois et hommes illustres de l'antiquité, Iconographie grecque* ii (Paris, 1811), 139, no. 7, pl. xlii (the rarest edition of this work—Paris, 1808—was inaccessible to us).

---

[1] This specimen is minted from the same pair of dies as no. 3, but the coin flan and all elements of obverse and reverse types are noticeably enlarged—though without any deformation of the details. We cannot understand or explain this strange fact (and analogies are unknown to us); therefore the authenticity of the coin no. 3*a* must be recognized as dubious.

H. K. E. Köhler, *Médailles grecques. Rois de Bactriane,* etc. (SPbg, *s.a.* (1823)), 506, no. 3 (reprinted in *Köhlers Gesammelte Schriften,* herausgegeben von L. Stephani, ii (SPbg, 1850), Serapis, mém. xviii, p. 218, no. 3).

G. Spasski, *The Cimmerian Bosporus* (Russ.) (Moscow, 1846), 62, pl. iii, 15.

Year 246 of the Pontic era (52/51 B.C.).

7.   **Pl. 2. 7.** Dies: αZ (Cast). Weight 8·15 gm.

Munich. Staatliche Münzsammlung. Mentioned by Berthier de la Garde (p. 104, no. 10/2).

Köhler, *Médailles grecques* 507, no. 4 (*Gesammelte Schriften* ii, p. 219, no. 4).

T. E. Mionnet, *Supplément,* etc. iv (Paris, 1829), 469–70, no. 24.

G. Kleiner, *Bildnis und Gestalt des Mithradates* (see above, p. 27 n. 1), S. 95, Abb. 7.

FIG. 2.

8.   **Pl. 2. 8 (Pl. 3. 3—enlarged).** Dies: αH; recoined (Mould). Weight 8·14 gm.

Vienna. Bundessamlung von Medaillen, Münzen und Geldzeichen. Mentioned by Berthier de la Garde (p. 104, no. 9/3; the date is read as 245 of the Pontic era).

J. Eckhel, *Catalogue musei Caesarei Vindobonensis numorum veterum,* etc. i (Vindobonae, 1779), 135, no. 1.

Köhler, *Médailles grecques* 506, no. 2 (*Gesammelte Schriften* ii, 219, no. 2). Mionnet, *Supplément* iv, 469, no. 23.

Sibirsky, *Catalogue,* pl. ix, 48 (true reading of the date).

A. A. Sibirsky, 'The Anonymous Tetrachalcs with the Scythian Gorytus' (Russ.), *ZOOID* x (1877), 31, 49, pl. ii, 6.

V. F. Gaidukevitch, *The Kingdom of Bosporus* (see p. 25 n. 3), 586, no. 53, pl. iii.

9.   **Fig. 2.** Uncertain dies (copper-plate engraving). Weight 8·21 gm.

Location unknown (at the beginning of the current century—Budapest. National museum). Mentioned by Berthier de la Garde (p. 104, no. 10/1; all authors except him had taken the date as 243 of the Pontic era).

*Wiczay Catalogue* (see p. 26 n. 3), 185, note, pl. xix, 425.

Köhler, *Médailles grecques* 506, no. 1 (*Gesammelte Schriften* ii, 218, no. 1).

Sestini, *Descrizione del museo Hedervariano* (see no. 4 of this list), p. 19, note.

Mionnet, *Supplément* iv, 469, 22.

10. **Pl. 2. 10.** Dies: γΘ (direct photo). Weight 8·18 gm.

Location unknown (Giel and Grand Duke colls.). Mentioned by Berthier de la Garde (p. 104, no. 9/1; the date reads as 245 of the Pontic era).

Chr. Giel, *Kleine Beiträge* (see p. 25 n. 2), S. 10, no. 21, Taf. ii.

A. N. Zograph, *The Antique Coins* (see p. 27, no. 2), pl. xliv, 3.

Year 247 of the Pontic era (51/50 B.C.).

11. **Pl. 2. 11.** Dies: γI (Cast). Weight 8·19 gm.

New York. Collection of the American Numismatic Society (Meynaerts coll., 1850–6; Prince Sibirsky coll., 1859; Giel coll., 1892; Grand Duke coll., 1913). Mentioned by Berthier de la Garde (p. 104, no. 8/1; the date reads as 244 of the Pontic era).

J. P. Meynaerts, *Notice* (see p. 25, no. 2), 209, pl. vi, 1.

*Description de la Collection de médailles antiques en or, grecques, romaines, byzantines et visigothes, recueillies par J. P. Meynaerts de Louvain* (Paris, 1856), 15, no. 46.

Koehne, *Description du Musée Kotschoubey* ii, 139.

Sibirsky, *Catalogue*, p. ix, 46.

Ch. Ch. Giel, *New Acquisitions* (see p. 25, no. 2), 353, no. 62, pl. vi.

Minns, *Scythians and Greeks*, pl. vi, 23.

12. **Pl. 2. 12 (Pl. 3. 7—enlarged).** Dies: γK (Cast). Weight 8·07 gm.

Vienna. Bundessammlung von Medaillen, Münzen und Geldzeichen. Mentioned by Berthier de la Garde (p. 104, no. 11/2).

Eckhel, *Catalogus musei Caesarei* (see no. 8 of this list), 135, no. 2.

Köhler, *Médailles grecques* 507, no. 5/1 (*Gesammelte Schriften* ii, 219, no. 5/1).

Mionnet, *Supplément* iv, 470, no. 25/1.

Sibirsky, *Catalogue*, pl. ix, 49.

13. **Pl. 2. 13.** Dies: γK (Mionnet Sulphur cast). Weight 8·10 gm.

Location unknown (at the beginning of the current century—Gotha. Herzogliches Münzkabinett). Mentioned by Berthier de la Garde (p. 104), no. 11/1.

*Gotha Numaria sistens Thesauri Fridericiani numismata antiqua*, etc. auctore Chr. Sig. Liebe (Amsteloedami, 1730), 10, no. 457.

Köhler, *Médailles grecques*, 507, no. 5/2 (*Gesammelte Schriften* ii, 219, no. 5/2).

Mionnet, *Supplément* iv, 470, no. 25/2.

Modern Forgeries

(*a*) G. F. Hill, *Becker the Counterfeiter* i (London, 1955), pl. v, 75 (copy of no. 7 of this list).

(*b*) P. Burachkov, *Catalogue of Coins of the Greek Colonies on the Coast of South Russia* (Russ.) i (Odessa, 1884), pl. xxv, 40 (copy of no. 11 but the date is changed).

(*c*) Köhler (*Médailles grecques* 507, no. 6 = *Gesammelte Schriften* ii, 219, no. 6) describes with references to many publications of the eighteenth century one silver stater (drachm?) similar to nos. 12–13; the authenticity of this coin is very doubtful.

38     K. V. GOLENKO AND P. J. KARYSZKOWSKI

## ABBREVIATIONS

CIRB     Corpus Inscriptionum Regni Bosporani. Moscow–Leningrad, 1956
         (Russian).

IOSPE    Inscriptiones antiquae orae septentrionalis Ponti Euxini Graecae et
         Latinae. Ed. B. Latyschev.

KS OAM   Kratkiye soobshcheniya Odesskogo Archeologicheskogo muzeya (Russian:
         Brief Reports of the Archaeological Museum Odessa).

MIA      Materialy i Issledovaniya po arkheologii SSSR (Russian: Materials and
         Researches on the Archaeology of the USSR).

NE       Numismatika i Epigrafika (Russian: Numismatics and Epigraphy).
         Moscow.

NS       Numizmaticheskiy sbornik (Russian: Numismatic Collection). Moscow.

OGIS     Orientis Graeci inscriptiones selectae. Ed. G. Dittenberger.

VDI      Vestnik drevney istorii (Russian: Journal of Ancient History). Moscow.

ZOOID    Zapiski Odesskogo Obshchestva istorii i drevnostey (Russian: Trans-
         actions of the Society of History and Antiquities at Odessa).

ZRAO     Zapiski Russkogo arkheologicheskogo Obshchestva (Russian: Trans-
         actions of the Russian Society of Archaeology).

## ADDENDUM

At the beginning of 1972 after this article had been sent for publication, we received, thanks to the kindness of Dr. Herbert A. Cahn, a cast of a new and unknown specimen of this coin (**Fig. 3**). Dr. Cahn informs us that the recently acquired gold stater was found near Trebizond.

FIG. 3.

The new coin belongs to the year 246 of the Pontic Era (52/51 B.C.) and was struck from obverse die α (the majority of gold coins of Pharnaces originate from that die). The reverse of this coin is of particular interest: the new, hitherto unknown difference-mark is placed on it—three pellets in the left field, near the tripod (not on the right as was usual).[1] Apparently the new starter must be considered to be one of the first issues of 246. Its weight is rather high—8·21 gm (it is equal to the weight of specimen no. 8).

The new coin is the second stater of Pharnaces, the find-spot of which is known; it seems to give the only trustworthy example of gold coins of the Bosporan Kings outside of the North and East coasts of Euxine. This last circumstance permits us to think that the coin was brought to the area of Trebizond at the time of the Asia Minor campaign of Pharnaces.

[1] The three pellets near the altar are known also on the Sassanian coins where they are considered as an old Iranian sacral symbol of power (H. Jänichen, *Bildzeichen der Königlichen Hoheit bei den iranischen Völkern*. Bonn, 1956, S.22, Taf. 24, 15). Such pellets, apparently with the same meaning, are also on the debased late staters of the Sarmatian King Thothorses of Bosporus (e.g. B. Köhne, op. cit., pp. 360ff., nn. 12–13, 17–18, 21; A. N. Zograph, op. cit., pl. L. 20).

# Epigraphical Notes on Hellenistic Bronze Coinage

J. R. MELVILLE JONES

DURING the Hellenistic period the use of bronze coinage spread further among the Greek city states, for reasons both political and economic. Increasing sophistication in financial matters encouraged the production of fiduciary coinages, from which the minting authorities could make a greater profit, and the growing importance for trade between states of the regal and cistophoric issues, with those of Rhodes, Athens, and perhaps Histiaea, may well have led to a decrease of interest in the production of silver coinage, even on the part of cities still nominally free. There is also some evidence for an increase in the price of silver in relation to copper.[1]

As a result, there seem to be some cases where denominations which had previously been struck in silver were now issued in bronze. A well-known inscription of the third century B.C. from Gortyn[2] declares that the city has decided to use bronze coinage in future, νομίσματι χρῆσθαι τῶι καυχῶι, τῶι ἔθηκαν ἁ πόλις, and that its citizens are now forbidden to accept silver obols, τὸδ δ' ὀδελὸνς μὴ δέκεσθαι τὸνς ἀργυρίος. There are two senses in which we may understand these lines. Either it was intended that no silver coinage at all should be used after the time of this proclamation, or the 'obols' of the second passage quoted here are to be taken literally, and it was only for this denomination that bronze was replacing silver. I believe that the latter interpretation is correct, because there seems to be an overlap in time between the first bronze issues of Gortyn, and the disappearance of silver coinage, and because in this inscription the fine for non-compliance with the terms of the

---

[1] For Egypt at any rate the evidence has been studied in detail; see A. Segrè, 'The Ptolemaic Copper Inflation' in *American Journal of Philology* 1942, 174–92, T. Reekmans, 'Monetary History and the Dating of Ptolemaic Papyri' in *Studia Hellenistica* 1948, 15–43, and 'Social and Economic Repercussions of the Ptolemaic Copper Inflation' in *Chronique d'Égypte* 1949, 324–42. For the beginnings of bronze coinage, and for emergency issues of bronze coinage with the denominations of silver, see E. S. G. Robinson, 'Some Problems in the Later Fifth Century Coinage of Athens', *MN* ix (1960) 1–15; E. S. G. Robinson and M. Jessop Price, 'An Emergency Coinage of Timotheos', *NC* 1967, 1–6; and M. Jessop Price, 'Early Greek Bronze Coinage', *Essays in Greek Coinage Presented to Stanley Robinson* (1968), 90–104. I should like to acknowledge help given by Price while this paper was being drafted. Some of the inscriptions discussed here were also studied by M. N. Tod, 'Epigraphical Notes on Greek Coinage', *NC* 1960, 1–24.

[2] Dittenberger, *Sylloge Inscriptionum Graecarum*³ 525 (Collitz and Bechtel, *Sammlung der griechischen Dialekt-Inschriften*, 5011), ll. 4–9.

decree is set at five staters of silver. The inscription is therefore to be dated c. 260–250 B.C., at the time when bronze was being introduced, and it is possible that the bronze coins which were struck at this time were reckoned as obols.[1]

Another inscription of 130–120 B.C., from Sestus,[2] uses almost the same phrase. The city has decided to make use of its own bronze coinage, νομίσματι χαλκίνωι χρῆσθαι ἰδίωι. Two reasons are given. There is firstly the aim of self-advertisement, of giving currency to the city's emblem (which seems to me to be the most likely rendering of the phrase χάριν τοῦ νομιτεύεσθαι τὸν τῆς πόλεως χαρακτῆρα),[3] and secondly, there is the profit which will accrue to public finances from striking such a coinage, τὸ δὲ λυσιτελὲς τὸ περιγεινόμενον ἐκ τῆς τοιαύτης προσόδου λαμβάνειν τὸν δῆμον. There is, however, no indication of the denominations which were to be struck.

Long before this, in the third century B.C., a bronze coinage had been in circulation in Boeotia. Two inscriptions survive which show us something of the way in which it was used. The first, the accounts of the agonothete Xenarchus, is dated to the period 221–216 B.C.,[4] which suggests that the minting of bronze started well before the end of the third century. Sums of money are listed separately, according to whether they are in bronze or in silver. The second, the *apologia* of the hipparch Pompidus, of second-century date, does the same, and also contains a conversion of a sum in silver into its equivalent in bronze, which makes it clear that the former commanded a premium of 25 per cent.[5] In neither case is there any indication of what any specific bronze coin might be worth. The similarity of the types used on silver and bronze of the Boeotian League at this period makes it possible that they were intended to represent the same denomination, the silver coins being either heavy drachms or very light didrachms; but there can be no certainty in this matter.

Coins themselves in the Hellenistic period occasionally declare their values. Some of these show that silver denominations were now being taken over by bronze, although most of such highly valued bronze coins belong to the time of the Roman Empire. At Metapontum there are the bronze coins marked ΟΒΟΛΟΣ, and perhaps ΤΕ(ταρτημόριον) and ΗΕ (μιτεταρτημόριον) (*HN*[2] pp. 79–80), and there is a ΤΡΙΩΒΟΛΟ from Samothrace (*HN*[2] p. 263).[6] This evidence is reinforced by passages from several

[1] For the introduction of bronze coinage at Gortyn, see G. le Rider, *Monnaies crétoises* (Paris 1966), 245, and A. E. Jackson, 'The Bronze Coinage of Gortyn', *NC* 1971, 37–51.
[2] *Orientis Graecae Inscriptiones Selectae* 339 (*Hermes* 1873, 113–39); first studied from a numismatic point of view by H. von Fritze in *Nomisma* i (1907), 1–13.
[3] The alternative translation, 'to give currency to the city's coinage', seems less appropriate here, although it is very close to the metaphorical use of the same phrase by Polybius (xviii, 34, 7), when he says that the practice of bribery is widespread among the Aetolians, τοῦ χαρακτῆρος τούτου νομιστευομένου παρ' Αἰτωλοῖς.          [4] *BCH* 1901, 365–75.
[5] *IG* vii, 2426, ll. 16–17.
[6] Coins of Aegium with ΗΜΙΟΒΕΛΙΝ, of Chios with ΟΒΟΛΟΣ, of Seleuceia Syriae

more inscriptions. A list of market-dues from Magnesia Ioniae of the second century B.C. uses the unit of the χάλκινος ὀβολός.[1] Two inscriptions of 156–153 B.C. include ὀβολοὶ χαλκοῖ among inventories in the Delian treasuries,[2] and a third, of 130 B.C., refers to Delian bronze tetrobols, . . . σὺν Δηλίοις τετρω-βόλοις χαλκοῖς.[3] Another Delian inscription dated shortly before 153 B.C. includes a reference to fifty-seven δραχ[μὰς] χαλκίνας,[4] and an almost illegible passage in an inscription of c. 200 B.C. from Priene has been restored by one editor at least to read δραχ]μὴν χαλκ[ῆν in one line.[5] There is no further evidence for bronze coins of the value of a drachma in the Hellenistic world outside Egypt,[6] so for the moment we must say that it was rarely if at all that a bronze coin was tariffed as highly as this before the Roman period.

As a result, the surviving references to bronze tetradrachms must be viewed with some suspicion, particularly since they are of the fourth and early third centuries B.C., when it is even less likely that coins so overvalued would have been in use in the Greek world. In 276/5 B.C. a [τ]ετράχμον χαλκοῦν was listed in an inventory from the Asclepieum in Athens,[7] and the - - - χμα χαλκᾶ of *IG* ii[2] 1487, 25, were also probably tetradrachms, appearing on this occasion in the accounts of the treasurers of Athena and the Other Gods at Athens for a year towards the end of the fourth century B.C. Even earlier than these, in a Delian inventory of 364 B.C.,[8] there appears the entry, Αἰγιναῖοι στατῆρες τρεῖς, τούτων [sic] χαλκὸς Ⅰ• | τετράδραχμα Ἀττικὰ ⲄⅡⅠ, τούτων . . . . . . α ⅠⅠⅠⅠ, ⲄⲈⲄ . . . μένον Ⅰ. In the matching lines from a similar inventory of about the same date, found at Athens,[9] the published version

with OBO, of Melos and Byzantium with ΔΡΑΧΜΗ and ΔΡΑΧΜΑ, and of Rhodes with ΔΙΔΡΑΧΜΟΝ, are of the Roman period. The large bronzes marked ΤΕΤΡΑΔΡΑΧΜΟΝ which were noted by Svoronos and Regling (*JIAN* 1906, 237–44 and 1908, 243–4), who discovered one and three examples respectively, remain a mystery, particularly if they really belong to the fifth century B.C. They were not plated, so can hardly be forgeries. If they were check-weights, as Svoronos suggested, it is surprising that so many survived. If they belong to the eastern Adriatic, as Regling supposed, the monogram of ΠΑ which appears on one of them might suggest that they came from Pale. But this does not help us to decide at what time they might have been made.

[1] Kern, *Inschr. von Magnesia am Maeander* 121, ll. 10, 15, and 19.
[2] *Inscr. de Délos* 1429 B ii, 45 and 1432 Bb i, 12.
[3] *Inscr. de Délos* 1450 B 5. This presents something of a problem. What coins could these have been? Issues of the Delian mint of this period do not seem to have included any bronze coin which we should be inclined to value as a tetrobol. The question is complicated by the fact that, as will shortly be made clear, this may have been a reference to counterfeit coins, silver-plated on a bronze core.
[4] *Inscr. de Délos* 1422, l. 7. The large number of coins in this instance makes it unlikely that they were forgeries.    [5] H. von Gaertringen, *Inschr. von Priene* 195, l. 20.
[6] Egyptian bronze coinage was certainly tariffed in drachmas, but we have no certain knowledge of the denominations represented by different coins. The pentadrachm spoken of by Heron, *Pneumatica* i, 21, which caused a machine to issue a measure of water for purification at a temple, was probably the smallest bronze coin in circulation, and the later bronze coins marked M and Π may have been of 40 and 80 drachmas.
[7] *IG* ii[2], 1534, l. 91.
[8] *BCH*. 1886, 461–75 (Michel, *Recueil* 815), ll. 60–1.    [9] *IG* ii[2], 1636, ll. 18–19.

reads, Αἰγιναῖο[ι στατῆρες τρεῖς, χαλκὸς Ι• τετράδραχμα Ἀττικὰ] | . . . . ΔΑ ὀκ[τ]ώ· τούτων χ[ίβδηλα? τέτταρα, τετριμμένον? ἕν. In each case, however, I think that the correct reading, allowing for some variation in spelling and line-division, must be: Αἰγιναῖοι στατῆρες τρεῖς, τούτων χαλκὸς Ι• τετράδραχμα Ἀττικὰ ὀκτώ· τούτων χαλκᾶ τέτταρα, τετριμμένον ἕν.[1]

These last two inscriptions help to clarify the situation a little. All the coins mentioned here could be described, it seems, as Aeginetan staters or Attic tetradrachms; but one of the former and four of the latter were 'bronze', and one of the latter was 'worn'. It looks as if the adjective χάλκεος referred to the condition, appearance, or nature of what might otherwise in each case have been classified as a legitimate silver coin.

Looking further, there is yet another inscription from Delos in which the same term appears twice,[2] and here it is possible, I think, to show exactly what it must have meant. On the first of the two occasions on which it is found, the presence of τετράδραχμα χαλκᾶ δύο καὶ παρερρινημένον ἕν is recorded. Later, when the grand total of temple offerings is recorded, the same coins are described simply as χαλκᾶ τετράδραχμα τρία. So 'bronze' might be used as a word to describe a tetradrachm which had been 'filed down' to test it. It seems clear that χάλκεος is in this instance no more than an equivalent for ὑπόχαλκος, the standard word to describe a plated coin or other object.

It is significant that the only inscriptions in which this term appears are all inventories of temple treasures. It is not likely that anyone would take the trouble to catalogue a counterfeit coin in any other circumstances; but the property of the gods would be recorded even if it was valueless.[3]

There may be some confirmation of this in the second century B.C. inscription from Dyme in Achaea which records the passing of the death sentence upon four men for counterfeiting and temple-robbery, ὅτι ἱεροφώρεον [καὶ

---

[1] The fact that eight tetradrachms were listed on one occasion and seven on another is not important; variations of this sort are not unknown in the Delian inventories. The editorial suggestion χίβδηλος is unlikely. This spelling is known from Suidas, the *Etymologicum Magnum* and the scholiast on Aristophanes, *Birds* 158, where an etymology is preserved which attempts to explain κίβδηλος as a reference to the naming of forged Athenian coins after the Chians.

The editors of the Attic inscription have assumed a *stoichos* of sixty letters, which would make my restoration too short; but so much of the line is missing that we must allow for the possibility of spaces being taken up by punctuation, or of syllabic division at the end of a line.

[2] *IG* xi (2), 158A, ll. 5 and 36.

[3] As examples of scrupulous care in recording items in inventories of sacred treasures, see *IG* ii², 1517 (*Hesperia* 1963, 170–5), where an 'obol which had been thrown away' is listed, also *Inscr. de Délos* 1408 A i, 26, where a triobol which had been found in front of one of the buildings is included (this entry is repeated in nos. 1428 and 1430). *IG* vii, 303, from the neighbourhood of Oropus, carefully lists coins and other objects which were to be melted down to replace worn-out sacred vessels, and forged coins are catalogued in *IG* ii¹, 1388 and 1400. O. Broneer, writing in *Hesperia* 1955, 135–6, reported the discovery of plated coins at the site of the temple of Poseidon at Isthmia; we cannot exclude the possibility that 'imitations' might have been accepted as gifts by temples.

νό]μισμα ἔκοπτον χάλ [κεον].[1] It was surely not the striking of coins in bronze only for which they were condemned, but the issuing of silver-plated forgeries which were internally of bronze.

It seems therefore that in some cases during the Hellenistic period bronze coins took on the denominations, as well as the role, of the silver coins which they replaced. But there is a distinction which must be made, when references to bronze issues of denominations traditionally struck in silver are being studied. Bronze obols, and perhaps even triobols, tetrobols, and drachmas, seem to have been in existence after c. 190 B.C., when some smaller denominations of silver coinage began to be replaced by bronze at a number of Greek mints. But with the exception of a very few emergency or obsidional issues, any earlier references to 'bronze' coins of higher value are not likely to have been to genuine coins, and are probably to plated forgeries.

[1] Dittenberger, *Sylloge Inscriptionum Graecarum*³ 530 (*BCH* 1878, 98).

# Architectura Numismatica

## Early Types: Greek, Roman, Oriental

An extended review of G. Fuchs, *Architekturdarstellungen auf römischen Münzen*[1]

BLUMA L. TRELL

[SEE PLATES 4–7]

GÜNTER FUCHS, like many other scholars who investigated and used the representations of architecture on coins as archaeological evidence, would have read a recent comment with mixed feelings. 'Particolarmente sensibile la mancanza di un corpus fotografico di tutte le monete con figurazioni dei monumenti di Roma, con un adeguato commentario archeologico. . . '.[2] The initiate would say of such a corpus: 'Fra il dire e il fare sta di mezzo il mare.'

Fuchs's study in *architectura numismatica*, published posthumously, is a valuable and careful work and demonstrates what enormous research is needed even for part of such a corpus. In fact, Fuchs's book covers only the early Imperial years, yet he has under study no less than fifty-four building-types with variations totalling close to an impressive 140. Even so, this does not include some monuments outside Rome. Fuchs studies the literary and archaeological evidence from the point of view of an art historian, but he also views and evaluates the various types of perspective, as an architect. Exceptional also is the chronological arrangement of the coins. The purpose is to establish die-makers' formulae and with these wherever possible to reconstruct the buildings represented. All the numismatic types investigated are of course in the British Museum catalogues.

Singularly characteristic of *architectura numismatica* is the fact that the researcher is trapped as it were in a circle. In many cases there is no saying what monument or even what type of monument is represented on the coin. In order to identify the coin-building, it is necessary to collect the archaeological evidence. But to collect the archaeological evidence, it is first necessary

---

[1] Günter Fuchs, *Architekturdarstellungen auf römischen Münzen der Republik und der frühen Kaiserzeit*, Deutsches Archäologisches Institut, *Antike Münzen und geschnittene Steine*, ed. Erich Boehringer, Bd. i (Berlin, 1969).

[2] Filippo Coarelli, 'Navalia, Tarentum e la topografia del Campo Marzio Meridionale', *Quaderni dell'Istituto di topografia antica della Università di Roma, V, Studi di topografia romana* (Rome, 1968), 27–37, at p. 27.

to identify the coin, which completes the circle. Finally, and by no means least importantly, it is the researcher's own scholarship that determines the validity of the identification, which indeed can be said of all research. Fuchs's work is a corpus; his pages, beyond their substantive contribution, make it clear that one cannot simply list the architectural coins, attach some archaeological commentary, and hope to call it a corpus.[1]

It is axiomatic that in numismatic research no varieties can be neglected. Especially is this basic to the study of architectural types. These often appear in a series over an extended period of time. Variations in the series invariably occur; too frequently these are not given proper evaluation. Fuchs himself did not present all the known varieties of the coins he covered. The only collection that can plausibly be called comprehensive is the unpublished dissertation of Donald F. Brown[2] and even this is limited to temples. His published monograph,[3] although an excellent study in art history, only inadequately carries over the research of his dissertation. For one thing, it scarcely gives a clue to the truly immense collection of types and varieties he made. We cite one example: the Jupiter Capitoline temple. How many varieties Fuchs collected we do not know. He publishes seven. Brown collected 150. His monograph publishes four.

Fuchs does not cite the Brown dissertation. The inference is that he did not see it, perhaps because it was unavailable to him. Today a few copies are in circulation. Although Brown was the first to use the painstaking method that resulted in this vast collection of coins,[4] subsequent excavations and numismatic studies have dated some of his conclusions. For example, he incorrectly assumed that the variations in the number of columns and steps and in some other respects necessarily signified that the monument had been altered or even rebuilt. He was not, indeed, is not alone in error. In my opinion the rule which has been found valid for Greek Imperials is valid for the Roman. I quote Professor Bellinger: '. . . decorations [i.e. variations] . . . are not mutually exclusive but exhibit the die-engraver's habit of selecting one detail or another when his field was too small to include them all.'[5]

Why did a moneyer or an emperor choose the building that appears on his coin? Both Fuchs and Brown looked for the answer to this problem.

[1] Numerous lists of this kind are available. A recent one by Balázs Kapossy has a significant bibliographical note: 'Es kann hier nur auf die wichtigsten Werke hingewiesen werden, die über die Einzelfragen weitere Auskunft geben.' ('Denkmäler des antiken Rom auf Münzabbildungen. Bemerkungen zur Antiken-Ausstellung im Bernischen Historischen Museum', *Schweizer Münzblätter* (1965), Heft 58, 54–9.)

[2] Donald F. Brown, *Architectura Numismatica*, Part I, *Temples in Rome, diss., unpublished*, New York University, 1941.

[3] Idem, *Temples of Rome as Coin Types*, NNM xc, 1940.

[4] This work was part of a project that was inspired and initiated under the title *Architectura Numismatica* by Karl Lehmann at New York University.

[5] A. R. Bellinger, *The Coins, The Excavations at Dura-Europos, Final Report VI* (New Haven, 1949), 160.

Brown in reviewing the representations of temples in Rome from the Volteius issue, now dated 78 B.C., to that of Alexander Tyrans, A.D. 311, claimed that 'most instances' can be classified as either: (1) representing actual building activity of the moneyer or the emperor, (2) commemorating some event important to the empire, (2) 'picturizing' a religious ceremony, or (4) commemorating an essentially political event. I am not entirely satisfied with any of the classifications and particularly not with no. 1 for the reasons stated in the last paragraph.[1] Brown does not associate any temple type directly with the commemoration of an ancestor. This motive, however, particularly interested Fuchs. Dealing specifically with the pre-Augustan coins, he found that some, not all, of the secular buildings were issued to honour an ancestor. By this show of Roman piety for an ancestor, the moneyer obliquely honoured himself.

According to Fuchs, the Romans hit on architectural types as the best means of showing their piety; this happened in the late second century B.C. About seventy-five years later the realistic portrait was adopted on coins. Fuchs believes that both the architectural type and the realistic portrait were tied up with *the cult of the individual* (words and italics mine).[2] Was the architectural type the result of the cultural climate in Rome in the second century B.C. and was it really 'von rein römischer Erfindung'?[3]

Fuchs takes note of the fact that there were architectural types issued before the Roman period. These were Oriental and could not, he claims, have directly influenced the Romans. The few early Greek types Fuchs leaves unexplained. These pre-Roman types are not illustrated by Fuchs. The earliest known temple on coins is well known from the British Museum handbook.[4] But another example from the same city, Hierapolis-Bambyce [Pl. 4. 1], shows the pitched roof of the temple more accurately.[5] There is some question whether the earlier Shrine of Ana at Tarsus is a temple [Pl. 4. 2]. There is no doubt the die-maker was attempting to show a sacred area of some sort. The flat roof would be appropriate to the East. It should be noted that there are more than three so-called antefixes, the number usually assumed to be on all examples. At least one coin clearly shows five. An early Syrian seal represents the same decorative element [Fig. 1]. Both coin and seal point

---

[1] The reason why a type was selected has been the preoccupation of numismatists since the sixteenth century. The difference between the early and the modern analyses can be seen in a charming article by Thomas Burgon, 'An Inquiry into the motive which influenced the Ancients in their choice of the various representations which we find stamped on their money', *Numismatic Journal* (September 1836), 1–35. For Mr. Thomas Burgon, religion was the sole motive.

[2] On the same subject see Margarete Bieber, 'The Aqua Marcia in Coins and Ruins', *Archaeology* 1967, 194–6.

[3] Fuchs, op cit., 9.

[4] B. V. Head, *A Guide to the Principal Coins of the Greeks* (London, 1932), pl. 28, 32.

[5] P. S. Ronzevalle, 'Les Monnaies de la dynastie de 'Abd-Hadad et les cultes de Hiérapolis-Bambycé,' *Mélanges de l'Université Saint Joseph*, Tome xxiii, fasc. i (1940), 5.

to the traditional stepped crenellations which we know from early Mesopotamian architecture, and recently used to interpret the later and more famous
Eastern coin of Bar Kochba of the Judaean revolt.[1] A small piece of Achaemenid art shows the moulding almost exactly as we know it from monumental
architecture [**Fig. 2**]. Another coin referred to by Fuchs can be described in
more detail. This is the Sandon shrine type of Tarsus. Professor Seyrig
published a reliquary which represents the building of the coins [**Pl. 7. 33**].
It was a pyramidal aedicula which housed the cult image of Sandon, set upon
a podium. The original building was undoubtedly made of wood.[2]

FIG. 1. Syrian Seal. Åbe Åkenström, 'Archi-
tektonische Terrakottaplatten in Stockholm',
*Skrifter utgivna av Svenska Institutet i Athen*
i (1951), Abb. 8, 2.

FIG. 2. Plaquette from Sardis. *McGraw-
Hill Encyclopedia of World Art* i,
pl. 540.

The pre-Roman examples from the Greek world have something in common which may explain their exceptionally early appearance. They are all
altars, not the very well-known small altars so often seen on coins, but monumental buildings. The issues are of Parium [**Pl. 4. 3**], Mantinea [**Pl. 4. 4**], and
Crimissa [**Pl. 4. 5**].[3] Rarely published, they are particularly important today
because of the increasing number of monumental altars coming to light in
the Near East. Significant also is the fact that monumental altars are definitely
Oriental in origin. Fuchs relies on the coins issued before Augustus not only

[1] M. Avi-Yonah, 'The Façade of Herod's Temple, an attempted reconstruction', *Reli-
gions in Antiquity, Essays in Memory of Erwin Ramsdell Goodenough*, ed. Jacob Neusner
(Leiden, 1968), 335, fig. 3.     [2] *Syria*, 1959, 43 ff.
[3] This coin of Crimissa is assigned by Fuchs to Sicily on the basis of B. V. Head, *The
Coins of Sicily* (London, 1903); it has alternatively been attributed to Crimissa, Lucania,
Italy in *NC* 1931, 87, 88.

to establish a case for his 'von rein römischer Erfindung' but to show some of the die-makers' formulae and failings. A dozen or so architectural types in a period of almost one hundred years can hardly serve as a basis of a statistical table. With Augustus came a much increased use of the architectural type, both in East and West. In fact, because of the large number of provincial local mints, the East led the empire in the production of these types. The problem of who introduced this convention is like that of the creation of the real dome. Perhaps it is not who invented something but who exploited it that is crucial. But more important, even after all this, no compelling reason is adduced by Fuchs, or, for that matter, by any one else why the Romans should have selected architectural types for their coins, to express their piety, politics, or personal vanity. This type of inquiry as it has been said 'dépasse l'histoire de l'art. Mais on peut établir ce que cherchaient les contemporains dans l'œuvre qui leur était destiné et par là remonter du public au créateur.'[1] Should we assume that the use of architectural types mark the beginning of what was a century later to become a special interest of the Roman world?

That some of the problems raised by Fuchs still fascinate and will continue to do so is evident from a recent title, 'Noch einmal Vesta auf dem Palatin'.[2] Kolbe offers a new reading of an inscription and interprets the well-known Sorrentine base as a representation of the temple of Vesta in the Forum. He concludes that there was no temple of Vesta on the Palatine. Fuchs comes to the opposite conclusion: the coin of Tiberius and the Sorrentine base refer to the shrine on the Palatine.[3] All those who have studied the numismatic evidence were troubled by the difference between the Tiberius coin and others in the Vesta-in-Forum series. To account for the difference between the Tiberius issue and an earlier one of the first century B.C. Kolbe is obliged to suppose that Augustus rebuilt the temple. Those who have studied the free-wheeling designs of Greek Imperial coins would find the Tiberius building nothing more than a different view of the same temple by a different die-maker. It is surprising that Fuchs did not keep this coin in the Vesta-in-Forum series yet is willing to entertain the possibility of including the coin of L. Rubrius Dossenus, now dated 91 B.C. This coin does not in fact show a round temple; the representation is that of a typical rectangular structure with pediment. Fuchs advances the argument that the die-makers were inexperienced with building types at this time and lacked the

---

[1] Pierre Lavedan, *Répresentation des villes dans l'art du moyen âge* (Paris, 1954), 9.

[2] Hans-Georg Kolbe, *RM* 1966/7, 94–104.

[3] Wartime publications were not available to many. Fuchs did not know the article in *NC*, 'Divus Augustus Pater; a study in the Aes Coinage of Tiberius' 1941, 97–116. Dr. Sutherland proves that the shrine on the Palatine near Augustus' house was dedicated not to Vesta but to Divus Augustus; the Tiberius coin represented this shrine. This study is also omitted by Ferdinando Castagnoli, 'Note sulla topografia del Palatino e del Foro Romano,' *Archeologia Classica* 1964, 173–99. It is suggested here that the coin represents the house of Augustus.

technique to delineate a round building. This is not convincing since the near-contemporary Volteius issue, now dated 78 B.C.,[1] exhibits a highly sophisticated technique.

It cannot be said that early die-makers lacked the skill to delineate buildings. A provincial type, for instance, of the early first century B.C. represents a two-storeyed building with startling realism [Pl. 4. 6–7]. The dome on a rectangular building and an unusual covered gallery are quite special. The dome is certainly not a real one. As far as I know there is no similar arrangement on a coin except on some issues of India [Pl. 4. 8–9]. These have been dated in the second half of the second century B.C.[2] David MacDowall has kindly informed me that not even a date in the first century can be proven; the early first century A.D. is more reasonable. Whatever the date, these are early examples of architectural types. The Graeco-Roman influence requires no comment. The monument represented is a stupa but exactly what the dome, gallery, and columned portion of the coin actually represent has not yet been fully explored. No one can reasonably question the skill of these early and 'provincial' die-makers.

Fuchs rejects the conventionally accepted identification of the Rubrius temple coin, affirming that the shape of a snake is in reality that of a flame. But at least one example, heretofore unpublished, clearly shows the presence of a snake [Pl. 5. 12]. Fuchs admits, of course, that there is a snake on Pl. 5. 10–11 but believes they are not identifiable as the object of the temple coin. I myself think the snake is wound around an omphalos as we find on a Tauromenium coin [Pl. 5. 15] and that in all cases of the Rubrius issues we have such an object upon a pedestal. As long as there are such sharp differences of opinion, one questions the possibility of making a definitive corpus of relevant coins.

I am far from suggesting Fuchs did not realize the importance of gathering all available examples. On the contrary, although he did not have as long a list of Egnatius coins as Brown, he had a better magnifying glass. Because there is no pediment shown, Brown concluded that the building represented was a portico, not a temple. Brown thought the entablature continued beyond the confines of the coin. Fuchs, on the other hand, explained the absence of the pediment and shows that the entablature was not in all cases cut off by the coin border. Beyond this, Fuchs points out a very distinctive series of vertical lines along the architrave. These he interprets as the representation of a Doric/Etruscan metope and triglyph frieze, appropriate to an Etruscan building. Another example shows two lines instead of one, which further strengthens Fuchs's conclusion [Pl. 5. 16]. The two-line design is

[1] M. H. Crawford, *Roman Republican Coin Hoards*, Table XIII; for the Rubrius Dossenus coin, *supra*, see Table XII.

[2] Kalyan Kumai Dasgupta, *The Adumbaras*, Calcutta Sanscrit College Research Series xliv (Calcutta, 1965).

a numismatic device known, for example, from an issue of Myrina, Aeolis [Pl. 5. 17].

The Palicanus coin [Pl. 5. 18] which Coarelli interprets is also part of the Fuchs study. At long last the handbooks are corrected. Both arrive at the same conclusion, each agreeing that the arched building with prows is not the rostra. It is a representation of part of a harbour. However, they disagree on another point, and here one must note the extreme divergence of opinion of two informed scholars. Fuchs identifies the object in the upper field of the coin as a bedstead. He frankly avoids accounting for the presence of this somewhat incongruous object in a maritime scene. But he equates it with an Etruscan funeral bed of the seventh century B.C. It does, indeed, resemble the Etruscan bed but it lacks the characteristic head-rest. Coarelli brushes aside the bedstead and identifies the object as one of the dockyard buildings, the ναυπάγια. In fact, he goes so far as to say that the curve of the ship-berths is a numismatic reference to the curve of the Tiber and he locates the port at the bend between the Circus Flamininus and the so-called Aedes Neptuni. Two objections stand in the way of this topographical interpretation. Fuchs convincingly demonstrates from paintings and other coins that the curve of the building is a traditional convention used to show harbours and not necessarily imposed on the design by the circular outline of the coin. One need only glance at harbour coin types to see the validity of this.[1] However, the British Museum coin has a detail (Fuchs's plate is not clear) that shows a straight section of land visible immediately above the superstructure of the shipberths [Pl. 5. 18]. The land is not curved at all.[2] The bend in the river on which Coarelli relies is absent. As for Fuchs's bedstead, it bears a precise resemblance to the bisellium of contemporary and near-contemporary coins [Pl. 5. 19–20]. Undoubtedly the bisellium refers to the moneyer who was a triumvir or to his father who was a tribune.[3] It may be a punning device[4] or an honorific symbol. In the absence of Palicanus' nomina and officia this cannot be determined.

Another arched building [Pl. 6. 22] to be seen on the coins of Censorinus, studied by Fuchs and Coarelli, is more than interesting. Fuchs could not have known either Coarelli's article or another by Alföldi with its rebuttal by Bertini.[5] The identification of the arches as the Aqua Marcia has been generally rejected. The coin is associated with the port of Ostia. It is apparent that although the column with statue is shown on some coins within one arch,

---

[1] For coins showing ports, see A. A. Boyce, 'The Harbour of Pompeiopolis, A Study in Roman Ports and Dated Coins', *AJA* 1958, 66–78, pls. 10–15.

[2] The B.M. coin is repeated here to show the detail of the shore.

[3] This is true if the father's name was L. Lollius Palikanus, tribune under Pompey.

[4] I owe this suggestion to Joan Martin of the Department of Coins and Medals, British Museum.

[5] Andrea Alföldi, 'La più antica rappresentazione del porto di Ostia', *Numismatica* 1964, 99–1–4; Antonio Bertini, ibid. 270–4.

the column did not actually stand there. It stood, in fact, on the shore [Pl. 6. 21]. Along with Bertini, I question Alföldi's interpretation. Alföldi relies upon the fact that the column is made up of 'punti irregolari', which for him is a numismatic device for representing reliefs on a spirally fluted column. One of the British Museum coins which he did not use [Pl. 6. 21] actually shows a spiral column. But the 'punti irregolari' are often very regular. There is no saying which of the die-makers was nearer reality except that I should assume the 'punti irregolari' were due to wear not to any artistic intent. It is, as I have said above, always necessary to collect and 'weigh' all available examples. The main thesis that the column was decorated with narrative reliefs and was therefore a prototype of Trajan's column was rejected by Bertini for other reasons, and rightly.

Much sharper difference of opinion exists about the denarius of Pompey the Younger. Spurning the identification as the Pharos of Messana, Fuchs suggests that the tower does not resemble a Pharos as depicted on reliefs and paintings: it lacks the multiple storeys and has only two windows where many more are usually indicated. Fuchs tentatively suggests it was more like the Tower of the Winds in Athens, the well-known octagonal Horologium. A provincial type [Pl. 6. 23], not in Fuchs, has been identified with the denarius.[1] Grant concludes that the building portrayed on both coins was the Pharos of Messana. If one compares the denarius with other lighthouse coins, the identification as a Pharos is inevitable. What is generally not emphasized is the die-makers' practice of abbreviating. Even some of the famous Alexandrian examples seem deliberately to have omitted details which we know existed from other coins in the series. A Cilician type with ship is a round tower with no upper zones much like the building on the Roman and provincial coins [Pl. 6. 24]. It is self-evident that this is a lighthouse; the legend confirms the identification.

Provincial architectural types of Sicily and Italy have yet to be given the importance in *architectura numismatica* that they deserve. For example, the coin of Caralis, Sardinia, could be profitably included in studying the Jupiter Capitoline series of Rome [Pl. 6. 25]. I see it as an exact copy of the Volteius Capitoline coin.[2] There can be no doubt that Roman types inspired the provincial, East and West, after the middle of the first century B.C. A coin of Corinth [Pl. 6. 26], for example, with round temple has its origin in a denarius with the Vesta-in-Forum shrine, of c. 50 B.C.[3] The Sardinian coin bears the legend VENERIS. Was the actual temple a copy of the Roman Capitolium? Did it have three divinities, i.e. Venus, Mars, Divus Julius? Did it have three cellae? Numismatic proof is available that the three doors of the Volteius coin meant there were three cellae on the interior.[4] On other

---

[1] Michael Grant, *From Imperium to Auctoritas* (Cambridge, 1946), 194.
[2] *BMCRR* pl. xlii. 1; Fuchs, pl. 2, 16–18.  [3] Grant, op. cit. 266.
[4] Of the well-known Aurelian relief in the Palazzo dei Conservatori, it is said: '. . . the

coins of the Capitolium series [Pl. 6. 27], the three cult statues were brought forward to the face of the building, together with their protective arches.[1] The three arches represent those that actually decorated the three aediculae of the interior. About the Sardinian coin, on the other hand, I have misgivings concerning the relevance of the three doors as evidence of three cellae. Because it is an out-and-out copy of the Roman die and because the legend indicated the dedication of the shrine to one divinity only, the three doors mean three doors and nothing more. The Sardinian copy, however, indicates how great an impression the ancient Etruscan shrine made on the first century B.C., and how provincial people built similar shrines in their own cities.

Another detail of the Volteius coin, the line of curves along the raking cornices, has been used as evidence for the Etruscan shrine. These, Gjerstad believes, represented the fictile spiral ornaments which were found in other, but contemporary, Etruscan sites.[2] Gjerstad uses similar evidence to reconstruct the friezes with horses and chariots. The quadriga of the elevation is based on literary evidence. I believe there is substantive backing for these details in the quadriga and the emphasis on horses and human figures which are found on some, not all, of the remaining coins of the Capitoline series.

But there are doubts about what coins belong in the Capitoline series. Brown had excluded a well-known coin said to have been minted in Ephesus in A.D. 82. Zucker, however, accepts it, suggesting that the head (?) in the tympanum is that of the god Summanus.[3] Literary evidence has a statue of this god decorating the Capitoline pediment in the third century B.C. But Zucker took no account of the fact that provincial cities built their own Capitolia which sometimes imitated the Roman Capitolium. Furthermore the eastern cities almost invariably exploited their own buildings on their coins. Böethius, commenting on Gjerstad's reconstruction of the Etruscan temple shows that he has no faith in the coins 'riguarda il numero ed il tipo

three cella doors signify three cults . . . an ideal representation of the Italic Etruscan three-cella temple. . . .' (Per Gustaf Hamberg, *Studies in Roman Imperial Art with Special Reference to the State Reliefs of the Second Century* (Uppsala, 1945), 96). Cf. the *Enciclop. dell'arte*, s.v. Frontone (1958, fig. 979), where a well-known Roman relief is described as the pediment of the temple of Juppiter Capitolinus (Bluma L. Trell, *The Temple of Artemis at Ephesos*, *NNM* cvii (1945), pl. xix). The three *portes-fenêtres* of the pediment represented in the relief was taken, I assume, to be a reference to the three doors of the temple itself. There is no evidence that the Capitoline had a pediment decorated with such openings. Nor is there any evidence, the relief itself apart, that such pedimental decoration was used in the West before the Early Christian period.

[1] Brown's dissertation lists this type but it is not illustrated in his monograph. It has not found its way into the handbooks, for example, E. Nash, *Pictorial Dictionary of Ancient Rome; Enciclop. dell'arte*, etc.

[2] E. Gjerstad, 'Early Rome, III, Fortifications, Domestic Architecture, Sanctuaries, Stratigraphic Excavations', *Acta Inst. Rom. Regni Sueciae*, xvii, 3 (Lund, 1960), 168–204; idem, 'Synthesis of the Archaeological Evidence', ibid. xvii, 4 (1966), 388–98.

[3] H. Zucker, 'Capitolium restitutum', *Jahrbuch des Bernischen Historischen Museums* (1959/60), 289–95.

delle colonne, sia per le sculture del timpano'.[1] In the light of this scepticism, it is surprising that he accepts as pertinent the evidence of another early coin, the issue of Plaetorius. Fuchs offers no identification whatever, suggesting merely that the contemporary Romans must have understood this strange representation. The coin shows a deep pediment, decorated by an anguipede monster, nothing more. Böethius maintains that the coin was issued to celebrate the rebuilding of the temple in the first century B.C. The coin, by showing only a pediment, emphasizes 'la parte forse più sensazionale del tempio ricostruito'.

While some scholars are sceptical about the coins as evidence, others assume that the Capitolium was rebuilt in the early imperial period and its style changed. As proof of this they point to the variations in the Capitoline series, as well as to the change in the style of the building shown on the coins. Variations usually indicate the disparate views of different die-makers. There is also an important reason for the difference in the style of the buildings which has considerable pertinence.

Here we have a remarkable fact, made more remarkable because seemingly it has never been noticed heretofore. The figures in the coin pediments duplicate exactly in much smaller size the cult images below on the façade. Moreover, the postures of the figures change from coin to coin. Where the cult images between the columns are standing, they are shown standing in the pediment. When Juppiter is shown sitting between the columns with the goddesses standing, the die-maker repeats exactly this composition in the pediment above. There are other similar changes and duplications. No one can possibly claim the actual cult images within the temple kept changing their positions. Nor was there any rule that required the divinities of the shrine to be represented in the pediment. The practice in fact was the opposite.

What has not been fully appreciated by those who would reject the coins completely as untruthful or who claim the changes in the series represent rebuilding is that Roman die-makers were artists. As artists they were subject to the same influences as their contemporary colleagues, the sculptors of Rome. Like the style of the Roman historical reliefs, for example, the style of the coins was both realistic, an inheritance from the Romano-Italic world, and also poetic, imaginative, an inheritance from the Greek. The playful design of the figures on the façade and in the pediment was the imaginative part of the die-maker's art. So also was the Greek look of the temples. But in all other respects I believe the coins were truthful, that they all represented the ancient Etruscan shrine (sixth or fifth century B.C.), the style of which was never changed.

---

[1] Axel Böethius, 'Veteris Capitoli humilia tecta', *Acta ad archaeologiam et artium historiam pertinentia, Inst. Rom. Norvegiae*, Oslo Universitetsforlaget 1962, 27–33 (see p. 27 n. 3); cf. Gjerstad's reply ibid., 'A propositio della ricostruzione del tempio arcaico di Giove Capitolino in Roma', 35–40.

Fuchs devotes a considerable portion of his book to the Villa Publica coin. He concludes that the coin shows a building of two storeys, where the upper storey was a recessed gallery, fronted by columns. But Fuchs is troubled by the columns in the second storey, an admittedly unusual structural arrangement. He therefore offers his reconstruction with reservations. Again another provincial coin comes to our assistance [Pl. 6. 28]. It presents an almost exact replica of the top portion of the building on the Villa Publica coin which Fuchs took or mistook for an upper-recessed gallery. There is no doubt in my mind that the row of columns with a half-pitched roof is a numismatic representation or an abbreviated view of a portico. The top section of the Villa Publica picture is also a portico. This part has found its way up by the numismatic formula of above instead of behind. It is shown smaller than the columned building below for the simple reason that it was actually further away. We would seem to have, therefore, an open area with a portico in the rear and an entrance columned building in front. This arrangement happily fits the functional requirements of the building in the Campus Martius as it is described in the literature[1] and particularly in Varro, *de re Rustica*, 3. 2. 4: 'praeterea cum ad rem publicam administrandam haec sit utilis ubi cohortes ad dilectum consuli adductae considant, ubi arma ostendant, ubi censores censu admittant populum'.

Another detail of the Villa Publica coins presents a problem. The short columns of the lower building have been interpreted as door- or gate-posts. But Fuchs has another theory. He makes two classifications of the coins, on which he bases his elevation. This shows the short columns as half-columns from which arches spring attached to taller columns. A horizontal entablature is carried by the tall columns. I find four main classes of types: two with short columns and two without. In one of these [Pl. 6. 29], the arches begin high above the capitals, springing as it were from the spandrels. There is no hint of the architrave suggested by Fuchs and the short columns are not attached to the tall columns; they are definitely free standing. Until we find a similar and controlled case of such free-standing columns I do not think we can settle this fascinating problem.

Fuchs's work is so comprehensive that it would be ungracious to cavil about the paucity of bibliography in some instances. But with respect to the well-known Curia coin [Pl. 6. 30], there is another and opposing theory.[2] A hint to this effect would have been useful. Also, as will appear below, another series of coins should have been included. It is generally assumed that the Augustan coin represents the Curia. From the Augustan period there is some literary evidence concerning the building, also a door and an

[1] For the relevant passages, see J. R. Hamilton, 'T. Didius and the Villa Publica', *NC* 1955, 224–8.

[2] E. Voerel, 'Die Darstellung eines Keltentempels auf einem Denar von Kaiser Augustus', *Jahrbuch der Schweizerischen Gesellschaft für Urgeschichte* 1939, 150–7; T. G. E. Powell, *The Celts* (London, 1958), 274.

Ionic capital. But we have no idea what the Curia looked like in the Julio-Claudian period. If we accept the usual identification of the coin, we must assume that there was no change in the style or appearance at any time between the first and the end of the third century A.D., although we know that the building was reconstructed twice, once under Domitian and again under Diocletian.

The opposing view makes out that the coin represents a Gallo-Roman shrine. I must confess that for this all the wrong reasons have been given. Yet there is some evidence that supports such an identification which I should like to offer here. A stele from Luxembourg [Pl. 7. 34] represents a fanum which appears to have a similar elevation. This shrine has been called an intermediate type between an 'altheimischen Umgangstempel der Treverer' and a typical Roman imperial building. Other sanctuaries are even closer to the coin: at Elst [Pl. 7. 36], Saint-Ouen-de-Thouberville [Pl. 7. 35], and the temple of Janus at Autun [Pl. 7. 37]. The core of the Autun monument is still standing and it bears a striking likeness to the Curia at Rome. It has similar windows and similar holes in the wall which must have held a pitched roof of a surrounding arcade.[1] But the question still remains: does the Augustan coin represent a temple like that of Autun which is dated to the first century A.D. or the Curia of Rome whose appearance we know but only as it was in the late third century A.D.?

In making a decision, as in a judicial procedure, all the evidence must be considered. This was not done, as far as I know, in the 'Curia case'. In the many studies, only one type was used, the Augustan issue. Although there are many examples of this type, they show no significant variations. The mint is considered 'uncertain' and probably 'Eastern'; Robert Carson assures me it is Roman. What has never been noted is that the same type appears on issues of Juba II [Pl. 6. 31–2]. The only difference is that instead of a Nike on the apex, there are crescent and star; instead of IMP CAES, the legend is AVGVSTI. Here there are surprising variations among the examples. At least one [Pl. 6. 31] proves beyond any doubt that Juba's die-makers copied the Augustan coin. On other examples, some of the surrounding colonnade has been removed, as it were, to give a view of the front of the building [Pl. 6. 32]. The windows are suppressed and the entrance enlarged so that details of the door can be engraved. The presence of the crescent and star as the top acroteria can be explained as a symbol of Juba's kingdom. The legend denotes a dedication to the emperor.

The admittedly unusual aspect of the building represented on the Augustan coin and on its copy has added to the difficulty of identification. But what

---

[1] A. Grenier, *Manuel d'archéologie gallo-romaine, III, L'Architecture* (Paris, 1958), fig. 151. A very recent excavation has produced a Gaulish temple with colonnade: W. Vanvin-ckenvoye, *Opgravingen te Tongeren in 1963/4. Publicaties van het prov. Gallo-Romeins Museum*, 8 (Tongeren, 1965), fig. 60.

we have learned from other provincial types indicates that the Juba coin represents a Curia built by the Numidian king in his own capital. To honour Augustus, his friend and patron, he made his Senate House an exact copy of the emperor's in Rome. Strictly speaking, the Curia in Rome was not Augustan. It had been planned and begun by Julius Caesar in the fateful year of 44 B.C. Augustus must have followed the plans of his great-uncle; the building is dedicated to him. I am convinced that these plans did not omit pronounced Celtic structural characteristics. In the long years Caesar spent in Gaul, and given his insatiable curiosity about all things, it is difficult to suppose that he was not aware of, and appreciative of, local architecture. Nevertheless, although some evidence of the peripteral columns has been found, we cannot say that the case of the Curia has been settled.

The Aqua Marcia has been the subject of many numismatic studies.[1] Fuchs rejects one early coin of the series said to represent the monument, stating that 'der Typ ist von M. Stuart überinterpretiert worden'. Fuchs himself analyses his material from more points of view than has ever been done. I would have expected him to appreciate the Stuart article since architectural coins have generally been neglected or under interpreted, if I may put it that way. Fuchs dates this early coin to the last part of the second century B.C. and offers a new interpretation of the legend. Because a dot follows the words Mn. AEMILIO, he believes this was in the dative case and that it was the name of the individual seated upon the horse above the building. LEP he takes as the nominative and as the name of the moneyer, Lepidus. The building, or the three arches below the equestrian figure, is tentatively identified as the base of the statue. Fuchs insists we know nothing about M'. Aemilius. He is equally sceptical about the equestrian figure on another coin in the series, a much less controversial coin because the arches are identified by the legend. He questions the identification of the statue as that of Marcius Philippus, the moneyer's ancestor, who is usually accredited with building the aqueduct. Because Stuart's article[2] has been relegated to a footnote in Fuchs or completely hidden in other works by our modern bibliographical shortcuts, it is well to summarize it here. Like Brown's dissertation, it was based on a comprehensive collection of the coins as well as the literary and archaeological evidence. Stuart dates the controversial coin to 90 B.C. and offers convincing proof that the aqueduct was begun in 179 B.C., not by Marcius Philippus but by an ancestor of Aemilius Lepidus, and that it was subsequently extended to the Capitoline by another ancestor. Marcius Philippus, the ancestor of Lucius Marcius who minted the coin of 56 B.C., completed the aqueduct; he did not initiate it. The arches on the coin of Aemilius Lepidus and on that of Lucius Marcius are absolutely identical.

[1] Fuchs, op. cit. 14 and 26.
[2] Meriwether Stuart, 'The Denarius of M'. Aemilius Lepidus and the Aqua Marcia', *AJA* 1945, 226–51.

Both therefore represent the Aqua Marcia. In both cases the coins were issued to honour ancestors whose statues appear as part of the coin design; these are not representations of the actual equestrian statues. It is interesting to note that Professor Bieber thought the statue of Lucius Marcius was a representation of the actual monument.[1] The equestrian figures differ because the ancestors were different. The Aemilius issues are amazingly reliable; they show the buttresses in the spandrels that actually existed. Only three arches are shown because only three were visible at the Via Praenestina: the ancient die-maker reproduced what the ancient traveller saw. But how does an Aemilius associate himself or his ancestor with a building known as Aqua Marcia? The answer is in the literary sources: before it got its famous name, it was called Aqua Fulvia or Aqua Aemilia Fulvia. The elder Aemilius and Professor Stuart, both neglected, can take consolation in the fact that even Marcius was forgotten. In the fifth century A.D., as Stuart shows, it was Marcus Agrippa who got the credit for the building.

Over and above his patient scholarship, it is his own professional, architectural designs—Fuchs himself was an architect—that make his book exceptional. Especially worth noting is the elevation of the Basilica Aemilia taken from a prior study which he summarizes in the present volume. It is of course impossible for me here to comment on all the building-coins he considers. I am sure it is now obvious that the making of a comprehensive corpus such as his, is 'laboriosum infinitumque'—'laboriosum' because every coin type and variation must be found and studied; 'infinitum' because archaeological excavations keep yielding what seems to be an infinity of material.[2]

## LIST OF ILLUSTRATIONS
### [PLATES 4–7]

1. Hierapolis-Bambyce. P. S. Ronzevalle, 'Les Monnaies de la dynastie de 'Abd-Hadad et les cultes de Hiérapolis-Bambycé' *Mélanges de l'Université Saint Joseph* 1940, pl. i, 3.
2. Tarsus. Pozzi-Naville, 1920, pl. lxxxiii, 2851.

---

[1] Professor Bieber believes the statue was placed above the great aqueduct in or near Rome, see *Archaeology*, loc. cit.

[2] It is equally obvious that the first and certainly possible step toward facilitating the use of Roman architectural coins is the making of a comprehensive bibliography in 'applied' numismatics. Cornelius C. Vermeule, who hit on this happy title, has set the pattern in his *A Bibliography of Applied Numismatics in the fields of Greek and Roman Archaeology and the Fine Arts*, London, 1956; *Classical Numismatics and Archaeology in Middle Eastern Studies, 1937–1957, Middle East Supplement to Research Bibliography*, 127–36. These should not only be brought up-to-date but considerably enlarged. Many non-numismatic journals and books, such as excavation reports, not only publish newly found coins, but also include valuable commentaries. Unfortunately, some of these are hidden as it were in the very pages that reveal other discoveries. I should like to suggest a similar bibliography for the Greek Imperial architectural coins, but more valuable now would be the publication of the coins themselves.

3. Parium. *BMC Mysia*, no. 42, pl. 21, 11.
4. Mantinea. *BMC Pelop.*, no. 6, pl. 34, 23.
5. Crimissa. G. F. Hill, *Coins of Ancient Sicily* (London, 1903), pl. xiii. 2.
6. Paestum. B.M., cf. *BMC Italy*, no. 77.
7. „ B.M.
8. Adumbara (Siradasa). *BMC Coins of Ancient India*, no. 2.
9. Adumbara (Siradasa). Ibid., no. 9.
10. Rome. *BMCRR*, no. 2459.
11. „ Ibid., no. 2461, pl. xxxviii, 5.
12. Rome. B.M.
13. Cast of coin of Rome in B.M., provenance unknown.
14. Cast of coin of Rome in B.M., provenance unknown.
15. Tauromenium. Hill, op. cit., pl. xiv, 7.
16. Rome. *BMCRR*, no. 3276.
17. Myrina. B.M. cf. *BMC Aeolis*, no. 44, pl. xxviii, 7.
18. Rome. *BMCRR*, no. 4011, pl. L, 18.
19. Rome. Ibid., no. 2465, pl. xxxviii, 7.
20. Augustus. *BMCRE*, no. 131, pl. 4, 17.
21. Rome *BMCRR*, no. 2417.
22. „ Ibid., no. 2419.
23. Panormus. *BMC Sicily*, no. 22.
24. Aegeao. F. Imhoef-Blumer, *Kleinasiatische Münzen* (Vienna, 1901), (Cilicia), pl. xvi, 19.
25. Caralis (Sardinia). B.M.
26. Corinth. Michael Grant, *From Imperium to Auctoritas* (Cambridge, 1946), pl. viii. 19.
27. Vespasian. *BMCRE*, no. 647, pl. 25, 10.
28. Paestum. *BMC Italy*, no. 61.
29. Rome. *BMCRR*, no. 3857.
30. Augustus. *BMCRE*, no. 631, pl. 15, 12.
31-2. Juba II. B.M. cf. Jean Mazard, *Corpus Nummorum Numidiae Mauretaniae-que* (Paris, 1955), nos. 144–54.
33. Reliquary. *Syria* 1959, pl. viii.
34. Stele from Luxembourg. A. Grenier, *Manuel d'archéologie gallo-romaine, III, L'Architecture* (Paris, 1958), fig. 157.
35. Reconstruction of the fanum at Saint-Ouen-de-Thouberville. Grenier, op. cit., fig. 955.
36. Reconstruction of temple II at Elst. J. E. A. Th. Bogaers, *De Gallo-Romeinse tempels te Elst in der Over-Betuwe* (The Romano-Celtic Temples at Elst in the Over-Betuwe District), (The Hague, 1955), pls. 44–5.
37. Reconstruction of temple at Autun. P. M. Duval et P. Quoniam, 'Relevés des monuments antiques d'Autun', *Gallia* 1963, fig. 34.

# The Manufacture of Celtic Coins from the La Marquanderie Hoard

F. C. THOMPSON AND M. J. NASIR

IN the early summer of 1968 one of the authors had the opportunity, through the kindness of Dr. J. T. Renouf, of inspecting some 250 coins from this hoard. Although the very similar coins from the Rozel hoard have been described and most excellently illustrated by Major N. V. L. Rybot,[1] little or nothing appears to be known with any certainty regarding the technique employed in their manufacture. Work in this field should have further value as an exploration of the possibilities for other metallurgical research on ancient series in general.

FIG. 1. Coin No. 3. Boar mint-mark (Scale 2:1).

A comparison of the beautiful drawings made by Major Rybot with the illustrations in De La Tour,[2] can leave no doubt that these hoards emanated from a mint or mints of the Coriosolites, a tribe from the Armorican peninsula. From the very large numbers of die varieties it is equally clear that the life of the dies must have been short, due either to the use of too soft a bronze (?) or of too brittle a metal. The absence of the characteristic marks on the coins due to cracked dies makes the latter alternative most improbable. There is, however, one *major* division amongst the coins in the use of two basic die-marks: (1), a debased boar, **Fig. 1,** and (2) the so-called 'lyre', **Fig. 2.**

[1] *Bull. ann. Soc. jersiaise* xiii (1937) and in a more extensive work published by the Société in 1952.          [2] *Atlas de monnaies gauloises,* pl. xxii.

From the specimens examined in 1968, fifteen were selected as worthy of detailed metallurgical investigation, and, with the approval of the Executive Committee of the Société Jersiaise, presented to us for this work. The authors take this first opportunity of expressing their thanks to them and to Dr. Renouf, the Curator of the Société's Museum, for this kindness. Of these

FIG. 2. Coin No. A3. 'Lyre' mint-mark (scale 2 : 1).

fifteen coins, all proved to be Groups I and II with the boar mint-mark. At a later date four further coins with the 'lyre' mark were selected for us by Dr. Renouf. The latter specimens will be discussed later, but so far as the former are concerned it is sufficient to say that we found no evidence of any significant difference in the mode of manufacture of the coins of the two sub-groups.

*Weights*

## TABLE I
### *Boar Mint-mark*

| Group I | | Group II | |
|---------|------|----------|------|
| *Our no.* | *gm.* | *Our no.* | *gm.* |
| 1 | 6·23 | 9 | 6·42 |
| 2 | 6·42 | 10 | 6·21 |
| 3 | 6·26 | 11 | 6·61 |
| 4 | 6·38 | 12 | 6·68 |
| 5 | 6·24 | 13 | 5·92 |
| 6 | 6·29 | 14 | 6·34 |
| 7 | 6·56 | 15 | 6·20 |
| 8 | 6·44 | | |

The wide variation in weight finds an explanation in the fact that, as the initial visual examination reveals, each coin showed, to a greater or lesser degree, a defect on the rim such as results when a casting is broken away from the runner through which the molten metal had entered the mould. This is well shown in the case of coin no. 3 [**Fig. 1**], and provides indisputable evidence that the coins had started their lives as cast rondels. Further, in some cases the specimens were so irregular in shape as to suggest that the casting was ill run and had not filled the mould completely. Although the evidence is not sufficiently definite to justify dogmatism, it is our strong opinion that the rondels were cast horizontally from a vertical runner as is shown in Akerman's illustration[1] [**Fig. 3.**] It is known that ancient coins were cast in this manner, and our evidence is entirely consistent with the view that this represents the method employed in producing these coins.

FIG. 3. Akerman's casting arrangements.

*Chemical composition*

Already from the visual examination it had become probable that the metal from which the coins were made was a silver-copper alloy. All specimens had a more or less silvery surface though the interior, when the coin was broken in two, had a characteristically coppery appearance. Before our receipt of the coins they had been cleaned in ammonia, a treatment which dissolves the copper compounds formed superficially during manufacture or subsequent corrosion in the soil, leaving a surface enrichment of silver.

Four coins from the very similar Rozel hoard were analysed by Dr. S. W. Smith at the Royal Mint and published by the Société.[2] It is not clear from the illustrations what were the mint-marks, a matter which as will be seen

[1] *Coins of the Romans Relating to Britain* (London, 1844).
[2] *Bull. ann. Soc. jersiaise* xii (1934), 321–7.

later is a matter of importance, but these results are reproduced here for comparison with our own, together with two analyses quoted by Evans,[1] both of which refer to specimens with the boar mint-mark.

TABLE II

| | Royal Mint analyses of coins from the Rozel hoard | | | | Analyses quoted by Evans. Boar mint-mark | |
|---|---|---|---|---|---|---|
| | 1A | B | 5C | 5D | A | B |
| Copper | 80·9 | 79·65 | 89·1 | 72·9 | 84·1 | 79·5 |
| Silver | 16·15 | 17·2 | 9·1 | 18·9 | 4·1 | 17·7 |
| Tin | 2·4 | 1·84 | 1·55 | 6·74 | 11·66 | 2·65 |
| Lead | Tr. | 0·84 | Tr. | 0·47 | .. | .. |
| Iron | Tr. | Tr. | Tr. | Tr. | 0·05 | 0·09 |
| Nickel | .. | Tr. | Tr. | Tr. | .. | .. |
| Cobalt | ND | ND | ND | ND | .. | .. |
| Zinc | 0·14 | 0·32 | 0·12 | 0·16 | .. | .. |
| Gold | 0·02 | 0·01 | 0·01 | 0·05 | 0·02 | 0·02 |

Any balance is accounted for by non-metallic inclusions [Fig. 4].
Tr. = Trace less than 0·01 per cent.
ND = Not determined.

FIG. 4. Inclusions of slaggy matter.

Of our fifteen specimens with the boar mint-mark, six were submitted to detailed chemical analysis, the results being recorded in Table III.

[1] *Ancient British Coins* (London, 1864).

Excluding our coin no. 4, Evans's specimen A, and coin 5C from the Mint figures, it will be evident that although the compositions do vary considerably, the metal is essentially a silver–copper alloy with around a fifth or a sixth of its weight of silver. The small contents of gold, which could not be separated 'industrially' from such material at the date when the coins were made, are without significance. The irregularity in the proportions of tin, and to a lesser extent the other impurities, strongly suggest the admixture of a certain amount of scrap metal to the melt of which some was bronze.

TABLE III

| | Coins with the boar mint-mark | | | | | |
|---|---|---|---|---|---|---|
| | 4 | 5 | 8 | 10 | 13 | 14 |
| Copper | 97·1 | 75·5 | 77·2 | 79·8 | 80·9 | 78·0 |
| Silver | 1·03 | 19·9 | 20·0 | 17·0 | 17·45 | 19·5 |
| Tin | 0·50 | 3·80 | 2·25 | 2·45 | 1·11 | 2·15 |
| Lead | 0·05 | 0·22 | 0·23 | 0·40 | 0·09 | 0·33 |
| Iron | 0·04 | 0·06 | 0·03 | 0·03 | 0·06 | 0·04 |
| Nickel | 0·02 | 0·11 | 0·03 | 0·02 | 0·03 | 0·02 |
| Cobalt | 0·04 | 0·15 | 0·04 | 0·04 | 0·01 | 0·14 |
| Zinc | 0·01 | 0·02 | 0·01 | 0·01 | 0·03 | 0·01 |
| Gold | 0·010 | 0·045 | 0·011 | 0·025 | tr. | 0·007 |

Our coin no. 4, Evans's coin A, and coin 5C from the Rozel find merit further consideration. The first contains only a twentieth of the silver normally present and the others less than a half. Irregularities of this magnitude cannot have been accidental and suggest that the mint-master or the melter was making a considerable illicit profit. Incidentally the figures for specimen no. 4 illustrate admirably the extent to which students of a series, particularly billon, can be led astray by relying too implicitly on the analysis of a single, or even a few coins. Regarding the two analyses quoted by Evans, both of which refer to specimens with the boar mint-mark, the composition of B is completely consistent with our own results, whilst considering our and the Mint's abnormal results analysis A need cause no surprise.

### The manufacture of the coins

We may now turn attention to the evidence, using normal metallurgical techniques, of the way in which the finished coin emerged from the cast rondel. Firstly, we may discuss the low-power micrograph shown diagrammatically in **Fig. 5**, where the flow lines show that the metal entered the mould at the right-hand side, flowed along the lower and, later, the upper surface and then curled round at the far end. There is, however, a curious feature of this figure. Instead of ceasing to enter the mould when it was filled, it is clear that even after this had occurred flow continued, the surplus liquid escaping through an orifice at the top. At first sight this suggested that a 'riser' had been incorporated in the mould through which entrapped air could escape.

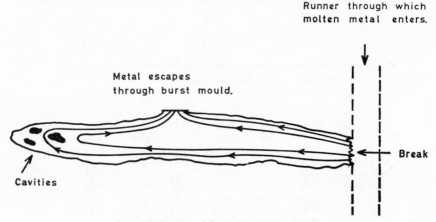

FIG. 5. Diagram of flow of metal in moulds.

Such a riser has not so far as we are aware been observed at the date when these coins were made and since no other specimen showed a similar structure, we suggest that it is more probable that the mould burst allowing the molten metal to flow through. The figure also illustrates the cross-section of a specimen from an ill-run mould, the spongy nature of the outer rim explaining both the deficiency in weight and the irregularity of some specimens. It is the presence of such spongy regions, or actual cavities, which may render measurements of density quite meaningless and, if used to get a rough measure of composition, highly dangerous.

Before being struck these cast blanks were reheated and the evidence for this will now be considered. Quite shortly, the laminated 'sandwich' structure shown in **Fig. 6** could not have originated in the initial casting; it is typical of a two-phase alloy which has been mechanically deformed. Further, the complete absence of 'slip-bands' or other strain markings characteristic of cold-struck coins—compare **Fig. 10** with **Fig. 6**—is equally conclusive evidence for the dogmatic statement that this striking was done hot. Quite apart from the structure which is adequate in itself, conclusive proof that these coins were in fact die-struck is provided by the existence of brokages in the British Museum collection.

The question then arises as to the temperature to which the blanks were reheated before being placed in the dies. This can be a matter of extreme difficulty; here fortunately it proved simple. At the surfaces of many of these coins the structure undergoes a sudden and profound change. This is shown, prepared so as to darken the melted parts and at a higher magnification, in

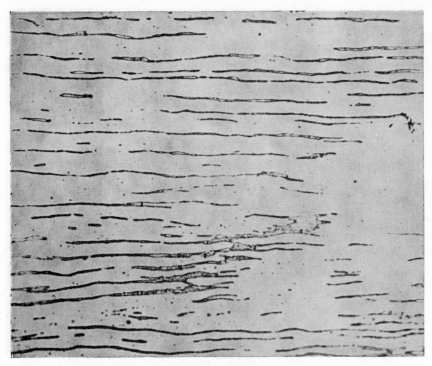

FIG. 6. Laminated structure typical of struck coin. Coin 5.

**Fig. 7.** This latter structure is quite typical of an alloy in the 'as cast' condition, i.e. one cooled down directly from the molten state. The reheating then had been carried out at a temperature sufficiently high to remelt the metal at the surface here and there, i.e. the flames had raised the temperature of the surface metal to some 750 °C. Further, here and there the melted structure was admixed with black, structureless oxide, whence the flames must have been highly oxidizing.

Since the degree of fusion—if any—and of oxidation varied greatly from point to point and from one coin to another, we are left with a picture of a pile of rondels heated in a primitive hot fire, the heating varying throughout the mass, the outer specimens, in more direct contact with the flames, being the more liable to superficial fusion and burning. So far as our evidence shows, however, all reached a temperature at least approximating to that at which melting commences, in an alloy of the average composition of these coins around 700 °C., though clearly no fixed temperature was attained.

There is another point which merits consideration in this connection. Many of the coins with the boar mint-mark show severe cracking at the edge

←—mel

not melted ↑

FIG. 7. Fused surface of Fig. 6 at higher magnification.

[Fig. 8]. This could be due to striking at too high a temperature or to impurities which form low-fusion constituents. No direct correlation could be found between the impurities and this form of cracking though it was not found in any of our specimens with the 'lyre' mint-mark coins which, as will be shown, were freer from impurities than those with the boar. There was, however, some relation between the tendency to crack and the degree of surface 'burning'. It would be consistent with our evidence, therefore, to believe that we have again evidence of too high a striking temperature for the boar coins, the cracking also being accentuated by higher contents of impurities. The sort of treatment which has been outlined offers a complete explanation of the silvery surface on the coins which has already been mentioned. The hot, oxidizing flames would preferentially burn out copper from the alloy resulting in surface enrichment in silver. One coin, no. 5, with an over-all silver content of 19·9 per cent had no less than 39 per cent silver in the surface after the removal in ammonia of the oxide, mainly of copper.

FIG. 8. Coin no. 7 showing edge cracking due to too high a striking temperature (scale 2 : 1).

*Subsequent changes*

The struck coin then cooled down, fairly quickly as later evidence shows, perhaps by being thrown in a heap on the shop floor, and the coin was ready for circulation. There is no evidence that the coins were subjected to any cleaning process at that stage.

That, however, was not the end of the story! There are many types of alloy, of which 'duralumin' is the best known, which after quick cooling undergo spontaneous hardening, slowly at ordinary temperature and more rapidly if somewhat reheated. Another group of alloys which also behaves in this way is the silver–copper alloys to which our coins belong and which includes the billon alloys in general. The common characteristic of the materials which show this 'age-hardening' phenomenon is that the solid solubility of one metal in another increases as the temperature is raised. As a result, a richer solution is formed which on quick cooling can be more or less retained in a state of supersaturation. These supersaturated solutions are inherently unstable and in the process of attaining equilibrium set up internal strains in the metal which in their turn cause an increase of hardness and usually an increase of brittleness. In the case of the (pure) silver–copper alloys the solid solubility of silver in copper is only some $\frac{1}{2}$ per cent at room temperatures but rises to about 8 per cent at a dull red heat. If the hot-struck coin of this composition is cooled quickly this excess silver is partly retained in such unstable solution and the slow relief of this instability will, in the 2,000 years or so since the coin was made, result in a harder and more brittle specimen than would be expected from a normal material. Some simple tests made on coin no. 5 showed the effects excellently. As received, this coin had a hardness of

163 V.P.H.[1] On reheating a portion to 750 °C. and cooling it in air—to simulate the conditions postulated—this hardness had fallen to 80, roughly the hardness of the coin as freshly struck. A short reheating followed by slow cooling raised the hardness to 94 and, as we have seen, 2,000 years at ordinary temperatures to 163.

Along with this age-hardening went a considerable embrittlement. When placed in a vice and given a blow with a light hammer the coin broke off short 'like a carrot'.

## (2) Coins with the 'lyre' mint-mark

Broadly the method of manufacture of these coins was the same as that for the boar coins just discussed. There were, however, differences in detail which in the aggregate seem to us to justify the statement that the coins with the 'lyre' mark were made under quite different conditions from the former.

In all, five specimens were available to us; four, as already mentioned, supplied by the Société jersiaise and the other, no. 16, from a private collection. The weights are collected in Table IV.

TABLE IV

| Our no. | Weight in gm. |
| --- | --- |
| 16 | 6·90* |
| A1 | 6·66 |
| A2 | 6·71 |
| A3 | 6·71 |
| A4 | 6·56 |

* This coin had a firmly adherent corrosion product.

Excluding no. 16, these weights are far more uniform than those for the boar coins.

Two of these specimens, no. 16 and A3, were analysed chemically with the results shown in Table V.

TABLE V

| | No. 16 | A3 |
| --- | --- | --- |
| Copper per cent | 72·2 | 73·9 |
| Silver ,, ,, | 21·4 | 21·7 |
| Tin ,, ,, | 5·86 | 3·85 |
| Lead ,, ,, | 0·24 | 0·28 |
| Iron ,, ,, | Tr. | Tr. |
| Nickel ,, ,, | Tr. | Tr. |
| Cobalt ,, ,, | Tr. | Tr. |
| Zinc ,, ,, | Tr. | Tr. |
| Gold ,, ,, | 0·086 | 0·12 |

[1] Vicker's pyramid hardness: a standard form of measurement.

These results are noteworthy (1) for the far greater uniformity of composition as compared with the boar coins, (2) in having a silver content higher than that of any of the others, and (3) in the most interesting freedom, less than 0·01 per cent, from all the minor impurities. They suggest most strongly they were made to a well-controlled standard.

FIG. 9. Coin A3 showing parallel lines due to striking stresses.

The microscopic examination also revealed some other interesting differences from the boar specimens. In the first place the fused, crozzled surfaces shown in **Fig. 7** were absent, and secondly, an occasional residue of strain marks was to be observed, **Fig. 9.** It is evident from these facts that the striking had been done at a temperature definitely lower than that of the boar coins, at a guess perhaps around 500–600 °C, the temperature at which the rondels would just begin to glow in a dark shop.

Taking all this evidence into consideration, the far more uniform weights, the equally uniform composition, the purer metal, the higher silver content, and finally the lower temperature of striking, we feel completely justified in our belief that the coins with the 'lyre' mark were made under far more rigid and skilled control than those with the boar mark, i.e. under different conditions of time or place.

In **Fig. 10** is shown an abnormal structure from one of these coins due beyond doubt to the deformation suffered by the metal when a coin was broken in a vice to prepare a specimen for the miscroscope. It is included here merely to show the sort of structure which would have been found had the coin been struck cold, for comparison with **Fig. 6** in the hot-struck state.

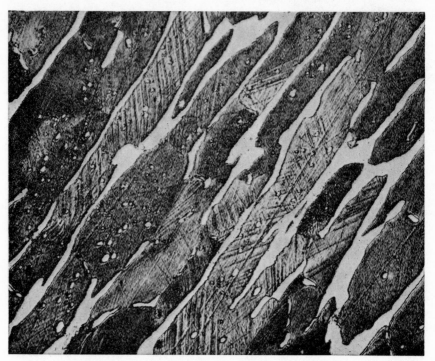

FIG. 10. Structure of same coin as Fig. 5 deformed cold.

We wish to express our most sincere thanks to those without whose assistance this work could not have been completed. First and foremost to the Leverhulme Trust for the award of an Emeritus Fellowship to one of us (F. C. T.); to Mr. L. H. Cope, F.I.M., for the analyses of coins nos. 5 and 13; to Professor R. B. Nicholson for the use of the facilities in the Department of Metallurgy of the University of Manchester, to Messrs. Alfred H. Knight, Ltd., for their skilled analytical work on the other coins; to Mr. Harry Spencer for making casts of the coins and photographs; to the Librarian of the British Non-Ferrous Metals Research Association who provided information on the ageing of copper–silver alloys, and to Dr. David Owen, Director of the Manchester Museum, for his continual forbearance during the whole period of the work. To the Trustees of the Museum of the Société jersiaise and to Dr. Renouf our thanks have already been expressed.

### CONCLUSION

Within the limits of our material, which included nineteen specimens, the work has shown that:

1. These coins, containing typically around 20 per cent of silver, were first cast as rondels. These were then reheated to a temperature such that at times the surface began to melt, i.e. around 700 °C., a low red heat. They were transferred to the dies and struck after which they cooled down in air. Subsequently the metal underwent a very slow, spontaneous hardening, the hardness being roughly doubled.

2. A particularly interesting aspect of the investigation is the evidence that specimens with the debased boar mint-mark were produced under quite different conditions from those with the so-called 'lyre' mark. The picture revealed is that the former were made carelessly, with no adequate control, in fact with clear evidence for deliberate fraud. Of the twelve full analyses available to us with the boar mint-mark, three, i.e. 25 per cent, contained less than one-half of the silver typically present, one of these being essentially silver-free. When, however, we come to those with the 'lyre' mark, the state of affairs is totally different. Uniform in weight and composition, well struck, and made from purer metal, they were the product of a mint under good, honest management.

It is not for us to offer an explanation for these facts; all we can say is that the two mint-marks represent coins struck at different times or in different localities.

# A Quinarius Hoard from Southern Italy

CHARLES A. HERSH

[SEE PLATES 8–11]

IN the course of 1971 three separate lots of related hoard material were brought to my attention: two of these were made up primarily of Roman Republican quinarii, while the third consisted entirely of quinarii. Although the information concerning these parcels of coins was made available to me by numismatists in three different countries, the batches were so very similar, both in their basic composition and the fact that each of them had a number of pieces which were at least partially covered by an identical greyish-black accretion, that I came to the obvious conclusion that all three groups of coins had come from one single hoard. Even more conclusive to this determination was the knowledge that each of these three accumulations consisted either wholly or primarily of quinarii, and all available records indicated that no sizeable find of Roman silver coins had as yet ever been recorded which was mainly composed of quinarii or even had a relatively large proportion of pieces of that denomination.[1] It would really have to stretch coincidence too far to treat each of these lots as a separate hoard, since all of these circumstances indicate the contrary.

The three parcels I have tabulated consisted of 204 coins, 13 denarii and 191 quinarii. I feel quite certain from the manner in which the material came to my attention that there were undoubtedly additional pieces in the find, although from the general uniformity of the three lots which I have examined it does not appear very likely that many, if any, additional quinarius issues might have been present in the hoard.

From all that I have been able to learn from the original purchasers of these coins, the hoard was discovered in southern Italy during 1970, near the port city of Taranto in Calabria—the site of the ancient Tarentum. Some of these coins were sold abroad by a Sicilian numismatist, which led at least one dealer-purchaser to the erroneous conclusion that the find was from Sicily, and that part of the find was referred to as the 'Sicilian hoard', at least for

---

[1] The most modern and complete study of the relevant find material has been collected by Michael Crawford in his *Roman Republican Coin Hoards*, London, 1969. This is a quite thorough, if flawed, résumé of much of the available information on this subject.

a time. However, the great weight of the coin evidence itself points to a southern Italian provenance, as all save a few pieces appear to come from that region of the peninsula; indeed there seems to be only one quinarius certainly from Sicily present.

As I previously noted, each of the three parcels of coins came from a different country and was shown to me by a separate correspondent: the Italian portion (69 coins) was photographed for me by an eminent collector, who made the first selection from this lot; the Swiss portions were from the same source and were sent to me by Münzen und Medaillen A.G. of Basel (54 coins) and Bank Leu & Co. A.G. of Zürich (3 coins), so that I was able to make the first selection; the English portion (78 coins) was handled by Spink & Son Ltd. of London, who showed me their pieces and permitted me the second choice, after the British Museum had made theirs. The quality and condition of the quinarii indicates that the Italian lot was the first selection made from the find, with the Swiss group of coins only slightly less fine; the English pieces were generally much less well preserved, but included some very rare quinarii. The fact that the few denarii discovered were sold with the Italian and Swiss selections of quinarii reinforces for me the view that they were the prime choices from the hoard.

Neither Sydenham[1] nor Crawford[2] is an ideal text to use to catalogue the hoard material. Sydenham, although much more explicit and detailed, is badly in error with regard to his dating of these early denarius and quinarius issues in the light of the latest researches on the subject; Crawford, on the other hand, has crowded and jammed so many of these issues into the three-year period from c. 211–208 B.C., in seeming disregard of all normal minting practices and procedures, that severe doubts are raised in my mind as to the validity of his whole basic arrangement of the coinage of this early period. On balance there is no question that at this point the Sydenham classification is far superior, if one discards his absolute chronology and uses only his relative chronology and arrangement.

This hoard seems also to go a long way towards confirming the basic correctness of Sydenham's concept of the ordering of the early denarii and quinarii issues by groupings, and appears to substantiate some of his area mint locations. The appearance in this find from southern Italy of precisely those quinarii which Sydenham had attributed to that region and the fact that other contemporary issues which he listed as having been struck outside that area were not present at all in the hoard is quite significant in my opinion. Not one of the quinarius issues that he ascribed to Sardinia,[3] Corcyra,[4] or

---

[1] E. A. Sydenham, *The Coinage of the Roman Republic* (London, 1952).

[2] Crawford, op. cit.

[3] Sydenham attributes three quinarii in Series 2 to Sardinia: S. 156 with a C mint-mark, 159 with an ΛΛ mint-mark, and 161 with an Λꝱ mint-mark.

[4] Sydenham lists one Corcyran quinarius; S. 185 in Series 5, which has the two mint-marks ⚥ and Λ on the reverse.

Rome[1] during this same period was present in this find, and only one quinarius with a Sicilian mint-mark or symbol[2] was found, while an almost complete range of quinarius issues which he assigned to southern Italy was discovered. Although the Sardinian, Corcyran, and Roman quinarii are very rare, even more so than indicated by the figures in the text of his corpus, so are some of the south Italian issues, notably those with the Ⲟ- (coin 142) and the ⱴ on the reverse (coins 125–33), while the Sicilian issue with the wheat-ear symbol (coin 191), of which only one specimen was found in this hoard, is as common as the most frequently found southern Italian issues.

A breakdown of the three parcels of coins which made up the hoard, according to their appropriate Sydenham classifications, shows the over-all similarity of the different lots:

| | | Italian parcel | Swiss parcels | English parcel | Total hoard |
|---|---|---|---|---|---|
| QUINARII | | | | | |
| *Anonymous issues* | | | | | |
| S. 141 | | 0 | 2 | 2 | 4 |
| S. 169 | | 33 | 13 | 30 | 76 |
| S. pre-176 | | 1 | 5 | 11 | 17 |
| S. 192 | | 6 | 5 | 4 | 15 |
| Sub-total | | 40 | 25 | 47 | 112 |
| *Issues with mint-marks and symbols* | | | | | |
| H | S. 174 | 4 | 5 | 3 | 12 |
| ⱴ (on reverse) | S. 176 | 2 | 4 | 3 | 9 |
| ⱴ (on obverse) | S. 176a | 3 | 3 | 2 | 8 |
| Ⲟ- | S. 181 | 0 | 0 | 1 | 1 |
| Ω | S. 181a | 2 | 5 | 12 | 19 |
| Ⲙ | S. 183 | 8 | 7 | 9 | 24 |
| Ⲙ | S. 184 | 1 | 3 | 1 | 5 |
| Wheat-ear | S. 194 | 1 | 0 | 0 | 1 |
| Quinarius total | | 61 | 52 | 78 | 191 |

[1] Only one of the early quinarii is given to the mint of Rome by Sydenham, S. 188 in Series 5 with the RÅ monogram.

[2] Apart from S. 194 in Series 6 which has the wheat-ear symbol as its mint-mark and which is present in this hoard, Sydenham attributes two other issues of quinarii to Sicily, namely S. 197 with the adze symbol and S. 200 with the moneyer's name, C·VⱤ (C. Terentius Varro). Both of these pieces are also from Series 6.

| | Italian parcel | Swiss parcels | English parcel | Total hoard |
|---|---|---|---|---|
| **DENARII** | | | | |
| *Anonymous issues* | | | | |
| S. 140 | 0 | 1 | 0 | 1 |
| S. 167 | 6 | 2 | 0 | 8 |
| S. 191 | 1 | 1 | 0 | 2 |
| *With symbols* | | | | |
| Anchor. S. 144 | 1 | 1 | 0 | 2 |
| Denarius total | 8 | 5 | 0 | 13 |
| Over-all total | 69 | 57 | 78 | 204 |

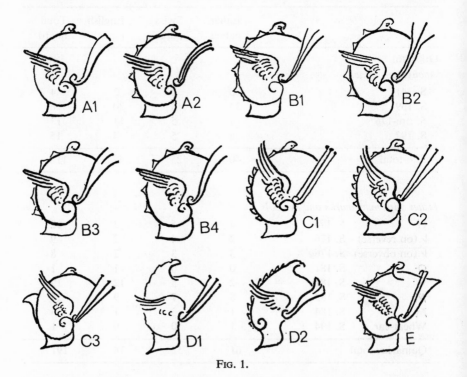

FIG. 1.

A more detailed analysis of the entire find follows, listing each coin by Sydenham classification number, hoard parcel, Sydenham helmet style (illustrated on **Fig. 1** above), obverse die numbers for the anonymous quinarius issues, and obverse and reverse die numbers for the quinarius issues with mint letters, monograms, or symbols, as well as all of the denarius issues. Present ownership of each coin is indicated when it is known. When this is left blank, my records indicate that the coin is in the hands of a professional numismatist. I was not able to classify further the reverse dies of the anonymous quinarius issues because the quality of some of the coin photographs that were available to me made exact identification very difficult, although such a study would have been desirable and might have been quite valuable and enlightening. Coins which are illustrated on the plates are indicated by an *.

| Quinarii | Coin number | Sydenham number | Parcel | Sydenham helmet style | Obverse die number | Reverse die number | In collection of |
|---|---|---|---|---|---|---|---|
| 1. Anonymous | 1* | 141 | English | A2 | I | | Author |
| (112) | 2* | ,, | Swiss | B1 | II | | ,, |
| | 3* | ,, | ,, | B1 | III | | ,, |
| | 4 | ,, | English | B1 | IV | | |
| | 5* | 169 | Swiss | B2 | V | | Author |
| | 6* | ,, | ,, | B2 | ⌐VI | | Richard Witschonke |
| | 7 | ,, | English | B2 | ⌐VI | | |
| | 8 | ,, | Swiss | B2 | VII | | A.N.S. |
| | 9* | ,, | ,, | B2 | ⌐VIII | | Author |
| | 10 | ,, | Italian | B2 | VIII | | Private collection G |
| | 11 | ,, | ,, | B2 | VIII | | Private collection G |
| | 12 | ,, | English | B2 | VIII | | |
| | 13 | ,, | ,, | B2 | ⌐VIII | | |
| | 14 | ,, | Italian | B2 | ⌐IX | | |
| | 15* | ,, | English | B2 | ⌐IX | | |
| | 16 | ,, | Italian | B2 | X | | |
| | 17 | ,, | English | B2 | XI | | |
| | 18 | ,, | ,, | B2 | XII | | |
| | 19 | ,, | ,, | B2 | XIII | | |
| | 20* | ,, | Swiss | B2 | ⌐XIV | | Author |
| | 21 | ,, | Italian | B2 | ⌐XIV | | |
| | 22 | ,, | Swiss | B2 | ⌐XV | | |
| | 23* | ,, | Italian | B2 | ⌐XV | | Private collection G |
| | 24* | ,, | Swiss | B2 | ⌐XVI | | A.N.S. |
| | 25 | ,, | English | B2 | ⌐XVI | | |
| | 26 | ,, | Italian | B2 | ⌐XVII | | Private collection G |
| | 27 | ,, | ,, | B2 | XVII | | |
| | 28 | ,, | English | B2 | XVII | | |
| | 29 | ,, | ,, | B2 | ⌐XVII | | |
| | 30 | ,, | Italian | B2 | XVIII | | |
| | 31* | ,, | ,, | B2 | ⌐XIX | | |
| | 32 | ,, | ,, | B2 | ⌐XIX | | |
| | 33 | ,, | English | B2 | ⌐XX | | |
| | 34 | ,, | ,, | B2 | ⌐XX | | |
| | 35 | ,, | ,, | B2 | XXI | | |
| | 36* | ,, | Swiss | B3 | ⌐XXII | | A.N.S. |
| | 37 | ,, | Italian | B3 | ⌐XXII | | |
| | 38 | ,, | Swiss | B3 | ⌐XXIII | | |
| | 39 | ,, | Italian | B3 | ⌐XXIII | | |
| | 40 | ,, | ,, | B3 | ⌐XXIII | | |
| | 41 | ,, | Swiss | B3 | ⌐XXIV | | |
| | 42* | ,, | ,, | B3 | ⌐XXIV | | Author |
| | 43* | ,, | Italian | B3 | ⌐XXV | | |
| | 44 | ,, | .' | B3 | ⌐XXV | | |
| | 45* | ,, | ,, | B3 | XXVI | | |
| | 46 | ,, | ,, | B3 | XXVII | | |
| | 47* | ,, | ,, | B3 | ⌐XXVIII | | |
| | 48 | ,, | English | B3 | ⌐XXVIII | | |
| | 49 | ,, | Italian | B3 | XXIX | | |
| | 50 | ,, | ,, | B3 | XXX | | |

| Quinarii | Coin number | Sydenham number | Parcel | Sydenham helmet style | Obverse die number | Reverse die number | In collection of |
|---|---|---|---|---|---|---|---|
| 1. Anonymous | 51 | 169 | Italian | B3 | ⌐XXXI | | |
| (continued) | 52 | ,, | English | B3 | XXXI | | |
| | 53 | ,, | ,, | B3 | ⌊XXXI | | |
| | 54 | ,, | ,, | B3 | XXXII | | |
| | 55 | ,, | ,, | B3 | XXXIII | | |
| | 56 | ,, | ,, | B3 | XXXIV | | |
| | 57* | ,, | ,, | B3 | XXXV | | British Museum |
| | 58* | ,, | Swiss | B3 | XXXVI | | Author |
| | 59* | ,, | Italian | B3 | XXXVII | | |
| | 60 | ,, | ,, | B3 | XXXVIII | | |
| | 61 | ,, | ,, | B3 | ⌐XXXIX | | |
| | 62 | ,, | ,, | B3 | ⌊XXXIX | | |
| | 63 | ,, | ,, | B3 | XL | | |
| | 64 | ,, | English | B3 | XLI | | |
| | 65 | ,, | ,, | B3 | XLII | | |
| | 66 | ,, | ,, | B3 | XLIII | | |
| | 67* | ,, | Swiss | B3 | XLIV | | Author |
| | 68 | ,, | Italian | B3 | XLV | | |
| | 69* | ,, | ,, | B4 | XLVI | | Private collection G |
| | 70 | ,, | ,, | B4 | ⌐XLVII | | |
| | 71 | ,, | English | B4 | ⌊XLVII | | |
| | 72 | ,, | Italian | B4 | XLVIII | | |
| | 73* | ,, | ,, | B4 | ⌐XLIX | | |
| | 74 | ,, | English | B4 | ⌊XLIX | | |
| | 75* | ,, | Italian | B4 | L | | |
| | 76 | ,, | English | B4 | LI | | |
| | 77 | ,, | ,, | B4 | LII | | |
| | 78 | ,, | ,, | B4 | LIII | | |
| | 79 | ,, | ,, | B4 | LIV | | |
| | 80 | ,, | ,, | B4 | LV | | British Museum |
| | 81* | Pre-176 | Swiss | D1 | ⌐LVI | | |
| | 82 | ,, | Italian | D1 | LVI | | |
| | 83 | ,, | English | D1 | LVI | | |
| | 84 | ,, | ,, | D1 | LVI | | |
| | 85 | ,, | ,, | D1 | ⌊LVI | | |
| | 86 | ,, | Swiss | D1 | ⌐LVII | | |
| | 87 | ,, | English | D1 | ⌊LVII | | |
| | 88 | ,, | Swiss | D1 | LVIII | | A.N.S. |
| | 89 | ,, | ,, | D1 | ⌐LIX | | |
| | 90* | ,, | English | D1 | ⌊LIX | | |
| | 91* | ,, | Swiss | D1 | LX | | Author |
| | 92 | ,, | English | D1 | LXI | | |
| | 93 | ,, | ,, | D1 | LXII | | |
| | 94 | ,, | ,, | D1 | LXIII | | |
| | 95 | ,, | ,, | D1 | ⌐LXIV | | |
| | 96 | ,, | ,, | D1 | ⌊LXIV | | |
| | 97* | ,, | ,, | D2 | LXV | | Author |
| | 98* | 192 | Swiss | C2 | ⌐LXVI | | |
| | 99 | ,, | Italian | C2 | ⌊LXVI | | |
| | 100 | ,, | Swiss | C2 | ⌐LXVII | | |
| | 101 | ,, | Italian | C2 | ⌊LXVII | | |
| | 102* | ,, | Swiss | C2 | ⌐LXVIII | | Author |
| | 103 | ,, | Italian | C2 | ⌊LXVIII | | |
| | 104* | ,, | Swiss | C2 | LXIX | | Author |
| | 105 | ,, | ,, | C2 | LXX | | A.N.S. |
| | 106 | ,, | Italian | C2 | LXXI | | |
| | 107 | ,, | ,, | C2 | LXXII | | |
| | 108 | ,, | ,, | C2 | ⌐LXXIII | | |
| | 109 | ,, | English | C2 | ⌊LXXIII | | |
| | 110 | ,, | ,, | C2 | LXXIV | | |
| | 111 | ,, | ,, | C2 | ⌐LXXV | | |
| | 112 | ,, | ,, | C2 | ⌊LXXV | | |
| 2. H (12) | 113* | 174 | Swiss | B3 | C | a | |
| | 114* | ,, | ,, | B3 | CI | b | |
| | 115* | ,, | ,, | B3 | CII | c | |
| | 116* | ,, | ,, | B3 | CIII | d | Author |

| Quinarii | Coin number | Sydenham number | Parcel | Sydenham helmet style | Obverse die number | Reverse die number | In collection of |
|---|---|---|---|---|---|---|---|
| 2. H (continued) | 117* | 174 | Swiss | B3 | CIV | e | |
| | 118 | ,, | Italian | B3 | CV | e | |
| | 119* | ,, | ,, | B3 | CVI | f | Private collection G |
| | 120* | ,, | ,, | B3 | CVII | g | |
| | 121 | ,, | ,, | B3 | CVIII | h | |
| | 122 | ,, | English | B3 | CIX | i | |
| | 123 | ,, | ,, | B3 | CX | j | |
| | 124 | ,, | ,, | B3 | CXI | ? | |
| 3. V (On Reverse) (9) | 125* | 176 | Swiss | D1 | CXII | k | Author |
| | 126 | ,, | Italian | D1 | CXIII | k | |
| | 127 | ,, | Swiss | D1 | CXIV | l | Richard Witschonke |
| | 128* | ,, | ,, | D1 | CXV | m | A.N.S. |
| | 129* | ,, | ,, | D1 | CXVI | n | Author |
| | 130* | ,, | Italian | D1 | CXVII | o | Private collection G |
| | 131 | ,, | English | D1 | CXVIII | p | |
| | 132* | ,, | ,, | D1 | CXIX | q | |
| | 133 | ,, | ,, | D1 | ? | r | |
| 4. V (On Obverse) (8) | 134 | 176a | Swiss | D2 | CXX | s | Richard Witschonke |
| | 135 | ,, | Italian | D2 | CXX | s | |
| | 136* | ,, | ,, | D2 | CXX | s | |
| | 137 | ,, | English | D2 | CXX | s | |
| | 138* | ,, | Swiss | D2 | CXXI | t | Author |
| | 139* | ,, | ,, | D2 | CXXII | u | Author |
| | 140* | ,, | Italian | D2 | CXXIII | v | |
| | 141* | ,, | English | D2 | CXXIV | w | |
| 5. O- (1) | 142* | 181 | English | B1 | CXXV | x | Author |
| 6. Ω (19) | 143* | 181a | Swiss | B3 | CXXVI | y | Author |
| | 144* | ,, | ,, | B3 | CXXVII | z | Author |
| | 145 | ,, | Italian | B3 | CXXVIII | z | |
| | 146* | ,, | Swiss | B3 | CXXIX | aa | Richard Witschonke |
| | 147 | ,, | English | B3 | CXXIX | aa | |
| | 148 | ,, | ,, | B3 | CXXIX | ab | |
| | 149 | ,, | ,, | B3 | CXXIX | ac | |
| | 150* | ,, | ,, | B3 | CXXX | ac | |
| | 151* | ,, | Swiss | B3 | CXXXI | ad | A.N.S. |
| | 152* | ,, | Italian | B3 | CXXXII | ae | |
| | 153 | ,, | English | B3 | CXXXII | af | |
| | 154 | ,, | ,, | B3 | CXXXIII | af | |
| | 155 | ,, | ,, | B3 | CXXXIV | ag | |
| | 156 | ,, | ,, | B3 | CXXXV | ag | |
| | 157 | ,, | ,, | B3 | CXXXVI | ah | British Museum |
| | 158 | ,, | Swiss | B4 | CXXXVII | ai | |
| | 159 | ,, | English | B4 | CXXXVIII | aj | |
| | 160 | ,, | ,, | B4 | CXXXVIII | aj | |
| | 161* | ,, | ,, | B4 | CXXXVIII | aj | |
| 7. M (24) | 162 | 183 | Swiss | B3 | CXXXIX | ak | |
| | 163 | ,, | ,, | B3 | CXXXIX | ak | |
| | 164* | ,, | Italian | B3 | CXXXIX | ak | Private collection G |
| | 165 | ,, | ,, | B3 | CXXXIX | ak | |
| | 166* | ,, | Swiss | B3 | CXXXIX | al | Author |
| | 167 | ,, | ,, | B3 | CXXXIX | am | A.N.S. |
| | 168 | ,, | ,, | B3 | CXL | an | Richard Witschonke |
| | 169* | ,, | ,, | B3 | CXL | an | |
| | 170 | ,, | English | B3 | CXL | an | |
| | 171 | ,, | ,, | B3 | CXL | an | |
| | 172 | ,, | Italian | B3 | CXL | ao | |
| | 173* | ,, | ,, | B3 | CXL | ap | |
| | 174* | ,, | Swiss | B3 | CXLI | aq | Author |
| | 175 | ,, | English | B3 | CXLI | aq | |
| | 176 | ,, | Italian | B3 | CXLI | ar | |
| | 177* | ,, | ,, | B3 | CXLII | as | Private collection G |
| | 178 | ,, | ,, | B3 | CXLII | as | |
| | 179 | ,, | English | B3 | CXLII | as | |
| | 180 | ,, | ,, | B3 | CXLII | as | |

| Quinarii | Coin number | Sydenham number | Parcel | Sydenham helmet style | Obverse die number | Reverse die number | In collection of |
|---|---|---|---|---|---|---|---|
| 7. ᛗ | 181 | 183 | English | B3 | CXLII | as | |
| (continued) | 182 | ,, | ,, | B3 | CXLII | as | |
| | 183 | ,, | ,, | B3 | CXLII | as | |
| | 184 | ,, | ,, | B3 | CXLIII | at | |
| | 185* | ,, | Italian | B3 | CXLIV | au | |
| 8. ᛗ (5) | 186* | 184 | ,, | B3 | CXLIV | av | Private collection G |
| | 187 | ,, | Swiss | B3 | CXLV | aw | A.N.S. |
| | 188* | ,, | English | B3 | CXLV | aw | Author |
| | 189* | ,, | Swiss | B3 | CXLV | ax | ,, |
| | 190* | ,, | ,, | B3 | CXLVI | ay | Author |
| 9. Wheat-ear (1) | 191* | 194 | Italian | C1 | CXLVII | az | Private collection G |
| *Denarii* | | | | | | | |
| 10. Anonymous | 192* | 140 | Swiss | A2 | CC | ba | Author |
| (11) | 193* | 167 | Italian | B2 | CCI | bb | ,, |
| | 194* | ,, | Swiss | B2 | CCII | bc | A.N.S. |
| | 195* | ,, | Italian | B3 | CCIII | bd | Private collection G |
| | 196* | ,, | ,, | B3 | CCIV | be | |
| | 197* | ,, | ,, | B3 | CCV | bf | |
| | 198* | ,, | ,, | B3 | CCVI | bg | |
| | 199* | ,, | Swiss | B4 | CCVII | bh | A.N.S. |
| | 200* | ,, | Italian | B4 | CCVIII | bi | Private collection G |
| | 201* | 191 | ,, | C1 (Probably) | CCIX | bj | |
| | 202* | ,, | Swiss | C3 | CCX | bk | A.N.S. |
| 11. Anchor (2) | 203* | 144 | ,, | A2 | CCXI | bl | A.N.S. |
| | 204* | ,, | Italian | A2 | CCXI | bm | Private collection G |

## I. THE ANONYMOUS QUINARIUS ISSUES (coins 1–112)

When Sydenham catalogued the anonymous quinarii for his corpus, he separated them into three groupings, each forming part of Series 1, 4, and 6. The first two groupings were attributed to mints in southern Italy, the third to a mint or mints in Sicily. I have felt for some time that his arrangement of all of the early anonymous silver issues was neither as complete nor as detailed and accurate as it might have been, so in order to be able to classify the anonymous quinarii in what I feel is as correct and precise a manner as possible, I have adjusted and reorganized his three listings into four new groups, which entail a number of changes:

### SERIES 1. SOUTHERN ITALY

| Number | Issue | Obverse | Reverse | References |
|---|---|---|---|---|
| 141 | Anonymous | Helmeted head of 'Roma' to the right; hair tied with band; on left, V. Helmets A2, B1. | Dioscuri on horseback to the right, holding couched spears; above, two stars; below, or in exergue, ROMᴧ or variants ROMᴧ, ROMᴧ, or ROMᴧ. | G.[1] pl. viii, 4 (A2 helmet); pl. viii, 5 (B1 helmet). |

[1] H. A. Grueber, *Coins of the Roman Republic in the British Museum* (London, 1910).

**SERIES 4. SOUTHERN OR SOUTH-EASTERN ITALY**

| Number | Issue | Obverse | Reverse | References |
|--------|-------|---------|---------|------------|
| 169 | Anonymous | Similar, but helmets B2, B3, B4. | Similar | G. pl. xii, 7 (B2 helmet); pl. xii, 6; pl. lxxxi, 5; pl. lxxxii, 1 (all B3 helmets). |

**SERIES 5. VARIOUS MINT AREAS**

| | | | | |
|--------|-------|---------|---------|------------|
| Pre-176 | Anonymous | Similar, but helmets D1, D2. | Similar | G. pl. lxxxii, 2 (D1 helmet). |

**SERIES 6. SICILY**

| | | | | |
|--------|-------|---------|---------|------------|
| 192 | Anonymous | Similar, but helmets C2, C3 (all without loops). | Similar | Haeberlin 131[1] (C3 helmet). |

The coins classed as S. 141 were almost certainly the earliest quinarii struck. Two different helmet styles are found: A2, a bowl-shaped helmet with a curved visor and with very slight splaying of the visor ends, and B1, which has much straighter lines forming the visor. A2 is closely related to A1, the style used on the earliest denarii, but the three lines which form the curved visor are clearly delineated and the small spikes at the back of the helmet are visible. In the B1 type helmet the three lines of the visor are much straighter than those in the A2 style helmets and there is considerable splaying of the visor ends. These are both quite scarce quinarius varieties. Only four coins which I have classified as S. 141 were found in this hoard, one A2 and three B1.

The quinarii catalogued as S. 169 have helmet types B2 and B3, which are further evolutions of the B1 style, and B4, which appears to have evolved from B3. The B2 visors show three straight visor lines which are greatly splayed at the ends. The B3 visors have the middle visor line much shorter than the outer lines, with this middle line beginning either as an off-shoot of one of the outer lines (coins 36 and 42) or merely indicated as a short line between the other two (coins 58 and 59). All the B3 visor lines are straight, not curved. The B4 style helmets have a visor made up of two straight lines, which are usually almost parallel to each other and generally unsplayed. The types of S. 169 are much more common than those of S. 141, especially the B2 and B3 helmets. Seventy-six quinarii in this over-all category were in the find, with many of the different obverse dies showing an almost infinite variety of visor shapes, within their classification.

[1] The Dr. Ernst J. Haeberlin collection, Adolf E. Cahn and Adolf Hess Nachf. Sale, 17 July 1933. The collection was catalogued by Herbert A. Cahn. There were 3,304 lots in the sale of the finest collection of Roman Republican coins ever to come under the hammer up to the present day.

The pieces which I have listed as S. pre-176 were included as part of S. 141 by Sydenham. The helmet here is a Phrygian type and not bowl-shaped, as were all the S. 141 and 169 quinarii, and as this style is very closely related to those quinarii with the $V$ mint-mark (S. 176 and 176a) I thought that it was reasonable to include them at this point. The D1 style anonymous coins are very close to the S. 176 quinarii, with the $V$ mint-mark on the reverse, while the D2 style anonymous piece with its peaked visor is quite similar to coins of S. 176a, with the $V$ mint-mark on the obverse. Both of these anonymous varieties are rare, especially the D2 style, which was unknown to me before I saw a quinarius of that type in the hoard (coin 97). There were sixteen specimens with D1 helmet among the anonymous quinarii in this find.

The anonymous quinarii classified as S. 192 are of a style almost always associated with the mints in Sicily. They have C2 and C3 type helmets, which are bowl-shaped as were those of S. 141 and 169. The C2 helmet has visor lines which are completely straight and its style apparently evolved from the C1 style (as on coin 191), which has a visor composed of three straight and parallel lines. The C1 style does not occur on anonymous quinarii, to my knowledge. The C3 helmet has a visor like those on the C2 coins, but it has one large spike at the back of the helmet instead of a number of small ones, as on all the other types of helmets on early quinarii. There are fifteen pieces with C2 style helmets in the hoard, normally a rare variety, while there are no C3 type coins at all in the find. This is quite surprising, as the C3 anonymous quinarii are probably the commonest variety of the whole issue, even less scarce than the B2 and B3 types of S. 169. My own feeling is that the rather uniform group of S. 192 coins from this find, which have a C2 type helmet but are quite unlike the general run of quinarii with C style helmets minted in Sicily, may be a variety which was struck in southern Italy. They are far below the usual quality of the C2 type helmet Sicilian quinarii, with a rather crudely designed obverse style, and they are generally weakly and poorly struck. Certainly they are very unlike the C2 style quinarius which was found during the Morgantina excavations in Sicily.[1] Of the eleven quinarii found in the sealed deposits at Morgantina which I have seen,[2] there was only one with a C2 type helmet, while nine had C3 styles and one was unattributable because of heavily encrusted material on the coin's surface. The C2 quinarius came from that group of nine coins, including three quinarii, found in a jar in the south sanctuary room proper; the other two quinarii uncovered there as well as seven others, evidently from the cistern of the private house across the Agora, were all of the C3 types so normal to Sicily, but completely lacking in this find from Calabria.

[1] The only publication to date of the Morgantina excavation material is T. V. Buttrey's article, 'The Morgantina Excavations and the Date of the Roman Denarius,' *CINR* ii (1961), 261 ff.

[2] Photographs of the silver coins found at Morgantina were supplied by my friend, Theodore Buttrey.

Obverse die-links among the 112 anonymous quinarii are quite frequent, but there are no really heavy concentrations of any single die, as in some of the issues with mint-marks from the find. Two obverse dies (nos. VIII and LVI) were found on five pieces, while one (no. XVII) was on four specimens. Two coins with obverse die VIII share a common reverse die also (coins 9 and 11), as do two with obverse die XVII (coins 28 and 29), while all five pieces with obverse die LVI (coins 81–5) share a common reverse die in addition.

## II. THE QUINARII WITH MINT-MARKS AND SYMBOLS
### (coins 113–191)

### A. S. 174. Mint-mark H (coins 113–24)

This is perhaps the most common of this group of quinarius issues with mint-marks and is the earliest issue of those found in this hoard. The twelve pieces here have no common obverse dies and only one reverse die-link (die e on coins 117 and 118). The coins also show more wear than any of the other series of quinarii with mint-marks. A very rare variety of this issue, S. 174*a*, which has the mint-mark on the left in the field instead of on the right below the horses on the reverse, was not found in this hoard. It probably was struck some time later than the H coins from this find, as its specimens always have a type of C2 style helmet. Coins of S. 174 almost always have a B3 shape helmet, as indeed do all of the dozen examples in this hoard, but a few very rare specimens exist that have the same type of C2 style helmet as the pieces of S. 174*a*. In fact an obverse die link between the two issues is known.[1]

### B. S. 176. Mint-mark ʋ (on reverse) (coins 125–33)

Until this present hoard was discovered this quinarius type was extremely rare, with probably less than a dozen specimens known. The nine coins from the find all show some wear and all were struck from different obverse dies, but two (coins 125 and 126) share a common reverse die. The Phrygian helmet (D1 type) used on this issue is quite different from the type (D2) used on S. 176*a*.

### C. S. 176*a*. Mint-mark ʋ (on obverse) (coins 134–41)

This issue, although rare, is more common than S. 176, and it has another variety of the Phrygian helmet, which is found on that issue also. The eight specimens of S. 176*a* from this hoard appear fresher and less worn than do the coins of S. 174 and 176. Four quinarii (coins 134–7) share both common obverse and reverse dies, but the other four have no dies in common at all.

---

[1] *BMCRR* ii, 194, no. 200 (S. 174); *BMCRR* ii, 194, no. 201 (S. 174*a*).

D. S. 181. Mint-mark o- (coin 142)

This excessively rare coin is scarcer even than S. 176, the other very rare issue of quinarii found in this hoard, and is known to me from only about half a dozen specimens. It is certainly an issue separate from S. 181a, where the obverses have a different style of helmet and a dissimilar variety of the letter Q is used as a mint-mark. This issue is certainly earlier than S. 181a because the B1 helmet used here is a precursor of the B3 type used on the S. 181a pieces. The style on S. 181 is also finer and more carefully executed than on the other group.

E. S. 181a. Mint-mark ∩ (coins 143–61)

The nineteen coins in this group show little wear and are later than the previous four series of quinarii with mint-marks. A number of pieces here share common dies, both obverse and reverse. As this is a scarce issue, the sizeable number and excellent condition of the coins found leads to the conclusion that this type was struck not very long before the burial of the hoard.

F. S. 183. Mint-mark Ж (coins 162–85)

Although this quinarius issue is quite common, the superb condition of the numerous specimens, which show very little or no wear at all, and the many common obverse and reverse dies shared by the pieces in the find indicate that they were minted almost immediately before the hoard was buried. Of especial interest is coin 185, which has an obverse die in common with coin 186, of the related S. 184 issue.

G. S. 184. Mint-mark Ж (coins 186–90)

The close similarity between this series and S. 183 has long been recognized. Evidence of a common mint for the two issues is indicated by the obverse die-link between coins 185 and 186. Although the obverse styles of the two issues were long regarded as very much alike, no common die-link for the two issues had previously been noted. The coins with the Ж monogram are much scarcer than the collateral series with the Ж. All five coins of this issue are in very fine condition and have a number of common die-links. They appear to have been struck shortly before the hoard was concealed, as were the S. 183 quinarii.

H. S. 194. Mint-mark wheat-ear (coin 191)

This piece, which has a C1 type helmet, was almost certainly struck in Sicily. Its symbol, the wheat-ear, has long been attributed to Sicily.[1] This probable attribution received further support from the evidence of the Morgantina excavations, where the one early Roman gold or silver coin with

[1] Sydenham, op. cit. 21, and C. A. Hersh, 'Overstrikes as Evidence for the History of Roman Republican Coinage', NC 1953, 42 f. and 49 f.

a mint-mark or symbol discovered in the sealed deposits was a gold twenty-As piece with a wheat-ear symbol (S. 234). This very rare coin was discovered in the cistern along with thirty-four anonymous quinarii and sestertii.[1] Although Sydenham placed this Mars/Eagle gold piece later in his chronology, and indeed the entire Mars/Eagle gold series, it is now generally accepted that this gold coin with the wheat-ear should be associated with S. 193 and 194. The above quinarius is generally quite common, although only one was found in this hoard; it is found with C1, C2, and C3 helmet types.[2]

### III. THE DENARII (coins 192–204)

Unlike any other published early Republican silver hoards of this period, which were composed either wholly or predominantly of denarii, the present hoard, as we have seen, was composed almost entirely of quinarii. Of the 204 coins found and noted only thirteen were denarii, but among these were some very interesting coins. Eleven of this group were anonymous denarii, while two had symbols. Eight of the anonymous denarii (coins 193–200) were pieces of the S. 167 series, a southern Italian issue with the ROMA legend on the reverse in semi-incuse letters; another two probably were of Sicilian origin, as they were of S. 191 type and had C type helmets (coins 201 and 202); indeed coin 202 has the C3 style helmet which was found on almost all of the Morgantina excavation quinarii, but which did not appear on any of the quinarii in this hoard. The only denarii with mint-marks or symbols are coins 203 and 204, which are examples of S. 144 with an anchor symbol which Sydenham attributed to southern Italy. These two denarii are in excellent condition and share a common obverse die.

This hoard from Calabria adds a good deal of weight to Sydenham's mint-area attributions of the various early Republican quinarius issues. Though it may not actually prove his attribution of a number of issues to southern and south-eastern Italy, it certainly offers strong support to his view. The absence from this hoard of some series of quinarii reinforces his attribution of them to other areas, even though it is not possible to speak of confirmation of his attribution of these issues to other mint-areas solely on the basis of their absence from one find, large though it may be and giving such a seemingly comprehensive picture of the quinarii which were circulating in southern Italy at the time of its burial. There is some good justification, however, for considering his mint-area attributions of quinarii missing from this find as well founded and sound, unless other criteria, based on more reliable information, not merely on intelligent supposition, can be advanced to upset these attributions.

[1] Buttrey, op. cit. 263 f.
[2] Published by the author in 'Sydenham in Retrospect', in *Mints, Dies, and Currency. Essays Dedicated to the Memory of Albert Baldwin* (London, 1971), 13, no. 10.

Sydenham postulated a chronology for the early denarius and quinarius issues based on 187 B.C. as the date for the inception of these coins and their parallel bronzes, but his dating has been subjected to considerable criticism in the twenty years since his book was published. I myself became disenchanted with the 187 B.C. date soon after the book appeared, as I felt there was an over-long period between the end of the quadrigatus issues (c. 215–212 B.C.) and Sydenham's proposed start of the denarius coinage in 187 B.C. This gap was too great to be occupied only by the early victoriati issues. The publication of some of the numismatic discoveries in connection with the Morgantina excavations resulted in the almost general acceptance of a date between 214 and 211 B.C. for the inception of the denarius and its associated coinages by Theodore Buttrey, Rudi Thomsen, Michael Crawford, and other leading students of this period. Sydenham's relative chronology, issue arrangements, and mint attributions for this era of the Roman coinage, however, have been challenged only in a few specific cases.

There is no question in my mind that this hoard from Calabria is later than the coins excavated at Morgantina. I feel that it probably dates from the years 205–195 B.C., if the now generally accepted date for the inception of the denarius issues to the period 214–211 B.C., based on the evidence of Morgantina, is to be followed.

Finally, I wish to thank the following for their substantial help and encouragement: Mrs. Silvia Hurter of Bank Leu & Co. A.G., of Zürich, Mr. Pierre Strauss of Münzen und Medaillen A.G., of Basel, Mr. George Muller of Spink & Son Ltd. of London, Mr. Robert Carson of the British Museum in London, and, perhaps most of all, my good friend and colleague in Italy who perforce must remain anonymous.

# Vespasian as Moneyer

## T. V. BUTTREY

[SEE PLATES 12–13]

MORE than half a century ago Laffranchi argued that some of the gold and silver coinage of Vespasian can be understood only as deliberately imitating types of Augustus. Laffranchi's thesis was that these types were repeated under Vespasian on the occasion of the centenary of the battle of Actium and after, and functioned as a memorial of that crucial event. More, they forced an analogy between Augustus and Vespasian, one both justified by the events and politically useful. 'Il mondo romano usciva allora da una guerra civile che aveva molta affinità con quella tra Ottaviano e M. Antonio, la cui cessazione accomunava Vespasiano ad Augusto, quale secondo restauratore dell'impero.'[1]

One could support this argument by turning to details beyond the coins: the emperor personally winning the support of the legions; returning from victory in the east to reign in a city of divided loyalties; undertaking the works of rebuilding in Rome, the financial reconstruction of the empire, the re-organization of the provinces. The so-called *lex de imperio Vespasiani* recognizes the analogy when it justifies some of the powers granted to Vespasian on the grounds that they had already been employed by Augustus, Tiberius, and Claudius.[2] Add to this that the dynastic principate was to continue; Vespasian could claim no ties to the Julio-Claudian family, but his own would provide the continuity necessary in future for peaceful succession rather than repeated civil war. No wonder then that the analogy with Augustus was pressed as well on the official documentation, the coins. No wonder too that Laffranchi's thesis has been absorbed into the literature as fact.[3]

But the thesis involves three difficulties. First, the revived Augustan types occur not at the beginning of the reign, where one would have expected their Actian message to have been most obvious and most necessary, but scattered through the reign. If they thereby indicate a continuing policy of back-reference to Augustus, they cannot be used to support the particular argument of the special reference to Actium on its centenary, for that passed with

---

[1] Lodovico Laffranchi, 'Un centenario numismatico nell'antichità', *RIN* 1911, 427–36.
[2] *CIL* 6, 930.
[3] e.g., *CAH* xi, 19. Most recently Enrico Bianco, 'Indirizzi programmatici e propagandistici nella monetazione di Vespasiano', *RIN* 1968, 145–224.

A.D. 70 while the Augustan types of Vespasian continued to be struck until his death in 79.

Second, hardly any of the Augustan types carries an overt reference to Actium anyway. We would welcome an imitation of Augustus' AEGYPTO CAPTA crocodile reverse, but instead there are vague and all-purpose representations of Neptune or of Victory. Some of Vespasian's coins bear Augustan types which patently have nothing to do with Actium, such as the laurel branches bestowed by the Senate in 27 B.C., or the kneeling Parthian on the recovery of the standards in 20 B.C. Still further types recall the person of Augustus himself—the capricorn, or the butting bull (if a reference to ancestral Thurium was intended on the Augustan coin). All in all, the imitative coins of Vespasian which Laffranchi cites do not seem to focus on anything special in Augustus' reign or life.

None the less, the thesis was taken up by Grant. 'The 100th anniversary of Actium fell in A.D. 70, that of the annexation of Egypt in 71, and that of *restituta respublica* in 74. Vespasian followed his predecessors Tiberius, Claudius and Nero in according numismatic celebration to these centenaries.'[1] Unfortunately, when he gets down to cases Grant has no evidence. His Appendix III, 'Vespasian's Centenary Issues of *c.* A.D. 69–71 and 73–74',[2] inspires no confidence when it begins with two issues of 69–70, (1) an *adlocutio* type in imitation of a piece described as 'shortly after Actium' here, but 'immediately preceding Actium' on p. 88; and (2) apparently Spanish aurei and denarii of *Divus Augustus* with reverse types of Concordia, Hispania, and Pax. None of this has any evident reference to Actium. Of the six 'centenary' types next listed by Grant, for A.D. 71, one is actually Vitellian,[3] two refer to the *Divus Augustus* coinage of Tiberius, one refers to the Parthian surrender of the standards. Only two have even a chance of including an Actian reference: the bronze with legend SPQR ADSERTORI LIBERTATIS PVBLICAE, whose Augustan analogue, however, is an eastern cistophoric tetradrachm; and the asses and dupondii bearing a Victory on prow with the legend VICTORIA NAVALIS, if they do not refer to Vespasian's victory on Lake Tiberias.[4] Even supposing this last type somehow to have been intended as an evocation of Actium, it was one of approximately fifty reverse types which occur on Vespasian's *aes* coinage of A.D. 71. If the reference is to Actium it is very thin indeed.

Similarly, for alleged references in A.D. 74 to the centenary of the *restituta respublica* Grant cites six types, of which the two laurel branches do recall

---

[1] Michael Grant, *Roman Anniversary Issues* (Cambridge, 1950), 88.

[2] Ibid. 179–80.

[3] More than half of Grant's treatment of Vespasian's 'centenary coinages' is concerned with the single type of Tutela, which has since been shown to have been a Vitellian innovation and so not relevant. See E. and F. Krupp, 'The *TUTELA* type of Vitellius', *NC* 1961, 129–30.

[4] Josephus, *Bellum Judaicum* 3, 522–31.

the Senate's gift of just 100 years before. But his other suggestions include (1) Vespasian's aurei and denarii with oak-wreath reverse, actually struck in A.D. 73, before the centenary and derived most recently from Vitellius in any case; (2) the rudder on globe, 'cf. coins of Augustus', which in fact appears as a type, and as this type, only on coins of Tiberius; and (3) the winged caduceus plainly imitated not from an imperial issue of Augustus ('the Roman coinage had last portrayed the *caduceus* in the hands of the herald-*ludio* of the Secular Games of 17 B.C.', p. 45), but, as a type, from denarii of Antony and Octavian struck probably in 43 B.C. If the evidence must be forced to this extreme to support Laffranchi's thesis, the case is hardly worth making.

The third and most serious difficulty is that while the gold and silver coinage of Vespasian is admittedly highly imitative, it is by no means specifically Augustan in reference. The types selected by Laffranchi make a coherent display of Augustan derivations, but in being selected they give a distorted picture of the total range of Vespasian's aurei and denarii, thus creating a further distortion in the alleged imitation of Augustus in Vespasian's policy. To give the complete picture of the coins and to re-examine the centenary thesis I have set out below the types of Vespasian's gold and silver coinage at the mint of Rome.[1] This synopsis is derived from the catalogues of Mattingly and Robertson, with a few additions. It does not claim to be complete in every detail; the final picture of the Flavian coinage will be at hand only when some martyr undertakes a full die study. But the table does illuminate the over-all structure of the types. Doubtful pieces are omitted. Coins struck outside Rome are not included: the mints are uncertain, the issues usually small, and most of the types are already represented at Rome. The types are shown in the order in which they occur in *BMCRE*, set against Mattingly's suggested dates of issue for convenience. In the right-hand column is my suggestion of the origin of the type, if it has a seemly antecedent. When more than one source is possible I give the most recent.

[1] Not the *aes*, which behaves entirely differently. All comments on Vespasian's coinage which follow refer to the gold and silver.

| Type | BMCRE ii Vespasian | 69/70 | 70/1 | 71/2 | 72/3 | 73 | 74 | 75 | 75/9 | 76 | 77/8 | 78/9 | 79 | Source |
|---|---|---|---|---|---|---|---|---|---|---|---|---|---|---|
| Titus and Domitian, busts | 1 [Pl. 12. 1] | V | | | | | | | | | | | | Vitellius (BMCRE i. 370, 12) [Pl. 12. 2] |
| Titus and Domitian, figures | 6 | V | | | | | | | | | | | | Galba (but rudder) (BMCRE i. 352, 241) |
| Fortuna stg. l. with prow | 7 | V | | | | | | | | | | | | Vitellius sesterce (BMCRE i. 58) |
| Mars r. | 10 | | V | | | | | | | | | | | |
| Neptune on prow stg. l. | 14 | | V | | | | | | | | | | | Otho (BMCRE i. 365, 5) |
| Aequitas stg. l. | 16 | | V | | | | | | | | | | | Otho (BMCRE i. 364, 1) [Pl. 12. 4] |
| Pax stg. l. | 20 [Pl. 12. 3] | | V | | | | | | | | | | | |
| Pax seated l., with branch and caduceus | 23 | | V | | | | | | | | | | | |
| Judaea and trophy | 31 | | | V | | | | | | | | | | |
| Judaea and palm | 43 | | | V | | | | | | | | | | |
| Titus and Domitian riding r. | p. 7, ‖ | | | V | | | | | | | | | | |
| Titus and Domitian seated | 45 | | | V | | | | | | | | | | |
| Sol/Vespasian | 47 [Pl. 12. 5] | | | V | | | | | | | | | | Obv. L. Mussidius Longus (Syd. 1094) [Pl. 12. 6] Rev. Octavian (BMCRE i. 100, 611) [Pl. 12. 6][7] |
| Concordia seated l. | p. 425 Addendum to p. 2 | | | | V | | | | | | | | | Nero[1] (BMCRE i. 209, 61) |
| Priestly implements, AVGVR, PON MAX, or TRI POT | 48 [Pl. 12. 8, 10] | | | | V | | V | | | | | | | Caesar (Syd. 1023) [Pl. 12. 9] |
| Neptune on globe stg. l. | 54 | | | | VT | V | | | | | | | | Octavian (BMCRE i. 100, 615) |
| Vesta seated l. | 55 [Pl. 12. 11] | | | | V | V | | | | | | | | Clodius Vestalis (Syd. 1134) [Pl. 12. 12] |
| Vesta stg. l. | p. 11, * [Pl. 13. 13] | | | | V | | | | | | | | | Lepidus/Regulus (Syd. 1105) [Pl. 13. 14] |
| Vesta temple | p. 11, † | | | | T | VT[2] | | | | | | | | |
| Victory r. on globe | 63 | | | | V | | | | | | | | | Octavian (BMCRE i. 99, 604) |
| Quadriga IMP CAESAR/Victory r. on prow | 147 | | | | | | V | | | | | | | Octavian (BMCRE i. 101, 617) |
| Vespasian in quadriga r., with or without IMP | 67 | | | | | V | | | | | | | | Octavian (BMCRE i. 101, 617) |
| Pax leaning on column l. | p. 12, * | | | | VT | VT | | | | | | | | Otho (without standard) (BMCRE i. 367, 21) |
| Victory r. crowning standard | 74 | | | | | VT | | | | | | | | |

[1] The same type occurs later under Vitellius, but Vespasian's legend CONCORDIA AVGVSTA reflects the Neronian CONCORDIA AVGVSTA rather than Vitellius CONCORDIA P R.

[2] Mattingly includes an unseen aureus of Domitian in the Vesta temple coins of A.D. 73 (BMCRE ii. 23, *), an anomaly in a system which regularly excludes Domitian from the shared reverse types of Vespasian and Titus. Such may not have been the case at Lugdunum where a piece of the same type is assigned (BMCRE ii. 84, 412). Robertson claims a copy of the Rome piece at Glasgow (RICHCC i. 245, 1), but its dies are the same as those of the British Museum aureus attributed to Lugdunum.

| Type | Page | Denomination marks | Parallel prototype |
|---|---|---|---|
| Judaea, palm, and emperor | 78 | VT | Vespasian sesterce of 71 (BMCRE i. 117, 543) |
| Titus in quadriga r. | p. 15, † | T    T    VT | Octavian (BMCRE i. 101, 617) |
| Clasped hands with winged caduceus and grain, poppies | 86 | | Civil Wars (BMCRE i. 290, 6) |
| SPQR in wreath | p. 16, † | VT   VT | Vitellius (BMCRE i. 370, 14) |
| Salus seated l. | 87 [Pl. 13. 15] | VT   VT | Nero (BMCRE i. 212, 87) [Pl. 13. 16] |
| Quinarius. Victory r. with wreath and palm | 91 | VTD   VD | Republic passim (Syd. 672, 956, 1079, 1284, 1291) |
| Quinarius. Victory seated l., wreath and palm | p. 17, * | VT   VD    D | M. Cato (Syd. 1053a, 1054) |
| Titus riding | p. 18, ‡ | T   T    V | Galba (BMCRE i. 311, 19) |
| Nemesis r. | 97 [Pl. 13. 17] | V | Claudius (BMCRE i. 165, 6) [Pl. 13. 18] |
| Vespasian seated r. | 98 [Pl. 13. 19] | VT   V   v | Tiberius[1] (BMCRE i. 124, 30) [Pl. 13. 20] |
| Titus seated r. | 114 | T   T | Tiberius (BMCRE i. 124, 30) |
| Domitian riding | 121 | D | Galba (BMCRE i. 311, 19) |
| Cow of Myron | 132 | V   VT   VT | Augustus (BMCRE i. 107, 661) |
| Laurel branches | 133 | VT   VT   VT | Augustus (BMCRE i. 58, 318) |
| Winged caduceus | 137 [Pl. 13. 21] | VT   VT   VT | Octavian/Antony (Syd. 1327a) [Pl. 13. 22] |
| Pax seated l. with branch | p. 425 (Addendum to p. 25) | V   V   VT | .. |
| Fortuna stg. l. on base with rudder | 145 | VT   VT   VT | Galba (but no base) (BMCRE i. 352, 241) |
| Spes l. | 154 | D | Vespasian aes of 72 (BMCRE i. 142, ‡) |
| Bull butting r. | 159 | V   VT   VT | Augustus (BMCRE i. 78, 450) |
| Eagle on base | p. 30, * | V   V | .. |
| Securitas seated l. | 165 | V   VT | Vespasian aes of 71 (BMCRE i. 129, *) |
| Victory l. on prow | 166 | V   V | Augustus quinarius (BMCRE i. 108, 670) |
| Victory on cista mystica | 168 | VT   VT | Augustus quinarius (BMCRE i. 105, 647) |
| Capricorn on globe, rudder, cornucopia | p. 32, † | T   VT   VT | Augustus (BMCRE i. 56, 305) |
| Aeternitas standing l. | 271 | T | .. |
| Jupiter stg. front | 276 | | Augustus (BMCRE i. 5, 23) |
| Pegasus | 193 | D | Octavian/Antony/Lepidus/ Mussidius Longus (Syd. 1100) |
| Cornucopia with fillet | 196 | D | |
| Mars stg. l. | 200 | VT | L. Valerius Flaccus (Syd. 565) |

1 A later Vitellian analogue holds patera rather than the branch common to the Tiberian and Flavian type. Vespasian's differs from both earlier types in placing the imperial figure on a curule chair instead of the high-backed seat.

| Type | BMCRE ii Vespasian | 69/70 | 70/1 | 71/2 | 72/3 | 73 | 74 | 75 | 75/9 | 76 | 77/8 | 78/9 | 79 | Source |
|---|---|---|---|---|---|---|---|---|---|---|---|---|---|---|
| Emperor crowned by Victory | 204 | | | | | | | | | | V | | V | Seleucus II (*BMC Seleucid Kings*, 6, 58) |
| Oxen | 206 | | | | | | | | | | VT | | | Octavian (with emperor) (*BMCRE* i. 104, 638) |
| Prow, star | 210 | | | | | | | | | | VT | | | Antony/Ahenobarbus (Syd. 1178) |
| Sow and young | 212 | | | | | | | | | | VT | | | :: |
| Modius | 216 [Pl. 13. 23] | | | | | | | | | | V | | | :: |
| Goatherd | 220 | | | | | | | | | | VT | | | :: |
| Roma seated r. | 223 | | | | | | | | | | T | | | Anonymous Republican (Syd. 530) |
| Barbarian and vexillum | 231 | | | | | | | | | | D | | | Augustus (*BMCRE* i. 3, 10) |
| Horseman r. | 234 | | | | | | | | | | D | | | :: |
| Wolf and twins | 237 | | | | | | | | | | D | | | :: |
| Annona seated l. | 290 | | | | | | | | | | | VT | | :: |
| Ceres stg. l. with grain and sceptre | 299 | | | | | | | | | | | VTD | | Nero (but torch) (*BMCRE* i. 204, 25) |
| Ceres seated l. with grain and torch | 243 | | | | | | | | | | | | V | Vitellius *aes* (*BMCRE* i. 381, 71) |
| Victory placing shield on trophy | 245 | | | | | | | | | | | | V | :: |
| Female with crown of towers | 249 | | | | | | | | | | | | V | Augustus (*BMCRE* i. 80, 465) |
| Capricorn on globe | 251 | | | | | | | | | | | | V | Octavian (*BMCRE* i. 103, 633) |
| Figure on rostral column | 253 | | | | | | | | | | | | V | Octavian (*BMCRE* i. 98, 599) |
| Venus with arms, leaning on column | 255 | | | | | | | | | | | | T | Augustus (*BMCRE* i. 7, 38) |
| Quadriga with modius | 256 | | | | | | | | | | | | T | C. Memmius (Syd. 920) |
| Trophy and captive | 258 | | | | | | | | | | | | D | Galba as (*BMCRE* i. 335, 159) |
| Vesta seated l. with palladium | 260 | | | | | | | | | | | | D | Galba as (*BMCRE* i. 361, 265) |
| Salus standing r. | 264 | | | | | | | | | | | | D | Mn. Fonteius (Syd. 724) |
| Goat in wreath | p. 47, * | | | | | | | | | | | | D | :: |
| Clasped hands with aquila | 267 | | | | | | | | | | | | | :: |

Two points emerge at once from this synopsis. There was a strong tendency in the Rome mint under Vespasian to employ a reverse type for a limited period, apparently one year. New types were introduced each year, the older ones being normally phased out. A few types were struck during two years, almost none for more than two.[1] Moreover, the new reverse types, constantly and regularly introduced, were normally copies or imitations of types on pre-Flavian coins. That this was standard mint procedure is clear from the whole run of Vespasian's coins.

A.D. 69–70

A number of original types, more than in any succeeding year, introduces the gold and silver of the new reign: a seated Pax, a standing Neptune,[2] and the two Judaea varieties which refer specifically to Vespasian's recent eastern campaign. In addition three of the dynastic reverses are only vaguely suggestive of earlier influence. The standing figures of Titus and Domitian might possibly have been imitated from the type of Nero and Poppaea (*BMCRE* i. 208, 52), while the seated figures with palms may recall the denarius of Sulpicius Platorinus (*BMCRE* i. 23, 115) which bears Augustus and Agrippa in a similar posture but without palms. Titus and Domitian riding r. may derive from a Republican Dioscurid type.

The remaining aureus and denarius types of this first year, those whose antecedents can be ascertained, do not support the theses of Laffranchi and Grant. The facing heads of Titus and Domitian [Pl. 12. 1] do go back originally to the denarius of Agrippa struck for Octavian in 38 B.C., with similar heads of Octavian and Caesar (Syd. 1330); but they here repeat the facing portraits of Vitellius' children, struck only a few months earlier [Pl. 12. 2]. Otherwise the borrowings are Republican, with one reverse of Octavian, or from the reigns of Galba, Otho [Pl. 12. 3–4], and again Vitellius. It doubtless was simpler for the engraver, or whatever official was responsible for the selection of types, to retain the inoffensively general figurations of the immediately preceding reigns, until Vespasian had returned to Rome and Flavian policy had been established. The optimistic reverses of the Imperial coinages do tend to be universally valid and easily carried over from one emperor to the next.

Thus the borrowed type was valid in itself, quite apart from an association with its original issuing authority. The imitation of the reverse of Vitellius' children is sufficient proof of that. But this then casts doubt on Laffranchi's basic, and unspoken assumption. He assumes that the imitation of an earlier

---

[1] Among the few exceptions the quinarius types seem to have been regarded as fixed to the denomination.

[2] 'The thought of the absent Emperor and the hope of his return are embodied in the types of Neptune and Fortuna' (*BMCRE* ii. xxxiii). But the legend of this issue is COS ITER TR POT, and only the second Neptune type, struck in A.D. 70–1, was identified as NEP RED.

coin type was meant to, and did in fact excite a memory of the meaning of that type in its context. The evidence of these few coins suggests the opposite: one was *not* supposed to balance Vespasian's children against those of Vitellius; the coin type merely happens to be convenient. Or again, *Concordia Augusta*, and the type of Concordia, are genuine expressions of Flavian publicity, without respect to the fact—or better, in spite of the fact—that the identical type with only a slightly different, more institutionalized legend, *Concordia Augusti*, had been struck for the egregious Nero.

A parallel case is the Sol/Vespasian denarius [Pl. 12. 5]. Here the engraver has combined elements of two earlier denarii which had nothing to do with one another [Pl. 12. 6–7]. On the reverse, copied from a type of Octavian, the earlier legend CAESAR DIVI F is replaced by VESPASIANVS in the same position, to convey the flavour of the original. The whole coin exudes an antique air, imposed on it through the general shape of the borrowed types, now more than a century old. This is to argue an antiquarian fascination with old coins, rather than an obsession with historical parallels cultivated to political ends. That such antiquarianism did in fact lie behind Vespasian's coins will be argued below, but the reverses of Concordia and the imperial children, however pointed politically, already support such a view.

A.D. 70–1

Only two of the first year's types were repeated, while six new types were introduced. Of the new types only one is original in any degree: the temple of Vesta, struck in quantity under Nero, appears in a larger design with the addition of a figure at either side. Otherwise the types are a deliberate imitation of earlier aurei and denarii of the Republic, Caesar, the Triumvirate, and Octavian. The most telling imitation is that of the denarius of Caesar [Pl. 12. 9], for it illustrates that the total type including legend where possible was taken over as a single conception. The legends AVGVR and PON(T) MAX were as applicable to Vespasian as to Caesar and so were retained, even though this is the only one of Vespasian's many coin types on which he is noted as augur. A single alteration in the type (aside from the omission of the inapplicable D(onativum) or M(unus) of the Caesarian prototype) is the change in reverse legend from PON MAX [Pl. 12. 8] to TRI POT [Pl. 12. 10], presumably to avoid the dittography of the first variety, since P M was already included in the title of the obverse die.

A second type of importance is that of the seated Vesta [Pl. 12. 11]. She had appeared most recently on aurei and denarii of Otho and Vitellius, with the legend denoting the pontifex maximus, as here. Her figuration, however, was slightly different in A.D. 69, for she held a patera and sceptre, and sat in a high-backed chair. That image was not the prototype of the Vespasianic, which actually derives from a Republican denarius of 43 B.C., struck by Clodius Vestalis (Syd. 1134) [Pl. 12. 12]. In each case she bears a simpulum lifted directly from the Republican. An exegesis of the Republican type has led to the identification of the lady not as the goddess herself but as Claudia Quinta, a Vestal Virgin. No matter; the similar figuration of god and priest is an ancient conceit and finds confirmation in the other Vesta type struck by Vespasian in A.D. 70/1 [Pl. 13. 13]. In this case the goddess is identified, but the type is a clear copy of another Republican coin, the aureus struck for Lepidus at Rome in 42 B.C. by the moneyer L. Livineius Regulus [Pl. 13. 14]. Lepidus' coin appears in a series struck by Regulus for all three members of the Triumvirate, each with a reverse referring to the mythological antecedents of their families—for Octavian, Aeneas, and Anchises; for Antony, Anton the son of Heracles; for Lepidus, the Vestal Virgin Aemilia who was, in Plutarch's version of the story, the mother of Romulus and Remus.[1] Thus the figure of the Republican priestess has provided the Imperial coin with the figure of the goddess herself.

The two reverse types of Neptune and Victory on globe are derived from the pre-Actian coinage of Octavian.[2] In each case the original identifying legend, CAESAR DIVI F, has been replaced by one identifying the divinity itself, NEP RED and VIC AVG.

Note that the Judaea types were not struck in A.D. 71, the year the triumph was actually celebrated.

### A.D. 71–2

A single, undated issue is assigned by Mattingly to this year. It is most unlikely that the coinage exhibited such a gap, which ought to be covered by issues now assigned to A.D. 70–1 and 72–3. There is no way to place the one coin in question, a copy in both its types of a denarius of Octavian.

### A.D. 72–3

The new types of A.D. 70–1 were, unusually, repeated, and five additional reverses introduced. The pre-Actian coinage of Octavian provides two of these, or rather one used for both Vespasian and Titus: the emperor, or the prince, in quadriga r. Some of the dies of this type bear no legend; those that do, read merely IMP in the exergue, precisely as Octavian's coin. The Victory r. with wreath and palm is a fair representation of the type which had appeared in A.D. 69 with the overtly hopeful legend VICTORIA OTHONIS, here altered to VICTORIA AVGVSTI; but Otho's standard is omitted. The Pax type was not seen before this year, although Galba's dupondii provide another form of the theme (significantly without purse?); and the Judaea type is a reproduction of a type already struck by Vespasian on sesterces of A.D. 71.

---

[1] Plutarch, *Romulus* 2. 3.

[2] Laffranchi's argument also falls partly on this point. The series of plain and forceful types of Octavian, attributed to 36–27 B.C. by Grueber (*BMCRR* ii, 8–17) and 31–27 B.C. by Mattingly (*BMCRE* i, 97–105) are now shown by Michael Crawford to be mostly pre-Actian (*Roman Republican Coin Hoards* [London, 1969], Table XVII and 41–2, note 8).

*A.D. 73*

Some of the coins last noted will probably have been struck in the first months of A.D. 73, before Vespasian entered on the censorship. The obverse dies of 73 which include that title for Vespasian or Titus appear with seven new reverse types of aurei and denarii, as well as two silver quinarii. Domitian also appears in this year of his second consulate with one type of aureus and denarius, and one of quinarius. The models for the types are again varied. The Republic supplies, at least indirectly, the reverse with clasped hands, etc. (Decimus Brutus, Syd. 942, 944), although only in the coinage of the Civil Wars, A.D. 68–9, do hands and caduceus appear with grain and poppies. The two quinarii types are also Republican, and do not imitate the most recent issues of this denomination, struck under Augustus. The figure of Titus or Domitian riding comes from Galba, who had apparently copied it from Octavian's pre-Actian coinage (Syd. 1317). Tiberius' enormous issues of aurei and denarii with reverse type of seated figure and PONTIF MAXIM are taken over by Vespasian legend and all, the figure now being the emperor rather than the ambiguous female (or Titus, with legend appropriately PONTIF TRI POT) [Pl. 13. 19–20]. The coins of Claudius provide a very familiar reverse, that of Nemesis r [Pl. 13. 17–18]. Nero's Salus seated l. is repeated exactly [Pl. 13. 15–16]. And finally the oak wreath with legend SPQR is taken from the coins of Vitellius and the Civil Wars.

*A.D. 74*

The coinage of A.D. 74 includes the repetition of a few types struck earlier (the Republican-inspired quinarii would remain standard for the rest of the reign), five new types for Vespasian and Titus, and one for Domitian. The winged caduceus had not appeared on denarii since the Republic, the latest of its appearances being the joint issue of Octavian and Antony [Pl. 13. 21–22].[1] Augustus also provided the originals of the other two types, the cow of Myron and the pair of laurel branches. Again the Augustan legends of AVGVSTVS and CAESAR AVGVSTVS have been altered to avoid the dittography with Vespasian's obverse legend. The Spes type of Domitian's aurei and denarii has no earlier prototype in these metals, but occurs on sesterces and asses of Vespasian and his sons from A.D. 72, in imitation of sesterces of Claudius.

*A.D. 75*

Again, two earlier types are continued into this year, but the bulk of the aurei and denarii are struck in six new types. Only two of these are identical with a pre-Flavian issue of the same module, but the others are of clearly identifiable origins. The bull butting r. derives directly from the aurei and

---

[1] The winged caduceus also appeared on Tiberian asses (*BMCRE* i, 135, 106) and is repeated on Vespasian's quadrantes (see below).

denarii of Augustus attributed to Lugdunum and struck during his tenth and twelfth imperatorships (*BMCRE* i, 78, 450; 81, 468). Both Titus and Vespasian employ the type, inserting their own number of imperatorial acclamation below the type in the reverse exergue, just as Augustus had done, or alternatively their consular numeration, not included in Vespasian's obverse titulature since COS IIII of A.D. 72–3. An Augustan original is also obvious for the capricorn with globe, rudder, and cornucopia.

The types of two Augustan quinarii were adapted to the larger flans of aureus and denarius, Victory l. on prow, and Victory l. on cista mystica with snakes to r. and l. The type of eagle on base is not precisely copied, but eagle on globe had been an important reverse in the series of Tiberius' DIVVS AVGVSTVS asses, and had been struck on Vespasian's asses since A.D. 71. Securitas seated l. had also appeared on Vespasian's dupondii of 71, imitated from *aes* of Nero, Galba, and Vitellius.

### *A.D. 75–9*

Mattingly includes under this half-decade a few issues of which the obverse legend offers no better chronological clue. Judging from the reverse types, however, it is pretty clear that they were struck in A.D. 75, or 76 at the latest. The Fortuna reverse repeats that of 74, as does the Pax type save for one detail. The two quinarii types, otherwise not attested for Vespasian after 74, are continued. Neither of the two new types of Aeternitas and Jupiter appears to have an antecedent.

### *A.D. 76*

Contrary to the usual pattern, the reverse types of Vespasian and Titus are all continuations from previous years, but two new types appear for Domitian. The Pegasus is taken from denarii of the Augustan moneyer Petronius Turpillianus (*BMCRE* i, 5, 23). The cornucopia with fillet had not appeared since even earlier, 42 B.C., when it was struck as a reverse type for each member of the Second Triumvirate by L. Mussidius Longus.

### *A.D. 77–8*

It is not possible to distinguish the products of these two calendar years, except that the sow and the goat-herd types appear with Titus' title IMP XIII and are therefore to be dated to A.D. 78. In any case during these two years all aurei and denarii are struck with new types, save for one possible repetition: the rider type of Domitian might be a view from the r. of the type struck for him and Titus in A.D. 73, though some details differ. Otherwise the types are derived from the Republic, or Augustus, or are of that style. The Mars figure is an exact copy of the Mars on a Republican denarius of L. Valerius Flaccus, with some dies even including the grain ear symbol at r.

The seated Roma is an equally faithful copy from an anonymous Republican denarius of the late second century B.C. Coins of Antony struck by Cn. Domitius Ahenobarbus provide the prow and star reverse. The denarius with yoke of oxen has a close parallel in a coin of Octavian, while the barbarian with vexillum struck as reverse for Domitian is of course taken directly from aurei and denarii of the Augustan moneyers P. Petronius Turpillianus, L. Aquillius Florus, and M. Durmius.

The remaining types of A.D. 77–8 are even more consciously antiquarian in origin. The emperor or victorious general crowned by Victory does not appear in this form earlier in the Roman coinage, although there are some types reasonably similar (cf. Syd. 561, 605). But it may well have a Greek origin. The type 'is either a derivative of bronze of Seleucus II or a remarkable coincidence'.[1] Moreover, the types of sow, modius [Pl. 13. 23], goat-herd, and wolf and twins are all of an archaistic style designed to be Republican *looking*, even though none of these is drawn from an original Republican coin. A representation of the wolf and twins (but not this one) goes back to the Romano-Campanian didrachm (Syd. 6); the modius, between grain ears, can be found on a denarius of L. Livineius Regulus (Syd. 1111), another of whose types had already been imitated in the coinage of A.D. 70–1. Here the legend runs across the field, in imitation of the pre-Actian issues of Octavian. The sow with young, and the goat-herd do not occur earlier at all among Roman coin types. All these types, in this form, actually originate with Vespasian, yet they are so designed as to suggest a late Republican origin, in that the field of the reverse is in each case left clear, with the brief legend falling in the exergue or across mid-field.

### A.D. 78–9

Two new types were introduced in this undated series. The Annona seated l. has no real prototype, but the standing Ceres with grain and sceptre has analogues in the coinage of Nero (grain and torch) and Otho (grain and cornucopia).

### A.D. 79

A dozen new types were introduced in this last year of Vespasian's reign, those of Vespasian and Titus at least being struck before Titus' accession on 23 June. Denarii of the Republic provided two of the new reverses, the trophy and captive (C. Memmius, Syd. 920), and the goat in wreath, a simplification of the type of Mn. Fonteius (Syd. 724). The types of Venus with arms, and figure on a rostral column come directly from denarii of

---

[1] Alfred R. Bellinger and Marjorie Alkins Berlincourt, *Victory as a Coin Type* (*NNM* 149), 58.

Octavian.[1] Capricorn with globe is taken from a denarius of the eleventh imperatorship of Augustus, where, however, the globe is held between the forepaws of the beast; and the quadriga with modius derives from a denarius type of the Augustan moneyers L. Aquillius Florus and M. Durmius. Bronze asses of Galba were the source of two types, Domitian's seated Vesta and standing Salus, while Vespasian's seated Ceres derives most recently from Vitellius. The three remaining types are new, although the clasped hands with standard has an analogue in a denarius of the Civil Wars.

This survey does not support Laffranchi's thesis. One cannot deny the Augustan reminiscences in Vespasian's coinage, but to focus on them to the exclusion of the other types is to misrepresent. A total of the types listed above according to derivation is as follows.

| | | | |
|---|---|---|---|
| Greek | 1 | Nero | 3 |
| Roman Republican | 12 | Galba | 6 |
| Octavian/Augustus | 20 | Otho | 3 |
| Tiberius | 2 | Vitellius | 4 |
| Claudius | 1 | Vespasian *aes* | 3 |

Now Mattingly saw that more than Augustan antecedents were present in Vespasian's coinage, and he argued that the range of imitations was intended to reflect Flavian achievements. 'The founder of the new dynasty is much concerned to establish connections with the old Republic and the first imperial house. Restored types are a persistent feature of the reign. . . . The selection of types to be restored was so made as to throw light on current events of the day' (*BMCRE* ii, xliii). Yet the Roman types selected for imitation covered a span of over 200 years prior to Vespasian's reign. Whatever their immediate significance in the A.D. 70s, the care with which the earlier figure was copied, and the fact that even the original legends, or at least the outward shape of the legends, was preserved when possible, suggests that what was being publicized was not an earlier event and Vespasian's putative connection with it, but the earlier coin itself. To observe this situation from another angle, it is noteworthy that types of Vespasian which might proclaim specific achievements are mostly wanting. Excepting only the *Judaea Capta* issues, they do *not* openly 'throw light on current events of the day'. Of all the buildings which Vespasian is known to have constructed or

---

[1] The identification of the figure and the column has long been argued. Eckhel opted for Nero's Colossus, whose portrait was removed by Vespasian and replaced by a head of Sol; and he noted only in passing, 'Typum, qualis in numo praesente est, non absimilem habes in numis Octaviani' (6,335–6). Mattingly accepted this reading (*BMCRE* ii, xlii). It is true that Vespasian's type differs from Octavian's in the one detail that the later figure on column is radiate. But if the statue originally was a dedication to Octavian (cf. *BMCRE* i, cxxiv and note 2), it could well have been rendered radiate after Augustus' death and deification, so that the coin of Vespasian, while copying an earlier type, will have brought its figuration up to date.

repaired, not one appears on any of his gold and silver.[1] The great so-called Forum Pacis is never shown on the coins, in contrast to Nero's Macellum or Titus' Colosseum. The grain supply was an immediate concern of Vespasian in late A.D. 69 or early 70,[2] yet Annona appears on his *aes* coinage first in 76, on gold and silver in 78/9. The roads, bridges, and aqueducts go unmentioned. Where at least some of Augustus' military successes are alluded to, only the vague suggestiveness of Mars, Pax, or Victoria decorates Vespasian's coins.

The question then is why the engravers at the mint preferred to ignore the real accomplishments of the reign, and to issue coins whose types were carefully copied from earlier pieces struck on many different occasions and under various authorities. The answer was already suggested by Mattingly when he recognized that Vespasian's gold and silver constitute a giant restoration coinage, the first series produced at Rome, although the legend *restituit* was not to appear on coin until the reign of Titus. We ought to be able to draw some comparisons between these issues and the admittedly restored coins of subsequent emperors. The greatest array, the restored aurei and denarii of Trajan, appear to present a cross-section of the Republican denarii and imperial aurei struck up to his reign. Mattingly saw their origin in two causes, '(a) the withdrawal of obsolescent coins from circulation and the wish to preserve some record of what is being lost; (b) the desire to explain and commend current policy by linking it to the record of the great past'.[3] Dio 68, 15 supports the first point when he notes that old coin was withdrawn by Trajan, and the silver hoards do show a remarkably high percentage of Republican denarii in circulation as late as Domitian and Nerva, with a sharp drop to almost nothing in the post-Trajanic hoards.[4] The second point is unexceptionable for a coinage whose whole history appears to be the purveying of imperial publicity.

But several problems remain. Dio does not justify the restoration of imperial aurei, for while he speaks of coins in general, the evidence supports him only for the denarii; the gold hoards show an entirely different pattern. The important break had been the reform of Nero in A.D. 64, whereby the weight of the aureus was reduced from 1/42 to 1/45 lb. The hoards show a drop in pre-reform aurei thereafter, but we have no reason to believe that Trajan took old gold from circulation. Further, the notion that the restored

---

[1] Thus the dedication of the Sodales Titii to Vespasian as *restitutor aedium sacrarum* (*CIL* 6,934). For further epigraphical evidence of Vespasian's building activity, see H. C. Newton, *The Epigraphical Evidence for the Reigns of Vespasian and Titus* (Ithaca, New York 1902), 46–50, and M. McCrum and A. G. Woodhead, *Select Documents of the Principates of the Flavian Emperors* (Cambridge, 1961), *passim*.

[2] Tacitus, *Histories* 4. 52.

[3] *BMCRE* iii, lxxxvii, a restatement of *BMCRE* ii, xxxviii and lxxvii commenting on restorations under Vespasian and Titus.

[4] For a survey of typical hoards see Sture Bolin, *State and Currency in the Roman Empire* (Stockholm, 1958), 335–57.

coins were somehow memorials to or replacements of original types no longer in circulation contains a number of improbabilities. Some of the restored denarii were copies not of pieces in frequent circulation but of considerable rarity, for example, the denarii of L. Servius Rufus, C. Numonius Vaala, and particularly Q. Cornuficius. One type was restored which had never existed in this form at all, the quadrigatus. Reduced to a denarius it now reappeared in the gallery of ancient types, although it is absolutely impossible that it had seen circulation for the previous 300 years.[1] But this confection of Trajan's engravers, and the small details in which some denarii differ from their originals, pale before the inventive talent which produced the restored Imperial aurei. Of twenty-five aurei in all, only six reproduce the original obverse legend, portrait, and reverse type. Thirteen alter the original obverse legend to DIVVS IVLIVS, DIVVS AVGVSTVS, etc., but even of these only three are matched to a reverse type appropriate to the emperor. Thus Caesar appears with two reverses, a standing Venus originated by Octavian and later taken over by Titus Caesar, and the Nemesis-Pax of Claudius. The restored aurei of Claudius, on the other hand, bear no reverse that actually had appeared on his aurei, but Spes (taken from Claudian sesterces), Concordia (from Nero and Vitellius), and a seated Vesta (Vitellius and the Civil Wars). Vespasian appears with reverses of Titus, and vice versa. Nerva is paired with a type of aquila and standards borrowed—if from his coinage at all— from a cistophoric tetradrachm. All this mixture, if bewildering, is quite deliberate, for the engraver had only to copy what was on the coin before him, and turn it over to reproduce the other side, if he had wished 'to preserve some record of what is being lost'. Even had he wanted to invent likely coins, as Ligorio invented likely inscriptions which had not yet been discovered, he could well have devised more than the three new reverses which this series holds—heads of Mercury and Jupiter (Vespasian), Mars and Minerva (Titus), emperor in elephant biga (Nerva). But novelty here is to be found not in the invention of new types, but in the scrambling of known obverses and reverses.

Thus Mattingly's argument that older coins were being replaced or memorialized is not sufficient. Trajan's coins include not only restorations of pieces which could not have been in circulation in his time, but 'restorations' of pieces which had never circulated in the memory of man. The other point, that restorations point up current policy, holds only when reference to that policy is explicit. A general evocation of the past, and an indication of imperial continuity are harmless enough, but, when we get down to cases, few of the types selected have anything specific to offer. Mattingly elsewhere argued that Trajan's mint exercised careful and deliberate choice;[2] but when

---

[1] The quadrigatus went out of circulation on the introduction of the denarius c. 212 B.C. Apparently only one hoard includes silver coins of the two systems mixed together (Crawford, op. cit., 66 no. 93, the Pisticci hoard).
[2] 'The Restored Coins of Trajan', *NC* 1926, 232–78.

he sees the types as selected '(a) for historical and legendary interest; (b) for general interest of type; (c) for religious interest; (d) for family references',[1] he is simply describing the Republican coinage itself. *Any* restoration of a Republican denarius will imitate an original derived from one of these categories. The inclination of our criticism is to extort some meaning from every type, but it is I think no accident that the very largest part of Mattingly's article is given to the discussion of the originals restored by Trajan, not to the meaning of the restorations themselves, for so little can be said about them. Trajan's current policy by no means emerges from them, and we cannot suppose it to be there simply by claiming that 'the main object of the restoration of Republican denarii seems to have been to revive the glorious memories of the old days and to link them up with the new glories of the Empire'.[2] On the contrary, the restored coins of Trajan are a random selection, their links to his empire doubtful, their types sometimes imaginary—as Bahrfeldt characterized them, 'eine antiquarische Spielerei'.

Two factors make restoration coins possible. First, there will have been in antiquity collections of coins, perhaps even a mint collection, which the engraver or the designer of types could consult.[3] Second, and more important, there must have been at the Rome mint (as no doubt at all mints) a tendency to look at the coins as products of a manufacturing process, not as purveyors of political, historical, religious, or aesthetic information. The entire tendency of our numismatic criticism, our use of coins, is to see coins as bearers of messages from the past, which happen to be conveyed to us through the types and legends of the money of the ancients but might as easily have reached us through literary, epigraphical, or other representational forms. But those who actually make the coins do so in a tradition of coins as complete physical objects, created through the arts of metal smelting and assaying, flan manufacture, die cutting, striking, and annealing—a multiplex manufacturing process of which one aspect only is the selection of the die types. Monetarily it is far more important that the aureus be of the proper weight, and the proper fineness, and bear some authorizing seal or legend, than that it commemorate this year's victory. Commemorate it may, but when it appears it will join a long series of coins of quite varying types which together constitute the history of mint production.

That history was known to the minters themselves, as earlier examples from Rome easily demonstrate. Under the Republic several doublets of type occur, the repetition usually remaining within the moneyer's family. Thus one of the earliest denarius types to appear after the succession of Dioscuri, bigas, quadrigas, etc., the column type of C. Augurinus (Syd. 463), is repeated a few years later by Ti. C. f. Augurinus (Syd. 494). L. Piso Frugi and C. Piso L. f.

---

[1] 'The Restored Coins of Trajan', *NC* 1926, 271.                                   [2] Ibid. 275.
[3] Thus the well-known passage in Suetonius, *Augustus* 75, which shows that the emperor had access to rare coins.

Frugi use the same Apollo/Horseman types about a quarter of a century apart (Syd. 650 ff., 840 ff.). Almost half a century separate the two issues of denarii and quinarii of the two M. Cato's, the later issue reproducing not simply the types but the legends and ligatures of the earlier (Syd. 596, 1052). Most mysterious is the repetition of three issues of Q. Fabius Maximus, M. Caecilius Metellus, C. Servilius (Syd. 478, 480, 483), all with Roma heads, which are found about forty years later with identical reverse types but now all with Apollo heads (Syd. 718-20). Under Augustus the moneyer L. Aquillius Florus restored two obverse types, heads of Virtus and Sol, and one reverse, the raising of Sicily, struck decades before by two putative ancestors (Syd. 557, 798; *BMCRE* i, 7, 36, 38; 9, 49). Not all repetitions derive from a family connection. Another Augustan moneyer, M. Durmius, restored the Republican reverse of Victory with palm and wreath r.; usually associated with the quinarius, it had been struck as a denarius with the head of Octavian in 42 B.C. by Livineius Regulus, and was restored by Durmius with the obverse portrait of Augustus. For a more illuminating instance of sheer antiquarianism note Durmius' rare denarius with Heracles obverse, the exact copy of the Heracles head on a coin long out of circulation, the third century B.C. Romano-Campanian didrachm (Syd. 6). Durmius even imitated non-Roman coins, striking denarii with types taken from Naples and Velia (*BMCRE* i, 12, 63; 12, 66).[1]

These last examples reveal no overt reference to the moneyer's family, in spite of Mattingly's conjecture (n. 1, below); and would be, even in that case, not references to 'the original home of his family' but at best to the *coins* of that supposed original home. The moneyer has preserved and transmitted to us not some overt notice of political or historical significance, but a recognition of the historicity of minting itself. The accumulated lore of the mint, deriving from the collection of dies and coins, from the examination of old and foreign coins submitted for melting and recoining, from the necessary records of bullion receipt and coin production, from the orders delivered to the engravers or from their design notebooks, and perhaps most of all from personal experience of the mint employees at all levels, handed down through the years—all this would have contributed to a sense of professional continuity, preserved by individuals or by the coins themselves even when the function of the institution was suspended (as when the mint of Rome appears to have abandoned gold and silver to Lugdunum under Augustus-Caligula). We will never know the motives of Durmius, for example, in choosing the types he did. But that he was able so to choose argues a tradition, not only

---

[1] And Capua or Paestum, according to Babelon i, 468 and Mattingly (*BMCRE* i, ciii–civ), but the boar type is actually copied only from the Republican denarius of Hosidius (Syd. 903). Mattingly also follows Babelon and others in stating that the Greek types 'appear to refer to Campania, which we may conjecture to have been the original home of his family', but there is no evidence for that at all. The *nomen* occurs epigraphically not in Campania but in Latium (*PIR*² D 209).

conceptual but physical, in terms of objects known and preserved, which we tend to underestimate. Certainly our habit of analysing the individual imperial coin type in terms of the contemporary history of the reign under which it was issued obscures traditional or even antiquarian tendencies on the part of the moneyers.

Furthermore, to return to Vespasian, the argument that part of the political force of his gold and silver types lies in their having been restored requires a public appreciation of the history of numismatic types. But it seems quite impossible that the public at large could have known that foreign types, or Roman types long out of circulation, were being revived on their current coin.[1] The large availability of Republican denarii in the late first century A.D. has its other side: could anyone at random really be expected to be familiar with all the types of this infinitely varied coinage, and to know, for example, not only that the types of trophy and captive struck for Titus Caesar in A.D. 79 was borrowed from an earlier model, but that the model was the first century B.C. denarius of C. Memmius who was preserving in his way the memory of the still earlier destruction of Corinth in 146 B.C.? These details are not of importance to people at large whose most pressing need, as far as coins are concerned, is to earn them and spend them. But they *are* matters of interest to the mint official, whose *métier* it is, and to the numismatist, whose study it is.[2]

All of this argues an antiquarian attitude in the Flavian mint which makes itself evident in the gold and silver types of Vespasian. What it does not yet reveal is the specific impetus behind this flowering of older types. For exactly the same materials were available to earlier emperors. Yet the aurei and denarii of Tiberius were churned out year after year with unaltering types, in stupefying dullness. Gaius' pious gallery of family portraits draws at least in part on the Augustan and Tiberian antecedents, and remains, with one additional wreath type, the standard for the reign. The innovations of Claudius' first year petrify in repetition, until his lucky fourth marriage is celebrated with coins of Agrippina and the adopted Ahenobarbus. Nero, after the customary recognition of family, produces a repeating series, then a new series, on the changing of the standard in A.D. 64. Galba, Otho, and Vitellius

---

[1] There are many analogies. How many Italians know, or care, that most of the types of the post-war aluminium coinage are free variations of specific ancient originals? Or how many Britons not coin collectors, that the seated Britannia derives from a sesterce of Antoninus Pius?

[2] Cf. A. H. M. Jones, 'Numismatics and History', in *Essays in Roman Coinage presented to Harold Mattingly* (Oxford, 1956), 15–16, who cites the analogy of the modern postage stamp: 'They throw a sidelight on the history of the period, but they mainly reflect the mentality of the post-office officials.' This may underrate the usefulness of the coins as evidence, or demean the authorities responsible for them; but he is right on insisting that coin types are selected by the bureaucracy, not by historians. Jones's less acceptable strictures on type interpretation are trenchantly dissected by C. H. V. Sutherland, 'The Intelligibility of Roman Coin Types', in *JRS* 1959, 46–55.

show more originality, partly because the repeated family references on the Julio-Claudian coins were not available to them; but in part the number of types of A.D. 68–9 is due to the innovations introduced by the extra-Roman mints in the west. No one can say where these aborted coinages might have led. But it is the Vespasianic mint of Rome which, for the first time since Augustus, and with even more regularity, produces a continuous and considered series of changing types, drawn for the most part not from the inventive imagination of the engraver or his superior but from the total fund of types elaborated at the Rome mint during the preceding 200 years and more.[1]

Nothing like this had been seen before. Vespasian's aurei and denarii mirror the coinage of the Republic in the general tendency toward annual alteration of type. In so far as they celebrate, or can be taken to celebrate, the emperor and his heirs, whose portraits normally occur on the obverse throughout, they mirror the usage introduced by Augustus who produced the most varied and interesting of the pre-Flavian coinages. But in so far as the Vespasianic coins deliberately copy earlier types and in this respect tend to avoid originality, they mirror the coinages not of Augustus but of Tiberius. The whole attitude toward typology reminds one of Tiberius' gold and silver, on which every single type was inherited from Augustus.

A further note of Tiberian reminiscence under the Flavians is to be found in the restored *aes* struck by Titus. Fully half the types derive from Tiberius; not one is Augustan. Of course several types of *Divus Augustus Pater* are restored, but they are plainly posthumous and must have been known in the Rome mint in Titus' time to have been struck under Tiberius. Similarly, of the ten restored *aes* types struck by Domitian, all repeated from the restorations of Titus, seven are restorations of Tiberius. One might conclude that at the Rome mint under Vespasian the Tiberian experience was remembered and emulated.

Now there is evidence of Imperial control in the selection of types—for example the Judaea series in all metals—and the use of types—for example the care with which Vespasian and Titus share common reverses, a sure sign of the heir, while Domitian is relegated to his own until the last year of Vespasian's reign.[2] This sort of arrangement depends from decisions

[1] Compare also the subsequent Flavian coinages. Titus' brief reign appears patterned on Vespasian's. Of his dated issues seven are struck for him as emperor in A.D. 79, eight in 80, with only one type overlapping. Domitian has a great many types during the first four years, with some innovation each year. The types are all carried over—'restored'?—from Vespasian, Titus, and Domitian Caesar, save that Germania Capta and most of the Minervas are original. After A.D. 84 he reverts to a pre-Flavian pattern. The types narrow to four versions of Minerva struck regularly each year until his death, the Germania Capta and quadriga types repeated sporadically, a brief nod at the Secular Games of A.D. 88, and a few novelties in 94–6.

[2] Ernst Kornemann, *Doppelprinzipat und Reichsteilung im Imperium Romanum* (Leipzig, 1930), 62–5, would have Vespasian and Titus virtually co-emperors, but he notes the incongruity of Titus simultaneously *princeps iuventutum* with Domitian.

attributable only to the imperial house itself, and it is not too much to suppose that Vespasian took as direct an interest in the coinage as had some of his predecessors.[1] If this is the reason for the particular flavour of Vespasian's coins, we can also suggest a possible source for it. Vespasian was known to be a man of a sentimental cast of mind. The villa of his grandmother at Cosa, where he had grown up happily, was preserved by him later in unaltered form. He kept a silver cup given him by his grandmother, from which he drank each year on particular occasions.[2] Perhaps it was in having had no family of particular public repute, and having succeeded to a rule whose emperors traced back their line through numberless generations to the gods themselves, that Vespasian felt the need of cultivating such roots as he had. The earlier part of his life had been spent in an unsought and a fairly undistinguished public career. The chronology of that career is not entirely certain, although we know that he served as military tribune and quaestor under Tiberius, aedile and praetor under Caligula.[3] But he must have served in yet one more office under Tiberius, for Augustus had made membership in the *vigintiviri* (who included the moneyers) obligatory upon anyone wishing to pursue a consular career.[4] It is not certain when Vespasian entered the vigintivirate, for there is evidence that it could be held either before or after the military tribunate.[5] The choices are c. A.D. 28 or 31–4. It is possible that at one of these two periods Vespasian filled the office of *triumvir monetalis*, and that the historical knowledge of Roman coinage which his own issues show, and the Tiberian flavour which we have noted above, derive from his earliest experience in office under Tiberius. That office would have continued to be filled even if no gold and silver was actually being struck at Rome. The undated *Divus Augustus Pater* asses were presumably issued continuously through the reign. No dated *aes* coinage is known from Rome c. A.D. 28, but some was struck there from 34–5 to the end of the reign. It is perhaps no coincidence that the two reverse types of as introduced at that time, namely the globe with rudder, and the winged caduceus, appear nowhere else in the subsequent imperial coinage until they are brought together in A.D. 74 on quadrantes of Vespasian (*BMCRE* ii, 162, 706).

That Vespasian had been a moneyer, and that the essential characteristics of his gold and silver typology derive from that experience, of course cannot

---

[1] Cf. the suggestion of Laura Voelkel, 'The Selection of Coin Types during the Reign of the Emperor Domitian', in *Studies Presented to David Moore Robinson* ii (Saint Louis, 1953), 243–7, who attributes the selection of Domitian's early types to the *procurator a rationibus*, Claudius. This attractive thesis unfortunately is supported by no evidence, and the argument takes on a certain circularity when the change in pattern after A.D. 84 is explained by the putative dismissal of Claudius by the emperor.

[2] Suetonius, *Vespasian* 2.

[3] Heinze Richard Graf, *Suetons Bild des Kaisers Vespasian*, diss. Halle-Wittenberg (Halle, 1937), 12–14.

[4] Theodore Mommsen, *Römisches Staatsrecht* i (Leipzig, 1876), 529.

[5] Ibid. 526.

be demonstrated. But whatever the reason, his coins show a strong sense of continuity on the part of the official who authorized them, and that a continuity not of historical reference as elicited from the various types and legends, but of the coins as artifacts. The continued existence of older aurei and denarii, bearing types which were of themselves attractive, suggestive, picturesque, excited as a response the 'restoration' of these old coins with their old types. This was not the recelebration of, say, the battle of Actium, but at most the restoration of a coin which had once meant to an earlier age the celebration of the battle. The wit that revived the ancient coin type, that manipulated it in celebrating Vespasian as augur by placing symbols and legend as only Caesar had, that substituted Vespasian or Titus for the anonymous seated female (Livia? Concordia?) of the Tiberian denarius, was rooted not in the exercise of a tendentious political mythology but in the love of numismatics itself.

### NOTE TO THE PLATE

For further comparative illustrations see Laffranchi, who presents most of the Augustan and a few Republican originals, with the Flavian imitations. My illustrations include additional Republican as well as a spread of originals derived from the other pre-Flavian emperors.

# Reattribution of the Milan Coins of Trajan Decius to the Rome Mint

## K. J. J. ELKS

[SEE PLATES 14–15]

THE pattern of issues for the coinage of Trajan Decius (A.D. 249–51) and his family attempted by Harold Mattingly in the reports on the Plevna hoard[1] and the great hoard from Dorchester,[2] and finally embodied in *Roman Imperial Coinage* iv, part iii, have never been completely satisfactory. Apart from the mint of Antioch he has identified two others, Rome and Milan. The distinction made is that at Rome there are two issues, the first lasting only a short while using the obverse legend IMP TRAIANVS DECIVS AVG on the silver and the second, which is far more common, IMP C M Q TRAIANVS DECIVS AVG. At Milan there are again two legends IMP CAE TRA DEC AVG and IMP CAE TRA DECIVS AVG and coins of this group are distinctly scarcer.

The original attribution of this latter group to Milan was made by Count de Salis in his arrangement of the coins in the British Museum, an attribution followed by Mattingly but not by everybody. Any suggestion by so eminent a numismatist as de Salis is always worthy of consideration and it is therefore much to be regretted that he left no written justification, but Mattingly does make the attempt. His reasoning is basically this:

1. The Milan coins comprise different legends and a distinct style of their own.

2. There seem to be only three substantive issues where six would be needed if the mint was Rome.

3. That at this time Milan was an important cavalry base which certainly issued coins later for Gallienus and maybe for previous reigns. There is a series of coins for Gallus and Volusian, and Valerian, which have been attributed to this mint.

4. As well as the coins of Decius there is the series of 'Divi' coins which are of the same style and also attributed to the Milan mint. This Mattingly finds particularly significant and recounts the story that Aurelian, some years later when receiving the envoys of the Juthungi at Milan, set out the effigies of the 'Divi' together with all the insignia of the army.

---

[1] *NC* 1924, 210 ff.  [2] *NC* 1939, 21 ff.

In addition to this there is the evidence of the Plevna hoard[1] which consisted for the most part of antoniniani of Decius which had every sign of having been moved straight from the Rome mint in bulk before deposit. This contained none of the Milan coinage and only two coins of the 'Divi' series.

In opposition, Professor Alföldi apparently expressed his opinion that he considered them to be the last issues of Rome while Laffranchi wanted to place them at Viminacium. This latter argument was not convincing and never fully accepted, especially when the coins of Philip I originally given to that mint were transferred to Antioch.

The chief argument against Mattingly's arrangement of the Rome mint issues is that they lack cohesion, a fact underlined by successive hoards. A discrepancy in the quoted numbers of one particular coin type in a hoard is not significant; when it occurs in every hoard then one must re-examine the attributions to see if there is a possibility of explanation.

The main problem of arranging the Rome coinage into issues is that the coins for members of Decius' family are altogether too numerous and varied to allow for any sort of cohesive pattern if this attribution to Milan is correct. Besides the one type of PVDICITIA (seated), which slots readily into place with 277 examples in the Dorchester hoard, Etruscilla has three other reverses which altogether total another 239 coins, while Etruscus (six types, 258 coins) and Hostilian (three types, 66 coins) enhance the problem. All these coins are left over after placing the one type of Etruscilla and all the acknowledged Rome mint coinage of Decius in the sequence of issues. It was probably the realization of this that caused Mattingly to give up the attempt to achieve a lucid arrangement (*RIC* iv, iii, 112).

One can agree immediately that the first issue of antoniniani was that small group of coins with the legend IMP TRAIANVS DECIVS AVG. Apart from one short-lived reverse type (VIRTVS AVG) all the remaining six types occur again in the second issue with legend IMP C M Q TRAIANVS DECIVS AVG. During the course of this issue they undergo some modification, two types being changed completely while a third (PAX AVGVSTI) ceases altogether and is replaced by a coinage for Herennia Etruscilla shortly after the change in obverse. The three types that remain in use are DACIA, PANNONIAE, and GENIVS EXERCITVS ILLVRICIANI and it is significant that it is these three types in their later variants that are used on the Milan coins. Taken as a whole, the progression of legend on the obverse of the coins of Rome to those attributed to Milan appears quite normal from what we know of the workings of the Rome mint in this period, so it is not inconceivable that they were the last issues from that mint as Alfoldi suggests.

Nor is the change of style as marked as would appear at first sight. The

[1] The last coins were of Decius and his family and numbered 1,659 out of 3,296 (i.e. approximately 50 per cent). They were in mint condition and many die-links were observed. There was no tailing off as one would expect in a normal hoard.

portrait is almost exactly the same and the greatest difference is in the lettering, though this is hardly surprising in a change from a cramped obverse legend of twenty-three letters to one of half that number. Mattingly himself admitted: 'The style is so close to that of Rome that one has to check the evidence closely to make sure that it is distinct', but he believed that the closeness was due to the formation of the mint from Rome personnel.

## TABLE I

*Change of Obverse Legend and Reverse Type on Coins of Decius*

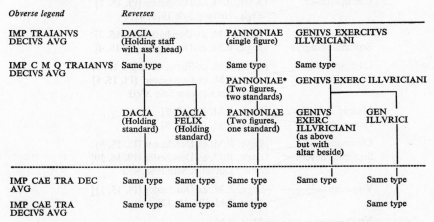

| Obverse legend | Reverses | | | | |
|---|---|---|---|---|---|
| IMP TRAIANVS DECIVS AVG | DACIA (Holding staff with ass's head) | | PANNONIAE (single figure) | GENIVS EXERCITVS ILLVRICIANI | |
| IMP C M Q TRAIANVS DECIVS AVG | Same type | | Same type | Same type | |
| | | | PANNONIAE* (Two figures, two standards) | GENIVS EXERC ILLVRICIANI | |
| | DACIA (Holding standard) | DACIA FELIX (Holding standard) | PANNONIAE (Two figures, one standard) | GENIVS EXERC ILLVRICIANI (as above but with altar beside) | GEN ILLVRICI |
| IMP CAE TRA DEC AVG | Same type | Same type | Same type | Same type | Same type |
| IMP CAE TRA DECIVS AVG | Same type | Same type | Same type | | Same type |

\* There are other minor variations on the Pannoniae type but they do not extend beyond the second issue.

The evidence for a mint at Milan under Decius is really extremely tenuous to say the least. The parading of images at Milan some twenty years later does not necessarily point to that city having been the source of a coinage devoted to them. If the operation of a mint distinctly separate cannot be traced any earlier than the following reign of Gallus and Volusian, then to attempt to separate the alleged Milan coins of Decius amounts to special pleading without any real justification. It may, therefore, be well to consider this point first.

At Rome there is a scarce, but well-defined, issue of coins for Trebonianus Gallus together with Decius' surviving son Hostilian, both as Augusti, with Gallus' son Volusian as Caesar. The second issue, and all others subsequently, feature only Gallus and Volusian as joint Augusti. The group of coins attributed to Milan is only for Gallus and Volusian as Augusti and the absence of the initial group is more than a little strange if one considers that Antioch, much further away, has a series with Hostilian as Augustus first. If it is accepted that the mint of Milan was not operating at the beginning of the reign the onus of proof is on anyone trying to establish that it first began operations earlier and not some time in the reign of Gallus and Volusian as can be clearly seen.

Table I shows that all the 'Milan' coins used, initially, reverse types featured on coins of Rome and it was this group which I examined to see if a definite link could be established by way of die-links. Although there is some

## TABLE II

### Die-links in the 'Divi' Coinage

Augustus — Altar, B.M. ex-Dorchester [Pl. 15. 1]
Commodus — Altar, B.M. ex-Dorchester [Pl. 15. 2]
Eagle, Helbing Sale 1929, 4276

Nerva — Eagle, B.M. ex-Dorchester [Pl. 15. 3]
Septimius Severus — Eagle, B.M. ex-Dorchester [Pl. 15. 4]

Hadrian — Altar, B.M. ex-Blacas Coll. [Pl. 15. 5]
Commodus — Altar, B.M. ex-Dorchester [Pl. 15. 6]
Eagle, Ars Classica Sale XVII

Marcus Aurelius — Eagle, B.M. [Pl. 15. 7]
Commodus — Eagle, B.M. [Pl. 15. 8]

Commodus — Eagle, B.M. ex-Dorchester [Pl. 15. 9]
Septimius Severus — Eagle, B.M. ex-Dorchester [Pl. 15. 10]
Altar, Schulman Sale 1968, 462

Vespasian — Eagle, B.M. ex-Dorchester [Pl. 15. 11]
Altar, B.M. [Pl. 15. 12]

Nerva — Altar, B.M.
Eagle, Ars Classica Sale VIII

Antoninus Pius — Altar, B.M. ex-Dorchester
Eagle, B.M. ex-Dorchester

Severus Alexander — Altar, B.M.
Eagle, Münzen und Medaillen Sale 1935, 779

evidence to believe that personnel were freely transferred between mints there is nothing to suggest that dies ever were, and therefore the use of the same die by coins supposed to be of different mints is to be accepted as more direct proof that they have a common mintage than any suppositions based purely on style which try to show otherwise. Die-links between coins in the British Museum of the two series are shown on **Plate 14**.

With the reattribution of these coins of Decius to Rome it followed that the 'Divi' series belonged there as well. In these last issues[1] there were two officinae operating exclusively for Decius, one shared with Etruscilla or Etruscus, one for Etruscilla alone, one for Etruscus and Hostilian, and one left over. This, I believe, produced the 'Divi' coins.

[1] The sequence of issues for this reign is outlined in my pamphlet *The Coinage of Trajan Decius* (privately published, 1971).

The 'Divi' coins cover eleven of Rome's more acceptable emperors and all have a common reverse legend of CONSECRATIO. Two reverse types are used, a large altar or an eagle, standing facing, with wings outspread. If the coins were indeed from one officina then considerable die-linking could be expected and this proved to be the case on examination. Many of the coins use the same pair of dies for obverse and reverse but a considerable number of others had either an obverse or reverse die in common. Of particular interest were those dies which linked an emperor with both types of reverse type (eagle or altar) and those where a particular reverse was used for more than one emperor. The material studied was again the British Museum collection embellished by recourse to illustrated sale catalogues over the last decades. Table II [**Plate 15**] illustrates some of the die-links observed and, although not pretending to be exhaustive, does tend to confirm what might be expected. With more coins available for study it should be possible to take this even further and determine the striking sequence for all of this series.

# Aspects of Coin Production and Fiscal Administration in the Late Roman and Early Byzantine Period

M. F. HENDY

IN the course of two recent articles the author has attempted to demonstrate the existence and trace the development of a close parallelism between the pattern of coin production and that of fiscal administration during the late Roman and early and middle Byzantine periods.[1] So far the years c. 292/3–324 and c. 400–c. 900 have been examined and, although it seems a plausible enough supposition that a parallelism existing both before 324 and after c. 400 should also have existed during the intervening period, it would clearly be convenient—as well as an additional strength to the argument as a whole—to have that supposition confirmed. Definition of this parallelism depends above all, from the numismatic point of view, on isolating the pattern of the comparatively regular and long-term production of coin and eliminating anomalous and temporary features. If this definition is to stand any chance of acceptance, however, it is clear that both elements of the process leading up to it must be justified: not only, that is, the retention of some features, but also the rejection of yet others. It is with these considerations in mind that the first section of this article has been written and has taken its particular form. The second and third sections will attempt to follow up points that, for reasons of space or relevance, it has hitherto been impossible to follow up more fully.

## I

In 324 the list of regular mints and major fiscal units was as follows: London (diocese Britanniae), Trier and Lyons (d. Galliae), Arles (d. Viennensis), Aquileia and Ticinum (d. Italia), Rome (d. Suburbicaria), Siscia (d. Pannoniae), Thessalonica (d. Moesiae), Heraclea (d. Thracia), Cyzicus (d. Asiana), Nicomedia (d. Pontica), Antioch (d. Oriens), Alexandria (provinces Aegyptus). There was thus a strong tendency for a major fiscal unit

---

[1] M. F. Hendy, 'Mint and Fiscal Administration under Diocletian, his Colleagues, and his Successors A.D. 305–24', *JRS* 1972 (forthcoming); idem, 'On the Administrative Basis of the Byzantine Coinage c. 400–c. 900 and the Reforms of Heraclius', *University of Birmingham Historical Journal* 1970, 129–54.

to possess a regular mint. Exceptions are provided by the existence of two mints in each of the dioceses of Gaul and Italy, and by the lack of mints in the dioceses of Africa and Spain.[1]

It seems to have been the decision to create at Byzantium an imperial residence (324)[2] and to endow it with appropriate institutions, including a mint (326),[3] that provoked the first major reorganization of the mint system since Diocletian. In 325 the mint of London was closed,[4] and in 326 that of Ticinum.[5] The former closure left the diocese of Britain without a mint, the future supply of copper coin apparently being undertaken by Trier and later Arles;[6] the latter left Aquileia as the sole mint of the diocese of Italy. At much the same time (325/6) the mint of Sirmium, which had been established by Constantine at the time of his final drift towards war with Licinius, was dismantled.[7] It seems reasonable to suppose that the closure of London and Ticinum at least was part of a consistent programme dictated by the redeployment of mint personnel at the expense of the western half of the empire and in favour of the eastern.[8]

At some stage prior to 327 the diocese of Moesia was split into two— Dacia and Macedonia—the former Moesian mint of Thessalonica falling to the new diocese of Macedonia. Dacia was left without a mint by much the same kind of process as resulted in the prefectural *scrinium* for the diocese of Oriens in fact continuing to deal with matters involving Egypt long after the latter had attained full diocesan status under Valens by being split off from Oriens, and had thus, in theory, become entitled to a *scrinium* of its own.[9]

After c. 327 the pattern of mints and fiscal units therefore stood as follows: Trier and Lyons (Galliae), Arles (Viennensis), Aquileia (Italia), Rome (Suburbicaria), Siscia (Pannoniae), Thessalonica (Macedonia), Heraclea (Thracia), Cyzicus (Asiana), Nicomedia (Pontica), Antioch (Oriens), Alexandria (Aegyptus). The city of Constantinople stood outside the normal pattern of regional administration to a greater extent even than Rome, for unlike the latter it had been superimposed upon the Diocletianic system and, for example, did not stand at the head of a diocesan unit.[10] It did, however, act as the main or only eastern imperial residence and focus of administration from

---

[1] Hendy, 'Mint and Fiscal Administration under Diocletian'.

[2] A. H. M. Jones, *The Later Roman Empire 284–602: a Social, Economic and Administrative Survey* iii, 11 (nn. 12, 13).                    [3] See below, p. 132 n. 3.

[4] *RIC* vii, 96.                                            [5] Ibid. 355, 359.

[6] C. H. V. Sutherland, *Coinage and Currency in Roman Britain* 74, 87. This switch in emphasis will then presumably have anticipated the transfer of the prefecture of the Gauls from Trier to Arles that seems to have taken place in c. 407 only.

[7] Sirmium is not listed above among the regular mints, operating on a long-term basis, for reasons that will become apparent. See below, pp. 126–9. For Serdica see below, p. 135 n. 2.

[8] The details of the operation remain obscure, but the consistency of the general programme seems clear; *RIC* vii, 19,359.

[9] Hendy, 'On the Administrative Basis of the Byzantine Coinage' 132, 137 (n. 39).

[10] Jones, *Later Roman Empire* iii, 11–12 (n. 13), 23 (n. 48).

now on, and its mint therefore came to occupy an increasingly predominant position. The dioceses of Britain, Spain, Africa, and Dacia remained without regular mints.

The same basic mint structure survived into the fifth century. The *Notitia Dignitatum* records the following *procuratores monetarum* at the disposition of the western *comes sacrarum largitionum*:[1]

> Procurator monetae Siscianae
> Procurator monetae Aquileiensis
> Procurator monetae urbis Romae
> Procurator monetae Lugdunensis
> Procurator monetae Arelatensis
> Procurator monetae Triberorum

The procurators at the disposition of the eastern *comes* are not recorded (*Or.* xiii, 18), but the coins themselves show the same mints to have been in operation as in 327 and earlier. The western section of this structure betrays a gradual disintegration from the first decade of the century onwards,[2] but the eastern survived, with remarkably few major interruptions, additions, or subtractions, into the seventh century, and has been dealt with elsewhere.[3]

The second half of the fourth century had nevertheless seen various developments of a temporary nature in the pattern of western monetary production. The usurpation of Magnentius in 350 resulted in the creation of a mint at Ambianum (Amiens) in the diocese of Gaul, bringing the number of mints in that diocese momentarily to three. Its function remains obscure: it has been suggested that it was intended as a potential relief for Trier in the case of that city coming under barbarian attack or control—but this would seem to presuppose a greater degree of foresight than was normal.[4] It is, on the other

---

[1] *Notitia Dignitatum Occidentalis* xi, 39–44. Sutherland (*RIC* vi, 89 [n. 1]) supposed Demetrius Catafronius *v(ir) p(erfectissimus) proc(urator) s(acrae) m(onetae) T(hessalonicensis)* of an undated inscription to have been an early holder of that office, but *CIL* vi, 1145, records the Constantinian Valerius Pelagius, who is coupled with a *v(ir) p(erfectissimus) rat(ionalis) s(ummae) r(ei)*, merely as *v(ir) e(gregius) proc(urator) s(acrae) m(onetae) u(rbis)*. Assuming the office of *procurator* to have held a uniform status at any given time, Catafronius must postdate Pelagius and have held office only when that status had shared in the inflationary movement typical of the fourth century and later. This is apparently confirmed by the career of the undated and anonymous *proc(urator) monetae Triverice* of *CIL* vi, 1641, who seems to have operated under the Gallic empire and in any case became *v.p.* only subsequently as *praeses* of Germania Superior. See H.-G. Pflaum, *Les Carrières procuratoriennes équestres sous le Haut-Empire romain* ii, no. 355, pp. 941–7; idem, 'La monnaie de Trèves à l'époque des empereurs gallo-romains', *CINP* ii, 273–80.

[2] For the copper coinage see edd. R. A. G. Carson, P. V. Hill, J. P. C. Kent, *Late Roman Bronze Coinage*, part ii, under the various mint headings.

[3] Hendy, 'On the Administrative Basis of the Byzantine Coinage' 147–52. The existence of the following eastern mints is independently attested or implied: Thessalonica—see above, n. 1; Heraclea—*Cahiers Archéologiques* 1956, 33 (n. 4); Cyzicus—Sozomen, *Historia Ecclesiastica* v, 15; Antioch—Julian, *Misopogon* 367–8; Alexandria—Ammianus Marcellinus xxii, 11, 9. I owe the Heraclean reference to the kindness of Mr. Michael Vickers.

[4] P. Bastien, *Le Monnayage de Magnence (350–353)* 34–5.

hand, known that Amiens was the birthplace of Magnentius and the alternative suggestion—that the creation of a mint there almost immediately after his accession might be taken as evidence of his favour or future intentions—is one that merits consideration.[1] That it owed its creation to personal rather than to strategic or organizational reasons seems confirmed by the fact that it was closed almost immediately after the recovery of Gaul by Constantius II in 353.[2] Whether or not Magnentius or his Caesar Decentius ever visited Amiens subsequent to their elevation seems unknown, but it may be significant that, despite its active role, the mint struck only in copper.[3] In this it resembled London throughout its career,[4] Lyons before 336,[5] and Alexandria after 314.[6] What Amiens, Lyons, and Alexandria (but admittedly not London) had in common was that they formed the second or third mint of their dioceses. This seems to indicate that, where a diocese possessed more than a single mint, the production of precious-metal coinage nevertheless tended to be confined to one.

Shortly before the brief occupation of Siscia by Magnentius in 351, an *officina* of its mint was detached and transferred to Sirmium where it remained (striking coinage in all metals) until early in the reign of Valentinian and Valens when some time between 364 and 367 it, and a second *officina* to which it had meanwhile given birth, were restored to Siscia.[7] Although its stay at Sirmium thus lasted over a decade both the circumstances of its departure from Siscia and its eventual return demonstrate the essentially political and *ad hoc* basis of its existence.

It seems likely that political reasons, in the form of revolts or the transfer of allegiances from west to east by Gildo the *comes et magister utriusque militiae per Africam* in 397, by Heraclian the *comes Africae* in 413, or by Boniface the *comes* in 427, lay behind the issue of a brief and minimal copper

---

[1] J. Bidez, 'Amiens, Ville natale de l'Empereur Magnence', *Revue des Études Anciennes* 1925, 312–18.

[2] Bastien, op. cit. 35. Relying on a passage in Sidonius Apollinaris (writing c. 465), it has been suggested that a fourth–fifth-century mint existed at Narbonne. The numismatic evidence, such as it is, is strongest for Magnentius and Constantius—but has, even so, quite rightly been discounted by R. A. G. Carson in 'A Roman Imperial Mint at Narbonne?', *NC* 1950, 144–8. The suggestion of a Roman (as opposed to Visigothic) mint at Narbonne is, however, a minor folly compared with that of a Byzantine mint at Cios under Leo, Basiliscus, and Zeno. See H. L. Adelson and G. L. Kustas, *A Bronze Hoard of the Period of Zeno I* (=*NNM* no. 148), 10–4.

[3] Ibid. 170–4.

[4] *RIC* vi, 113, 123–40; *RIC* vii, 97–116. Both gold and silver had, of course, been struck under Carausius and Allectus, but under entirely different political and administrative circumstances; nor can the probable issues of Magnus Maximus (see below, p. 122 n. 2) be regarded as anything but anomalous.

[5] *RIC* vi, 229, 241–65; *RIC* vii, 121, 122–42.

[6] *RIC* vii, 698, 702–12; *RIC* ix, 296, 298–304.

[7] For its copper coinage, see Carson, Hill, Kent, *Late Roman Bronze Coinage*, part ii, 76–7. For examples of its precious metal coinage, see O. Ulrich-Bansa, *Moneta Mediolanensis (352–498)*, 9–10; and *RIC* ix, 145–7.

coinage at Carthage at some point late in the fourth century or early in the fifth.[1]

Mints, or at least the more regular mints, tended—for obvious reasons of convenience—to be accompanied by treasuries (*thesauri*) with stocks of metal, whether in coined or bullion form. The *Notitia* records the following *praepositi thesaurorum* at the disposition of the western *comes sacrarum largitionum*—*thesauri* that were, or might originally have been paired with *monetae*, being marked with an asterisk:[2]

| | |
|---|---|
| Praepositus thesaurorum Salonitanorum, Dalmatiae | ⎫ Per |
| Praepositus thesaurorum Siscianorum, Saviae* | ⎬ Illyricum |
| Praepositus thesaurorum Sabarensium, Pannoniae primae | ⎭ |
| Praepositus thesaurorum Aquileiensium, Venetiae* | ⎫ |
| Praepositus thesaurorum Mediolanensium, Liguriae* | ⎬ Per |
| Praepositus thesaurorum urbis Romae* | Italiam |
| Praepositus thesaurorum Augustae Vindelicensis, Raetiae secundae | ⎭ |
| Praepositus thesaurorum Lugdunensium* | ⎫ |
| Praepositus thesaurorum Arelatensium* | ⎬ Per |
| Praepositus thesaurorum Remorum | Gallias |
| Praepositus thesaurorum Triberorum* | ⎭ |
| Praepositus thesaurorum Augustensium* | ⎱ In Britannis |

The stage at which this pattern of *thesauri* was brought into being remains uncertain, but comparison with that of *monetae* suggests it to have been an early and probably an essentially Diocletianic feature. It is clear in the first place that, although by no means all *thesauri* will have coincided with early *monetae*, each early *moneta* will nevertheless have readily coincided with a *thesaurus*. London (Augusta)[3] will thus have lost its *moneta* in 325,[4] but retained its *thesaurus*. Evidence about to be discussed suggests that if the *thesaurus* at Milan was ever connected with a *moneta*—and was not merely, for instance, a superseded adjunct of the tetrarchic residence—nearby Ticinum, which was closed in 326, is a more likely candidate than Milan itself.[5] According to Lactantius, the old Maximian, attempting a coup against Constantine at Arles in 309 'repente purpuram sumit, thesauros invadit, donat ut solet large',[6] which—if Lactantius is using the term technically—must mean that the *thesaurus* there antedated the mint established in 313. If the *res summa* was confronted with the problem of what to do with the mint of Ostia after the defeat of Maxentius in 312, and yet, in view of the

---

[1] Carson, Hill, Kent, *Late Roman Bronze Coinage*, part ii, 58.

[2] *N. Dig. Occ.* xi, 21–37.

[3] Ammianus Marcellinus, xxviii. 3 ('. . . ab Augusta . . , quam veteres appellavere Lundinium . . .').          [4] See above, p. 118 n. 4.

[5] See below, pp. 124–5 n. 6. Ticinum: see above, p. 118 n. 5.

[6] Lactantius, *De Mortibus Persecutorum* xxix, 3–8; *Panegyrici Latini* vii (vi), 14–20, esp. 18; Eutropius, *Breviarium* x, 3.

recent episode involving Domitius Alexander, was unwilling to restore it to its original site at Carthage, its pairing with the hitherto mintless *thesaurus* at Arles may have appeared an obvious solution.[1] Just as possession of the treasury at Arles allowed Maximian to distribute largesse, so possession of that at London may well have allowed Magnus Maximus to issue a precious-metal coinage at the commencement of his usurpation against Gratian in 383. Augustodunum (Autun) as an alternative identification of the mint signing itself AVG on its products provides no such attractive explanation.[2] It is clear in the second place that dioceses notably lacking mints also lacked treasuries. Neither Africa nor Spain is represented in the list. This may be the result of accident, as suggested by Jones,[3] but could well have been the true state of affairs. For the Diocletianic mint of Carthage had been removed, apparently as an act of political precaution, in 307.[4] It seems reasonable to suppose that any African *thesaurus* would have been removed at the same time. The mint of Carthage was not reopened on anything but the most temporary and anomalous of bases until the Vandal period:[5] it is therefore quite possible that Africa continued without a treasury as it continued without a mint. Spain had never possessed a mint: it may never have possessed a treasury either.

It is noticeable that none of the more temporary mints that have been mentioned, whether Ostia, Ambianum, or Sirmium, can be shown to have been paired with a *thesaurus* or to have left any mark on the list in the *Notitia*.[6]

The *praepositi* at the disposition of the eastern *comes* are not listed by the *Notitia* (*Or.* xiii, 10), although it is known independently that *thesauri* existed at Philippopolis and Nicaea—neither, however, exactly coinciding with a mint.[7]

For well over a century in the west, and for well over three centuries in the east, the regular production of coin—if increasingly that of copper coin only —was therefore the responsibility of a group of mints of which two features, its constant composition and its reflection of the pattern of regional fiscal

---

[1] For references to the Carthaginian-Ostian interlude: Hendy, 'Mint and Fiscal Administration under Diocletian'.

[2] *RIC* ix, 1. It was doubtless similar circumstances that dictated the issue of a gold coinage at Antioch by the usurper Leontius in 484–8. See J. Tolstoi, *Monnaies byzantines*, ii, 168–9.                                            [3] Jones, *Later Roman Empire* i, 429.

[4] See above, n. 1.

[5] See above, p. 121 n 1.; *BMC Van.* 1–16.

[6] Ostia: Hendy, 'Mint and Fiscal Administration under Diocletian'. Ambianum and Sirmium: above, pp. 119–20. This class of mint seems comparable with the later one comprising Seleucia and Isaura, Alexandretta, and Cyprus: Hendy, 'On the Administrative Basis of the Byzantine Coinage' 148.

[7] Jones, *Later Roman Empire* iii, 105 (n. 44). *Thesauri* or *arcae* of uncertain status are also known to have existed (from the gold ingots that their personnel signed) at Sirmium, Naissus, and Thessalonica. See G. Elmer in *Numizmatičar* 1935, 17–21; O. Iliescu in *Revue des études sud-est européennes* 1965, 269–81.

administration, were characteristic. Mints were occasionally created outside
this group, but in that case tended neither to exhibit the quality of per-
manence nor to bear any clear relation to the administrative pattern, their
temporary existence frequently having some obvious and specific political or
military basis.

## II

The omission of two further western mints by the *Notitia*, those of Milan
and Ravenna, provides a convenient point of departure for the second
section of this article.

The mint of Milan came into existence in 352/3, on the occasion of the
presence there of Constantius during his campaign against Magnentius.[1]
Its reputation as an *opulens moneta* is independently confirmed by Ausonius.[2]
That of Ravenna seems to have commenced production under Honorius in
402/3, its inception presumably reflecting the transfer of the western *comitatus*
from Milan at that date. The connection between the two seems clear: before
402/3 Milan was both a main—frequently the main—western residence, and
a major centre of coin production; after that date Ravenna was both, production at Milan thereafter becoming much more sporadic although it ceased
entirely only with the Ostrogothic period.[3] Now the date of the *Notitia* or
of its component parts is a question on which an enormous amount of
scholarly energy has been expended, and to which it is not intended that this
article should in any way form a contribution. Nevertheless, whatever
attitude towards the date and composition of the *Notitia* is adopted, it seems
clear that there is a good prima facie case for supposing that it should mention either the mint of Milan, or that of Ravenna, or both, along with the
others listed above. In fact it mentions neither—at least by name.

The omission of Milan, at least, has been convincingly explained by Kent
who points out that, unlike the products of the *monetae* listed in the *Notitia*,
those of Milan are—with minimal exceptions—confined to the precious
metals, at first to gold then to gold and silver. There seems furthermore to
have been a marked tendency for the mint's operation to have coincided with
the presence of the emperor and his *comitatus* in the city. These distinctions
carry over into the products of Ravenna as, by and large, the successor to
Milan. Kent therefore concludes that the operation of Milan represents the
activity not of a *moneta* of the kind listed by the *Notitia* but of the comitatensian

---

[1] Ulrich-Bansa, *Moneta Mediolanensis* 8–9.

[2] Ausonius: *Ordo Urbium Nobilium* ('Templa, palatinaeque arces, opulensque moneta').

[3] The connection between the falling production of Milan and the inception of Ravenna
has been denied by Ulrich-Bansa (*Moneta Mediolanensis* 171, nn. 12, 13) but against all
historical probability. The details of the connection are open to discussion: the existence
of the connection itself is not. For the latest products of Milan (in the name of Anastasius)
see Ulrich-Bansa, *Moneta Mediolanensis* 346; *BMC Van.* 59; J. P. C. Kent, 'The Coinage
of Theodoric in the Names of Anastasius and Justin I', in *Mints, Dies and Currency* 67–74.

*officium* of the *comes sacrarum largitionum*. The same should, then, presumably hold good for Ravenna.[1]

Examination of the internal structure of this same *officium* as described in the *Notitia* and in a law of 384 preserved in the *Codex Justinianus* suggests it to have been capable of functioning independently as both *thesaurus* and *moneta*. The relevant departments may be arranged as follows:[2]

| | |
|---|---|
| Scrinium auri massae | (Scrinium auri ad responsum?) |
| Scrinium ab argento | Scrinium a miliarensibus |
| | Scrinium ad pecunias |

Aurifices solidorum
(Sculptores et ceteri artifices?)

It seems clear that bodies of technicians, such as *aurifices* (goldsmiths), *argentarii* (silversmiths), *barbaricarii* (gilders), and *sculptores* (engravers),[3] were not classed as *scrinia*—a designation apparently reserved to administrative and clerical departments. Of these latter the *scrinium auri massae* will obviously have dealt with gold bullion, that *ab argento* possibly with silver bullion. The *scrinium a miliarensibus* will have dealt with silver coinage, that *ad pecunias* with copper coinage.[4] The function of the *scrinium auri ad responsum* remains obscure: Jones supposed it to have dealt with the returns of gold stocks in regional *thesauri*, and this may well have been the case, but it could equally well have formed the equivalent of the two monetary *scrinia* and thus have dealt with some aspect of gold coinage.[5] The *aurifices solidorum* will obviously have concerned themselves with the actual manufacture of gold coin.

This capacity of the comitatensian *officium* to function as an independent *thesaurus* renders it likely that the unit at Milan, the *praepositus* of which is listed in the *Notitia* along with and on exactly the same footing as the others, should be distinguished from the comitatensian.[6]

---

[1] Milan: *RIC* ix, 71, 75–84; Carson, Hill, Kent, *Late Roman Bronze Coinage*, part ii, 58. Ravenna: Carson, Hill, Kent, loc. cit. Comitatensian *officium*: J. P. C. Kent, 'Gold Coinage in the Later Roman Empire', in *Essays in Roman Coinage Presented to Harold Mattingly* at 201.

[2] *N. Dig. Occ.* xi, 88–99; *Or.* xiii, 22–34. *Codex Justinianus* xii, 23, 7 (= the corrupt *Codex Theodosianus* vi, 30, 7).

[3] The *sculptores* may have been or have included die-engravers (cf. the *scalptores sacrae monetae* of *CIL* vi, 8464), although the latter may equally well have been included among the undifferentiated *aurifices solidorum*. M. R. Alföldi (*Die constantinische Goldprägung* 20) in fact finds the senior *sculptor* in the *ducenarius* of the *aurifices*—but it is wildly unlikely that an officer of high equestrian grade would have indulged in manual labour of this kind. If there was such a person he is probably to be found among the workmen of the *formae*.

[4] For this restricted meaning of *pecunia* see below, p. 137 n. 1.

[5] Jones, *Later Roman Empire* i, 428—representing a change from his former opinion (in 'Numismatics and History' in *Essays in Roman Coinage* at 28, n. 1).

[6] It may be suggested that the *thesaurus* was originally intended to perform a dual function and was sited at Milan in the presence of the imperial residence (that of Maximian),

The structure outlined above is to be understood against the background of a series of reforms in fiscal procedure undertaken by Valentinian I and Valens in 366–7, the details of which have been admirably elucidated by Kent. The result of these reforms was formally to limit the normal minting of gold coin to the *comitatus*. There is little doubt that an effective concentration of this kind had in any case long existed, for the widespread and simultaneous coining of gold had become virtually confined to the accessional or quinquennial issues that marked the taxation and donatives appropriate to such occasions. After the reforms of 366–7 regional mints (termed *monetae publicae* in a law of 369) were normally used for the production of gold coin only in the presence of the *comitatus* and therefore on the occasion of an imperial visit or propinquity.[1]

The major numismatic difficulty in attempting to define the role of the comitatensian mint, the nature of its products, and the implications of its presence or absence—other than in the cases of Milan and Ravenna—is that very few issues of coin, whether of precious or base metal, are sufficiently closely datable. The major historical difficulty is that insufficient documentation survives to give a detailed and consistent knowledge of imperial movements. It is thus all too frequently impossible to isolate coinage produced by a regional *moneta* on the occasion of even a known comitatensian visit from that produced in the normal course of affairs. This does not mean that the general effects of a prolonged comitatensian presence or absence invariably remain obscure. While Trier acted as the main residence for Valentinian I and Gratian between 367 and 381 the coining of gold was at least strongly concentrated there.[2] While Antioch performed that service for Valens between 371 and 378 the same phenomenon is observable.[3] Then even the mint of Constantinople was affected, for little or no gold coinage is attributable to the city during those years.[4] A more detailed definition than this is nevertheless feasible on rare occasions. These occasions tend to have occurred when an emperor was required—generally by some emergency—to mount an expedition involving his own presence, and therefore that of his *comitatus*, at several cities with *monetae publicae* within a relatively short space of time.

the pre-existing mint at Ticinum being so near as to be not worth moving. It would have lost its special status in the absence of a resident emperor and the growth of independent palatine bureaux.

[1] Reforms of 366–7: Kent, 'Gold Coinage in the Later Roman Empire' 199–200; Hendy, 'On the Administrative Basis of the Byzantine Coinage' 141–2.
[2] *RIC* ix, 3, 15–8, 20–1, 23–4.                                    [3] Ibid. 202, 275–9.
[4] Ibid. 202, 217, 222. If the silver issue VOT XX MVLT XXX with mint-mark CONCM or CNCM of p. 222 (no. 42 *bis*) really is to be dated to this period and the *quindecennalia* of Valens (from 28 March 378), it will probably have been struck during his brief stay in the capital (late May–early June: Seeck, *Regesten* 251) before his fatal Gothic campaign. The mint-mark will then contain elements of Con(stantinopolis) and *c(o)m(itatus)*. Cf. Kent, 'Gold Coinage in the Later Roman Empire' 202, for the similar gold mint-mark, COMTM* or COMM*.

When similar issues of coin are found at all or a number of these cities, and no others, and the exact date of the expedition as provided by documentary sources is found to lie within the approximate dating provided by the coins, then some fairly direct connection between the two may reasonably be assumed. On the even rarer occasion of the *comitatus*, or at least its fiscal components, becoming resident at a centre where the services of a *moneta publica* were not available, the products of its own mint are readily distinguishable—for they are not, as usual, masked by a mass of largely undifferentiated material. Four instances of these kinds of situation seem instructive.

The first has already been mentioned. Between 319 and 324 Constantine seems to have been frequently at Sirmium, sometimes over an extended period of time. He was also there, more briefly, in 326. A mint was brought into operation there in 320 and continued in operation until 326. Its products are very heavily concentrated in favour of gold—silver and copper achieving a minimal representation only.[1]

At the end of 378 Gratian moved hurriedly into Illyricum in an attempt to restore the grave situation resulting from the death of his colleague Valens in August of that year at the hands of the Goths. He seems to have been at Sirmium on 6 December,[2] was certainly there by 19 January when Theodosius was proclaimed as successor to Valens,[3] and was still there on 24 February.[4] He is known to have returned subsequently through Aquileia (2, 5 July), and Milan (31 July, 3 August), to Trier (14 September).[5] Theodosius spent the rest of 379 and most of 380 at Thessalonica before moving on to Constantinople where he arrived in November.[6]

The brief reactivation of the mint of Sirmium (closed since 364–7) at about this time was therefore very plausibly connected by Pearce with the presence of the *comitatus* in early 379.[7] It proceeded to strike certainly in gold, and perhaps in silver, but not at all in copper. The reverse type used for the gold— two seated emperors with inscription VICTOR IAAVGG and mint-mark SIROB—was used for similar issues from Aquileia (AQOB), Milan (MDOB), Trier (TROB), and Thessalonica (TESOB). The western issues, or at least those from Aquileia and Trier, were connected by Pearce with Gratian's presence on his return journey: the eastern with Theodosius' prolonged residence at Thessalonica.[8]

On this occasion Gratian's *comitatus* seems not to have included the full range of technical staff, for it was evidently necessary to transfer at least die-

---

[1] *RIC* vii, 462, 467–77.

[2] O. Seeck, *Regesten der Kaiser und Päpste 311–476* 250 (*C. Th.* vi, 30, 4).

[3] Seeck, *Regesten* 250, 251.

[4] Ibid. 250.　　　　　　　　　　　　　　　　　　　　　　　　[5] Ibid. 250, 252.

[6] Ibid. 251, 253, 255.　　　　　　　　　　　　　　　　　　[7] *RIC* ix, 156, 159–60.

[8] Aquileia: *RIC* ix, 87, 98–9, where AQOBF is made to precede AQOB. Trier: ibid. 24. Thessalonica: ibid. 165, 180. Milan: ibid. 76–7.

engravers from Siscia to Sirmium, their influence being visible on the products of the reactivated mint. Dies for the Aquileian, Treveran, and Thessalonican issues seem also to have been engraved by the regular staff of those mints.[1] Contemporary western practice, on the other hand, by no means excluded the movement of comitatensian engravers: Treveran staff of this class seem to have been active at both Aquileia and Milan on at least one occasion, and a connection between the last two mints is confirmed by the existence of an obverse die-link. If Pearce's chronology is correct this particular movement will have occurred when Gratian transferred his main residence from Trier to Milan in 381.[2]

Much the same kind of process is to be seen at work on the occasion of Theodosius' expedition against the western usurper Magnus Maximus. Theodosius met his largely dispossessed colleague Valentinian (II) at Thessalonica in late 387.[3] He defeated Maximus in two battles before taking him prisoner near Aquileia on 28 August 388. He was still at Aquileia on 22 September, but by 10 October was at Milan and presumably wintered there.[4] He is known to have been at Rome between 13 June and 30 August 389 and then to have returned to, and wintered at, Milan.[5] 390 was spent at Milan, as was the first part of 391 (at least until 15 April).[6] By 16 June he was at Aquileia, but appears not to have reached Constantinople until late in the year (possibly on 10 November).[7]

At about this time a number of gold issues with eastern reverse types appeared at western mints. That of Constantinopolis seated, with the inscription CONCORDI AAVGGG, appears at Thessalonica (mint-mark CONOB or COMOB), Aquileia (AQOB), and Milan (MDOB).[8] That of Roma and Constantinopolis seated together, with the inscription GLORIA RO MANORVM (mint-mark ROMOB), appears at Rome only.[9] Although there is little or no trace of workmanship other than that appropriate to the various mints in the dies engraved for these issues, not only the reverse types but also the form of mint-mark and the sporadic *officina* numbering are eastern in character.[10] Despite supposed difficulties in the interpretation of the *vota* figures found on the shield held by Constantinopolis, and on the reverses of the accompanying silver, it is hard to resist the straightforward proposition that these issues reflect the western presence of Theodosius' *comitatus*

---

[1] *RIC* ix, 156.    [2] Seeck, *Regesten* 256; *RIC* ix, 72, 76–7.
[3] Seeck, *Regesten* 273 (*C. Th.* i, 32, 6 [31 Dec.]).
[4] Seeck, *Regesten* 273, 275.    [5] Ibid. 275, 277.    [6] Ibid. 277–8.
[7] Ibid. 279. Probably travelling via Thessalonica. The three laws of 18, 28 July, and 17 September—all given at Constantinople and addressed to Tatian (*ppo. Or.*)—would then have emanated from Arcadius.
[8] Thessalonica: *RIC* ix, 184–5. Aquileia: ibid. 102. Milan: ibid. 77–8.
[9] *RIC* ix, 132.
[10] S and B sporadically at Thessalonica (loc. cit.). Θ invariably at Aquileia and Milan (locc. citt.) seems to have a different significance implicit in its disappearance at Rome (loc. cit.). See below, p. 139.

between 387 and 391. Pearce's suggestion that the adoption of the eastern features signified Valentinian's acceptance of an eastern protectorate in the few months preceding his dispossession by Maximus seems historically much less plausible—even supposing that the general case for such minutiae having been regulated in so immediate and positive a way were a sound one. It is noticeable that the Constantinopolitan mint struck no gold during this period, but did perhaps strike a little silver, and copper certainly as normally.[1]

The organizational details of the expeditions of 379 and 387 contrast somewhat with those of the expedition of 394 undertaken by Theodosius against the western usurper Eugenius. The emperor left Constantinople in May of that year, taking with him his younger son Honorius but leaving behind his elder Arcadius, and travelling by way of Heraclea and Adrianople.[2] The defeat of Eugenius in September was followed by Theodosius' establishment at Milan, where he died on 17 January 395.[3] About this time there appeared an appreciable issue of gold coin (and gold coin only) in the names of the eastern emperors but with the mint-mark $\dfrac{S \mid M}{COMOB}$. It commenced by employing a Thessalonican style—confirmed by the existence of obverse die-links with a Thessalonican issue—but soon developed into one employing an exclusively Constantinopolitan style in which the reverse inscription was followed by an *officina* number ranging from A to I, just as the products of the metropolitan mint had done since shortly after 379.[4]

The conclusion towards which this evidence points seems clear, and has in fact long been drawn if not unanimously accepted. Staff from first the mint of Thessalonica, then from that of Constantinople, had been transferred to Sirmium. The implications of the latter transfer at least are remarkable, involving as it did the entire staff of the ten *officinae* into which the eastern *officium* was divided for the manufacture of gold coin. As might be expected in the circumstances there is no contemporary gold coinage with the customary eastern form of mint-mark CONOB and therefore attributable to Constantinople itself: there is, on the other hand, perhaps a little silver, and the production of copper certainly continued without interruption or even diminution.[5]

---

[1] See below, pp. 137–9 ('Appendix'). Constantinopolitan copper: *RIC* ix, 234.

[2] Seeck, *Regesten* 283–4 (29 April Constantinople, 20 May Heraclea, 20 June Adrianople).

[3] Seeck, *Regesten*, 284.

[4] Sirmium: *RIC* ix, 157, 160–2. Thessalonica: ibid. 167, 188.

[5] The coin issues involved in this episode, and probably the interpretation to be placed upon them, are of the greatest complexity. Pearce's attribution to Sirmium has been challenged by Kent ('Gold Coinage in the Later Roman Empire' 202), and by Ulrich-Bansa (*Moneta Mediolanensis* 156–9; *NC* 1952, 155–6; 'Note di numismatica teodosiana: il solidus aureus dal 392 al 395', *RIN* 1966, 113–15): but in this author's opinion will be found substantially correct. Ulrich-Bansa regards the SM of the mint-mark as standing merely for S(acra) M(oneta)—which it had of course done at an earlier period—and the coins themselves as normal issues of Thessalonica and Constantinople. Kent regards SM as

It was presumably Theodosius' presence at Milan 394–5, after the defeat of Eugenius, that lay behind the issue of a type similar to and no doubt supplementing that from Sirmium but with mint-mark $\dfrac{\text{M} \mid \text{D}}{\text{COMOB}}$ and in a style appropriate to the mint. The existence of an equivalent issue from Aquileia (mint-mark $\dfrac{\text{A} \mid \text{Q}}{\text{COMOB}}$) also seems a possibility.[1]

The burden of the numismatic evidence seems to be that the coining of gold was at least very heavily influenced by, and concentrated upon, the current position of the imperial *comitatus*, and is therefore entirely in conformity with that of the documentary evidence. This seems to have been the case both during periods of rapid movement such as those brought on by emergencies, and during periods of prolonged residence at Trier, Milan, or Ravenna in the west, or at Constantinople or Antioch in the east. During periods of rapid movement comitatensian progress is reflected in issues from the various *monetae publicae* that lay in its path. It then seems to have been normal practice for dies to be engraved by the staff of those *monetae*, although once engraved custody of the dies doubtless appertained to the *comitatus*. That this was so seems confirmed by the existence of obverse die-links between the products of different mints and of reverse dies engraved for use at one mint subsequently recut for use at another.[2] A skeleton mint staff nevertheless presumably accompanied the *comitatus* even on these occasions, for indeed forming the elements of a mint-name, but proposes Selymbria in place of Sirmium. Neither carries conviction. Against Ulrich-Bansa it should be pointed out that the issues with Thessalonican and Constantinopolitan features appear to form successive parts of a series: in other words, that they at least cannot be the contemporaneous products of different mints. If, as he would not deny, SM by its very position in the design acts as a parallel to MD and perhaps to AQ as well (see below, n. 1), then SM should form the elements of a mint-name just as they do. Kent argues that the supposedly treasonable activities of Rufinus in 395 imply the metropolitan presence of staff for the minting of gold (Claudian, *In Rufinum* ii, 341–2: '. . . quod post vota daretur/insculpi propriis aurum fatale figuris'). But Rufinus' activities (if accurately reported by Claudian, a creature of Stilicho) were so flagrantly illegal that it may be doubted whether he would have had recourse to the services of regular moneyers: if he had, then those of the staff of the *moneta publica* would still have been available (below, pp. 131–3; cf. *RIC* ix, 235–6). But what, in any case, was a praetorian prefect doing interfering with the staff of the *comitivae*? He further argues that an attribution to (western) Sirmium would leave the eastern half of the empire without a mint after Theodosius' death. It is not, however, necessary to suppose that Theodosius would have anticipated the inconveniences caused to monetary production by that event. And while a mint at Sirmium would undoubtedly have found itself on western territory in 395 (cf. below, p. 136 n. 1), neither its use by eastern officials, nor its subsequent return to the east in the same way as the army, would thereby have been precluded.

[1] Milan: *RIC* ix, 84. Aquileia: Ulrich-Bansa, *Moneta Mediolanensis* 159; idem, 'Note di numismatica teodosiana' 116; Seeck, *Regesten* 284. Kent ('Gold Coinage in the Later Roman Empire' 202–3) also connects certain solidi of Theodosius II (IMPXXXXIICOS XVIIPP / CONOB or COMOB: Tolstoi, *Monnaies byzantines* i, 68–9, nos. 18–24) with the *expeditio Asiana* of 443 (Seeck, *Regesten* 373).

[2] See above, p. 127 n. 2 and p. 128 n. 4, below, p. 139; Kent, 'Gold Coinage in the Later Roman Empire' 200 (n. 5).

only something of the kind would explain the standardization of mint-marks on Gratian's expedition of 379 or of reverse types on Theodosius' of 387. It is possible, for example, that some or all of the *aurifices solidorum* were included, but the relevant *sculptores* excluded. A similar practice presumably held good for the staff of the various *scrinia* of the *officium*—the bullion needed, for example, might well have come from regional *thesauri* rather than from comitatensian stocks. On the occasion of longer-term changes in residence, on the other hand, the entire *officium* seems to have been transferred, as when Gratian moved from Trier through Aquileia to Milan in 381, or when Theodosius moved west in 394—although in the latter case the mint, at least, ended up not at Milan but at Sirmium which held a convenient strategic situation on the borders of the two Illyrian dioceses. Whenever the products of the comitatensian mint itself are distinguishable at Milan, Ravenna, or Sirmium, and however its personnel was constituted—whether by the temporary secondment of at least some staff from nearby regional *monetae*, or by the wholesale transfer of its own staff—they are overwhelmingly weighted first in favour of gold alone, then in favour of gold and silver, but always to the exclusion of copper. It is therefore probably significant that, with the possible exception of the *scapltores*, the only comitatensian mint technicians mentioned by the *Codex* are the *aurifices solidorum*. While it is conceivable that equivalent staff for the manufacture of silver and copper coin are disguised under some such general designation as 'ceteri artifices' it may well be wondered whether the staple comitatensian product was not indeed just gold solidi, with such silver and minimal copper as was required also being produced by the *aurifices solidorum*.

## III

An apparent anomaly nevertheless remains to be explained. Although Milan, Ravenna, and Sirmium, as sites *par excellence* for the comitatensian mint, duly coined virtually in precious metals only, both Trier in the west and Constantinople in the east coined in copper throughout.[1] Now the administrative difference between Trier, on the one hand, and Milan, Ravenna, and Sirmium, on the other, is that the first was basically a *moneta publica*, and is listed as such in the *Notitia* where the others are ignored. Where Trier effectively differed from the remaining *monetae publicae* was that it happened to provide the imperial residence—therefore becoming comitatensian or rather having comitatensian staff superimposed on it—far more frequently and for longer periods of time than they.[2] The nearest to an equivalent was probably Antioch in the east.[3] The question obviously arises as to whether Constantinople was, in theory at least, merely a more extreme example of this kind of situation than either Trier or Antioch.

[1] *RIC*, under relevant reigns and mint headings.
[2] See for instance above, p. 125.                    [3] See for instance above, p. 125.

The implications of this question have been taken to their logical extreme by Kent who suggests that the comitatensian mint and the *moneta publica* at Constantinople were in fact separate institutions—not only administratively but even physically.[1] The former, as an integral section of the *largitiones comitatenses*, might by definition have been expected to be located in or near the palace itself, and for what it is worth a scholium on Constantine Porphyrogenitus' *De Caerimoniis* does indeed place, ἡ παλαιὰ χαραγή there.[2] This is also known to have been the case at Ravenna where, in 572, a certain Flavius Johannis is recorded as owning a *statio* (stall) 'ad Monitam auri in porticum sacri Palati(i)'.[3] Yet, according to the *Notitia Urbis Constantino-politanae*, which is datable through its dedication to Theodosius II, 'Regio duodecima . . . continet in se . . . monetam'.[4] The twelfth region ran more or less parallel to the shore of the Marmora, its extreme western end reaching out to the *porta aurea* (probably the Constantinian one). Between its eastern end and the first region, which contained the *palatium magnum*, lay the ninth and the third regions.[5] In other words, the mint in the twelfth region was just about as far from the Great Palace as it could possibly be. Its identification as a *moneta publica* quite separate from that formed by the comitatensian *officium* clearly provides an ingenious solution to the problem.

A physical separation of mints such as that suggested by Kent would in fact go far towards explaining several features of the metropolitan coinage. The organizational structure producing gold coin seems, for instance, to have for long differed from that producing both most of the silver and all of the copper. While gold was, with rare exceptions only, not marked with the

---

[1] Kent, 'Gold Coinage in the Later Roman Empire' 201.

[2] Constantine Porphyrogenitus, *De Caerimoniis* i, 1 (ed. Vogt i [*texte*], p. 5, n. 1). The location of the ὀκτακίονος θόλος that seems formerly to have housed this mint is given by the scholium as εἰς τὴν α' σχολήν. More particularly it seems to have been in that part of the *scholai* termed αἱ κορτῖναι. For the *tholos*: R. Guilland, 'Autour du Livre des Céré-monies. Le Grand Palais. Les quartiers militaires', *Byzantinoslavica* 1956, 89–91. For the *scholai*: ibid. 91–5. For the *kortinai*: ibid. 85–7. The *tholos* was, by tradition, of Constantinian origin: ibid. 87–8. The *scholai* were themselves adjacent to the entrance of the Great Palace (ἡ χαλκῆ), for which: C. A. Mango, *The Brazen House* (Arkæol. Kunsthist. Medd. Dan. Vid. Selsk. iv⁴ [1959]). For the latest general plan of the Great Palace: that by S. Miranda accompanying R. Guilland, *Études de topographie de Constantinople byzantine* ii (fold-out at back). It seems clear that the palace at Ravenna was constructed on lines similar to those of the Great Palace, having for instance according to Agnellus its own *chalce* ('. . . in fronte regiae quae dicitur Ad Calchi.., ubi prima porta palatii fuit'), and that an equivalent position should therefore probably be sought for the former's *moneta auri* 'in porticum sacri Palati(i)': Agnellus, *Liber Pontificalis Ecclesiae Ravennatis* c. 94 (MGH *Scriptores Rerum Langobardicarum et Italicarum Saec. VI–IX* 337); E. Dyggve, *Ravennatum Palatium Sacrum* (Arkæol. Kunsthist. Medd. Dan. Vid. Selsk. iii² [1941]), 44–9.

[3] G. Marini, *I papiri diplomatici raccolti ed illustrati*, no. 120, p. 185. The *monitarius auri* Paschalis of this document was in fact *v. d(evotissimus)* not *v. c(larissimus)* as described in my previous article ('On the Administrative Basis of the Byzantine Coinage' 142).

[4] *Notitia Urbis Constantinopolitanae* xiii, 12.

[5] *Palatium*: *N. Urb. Const.* ii, 8. The regions: R. Janin, *Constantinople byzantine* 43–58.

number of the *officina* producing it until after 379, and was then consistently marked by a total of ten officinae,[1] silver (or at least extensive issues of silver) and copper were so marked from a very early stage by a varying total of *officinae* that was nevertheless common to both.[2] It would also help to explain why the Codex mentions *aurifices solidorum* only as the mint technicians of the comitatensian *officium*; why little or no gold was struck at Constantinople during Valens' absence 371–8, and none at all during Theodosius' absence 387–91; and why and how the Constantinopolitan *aurifices* were transferred to Sirmium in 394 without affecting the metropolitan production of copper.

A degree of support for this suggestion may perhaps also be had from a consideration of the circumstances surrounding the foundation of the metropolitan mint(s). A *terminus ante* for the creation of that identified as a *moneta publica* is provided by its having struck momentarily for Crispus and Fausta, both of whom were executed during the course of 326 and probably towards the end of that year.[3] Constantine is recorded as having been at Heraclea in February 326, and was probably at Constantinople on 8 March, but was in any case already at Aquileia on 4 April on the way to Rome for the celebration of his *vicennalia* on 25 July.[4] He is not again recorded at Constantinople until 11 June 327, having been at Thessalonica as late as 27 February on his way back from Rome.[5] It is therefore quite possible, even probable, that the mint came into service actually in the absence of the *comitatus* and there can in any event have been little connection between the two for the first several years of its existence.[6] It proceeded to strike in copper, silver, and—at this early stage—very sparsely indeed in gold.[7] The pattern of its products thus conformed to that of any other regional *moneta*, and certainly contrasted with that of near-contemporary Sirmium which has been shown above to have formed an early instance of the comitatensian mint at work.[8] It may therefore be suggested that the creation of a *moneta publica* formed an integral part of that programme of public building by which Byzantium was transformed into Constantinople and New Rome. It was only with the dedication of the city (11 May 330) and Constantine's increasingly frequent and lengthy periods of residence there that its production of gold became

---

[1] *RIC* ix, 223.

[2] e.g. Constantine—*RIC* vii, 578 (Æ) A–IA, 579 (Æ) A–IA; 587–8 (Æ) A–IA, 589–90 (Æ) A–IA. Constantius II—*Coh.* vii, p. 492, no. 343 (Æ) A–IA, Carson, Hill, Kent, *Late Roman Bronze Coinage* ii, 86–7 (Æ) A–IA. Jovian—*Coh.* viii, p. 79, no. 33 (Æ) A–Δ, Carson, Hill, Kent, op. cit. 42, 86–7 (Æ) A–Δ. Valentinian, Valens—*RIC* ix, 211–13 (Æ) A–Z (H exists, but is rare), 214–16 (Æ) A–Z. This correspondence seems to cease under Valentinian, Valens, and Gratian (*RIC* ix, 216–21), and officina numbers in any case thereafter disappear from the silver. See below, p. 133 n. 2.

[3] *RIC* vii, 71–2, 569–71.

[4] Seeck, *Regesten* 176–7.                                                   [5] Ibid. 178.

[6] Constantine's prolonged residences at his new capital date from c. 330 only. See below, p. 133 n. 1.

[7] See above, n. 3.                                                   [8] See above, p. 126.

intense.[1] It is then, in the circumstances, legitimate to connect this change of emphasis with the arrival and prolonged presence of the *comitatus* with its mint.

If the case for separate mints at Constantinople has any validity, it may be surmised that the comitatensian mint will normally have produced gold and such silver as had an occasional character and medallic function. The *moneta publica* will normally have produced copper and, at least up until the reforms of 366–7, the more extensive issues of silver—particularly the small denomination now commonly misnamed 'siliqua'.[2] It will also, in theory at least, have been capable of the occasional issue of gold until 366–7. The distinction between the metals used by the two mints will thus at first not have been absolute but, with the reforms of 366–7 effectively bringing the striking of gold by *monetae publicae* to an end, and with the virtual disappearance of a silver coinage at the commencement of the fifth century, it will eventually have become so. From quite early on in the fifth century gold alone will have been produced in the palace, copper alone in the twelfth region. This would in itself explain the appreciable differences in organization still evident in the production of the two metropolitan coinages during the later fifth and the sixth centuries.[3]

Evidence for the separate existence of two mints, one (the *moneta aurea* or *auri*) producing gold, the other (the *moneta publica*) producing copper, is even stronger in the case of Ravenna than in that of Constantinople.

The mint that had produced the almost entirely precious-metal coinage of the western emperors achieves a casual mention as *moneta aurea* in an

[1] Seeck, *Regesten* 180–4; *RIC* vii, 565, 576–90.

[2] Kent ('Gold Coinage in the Later Roman Empire', 200) supposes the production of silver to have become assimilated to that of gold as a result of the reforms of 366–7. The evidence of the metropolitan mint(s) tends to support him; see above, p. 132 n. 2. 'Siliqua': Jones, 'Numismatics and History', 28 n. 2.

[3] Gold coinage was then, as it had long been (see above, p. 132 n. 1), produced by ten *officinae* (A–I); copper of the Anastasian reform and after by five *officinae* (A–Є). *Officina* numbers seem to have been imposed on the gold well after the engraving of the rest of the reverse die and, it seems, often by a different hand. They were also altered on occasion to denote use in an *officina* other than that for which they were originally intended. The implication seems to be that reverse dies were engraved and kept centrally—outside, that is, the individual *officinae*. This seems confirmed by the existence of obverse die-links between different *officinae*. See P. Grierson, 'Coins monétaires et officines à l'époque du Bas-Empire', *SMzB* xi, 1–8; cf. C. H. V. Sutherland, 'Coins monétaires et officines à l'époque du Bas-Empire: note supplémentaire', *SMzB* xi, 73–5 (but using non-Constantinopolitan and base-metal material). *Officina* numbers on the copper, by contrast, were an integral part of the design and appear to have been engraved at the same time as the rest of the reverse die. They do not appear to have been altered for use in other *officinae*. The implication seems to be that reverse dies were engraved and kept in the individual *officinae*. This is surely confirmed by the well-known fact that in the sixth century each *officina* tended to differentiate its reverse dies not only by the imposition of its own number but also by use of variations in the form of stars, or by combinations of crosses and stars, etc., that were peculiar to itself. See D. M. Metcalf, 'Organization of the Constantinople Mint for the Follis of the Anastasian Reform', *NC* 1961, 131–2; *DOC* i, under appropriate headings from Anastasius to Justinian.

undated source describing the building activities of Odovacer and Theoderic —with reference to the former in this instance. Although there seems to have been an hiatus in its production under the Ostrogothic kings, whose gold coinage seems increasingly to have been struck at Rome, it was presumably identical with that described as *moneta auri* and located 'in porticum sacri Palati(i)' in 572.[1]

As noted above, the city is not listed as possessing a *moneta publica* by the *Notitia*, and since it produced virtually no copper at that time is indeed unlikely then to have done so. Nevertheless, Agnellus' *Liber Pontificalis*, written towards the middle of the ninth century, records of the thirty-fifth archbishop, Reparatus (671–7), that: 'De monasterio sancti Apolenaris quaesitus est, hic Ravenna non longe a posterula Ovilionis in loco qui vocatur Moneta publica.'[2] Now it seems clear that Agnellus' reference, on the one hand, can only have been to a former late Roman or Byzantine mint— for very little coinage seems to have been struck since the destruction of the exarchate in 751[3]—and that, on the other, the mint in question cannot have the palatine *moneta auri*—for not only the terminology employed but even the locations cited are incompatible with such an identity.[4] At some stage between 402/3 and 751 Ravenna had therefore acquired a *moneta publica*: is that stage identifiable with any precision? It should, on the face of it, be identical with that at which the regular copper coinage characteristic of such a mint first appeared at Ravenna. An Ostrogothic or more likely a post-540 dating therefore seems likely, for as already observed there are virtually no Ravenna copper coins of the western emperors, and although a small series of 'quasi autonomous' coins is known for the Ostrogothic period,[5] regular production commenced only in 552/3.[6] This last event seems to have been connected with the arrival of Narses who had himself held the office of *sacellarius* and was then, despite his military command, still *praepositus sacri cubiculi*, both posts entailing either the actual performance or the general oversight of financial functions.[7] That functions of the kind and order required were indeed ultimately within Narses' competence is demonstrated

---

[1] *Moneta aurea*: source cited in MGH *Scriptores Rerum Langobardicarum et Italicarum Saec. VI–IX*, at p. 267 (n. 2). *Moneta auri*: see above, p. 131 n. 3.

[2] Agnellus, *Liber Pontificalis Ecclesiae Ravennatis*, c. 115 (MGH *Scr. Rer. Lang.* 353). In c. 164 (ed. cit. 383) the same mint is termed *moneta vetus*—presumably because no longer used. Cf. above, p. 131 and n. 2.

[3] *CNI* x, 680–2; cf. M. Thompson, 'The Monogram of Charlemagne in Greek', *MN* 1966, 125–7.

[4] *Enciclopedia dell'arte antica classica orientale* vi, 616.

[5] *BMC Van.* 106–7.

[6] *DOC* i, 184–5 (decanummia). The first coins actually bearing a mint-name occur as late as 559/60, 560/61 (*DOC* i, 183–4; half folleis, folleis).

[7] For Narses: Jones, *Later Roman Empire* iii, 163 (n. 7)—as *sacellarius*; 56 (n. 55)—as *praepositus*; 56 (n. 51)—invasion of Italy. For the offices: E. Stein, 'Untersuchungen zum Staatsrecht des Bas-Empire', *Zeitschrift der Savigny-Stiftung für Rechtsgeschichte*, Romanistische Abteilung, 1920, 240–51.

by the terms of the *Constitutio Pragmatica* by which, in 554, Justinian regulated the affairs of Italy. Among others, clause 19 is entitled *De Mensuris et Ponderibus*, clause 20 *De Mutatione Solidorum id est Monetae*, and 25 *Ut Fabricae Publicae Serventur*. The whole is addressed: *Narsi viro ill. praeposito sacri cubiculi, Antiocho viro magnifico praefecto per Italiam*.[1] It is, therefore, not inconceivable that the *moneta publica* at Ravenna owed its construction to a programme influenced, but not necessarily specifically directed, by him.

## IV

Despite the unchanging appearance of its external structure the production of coin during the late Roman and early Byzantine period can therefore be shown to have undergone shifts of internal emphasis that conform to, and probably reflect, similar trends known to have occurred in the general fiscal administration of the empire. The Diocletianic situation, with its single tier of regional mints producing gold and silver sporadically, and copper with some degree of continuity, survived the abdication of that emperor by a considerable time. Although there are even then unmistakable signs of a tendency for gold coining to concentrate upon the current position of the emperor and his *comitatus*, it is only well into the reign of Constantine, with the brief operation of the mint of Sirmium, that this tendency can be shown to have achieved some kind of formal embodiment.[2] At much the same time and during the years following it seems clear that the widespread and simultaneous coining of gold at mints other than that currently occupied by the *comitatus* becomes institutionalized and virtually confined to the occasion of accessional and quinquennial celebrations. The first permanent sign of the emergence of a double tier of mints, a regional one for copper and a comitatensian one for gold, occurs with the opening of the mint of Milan under Constantius II, producing first gold alone then gold and silver, and operating only in the presence of the *comitatus*. This development was taken to its logical conclusion with the reforms of Valentinian and Valens confining the coining of gold to the comitatensian *officium* of the *comes sacrarum largitionum*. It is this situation that is reflected by the *Notitia*, mentioning as it does all the western regional *monetae publicae* from Trier to Siscia, but none of the mints used by the comitatensian *officium* alone, whether Milan or Ravenna or Sirmium.

The first sign of a reaction against the comitatensian monopoly of gold coining dates from the turn of the fourth century, and although the trend of which it formed part is obscured by the disintegration of the western empire and the emergence of independent barbarian states—most having their own

---

[1] Justinian, *App.* vii, 1–27.

[2] Unless perhaps slightly anticipated by the even briefer reopening of Serdica for the production of gold only under Licinius in 313/14: *RIC* vii, 478–80.

pseudo-imperial coinages—its extent and limitations become relatively clear in the arrangements adopted for the areas reconquered under Justinian. The regional praetorian prefectures are by then each permitted the regular, if inevitably small-scale, minting of gold coin: first that of Illyricum at Thessalonica, then those of Africa and Italy at Carthage and Ravenna respectively.[1] It appears probable that this function was performed by drafts of comitatensian moneyers seconded for the purpose, witness the *palatini sacrarum largitionum* at Ravenna in 572, thus allowing the theory of a central monopoly to stand. The essential distinction between the gold and copper coinages nevertheless persisted and is to be seen enshrined in the continued existence of separate mints for gold and copper at both Constantinople and Ravenna, the latter probably being a late, and post-reconquest, foundation. At this stage the situation appears to have become stabilized and to have lasted more or less unchanged until the final disappearance of the late Roman and early Byzantine administrative structure during the seventh century.

The establishment or evolution of all three major elements of this structure had therefore by then been reflected—however imperfectly—in contemporary coinage: the establishment of regional, largely diocesan, fiscal units in the late third century; the evolution of the *comitatus*, with its permanent offices and bureaux, during the fourth century; and finally the emergence of the

---

[1] Kent, 'Gold Coinage in the Later Roman Empire', 203; Hendy, 'On the Administrative Basis of the Byzantine Coinage', 142–5. Thessalonican gold issues will, of course, have commenced well before the city became the seat of the prefect of Illyricum, but its mint will even at that early stage have been the only regular one available to him—in terms of monetary production much the same thing. It seems that the prefecture of Illyricum (i.e. the dioceses of Dacia and Macedonia) was allotted to Honorius in 395, but that very soon after (probably in 396) it was transferred to Arcadius, and that—despite the machinations of Stilicho—it never reverted to the west. See E. Demougeot, *De l'unité à la division de l'Empire romain 395–410*, 119–375. The seat of the prefect at this stage remains unknown. Justinian (*Nov.* xi [535]) and Theodoret (*Historia Ecclesiastica* v, 17) both mention that he resided at Thessalonica—after having been forced to move there: 'Attilanis temporibus . . . de Sirmitana civitate', according to the former. These *Attilana tempora* are now generally dated to 441/2 (e.g. Jones, *Later Roman Empire* i, 193; iii, 37 [n. 48]). But how long had Pannonia Secunda, in which Sirmium stood, been part of the (eastern) Illyrian prefecture? J. B. Bury (*A History of the Later Roman Empire from the Death of Theodosius I to the Death of Justinian [395–565]* i, 225–6 [n. 5]) suggested that the province was ceded to the east as late as 437, on the occasion of Valentinian III's marriage to Licinia Eudoxia. It is therefore probably significant that it is listed in Hierocles' *Synecdemus*—which is an eastern document and, according to Jones (*Later Roman Empire* iii, 381), basically datable to the reign of Theodosius II. J. R. Palanque supposed that, before 437, the prefect of Illyricum had resided at either Naissus or Serdica, both in the diocese of Dacia (*Essai sur la préfecture du prétoire du Bas-Empire* 123 ['à Naissus'], *Errata* facing p. 144 ['Au lieu de: Naissus; lire: Sardique']). Certainly it is clear that the *Notitia* regards the whole of the diocese of Illyricum (i.e. the former Pannonia), including Sirmium, as part of the (western) prefecture of Italy (*Occ.* ix, 18; xi, 47; xxxii, 49, 50, 54), and it also seems clear that, in omitting an entry for a *vicarius Daciae* and his *officium*, the *Notitia* implies that the prefect was then resident in that diocese (e.g. Jones, *Later Roman Empire* iii, 79 [n. 18]). Sirmium was itself, at any rate, still regarded as eastern in 505, when Theoderic occupied it: recaptured from the Gepids in 567, it was finally lost to the Avars in 582 (refs. Jones, *Later Roman Empire* iii, 44 [n. 20], 57 [n. 3], 58 [n. 11].)

regional prefecture, with its fixed territorial boundaries, during the late fourth and the fifth centuries.

It may well be asked, in conclusion, whether considerations of public convenience ever entered into this scheme. The answer would seem to be that they did not, or that they played so minor a role as now to be invisible. Constantius II might refer to 'pecunia in usu publico constituta' in a law of 356, but in doing so was employing the term 'pecunia' in a restricted sense that referred to copper coin alone: indeed that same law placed severe restrictions on the movement of copper coinage,[1] and it was production of precisely that coinage that can most easily be shown to have conformed to the pattern of regional fiscal administration and to have fulfilled fiscal and military needs rather than the demands of public convenience.[2] In view of what is known of late Roman and early Byzantine civilization, nothing else should really have been expected.

## APPENDIX

### *The Sequence of Main Precious-metal Issues c. 387–91*

Constantinopolitan issues of the period bear the *vota* figures V/X, X/XV, and X/XX. These are of the traditional *soluta/suscepta* type, and will thus have referred to vows celebrated and undertaken at the opening of or during the final year of the current quinquennium, the cycle as a whole being reckoned from the day of accession. V/X will thus have been appropriate to Arcadius' quinquennial year from 19 January 387 onwards, and X/XV to Theodosius' decennial year from 19 January 388. It would nevertheless have been an obvious convenience, given the administrative context, to have combined the necessary taxation and resultant ceremonies. An excellent example of such an occurrence is to be found in Marcellinus Comes' report that: 'Theodosius iunior decennalia, Honorius Romae vicennalia dedit' (*Chronicon*, s.a. 411). Theodosius' *decennalia* were indeed due in 411, but Honorius' *vicennalia* in 412 only: the two had been combined. Theodosius' later quinquennial celebrations are notoriously anticipated by a year, or even two. The *Consularia Constantinopolitana* in fact records (s.a. 387) that: '. . . quinquennalia Arcadius Aug. propria cum Theodosio Aug. patre suo . . . celebravit die xvii kal. Feb.'; and Libanius connects rioting at Antioch in 387 with taxation for both *quinquennalia* and *decennalia*, also identifying the military basis of such exactions (*Oratio* xxii, 4; cf. Browning in *JRS* 1952, 13–20). Whether this is in itself sufficient to justify the assumption of combined ceremonies is doubtful, but the phenomenon is effectively probable. It is in any case clear that the dynastic ceremonial of the Theodosian house was most effectively 'managed'. Arcadius' elevation in 383 seems to have been designed to coincide with the opening of the final year of his father's first quinquennium, Honorius' elevation on 23 January 393 with that of his third

---

[1] Constantius: *C. Th.* ix, 23, 1. Pecunia: Augustine, *Sermo* cxxvii, 3 ('. . . aurum, vel argentum, vel pecuniam . . .') (in *Patrologia Latina* xxxviii, at col. 707); see also above, p. 124 n. 2. Both headings are discussed by P. Grierson, 'The Roman Law of Counterfeiting', in *Essays in Roman Coinage* at 240–61.

[2] Hendy, 'Mint and Fiscal Administration under Diocletian'.

quinquennium, and Theodosius II's elevation on 10 January 402 with that of his father Arcadius' fourth quinquennium. Marcellinus even records of the last two: 'Honorium pater suus Theodosius in eodem loco [i.e. Hebdomon] quo fratrem eius Arcadium Caesarem fecit' (s.a. 393), and 'Theodosius iunior in loco quo pater patruusque suus Caesar creatus est' (s.a. 402).

V/X for Arcadius and X/XV for Theodosius were accompanied by a third set of figures. This surely suggests that it was intended that the whole of the current imperial college should be commemorated and therefore that the third set refers to Valentinian. Now Valentinian's elevation occurred on 22 November 375: his *decennalia* had therefore been celebrated in 384/5 (Symmachus, *Relatio* xiii); his *quindecennalia* were not due until 389/90. In 387 his appropriate *vota* figures would still have been X/XV—the same, that is, as Theodosius'. Ambiguity was avoided by granting him—as theoretically senior to Theodosius—a decennial reckoning thus: X/XX. The figures for the two eastern emperors virtually monopolize the gold coinage, those for the western one monopolize the silver: a deliberate but not necessarily significant division. That the gold in the names of Valentinian, Theodosius, and Arcadius, and bearing the *vota* figures of the last two, was struck contemporaneously rather than as part of a series over the two years 387-8, is confirmed by the division of *officinae* (*RIC* ix, 208: Th. A–Δ; Val. Є, S; Arc. Z–I).

The silver *missorium* at Madrid bearing the inscription D N THEODOSIVS PERPET AVG OB DIEM FELICISSIMVM X (R. Delbrueck, *Die Consular-diptychen und verwandte Denkmäler* i, no. 62, pp. 235–42) has a clear potential relevance to the subject under discussion.

It is surely an official product and gift, one of a recognizable series of such, and will therefore have been manufactured by the *argentarii comitatenses* of the *officium* of the *c.s.l.* Its iconography should be comparable to that of the contemporary precious-metal coinage which was produced by another section of the same *officium*. The three seated figures—all diademed—can thus only be Theodosius himself (the large central figure), Valentinian (smaller, to his right), and Arcadius (smallest, to his left). The suggestion that they represent Theodosius, Arcadius, and Honorius, is improbable simply because at the time—whether 387 or 388—Honorius would not have been portrayed as diademed on official products.

The dominance of Theodosius in the design shows it to have been executed under his jurisdiction, and the Greek inscription on the back recording its weight (50 lb.) suggests that it was, moreover, an eastern product—or at the very least that it was made by eastern craftsmen. If, as seems likely, Constantinopolitan, it will have been made in 387—either because his *decennalia* were celebrated in that year as suggested above, or well in anticipation of a celebration in January 388. It is, in other words, unlikely to have been made, and *a fortiori* a decennial celebration to have taken place, in the metropolis after Theodosius' departure westwards in late 387. It is of course possible, but much less probable, that it was made elsewhere (for instance at Thessalonica as Theodosius' base in early 388) but by metropolitan craftsmen travelling with the *comitatus*. Since it was found in the west (near Mérida/Emerita, Spain) it may well, in one way or another, have travelled with the *comitatus* on that occasion.

This, then, would have been the situation, and these the current *vota* figures, when Theodosius left the capital for Thessalonica in late 387. The same figures (which would remain appropriate until the next quinquennial celebration), and much the same kind of division, are both evident in the (subsequent) products of the mints of Thessalonica, Aquileia, and Milan. At Rome a new set of figures (XV/XX) also appears. Now Marcellinus records (s.a. 389) that: 'Theodosius imperator cum Honorio filio suo Romam . . . introivit, congiarium Romano populo tribuit.' This visit is known to have taken place between 13 June and 30 August 389 (see above, p. 127 n. 5). If the new figures appeared towards its end they will have anticipated only slightly the celebration of Valentinian's *quindecennalia* (due 22 November 389) —for which they are in fact entirely appropriate. XV/XX also occurs on the gold coinage of Thessalonica, which Theodosius probably visited in the summer of 391 on his way back to Constantinople (see above, p. 127 n. 7), and on Valentinian's own silver coinage from the mint of Lyons (*RIC* ix, no. 42, p. 51).

It seems probable that these gold and silver issues which, it is suggested in the text above, were produced for or by Theodosius' eastern *comitatus* while in the west 387–91, were paralleled by contemporary issues from Valentinian's western *comitatus*. Limitations of space forbid a detailed listing but the solidi concerned are probably to be found among the VICTOR IAAVGG issues from Thessalonica (m.-m. COM), Aquileia ($\frac{A \mid Q}{COM}$), and Milan ($\frac{M \mid D}{COM}$), as well as subsequently from Lyons ($\frac{L \mid D}{COM}$), and Trier ($\frac{T \mid R}{COM}$), both of which were assigned to Valentinian by the 'settlement' of 388/9 (*RIC* ix, 185, 103, 80, 50, 30, etc.). Significantly enough, VRBS ROMA silver pieces of this group from Lyons are linked by obverse dies with VIRTVSRO MANORVM pieces from Aquileia, while other pieces of the former type also have aberrant and composite mint-marks containing elements both of the LVG of Lyons and the MD of Milan (Pearce, in *NC* 1944, 46–8).

It seems probable that this contemporaneity will also explain the letter Θ that terminates the reverse inscription of the CONCORDI AAVGGG issues of Aquileia and, above all, Milan (see above, p. 127 n. 8). Possible explanations, some of them belonging to the world of fantasy, have been listed by Ulrich-Bansa (*Moneta Mediolanensis* 66–8). The simplest and most plausible in the circumstances is surely that it was intended—as the initial letter of Θεοδόσιος—to distinguish and indicate the ultimate ownership of dies engraved and perhaps used alongside those of Valentinian. Θ is noticeably absent from the issues that seem to have marked Theodosius' presence at Rome in 389 (see above, p. 127 n. 9), simply because, Valentinian no longer being present (Seeck, *Regesten*, 274, 276), the question of distinction did not arise.

If the essentials of this sequence and its implications are accepted, then the probable context of an earlier group of gold coins, VICTOR IAAVGG (m.-m. COM) from the mints of Milan, Aquileia, and Thessalonica, becomes clear. It will have emanated from Valentinian's *comitatus* between 380 and 387 while that emperor had Gratian then Maximus, mainly at Trier, and Theodosius, mainly at Constantinople, as his colleagues, and while he was in theoretical or actual control of Illyricum, Italy, and Africa (*RIC* ix, 76–8, 180; *Revue des études byzantines* 1951, 11–17; *Byzantion* 1951, 8–12).

# A Hoard of Constantinian Reduced Folles from Brentford, Middlesex

JOHN CASEY

THE coins listed and discussed below were brought to the author's attention when they were offered for sale in a London auction room. The provenance assigned to them has no authority beyond the tradition that they were found in Brentford, Middlesex, and no circumstantial account has survived of the date of the find or of the archaeological context from which it was recovered. The coins had been cleaned in acid so that similarity of patina or corrosion could not be used to supplement the evidence of their hoard status, though the internal evidence puts this beyond question.

Reference throughout is to *RIC* vii. The number in brackets after the *RIC* reference indicates the number of specimens and the number for each mint *officina* when this is other than the first *officina*.

## LONDON

| | | | | *RIC* |
|---|---|---|---|---|
| 1–12. | Crispus | $\frac{\text{F} \mid \text{B}}{\text{PLON}}$ (322–3) | BEAT TRA-NQLITAS  VOT/IS/XX | 250 (12) |
| 13. | ,, | ——,, | ,, | 251 (1) |
| 14–17. | ,, | PLON (323–4) | ,, | 279 (4) |
| 18–19. | ,, | ,, | ,, | 281 (2) |
| 20–1. | Constantine II | $\frac{\mid}{\text{PLON}}$ (324–5) | PROVIDEN-TIAE CAESS | 296 (2) |

## LUGDUNUM

| | | | | |
|---|---|---|---|---|
| 22–4. | Crispus | $\frac{\text{C} \mid \text{R}}{\text{PLG}}$ (322–3) | BEATA TRAN-QVILLITAS. VO/TIS/XX | 166 (3) |
| 25–37. | ,, | ,, | ,, | 168 (13) |
| 38. | ,, | ,, | ,, | 171 (1) |
| 39–42. | ,, | PLG (323) | ,, | 202 (4) |

## TRIER

| | | | | |
|---|---|---|---|---|
| 43. | Licinius I | PTR (320) | VIRTVS EXERCIT VOT/XX | 267 (1) |
| 44–5. | Crispus | PTR (320) | BEATA TRAN-QVILLITAS. VO/TIS/XX | 308 (2) |
| 46. | ,, | ,, | ,, | 322 (1) |

## ARLES

| | | | | |
|---|---|---|---|---|
| 47–50. | Constantine I | PX̄AR (322–3) | SARMATIA DEVICTA | 257 (P 2, S 2) |
| 51. | Constantine II | PX̄AR (324–5) | PROVIDEN-TIAE CAESS | 274 (Q 1) |
| 52. | ,, | PAURL (325–6) | VIRTVS CAESS | 297 (1) |

### ROME

| 53. | Constantine II | $\overline{RP}$ (321) | CAESARVM NOSTRORVM VOT/X | 242 (T 1) |
| 54. | Constantius II | R⚬P (326) | PROVIDEN-TIAE CAESS | 290 (Q 1) |

### TICINUM

| 55. | Licinius I | $\overline{P\smile T}$ (319–20) | VIRTVS EXERCIT VOT/XX | 123 (S 1) |

### AQUILEIA

| 56. | Licinius I | $\frac{S \mid F}{AQS}$ (320 | VIRTVS EXERCIT VOT/XX | 51 var. (1) |
| 57. | Constantine II | ·AQT· (320) | CAESARVM NOSTRORVM VOT/X | 101/(1) |
| 58. | ,, | ⚔\|⚔ (322 AQT | ,, | 115 (1) |

### SISCIA

| 59 | Licinius I | S $\mid \frac{F}{H}$ (322) ASIS✳ | VIRTVS EXERCIT. VOT/XX | 121 (1) |

### THESSALONICA

| 60–4. | Constantine II | $\overline{TSBVI}$ (324) | CAESARVM NOSTRORVM. VOT/X | 128 (5) |
| 65. | ,, | SMTSA (326–8) | PROVIDEN-TIAE CAESS | 157 (1) |

### UNASSIGNABLE

| 66. | Licinius I | | VIRTVS EXERCIT. VOT/XX | cf. Trier 267 (1 |

### IRREGULAR

| 67. | Constantine II | *Obv.* CONSTANTINVS IVN NOB C |
| | | Bust, laureate, bare right, seen from the rear. |
| | | *Rev.* PROVIDE- NTIAE CS STR. |

Copies of the issues of 324–5 of the Trier mint are not uncommon (cf. *RIC* vii, 205, etc.) and, though the style and lettering of the present specimen are good it probably falls into this class.

### *Distribution by Mints*

| LONDON | LUGDUNUM | TRIER | ARLES | ROME | TICINUM | AQUILEIA | SISCIA | THESSALONICA | UNASSIGNABLE | IRREGULAR | TOTAL |
|---|---|---|---|---|---|---|---|---|---|---|---|
| 21 | 21 | 4 | 6 | 2 | 1 | 3 | 1 | 6 | 1 | 1 | 67 |

If the hoard is complete as we have it, then the predominance of coins of the Lugdunum mint over those of the Trier mint is an unusual feature. Comparison with other hoards which consist predominantly of the PRO-

VIDENTIAE CAESS and BEATA TRANQVILLITAS issues indicates a preponderance of the more western mint. The distribution in the Brentford hoard may perhaps indicate that we are here dealing with part of a consignment which had little time to be distributed before being hoarded, though the absence of any die-links, either obverse or reverse, may militate against this suggestion.

|  | London | Trier | Lugdunum |
|---|---|---|---|
| Llanberthery[1] | 17·4% | 62·3% | 20·3% |
| Canterbury[2] | 51% | 43% | 6% |
| Guilsfield[3] | 62% | 36·6% | 1·5% |
| Brentford | 45·5% | 9·0% | 45·5% |

### Date of Deposit

The absence of *Gloria Exercitus* issues provides a *terminus ad quem* for the closure of the hoard by A.D. 330.

Individually the coins call for little comment. One, however, is of some interest and fills a lacuna in the coinage of the mint of Aquileia which has been created in *RIC* vii.

56. *Obv.* IMP LIC - INIVS AVG
Helmeted bust, cuirassed right.

*Rev.* VIRTVS EXERCIT VOT/XX $\dfrac{S \mid F}{AQS}$

Bruun, *RIC* vii, 400, omits this issue with its abbreviated imperial title noting that 'The short obverse legend for the S | F mark has yet to be confirmed, in the author's opinion.' Maurice,[4] however, specifically records the short legend type 'avec et sans S | F, Off. S' and quotes specimens in London and Paris. Examination of the British Museum collection confirms the evidence of Maurice and, with the present specimen, we may restore this type to the issues of A.D. 320; At the same time the removal of the long legend IMP LICINIVS PF AVG quoted by Bruun (*RIC* vii, Aquileia 50, 51) from these issues may be proposed on the evidence of its absence from the B.M. collection, although it is this collection which is quoted as substantiating the type. It is clear that the long legend has been inadvertently transcribed and that the short legend type is the norm.

---

[1] G. C. Boon, 'A Constantinian Hoard from Llanberthery, near Barry, Co. Glamorgan', *NC* 1960, 253–65.
[2] R. A. G. Carson, 'The Canterbury Hoard', *NC* 1957, 249–57.
[3] B. O'Neil, 'The Guilsfield coin hoard', *Bulletin of the Board of Celtic Studies* 1936, 255–70.     [4] J. Maurice, *Numismatique constantinienne* i, 323.

# A Hoard of Constantinian Coins from Freston, Suffolk

E. OWLES, N. SMEDLEY, AND H. WEBB

In April 1959 Mr. R. Thompson ploughed up a hoard of over 3,000 fourth-century coins on Potash Farm, Freston (TM/16493758). The coins were afterwards purchased from the landowner, Mr. A. Suckling, and are now in Ipswich Museum (reg. no. 963–95).

Subsequent examination of the site by the writers showed that the hoard had been placed in a large pot sealed by a smaller one. No other evidence of Roman occupation could be seen in the vicinity and none has been reported from Freston, though the neighbouring parishes of Wherstead and Holbrook have both produced Roman pottery. In 1803 a hoard of exactly 2,000 third-century coins was found at Wherstead 1½ miles north of Potash Farm,[1] and in 1841 a large quantity of coins of Diocletian, Maximian, Constantine, Constans, and Constantius was found at Holbrook on the marshes by the Stour some two miles to the south.[2]

The pots in which the hoard was concealed had been broken and scattered in the plough-soil, but they were capable of reconstruction. The larger pot (Fig. 1) is slate grey with scribbled zigzag decoration on the shoulder, and three burnished bands below and one above. The inside, and especially the bottom 3 inches, is heavily encrusted with bronze corrosion. The rim is missing, destroyed by previous ploughings, but one fragment which has survived indicated that the opening was about 6½ inches in diameter. This corresponds with the maximum diameter of the smaller pot which shows traces of bronze corrosion on the outside of the base. It is black with a metallic lustre decorated with horizontal burnished lines, a groove on the shoulder and a flattened cordon on the neck. There is a shallow depression in the base.

The hoard consists of 3,118 coins. With the exception of an antoninianus of Tetricus I (A.D. 270–3), a commemorative coin of Claudius II (A.D. 268–70), one SOLI INVICTO COMITI of A.D. 317, and a barbarous VICTORIAE LAETAE P(R)INC P of A.D. 319, all the coins were struck between the years 324 and 348 covering the reigns of Constantine I and his family. Eleven

---

[1] *Victoria County History* 319, and F. Barham Zincke, *Some Materials for the History of Wherstead* 130 ff. Five coins in Ipswich Museum (reg. no. 969–24).

[2] *Victoria County History* 309, and *NC* 1841, 64. Pottery in Ipswich Museum (reg. no. 970–118).

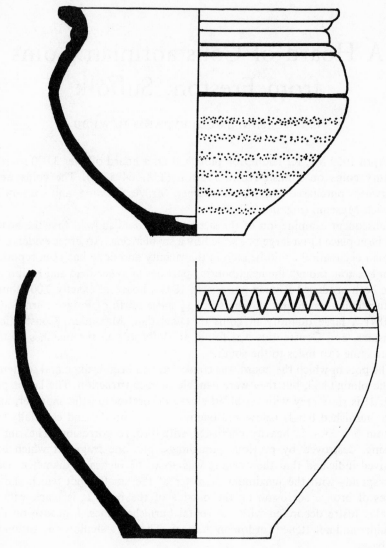

FIG. 1. Scale 1:2.

mints are represented, though naturally the bulk of the coins comes from Gaul: Trier 68 per cent, Lyons 19 per cent, Arles 9 per cent, Rome 2 per cent, with Siscia, Aquileia, Constantinople, Cyzicus, Thessalonica, Nicomedia, and Heraclea between them making up the remaining 2 per cent. The types represented are GLORIA EXERCITVS 43 per cent (1 standard 27 per cent, 2 standards 16 per cent), VICTORIAE DD AVGGQ NN 28 percent, Wolf and Twins 11 per cent, Victory on Prow 8 per cent, PAX PVBLICA 5 per cent,

PIETAS ROMANA 4 per cent, Quadriga 15 examples, VIRTVS AVGVSTI 11, SECVRITAS REIPVBLICE 4, D N CONSTANTINI MAX AVG—VOT XXX 2, and one example each of CONSTANTINVS CAESAR, CONSTANTIVS CAESAR, Star in Wreath, and AETERNA PIETAS.

The hoard contains one brockage obverse 3fQ and the following coins not listed in *Late Roman Bronze Coinage*:[1] Constantine I, all GLORIA EXERCITVS (2 standards) two coins no. 67 and one no. 72 with the bust type Q instead of N; and one coin no. 367 with the bust type K instead of N. An Arles Quadriga 21aR with the mint-mark $\frac{\text{x}|}{\text{PCON}}$. A similar coin may also be of Arles, but the mint-mark is not clear. A Constans, VICTORIAE DD AVGGQ NN no. 257 has obverse legend 3d instead of 3e.

Some coins are certainly imitations identifiable by their irregular die-axes or mint-marks. Others, less obvious, may also be imitations but have escaped detection.

The writers are greatly indebted to Mr. R. A. G. Carson of the British Museum for his invaluable assistance in the preparation of this paper, and to Messrs. Suckling and Thompson for reporting and handing over the coin hoard.

| Ruler | Mint-mark | Reverse | | Quantity | Reference RIC |
|---|---|---|---|---|---|
| | | **270–3** | | | |
| Tetricus I | | LAETITIA AVG | | 2 | 86 |
| | | **TREVERI**<br>**317** | | | |
| C I | $\frac{\text{T}|\text{F}}{\text{BTR}}$ | SOLI INVICTO COMITI | | 1 | 135 |
| | | **DIVUS**<br>**320–1** | | | |
| Claudius | ///TR | REQVIES OPT MER | | 1 | 297 |

| Ruler | Mint-mark | Reverse | *Officina & Quantity* | | |
|---|---|---|---|---|---|
| | | **324–30** | P | S | LRBC |
| C II | PTR | Star/CONSTAN/TINVS/CAESAR | | 1 | 20 |
| Cs | ,, | Star/CONSTAN/TIVS/CAESAR | | 1 | 24 |
| | | **330–5** | | | |
| C I | TRP | GLOR—IA EXERC—ITVS<br>(2 standards) | 1 | 4 | 48 |
| C II | ,, | ,, | 4 | 1 | 49 |
| Cs | ,, | ,, | 1 | 1 | 50 |
| U.R. | ,, | Wolf and Twins | 3 | 5 | 51 |
| Cp. | ,, | Victory on Prow | 19 | 11 | 52 |
| C I | TRP· | GLOR—IA EXERC—ITVS<br>(2 standards) | | 5 | 53 |
| ,, | ,, | ,, | | 2 | 53a |
| ,, | ,, | ,, | 13 | 1 | 54 |

[1] R. A. G. Carson, J. P. C. Kent, and P. V. Hill, *Late Roman Bronze Coinage*.

| Ruler | Mint-mark | Reverse | Officina & Quantity P | S | Reference LRBC |
|---|---|---|---|---|---|
| C I | TRP· | GLOR—IA EXERC—ITVS | 2 | | 55 |
| | | (2 standards) | | | |
| C II | ,, | ,, | 17 | 18 | 56 |
| Cs | ,, | ,, | 6 | 9 | 57 |
| U.R. | TRP· | Wolf and Twins | 17 | 15 | 58 |
| Cp. | ,, | Victory on Prow | 22 | 21 | 59 |
| C I | TR·P | GLOR—IA EXERC—ITVS | 7 | 6 | 60 |
| | | (2 standards) | | | |
| ,, | ,, | ,, | 9 | | 61 |
| C II | ,, | ,, | 16 | 9 | 63 |
| Cs | ,, | ,, | 4 | 10 | 64 |
| U.R. | ,, | Wolf and Twins | 11 | 11 | 65 |
| Cp | ,, | Victory on Prow | 20 | 19 | 66 |
| C I | TRP★ | GLOR—IA EXERC—ITVS | 1 | | 67 |
| | | (2 standards) | | | |
| ,, | ,, | ,, | 2 | | ,, (2a Q) |
| C II | ,, | ,, | 5 | 9 | 68 |
| Cs | ,, | ,, | 4 | 5 | 69 |
| U.R. | ,, | Wolf and Twins | 26 | 13 | 70 |
| Cp | ,, | Victory on Prow | 21 | 10 | 71 |
| C I | ⓧ TRP | GLOR—IA EXERC—ITVS | 3 | | 72 |
| | | (2 standards) | | | |
| ,, | ,, | ,, | 1 | | ,, (2a Q) |
| C II | ,, | ,, | 9 | 8 | 73 |
| Cs | ,, | ,, | 5 | 5 | 74 |
| Cn | ,, | ,, | 1 | 2 | 75 |
| U.R. | ,, | Wolf and Twins | 15 | 19 | 76 |
| Cp | ,, | Victory on Prow | 13 | 8 | 77 |
| C I | ⚘ TRP | GLOR—IA EXERC—ITVS | 1 | | 78 |
| | | (2 standards) | | | |
| ,, | ,, | ,, | 1 | | 79 |
| ,, | ,, | ,, | 1 | | 80 |
| C II | ,, | ,, | 1 | 4 | 81 |
| Cs | ,, | ,, | 2 | 3 | 83 |
| Cn | ,, | ,, | 3 | 1 | 84 |
| U.R. | ,, | Wolf and Twins | 16 | 14 | 85 |
| Cp | ,, | Victory on Prow | 11 | 3 | 86 |

335–7

| Ruler | Mint-mark | Reverse | P | S | LRBC |
|---|---|---|---|---|---|
| C II | TRP | GLOR—IA EXERC—ITVS | 1 | | 88 |
| | | (1 standard) | | | |
| Cs | ,, | ,, | 1 | | 89 |
| D | TRP | GLOR—IA EXERC—ITVS | | 1 | 91 |
| | | (1 standard) | | | |
| C I | ·TRP· | ,, | 11 | 1 | 92 |
| C II | ,, | ,, | 29 | 43 | 93 |
| Cs | ,, | ,, | 26 | 26 | 94 |
| Cn | ,, | ,, | 15 | 14 | 95 |
| D | ,, | ,, | 3 | 1 | 96 |

337–41

| Ruler | Mint-mark | Reverse | P | S | LRBC |
|---|---|---|---|---|---|
| Cn | + TRP | GLOR—IA EXERC—ITVS | 1 | | 103 |
| | | (1 standard) | | | |
| H | ,, | PA—X PV—BLICA | 5 | 4 | 104 |
| T | ,, | PIETAS—ROMANA | | 3 | 105 |
| C I | ·TRP· | Quadriga | 1 | 2 | 106 |
| C II | ,, | GLOR—IA EXERC—ITVS | 1 | 2 | 107 |
| | | (1 standard) | | | |
| Cs | ,, | ,, | 6 | 7 | 108 |
| Cn | ,, | ,, | | 3 | 110 |
| H | ,, | PA—X PV—BLICA | 31 | 10 | 112 |

| Ruler | Mint-mark | Reverse | P | S | LRBC |
|---|---|---|---|---|---|
| T | ·TRP· | PIETAS—ROMANA | 30 | 9 | 113 |
| C I | TRP | Quadriga | 5 | 5 | 114 |
| Cs | „ | VIRTVS—AVGG NN | 3 | 3 | 116 |
| Cn | „ | „ | 2 | 2 | 118 |
| H | „ | PA—X PV—BLICA | 9 | 3 | 119 |
| T | „ | PIETAS—ROMANA | 13 | 9 | 120 |
| C II | TRP⚡ | GLORI—A EXER—CITVS (1 standard) | 2 | | 125 |
| Cs | „ | „ | 28 | 42 | 126 |
| Cn | „ | „ | 6 | 14 | 127 |
| H | „ | PA—X PV—BLICA | 23 | 13 | 128 |
| T | „ | PIETAS—ROMANA | 25 | 13 | 129 |
| Cn | TRP⌣ | GLORI—A EXER—CITVS (1 standard) | 1 | | 131 |
| Cs | M / TRP⌣ | „ | 20 | 22 | 132 |
| Cn | „ | „ | 41 | 25 | 133 |
| Cn | N / TRP | „ | 2 | 1 | 134 |

**341–6**

| Ruler | Mint-mark | Reverse | P | S | LRBC |
|---|---|---|---|---|---|
| Cs | M / TRP | VICTORIAE DD AVGGQ NN | 4 | 6 | 137 |
| Cn | „ | „ | 15 | 13 | 138 |
| Cs | ⚲ / TRP | „ | 10 | 8 | 139 |
| Cn | „ | „ | 65 | 60 | 140 |
| Cn | „ | „ | | 6 | 140a |
| Cs | ★ / TRP | „ | 2 | | 141 |
| Cn | „ | „ | 11 | 12 | 142 |
| Cn | „ | „ | 2 | 1 | 142a |
| Cn | C / TRP | „ | | 1 | 143a |
| Cs | D / TRP | „ | 10 | 3 | 145 |
| Cs | „ | „ | 5 | 4 | 146 |
| Cs | „ | „ | 5 | 6 | 147 |
| Cn | „ | „ | 75 | 78 | 148 |
| Cn | „ | „ | 27 | 28 | 149 |
| Cn | „ | „ | 25 | 37 | 150 |
| Cs | Є / TRP | „ | 4 | 1 | 152 |
| Cs | „ | „ | 1 | 1 | cf. 152Є |
| Cn | „ | „ | 1 | 1 | 153 |
| Cn | „ | „ | 7 | 3 | 154 |
| Cn | „ | „ | 10 | 9 | 155 |
| Cn | ⚘ / TRP | „ | 4 | 2 | 159 |
| Cn | „ | „ | 1 | 2 | 160 |
| Cs | ⚘ / TRP· | „ | 2 | 1 | 161 |
| Cn | „ | „ | 1 | | 162 |
| Cn | „ | „ | 1 | 4 | 163 |
| Cn | „ | „ | 1 | 1 | 164 |

**LUGDUNUM**
**330–5**

| Ruler | Mint-mark | Reverse | P | S | LRBC |
|---|---|---|---|---|---|
| C I | PLG | GLOR—IA EXERC—ITVS (2 standards) | 4 | 1 | 180 |

| Ruler | Mint-mark | Reverse | Officina & Quantity P | S | Reference LRBC |
|---|---|---|---|---|---|
| C II | PLG | GLOR—IA EXERC—ITVS (2 standards) | 9 | | 181 |
| Cs | ,, | ,, | 7 | | 182 |
| ,, | ,, | ,, | 1 | | 183 |
| U.R. | ,, | Wolf and Twins | 6 | 1 | 184 |
| Cp | ,, | Victory on Prow | 16 | 2 | 185 |
| C I | ·PLG | GLOR—IA EXERC—ITVS (2 standards) | 2 | | 186 |
| C II | ,, | ,, | 24 | 5 | 187 |
| Cs | ,, | ,, | 9 | | 188 |
| U.R. | ,, | Wolf and Twins | 19 | 5 | 190 |
| Cp | ,, | Victory on Prow | 15 | | 191 |
| Cs | ⌣PLG | GLOR—IA EXERC—ITVS (2 standards) | 1 | | 194 |
| U.R. | ,, | Wolf and Twins | 2 | 2 | 195 |
| Cp | ,, | Victory on Prow | 2 | 1 | 196 |
| C I | ⌣PLG | GLOR—IA EXERC—ITVS (2 standards) | 2 | | 197 |
| C II | ,, | ,, | 17 | 2 | 198 |
| Cs | ,, | ,, | 7 | | 199 |
| U.R. | ,, | Wolf and Twins | 9 | 2 | 200 |
| Cp | ,, | Victory on Prow | 10 | 1 | 201 |
| C I | ★PLG | GLOR—IA EXERC—ITVS (2 standards) | 2 | 1 | 202 |
| C II | ,, | ,, | 11 | 1 | 203 |
| Cs | ,, | ,, | 1 | | 204 |
| U.R. | ,, | Wolf and Twins | 13 | 6 | 205 |
| Cp | ,, | Victory on Prow | 3 | 3 | 206 |
| C I | ⚓PLG | GLORI—A EXER—CITVS (2 standards) | | | 212 |
| Cn | ,, | ,, | 1 | | 216 |
| U.R. | ()PLG | Wolf and Twins | 1 | | 220 |
| Cp | ,, | Victory on Prow | 1 | | 221 |

### 335–7

| Ruler | Mint-mark | Reverse | P | S | LRBC |
|---|---|---|---|---|---|
| C I | PLG | GLOR—IA EXERC—ITVS (1 standard) | 3 | 2 | 222 |
| C II | ⌣PLG | ,, | | 2 | 226 |
| C I | ★PLG | ,, | 1 | | 228 |
| C II | ,, | ,, | 11 | 3 | 229 |
| Cs | ,, | ,, | 4 | | 230 |
| C I | ⚓PLG | ,, | 1 | 3 | 231 |
| C II | ,, | ,, | 11 | 3 | 232 |
| C II | ,, | ,, | 1 | 1 | 233 |
| Cn | ,, | ,, | 1 | | 236 |
| D | ,, | ,, | 1 | 3 | 237 |
| C II | ✠B / PLG | ,, | 2 | 1 | 240 |
| C II | ,, | ,, | 14 | 2 | 241 |
| Cs | ,, S | ,, | 8 | 1 | 242 |
| C II | ⚓PLG | ,, | | 1 | 246 |
| Cs | ,, | GLORI—A EXER—CITVS (1 standard) | 1 | | 248 |
| Cn | ,, | ,, | 1 | 1 | cf. 248 3eN |
| Cs | Y / PLG | ,, | 3 | 2 | 250 |
| Cn | ,, | ,, | 10 | | 251 |
| Cs | I / PLG | ,, | 8 | 2 | 252 |
| Cn | ,, | ,, | 6 | 2 | 253 |

| Ruler | Mint-mark | Reverse | Officina & Quantity P | S | Reference LRBC |
|---|---|---|---|---|---|
| | | **341–6** | | | |
| Cn | PLG | VICTORIA—AVGVSTORVM | 3 | | 255 |
| Cs | ,, | VICTORIAE DD AVGGQ NN | 8 | 7 | 256 |
| Cn | ,, | ,, | 1 | | 257 (3dn) |
| Cn | ,, | ,, | 1 | 3 | 258 |
| Cs | ★/PLG | ,, | 2 | | 259 |
| Cs | S T/PLG | ,, | 15 | 2 | 260 |
| Cn | ,, | ,, | 2 | | 262 |
| Cs | Ph/PLG | ,, | 5 | 6 | 266 |
| Cn | ,, | ,, | | 2 | 268 |
| Cs | HR/PLG | ,, | 1 | 1 | 269 |
| Cn | ,, | ,, | 1 | 1 | 270 |
| Cs | /PLG | ,, | 1 | 1 | 273 |
| | | **ARELATE** | | | |
| | | **330–5** | | | |
| C I | ★/PCONST | GLOR—IA EXERC—ITVS (2 standards) | 6 | | 352 |
| C II | ,, | ,, | 1 | 3 | 353 |
| Cs | ,, | ,, | 1 | 6 | 354 |
| U.R. | ,, | Wolf and Twins | 1 | 3 | 355 |
| Cp | ,, | Victory on Prow | 1 | | 356 |
| C II | ∪/PCONST | GLOR—IA EXERC—ITVS (2 standards) | | 1 | 358 |
| Cs | ,, | ,, | | 1 | 359 |
| U.R. | ,, | Wolf and Twins | 1 | | 360 |
| Cp | ,, | Victory on Prow | | 1 | 361 |
| C I | /PCONST | GLOR—IA EXERC—ITVS (2 standards) | 1 | | 362 |
| Cs | ,, | ,, | | 2 | 364 |
| C I | /PCONST | ,, | 6 | 2 | 367 |
| C I | ,, | ,, | 1 | | 367 (2ak) |
| C II | ,, | ,, | 1 | | 369 |
| U.R. | ,, | Wolf and Twins | | 3 | 371 |
| Cp | ,, | Victory on Prow | 1 | 2 | 372 |
| C I | /PCONST | GLOR—IA EXERC—ITVS (2 standards) | 2 | 1 | 373 |
| C II | ,, | ,, | 3 | 2 | 374 |
| Cs | ,, | ,, | 1 | | 375 |
| U.R. | ,, | Wolf and Twins | 4 | 1 | 376 |
| Cp | ,, | Victory on Prow | | 4 | 377 |
| C I | /PCONST | GLOR—IA EXERC—ITVS (2 standards) | 1 | 1 | 378 |
| C II | ,, | ,, | 2 | | 379 |
| Cs | ,, | ,, | | 3 | 380 |
| Cn | ,, | ,, | | 2 | 381 |
| U.R. | ,, | Wolf and Twins | 3 | 1 | 382 |
| Cp | ,, | Victory on Prow | 2 | 2 | 383 |
| Cr | /PCONST | GLOR—IA EXERC—ITVS (2 standards) | 1 | | 391 |
| C II | ,, | ,, | 3 | | 392 |
| Cs | ,, | ,, | | 2 | 393 |

| Ruler | Mint-mark ◊ | Reverse | Officina & Quantity P | S | Reference LRBC |
|---|---|---|---|---|---|
| U.R. | PCONST | Wolf and Twins | 2 | | 396 |
| Cp | ,, | Victory on Prow | 2 | | 397 |

**335–7**

| Ruler | Mint-mark | Reverse | P | S | LRBC |
|---|---|---|---|---|---|
| C I | ✶ / PCONST | GLOR—IA EXERC—ITVS (1 standard) | 6 | | 398 |
| C II | ,, | ,, | 5 | | 399 |
| Cs | ,, | ,, | 1 | 2 | 400 |
| Cn | ,, | ,, | 1 | 1 | 401 |
| D | ,, | ,, | 1 | 1 | 402 |
| U.R. | ,, | Wolf and Twins | | 5 | 403 |
| Cp | ,, | Victory on Prow | 2 | | 404 |
| C I | X / PCONST | GLOR—IA EXERC—ITVS (1 standard) | 1 | | 405 |
| D | ,, | ,, | 1 | | 408 |
| Cp | ,, | Victory on Prow | | 1 | 410 |
| C II | O / PCONST | GLOR—IA EXERC—ITVS (1 standard) | 1 | | 411 |
| Cs | ,, | ,, | | 1 | 412 |
| U.R. | ,, | Wolf and Twins | 1 | 2 | 414 |
| Cp | ,, | Victory on Prow | 1 | | 415 |

**337–41**

| Ruler | Mint-mark | Reverse | P | S | LRBC |
|---|---|---|---|---|---|
| C II | O / PCONST | GLOR—IA EXERC—ITVS (1 standard) | 1 | | 416 |
| Cs | ◡ / PCONST | ,, | 1 | | 420 |
| Cn | X / ,, | ,, | 3 | 3 | 421 |
| Cs | X / PCONST | ,, | 1 | | 423 |
| Cn | X,, / ,, | ,, | 1 | | 424 |
| C I | X,, / PCON | AETERN—A PIETAS | | 1 | 429 |
| C II | ,, | GLORI—A EXER—CITVS (1 standard) | 1 | | 430 |
| Cs | N / PCON | ,, | | 1 | 434 |
| Cs | I,, / PCON | ,, | 1 | | 435 |
| Cs | I / PARL | ,, | 3 | | 438 |
| Cn | ,, / | ,, | | 1 | 440 |
| Cs | G / PARL | ,, | 22 | 1 | 441 |
| Cn | ,, | ,, | | 3 | 442 |
| Cn | ,, | ,, | | 3 | 443 |
| C I | X⏐ / PCON | Quadriga | 1 | | — |

**341–6**

| Ruler | Mint-mark | Reverse | P | S | LRBC |
|---|---|---|---|---|---|
| Cs | G / PARL | VICTORIAE DD AVGGQ NN | 8 | | 444 |
| Cs | P / PARL | ,, | 3 | | 448 |
| Cn | ,, | ,, | 1 | 1 | 449 |
| Cs | ΛΆ / PARL | ,, | 18 | 6 | 455 |
| Cn | ,, | ,, | 2 | 12 | 456 |

| Ruler | Mint-mark Reverse | | Officina & Quantity P S | | Reference LRBC |
|---|---|---|---|---|---|
| Cn | $\frac{\text{ΛΛ}}{\text{PARL}}$ | VICTORIAE DD AVGGQ NN | 1 | | 457 |
| Cs | $\frac{⚘}{\text{PARL}}$ | ,, | 2 | | 458 |
| Cn | ,, | ,, | | 2 | 460 |

ROME
330–5

| | Mint-mark and officina | | Officina | Quantity | |
|---|---|---|---|---|---|
| U.R. | RFP | Wolf and Twins | Q | 2 | 535 |
| Cp | ,, | Victory on Prow | P | 2 | 536 |
| C I | RBP | GLOR—IA EXERC—ITVS (2 standards) | P | 2 | 537 |
| C II | ,, | ,, | P | 1 | 538 |
| Cs | ,, | ,, | P | 4 | 539 |
| U.R. | ,, | Wolf and Twins | P | 2 | 540 |
| Cp | ,, | Victory on Prow | P | 4 | 541 |
| Cs | R◉P | GLOR—IA EXERC—ITVS (2 standards) | P | 1 | 544 |
| Cn | ,, | ,, | P | 1 | 545 |
| Cp | ,, | Victory on Prow | P | 3 | 547 |

335–7

| | | | | | |
|---|---|---|---|---|---|
| Cs | R★P | GLOR—IA EXERC—ITVS (1 standard) | P | 1 | 568 |
| U.R. | ,, | Wolf and Twins | P | 2 | 571 |
| Cp | ,, | Victory on Prow | P | 5 | 572 |
| Cs | R✧P | SECVRI—TAS REIPVB | P | 1 | 578 |

337–41

| | | | | | |
|---|---|---|---|---|---|
| C II | R✦P | VIRTVS AVGVSTI | P | 1 | 602 |
| Cs | R★P | GLOR—IA EXERC—ITVS (1 standard) | P | 1 | 614 |

341–6

| | | | | | |
|---|---|---|---|---|---|
| Cn | R·P | VICTORIAE DD AVGGQ NN | P | 1 | 633 |
| Cs | R◯P | ,, | P | 1 | 637 |
| Cn | ,, | ,, | P, Q, T, E | 2, 4, 3, 5 | 638 |

AQUILEIA
334–5

| | | | | | |
|---|---|---|---|---|---|
| Cp | AQP | Victory on Prow | S | 1 | 655 |
| C II | $\frac{+}{\text{AQP}}$ | GLOR—IA EXERC—ITVS (2 standards) | P, S | 1, 1 | 657 |
| U.R. | ,, | Wolf and Twins | P | 1 | 660 |
| Cs | $\frac{\text{F}}{\text{AQP}}$ | GLOR—IA EXERC—ITVS (2 standards) | P | 1 | 664 |

335–7

| | | | | | |
|---|---|---|---|---|---|
| Cs | ·AQP | GLOR—IA EXERC—ITVS (1 standard) | P | 1 | 676 |

| Ruler | Mint-mark | Reverse | Officina | Quantity | LRBC |
|---|---|---|---|---|---|
| | | 337–41 | | | |
| Cs | AQP✿ | GLOR—IA EXERC—ITVS | P | 1 | 684 |
| | | (1 standard) | | | |
| Cn | ✿\|✿ AQP | ,, | P | 4 | 688a |
| Cs | ◊ AQP | ,, | P | 1 | 691 |
| Cn | AQP | ,, | P | 1 | 692c |
| Cn | ⚸ AQP | ,, | P | 1 | 694 |
| | | 341–64 | | | |
| Cs | AQP | VICTORIAE DD AVVGGQ NN | P | 1 | 701 |
| Cn | ,, | ,, | S | 1 | 702 |
| Cn | ◊ AQP | ,, | P | 1 | 709 |

SISCIA

330–5

| Ruler | Mint-mark | Reverse | Officina | Quantity | LRBC |
|---|---|---|---|---|---|
| Cs | ASIS | GLOR—IA EXERC—ITVS | A, Δ, Є | 1, 2, 1 | 744 |
| | | (2 standards) | | | |
| U.R. | ,, | Wolf and Twins | Γ | 1 | 745 |
| Cp | ,, | Victory on Prow | B | 1 | 746 |
| C II | ·ASIS· | GLOR—IA EXERC—ITVS | Є | 2 | 748 |
| | | (2 standards) | | | |
| Cs | ,, | ,, | A | 1 | 749 |
| U.R. | ,, | Wolf and Twins | A, Γ | 1, 1 | 750 |

335–7

| Ruler | Mint-mark | Reverse | Officina | Quantity | LRBC |
|---|---|---|---|---|---|
| C I | ASIS | GLOR—IA EXERC—ITVS | ? | 1 | 754 |
| | | (1 standard) | | | |
| C II | ,, | ,, | A | 1 | 755 |

337–41

| Ruler | Mint-mark | Reverse | Officina | Quantity | LRBC |
|---|---|---|---|---|---|
| Cn | ⚸ ASISᴗ | GLOR—IA EXERC—ITVS | B | 1 | 775 |
| | | (1 standard) | | | |
| Cn | ·ASIS★ | ,, | Γ | 1 | 778 |
| Cs | ⚸ ASIS | ,, | A | 1 | 780 |

341–6

| Ruler | Mint-mark | Reverse | Officina | Quantity | LRBC |
|---|---|---|---|---|---|
| Cs | ⚸\| ★ASIS★ | VICTOR—IA AVGG | Є | 1 | 785 |
| Cs | ASIS | VICTORIAE DD AVVGGQ NN | A | 1 | 790 |
| Cn | ,, | ,, | A, Γ | 2, 1 | 791 |
| Cs | ·ASIS· | ,, | A | 1 | 792 |

THESSALONICA

330–5

| Ruler | Mint-mark | Reverse | Officina | Quantity | LRBC |
|---|---|---|---|---|---|
| U.R. | SMTSA | Wolf and Twins | Є | 2 | 838 |

337–41

| Ruler | Mint-mark | Reverse | Officina | Quantity | LRBC |
|---|---|---|---|---|---|
| Cn | ,, | GLORI—A EXER—CITVS | B | 2 | 856 |
| | | (1 standard) | | | |

| Ruler | Mint-mark | Reverse | Officina | Quantity | LRBC |
|-------|-----------|---------|----------|----------|------|

### HERACLEA
#### 330–5

| Ruler | Mint-mark | Reverse | Officina | Quantity | LRBC |
|-------|-----------|---------|----------|----------|------|
| U.R. | SMHA | Wolf and Twins | Δ | 1 | 902 |

#### 337–41

| C II | ,, | GLOR—IA EXERC—ITVS<br>(1 standard) | Є | 1 | 944 |
|------|-----|---------|----------|----------|------|

### CONSTANTINOPLE
#### 326–30

| C I | CONS | SPES \| PUBLIC | A | 1 | 978 |
|-----|------|---------|----------|----------|------|

#### 330–5

| C I | CONSA· | GLOR—IA EXERC—ITVS<br>(2 standards) | A | 1 | 1010 |
|-----|--------|---------|----------|----------|------|
| C II | ,, | ,, | Θ | 1 | 1011 |
| Cp | ,, | Victory on Prow | Z | 2 | 1014 |
| C I | ·CONSA· | GLOR—IA EXERC—ITVS<br>(2 standards) | H | 1 | 1017 |

#### 337–41

| Cs | CONSA | GLOR—IA EXERC—ITVS<br>(1 standard) | Θ | 1 | 1043 |
|----|-------|---------|----------|----------|------|

#### 341–6

| POP<br>ROMANUS | CONSA | Star in Wreath | H | 1 | 1067 |
|----------------|-------|---------|----------|----------|------|

### NICOMEDIA
#### 330–5

| C I | SMNA | GLOR—IA EXERC—ITVS<br>(2 standards) | A, B, | 1, 2 | 1117 |
|-----|------|---------|----------|----------|------|

#### 337–41

| Cs | SMNA | GLOR—IA EXERC—ITVS<br>(1 standard) | B | 1 | 1139 |
|----|------|---------|----------|----------|------|

### CYZICUS
#### 330–5

| U.R. | SMKA· | Wolf and Twins | Є | 1 | 1218 |
|------|-------|---------|----------|----------|------|
| C I | SMKA | GLOR—IA EXERC—ITVS<br>(2 standards) | A | 1 | 1221 |
| Cs | ,, | ,, | A | 1 | 1227 |

#### 335–7

| C II | SMKA | GLOR—IA EXERC—ITVS<br>(1 standard) | A | 1 | 1264 |
|------|------|---------|----------|----------|------|

## IMITATIONS (BARBAROUS)

s  = small size
da = irregular die-axis
m = irregular mint-mark

### TRIER

| Ruler | Mint-mark | Reverse | Remarks | Quantity |
|-------|-----------|---------|---------|----------|
| C I | STR | VICTORIAE LAETAE P(R)INC P VOT<br>PR<br>Two Victories | cf. *RIC* vii, pl. 4,<br>231<br>Barbarous helmeted<br>head left | 1 |

| Ruler | Mint-mark | Reverse | Remarks | Quantity |
|---|---|---|---|---|
| Cp | TRP | Victory on Prow | da s. | 1 |
| " | TRS | " | " | 3 |
| U.R. | PTR | Wolf and Twins | m | 1 |
| C I | TRP | GLOR—IA EXERC—ITVS (2 standards) | da. s. 2aK | 1 |
| " | TRS | " " | da. s. 2aK | 2 |
| C II | TRP | " " | da. 1b. | 1 |
| " | " | " " | Head left and no paludumentum | 1 |
| Cs | TRS | " " | da. s. | 1 |
| Cn | TRP | GLOR—IA EXERC—ITVS (1 standard) | da. s. | 1 |
| " | RS | " " | da. s. | 1 |
| " | PTR | " " | m. Rough inscrip. | 1 |
| " | ЯRT | " " | da. m. | 1 |
| " | TR | " " | da. s. | 3 |
| " | TRS | " " | m. s. Rough inscrip. | 1 |
| Cp | TR·S | Victory on Prow | da. s. | 1 |
| " | $\frac{\text{🦅}}{\text{PTR}}$ | " | m. | 1 |
| C I | TR·S | GLOR—IA EXERC—ITVS (2 standards) | da. s. | 1 |
| " | TR·P | " " | da. 2aP | 2 |
| " | P·TR | " " | m. s. | 1 |
| C II | TR·S | " " | da. s. 1b | 2 |
| " | ·TRS· | " " | m. 2aK | 1 |
| Cs | ·TRS | " " | m. Rough inscrip. | 1 |
| U.R. | $\frac{\text{XX}}{\text{TRZ}}$ | Wolf and Twins | m. | 1 |
| Cs | $\frac{\text{N}}{\text{TRP}}$ | GLOR—IA EXERC—ITVS | da. m. s. | 1 |
| " | $\frac{\text{V}}{\text{TR·}}$ | " " | da. m. | 2 |
| " | $\frac{\text{M}}{\text{TRS}}$ | " " | da. m. | 1 |
| " | $\frac{\text{☉}}{\text{TRP}}$ | " " | da. m. | 1 |
| " | ·TA◡ | " " | da. m. | 1 |
| " | $\frac{\dot{\text{M}}}{\text{TRS}}$ | " " | da. m. | 1 |
| " | $\frac{\text{·}}{\text{IRP}}$ | " " | s. m. | 1 |
| Cn | $\frac{\text{M}}{\text{TRP}}$ | VICTORIAE DD AVGGQ NN | m. da. s. | 1 |
| " | $\frac{\text{·◊}}{\text{TRS}}$ | " | m. da. s. | 2 |
| " | $\frac{\text{◊}}{\text{TRP}}$ | " | m. s. | 1 |
| " | $\frac{\text{D}}{\text{TRP}}$ | " | da. m. s. | 1 |
| " | TR·P | " | mis-shapen | 1 |
| C II | $\frac{\text{✳}}{\text{STRE}}$ | PROVIDENTIAE AVGG | da. | 1 |

**LUGDUNUM**

| | | | | |
|---|---|---|---|---|
| U.R. | PLG | Wolf and Twins | da. s. | 3 |
| " | SLG | " " | da. Rough Wolf | 1 |
| " | $\frac{\text{☢}}{\text{PLVG}}$ | " " | m. da. | 1 |
| " | ·PLG· | " " | m. | 1 |
| C I | PLG | Quadriga | m. s. | 1 |

| Ruler | Mint-mark | Reverse | Remarks | Quantity |
|---|---|---|---|---|
| C I | PLG | GLOR—IA EXERC—ITVS (2 standards) | da. 2a $Q$ | 1 |
| ,, | SLG | ,, | da. 2a $Q$ | 1 |
| C II | PLG | ,, | da. s. | 1 |
| ,, | PL·G | ,, | da. m. | 1 |
| ,, | ·PLG· | ,, | s. m. | 1 |
| ,, | ◡PLG | ,, | da. 1bN | 1 |
| ,, | ⚘ / PLG | ,, | m. 1bQ. | 1 |
| ,, | +VG | ,, | m. s. da. | 1 |
| Cs | ☧ / PLG | GLOR—IA EXERC—ITVS (1 standard) | da. Rev. inscrip. irreg. | 1 |
| Cn | PLG | VICTORIAE DD AVGGQ NN | da. s. | 1 |
| ,, | i–i / PLG | ,, | da. m. s. | 1 |
| ,, | Ṁ / PLG | ,, | m. s. | 1 |
| ,, | T S / SLG | ,, | m. Face rough | 1 |
| ,, | :: / SLG | ,, | m. s. | 1 |

### ARELATE

| Ruler | Mint-mark | Reverse | Remarks | Quantity |
|---|---|---|---|---|
| D | ˙ / PCONST | GLOR—IA EXERC—ITVS (1 standard) | · instead of ☧ | 1 |
| C I | ❂ / SCONST | GLOR—IA EXERC—ITVS (2 standards) | m. 2a $K$ | 1 |
| ,, | ❂ / PCONST | ,, ,, | da. Rough inscrip. | 1 |
| Cn | Ph / ARII | VICTORIAE DD AVGG QNN | m. s. | 1 |

### UNCERTAIN

| Ruler | Mint-mark | Reverse | Remarks | Quantity |
|---|---|---|---|---|
| C I | | GLOR—IA EXERC—ITVS (2 standards) | da. s. | 5 |
| Cs | | ,, (1 standard) | ,, | 5 |
| Cn | | ,, ,, | ,, | 1 |
| U.R. | | Wolf and Twins | ,, | 9 |
| Cp. | | Victory on Prow | ,, | 3 |
| | | VICTORIAE DD AVGG QNN | ,, | 3 |
| | | GLOR—IA EXERC—ITVS (2 standards) | ,, | 3 |
| | | ,, (1 standard) | ,, | 14 |

# Roman Coins in Northern France and the Rhine Valley

## RICHARD REECE

THIS is the third report on groups of Roman coins in continental museums. The first report (*NC* 1967), dealt with material in the southern half of France, the second report (*NC* 1971), recorded material in Italian museums north of Rome, while this report lists coins in collections in the north-east of France and in four in Germany near to the Rhine. Details of the sixteen French collections were collected personally during September 1970 while the four German sites added for comparison were chosen from those published in the magnificent volumes of *Die Fundmünzen der römischen Zeit in Deutschland*.

The method of recording and presentation, which changed substantially between reports one and two, has now settled into the form expressed in the second report. The coins listed in the various museums have been divided up into five categories—gold, silver (up to 259 and after 294), large bronze (in this case all sestertii since Æl of the fourth century do not appear in the north of France), medium bronze (including asses, dupondii, folles, and fourth-century Æ2), and small bronze (Æ3–4).

Within these categories the coins have been divided into the usual twenty-one periods with the following date limits: I 27 B.C. to A.D. 41, IIa 41 to 54, IIb 54 to 69, III 69 to 96, IV 96 to 117, V 117 to 138, VI 138 to 161, VIIa 161 to 180, VIIb 180 to 193, VIII 193 to 222, IXa 222 to 238, IXb 238 to 259, X 259 to 275, XI 275 to 294, XII 294 to 317, XIIIa 317 to 330, XIIIb 330 to 348, XIV 348 to 364, XVa 364 to 378, XVb 378 to 388, XVI 388 to 402.

Table I gives details of the sixteen French sites and four German sites for the whole of the Roman period; Table II gives details of the collections by emperors from 259 to 294. In the tables any material suspected to contain hoard material is marked by *, and these results are therefore expected to be aberrant. Where hoards could be completely isolated they do not intrude into the tables, but are mentioned in the text.

Brief details of the groups and collections seen and listed, or manuscripts consulted, with mention of their possible archaeological reliability, are as follows:

*Soissons.* Civic Museum in the former monastery of Saint-Léger. The museum houses a small collection of 122 coins which have no provenances in the majority of cases, but from their type and condition are likely to be local finds. The impression of the curator is that they represent the tail-end of a once large and extensive municipal collection. They may therefore be the poor local finds which were not judged worthy of display. Seen against the background of all the groups of coins from the area this impression seems likely to be true.

*Condé-sur-Aisne.* A ford on the river Aisne about 11 km. east of Soissons produced a group of well over 3,000 coins during operations to straighten and dredge the river. Some of these are now conserved in the museum at Soissons, but M. Giard has studied and published these, and others now in private hands (*RN* 1968, 76 and 1969, 62). For the purposes of these lists some 2,989 coins are legible. There is no real evidence that the group contains hoard material from the reigns of Augustus and Nero, except for the remarkably large percentage of these coins, so that they should probably be treated as an accumulation. In general the group must reflect to some extent the coins in use and available for loss in the Roman period, and invites comparison with the Tiber finds described in the second report.

*Sens.* Two collections are housed in the Municipal Museum. One, containing 897 coins, belongs to the Archaeological Society of Sens; the other, containing 231 coins, belongs to the museum. In general few coins have any provenance, but there is no *a priori* reason to suspect large-scale contamination by imports, and close study confirms this.

*Autun.* The 206 coins listed are on display, and are probably only a selection from a larger reserve collection. It has unfortunately been impossible to obtain confirmation of this point, and the material is included mainly to list what was actually seen. It also has the function of providing a 'control', for detailed study shows that its composition is completely aberrant and can be paralleled in no other collection known to me. It therefore provides welcome confirmation that rigorous selection on the part of collectors or recorders can be detected by close study.

*Avallon.* Due to the removal of the Library and the Museum at Avallon it was not possible to list the some 1,175 coins in the museum with the fullest accuracy: some details are therefore a little uncertain. In general the coins have no provenances, and a series of aes grave and some Republican denarii are known to come from Italy, so that it is only fair to record the curator's feeling that the whole collection is suspect. In practice, however, the obvious collector's pieces can usually be spotted, and the results when these are ignored are consonant with other collections in this area of France.

*Auxerre.* A large and important collection disappeared from Auxerre some time between 1905 and about 1912, leaving the present remnant of 507 coins in the Musée Historique, and twenty-four coins in the Musée Archéologique. Since the two groups are thought to be purely local in origin they have been

## TABLE II

| | Gallienus | Salonina | Claudius II | Quintillus | Aurelian | Severina | Postumus | Laelian | Victorinus | Marius | Tetricus I | Tetricus II | Tacitus | Florian | Probus | Carus | Carinus | Numerian | Diocletian | Maximian I | Constantius I | Galerius | Carausius | Allectus | Barbarous |
|---|---|---|---|---|---|---|---|---|---|---|---|---|---|---|---|---|---|---|---|---|---|---|---|---|---|
| Soissons | 11 | 1 | 1 | | | | | | 1 | | 1 | 1 | | | | | | | | | | | | | 4 |
| Condé-sur-Aisne | 20 | | 22 | 2 | 1 | | 2 | 1 | 3 | 1 | 10 | 8 | | | 2 | | | | 1 | 2 | | | | | 66 |
| Sens A | 13 | 13 | 35 | 7 | 10 | 1 | 6 | 1 | 18 | | 20 | 18 | 7 | 2 | 22 | 7 | 2 | 4 | 4 | 1 | 2 | 5 | | | 14 |
| Sens M | 3 | 2 | 8 | | 1 | | 13 | | 5 | 3 | 13 | 3 | | | 2 | | | | 2 | 2 | | | 1 | | |
| Autun | 56 | 1 | 5 | 1 | 2 | 1 | 1 | | 3 | | 3 | 7 | 1 | 2 | 3 | 1 | 2 | 3 | 2 | 2 | 3 | 2 | 1 | | 10 |
| Avallon | 119 | 2 | 75 | 6 | 12 | 1 | 29 | | 9 | | 17 | 19 | 1 | | 19 | 2 | 4 | 2 | 6 | 5 | 1 | 3 | 1 | 1 | 1 |
| Auxerre | 3 | 12 | 37 | 3 | 3 | 2 | 33 | | 25 | 1 | 31 | 2 | 1 | | 4 | 1 | | 1 | 2 | 1 | | | | 1 | 1 |
| Châtillon | 19 | 18 | 2 | | 2 | | 2 | | | | 5 | 9 | 2 | | 4 | | 1 | | 5 | 5 | 4 | | 1 | | 15 |
| Langres A | 37 | | 10 | 1 | | | 5 | | 2 | | 5 | 12 | | | | 1 | | | 2 | 1 | 1 | 2 | 1 | | 1 |
| Langres B | 22 | 4 | 27 | 7 | 11 | | 27 | | 12 | 6 | 17 | 3 | 6 | | 26 | 1 | 5 | 2 | 12 | 13 | | | | | |
| Langres C | 52 | 3 | 54 | 3 | 4 | 1 | | | 6 | | 6 | 29 | 1 | | 9 | 1 | 1 | | 7 | 1 | 3 | 4 | | 1 | |
| Verdun | 11 | 4 | 6 | 8 | 15 | | 21 | | 27 | | 30 | | 6 | | 20 | | 2 | 4 | 11 | 12 | | | | | |
| Belfort | 11 | 5 | 7 | | | | 8 | | 5 | | 4 | | 1 | | 2 | 1 | | 1 | 2 | 2 | | | | | 36 |
| Sélestat | 3 | 2 | 2 | | 1 | | | | | | 1 | | | | | | | | 5 | 1 | | 1 | | | 3 |
| Haguenau | 22 | 2 | 6 | | 2 | | 2 | | | | | 9 | 1 | | 18 | 5 | 4 | 3 | 2 | | 2 | | | | 8 |
| Rhine | 7 | 15 | 15 | 4 | 21 | 1 | 13 | | 10 | | 4 | 4 | 3 | | 1 | | | | 9 | 5 | | | | | 15 |
| Rheinzabern | 9 | 3 | 15 | 1 | 5 | | 3 | | 1 | | 16 | 3 | 1 | 1 | 2 | | | 1 | 1 | | | | | | 8 |
| Speyer | 5 | 1 | 21 | | 2 | | 3 | | 2 | | 13 | 3 | 3 | | 4 | | | | 3 | 4 | | 1 | | | 12 |
| Pachten | | | 17 | | 3 | | | | 5 | | 10 | | | | | | | | 3 | 1 | | | | | 8 |
| Mainz | 27 | 9 | 24 | 1 | 17 | | 21 | | 9 | | 45 | 8 | 1 | | 8 | 1 | 1 | | 14 | 9 | 2 | 2 | | | 40 |

M

combined in this record. Three small copper hoards in the Musée Archéologique deserve brief mention. The first consists of three asses of Tiberius, the second of about fifty radiate coins of Gallienus and Tetricus, and the third is attributable to the middle of the fifth century. It consists of a barbarous copy of the *Fel Temp Reparatio* reverse showing the Fallen Horseman, eighteen *Victoria Auggg* of the House of Theodosius, and one of Valentinian III with reverse showing a cross in a wreath, from the mint of Cyzicus.

*Châtillon-sur-Seine.* The museum contains, apart form the great Vix treasure, most of the finds excavated from the Roman town of Vertilium (modern Vertault 20 km. west of Châtillon). One hundred and fifty-nine coins have been integrated into a collection, but there are other finds which deserve future detailed study. The museum also houses four hoards from Vertilium—33 antoniniani all of the period 214 to 222, 45 antoniniani from Elagabalus to Valerian, 170 sestertii from Augustus to Postumus, and 104 Æ3 of the House of Constantine to c. 348. Two other hoards which are perhaps not well known are the Gomméville hoard (1938) of 4,913 antoniniani from Valerian to Probus, and the Montliot hoard (1958) in which sixteen antoniniani from Philip I to Gallienus are mixed with fifty-five sestertii from Trajan to Commodus. These come from the immediate neighbourhood of Châtillon.

*Langres.* Although the process of reclassification meant that the coin collection at the Musée du Breuil-de-Saint-Germain was not open for inspection it was possible to consult several nineteenth-century manuscript catalogues which not only gave adequate descriptions of the coins, but in almost all cases the provenances from which they derived. The group called Langres A comprises 432 coins from the Collection Colson. Most of these are recorded as coming from 'Châtelet'. This is probably to be identified with the Bois du Chatelet 28 km. east-south-east by east of Langres. A few coins in this collection are recorded as coming from Langres itself, and an even smaller number from surrounding hamlets. Langres B consists of 1,120 coins from the 'Médailler de M. l'Abbé Fourot'. Most are recorded as coming from Langres itself with a minority from Perthes (possibly the village 10 km. west of Saint-Dizier). Langres C is a composite group drawn from a list which aimed to summarize the coins given to the Society, to which the museum belongs, before 1860. The 371 coins listed come from many donors, and mainly unknown origins. The only blemish which prevents the first two groups claiming perfection is the faint suggestion that the Abbé Fourot indulged in the exchange of duplicate reverses. This is only suspected for the common Consecratio reverses of Claudius II, and is most unlikely to have any effects on the large comparisons for which this study is intended.

*Verdun.* The Municipal Museum in the Hôtel de la Princerie has on show a collection of 1,494 coins without record of provenances. All the indications are that the coins are mainly archaeological finds rather than imported collector's pieces, but the matter must remain open. Two hoards were recognized and isolated from the lists. One consists of fourteen mint antoniniani from 250 to 259, and the other includes sixty Æ3 of 317 to 330 of uniform wear and patina.

*Belfort.* A collection of 306 coins was listed in the museum from a manuscript catalogue which, in the minority of cases when a provenance was given, suggested a collection formed by gifts of casual finds in and around Belfort.

*Mulhouse.* No group of locally found coins exists as yet in the Musée Historique, but M. Roger Schweitzer kindly gave me some unpublished information which has been incorporated in the composite group 'Rhine Valley'. The curator of the museum, Mme Stahl, kindly allowed me to examine and record an unpublished hoard from Hirtzbach, 20 km. southwest by south of Mulhouse. This hoard of fifty-three sestertii ends with Antoninus Pius and Faustina I, with one coin of Marcus Aurelius unbearded. It is interesting that nine of the twenty hoards listed as found in the neighbourhood of Mulhouse in the *Bulletin du Musée Historique Mulhouse* 1926, belong completely to the fourth century.

*Colmar.* A few coins found locally, and information on others, are on display in the archaeological section of the Musée d'Unterlinden. These details have been incorporated into the 'Rhine Valley' group.

*Sélestat.* A small collection of 157 coins is kept in the great Humanist library, now housed in the Bibliothèque de la Ville. They are thought to be local finds, and there seems no reason to question this. The library also has five folles of 307 to 313 which must come from a local hoard of the type frequently recorded around Strasbourg and further North, but not to the South, for example around Mulhouse. A hoard of sixty-nine antoniniani from Gordian III to 259 is recorded as having been found locally and is kept separately.

*Strasbourg.* Due to the exigencies of time it was unfortunately not possible to examine the local finds in detail. Such information as was gleaned has been incorporated into the 'Rhine Valley' group.

*Haguenau.* The municipal library and museum has a small, but excellent, collection of 174 coins, all with recorded provenances, which show it to be a purely local collection.

*Wissembourg.* Although there were no sporadic finds two local hoards were noted. One consists of forty-eight sestertii from Vespasian to Marcus Aurelius ending in about 170, the other comprises 100 folles all struck between c. 306 and 308 which come from the Rhine fortress of Seltz, 20 km. south-east of Wissembourg.

*Rhine Valley.* This composite group of 472 coins is of only medium reliability since it is the sum of sporadic finds and small collections noted on the west bank of the Rhine from Mulhouse to Wissembourg. The high incidence of aurei of Nero recorded around Strasbourg as individual chance finds from a wide area shows that one should not be too sceptical of gold coins when they turn up in unprovenanced local collections.

### German sites

*Rheinzabern* (the coins are listed in *FMRD* iv, pt. 2 (Pfalz), nos. 2073 and 2074). This site is well known for its flourishing fine pottery industry of the second and third centuries, and is one of the few sites on the west bank of the Rhine in Germany to produce more than around 200 coins, with a total of 995.

*Speyer* (*FMRD* iv, pt. 2, no. 2317). The 746 coins come almost entirely from the fairly small area covered by the river frontier town and the successive fortresses or Kastellen.

*Pachten* (*FMRD* III (Saarland) no. 1143). The importance of this small settlement, now 24 km. north-west by west of Saarbrücken, depends on its position on a Roman cross-roads. It stands where the main route from Metz to Mainz crosses that from Trier to Strasbourg. Even so, the total of 313 coins listed is not very great by the standards of Metropolitan France, Italy, or England.

*Mainz* (*FMRD* iv, pt. 1 (Rheinhessen)). A great fortress such as that which stood near the confluence of the Main and the Rhine inevitably shows finds of Roman coins extending over a large area which included the successive Kastellen, their attendant vicus and satellite settlements. The 2,188 coins summarized here include those with known findspots in and around the fortress area (no. 1148), together with those from the centre of the modern town (no. 1157), those found in the river (no. 1173), and those from the general area (no. 1174).

Full references and descriptions of the coins from the four German sites, together with details of the history of the coins quoted, and some archaeological details of the sites will be found in the references to *Die Fundmünzen der Römischen Zeit in Deutschland* quoted for each site.

As in earlier reports there is no intention here to offer methods for the study of these coins listed, or to present results obtained from such study. References in the text to 'further work' will have suggested that such research is being pursued, and it is hoped to present this in print shortly. A list of Roman coins on sixteen sites in Britain will be submitted for publication in *Britannia*, and should appear in 1972 or 1973. This will complete the survey of groups of coins from Rome to Hadrian's Wall and there will then be a wide enough view to produce useful conclusions. A survey of the four areas covered (Italy, south France, north France, England) together with the methods of study used will appear in *Britannia* iv (1973). Further work, the material for which is already collected, will involve a study of the actual coin-types found in British hoards and site-finds, and after the more archaeological excursuses mentioned above, this should bring the study back within the scope of this journal.

# Stefanus R

B. H. I. H. STEWART

[SEE PLATE 16]

THE forms of obverse inscription found on coins of the first type of Stephen (1135–54) have recently been the subject of renewed attention. Mr. Seaman[1] has revived the division, first proposed by W. J. Andrew more than half a century ago but since largely overlooked, into three varieties according to the spelling of the king's name and title:

A. STIFNE REX
B. STIEFNE RE or R
C. STIEFNE

Mr. Dolley and Mr. Goddard[2] have adduced evidence to confirm the correctness of this sequence, and discussed (as Andrew had done) the unusual spelling of the king's name on the coins as *Sti(e)fne*.

Neither Seaman nor Dolley-Goddard, however, is concerned with the most striking anomaly in the list of obverse inscriptions on type I, the reading STEFANVS R. This form was passed without mention by Brooke in the *British Museum Catalogue* and we have to look back to Andrew for comment. He writes: 'The error [the spellings *Stifne* and *Stiefne*] did not pass unnoticed at the time, for although the later form +STIEFNE was retained upon the official money until the end of the reign, the Abbot of Reading, for example, corrected the legends on the dies he used to +STEPHANVS R . . .' This is a remarkable assertion. The source is his unfinished *Numismatic History of the Reign of Stephen*, a work overtaken by Brooke's great *Catalogue*, and of which three parts only, scarcely reaching the subject itself, were published in the *British Numismatic Journal*, although much further material was subsequently laid before the British Numismatic Society and is recorded by extensive notes in the Proceedings.[3]

---

[1] R. Seaman, 'King Stephen's First Coinage, 1135–1141', Seaby's *Coin & Medal Bulletin*, Feb. 1968, 60–2. I am grateful to Mr. Seaman for providing me with several references in connection with this paper.

[2] M. Dolley and K. A. Goddard, 'The A. N. Spellings "Stifne", "Stefne" and "Stiefne" found in the obverse legends of English coins of Stephen's first substantive type', *Proc. R.I.A.* vol. 71 (1971), section C, 19–34.

[3] The three published parts are in *BNJ* vi (177–90), viii (87–136), and x (43–69); see also *Proceedings* in vols. xi, xv, xvi, xvii, and xviii. The quoted passage is on p. 60 of *BNJ*.

We therefore need to look elsewhere in Andrew's writings to discover what he means. We must consult his *Numismatic History of the Reign of Henry I*, which comprises the *Numismatic Chronicle* volume for the year 1901, and a note on 'Some coins of the Reign of Stephen A.D. 1135–1154', which appeared in the *Numismatic Circular* for 1914 in connection with the then forthcoming Carlyon-Britton sale and in which, to quote the writer's own words, he ventured 'to anticipate a few pages of my numismatic history of that reign, now running through the *British Numismatic Journal*, by the following notes, in the hope that they may explain away and dispel some, at least, of the time-honoured fallacies that still cling to the medallic records of the period.'

The first of the notes reads as follows:

In 1129 the Abbot of Reading received a grant of the use and profits of one moneyer, Edgar, coining at London 'as if he were at Reading'. This was because such a privilege in the Metropolis was far more valuable than if it had been restricted to the rural conditions then surrounding the new monastery. The Abbot had power to appoint a successor 'after Edgar or in his place', and subsequent records show that he had the right to order special dies, varying 'the impressions and inscriptions.' When, therefore, we find some half dozen coins extant, bearing the reverse legends +LIEFRED:ON LVND and +SMEPINE:ON LVN, which differ from the regal issues in the 'impression' of an arched crown and a profusion of the ecclesiastical symbol—the annulet, coupled with a correction of the doggerel legend +STIFNE REX to +STEFANVS R, we may be quite certain that they represent the Abbot's money. In *Henry I* I identified the moneyer Edgar's issue in that reign. Possibly he died and Liefred and Smewine were successively appointed by the Abbot under his powers.

In his *Numismatic History of the Reign of Henry I* Andrew gives the text of the charter granting the abbot a moneyer, and later lists certain coins of the last type of the reign, *BMC* type XV, by the moneyer Edgar who held the appointment for the abbot. His argument runs in the following way: Edgar's coins are unornamented; therefore he had never coined, at least in type XV, for the king. His name does not occur in the next reign; so he had died or retired by 1135. The abbot would then appoint another London moneyer whose coins would thereafter carry a distinguishing mark, probably an annulet. Such a mark is found on a few coins of Baldwin who continued to coin under Stephen and was succeeded by Smewine. Andrew justifies his assumption of the use of marks by reference to an equally hypothetical case under Peterborough and to a writ of 1338 in relation to the Reading coinage of Edward III.[1]

This ingenious theory has been widely accepted—though Brook is significantly silent—and sale catalogues and other literature have often referred to it during and since Andrew's time. To cite two examples, Andrew's remarks to the British Numismatic Society on the subject are quoted in connection

---

[1] *NC* 1901, 371–8; Peterborough, ibid. 363.

with Carlyon-Britton's *Stefanus* and the Reading attribution is fully described with reference to a Stephen penny of Roth's, by Baldwin of London, 'with annulet in front of crown'. Commander Mack, though mentioning the theory in his monograph on the coinage of *Stephen and the Anarchy*,[1] tells me that he has never been entirely happy with it.

The Stefanus variety was first described by Rashleigh in his report on the 1818 Watford hoard in *NC* 1850. With regard to the king's name and title he observed that 'on four coins it is written STEFANVS R, a way of spelling the name (with an F) which has hitherto been unknown; and the Latin termination is extremely rare'. Of the four coins, three were by the moneyer Liefred of London and one by Smewine. On Rashleigh's plate a Liefred coin (composite?) is illustrated as no. 11 and the Smewine is no. 12.

Examples of the variety of which I have record are:

Liefred (*a*) British Museum, *BMC* no. 68. Rashleigh acquired the Watford coins on the death of their original owner, and this is one of the many Watford coins acquired from him by the museum in 1849. Weight 22·8 gr. [**Pl. 16. 10**]

(*b*) R. P. Mack (Sylloge no. 1605), ex W. J. C. Youde, ex Carlyon-Britton, lot 1492 (illustrated). Weight 19·4 gr. [**Pl. 16. 11**]

(*c*) N. P. Ballingal ex Lockett lot 3926, ex S. M. Spink, ex Watford hoard. Weight 22·5 gr. [**Pl. 16. 12**]

(*d*) Stewart, without known pedigree. Weight 20·0 gr. [**Pl. 16. 13**]

Smewine (*e*) Ballingal, ex Ryan lot 911, ex Wheeler lot 179, ex Reynolds lot 67. Weight 18·2 gr. [**Pl. 16. 8**]

(*f*) Ballingal, ex Lockett lot 3926, ex S. M. Spink, ex Rashleigh lot 609, ex Watford hoard. Illustrated *NC* 1850, plate opp. p. 138, no. 12; Rashleigh sale catalogue (Sotheby, 25 June 1909); *BNJ* xxxv (1966), pl. i no. 22 (*o*). Weight 22·1 gr. [**Pl. 16. 9**]

Coins *a–d* read on the reverse LIEFRED: ON: LVND:; coin *e*, SMEPINE: ONL (. . .) and coin *f*, SMEPINE (:?) ON: LVN: (the NE joined in both cases).

It can be seen from **Plate 16** that all six coins are from the same obverse die, and that the two by Smewine are from an earlier state of it than those of Liefred. The die was in a clean condition when used for Smewine and the impressions are in full relief. For the Liefred strikings the die had evidently been rubbed or polished down, so that the elements of the design are thinner and there is less depth to them.[2] Smewine's two coins are from different reverse dies but the reverse of all four of Liefred is the same (note the blobs at VN

[1] *BNJ* xxxv, 43.
[2] I have described this effect in *Mints, Dies and Currency* (ed. Carson, 1971), 259.

in LVND). Coin *e* shows marks on the reverse die under the earlier letters of the moneyer's name, but it is impossible to determine what has been removed, if recutting has taken place. We do not know enough about the pairing of dies in Stephen's time to be able to draw any conclusions from the fact that this particular obverse was used by one moneyer with two dies and later, and perhaps more extensively, by another with one. Both these moneyers were active in Henry's last type and in Stephen's first, but so far as we know not earlier or later.

So far from the *Stefanus* die having been altered as to the crown and inscription to satisfy the abbot of Reading, my contention is that it is an altered die of Henry I which preserves some of its original features.[1] The crown is intact as in effect it alone could be in such a transformation of type. It is of the arched form as on the last type of Henry I, on which the inscription is normally hENRICVS, rarely hENRICVS R. No. 4 on **Pl. 16** is a London coin of this type by the moneyer Estmund (*BMC* 249) showing the crown with a broad, flat shape very similar to that on the *Stefanus* die. Another coin of this issue, by Smewine (*BMC* 267), though with a narrower and dumpier crown, is a splendid example of the type and reads hENRICVS R [**Pl. 16. 5**].

Comparison with a typical London coin (*BMC* 67) by the moneyer Liefred of Stephen's first type [**Pl. 16. 7**] reveals many points of difference, in addition to the crown and inscription, such as could have arisen from an engraver's attempts to adapt the nearly facing portrait, with sceptre to the left, of Henry's type XV to the right facing profile, with sceptre before, of Stephen's type I. There are traces of other letters beneath STEFAN and the letters ST are out of alignment with those that follow.

Parts of the design which suggest alterations are the facial features, the drapery round the neck, and the bust and arm. Eye, nose, mouth, and chin may be compared with those of normal type I portraits where the profile face is more of an integrated whole. One of the coins (*f*) shows a blob at the back of the face which could perhaps be the trace of a nose from type XV. The drapery between the chin and wrist is curious for a profile bust. Normal type I obverses have the collar in a shallow curve, with the ends more or less level, from the shoulder to beneath the chin; on the *Stefanus* die the collar curves upwards at the front and has an extra line of drapery below, an arrangement inappropriate to the side view but like that on the near-facing bust of type XV. The upper arm on the *Stefanus* die comes rather sharply down from the neck, with a good deal of bust behind it, in contrast to the depiction on normal Stephen dies, where the arm is flatter and comes from the shoulder at the left.

---

[1] After coming to this conclusion, I have found that there is with coin *e* a ticket in the hand of Mr. Peter Seaby who some years ago had noted '? altered from Henry I type XV, for Abbot of Reading . . . crown of last type of Henry I. . . . King's name and moneyer's name recut?' There was also a coin (lot 126*a*) in the Walters sale (1932), probably one of the six here listed, which is described as having 'three annulets on the crown and the legend appears to have been erased in the die'.

It may not be a coincidence that the line of the upper arm coincides with the position of the sceptre of type XV and it could be that the one contains the shadow of the other.

For all these reasons I am inclined to think that the *Stefanus* die is the result of skilful alteration of a complete die of Henry I, unused or little used in that reign. I accept that this may not be so apparent to others' eyes as it is to mine. It could be argued, for example, that this was a die left unfinished at Henry's death and in due course completed with the type of the new reign; or even that it was an early production of the Stephen type by a die-sinker still influenced by features of the previous issue. However, having examined all the specimens with great care I do not think that either of these explanations would adequately account for the peculiarities described above.

On the other hand, it is not easy to account for die-alteration of the kind and extent which would have been involved, if such is the correct explanation. It seems doubtful whether economy or shortage of dies would have necessitated it at London itself. It could hardly have taken much less long, if at all, to make the alteration than to engrave a new die altogether. It is likely that the die was reworked early rather than late in the period of Stephen's first type. The adaptation of one type to the next presupposes, I think, the existence of dies (if not coins) of the new design as a model, so that it would not have been absolutely the earliest. A terminal date of c. 1141 is, of course, provided by the context of the Watford hoard, but this is of little value since regular issues of the first type were probably complete by about that time. The occasion and the cause of the alteration must therefore remain a mystery.

Instances of the wholesale alteration of the type or inscription on a die are naturally very rare. In English hammered coinage, although all kinds of die-alteration are uncommon, those relating to small parts of the inscription are least infrequently found. Names might need to be altered when a die was moved from one mint to another or if the wrong mint-name had been engraved in error: examples are Winchester to Wilton and London to Exeter in the 1180 recoinage. Rulers' names or initials were occasionally altered, as Edward to Richard in 1483 or R to E in 1377. In the later hammered period, a mint-mark or date could easily be brought up to date by overpunching in a single place on the die.

More drastic alterations are, of course, generally to be found at periods when the coin-types themselves were frequently and substantially altered. In the case of English coinage this situation applied particularly from late in the reign of Edgar (959–975) until the system of periodic recoinages broke down in the administrative anarchy of Stephen's time. The more important type appears to have been the reverse, and it is therefore this which normally belongs to the later issue where muling occurs between one type and another. In the very few cases where the obsolete type of a muled coin has been altered to make it resemble the current one, it is therefore usually the obverse which has been brought up to date. Examples are to be found in Ethelred's Hand issue, where a Rochester First Hand obverse has a sceptre added to conform to the type of Second Hand,[1] and in the reign of William I where rather more elaborate adjustments were made in order to make the second type (Bonnet) resemble the third (Canopy), and the third type the fourth (Two Pillars).[2] A case of reverse type alteration is, I believe, to be found with the conversion of an Intermediate Small Cross reverse to the Crux type,[3] a major change but not a difficult one, since the original type occupied such a small part of the field. Alteration of an obverse of Henry I to Stephen's first type would have involved altogether a more fundamental reworking of the die, not only because the name is changed as well as the type, but also because so little of the earlier design could be adapted simply to the later.

If die-alteration is the basic explanation of the *Stefanus* coins, it undermines a number of Andrew's assumptions about the coinage of the period. It is proper to remark that Andrew's work, though full of diverse and often useful information, has frequently been found, where independently tested, to contain extravagant theories based on nebulous or incorrectly interpreted evidence. As regards his general approach to historical numismatics, Crump and Johnson's verdict on the central theme of his *Henry I* (that the mints were generally in private hands and could only coin when their lord was in England) was that it seemed to them 'wholly impossible to find evidence for or against such a theory' and they demonstrate with devastating effect a few examples of how 'deficient evidence has frequently produced bad history'.[4] I will cite, by way of example, only one instance of Andrew's technical numismatics. His comment on the occurrence of the name Rodbert as a Canterbury moneyer of Henry I's last type is that 'Robert was probably father of '+ROGER OF R' (ROGER FILIVS ROBERTI) who coined here for Henry II.'[5] Unhappily for this proposal, a moneyer named Roger of R does not appear on the Short-Cross coinage until the class numbered V (and last in the series) by Evans[6] which, as Andrew was in a position to know, was not struck until more than a quarter of a century after Henry II's death. Moreover, even though it is no discredit to Andrew to have been unaware of the entry in the Rolls relating to the appointment of Roger of Rochester as an archbishop's moneyer at Canterbury in 2 Henry III (1217/18), it is simply perverse to treat the invariable OF R as if it were the same as, or an error for, F. R.

We ought therefore to reconsider the strength of the evidence on which the attribution to the abbot of Reading is based. The case rests on the occurrence

---

[1] J. D. Brand, 'A link Between the First and Second Hand types of Aethelred II', *Num. Circ.* 1965, Sept.      [2] *BMC Norman Kings* I, xxxvii–ix.
[3] *BNJ* xxxvii (1968), 18.      [4] *NC* 1902, 373.
[5] *NC* 1901, 136.
[6] Lawrence's standard classification of the series (*BNJ* xi) had not yet appeared. Evans class V is more or less equivalent to Lawrence class VII.

of annulets in the design of certain coins of the period of the London mint and the assumption that they denote special dies for the abbot. That the annulet was used as an ecclesiastical symbol on English coinage is itself beyond doubt. The coins of Stamford under Edward the Martyr and Ethelred II[1] and of York under the Confessor are sufficient proof of this. But the Norman evidence is much less satisfactory. It consists, so far as I know, of the following:

(a) two coins of Canterbury, one of London, and one of Stamford [Pl. 16. 1–3] in type XIV of Henry I, with an annulet on the king's shoulder;[2]

(b) a London coin of type XV of Henry I by the moneyer Baldwin with an annulet on the king's right cheek (Lockett 2940c; Pl. 16. 6);

(c) the Stefanus die, here discussed, with an annulet at the foot of each arch of the king's crown and beneath the wrist;

(d) also in Stephen type I, on otherwise normal dies, annulets are sometimes to be found: there is, for example, one of variety A reading— —DEPIN: ON—, perhaps of Baldwin, with an insignificant annulet at the front of the crown.[3]

All these cases, it should be noted, are of annulets on the obverse, not on reverse dies as in the Saxon period. The argument would therefore be that certain obverse dies were specially marked to be used by the abbot's moneyer, with the implication that a nominated moneyer who had never struck for the king would not need to have his abbatial die marked but that a royal moneyer transferred to the abbot would need a mark on his obverse die thereafter. This theory permitted Andrew to assign all Edgar's coins of type XV to the abbot, though none has an annulet, and to assume that he was succeeded by Baldwin just before the end of the type and that the moneyers Smewine and Liefred were assigned to the office in type I of Stephen.

Mr. Elmore Jones raised the question of whether the annulets on the type XIV coins of Canterbury and Stamford should be associated with the abbots of St. Augustine and of Peterborough respectively, both of whom are known to have enjoyed rights of coinage at one time or another. His later discovery of another annulet coin of the same type, by Blacaman of London, could have been thought to strengthen the case, since London was also a mint where an abbot's privilege was exercised. The difficulty here, however, is that the charter appointing the Abbot of Reading's moneyer refers to 'Edgarus et quicunque post eum monetarius fuerit' in terms implying that Edgar, whose

[1] Stewart, 'Peterborough and Stamford', Seaby's Coin & Medal Bulletin, April 1970, 117–20; also BNJ xxviii (1956), 106–10.

[2] F. Elmore Jones, 'New Light on the Abbot of Peterborough in the Norman Period', BNJ xxvii (1954), 179–81. For the Canterbury coin of Algar see BNJ xxvi, pl. B. 5. I am indebted to Mr. Elmore Jones for many helpful comments in relation to this paper.

[3] Drabble (1939), 699 (illustrated), ex Wheeler (1930), 181, ex Roth (1918), 141.

London coins are only of type XV, was the first appointee. Mr. Elmore Jones's caution in relation to the Canterbury and Stamford coins was therefore probably justified, and the annulets in this type may be no more than ornamental additions. Annulets on the shoulder forming part of the design are also, for example, sometimes found in variety C of Stephen type I and at various mints.

Baldwin is only recorded in Henry's last type and Stephen's first; his coins of Stephen seem generally to be of the earliest variety (A) reading REX. In each type his annulet die is the exception, and most of his coins are without. Yet, if a case for the significance of annulets were to be made out, the occurrence of dies so marked in successive types by the same moneyer (that is if the Stephen coin is his) must be accounted as potentially in its favour. Mr. Elmore Jones has suggested that the annulet in type XV is a die-flaw or even an eye punched in the wrong place. It may be so, though it is a little large.

But what of the annulets on the *Stefanus* die? That at the wrist could be no more than a typological ornament, meant to be a sceptre-terminal perhaps. But those in the crown are certainly abnormal and I know of no coin of Henry's last type with this feature. Again they may be no more than decoration, but if so it is remarkable that only this die, one thought worthy of decoration, should have them.

Curious as these annulet coins may be, however, their attribution to the abbot of Reading seems to me to require a series of assumptions which cannot be substantiated and which, on balance, I do not think the circumstantial evidence supports. The proposed sequence of moneyers—Edgar, Baldwin, Smewine, Liefred—seems somewhat unlikely within so comparatively short a period and it must be remarked that the dies of known abbatial moneyers, Edgar at this time and Alferg at Canterbury under Henry II, do not carry an annulet or any other mark. We can only admit that if there was some significance in the annulets at this period we still do not know what it was.

It would be wrong in this context to omit mention of the annulet on some London coins of Edward I. This occurs on a few dies at a very early stage in the recoinage of 1279 (Fox class I*d*) and also soon after the recoinage of 1300. The later issue is represented at the present time by two coins only, so far as I know. Both are from the same obverse die of Fox class X*a*, one being a X/IX mule [Pl. 16. 14] and the other a coin of pure class X [Pl. 16. 15]. The Fox brothers, knowing only the coins of class I*d* and influenced by Andrew's theories, suggested that the annulet might denote the abbot of Reading's die;[1] the attribution has since become an accepted piece of orthodoxy in English numismatic literature. Except in one case, that of the quatrefoil on the archbishop of York's coins in class III, marks found on the breast in the

---

[1] *BNJ* vii, 108.

Edwardian series—pellets in classes IV and V, rosettes in class VII and stars in class IX—are common to all mints. The annulet is presumably, therefore, to be regarded as a deliberate mark in relation to certain coins struck at London, the more especially since it is now known to have been used in the second as well as in the first recoinage of Edward I's reign. Although there is no reference in the London mint accounts or other coinage records of the period to a die for the abbot, his coinage under Edward III, struck at Reading itself, is both documented and identifiable. Furthermore, Mr. M. R. Broome has recently brought to notice the fact that Edward II's confirmation of the abbot's privileges excluded the right of coinage, which could be understood to suggest that this had recently been exercised.[1] The Reading theory must, however, be recognized as no more than a conjecture, though a rather more plausible one, ironically, than that relating to the annulet coins of the 1130s which suggested it.[2]

[1] Mr. Broome's paper on 'The Coinage of Reading' was read to the Numismatic Congress held there in 1969.

[2] I am grateful to the Keeper of Coins, the British Museum, for providing casts of the coins on Pl. 16 and to their owners for permission to illustrate them: British Museum, nos. 4, 5, 7, and 10; A. H. Baldwin & Sons Ltd., no. 6; N. P. Ballingal nos. 8, 9, and 12; C. E. Blunt, no. 14; F. Elmore Jones, nos. 1 and 2; R. P. Mack, no. 11; and P. Woodhead, no. 15. No. 3 is illustrated from a cast in the British Museum.

# The Billon Coinages of James VI of Scotland

## J. K. R. MURRAY

THERE were three separate issues of billon coins during the period 1583–94 and they have been described in detail both by E. Burns in *The Coinage of Scotland* and by Mr. Ian Stewart in *The Scottish Coinage*. Neither writer, however, made use of the additional information concerning these issues contained in the *Compt of the Coynzehous*, of which only a very small part was transcribed by R. W. Cochran-Patrick in his *Records of the Coinage of Scotland*.[1] It is with the object of repairing this omission that this note has been written. The *Compt*, of which the original is in the Scottish Record Office, Edinburgh,[2] consists of an account of the receipts and expenditure at the Scottish mint and includes the quantities of metal coined. It covers the years 1582–1627, although it is not complete for this period.

A brief outline of each issue is given below so that the information given in the *Compt* can be seen in its right context. As with certain other Scottish coins, the names now used for these billon coins do not correspond to the names found in the old Acts and other records. The modern names seem to date from the publication in 1845 of John Lindsay's *A View of the Coinage of Scotland* and have been retained by subsequent writers. I have used the original names at the beginning of each section, putting the modern names in brackets after them. The eightpenny groats were also known as *achesons* or *atkinsons* after the mintmaster, Thomas Achesoun (1581–1611). The name *bothwell*, later corrupted to *bodle*, was used for a Scottish twopenny piece and probably dates from this period. It is not known whether the name was first applied to twopences of billon (struck during 1588–90) or to those of copper (struck in 1597). The Bothwell after whom the coins were named is also not known.[3]

EIGHTPENNY and FOURPENNY GROATS (placks and half-placks) (**Fig. 1, 1**)

An Act of Privy Council dated 24 December 1583 ordered a coinage of eightpenny and fourpenny groats, 3 deniers fine, of which there were to be

---

[1] Vol. ii, 313–17. Afterwards cited as C–P.

[2] Reference E 101/2–3.

[3] The earliest known reference to bothwell as a coin name occurs in British Museum Add. MS. 28566, fol. 29*b*. This is dated c. 1639. A transcript of this folio is given in *BNJ* xxxix, 130.

270 eightpenny groats to the pound weight.[1] The face value of one pound of coin was thus £9.

*Obv.*   IACOBVS·6·D: G.R.SCOTOR⸍   Crowned shield.
*Rev.*   OPPIDVM·EDINBVRGI   Crowned thistle.

Other varieties have IACOB, SCO, OPPID, and EDINB. Fourpenny groats are similar, but always have IACOB, etc.

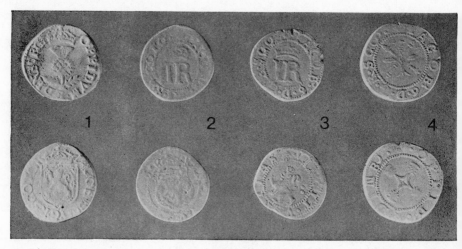

FIG. 1.

The Privy Council also ordered that all old billon money coined in the reign of Mary and earlier was to be brought to the mint where it would be exchanged, shilling for shilling, for the new alloyed money. The intrinsic value of the old billon money was by then greater than the currency value, so little was brought in, since it was more profitable to melt it down. Several further Acts of Privy Council complained about this practice which deprived the king of his profit.

Striking commenced in January 1583/4[2] and was continued until 1587. By 7 August of that year 2,491 stone of groats had been struck, giving a useful profit of nearly £42,000 Scots. At this stage minting ceased because it was felt that too much base money had been issued. Indeed an Act of Parliament of July 1587 stated that the country had sustained great harm through the over-abundant issue of base coin and appointed a commission to consider the matter and also the question of coining new gold and silver money.[3] Nevertheless, in October of the same year a further 140 stone was ordered

---

[1] C–Pi, 158.     [2] C–Pi, 168, and *Compt*, fol. 7v.     [3] C–Pi, 116.

and struck.[1] In July 1588 yet another 80 stone was ordered which was to provide the Earl of Bothwell with funds to purchase powder, shot, victuals, and other necessaries for an expedition against some insurgents in the north isles.[2] The *Compt* informs us that, of this 80 stone, 77 st. 15 lb. was actually struck. No profit was credited to the mint in the accounts for this last issue. Including these two lesser quantities, the total weight of coin struck was 2,708 st. 15 lb., having a face value of £390,087 Scots.

Mr. Stewart considers that the groats with IACOBVS and SCOTOR are the earliest, a matter about which the *Compt* gives us no enlightenment.

Of the moves by the mint to Dundee and Perth which the Privy Council ordered in 1585 on account of the plague raging throughout Scotland,[3] the *compt* records the expenditure of £551. 15s. 9d. for repairing the Dundee mint and transporting the mint staff and equipment to Dundee and back to Edinburgh (fol. 13). There was no expenditure for moving the mint to Perth, so it seems unlikely that any such move took place.

TWOPENNY and PENNY PLACKS (hardheads and half-hardheads)

Only a month after the Privy Council had ordered the 80 stone for the Earl of Bothwell, another Act of 30 August 1588 ordered a new coinage of twopenny and penny placks, half a denier fine, of which there were to be 320 twopenny placks to the pound, giving a face value of £2. 13s. 4d. per pound [**Fig. 1, 2**].[4] Forty stone of fine silver was to be used for this issue—a total of 960 stone of coin. This coinage was intended to fulfil the need for coins of very small value.

*Obv.* ·IACOB·6·D·G·R·SCOTO· IR crowned.
*Rev.* ·VINCIT·VERITAS· Crowned shield.

No pennies are known for this issue.

Since the twopenny plack was about the same size and weight as the eightpenny groat, it had been found that some people were cheating the ignorant by giving placks for groats. To counter this, an Act of Privy Council of November 1588 altered the design of the reverses so as to make the coins more easily distinguishable from those of the preceding issue [**Fig. 1, 3**].[5]

*Obv.* As before, but with SCOTO or SCO.
*Rev.* ·VINCIT·VERITAS· Crowned lion rampant to left; two pellets behind to indicate the value.

The pennies are similar, but do not have a pellet behind the lion; the letters IR are in monogram.

After the 960 stone originally ordered had been struck, the Privy Council ordained in March 1589/90 that the coining of gold, silver, and alloyed money,

[1] C–Pi, 168–9    [2] C–Pi, 170.    [3] C–Pi, 165–6.
[4] C–Pi, 170–2.    [5] C–Pi, 173.

particularly eightpenny groats and twopenny placks, be continued until further notice owing to the need to provide additional funds for the treasurer-depute, Sir Robert Melville.[1] As a result of this prolongation the total weight of placks was increased to 1,198 st. 5 lb., all of which was struck during the accounting period from 7 August 1588 to 1 September 1590. In spite of the reference to eightpenny groats in the Act of Privy Council just quoted, the *Compt* does not mention the striking of any more of them after the 80 stone for the Earl of Bothwell. It seems certain, therefore, that no more were struck.

FOURPENNY PLACKS (saltire placks) [**Fig. 1, 4**]

The coining of twopenny placks was completed by June or July 1590 and thereafter no billon money was minted until Parliament ordered a new coinage on 27 December 1593 owing to the great scarcity of silver and alloyed money, particularly small money.[2] The shortage had been brought about by calling in all base money, apart from the recent issue of penny and twopenny placks, and by the unlawful melting down and transporting abroad of coined silver and alloyed money. The new coinage was to consist of fourpenny placks, one denier fine, of which there were to be 320 to the pound weight, having a face value of £5. 6s. 8d. per pound. Two hundred stone of fine silver was to be used which would have given 2,400 stone of alloyed coin.

*Obv.* ·IACOB'·6·D·G·R·SCO'· Leaved thistle over two sceptres in saltire.
*Rev.* ·OPPID'·EDINB'· Lozenge with a thistle head on each point.

In January 1593/4 a contract was signed whereby the town council of Edinburgh was to undertake the responsibility for striking a new coinage of gold riders and half-riders, and silver ten-shilling, five-shilling, thirty-penny, and twelve-penny pieces which had just been ordered.[3] One of the terms of the contract was that all current gold, silver, and alloyed coin, except twopenny and fourpenny (saltire) placks, was to be called in and melted down. It was further stipulated that neither the king nor any other persons were to be permitted to coin money while the contract was in force. One result of this contract being given to Edinburgh town council is that the full amount of gold and silver 'passing the irons' is not recorded in the *Compt*. There is a warden's register in the British Museum which to some extent remedies this deficiency.[4] This shows that striking began on 4 February 1593/4. By 30 April 1596, when the mint was closed for some eighteen months, there had been struck about 100 stone of gold coin and 1,150 stone of silver. This was an exceptionally high output of Scottish coin in such a short time and was entirely due to the recoining of old money.[5]

[1] C-Pi, 173–4.    [2] C-Pi, 120–2.    [3] C-Pi, 182.    [4] Add. MS 33517.
[5] The money called in would have included a large proportion of English and other foreign coin. In 1584 little but foreign gold was circulating in Scotland (see C-Pi, 164–5), but the striking of thistle nobles (43½ st.) and hat pieces (14¾ st.) should have greatly improved the position by early 1594.

According to an entry in Cochran-Patrick's *Records*, the fourpenny placks were proclaimed on 7 January 1593/4 (about ten days after the order for the coinage had been ratified by Parliament), but on 19 January the issue was stopped.[1] By this time only 26 st. 11 lb. had been struck—a figure provided by the *Compt*. The decision to stop striking placks was certainly due to the terms of the above-mentioned contract preventing the king from coining money. Although the silver issue was a substantial one, it could not wholly remedy the shortage of small money, since the smallest coin was the twelve-penny piece. This was much too large at a time when the poorest people needed coins of a penny and twopence. When Parliament ordered a coinage of copper turners and pennies in 1597 it commented on the scarcity of small money then current.[2] This lack would not have been entirely made good even if the full amount of 2,400 stone of fourpenny placks had been minted.

| Accounting period | Denomination | Fineness den. gr. | | Weight st. | lb. | Profit (in Scottish pounds) | Face value | Reference in compt. |
|---|---|---|---|---|---|---|---|---|
| 1 May 1583 to 21 April 1586 | Eightpenny and fourpenny groats | 3 | 0 | 1,925 | 1 | £32,580 | £277,209 | fols. 7ᵛ and 8 |
| 21 April 1586 to 7 Aug. 1587 | ,, | | ,, | 565 | 15 | £9,390 | £81,495 | fols. 14ᵛ and 15 |
| 7 Aug. 1587 to 7 Aug. 1588 | ,, | | ,, | 140 | 0 | £2,400 | £20,160 | fol. 17 |
| 7 Aug. 1588 to 1 Sept. 1590 | ,, | | ,, | 77 | 15 | .. | £11,223 | fol. 19 |
| ,, | Twopenny and penny placks | | 12 | 1,198 | 5 | £10,505 | £51,128 | fol. 19ᵛ |
| 1 Nov. 1592 to 1 Feb. 1596 | Fourpenny placks | 1 | 0 | 26 | 11 | £533 | £2,280 | fol. 26ᵛ |

Mr. Stewart has drawn my attention to the fact that the punch used for the design on the obverse of the saltire plack is the same one as used for the centre of the reverse of the thistle noble. The latter had been issued during 1588–90, with a very few struck probably in 1592. This reusage is typical of the economy exercised at the Scottish mint with regard to punches and dies, and many examples could be cited.[3] Perhaps the main interest of the saltire placks is that they were the last billon coins to be struck in Scotland. From now on pure copper was used for coins worth one penny, twopence and, from Charles II's reign, sixpence. A silver sixpenny piece (equivalent to one half-penny sterling) was issued after the union by James VI and also during the first coinage of Charles I. Thereafter the value of the smallest silver coin rose steadily to 20*d*. (later 24*d*.) by Charles I, 40*d*. by Charles II and 60*d*. (equal to 5*d*. sterling) by William and Mary.

[1] C–Pi, introduction, clix.
[2] C–Pi, 132.
[3] e.g. the monogrammed IR on the penny plack has been borrowed from the gold two-thirds lion noble (1584–8).

The table on p. 181 is a summary of the billon issues. The details given by the *Compt* include the fineness, the amount of coin struck, the profit on each stone and total profit. The face values have been calculated by me from the weights.

## ACKNOWLEDGEMENT

My thanks are due to the Keeper, Dept. of Coins and Medals, British Museum, for supplying plaster casts to illustrate this paper.

# Echoes of the Name of Lorenzo Tiepolo

## IMITATIONS OF VENETIAN GROSSI IN THE BALKANS

### D. M. METCALF

[SEE PLATE 17]

THE purpose of this note is to gather together a number of scattered references to a puzzling variety of coinage struck in the name of the doge Lorenzo Tiepolo (1268–75), but often much reduced in weight and size from the normal grosso. It was once thought that such coins were half-grossi; but they are in fact imitations, belonging to the territories of present-day Yugoslavia and Greece, and they are certainly not official Venetian issues. Thirty new specimens are published here. The significance of their chronology is explored, along with their metrology. Most of these coins were struck long after the time of L. Tiepolo, indeed after his grossi had fallen out of circulation, and it is curious that his name should have been perpetuated in preference to those of other doges. There are, however, a few imitations in the names of later doges, up to P. Gradenigo (1289–1311) in the earlier part of the imitative series, and up to F. Dandolo (1329–39) in a related series of imitations which are of normal size and weight.

Kunz, as long ago as 1869, published five specimens in the Museo Bottacin, Padua; and even earlier Cumano had suggested that the variety was a half-grosso. Kunz rejected this view for various good reasons, in particular the variability of weight among the smaller-module coins. The Bottacin specimens (reproduced as **Fig. 1**) weighed 1·55, 1·50, 1·29, 1·24, and 1·19 gm. respectively[1] —as compared with 2·18 gm. for the authentic grossi, which are carefully weight-adjusted.

Stockert in 1923 described three types of imitative Serbian coinage modelled closely on the Venetian mezzanini of the fourteenth century.[2] Their prototype, valued at 16 denari, was first struck by the doge F. Dandolo (1329–39) on a weight-standard of 1·242 gm. and a reduced fineness of 70 per cent silver.

---

[1] C. Kunz, 'Il Museo Bottacin, annesso alla Civica Biblioteca e Museo di Pavia', *Periodico di num. e sfragistica per la storia d'Italia* ii (1869), 73–94. The weights are given as 30, 29, 25, 24, and 23 Venetian grains—of which 1 grano = 0·05175 gm.

[2] K. Stockert, 'Beiträge zur serbischen Münzkunde, 3. Venezianische von Serbien im Mittelalter gefälschte Mezzanini', *NZ* 1923 13–15.

The mezzanino was unfavourably received, and a modified version was introduced during the dogate of A. Dandolo: it was a coin of 0·80 gm. weight, and
of the traditional fineness of 96·5.[1] It seems never to have gained a role in the
Venetian currency, its function as a petty coinage being fulfilled by the
soldino. (This coin, valued at 12 denari, was also introduced by F. Dandolo—
and was swiftly counterfeited 'in partibus Slavonie', i.e. in the west Balkans.[2])
All except one of Stockert's eleven 'falsifications' showed the kneeling doge

FIG. 1.

and the standing Christ, as on the coins of A. Dandolo. Their average weight
was quite closely controlled at about 0·65–0·66 gm. There was reason to suppose that they came from a hoard of the later part of the fourteenth century.
The odd coin, which Stockert designated as his group 1, was quite different;
its types were those of the original Venetian grosso, and it was larger than
groups 2 and 3 (although still of course much smaller than a grosso) and of
rougher workmanship than the others, and weighed 0·885 gm. Its appearance,
and its provenance, gave no reason to doubt but that it was from the same
hoard; and Stockert, while noting that its weight was in excess of that of the
Venetian mezzanino, was evidently of the opinion that it too was from the late
fourteenth century. His line drawing is reproduced as **Fig. 2.** From it one can
see that there is no inscription (IC XC) on the obverse, and that the reverse
inscription is a series of meaningless symbols, such as large annulets, or a V
with dotted ends. No doge's name could be read into them, and the coin is
thus distinct from those published by Kunz, which are quite literate. There is
apparently a large annulet on the obverse, by Christ's elbow, similar in workmanship to those on the reverse.

Stockert's note was quickly followed up by an important article by Saria
on the Kičevo hoard, which was found in or before 1921, at a locality about

---

[1] N. Papadopoli, *Le monete di Venezia* (Venice, 1893), 173–4, 181–2. A chemical analysis,
as reported by Papadopoli, showed that a mezzanino was 96·8 per cent fine.
[2] Ibid. 160–1.

45 km. north of Ohrid. The Belgrade museum acquired a total of 345 coins, including 2 Venetian grossi of G. Soranzo and F. Dandolo, and 41 lightweight imitations. The average weight of the latter was 0·97 gm. Saria distinguished 13 varieties, some of which had a more or less blundered version of LA. TEVPL (Lorenzo Tiepolo) as their legend.[1] The date of concealment of the hoard is c. 1371, and the imitations are, in Saria's view, the product of an official mint in the time of the Serbian ruler Vukašin.[2]

FIG. 2.

The evidence of the Kičevo hoard is confirmed by the slightly later Sofia hoard, in which Serbian coins of Vuk Branković were predominant. Found also in 1921, it contained 506 pieces, including 136 genuine Venetian grossi from J. Tiepolo to A. Dandolo, and 103 imitations. Of these 103, as many as 91 were of L. Tiepolo, with numerous die-identities among them, and an average weight, according to Nuber, of 0·805 gm.[3] Most important, one of the coins was die-linked to a coin of Vukašin (1365–71) from the same hoard.[4] This die-link demonstrates conclusively both the date and the official character of the light-weight imitations.

Two more specimens are recorded from the Knyazhevo hoard of 1934, from Bulgaria, concealed at about the same date.[5]

More recently, Marić published four more similar little pieces in his *Studije iz srpske numizmatike*, describing them as 'falsifications of Venetian matapans', from the Belgrade museum's 1935 hoard from 'an unknown findspot in southern Jugoslavia'.[6] Dimitrijević has subsequently identified this parcel of coins as coming from the Dobrište hoard, concealed c. 1310.[7] The crucial importance of the hoard-context is that it shows that the imitative pieces were already in existence at that date, and that they could be hoarded along with regular Venetian, Serbian, and Bosnian coins of good weight. It also suggests that the very intriguing phenomenon of the use of the name of

---

[1] B. Saria, 'Iz numizmatičke zbirke Narodnog Muzeja u Beogradu, IV. Der Fund von Kičevo. Ein Beitrag zur altserbischen Numismatik', *Starinar* 3/iii (1924/5), 73–91. There is a further discussion in B. Saria, 'Die Entwicklung des altsersbischen Münzwesens', *Südost-Forschungen* xiii (1954), 22–61. See also S. Dimitrijević, 'Problemi srpske srednjovekovne numizmatike, II', *Istoriski Glasnik* 1957/3–4, at 126–7.

[2] Saria, op. cit. 1954, 43, 50, 51–2.     [3] Ibid. 54.     [4] Ibid. 52.

[5] T. Gerasimov, 'Kolektivni nakhodki na moneti prez 1934–1936 g.', *Izvestiya na Bulgarskiya Arkheologicheski Institut* xi/1 (1937), 315–24.

[6] R. Marić, *Studije iz srpske numizmatike* (Srpska Akademija Nauka, Posebna Izdanja, no. 259), Belgrade, 1956.     [7] Dimitrijević, op. cit. 126.

L. Tiepolo on Serbian coins almost a hundred years after his death may have rested on a tradition of doing so, which can be traced back at least to a time when the genuine coins of that doge were still circulating freely in the Serbian currency. The four important coins from Dobrište, which are illustrated on plates xl/xli of the *Studije*, are as follows:

*Marić*

181  Imitation of grosso of L. Tiepolo (1268–75). LAA . . . VLL, etc. *Obv.* Star beneath left elbow (this is a secret mark not found on the Venetian coins; but it occurs on early Serbian grossi in the Verona hoard, concealed c. 1284). 20–1 mm. 1·95 gm. In the view of Marić, this specimen was struck at Brskovo.

182  Another. ·ATEVPL. 19 mm. 1·77 gm.

183  Imitation of grosso of P. Gradenigo (1289–1311). Secret marks *symmetrically* to left and right of the throne (dots, which are not found on the Venetian coins in exactly this form). 16–18 mm. 1·55 gm. (flan smaller than dies).

184  Imitation of grosso, of uncertain doge. Secret marks arranged as on 183 (x to l., dot to r.; not found on Venetian coins: note the symmetrical arrangement). Characteristic sloping top to the back of the throne. 16–17 mm. 1·52 gm.

The first two imitations are exceptionally heavy, and the others are equivalent to the heaviest at Padua. This serves to confirm their relatively early date as attested by their hoard context. From the evidence of the Dobrište hoard we may be sure that imitations were being made from current Venetian models at least as *late* as 1289 (i.e. into the time of P. Gradenigo); and we may postulate that some of the (very heavy) imitations in the name of L. Tiepolo are earlier than Marić no. 183, and may have been struck within a very few years of the death of that doge. Certainly, the hoard proves that imitations in his name were being made at a time when the prototype could still be found in circulation in the west Balkans. Secondly, it proves that light-weight copies were being made at a time (1289 and later) when the official Serbian royal coinage was fully established and flourishing. Also, the copies imitate the little secret marks on the obverse, which are found especially on the Serbian coins struck before c. 1281. One's over-all impression, therefore, is that they originated in the 1280s or even the late 1270s—that is, at almost the same moment as the Serbian coinage, from which they borrow elements in their design. Yet they can hardly be part of that coinage. To which region might they belong? The hoards from seventy to ninety years later, which locate the imitations of that date firmly in western Macedonia and the adjoining areas, offer only indirect evidence; and the Dobrište hoard, from the same part of the Balkans, is unconfirmed by other provenances. The fact that it contained Bosnian coins is, however, unusual. Also, the genuine coins of L. Tiepolo and J. Contarini are over-represented at Dobrište, in comparison with their proportions among the Venetian grossi in other hoards, and it may be that there was an element in the currency of the region where the Dobrište hoard was assembled, consisting of Venetian coins that had been brought there in the 1270s, and which had tended to remain in circulation there. Those of L. Tiepolo may have been the first to become familiar there, and this might explain their choice as a prototype. The imitations are evasive, or perhaps one might say unforthcoming as regards any political guarantee; yet they have too long a history to be dismissed as the work of individual counter-feiters. They are better interpreted as a substantive coinage—and if they are scarce today, they are certainly no more so than the earliest Bosnian coinage, consisting of imitations of Venetian grossi (but of good weight) issued by rulers of the Šubič dynasty at Bribir in the north Dalmatian coastlands, in the first years of the fourteenth century.[1] By analogy, one may speculate that the imitations in the name of L. Tiepolo were begun by the effective ruler of some semi-independent territory, controlling, perhaps, a routeway from the Adriatic into the interior, such as the Neretva valley, or some part of southern Bosnia. Two specimens have been analysed and have been shown to have unusually large traces of gold in their silver. This suggests that the source of their metal was not Brskovo, the mine from which Serbia derived most of its silver in the late thirteenth and early fourteenth century.[2]

The imitations from the second half of the fourteenth century have sur-vived in quite large numbers, thanks to the Kičevo and Sofia hoards, in which their average weight was 0·97 and 0·805 gm. respectively. The earliest imita-tions, weighing over 1·5 gm., are relatively scarce, and more evidence is needed to establish whether they were originally any more plentiful, and to bridge the gap in what appears to be a progressively declining series of weights, with specimens in the range 1·0–1·5 gm. Such specimens can be found, although unfortunately without exact provenances attaching to them. The *Corpus Nummorum Italicorum* catalogues one, which is described as 'tutto come nel grosso, ma in dimensioni minori'. The legend is given as ·LATEVPL⁄ SMVENETI, a slight but significant variation from the normal ·LA·TEVPL⁄ ·S·M·VENETI. The coin, which was then in the collection of the Count Zoppola, at Udine, weighed 1·20 gm. and was 17 mm. in diameter.[3] Another similar piece in the Italian royal collection weighed 1·32 gm. and was 19 mm. in diameter.[4] Among the coins of G. Dandolo, *CNI* includes one weighing 1·09 gm. (if the text is correct) but apparently of normal dimensions.[5]

The weights of the official Venetian grossi were very carefully controlled, in comparison with most medieval coinages. Individual coins varied somewhat,

---

[1] G. Krasnov, 'Prilog istraživanjima novaca Šubića Bribirskih', *Num. Vijesti* 27 (1969), 21–7.

[2] A. A. Gordus and D. M. Metcalf, 'The Metal Contents of the Early Serbian Coinage', *RBN* 1969, 57–82.          [3] *CNI* 23.          [4] *CNI* 22.          [5] *CNI* 7.

of course, but in general the reputation of the grosso was well deserved. This may be illustrated from a sample of currency as found in the Dobrište hoard (nos. 163–80), where the weights, even after wear, are mostly within 5 per cent of the intended 2·18 gm.: 2·18, 2·17 (3 specimens), 2·14 (4), 2·13, 2·12 (3), 2·10 (6), 2·08 (2), 2·02 (3), 1·96, 1·90 (2).

If the weight of a little-worn coin falls much below this range, there is reason to suspect that it may be a counterfeit. Ljubić recorded the individual weights of some Venetian grossi in the Zagreb museum (which are likely to have been found in Jugoslavia), in the section on metrology in his *Opis*:[1]

| | |
|---|---|
| P. Ziani (1205–29) | 2·05 |
| J. Tiepolo (1229–49) | 2·15, 2·06 |
| R. Zeno (1253–68) | 2·07, 2·05, 1·91 |
| L. Tiepolo (1268–75) | 2·04, 1·65 |
| J. Contarini (1275–80) | 2·06, 2·03 |
| G. Dandolo (1280–9) | 2·15, 1·78 |
| P. Gradenigo (1289–1311) | 2·18, 2·15, 2·02, 2·00, 1·90 |
| G. Soranzo (1312–28) | 2·20, 2·12, 2·05, 1·99, 1·82 |
| F. Dandolo (1329–39) | 2·07, 2·05 |

The range corresponds very closely with that given by the Dobrište hoard, and the lightest coin (giving no occasion for surprise!) is of L. Tiepolo, and almost certainly an imitation.

Two specimens of small module in the Ashmolean Museum are said to have been 'found in a mine somewhere in eastern Europe many years ago'. They were part of a small group of Serbian medieval coins, which were mixed with a larger number of Roman denarii. There is reason to suspect that they came from a collection that was dispersed at the time of the First World War, and it can hardly be doubted that their original provenance is Serbian:

1. Imitation of grosso of L. Tiepolo (1268–75). *Obv.* Secret marks:+to l., within a small fold of drapery; and an identical+to r., beneath the elbow. Flat-topped back to throne. *Rev.* L·ATЄVPL to l., SMVЄNЄ [ . . .] to r.; DVX 16–17 mm. Carefully die-adjusted. 1·235 gm. Quite close in style to Marić III, 183. [Pl. 17. 1.]

2. Imitation of grosso of G. Dandolo (1280–9). *Obv.* Throne with sloping back. Poor, linear style. Note the stylized beard and moustaches. *Rev.* IODADVI to l., SMVЄNЄTI to r.; DVX. Faces in the same style as on the obverse. 19 mm. (part of margin broken away). Reversed die-axis (12 o'clock position). 1·22 gm. [Pl. 17. 2.]

The first coin is 75 per cent silver (an alloy used in Serbia in the period 1331–46), and the second is 53 per cent silver.[2]

[1] S. Ljubić, *Opis Jugoslavenskih Novaca* (Zagreb, 1875), p. X.
[2] Gordus and Metcalf, op. cit.

A third coin at Oxford is of normal module, but light weight. It was purchased for the Bodleian Coin Room through Sir Charles Oman in 1897, and its provenance is unknown:

3. Imitation of grosso of L. Tiepolo. *Obv.* Secret marks: 5-pointed star between feet; sketchy lozenge-shaped marks beneath right elbow (to observer's left) and also beside right knee. Square-topped throne. The cross in the nimbus is dotted. The pyramidal groups of three dots at the corners of the throne are upside-down. *Rev.* ·LⱭTIIЄVIL to l., SMVЄNЄTI to r.; DIIX. There is a secret mark consisting of a five-pointed star at the foot of the staff of the banner, to the l.; its form suggests that the star on the obverse, which at first sight might be a star and circle combined, is intended to be simply a star outlined by five intersecting lines. 19–20 mm. Die-adjusted. 1·56 gm. [Pl. 17. 3.]

A hoard may well be the source for a further group of twenty-five coins, comprising twenty-four imitations and one genuine Venetian grosso cut down to the same size and weight. These coins, which are illustrated on **Pl. 17. 4–28,** were kindly made available for study by Mr. C. H. Subak, and represent a substantial addition to the available evidence. All their dies are different, which is a pointer to the scale on which the LA.TEVPL imitations were struck. Inspection suggests that they can be divided into two modules; and the pattern of their weights shows that the two groups are on different standards, and hardly overlap. They are all fairly carefully die-adjusted ↑↓, except nos. 6, 13, 18, and 23, which are ↑↑:

*Larger module*

| | | |
|---|---|---|
| 4. 1·39 | 8. 1·25 | 12. 1·31 |
| 5. 1·64 | 9. 1·70 | 13. 1·38 |
| 6. 1·41 | 10. 1·51 | 14. 1·06 |
| 7. 1·48 | 11. 1·17 | 15. 1·44 |

*Smaller module*

| | | |
|---|---|---|
| 16. 1·01 | 20. 0·97 | 24. 0·85 |
| 17. 1·10 | 21. 0·83 | 25. 0·87 |
| 18. 1·04 | 22. 1·13 | 26. 0·95 |
| 19. 1·15 | 23. 1·00 | 27. 0·87 |

*Venetian grosso*
28. 1·03

There are imitative secret-marks on some of these coins, in particular crosses to left and right on nos. 6–11, with the addition of an annulet between the feet on no. 6, and a letter ⵜ on nos. 7–8 (cf. nos. 2 and 1 respectively among the Bottacin specimens). Nos. 6–11 are a compact stylistic group; the more sketchy obverse style of nos. 12–13 is linked with it through the very similar reverses, nos. 11–12. Nos. 14–15 are coarser. Among the small-module coins, two have a five-pointed star under the elbow (nos. 22 and 27), one has a monogram with a letter ⊘ on the reverse (no. 24; there is perhaps also a cross on the obverse, which is a near-duplicate of no. 22), and one has the more than usually blundered reverse inscription ΗΟΠΤVΘΙ (no. 27).

There exists also a quite different class of 'falsifications', again mostly in the name of L. Tiepolo, but of normal module and good weight. They were produced not earlier than the 1330s, and may in fact belong to the second half of the fourteenth century. The Stobi hoard of 1937 consisted, as published by Marić, of ninety coins of which the latest were (again) of King Vukašin (1365–71). There were among the total four authentic Venetian grossi of P. Gradenigo, G. Soranzo (two specimens), and F. Dandolo (1329–39), and twenty-two further coins which Marić catalogued, quite correctly, as imitations.[1] Their module and style, so far as can be judged from the quality of the illustrations, are quite acceptable, but the legends are all more or less blundered. The doges to which they are referred, and the weights of the individual specimens, are as follows:

L. Tiepolo: 2·37, 2·36, 2·25, 2·01, 2·00 (2 specimens), 1·92, 1·88, 1·78, 1·68, 1·64, 1·63;
J. Contarini: 1·79;
F. Dandolo: 2·20, 2·18, 2·10, 2·09 (2), 2·04, 2·02, 1·97, 1·96.

No hoard-group of a dozen genuine coins of L. Tiepolo would include three weighing as much as the three heaviest here—quite apart from any consideration of loss of weight by wear in coins ostensibly ninety years old at the date of concealment. The *spread* of weights is wider than it would be among Venetian issues, even though the *average* is quite close to an acceptable figure (1·96 gm.). Most of the imitations attributed by Marić to F. Dandolo are very blundered and could equally well have been read as IODANDVL (G. Dandolo, J. Contarini's immediate successor). But a few read clearly FRADAN, etc. Two or three of the coins of L. Tiepolo have secret-marks, including a Θ, which occurs also on the reverse of one of the Bottacin coins. As the hoard is from as far south as Stobi, could this possibly stand for Thessalonica? And in order to suggest an interpretation for the letter Π which occurs on three of the Subak coins and again on one at Padua, ought one to be looking much further south in the Adriatic coastlands, for example to Arta?

Evidence from Greece is limited to the 'Stobi' type of imitations. A coin which seems to be in the same style was acquired in 1956 by the Athens cabinet, in a hoard that was confiscated by the Greek authorities from a Swiss scholar, who insisted, however, that he had not bought it in Greece.[2]

---

[1] Marić, op. cit. 420–7.

[2] D. M. Metcalf, *Coinage in the Balkans, 820–1355*, Thessalonica, 1965, and information kindly conveyed by Mrs. I. Varoukha-Khristodhoulopoulou as Keeper of the Greek National Coin Collection.

The hoard was dated by a coin of B. Gradenigo (1339–43), yet many of the twenty-six Serbian coins in it were evidently of thirteenth-century date:

29. *Obv.* Secret-marks: 5- or 6-pointed star below left elbow; two very sketchy lozenges (cf. no. 3 above) by right elbow and right knee. *Rev.* ·IΛNΛNƆVLL: to l., ·SMVCNCTI· to r.; DVX. Doge with long hair. 21 mm. Die-axis c. 5 o'clock. 2·0 gm. [Pl. 17. 29.]

A related coin in much the same style (note the rather heavy lettering) was bequeathed to the Ashmolean Museum by E. S. Bouchier in 1930:

30. *Obv.* Secret-marks: nothing visible below the left elbow, but the coin is obscure at this point. Two very sketchy lozenges as in no. 29. *Rev.* I·ADN·DVL·O to l., SMVЄNЄTRI· to r.; DVX. 20–1 mm. Die-axis c. 5 o'clock as on no. 29. 1·93 gm. [Pl. 17. 30.]

It is difficult to say whether these two coins are to be referred to G. Dandolo or F. Dandolo. They may be deliberately ambiguous.

Yet another imitation was published by Lambros as an Achaian coin of Robert of Anjou. It reads RANDVIO—R supposedly for Robert, and ANDVIO as a blundered copy of A DANDVL. The weight is 2·044 gm.[1] We may reject Lambros's interpretation, and see the coin as part of the same series as the preceding two specimens. Lambros wrote: 'J'ai vu dans le temps plusieurs de ces gros, mais je ne les collectionnais pas, ne leur attribuant pas alors l'importance qu'ils avaient.' Schlumberger, who included the coin in his *Numismatique de l'Orient Latin*, added (on what authority is not specified, but perhaps information from Lambros) that it was found in the Peloponnese.[2] Eighteen similar coins, without provenance, were carefully described (but not illustrated) by Le Hardelay.[3]

Finally, there is a coin which is not of the Venetian type at all, and which comes from north Serbia. It indicates that LA TEVPL, SMVENETI became a traditional formula with little or no meaning. Valtrović, in a note entitled 'An unpublished Serbian coin',[4] describes how some Serbian silver coins had been found when a new road was built 'na Rašku': one specimen which came into his hands was similar to that illustrated by Ljubić, pl. xv, 24, except that the legend was SЄMЄЄTS LЄTCVЄL. The weight was 1·14 gm. This coin gives a distant echo of the name of Lorenzo Tiepolo.

[1] P. Lambros, 'Monnaies inédites en or et en argent frappées à Clarence, à l'imitation des monnaies vénitiennes, par Robert d'Anjou, prince du Péloponnèse', *BCH* 1877, 89–99, pl. i, 11.                                                                    [2] Loc. cit. 321.

[3] C. Le Hardelay, 'Contribution à l'étude de la numismatique vénetienne', *RN* 1913, 218–21 (nos. 17–30), 223–4 (nos. 37–40). These imitations were identified as 'levantine' (i.e. Aegean area?) by V. Padovar, *La nummografia vereziana. Sommario documentuto*, 1882, 327–8.

[4] M. Valtrović, 'Srpski novac još ne pročitan', *Starinar* i (1884), 42.

# Analyses of Lombardic Tremisses by the Specific-Gravity Method

W. A. ODDY

[SEE PLATES 18–19]

## 1. *The method of analysis*

ANALYSES have been carried out of eighty-nine Lombardic tremisses by the specific gravity method using perfluoro-1-methyl decalin as the immersion liquid.[1] The results are presented in Tables I to VI. The gold content has been calculated assuming that the main elements present are gold and silver, and that copper is not present in a significant amount. By analogy with other Barbarian coinages of the Dark Ages this is most probably true[2, 3, 4] and it is supported by the published analysis of a coin of Desiderius which contained 33·1 per cent gold, 63·5 per cent silver, and 3·3 per cent copper.[5] In any case theoretical considerations suggest that the presence of up to 5 per cent of copper in a gold/silver alloy only introduces an error of up to 2 per cent in the gold content as determined by the specific-gravity method.[6]

The experimental accuracy of this method of analysis has been estimated to be ±1 per cent,[1] but recent comparisons with analyses carried out by other non-destructive methods[7] and with the results of chemical analysis[8] suggest that the error can be as much as ±3 per cent. In fact the specific-gravity result is usually systematically slightly lower than that found by other methods and so it is probably fairly safe to assume that the actual gold content lies somewhere between the value given in the tables and a figure which is 2 or 3 per cent higher.

## 2. *Classification of the coins*

On the basis of stylistic considerations the coins, which are all tremisses, can be divided into six classes. These major divisions of the Lombard coinage are now generally accepted by most scholars (e.g. Bernareggi[9, 10] and Grierson[11]) and have superseded the classification of Wroth.[12] Photographs of casts of all the coins, with the exception of those which were illustrated in the *British Museum Catalogue*,[12] are on **Pls. 18** and **19**.

*Lombardy*

Class I (Fig. 1)  Pseudo-imperial coins of increasingly large flan having diademed imperial bust to right on obverse and facing Victory on reverse. The name of the emperor in the obverse legend is at first recognizable.

O

Class II    Coins of similar fabric, but with the name and bust to right of the Lom-
(Fig. 2)    bard king on the obverse and with the Victory replaced by a standing
            figure of St. Michael on the reverse. This group also includes coins of
            Ratchis with facing bust and of Ratchis, Aistulf and Desiderius with a
            monogram replacing the profile bust on the obverse, but none of these
            was available for analysis.

*Tuscany*

Class III   Pseudo-imperial coins having diademed imperial bust to right on obverse
(Fig. 3)    and cross potent on reverse. The fabric is similar to that of the coins of
            class I and the name of the emperor in the obverse legend is at first
            recognizable.

Class IV    Pseudo-imperial coins having a much smaller flan than Class III and
(Fig. 4)    neater in appearance. On the obverse is a diademed bust to right and on
            the reverse is a cross potent but the legends are completely blundered and
            consist of few letters repeated several times.

Class V     Coins initially with a monogram on the obverse, but later with the name
(Fig. 5)    of a city surrounding a star. On the reverse is a cross potent surrounded
            by a continuous repetition of either the letters VI or VΛ.

*Lombardy and Tuscany*

Class VI    Coins of Lombard kings having the name of the mint surrounding a star
(Fig. 5)    on the obverse and the name of the king surrounding a cross potent on the
            reverse.

**Figs. 1** to **5** show a diagrammatic representation of the analytical results
for each class, in which the weight of each coin is plotted against its gold
content. Damaged and repaired coins are omitted from these diagrams. On
the basis of these graphs the six classes have been tentatively subdivided into
ten groups, which are discussed below. On all the diagrams a black spot
indicates that the Lombard attribution of the coin is certain, while a circle
is used to indicate results on coins which may not be official Lombard issues.
These doubts are amplified in the table of results.

The first column on pages 202–14 records the number of the analysis and
the present location of the coin. The analysis numbers are continued from the
various tables in the volume of *Proceedings of the Royal Numismatic Society
Symposium* on coin analysis which was held in December 1970. Almost all
the coins can be seen in one of three places; the British Museum, London
(BM); the Grierson Collection in the Fitzwilliam Museum, Cambridge (PG);
and the Ashmolean Museum, Oxford (AM). The second column contains
the legends, and a reference is given to the *British Museum Catalogue*[12] and
to Bernareggi[10] where appropriate in the third column. This is followed by
the weight in grammes, specific gravity, and gold content.

3. *Class I. Pseudo-imperial coins of Lombardy in the names Justinian I, Justin II and Maurice*

Although there are very few coins in this class which were available for analysis, some of which are only doubtfully attributed to the Lombards, one can postulate the existence of two different groups, the first (group 1) having a gold content of more than 92 per cent and the second (group 2) a gold content between 73 and 85 per cent. The coins of group 1 are obviously struck to the same weight standard as the regular imperial issues, and are as near to 'pure gold' as the Lombard moneyers could attain. Half the coins in group 2 are lighter in weight but because of the small number of specimens involved it is not possible to determine whether this represents an official reduction in weight.

The average composition of the coins of group 1 is 96·2 per cent and of group 2 is 79·3 per cent. The difference represents one step in the process of debasement, but the results are too few to be certain that an interval of about 17 per cent was the aim of the Lombard moneyers.

4. *Class II. Coinage of Cunincpert (688–700) to early in the reign of Desiderius (756–74) struck in Lombardy*

These coins were the successors in Lombardy of those 'anonymous' issues described above. An examination of **Fig. 2** shows that these regal coins can be divided into two groups. Group 3 contains the issues of Cunincpert and Aripert II, who struck what is essentially undebased gold, the average composition of the six coins of these two reigns being 95·5 per cent. However, the coins of Liutprand, group 4, are considerably debased and it seems likely that at least two stages in the debasement process (about 70 per cent and about 50 per cent) are represented by these analyses. Unfortunately there are too few results to draw any firm conclusions about the size of the steps in which the process took place. It should be noted that the average weight of the coins of Cunincpert and Aripert II is 1·36 gm., which represents a reduction in weight from that of the coins in group 1 of class I, which imitate the regular imperial tremisses in weight. This weight change would be expected to follow that of the regular imperial series of Sicily, which Grierson suggests took place in the late seventh century,[13] and this agrees with its occurrence in Lombardy in the reign of Cunincpert (688–700), or possibly in the late pseudo-imperial issues which immediately preceded his reign. The average weight of the three coins of Liutprand is 1·20 gm., and thus his long reign saw not only a debasement of the alloy, but also a reduction in weight of the coins.

5. *Class III. Pseudo-imperial coins of Tuscany in the names of Heraclius and Constans II*

Examination of **Fig. 3** suggests that these coins can also be divided into two groups of similar average compositions to groups 1 and 2 of class I.

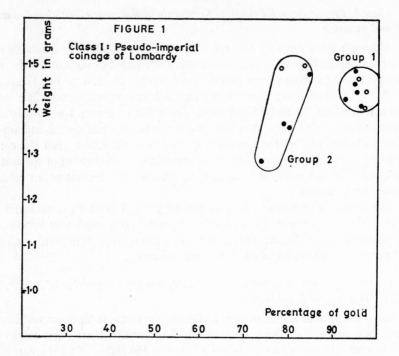

FIGURE 1

Class I: Pseudo-imperial coinage of Lombardy

Group 1

Group 2

Weight in grams

Percentage of gold

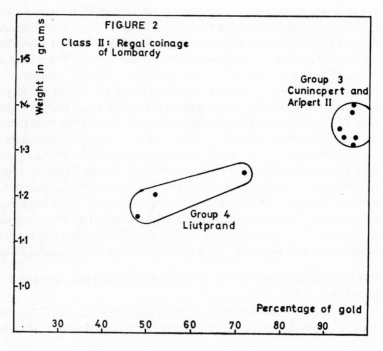

FIGURE 2

Class II: Regal coinage of Lombardy

Group 3
Cunincpert and
Aripert II

Group 4
Liutprand

Weight in grams

Percentage of gold

Group 5 contains those coins with a gold content greater than 91 per cent, which are presumably struck to the same weight standard as group 1 of class I and as the official contemporary imperial Byzantine issues. Group 6 is somewhat more diffuse, although if the five most debased coins are omitted (only four of them appear on **Fig. 3** as one is damaged and so cannot be plotted) the group would be much more compact. Examination of these five coins suggests that three of them may be contemporary forgeries, and a fourth is only doubtfully attributed to the Lombards. This leaves only one definitely Lombard coin of class III which has a gold content of less than 80 per cent. The average composition of group 5 is 94·5 per cent and of the whole of group 6 is 79·7 per cent, although if the five most debased coins are omitted the latter becomes 83·8 per cent. Although group 6 is obviously the result of a debasement of the coinage alloy, it would be unwise to be too specific about its intended magnitude because of the heterogeneous nature of the coins.

### 6. *Class IV. Anonymous pseudo-imperial coins of Tuscany*

Although it is thought that this is the coinage which followed after that described in the previous section, the change in style is very marked. Once again an examination of a diagrammatic representation of the analytical results [**Fig. 3**] suggests the division into groups within the general heading of Class IV.

The coins can also be divided according to the symbol placed in front of the face on the obverse, and Wroth suggested[12] that these may indicate different mints. Grierson is of the opinion[11] that the three coins marked with the symbols ??, ??? and ?? respectively are contemporary forgeries, but only the one bearing the symbol ?? is very base, and the other two are as good in the quality of their gold as some of the undoubtedly genuine coins. Hence the three are included in the following discussion, although they could be omitted without materially affecting the suggested scheme.

An examination of the analytical results suggests that more than one symbol was current at the same time and it seems likely that the symbols may have had a chronological significance as well as a geographical one. Consideration of **Fig. 4** in which the weight of each coin has been plotted against its gold content shows that the coins can be divided into four groups. Group 7 corresponds, in its analytical figures, to group 6 of the previous class, having a composition range of 76 per cent to 88 per cent. The coins of this group are struck at the regular imperial weight of between 1·4 and 1·5 gm. The next significant group consists of four coins (group 9) which have suffered both a debasement to between 56 per cent and 67 per cent and a reduction in weight to between 1·25 and 1·37 gm.

Between groups 7 and 9 are two coins with a similar composition but one of which is struck to the old weight standard and the other to the new one (group 8). These may only be outlying members of groups 7 and 9, but it is

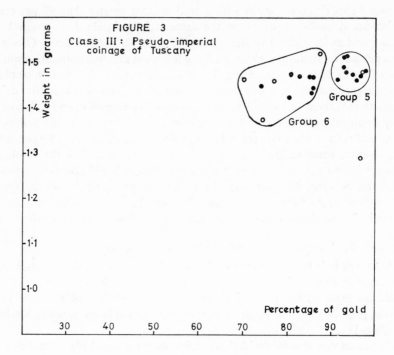

FIGURE 3

Class III : Pseudo-imperial coinage of Tuscany

Weight in grams

Percentage of gold

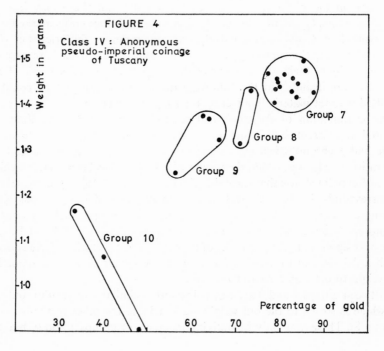

FIGURE 4

Class IV : Anonymous pseudo-imperial coinage of Tuscany

Weight in grams

Percentage of gold

tempting to suggest that they represent a further debasement from group 7, and when this had taken place, a weight reform was instituted as a further method of strengthening the economy. An examination of these two coins does reveal one significant difference between them. The lighter one (i.e. weight reformed) has the symbols •— and —• as part of the obverse legend. This distinguishes it from the other member of group 8 and all those of group 7 without a 'mint-mark' before the face. However, it does resemble most of the coins which do have a symbol in front of the face.

Group 9 would then represent the result of another step in the debasement at the new weight standard of slightly more than 1·3 gm. The average compositions of groups 7, 8, and 9 are 81·8 per cent, 72·2 per cent, and 62·3 per cent respectively, but little can be deduced from the gaps between them when the groups are so diffuse and usually have very few coins in them.

Finally, group 10 consists of three very light and much-debased coins but the intended values of weight and fineness are obscure. This leaves one anomalous coin, which has the symbol ⟨ before the face. It has a composition placing it in group 5, but a weight appropriate to group 7. In the absence of more results on similar coins it cannot be further assigned, and indeed it may not be an official Lombard issue.

One possible interpretation of these results is that at the inception of the coinage of class IV there were two mints in operation (called A and B below). Both initially struck coins of the same weight and fineness as group 6 of class III, but to distinguish between the two outputs, one of the mints placed a letter B before the face on the obverse (mint B) while the other left this part of the field blank (mint A). Then, if the evidence of group 8 is to be believed, the output of mint A was first debased by about 10 per cent and then suffered a weight reduction of about 0·1 gm.

It seems likely that this weight reduction followed that of the imperial series of Sicily which took place in the late seventh century.[13] Hence this weight reduction acts as a fixed point for the dating of class IV. (See also Section 4 above.) After a further debasement to a mean composition of 61·7 per cent, mint B continued in production (group 9) but there is no further activity at mint A, unless the single coin with the symbol ε before the bust on the obverse represents renewed output from this source. Finally there are the three poor-quality coins of group 10. These seem to represent the result of another debasement after which mint B still continued in production. Again a single coin in this group, having the symbol ϒ on the obverse, may originate in mint A, or may be a contemporary forgery. These conclusions are very tentative and are based on too few analyses to be regarded as proven. However, they do provide a basis for further discussion on stylistic grounds.

### 7. *Class V. So-called quasi autonomous coinage of Tuscan cities*

Only seven coins of this class were available for analysis, three of them having a monogram on the obverse and three a star. Unfortunately two of the coins with monograms are fragmentary and one with a star has been repaired and so they cannot be plotted on **Fig. 5.** The analysis results are randomly scattered between 40 per cent and 53 per cent of gold and do not suggest any further subdivions of this class, however, on stylistic grounds. Grierson is of the opinion[11] that the coins with a monogram precede those with a star on the obverse.

## 8. *Class VI. The final phase of the Lombard coinage—Aistulf and Desiderius*

Early in the reign of Desiderius the coinage of Lombardy and Tuscany was unified. It is perhaps surprising that the design chosen for this coinage copied the quasi-autonomous issues of Tuscany, rather than the concurrent issues of Lombardy which has the king's bust on the obverse and a figure of St. Michael on the reverse.

The issues of Aistulf of Tuscan type and what are presumably the earlier pieces of Desiderius of the same type were struck in an alloy about 55–60 per cent fine, but later in the reign of Desiderius serious debasement took place until the coinage was very pale. Isolated results of 41, 35, and 27 per cent do not suggest any reliable figure for the magnitude of this debasement, but are an indication of the poor quality of the coinage when the Lombard kingdom was subdued by Charlemagne in 774.

## 9. *Conclusions*

It must be stressed that the deductions which have been made from these analytical results are perforce very tentative because of the small number of coins in many of the groups. However, it is hoped that these analyses will provide a basis for future numismatic study of the Lombard series, backed up where possible by more analyses to prove or disprove the validity of the groupings which have been suggested above.

## *Acknowledgements*

I am deeply indebted to Professor P. Grierson for his encouragement of this work and for generously making available both his own collection of Lombard coins and the results of his own researches prior to their publication; and to Dr. A. E. Werner for his support of an analytical programme of work on Dark-Age coinage, of which the above results form a part. I am also grateful to the Keepers of Coins in the British Museum and the Ashmolean Museum for access to the coins in their care, to Dr. D. M. Metcalf for information about the Oxford coins, to B. A. Nimmo for making the casts for the illustrations, and to Miss Ann Bugden for assistance with calculating the results.

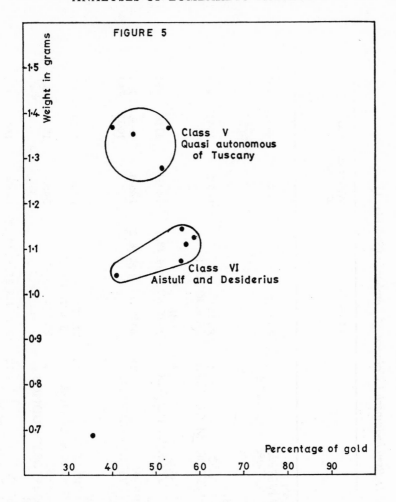

FIGURE 5

Weight in grams

Class V
Quasi autonomous
of Tuscany

Class VI
Aistulf and Desiderius

Percentage of gold

TABLE I

*Class I: Pseudo-Imperial Coinage of Lombardy* (See **Fig. 1**)

| Analysis number and location of coin | Legend | | Reference | Weight in grammes | S.G. | % Au |
|---|---|---|---|---|---|---|
| In the name of Justinian I (527–65) | | | | | | |
| SG. 291<br>PG | DNIVSTINI ANVSPFAVI<br>VICTORIΛΛVIVCTORVH CONOB<br>Possibly Lombard | ↑↓ | **Pl. 18** | 1·4046 | 18·91 | 97·3 |
| In the name of Justin II (565–78) | | | | | | |
| SG. 292<br>PG | DNIVSTI NVSPPΛVC<br>VICTORIΛΛVCVSTORVM CONO∩<br>Probably Lombard | ↑↓ | **Pl. 18**<br>Cf. *BMC* 123, 1 | 1·4372 | 18·92 | 97·4 |
| SG. 293<br>BM | DNIVSTI NVSPPAVC<br>VICTORIΛΛVCVSTORVN CONOB<br>Probably Lombard | ↑↓ | **Pl. 18**<br>*BMC* 123, 1; pl. 18, 1 | 1·4984 | 17·00 | 83·5 |
| SG. 294<br>BM | DNIVSTI NVSPPΛV<br>VICTORIΛΛ IVƆVSTRVII CONOII<br>Probably Lombard | ↑↘ | *BMC* 124, 2; pl. 18, 2 | 1·4944 | 16·39<br>16·37 | 78·4<br>78·3 |
| In the name of Maurice (582–602) | | | | | | |
| SG. 295<br>BM | VN∩ΛVR CTIbPPVI<br>VIITORIΛΛVIVITORVN CONOR | ↑↓ | **Pl. 18**<br>Cf. *BMC* 128, 22 | 1·4085 | 18·79 | 96·7 |
| SG. 296<br>PG | RmΛVRC TIbPPΛVI<br>VICTORIΛΛVCVITORVN CONOB<br>Probably Lombard | ↓↑ | **Pl. 18** | 1·4692 | 18·66 | 95·7 |
| SG. 297<br>BM | DNmΛVR CTbPPVI<br>VICTORIΛΛVIVITORV IONOR | ↑↘ | *BMC* 128, 25; pl. 18, 23 | 1·4404 | 18·61 | 95·4 |

| | Inscription | | Reference | | | |
|---|---|---|---|---|---|---|
| SG. 298 BM | DNMΛVR CTbPPVI VNTOVRIΛΛVIVITORVN CONOR | ↑↓ | Pl. 18 BMC 128, 24 | 1·4886 | 18·55 | 95·0 |
| SG. 299 PG | DNΠΛVR CTIbPPVI VIITORIΛΛVIVITORVN CONOR | ↑↓ | Pl. 18 Cf. BMC 128, 22 | 1·4590 | 18·55 | 95·0 |
| SG. 300 BM | DNMΛVR CTIbPPVI VIITORIΛΛVIVITORVN CONOR | ↑↓ | Pl. 18 BMC 128, 22; pl. 18, 22 | 1·4245 | 18·21 | 92·7 |
| SG. 301 AM | DVMΛVR CTbPPVI VICTORIΛΛVIVITORVII CONOR | ↑↓ | Pl. 18 Cf. BMC 128, 25 | 1·4791 | 17·11 | 84·4 |
| SG. 302 AM | DIMΛVR CTbPPVꟄ VIITORIΛΛVIVITIORVꟄ COMOI | ↑↓ | Pl. 18 | 1·3627 | 16·55 | 79·9 |
| SG. 303 BM | MΛVI CTԀPPV· VIITORIΛΛVITORV COIIOR | ↑↓ | BMC 129, 26; pl. 18, 24 | 1·3706 | 16·43 | 78·8 |
| SG. 304 BM | DIMV· ·OPPVI UIIꓤOTVIVITO IOИO | ↑↓ | BMC 129, 27; pl. 18, 25 | 0·7876 | 16·17 16·20 | 76·5 76·7 |
| | This coin has been clipped and is not included on **Fig. 1.** | | | | | |
| SG. 305 BM | DVMΛVR CTIbPPVI IVICTOΠIΛΛVIVITOꟼΛꟼ COHOV | ↑↓ | Pl. 18 BMC 128, 23 | 1·2902 | 15·86 15·85 | 73·6 73·5 |

## TABLE II

### Class II: Regal Coinage of Lombardy (See **Fig. 2**)

| Analysis number and location of coin | Legend | Reference | Weight in grammes | S.G. | % Au |
|---|---|---|---|---|---|
| **Cuincpert 688–700** | | | | | |
| SG. 306 BM | DNCVNI NCPER ↑← / D before face. / SCSHI HΛHIL | BMC 138, 1; pl. 20, 1 Bernareggi 141, 37b | 1·4046 | 18·75 | 96·4 |
| SG. 307 PG | DNCVII NICPER ↑↑ / M before face. / SCSIII HΛHIL | Pl. 18 | 1·3340 | 18·44 | 94·2 |
| SG. 308 BM | DMCVNI HCPER ↑↑ / M before face. / SCSMI HΛHIL | BMC 138, 2; pl. 20, 2 Bernareggi 139, 24a | 1·3529 | 18·29 | 93·3 |
| **Aripert II 701–12** | | | | | |
| SG. 309 PG | DHΛR IPGR ↑← / G before face. / SCSHL HΛHIL / Same dies as SG. 311 | Pl. 18 | 1·3171 | 18·79 | 96·7 |
| SG. 310 BM | DNΛ RIPER ↑↗ / M before face. / SCSMI HΛHIL | BMC 141, 1; pl. 20, 3 Bernareggi 145, 57b | 1·3327 | 18·80 | 96·7 |
| SG. 311 Trade | DHΛR IPGR / G before face. / SCSHL HΛHIL / Same dies as SG. 309 | Pl. 18 | 1·3881 | 18·69 | 96·0 |

**Liutprand 712–44**

| | | | | | | |
|---|---|---|---|---|---|---|
| SG. 312￼ BM | DNΛV TPRΛIIX￼ T before face.￼ SCSH HΛHIL | ↑↑ | **Pl. 18**￼ *BMC* 144, 3; pl. 20, 6￼ Bernareggi 154, 107 | 1·2536 | 15·68 | 71·9 |
| SG. 313￼ BM | DILVT [M]RIP￼ S before face.￼ SCS IIIIL | ↑↗ | **Pl. 18**￼ *BMC* 144, 2; pl. 20, 5￼ Bernareggi 153, 98 | 1·2031 | 13·81 | 51·8 |
| SG. 314￼ BM | DIIIV /////////////￼ M before face.￼ ·SCS IIIIL | ↑↑ | *BMC* 143, 1; pl. 20, 4￼ Bernareggi 150, 76*a* | 1·1552 | 13·50 | 47·7 |

## TABLE III

*Class III: Pseudo-Imperial Coinage of Tuscany (See* **Fig. 3***)*

| Analysis number and location of coin | Legend | Reference | Weight in grammes | S.G. | % Au |
|---|---|---|---|---|---|
| **In the name of Maurice or Heraclius** | | | | | |
| SG. 315 PG | ONNΛRΛHI VIPPΛVI VNTOΛIVΛVITOΛVH IONOB  ↑↓ | **Pl. 18** | 1·5130 | 18·21 18·22 | 92·6 92·7 |
| SG. 316 BM | DII[M]ΛVI[?]T TII9PΛVI VIITOR•:•HIIOIRVII IONO  ↑↑ Probably a contemporary forgery. | *BMC* 154, 3; pl. 21, 3 | 1·4750 | 16·61 | 80·4 |
| **In the name of Heraclius (610–41)** | | | | | |
| SG. 317 AM | DNNERΛC LIVSPPΛVC VICTORIΛΛVCVSTORVN CONOB  ↑↓ Same obverse die as SG. 318. Probably Lombard, but perhaps imperial of Ravenna. | **Pl. 18** | 1·4787 | 18·82 | 96·8 |
| SG. 318 PG | DNNERΛC LIVSPPΛVC VICTORIΛΛVIVSTORVN CONOB  ↑↓ Same obverse die as SG. 317. Probably Lombard, but perhaps imperial of Ravenna. | **Pl. 18** | 1·2913 | 18·77 | 96·5 |
| SG. 319 BM | DNHERΛCL IVSPPΛVCCC VICTORIΛΛVIVSTORVM CONOB  ↑↓ | **Pl. 18** *BMC* 131, 35 | 1·4748 | 18·76 | 96·4 |
| SG. 320 BM | DNHERΛCL IVSPPΛVCCC VICTORIΛΛVIVSTORVI CONOB  ↑↓ | *BMC* 131, 34; pl. 19, 1 | 1·4759 | 18·49 | 94·6 |
| SG. 321 BM | ONIIIRΛCL IDERPΛVI VIITORIΛΛVCVSTORVN IOHOΘ  ↑↓ | *BMC* 130, 31, pl. 18, 29 | 1·5138 | 18·27 | 93·1 |
| SG. 322 PG | DNCRΛC LIVΘPPN VICTORIΛΛVCVITOΛV CONOB  ↑↓ | **Pl. 18** | 1·4904 | 18·19 | 92·5 |

| No. | Coll. | Legend | Axis | Reference | S.G. | Weight | % |
|---|---|---|---|---|---|---|---|
| SG. 323 | BM | HEHAIL VSPPAVC / VITORIAAVIVITORVH IONO | ↑↓ | *BMC* 131, 33; pl. 18, 31 | 1·4643 | 18·04 / 18·01 | 91·5 / 91·2 |
| SG. 324 | BM | AHHIA/////// A SHAVII / VIIOAIAAVVITOIVNO IONO  Possibly Lombard. | ↑↓ | *BMC* 131, 37; pl. 19, 3 | 1·5207 | 17·45 / 17·43 | 87·1 / 86·9 |
| SG. 325 | BM | •NIAIVGI OVSPPAV / PIAA•ATIMAATOAAAI9 OHO | ↑↓ | *BMC* 132, 40; pl. 19, 6 | 1·4695 | 17·23 / 17·28 | 85·4 / 85·9 |
| SG. 326 | BM | DNHIRA•:• CIVIPAVC / VIIONINVIVIIONVII CONOD | ↑↓ | *BMC* 131, 38; pl. 19, 4 | 1·4354 | 17·21 | 85·3 |
| SG. 327 | BM | DHIIERACLI VSPPAVSI / VICTORIAAVSTOIII CONOB | ↑↓ | *BMC* 131, 32; pl. 18, 30 | 1·4698 | 17·14 | 84·7 |
| SG. 328 | BM | CAIIFI AOVII / IVIITORVAITIOIRVII ONO | ↑↑ | *BMC* 131, 39; pl. 19, 5 | 1·4720 | 16·76 | 81·5 |
| SG. 329 | BM | DINIERA CLIVSPPAV / VICTORIAAVIVSTORVII CONO  Possibly Lombard. | ↑↑ | *BMC* 131, 36; pl. 19, 2 | 1·4619 | 16·20 / 16·20 | 76·7 / 76·7 |
| SG. 330 | PG | ON/////AC L/////PAVC / VITORAAVIPITCVI IONO | ↑↓ | **Pl. 18** | 1·4505 | 15·93 / 15·91 | 74·2 / 74·0 |

In the name of Constans II (641–68)

| No. | Coll. | Legend | Axis | Reference | S.G. | Weight | % |
|---|---|---|---|---|---|---|---|
| SG. 331 | BM | •STANCON•:•9INP5P / ICTORIAAVSTO CONOB | ↑↓ | *BMC* 133, 45; pl. 19, 10 | 1·4816 | 18·88 | 97·2 |
| SG. 332 | BM | VITONIA VATINSVI / ITORIA IVSTO CONOB | ↑↓ | **Pl. 19**  *BMC* 133, 47; pl. 19, 12 | 1·4634 | 18·63 | 95·5 |
| SG. 333 | BM | VATONV VATINSTI / ICTORIA AVSTOS CONOB | ↑↓ | *BMC* 133, 46; pl. 19, 11 | 1·4798 | 18·31 | 93·3 |
| SG. 334 | BM | ONAAVIC AAVINP / VIOTIVIVINBOTVI OONO | ↑↓ | *BMC* 133, 48; pl. 19, 13 | 1·4454 | 17·25 | 85·6 |
| SG. 335 | BM | DNIOITA NTINVI / VICTIRIAAVIVITI IOIIOA  Same dies as SG. 337 | ↑↑ | **Pl. 19**  *BMC* 133, 44; pl. 19, 9 | 1·4238 | 16·60 | 80·3 |

TABLE III (*cont.*)

| Analysis number and location of coin | Legend | | Reference | Weight in grammes | S.G. | % Au |
|---|---|---|---|---|---|---|
| SG. 336 PG | OINIO[R/////] SIIINTVI VIOITIVIOΛHVΛOTI IIOHO | ↑→ | Pl. 19 | 1·4974 | 17·13 | 84·6 |
| | This coin has been repaired and is not included on Fig. 3. It obviously belongs to group 6. | | | | | |
| SG. 337 PG | DNIOITΛ NTINVI VICTIRIΛΛVIVITI IOIIOΛ | ↑↑ | Pl. 19 Cf. *BMC* 133, 44 | 1·4516 | 16·70 | 81·1 |
| | Same dies as SG. 335. This coin has been repaired and is not included on Fig. 3. It obviously belongs to group 6. | | | | | |

Blundered legends. Possibly contemporary forgeries

| | | | | | | |
|---|---|---|---|---|---|---|
| SG. 338 BM | U••• •:•••••• VITIIOITIIMΛTIOVII OMOꓕ | ↑↓ | Pl. 19 *BMC* 153, 2; pl. 21, 2 | 1·3746 | 15·91 | 74·0 |
| SG. 339 BM | V-I·III TOꓒOꓒ VNIVIINIIVIIIVNIIVIIII | ↑↓ | *BMC* 153, 1; pl. 21, 1 | 1·2489 | 15·61 | 71·2 |
| | This coin is damaged and is not included on Fig. 3. | | | | | |
| SG. 340 BM | VINIII//////// IꓩΛIꓵV VOИOVIΛTOИIOΛꓕ | ↑↖ | Pl. 19 *BMC* 154, 4; pl. 21, 4 | 1·4624 | 15·46 | 69·8 |

# TABLE IV

*Class IV: Anonymous Pseudo-Imperial Coinage of Tuscany (See **Fig. 4**)*

| Analysis number and location of coin | Legend | Reference | Weight in grammes | S.G. | % Au |
|---|---|---|---|---|---|
| No symbol before face | | | | | |
| SG. 341 BM | ·ΛΙΙVΛ ·VΛOHI / VIIIOΛVIVΛOIIIVΛ | *BMC* 135, 13; pl. 19, 24 | 1·4256 | 17·54 | 87·8 |
| SG. 342 AM | ΙVΙΙCΙΛ· VIHOVΛ / ΙCΛIHΛVΛΛVOIVVIΛ | **Pl. 19** | 1·4708 | 17·26 | 85·6 |
| SG. 343 AM | ΙVHIV· VHOVI / VIIIOHVIVNOIIIVVI | **Pl. 19** | 1·4152 | 16·98 | 83·4 |
| SG. 344 BM | ΙVIIVΛ· VHOIV / VΠΙOLΙVΛHOLΙVVI | *BMC* 135, 14; pl. 19, 25 | 1·4266 | 16·87 | 82·5 |
| SG. 345 AM | IHᴙ· ·VᴙHI / VΠΙONΛVΛNONVN | **Pl. 19** | 1·4560 | 16·84 | 82·3 |
| SG. 346 PG | IIIV[N]V VIOHVI / VIIIOIIVIVIIIOIIIVII | **Pl. 19** | 1·4586 | 16·49 | 79·3 |
| SG. 347 Fitzwilliam Mus. | VΛOIV VHOΛV / VΠΙONΛVΛVHOIHVΛ | **Pl. 19** | 1·4352 | 16·42 / 16·46 | 78·7 / 79·0 |
| SG. 348 BM | IIIVHV VIOHVI / VIIIOHVIVHOIIIVVI | *BMC* 135, 12; pl. 19, 23 | 1·4013 | 16·39 | 78·4 |
| SG. 349 PG | ΛVIVO TIVIITΛ / VIIIOIIVΛVIIOIIIVIVI | **Pl. 19** | 1·4343 | 15·85 | 73·5 |
| SG. 350 BM | IIIV▬▬▬VZII / VIOIVVVIOIIIVI | **Pl. 19** | 1·3118 | 15·57 | 70·8 |

TABLE IV (cont.)

| Analysis number and location of coin | Legend | Reference | Weight in grammes | S.G. | % Au |
|---|---|---|---|---|---|
| **B before face** | | | | | |
| SG. 351 BM | IVIIV——•VIHVI ↑↙ VΠΙΟΗVΛΗΟΙΗVΠ | BMC 134, 3; pl. 19, 16 | 1·4941 | 17·18 | 85·0 |
| SG. 352 BM | IVHV—•IVOHVI ↑↖ VΠΙΟΗVΛΗΟVΗVΠ | BMC 134, 4; pl. 19, 17 | 1·4423 | 17·16 | 84·8 |
| SG. 353 BM | IVHV—•VHONV ↑↖ VΠΙΟΙΙVΛVΙΙΟΙΙΙVΙΙ | Pl. 19 | 1·4426 | 16·70 | 81·1 |
| SG. 354 PG | IVHV—•VHOVI ↑→ VΠΙΟΗVΛΗΟΤΗVΠ | Pl. 19 | 1·4630 | 16·65 | 80·7 |
| SG. 355 BM | IVIIV—•VUOVI ↑→ VΗΙΟΙΙVΛVΝΟΙΙΙVΝ | BMC 134, 1; pl. 19, 14 | 1·4404 | 16·50 | 79·4 |
| SG. 356 BM | IVHVΛ—•ΛVIHVII ↑↓ VΠΙΟΗVΛΗΟΙΗVΝ | Pl. 19 BMC 135, 5 | 1·4607 | 16·27 | 77·3 |
| SG. 357 PG | ΤΙΙΤ—•VI–ИΤ ↑→ VOIVVNOVII—I | Pl. 19 | 1·3265 | 15·11 | 66·3 |
| SG. 358 BM | IVIIV—•VIIOVI ↑↗ ΠΙ••ΟΠΙΛΠΙΟΙΙΙΠΝ | BMC 134, 2; pl. 19, 15 | 1·3738 | 14·76 | 62·6 |
| SG. 359 BM | VΛVI—•VΛVΛ ↑→ VΛΙΟVΛVΛVΙΟΛVV | Pl. 19 BMC 135, 7 | 1·2504 | 14·17 | 56·1 |
| SG. 360 BM | VΛV—•VIIΛV ↑↓ VIVOIΛIIVOΛVΛ | BMC 135, 6; pl. 19, 18 | 0·9050 | 13·52 | 48·0 |
| SG. 361 BM | VΛV—•VΛIV ↑↗ VVOVVVVVIOVVV | BMC 135, 8; pl. 19, 19 | 1·0636 | 12·91 | 40·0 |

**Ꝛ before face**

| SG. 362 | VI··II· VIIOVΛ | ↑↙ | **Pl. 19** | 1·3696 | 14·89 | 64·0 |
| BM | VIVOIVVIOIVIII | | BMC 135, 10; pl. 19, 21 | | | |

**⊀ before face**

| SG. 363 | VI⊢—⌐IVIVI | ↑↑ | BMC 135, 9; pl. 19, 20 | 1·1682 | 12·45 | 33·7 |
| BM | VIOVIVVIOVΛV | | | | | |

**⟨ before face**

| SG. 364 | ΛVΙΙΙΙΙ VNOVΛ | ↑↗ | **Pl. 19** | 1·2793 | 17·04 | 83·8 |
| BM | VIIIO[Ⅲ]VΛΛΠVN | | BMC 135, 11; pl. 19, 22 | | | |

## TABLE V

### Class V: So-called 'Quasi-Autonomous' Coinage of Tuscan Cities (See Fig. 5)

| Analysis number and location of coin | Legend | Reference | Weight in grammes | S.G. | % Au |
|---|---|---|---|---|---|
| **Monogram obverse** | | | | | |
| SG. 365 PG | [monogram] ↑↑ ΛΛΛΛΛΛΛΛΛΛ | Pl. 19 / Cf. Bernareggi 187, 200 | 1·2794 | 13·78 | 51·4 |
| SG. 366 BM | [monogram] ↑↙ ΛΛΛΛΛΛΛΛ | Pl. 19 / BMC 151, 4; pl. 20, 16 / This coin is damaged and is not included on **Fig. 5.** | 1·3056 | 13·58 | 48·8 |
| SG. 367 BM | [monogram] ↑→ VIVIVIVIVIVIVIVI / This coin is damaged and is not included on **Fig. 5.** | Pl. 19 / BMC 151, 3; pl. 20, 15 / Cf. Bernareggi 187, 201 | 1·2182 | 13·13 | 42·9 |
| **Star obverse. Mint of Lucca** | | | | | |
| SG. 368 BM | +FLAVIALVCA ↑↑ ·VIVIVIVIVIVIVIV | BMC 150, 1; pl. 20, 13 / Cf. Bernareggi 189, 204 | 1·3677 | 13·92 | 53·1 |
| SG. 369 AM | +FLAVIALVCA ↑↙ ·VIVIVIVIVIVIVIV | Pl. 19 / Cf. BMC 150, 1 / Cf. Bernareggi 189, 204 | 1·3686 | 12·92 | 40·1 |
| SG. 370 BM | +FLAVIALVCA ↑↙ *VIVIVIV*VIVIV / This coin has been repaired and is not included on **Fig. 5.** | Pl. 19 / Cf. Bernareggi 189, 206 | 1·3383 | 12·55 | 35·1 |
| **Star obverse. Uncertain mint** | | | | | |
| SG. 371 BM | +FLAVIVCLrV ↑↙ ·VIVIVIVIVIVIV | Pl. 19 / BMC 150, 2; pl. 20, 14 / Bernareggi 193, 215 | 1·3526 | 13·28 | 44·9 |

## TABLE VI

### Class VI: Regal Coinage of Lombardy and Tuscany Together (See Fig. 5)

| Analysis number and location of coin | Legend | Reference | Weight in grammes | S.G. | % Au |
|---|---|---|---|---|---|
| **Aistulf 749–56. Mint of Lucca** | | | | | |
| SG. 372 BM | +FLAVIALVCA / D⁻NAISTVLFREX ↑↗ | **Pl. 19** / *BMC* 148, 1; pl. 20, 9 / Cf. Bernareggi, 194, 219 | 1·1263 | 14·41 | 58·9 |
| SG. 373 PG | +FL·AVIA·LVCA / +D·VAIωTVL·F·RE ↑↓ | **Pl. 19** / Bernareggi 195, 224 | 1·1451 | 14·17 | 56·1 |
| **Desiderius 756–74. Mint of Lucca** | | | | | |
| SG. 374 BM | +FLAVIALVCA / +D·VDESIDERREX ↑↑ | *BMC* 149, 2; pl. 20, 11 / Bernareggi 196, 228 | 1·1105 | 14·24 | 57·0 |
| SG. 375 PG | +FL·AVIALVCA / D⁻NDESIDERREX ↑→ | **Pl. 19** / Cf. Bernareggi, 196, 230 | 1·0430 | 12·98 | 41·0 |
| SG. 376 BM | +FL·AVIAL·VCA / +DNDESIDER·R ↑↓ | *BMC* 149, 1; pl. 20, 10 / Bernareggi 196, 227 | 0·6873 | 12·58 | 35·5 |
| This coin is exceptionally light but does not appear to have been clipped. | | | | | |
| **Mint of Piacenza** | | | | | |
| SG. 377 BM | +FL·A·PLACENTIAG / +DNDESIDERIVSR· ↑↓ | **Pl. 19** / *BMC* 149, 3; pl. 20, 12 / Bernareggi 174, 172 | 1·0723 | 14·11 | 55·8 |
| SG. 378 BM | /////ILAIIAPLA////// / /////ESIDER·R//// | **Pl. 19** / Bernareggi 174, 172 *bis* | 0·5576 | 13·14 | 43·0 |
| This fragment has been repaired and is not included on **Fig. 5.** | | | | | |

TABLE VI (*cont.*)

| Analysis number and location of coin | Legend | Reference | Weight in grammes | S.G. | % Au |
|---|---|---|---|---|---|
| SG. 379 PG | Uncertain mint /////OVAT·ARI+////// ⇑ +DN©SI////// | **Pl. 19** Bernareggi 182, 198 | 0·5768 | 12·05 | 27·7 |

This coin is broken and is not included on **Fig. 5.**

## REFERENCES

1. M. J. Hughes and W. A. Oddy, 'A Reappraisal of the Specific Gravity Method for the Analysis of Gold Alloys', *Archaeometry* xii, 1 (1970), 1–11.

2. R. F. Coleman and A. Wilson, 'Activation Analysis of Merovingian Gold Coins', *Proceedings of the Royal Numismatic Society Symposium on the Analysis of Coins*, 1972.

3. A. A. Gordus, 'Neutron Activation of Coins and Coin Streaks', *Proceedings of the Royal Numismatic Society Symposium on the Analysis of Coins*, 1972.

4. S. C. Hawkes, J. M. Merrick, and D. M. Metcalf, 'X-Ray Fluorescent Analysis of some Dark-Age Coins and Jewellery', *Archaeometry* ix (1966), 98–138.

5. F. Jecklin, 'Der langobardisch-karolingische Münzfund bei Ilanz', *Mitteilungen der Bayerischen Numismatischen Gesellschaft* xxv, (1906–7), 28–79.

6. W. A. Oddy and M. J. Hughes, 'The Specific Gravity Method for the Analysis of Gold Coins', *Proceedings of the Royal Numismatic Society Symposium on the Analysis of Coins*, 1972.

7. W. A. Oddy, 'The Analysis of Gold Coins—A Comparison of Results obtained by Non-Destructive Methods', *Archaeometry* xiv. 1 (1972), 109–17.

8. W. A. Oddy and F. Schweizer, 'A Comparative Analysis of some Gold Coins', *Proceedings of the Royal Numismatic Society Symposium on the Analysis of Coins*, 1972.

9. E. Bernareggi, *Il sistema economico e la monetazione dei longobardi nell'Italia Superiore*, Milan, 1960.

10. E. Bernareggi, 'Le monete dei longobardi nell' Italia padana e nella Tuscia', *RIN* 1963, 35–142.

11. P. Grierson, Unpublished researches. I am very grateful to Professor Grierson for discussing his own work with me, and in particular for suggesting the final form of the classification used in this paper.

12. W. Wroth, *Catalogue of the Coins of the Vandals, Ostrogoths and Lombards in the British Museum*, London, 1911.

13. P. Grierson, *Catalogue of the Byzantine Coins in the Dumbarton Oaks Collection and in the Whittemore Collection*, Vol. II, Part I, Washington, 1968, 16–17.

One has to compare the coins with those of Sicily, since the products of Rome and Ravenna, whose pattern is much more likely to have been followed by the Lombard coinage, cannot be precisely identified. It will probably be shown eventually that the closer parallel is with one or both of these mints.

# A Neglected Scillonian Circulation of Wood's Halfpence

## MICHAEL DOLLEY

As is well known, a patent to strike copper halfpence and farthings for Ireland was granted to the Englishman William Wood in 1722, but was surrendered by him in August 1725 as a consequence of popular opposition to the new coins which had found its most devastating if not perhaps its most politically decisive expression in Jonathan Swift's *Drapier Letters* of 1724. In the event, very considerable quantities of the halfpence in particular were left on Wood's hands, and the English entrepreneur displayed considerable ingenuity and resource in attempting to foist them on the American colonies, a proceeding that could be thought the more reprehensible inasmuch as he had negotiated generous compensation in respect of the abandoned patent. To the best of the present writer's knowledge, however, there has never appeared in any numismatic work or journal a statement to the effect that the withdrawn Anglo-Irish coins were given a new lease of life, if not official or strictly legal currency, in an area that is still an integral part of the United Kingdom.[1] My colleague Dr. Nicholas Round, however, has been kind enough to draw my attention to a passage that occurs on p. 44 of Robert Heath's *A Natural and Historical Account of the Islands of Scilly etc.* (London, 1750) which has recently been the subject of a facsimile reprint under the title *The Isles of Scilly* (Newcastle upon Tyne, 1967). Heath had served as an officer in the Scillonian garrison in the 1740s, and his notes were being made within two decades of the importation into the islands of the offending specie. The critical passage runs as follows:

> The Coin is of the same Kind and Value here with the current Coin of *England*, except the *Irish* [*sic*] Half-pence, which are the only Change in the Islands for Silver, not intrinsic Value, but of smaller Size than the *English* half-pence, and are not current elsewhere. These Half-pence were first introduced by *Irish* Traders hither, (some of *Wood's* Agents, employ'd by their honest Proprietor.) At which Time, an Inhabitant or two, more avaricious than honest, favouring the Imposition, made a considerable Purchase of them by Weight, (some say at the Rate of about one third Currency) and so stocked the Islands.

[1] There is no reference to Scilly in such standard works as H. Davis, *The Drapier's Letters to the People of Ireland* (Oxford, 1935) and O. W. Ferguson, *Jonathan Swift and Ireland* (Urbana, 1962), nor in P. Nelson, *The Coinage of William Wood 1722–1733* (2nd edn., London, 1959).

The reference to the smaller size of the Wood's halfpence is well justified. The Anglo-Irish pieces in question were only four-fifths of the weight of their English counterparts. It is doubtless this conspicuous inferiority that explains their ultimate disappearance from the Scillonian scene. In a letter, the Honorary Secretary of the Isles of Scilly Museum Association, Mrs. R. MacLaran, has kindly informed the present writer that the Anglo-Irish coins in the museum's collections are limited to 'one George I halfpenny dated 1723' and 'two George III halfpennies dated 1805'. The letter goes on to say that 'the enquiries I have made do not show that many of these coins were found in Scilly and we assume that the one we have was probably lost by a seaman visiting the Islands'. Wood's halfpence, of course, never in fact achieved in Ireland the wide currency which would make plausible the implied casual occurrence in a mariner's change, and Heath's almost contemporary account of their systematic introduction into Scilly makes it far more likely that the specimen in the local museum is a lone survivor from the batch bought up by the enterprising merchants of the islands at a discount which must suggest that the transaction belongs no earlier than the summer of 1725. Wood, incidentally, had been under an obligation to redeem his Anglo-Irish pieces, and it is no obstacle to our acceptance of Heath's account that the specimen in the local museum should be dated 1723. Circulated pieces, and not just proofs, dated 1722 and even 1724 are not unknown, but the one really common date for the series is 1723, and coins with this last date would have predominated in the stocks of recalled halfpence which the unfortunate 'hardware dealer' was seeking to unload on new markets.[1] Another question, of course, is when the circulation of Wood's halfpence on Scilly came to an end, and there is the further problem of whether there was ever the formal demonetization that the apparent rarity of the pieces on Scilly today would seem to indicate. Research into these loose ends, however, is something best left to a Scillonian resident with time and opportunity to peruse the totality of the eighteenth-century archives as well as inspect the representation of English as well as Anglo-Irish coppers in all the local cabinets.

While on the subject of Heath's *Natural and Historical Account*, though, mention may also be made of a further passage which could be thought to be of numismatic interest inasmuch as it gives an account of a hoard which seems to have escaped the net of the Royal Numismatic Society's recent

[1] The National Museum of Ireland has 5 halfpence dated 1722, including 2 of the HIBERNIÆ patterns; 14 halfpence with the date 1723, including some proofs; and 3 halfpence of 1724 of which at least 1 is only doubtfully uncirculated. The position at the Ulster Museum is 6 halfpence dated 1722, again including 2 of the HIBERNIÆ patterns; 12 of the halfpence of 1723; and 2 of those of 1724. In the case of this collection it is particularly noticeable that it is only the 1723 halfpence which evidence circulation to any marked degree. We do well to remember, too, that public collections of their nature tend to give over-representation to the uncommon at the expense of the normal, and particularly when the condition of the bulk of the latter leaves so much to be desired.

bibliography of post-1500 coin-hoards from Great Britain and Ireland. The passage in question occurs on p. 38, and runs:

> In the year 1744, as a Mason was repairing an old House in this Island [i.e. Trescol], a Sum of King *Charles's* Half Crowns were found hid in the walls by a deceased Dweller; the Number of which appeared to be about five hundred. The Workman was taken into Custody by the Agent, who promised him a Share to discover the Number he had found, but he had Sense enough to keep the whole Prize to himself.

One cannot but be struck by the alleged size of the hoard, and it is also to be observed that the coins seem all to have been of the one denomination, the largest to have enjoyed general currency. There is, however, an obvious historical occasion for the treasure's concealment, one, too, which is entirely consonant both with its apparent magnitude and with its seemingly uniform composition. After the death of Charles I, Scilly remained a royalist outpost and naval base, and a major expedition would be needed under Admiral Blake in 1651 before the Commonwealth could winkle out the defenders. The principal royalist garrison was on St. Mary's, but significantly the attack on it was mounted through Tresco (or Trescaw) where there was an important outwork. It is reasonable to suppose that the coins found in 1744 had formed the whole or part of a royalist war-chest, and that they had been concealed in the walls of a private dwelling-house when it became clear that the position of the garrison had become hopeless. The construction of a new battery by the Commonwealth with the consequent stationing of a picket must effectively have prevented any clandestine royalist recovery of the specie, and with the deaths within the next decade of the officer or officers concerned the secret was safe. The fate of the coins after their discovery in 1744 is not reported, but the probability is that most if not all found their way to a jeweller's crucible, and it is perhaps idle to speculate on the likely proportion among them of the coins of the West Country mints which are so prized by collectors today.

# The 1780 Restrike Talers of Maria Theresia

## M. R. BROOME

[SEE PLATES 20-3]

THIS paper is concerned with the series of coins now known as Maria Theresia Talers. These silver pieces, some 40 mm. in diameter and bearing the date 1780, purport to be struck on the authority of Maria Theresia Valperga Amelia Christina, Archduchess of Austria, Queen of Hungary and Bohemia, and daughter, wife, and mother respectively of four emperors of the Holy Roman Empire. The reverse carries the double-headed Imperial Eagle displaying a quartered coat of arms with, in the fourth quarter, in most cases, the arms of Burgau, a Margravate near Augsburg which belonged to the Habsburghs until 1805. On the obverse, under the bust of Maria Theresia, appear the initials of the surnames of the mint-master and the mintwarden respectively of the mint of Günzburg then the chief town of Burgau. These coins are still being minted in Vienna, albeit as souvenirs, and their issue seems to have been almost continuous over the whole of the intervening 190 years.

The pedigree of the Maria Theresia taler can be traced back to the original Joachimstalers of the Counts of Schlick which were themselves just one of the series of silver guldiners first issued in 1486 by Archduke Sigismund of the Tyrol with a value equivalent to that of the gold gulden.

The earliest comprehensive description of the Maria Theresia taler was given by Peez and Raudnitz in 1898.[1] A more recent outline of the historical background has been given by Stride[2] and a description of the economic forces ensuring continuity, by Hans.[3] This present paper is an interim report on an attempt to assign the approximate date of issue and mint of origin to the different varieties which can be distinguished.

## The historical background

The reasons for the initial restriking of this coin of 1780 are given in an interesting paper by Carl von Ernst[4] who explains that Günzburg mint was

---

[1] C. Peez and J. Raudnitz, *Geschichte des Maria-Theresien-Thalers*, Vienna, 1898.

[2] H. G. Stride, 'The Maria Theresa Thaler', *NC* 1956, 339–43.

[3] J. Hans, *Maria-Theresien-Taler*, Leiden, 1961.

[4] C. v. Ernst, 'Die Münzbuchstaben S. F., F.S., T.S.–I.F. auf Thalern der Kaiserin Maria Theresia mit der Jahreszahl 1780', *NZ* 1896, 305–8.

opened in 1764 specifically to mint talers for the use of the Augsburg bankers in their financing of trade with the East. This export of 'Imperial dollars' had been steadily increasing for some years and those destined for Turkey were controlled by a monopoly as early as 1751.

The coinage of the Holy Roman Empire for the second half of the eighteenth century is complicated by the fact that, from 1745 to 1765 there were two parallel issues, one with Maria Theresia's name and bust, and the other with those of her husband Francis, estwhile Duke of Lorraine and now perforce Duke of Milan, and Holy Roman Emperor. When Francis died in 1765 and his son Joseph was elected in his stead, the dualling of the coinage continued, but was further complicated by the issue of a third set of coins bearing Francis's bust and name but with the constant date 1765.

Maria Theresia died in November 1780 and by then it had become apparent that talers bearing the bust of the empress were valued more highly in Arabia and the Yemen than those with the bust of the emperor. Early in 1781 one of the banking firms sent a consignment of bullion to Günzburg mint with the request that it be coined into Maria Theresia talers. The request was passed to Vienna and on 22 February 1781 the 'Hofkammer' gave permission for the use of the existing dies for this purpose until they wore out. By November 1783 when new supplies of bullion were brought in, these dies had become unusable and on 1 December new dies were authorized by Vienna.

The picture painted by Ernst is seemingly that of a continuing issue of Günzburg talers during the few years before and after 1780. The only Günzburg mint statistics available for this period relate to 1765 when 2,512,905 talers were struck and to 1785 when the figure was 856,257[1] but an examination of the available evidence helps to establish more clearly the origins of the ubiquitous restrike.

An assessment of the frequency of occurrence today of the coins dated prior to 1780 provides an interesting comparison. Four main types of taler were struck at Günzburg during the first seventeen or so years of activity, viz. an 'armoured' bust, a heavily veiled bust, a lightly veiled bust, and a 'Convention taler' bearing the arms of Burgau but no bust. A very rough guide to the scarcity of each date of these types is given in Table I using Davenport's[2] reference numbers. Some idea of the numbers of coins involved can be obtained from Table II where the mintage figures for Vienna talers for the period 1753–65 are compared with their relative scarcity on the same basis.

Whilst it would be dangerous to read too much into such comparisons, it might be said that a 'C' assessment represents over a million specimens, an 'S' assessment between half a million and three-quarters of a million, and an 'R' would indicate under half a million talers of that date.

[1] Hans, op. cit. 16.
[2] J. S. Davenport, *European Crowns 1700–1800*, Galesburg, 1961.

## TABLE I

### *Günzburg Talers*

| Davenport Nos. | D1147 | D1148 | D1149 | D1150 |
|---|---|---|---|---|
| Date on coin | | | | |
| 1764 | R | — | — | — |
| 65 | VC | — | R | — |
| 66 | — | C | — | — |
| 67 | — | C | R | — |
| 68 | — | — | S | — |
| 69 | — | — | R | — |
| 70 | — | — | S | — |
| 71 | — | — | R | — |
| 72 | — | — | S | — |
| 73 | — | — | — | R |
| 74 | — | — | — | S |
| 75 | — | — | — | VR |
| 76 | — | — | — | VR |
| 77 | — | — | — | S |
| 78 | — | — | — | — |
| 79 | — | — | — | — |
| 80 | — | — | — | VC |

D1147 = Armoured Bust
D1148 = Convention Taler
D1149 = Heavily veiled bust
D1150 = Lightly veiled bust

VC = Very Common
C = Common
S = Scarce
R = Rare
VR = Very Rare
— = Not Known

## TABLE II

### Vienna Talers

| Date | Mintage ex Hans (1) | Relative Scarcity (2) |
|------|---------------------|------------------------|
| 1753 | 155824 | R |
| 54 | 272611 | R |
| 55 | 363963 | R |
| 56 | 605824 | S |
| 57 | 558572 | S |
| 58 | 382057 | S |
| 59 | 320920 | VR |
| 60 | 528082 | R |
| 61 | 766473 | R |
| 62 | 503771 | S |
| 63 | 401244 | R |
| 64 | ? | S |
| 65 | 1,488115 | C |

1. It is likely that these figures represent the coins struck during a particular accounting period. For 1785 to 1789 this ran from 1 November to 31 October.
2. The relative scarcity of pieces offered for sale during 1968–70.

For Günzburg then, the period of 1768–74 might average half a million pieces each year, whereas for the period 1775–9 there was considerably less. More specifically, there seems to have been little production in 1775 and 1776 (both these coins are very rare indeed), some activity in 1777, and none at all in 1778 and 1779. Overdates in this series are unusual and no doubt dies were used at later dates than that shown on the die, but it seems clear that the demand for talers from this mint between 1775 and 1779 was very small. Furthermore, if the dies existing in February 1781 (and dated 1780) could be used for a further two and a half years, they also could have had very little use in 1780, and it would appear that genuine Günzburg 1780 talers, struck in that year, represent a minute fraction of the coins bearing that date.

*Major varieties*

Leaving for a moment the pre-1780 coins, a first look at the 1780-dated restrikes shows that there are two main varieties in circulation, which by reference to Davenport's *European Crowns 1700–1800*[1] can be referred to as D1150 and D1151, the present-day strikings being of the latter type. Although the types are similar, the main variation occurs on the obverse where two different busts are found, easily separable by the presence (D1151) or absence (D1150) of pearls surrounding the shoulder brooch. It is interesting to note in passing that Davenport does not list the date 1780 under D1150 although these coins are fairly common; an indication perhaps of the scant attention given to any such coin bearing that date. The 'plain brooch' type is also found with minor variations on talers bearing the mint officials' initials for Vienna (1773–9), Hall (1772–6), and Günzburg (1773–7) and for Karlsburg (where restrikes are recorded in 1785), dated 1780 only. It is also to be seen on the very rare 1777 scudo of Milan which might possibly be considered to be a pattern.

It is significant that the first three mints mentioned above are those listed by Miller zu Aichholz[2] as producing talers for export. Ernst reports in another paper[3] that the issue of coins with the heavily veiled bust instigated in 1765 with the death of Francis 1, was replaced by a 'lightly veiled' design by an Order dated 5 May 1770. Pressure had been brought to bear by the Augsburg bankers who found that the Turks would not easily accept the coins with the 'widow's veil,' and evidence of this pressure can be seen in the large numbers of the original Günzburg type bearing an 'armoured' bust and dated 1765 which were produced in 1767 some two years *after* the first heavily veiled issue from this mint.

Heavily veiled coins dated 1771 and 1772 are not rare and unless the Order of 1770 was ignored by the mint officials it must be assumed that they were using up stocks of existing dies first. It might then be argued that the dies were issued undated and the correct date added when a particular die was about to be used. A contrary indication comes from the fact that no die duplicates with differing dates have yet been noted. In fact there seem to be considerable variations from one year to the next and, for one of the scarcer issues, that of Vienna dated 1772, there are at least three quite different busts in use which are not found elsewhere or with other dates.

The earliest coin with the new design found so far, is a taler of Hall mint dated 1772 (and apparently a rare piece) and there seems little doubt that the 'plain brooch' issues from these three mints were regular issues and were

---

[1] Davenport, op. cit. 60.
[2] V. von Miller zu Aichholz, A. Loehr, and E. Holzmair, *Österreichische Münzprägungen 1519–1938* 282.
[3] C. v. Ernst, 'Münzzeichen und Münzmeisterbuchstaben auf österreichischen Münzen', *NZ* 1894, 492.

struck at a date close to that given on the coins. The change of mint officials in 1774 is reflected in the initials they bear and the style is consistent.

Examination of similar coins dated 1780 shows no evidence of lack of continuity with issues of earlier dates and it seems reasonable to suppose that this type represents the 'original' Maria Theresia Taler.

The 'pearly brooch' type of D1151 first appears on a very rare taler of Prague mint dated 1773. The use of a pearled or jewelled brooch, however, had been extensive and all issues between 1741 and 1765 bore one prominently in the design. With the issue of the 'widow's veil' type in 1765 it was dropped, but significantly it reappeared on the coins of Vienna two years later when the shoulder drapery was also rearranged to resemble more closely the pre-1765 issues.

It has been reported from the Yemen that until recently coins were rejected by the Arabs of the interior if the brooch could not be felt with the thumb. If this test were applied in 1765 it is possible that the 1767 Vienna issues were an unsuccessful attempt to meet it.

The Prague talers of 1773/5 are all scarce and no evidence has yet been found that they were ever exported in quantity. The obverse type does not seem to have been adopted by any other mint before 1780 but it apparently provided the pattern for most of the succeeding restrikes. It is possible that this type was deliberately used to separate restrikes from earlier issues when the authorities became aware that demand was not diminishing.

The vast majority of restrike talers are copies of coins from the Günzburg mint in that they show the arms of Burgau in the fourth quarter of the simplified imperial arms on the reverse and bear, under the bust on the obverse, the initials S.F. for the Günzburg mint officials Tobias Schöbl and Josef Faby. There are a number of varieties, however, with initials on the reverse and no initials (or, in one case, a B) on the obverse. While some of these show a pearled brooch and others do not, they all have the arms of Upper Austria in the fourth quarter, unlike the normal pre-1780 Günzburg issues, and one might assume that the dies were cut in Vienna and then issued to the various mints with the appropriate initials added.

The reverse of the Günzburg type coins can be divided into two main types parallel with the obverse types. Here the 'recognition symbol' is the form of the second letter in the abbreviation AUST. Coins of type D1150 use U and coins of type D1151 use V. A check of the smaller imperial coinage of the time shows that the U–V transition began in 1780 and was complete by 1790 except in the Austrian Netherlands and Milan. A useful 'mule' is known of a 1780 taler with obverse D1150 and reverse D1151, pointing to a close connection in time between the introduction of the pearled brooch and the use of V in place of U. It is perhaps worth noting at this point that the illustration set against D1151 by Davenport is that of a twentieth-century restrike.

One of the most interesting details of this series, and one of the least documented, is the edge inscription and the variety of decorative arabesques which separate the words *Justitia et Clementia*. Maria Theresia had chosen as her official motto the two principles on which she based the whole of her life, and these words appear on most of taler and half-taler size coins of her reign. If one compares the edge inscription of coins struck before 1780 two factors soon emerge. The earlier coins have the letters wider apart within each word, and for the later issues at least, each mint uses a different symbol to separate the words, although often combined with stars or rosettes. From an examination of the edge inscription only, it then becomes possible to allocate coins to their mint of issue and to place them approximately in chronological order (**Fig. 1**).

One interesting result of such an exercise is that the 'Convention' talers of Günzburg fall into two quite separate groups; one with the word IVSTITIA occupying some 30 mm and another at about half this length. According to Miller zu Aichholz[1] these talers were restruck in 1792 to pay the army and the second group might well consist of these restrikes.

If the edge markings of 1780 Günzburg talers are compared, two new groups appear, one with typically Günzburg arabesques and the other equally typically from Vienna and very similar to those used today. The first group, however, includes coins with both plain and 'pearly' brooches and the assumption could be made that all this group were struck at Günzburg before it closed in 1805. These coins are scarce but not rare and this would be in agreement with the mintage of 15 million pieces for Günzburg between 1785 and 1803 given by Hans.[2]

More precise dating of this series is possible with the aid of two rare varieties, listed by Davenport as D1151C and D1151D. According to Ernst[3] in the last quarter of 1793, talers were struck at Günzburg with dies carrying the letters F.S. under the bust instead of S.F. This change arose as a result of the death of Tobias Schöbl in April 1789. Josef Faby became mint-master and the cashier Franz Stehr was promoted to mint-warden. When the next set of dies became needed, the Günzburg officials apparently decided to change the initials without approaching Vienna. Imperial approval, however, was not forthcoming and most of the coins were melted. A specimen exists in the National Collection in Vienna and this provides a useful key to the dating of the early part of this series as it is, presumably, typical of the Günzburg issues of the time. The coin carries the 'pearled' brooch on the obverse and has a V in 'Aust' on the reverse. The edge markings, however, are typically Günzburg in style and on the basis of this coin one must assume that the U–V shift and the change to the 'pearled' brooch both took place in 1793 or earlier.

---

[1] Miller zu Aichholz, op. cit.
[2] Hans, op. cit.                        [3] Ernst, op. cit., *NZ* 1896, 307.

# EDGE ARABESQUES.
## 1742 – 1778.

  Vienna 1742

 Kremnitz 1743

  Vienna 1755

  Vienna 1778

  Hall 1774

 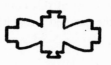 Günzburg 1771

FIG. 1.

The second variety which provides a checkpoint in time is D1151D. This coin has no initials on the obverse and has the arms of Upper Austria in the fourth quarter of the reverse with T.S.–I.F. at the sides of the eagle's tail. Ernst[1] quotes correspondence between Vienna mint and Günzburg mint indicating that six pairs of dies of this type were issued in the second half of 1797. The coins themselves are quite rare but two distinct varieties exist, plain brooch and pearled brooch. There are marked differences in style but the later type has the same key points as D1151C. It is extremely interesting to note that D1151C and D1151D have almost identical edge arabesques [Pl. 22, E 2 and E 1] in spite of the Upper Austria arms in the fourth quarter of D1151D. It would appear then that either Vienna was using similar arabesques to Günzburg at the time, or more likely, that specifically Günzburg collars were used with the nominally Vienna dies for this issue.

Support for the hypothesis of specific arabesques for each mint comes from the 1780 talers of Kremnitz (D1134) where over a million were reputed to have been struck between 1781 and 1786, and Karlsburg (D1146) with half a million between 1785 and 1803. The Kremnitz coins are extremely rare and it is possible that the mintage figures include the 1780 'Madonna-talers'. The arabesques do not show either the Günzburg or the Vienna symbols but are quite consistent with those used at Kremnitz since 1765. The Karlsburg coins, on the other hand, are relatively common and show two major varieties and several minor ones, consistent perhaps with a period of issue of eighteen years, but unlikely with a mintage of only half a million pieces. The edge arabesques again include a symbol used only at this mint and exclude the symbols of all other mints.

An interesting comment on these coins is provided by Forrer[2] who quotes the Vienna Mint Catalogue as stating that Karl Wurschbauer, Engraver at Karlsburg from 1805 to 1841, was reprimanded in 1814 for neglect in the execution of dies for the 'Levant talers'. Chief engraver Harnisch complained that the dies from Karlsburg are the worst of all the mints. One might assume therefore that Karlsburg dies were engraved at Karlsburg and that 'Levant talers' were still being struck there, and at least two other mints in 1814. If the figures quoted by Hans[3] for 1785 are correct, Karl Wurschbauer could not have engraved the original Karlsburg dies as his apprenticeship did not begin until 1793.

An interesting piece is the rare taler bearing the initials of the Prague mint officials (D1140) which, according to Hans[4] was issued between 1836 and 1842 to a total of nearly a quarter of a million pieces. Two varieties are listed by Davenport having initials on the reverse of either EvS–I.K. or P.S.–I.K., both types having the arms of Upper Austria in the fourth quarter unlike the earlier issues from Prague. The mint-master from 1755 to 1784 was Paul

---

[1] Ibid.
[2] L. S. Forrer, *Biographical Dictionary of Medallists* vi, 562–4.
[3] Hans, op. cit.
[4] Ibid. 17.

Erdmann von Schwingerschuh and coins from 1766 to 1780 are found with the abbreviation EvS or sometime VS. The P.S. variety illustrated by Davenport presumably refers to the same man but it seems possible that this abbreviation was chosen for the 1836–42 restrikes as being more in keeping with the style of other mints then in use.

Mint statistics for the crucial period 1767–84 are mostly unavailable and the Prague mint was closed during the period 1784–95 presumably due to a lack of demand for its services, but a possible explanation of the EvS variety could be that this was struck during von Schwingerschuh's period of office or shortly after. An examination of the style and edge reading of this very rare variety would support or demolish this hypothesis but so far this has not been possible.

The same restraints have prevented the attribution of the coin listed by Davenport as D1151E which has on the reverse the initials P.S.–I.F. Davenport lists this under Günzburg presumably as a variety of T.S.–I.F. but it could also be a variety of the Prague coin P.S.–I.K. mentioned above, in which case its style should be that of the 1840s rather than the 1800s. Herinek,[1] however, does not mention this variety, and the National Collection in Vienna does not have a specimen.

*Tentative classification*

A comparison of available specimens, ranging from coins bearing dates prior to 1780, to the current productions of Vienna mint, enables a number of groupings to be made, both for the obverses and for the reverses.

Although the two main types of bust seem at first sight to provide a primary division, it soon becomes obvious that this would cut across many other similarities. A more useful division can be based on the treatment of the fourth quarter of the reverse arms, and therefore all coins showing the arms of Upper Austria have been called class I, and those with the arms of Burgau, class II. Talers are also known with other arms in the fourth quarter but none so far are dated 1780.

There are five major varieties of obverse die to be found used for class I coins [Pl. 20] and when these are compared with other Habsburgh issues of the period 1775–1850, a clear development of style is apparent. Obverse I is very similar to the Günzburg talers of 1774–7 with heavy irregular lettering and a characteristic treatment of the truncation. Obverse 2 seems of finer engraving but has clear affinities with the Vienna talers of 1774–9. Obverses 3 and 4 both have pearls around the shoulder brooch and use a new and heavier bust. Obverse 5, although modelled on 4, has a different touch and some of its varieties are very similar to the current issues.

The reverse dies of class I [Pl. 21] all show initials of mint officials, and if they are separated according to these initials the groups correspond to the

---

[1] Ludwig Herinek, *Österreichische Münzprägungen von 1740–1969*, Vienna, 1960.

obverse varieties just mentioned. If an attempt is made to order the reverses into a stylistic progression, although one is discernible, it does not coincide with that indicated by the obverse side.

It is likely that the design and spacing of the edge arabesques might help to clarify the sequence, but many of these coins are rare and have not been available for detailed examination. The table at the end of this paper therefore lists the varieties but makes no pretence that the order shown is necessarily chronological.

Considering now the coins with the Burgau arms, which have been designated as class II [**Pls. 22–23**], both obverse and reverse designs can be separated into several fairly clear varieties. Obverse 6 is similar in style to the pre-1780 issues from Günzburg and is likely to be the earliest of the class. Apart from the initials under the bust, it is also very close to obverse 1 thus tending to show that that die also is early in the series. Obverse 10 is very similar to obverse 5 and to the issues of the present day but obverses 7, 8, and 9 have a style not found amongst class I coins.

The evidence regarding obverse 7 quoted by Ernst[1] seems clear that these dies showing F.S. under the bust were made at Günzburg in 1793 using the 'Punzen und Matrizen' sent from Vienna, and presumably on the authority of Josef Faby who was then the senior mint official there. These coins are very rare as they were mostly melted down at the mint, but the obverse design seems to have guided the engraver of obverse 8. If so this could be an indication that coins of the latter type could be dated 1794–1805. Support for this dating is provided by Ede[2] who illustrates an example of a current taler in a plate published on 1 September 1808. One pearl is missing from both diadem and brooch but the drapery is quite clearly copied from a coin of obverse 8. Several of the coins in this book show dates of the first six or seven years of the nineteenth century so that publication must have followed shortly after the engraving.

An enigma which has puzzled writers on the subject for the last century is the coin listed as type 15 (obverse 9). The style of this coin is completely at variance with all other restrike talers and indeed with all other Habsburgh issues, yet the underlying design is very similar to obverse 8. The resemblance is even more acute on the reverse. So far no very firm suggestion has been put forward for the interpretation of the letters ST, found, as an obvious addition to the design, above the normal initials S.F. under the bust. Ernst[3] very tentatively mentioned Milan as a possible mint but no coins of comparable style are apparent from this mint. Schlickeysen[4] lists a number of German engravers of the period 1780–1820 who are known to have used these initials.

[1] Ernst, op. cit., p. 221, n. 4, above.
[2] James Ede, *A Complete View of the Gold and Silver Coins of All Nations*, London, 1808.
[3] Ernst, op. cit., *NZ* 1896, 308.
[4] F. W. A. Schlickeysen, '*Erklaerung der Abkuerzungen auf Muenzen der neueren Zeit*, Berlin, 1896.

German copies of Austrian talers would indeed have been a possibility, but so far there is no proof that this theory is more valid than any other.

The six reverses of class II [Pl. 23] are in far better agreement with their obverses than those of class I. Reverse J shows the spelling AUST and is only found associated with obverse 6. It has many points of similarity with pre-1780 Günzburg coins, particularly in the treatment of the nimbi to the eagle's heads and of the tapes descending from the Habsburgh crown.

Reverse K seems to be a transition between J and L with the latter progressing to reverse M with its characteristically narrow digits in the date. An illustration given by Ambrosoli[1] in a publication dated 1891 shows a coin with obverse 8 and reverse M, presumably as an example of a typical taler of the period. Coins of this type are not rare even now and must have been produced in considerable quantities. Reverses L and M show one feature not to be found on class I coins and that is the arrangement of the feathers in the eagle's tail in two rows with an upper row of five feathers.

Reverse N has the same feature although the coarse flat engraving is out of character with the whole sequence. The date and Burgundian cross on this reverse are also much smaller than the remainder of the legend.

Reverse O is the design used for all the more recent coins and seems to have been in use for over 100 years. A specimen in the British Museum collection carries a ticket noting that it was from Vienna mint and produced in 1867–8.

One very definite division of the class II issues is provided by the arabesques on the edge. All coins so far found of obverses 6–9 and reverses J–N use arabesques of type $b$ and $c$ (or derivatives thereof) together with a rosette of 4, 5, or 6 petals. All coins with obverse 10 and reverse O, on the other hand, have arabesques type $a$ and $d$ together with a rosette of eight petals and one or more pellets [Pl. 22, E 3]. An examination of talers from Günzburg mint and dated 1765–77 showed that each one carried arabesques of types $b$ and $c$ whereas coins of a similar period from Vienna mint carried very obvious predecessors of types $a$ and $d$. (Similar arabesques are also found on issues from Vienna in the name of Joseph II although the system was changed in 1790 when Leopold II came to the throne). The style of these two subgroups is quite different indicating a separation not apparent in the continuity of class I.

## Nineteenth-century talers

During the period 1820 to 1866 talers were struck at Vienna, Milan, and Venice at an annual rate varying from under 100,000 in 1846 to 4,000,000 in 1864 when the American Civil War cut the supply of American cotton to Europe. So far no progress has been made in separating the issues of these

---

[1] Solone Ambrosoli, *Numismatica* (Milan, 1891), 161.

three mints, possibly because the dies were all made in Vienna. In 1787, for example, Miller zu Aichholz[1] records that Vienna dies were issued to the Milan mint. Neither Venice nor Milan had previously struck coins for Austria bearing the initials of their own mint officials so there was no precedent for introducing a new variety of taler.

Many of the coins bearing the arms of Upper Austria in the fourth quarter of the reverse and the initials I.C.–F.A. for Johan Aug v Cronberg and Franz Aicherau, at the sides (D1117) seem to be of this period. They are met with quite frequently and according to Hans[2] were issued until 1856, although Ernst[3] suggests 1823. In style they are closer to the modern restrikes than to the coins discussed so far. One very clear characteristic is the shape of the saltire or Burgundian cross which appears after the date. This mark, originally introduced on Austrian coins in 1751 to show that they complied with the standards of the Austro-Bavarian Monetary Convention, takes the shape of a flattened cross on pre-1780 coins, i.e. the left-hand angle between the arms is less than a right angle. With the later D1117 issues, however, this angle has become more than a right angle and the whole cross has become tall and thin, similar to the shape now in use. For the regular Austrian issues this type of cross first appears on talers with the accession of Leopold II, in 1790, the change coinciding with the termination of the use of specific edge arabesques for each mint (**Fig. 2**).

According to Hans[4] although some 5 million talers were struck in Vienna between 1785 and 1790, none at all were struck from 1792 to 1796 (figures for 1791 are missing) and only just over half a million for the period 1797–1803. It seems possible, therefore, that the later D1117 type represents the coins struck after the French Revolution and after Günzburg mint had closed down.

One mystery at the moment is the reason for the reintroduction of coins bearing the arms of Burgau, presumably at a time when this area was part of Bavaria. Possibly they were originally the issues of Milan and Venice only, these mints providing over half the total output of some 30 million pieces during 1820–66. Ernst[5] considers that all strikings after 1823 were of the Burgau type, but gives no evidence to support his opinion.

In 1857 Austria changed the basis of her currency to comply with the standards of the German Currency Union. Venice Mint was lost in 1866 and Milan in 1859. It may therefore have seemed apposite about 1860 to suspend production of the traditional Vienna-type coins and to concentrate all work on the Günzburg type. No doubt research into documents of the period would establish the truth or otherwise of this supposition. The evidence

---

[1] Miller zu Aichholz, op. cit.     [2] Hans, op. cit. 12.
[3] C. Ernst, 'Der Levantinerthaler', *NZ* 1872, 271–95.
[4] Hans, op. cit.
[5] Ernst, op. cit., p. 221, n. 4, above.

# SALTIRES.

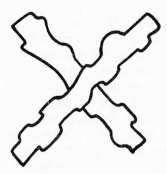

Vienna 1778

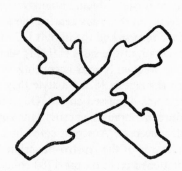

Günzburg ca 1805

Vienna ca 1830

Vienna ca 1900

Vienna 1960

Brussels

London

Paris

Fig. 2.

provided by the coins is limited to the fact that the class I Vienna productions seem to provide a fairly continuous series from c. 1773 whereas the class II coins fall into two sharply separated stylistic groups.

*Nineteenth-century countermarked coins*

From 1867 until 1934 it would appear that coins were struck nearly every year at the Vienna mint and, although there are very few clues available from which to date particular specimens, a little help is provided by counter-marked coins.

The export of talers to the Near East was well under way by the time the Günzburg mint began to operate in 1764 and counter-marks on pre-1780 coins are known for Java, Soumenep,[1] and Mozambique. For post-1780 coins Folgosa[2] quotes documents for Mozambique showing that, between 5 and 18 January 1889 a countermark consisting of a crown over P.M. was applied to the majority of the silver coins to be found on the island and that the punch was destroyed the following day. On the assumption that one punch only was used, he estimated that between 120,000 and 160,000 coins were marked of which some 40 per cent were Maria Theresia talers.

Countermarked coins eventually circulated at a premium of 60 per cent over normal coins and contemporary forged countermarks exist, but presumably most coins thus marked were struck prior to 1900.

Talers are also found countermarked P.M. with no crown and although Folgosa[3] discusses these coins he is less precise on their origin and dating. It seems likely, however, that they are of the same general period of the last decade or so of the nineteenth century and Funch-Rasmussen[4] suggests dates of 1889/92.

Countermarking seems to have been used fairly frequently in the Portuguese colonies, for talers and other coins are found with a (Portuguese) crown, reputedly for the Azores; a crown over G.P. and a crown over L.M. (Lorenquo Marques?).[5] There is also a monogram MR which Folgosa[6] dates to May 1767.

A full discussion of these countermarks is beyond the scope of this paper, but if those attributed to Mozambique are accepted as late nineteenth century, a guide is provided to the latest date of issue of the talers themselves. Most of them are of the general type 16 (*obv.* 10, *rev.* O) although a few are earlier.

An indication of the original date of this type is provided by the occasion of the British invasion of Abyssinia in 1867/8 when, to provide for local

[1] E. Netscher and J. A. van den Chijs, *De munten van nederlandisch Indië* (Batavia, 1863), 158.

[2] J. M. Folgosa, *As moedas da África oriental portuguesa: Mozambique* (Oporto, 1956), 36.

[3] Folgosa, op. cit. 40.

[4] C. F(unch)-R(asmussen), 'Marie-Theresia-Thaleren', *NNUM* 1959, 130.

[5] J. S. Davenport, *The Dollars of Africa, Asia, and Oceania* (Galesburg, 1969), 191.

[6] Folgosa, op. cit. 14.

purchases the British Government ordered a large number of talers from Vienna. The B.M. collection contains a specimen from the Parkes Weber collection which has a ticket noting that it was struck on this occasion. Interestingly, Holzmair[1] mentions that these coins had to be obtained through bullion merchants in Vienna and Trieste.

If the coins of the little group which has been tentatively assigned to the late nineteenth century are compared, they are found to show certain characteristics in common, which are not seen on earlier issues. The most obvious is the presence of an irregular circumferential line, running generally through the base of the legend, and appearing on both faces of the coin. Hans[2] describes this as a die flaw caused by striking the blanks with no edge collar. The line certainly shows in relief on the coin but is never very pronounced. Its origin is puzzling and may be more complex than Hans indicates, but its existence on a coin seems to indicate a product of the late nineteenth or early twentieth century.

*Twentieth-century issues*

The issues of the twentieth century began by being remarkably consistent. Where a piece can be dated, as, for example, the striking in gold in the British Museum collection made for presentation to the Emperor of Abyssinia in 1926, little variation can be found from earlier issues. In 1935, however, a new development appeared. Although demand had virtually vanished during the preceding few years, the coins were still the only acceptable currency in certain parts of the world including Abyssinia. When Italian preparations began for the invasion of this country it became apparent that the control of production was an important economic weapon. An agreement was therefore negotiated with the Austrian Government on 9 July 1935[3] whereby a pair of dies and a set of collars were handed over to the Italian mint of Milan. Interestingly, Klein[4] quotes at third hand the Vienna Ministry of Finance to say that a contract had once been concluded with an English company to mint Maria Theresia talers under its own authority. There was, therefore, a precedent for striking the coins outside Austria. No facts have so far been uncovered to disclose which company was involved or whether any coins were actually struck abroad before 1935.

The mint of Milan had been closed since the end of the nineteenth century when the authority to mint coins was transferred to Rome. This authority was now invoked and 19,445,000 talers[5] were produced there between 1935 and 1939. One of the provisos of the agreement was that Vienna should not

[1] Eduard Holzmair, 'Der Levantinertaler', *CINR* 1961, ii.      [2] Hans, op. cit.
[3] J. Abseher, 'Ablauf der Vereinbarung zwischen Österreich und Italien betreffend das Prägerecht für Maria-Theresien-Talern', *Mitteilungen der Öst. Num. Gesellschaft*, Bd. xii, 2, ii.
[4] Friedrich Klein, 'Der Maria-Theresien-Taler und seine internationalen Schicksale', *MÖNG* (June 1947), 33–8.      [5] Hans, op. cit. 19.

strike more than 10,000 pieces each year. Other countries needing supplies had perforce to obtain them from Italy and in consequence of pressure from the bullion brokers,[1] the mints of London, Paris, and Brussels prepared their own dies and struck several million pieces each in the period 1935–41.

It is interesting to examine the detailed comparison made at the Royal Mint, between their own strikings and the issues of Rome and Brussels. From these notes and from the examination of specimens preserved in other mints it has been possible to separate some varieties and to attribute them to their mint of origin. Apart from those mentioned already, three other mints are known to have struck talers, namely Utrecht,[2] Bombay, and Birmingham. Other mints alleged to have been involved at one period or another, include Antwerp,[3] Florence,[4] Leningrad,[5] and Marseilles,[6] but so far little evidence has been forthcoming.

*British strikings*

The London issues began according to Tilger[7] at the end of 1936 and Stride[8] notes that 8¾ million had been issued up to the beginning of the Second World War. The terms of the contract required that the necessary bullion be supplied to the mint by the purchasers who then paid the agreed charges for coining, a reversion to the traditional role of the mint of a 'worker in other people's metals'. It would appear that the dies were engraved to produce a close similarity to the Austrian coins but not an identical copy, a feat which was no doubt within the engraver's power. The style of the London coins is more regular and balanced, particularly the lettering, and one of the central tail feathers on the reverse is missing. An illustration of a 'London' taler will be found on Plate A of the Royal Mint report of 1961. An interesting specimen in the British Museum collection ticketed as Royal Mint 1936, shows at the top of the reverse what appears to be an incipient circumferential die flaw, a feature notably absent from the normal British strikings but common on early coins from Vienna [**Pl. 23**].

By 1940 the wartime blockade of England made it expedient to reserve an alternative source, and matrices and dies were sent to Bombay where supplies of silver could be better ensured.[9] Some 18 million pieces were struck there in 1940 and 1941, but demand then slackened off and at the end of 1941 Bombay

---

[1] *Annual Report of the Deputy Master and Comptroller of the Royal Mint (1937)*, 78.

[2] Hans, op. cit. 15 n.

[3] Peez und Raudnitz, op. cit. 72.

[4] Antonio Alessandrini, 'Florence Struck Maria Theresia talers in 1814', *World Coins* (August 1969).

[5] Robert H. Behrens, 'Maria Theresia's Invisible Empire Survives with Coins Tradition', *World Coins* (August 1969), 824 ff.

[6] E. Zay, *Histoire monétaire des colonies françaises* (Paris, 1892), 242.

[7] G. Tilger, 'The Maria Theresa Thaler' (unpublished (?) paper dated 17 December 1938).

[8] Stride, op. cit. 342.

[9] *Annual Reports of the Deputy Master and Comptroller of the Royal Mint 1939–1944*, 28.

still had nearly 4 million pieces in stock. Assay reports from the Royal Mint comment that the metal from these coins has a slight gold content, consistent with the use of Indian rupee silver.

An early specimen of the Bombay strikings exists in the Royal Mint which has a weakly struck 'M' on the obverse and a peculiar 'S' in the mint officials' initials. Only one other specimen has so far been found showing these variations and it is possible that the 'error' was rectified.

The coining of 30 million talers in London and Bombay satisfied demand until 1949 when an order for one million pieces apparently found the Royal Mint too busy and half the order was sub-contracted to The Mint (Birmingham) Ltd.[1] Again silver was supplied by the purchaser and some was returned when the last few pieces of the order were cancelled. The dies for the Bimingham issue seem to have been supplied by the Royal Mint and the record specimen at Birmingham is virtually indistinguishable from the contemporary London issues. In 1953, however, when a similar situation occurred, Birmingham apparently cut their own dies, as the record specimen shows several points not found in the London issues. The most obvious ones are the length of the word IVSTITIA and the use of three central tail feathers on the reverse.

This particular spate of activity produced some 6 million pieces which satisfied the market and the total had risen only another million by the time the taler treaty was rescinded in 1960. The following year Austria regained, by consent, the sole right to strike these interesting relics of her past.

Table III collects together the recorded mintage figures, mainly from Royal Mint Reports, for the mints of London, Bombay, and Birmingham.

*European strikings outside Austria*

Although it is clear that a set of Vienna dies was in fact sent to Rome it would appear that new dies were engraved there as specimens from this mint show many differences of detail. The two most obvious are the size of the coin, which is a good millimetre less in diameter than normal, and the rough condition of the edge markings. On close inspection it seems likely that the coins were blanched after striking, possibly to obviate the use of 'red' copper in the alloy, and worn specimens look remarkably dull in places. According to Hans[2] the pieces were struck between August 1935 and May 1937 and were, unaccountably, at a slightly enriched fineness of 0·835. This was confirmed by assay at the Royal Mint where a figure of 0·8345 was noted.

Of the remaining three mints, Utrecht is noted by Hans[2] as striking talers in 1939 but the whole consignment was melted owing to the outbreak of war. Brussels produced nearly 10 million talers in 1937/8 specifically for the Yemen and parts of Arabia, but for some reason omitted one of the pearls in

---

[1] *Annual Report of the Deputy Master and Comptroller of the Royal Mint 1949*, 9.
[2] Hans, op. cit.

the diadem with the result that these coins were often rejected by the Arabs. According to Behrens[1] a further 11½ million pieces were struck at Brussels between 1954 and 1957.

TABLE III

*Output from British-controlled Mints*

| Year | Royal Mint | Bombay | The Mint Birmingham |
|------|-----------|--------|---------------------|
| 1936 | 150,125 | .. | .. |
| 1937 | 3,719,415 | .. | .. |
| 1938 | 5,086,085 | .. | .. |
| 1940 | 3,766,391 | .. | .. |
| 1941 | 2,002,000 | 16,344,523 | |
| 1949 | 500,000 | .. | 475,000 |
| 1953 | .. | .. | 180,000 |
| 1954 | 2,560,000 | .. | 2,434,000 |
| 1955 | 800,000 | .. | 399,500 |
| 1957 | 272,429 | .. | .. |
| 1958 | 340,171 | .. | .. |
| 1959 | 202 | .. | .. |
| 1960 | 213,180 | .. | .. |
| 1961 | 749,072 | .. | .. |
| Totals: | 20,159,070 | 16,344,523 | 3,488,500 |

Paris, whose taler production commenced soon after the Italians, went on striking intermittently up to 1959 and produced nearly 12 million pieces. In fact, the mint was still selling the coins as examples of medallic art in 1966. These specimens all have a very characteristic saltire after the date. It seems to be formed of two crescents rather than a genuine cross. There are several other details typical of this mint, and in particular the main edge arabesque is longer than usual and has a large terminal annulus (**Fig. 3**).

*Twentieth-century Austrian issues*

It would appear that Austria did not exercise her nominal right to strike talers until 1946 and, if Behren's figure of over 12 million pieces in 1954[1] is excluded, did not substantially exceed the 10,000 pieces per annum laid down in the Italian taler treaty until 1957. The eleven-year period 1946–56 saw the production of a total of under 150,000 talers whereas the twelve-year period 1957–68 produced nearly 7 million.

If a group of type 16 coins is sorted to exclude varieties known to come from mints outside Austria, the residue is composed of two varieties, separable primarily by the shape of the saltire. Comparison with present productions of the Vienna mint and with countermarked specimens of the nineteenth

---

[1] Behrens, op. cit.

# EDGE ARABESQUES
# 1860- 1960

 Vienna pre 1900

 Brussels

 Paris

 London

 Vienna ca 1960

FIG. 3.

century indicate that both varieties are from Vienna, with the larger more regular saltire apparently identifying the earlier type.

Some guidance on the date of changeover is provided by countermarked talers used in the Arab States mostly for the period 1916 to 1924 when the states of Hejaz and Nejd had a brief period of independence. Talers are found heavily countermarked on the obverse with the Arabic word Nejd or Al Hejaz. Davenport[1] considers the former to date from as early as 1906.

The earliest countermarks from this area known on Maria Theresia talers (and on various other coins) are dated A.H. 1307 and were apparently issued by Sultan Monasar Ibn Abdullah of Qua'iti.

Yet other pieces are known countermarked on each side with the die of a five-sided Yemeni coin dated A.H. 1371 and, of the same period, 'holey talers' from which a centre blank has been removed and the rim marked in Arabic.

Of the pieces examined so far only those dated A.H. 1371 (A.D. 1952) show the later version of the Vienna saltire and, if the assumption is made that these countermarks are genuine, this date might represent the latest time for the new design to be introduced.

### Conclusions

As this paper is an interim report on work which is still proceeding, it is not possible to draw many firm conclusions. It would, however, seem likely that the coins struck from the original 1780 Günzburg dies were produced between 1780 and November 1783 and were of similar design to the 1777 coins from the same mint. As the latter issue is now considerably scarcer than the 1780 coins of the same appearance it is probable that the new dies authorized on 1 December 1783 were of the same design again (type 9). The unprecedented demands on Günzburg for over 13 million talers in the period 1785 to 1790 may well have occasioned the new designs of type 13 which seem to have been used at least until the close of the mint in 1805.

The style of type 12, dated by Ernst to 1793, then falls into place and the dies marked T.S.–I.F. provided by Vienna at least twice between 1780 and 1797, reflect the development of style during this period.

If it can be argued that the Vienna coins of type 8 form a continuous series from perhaps 1805 to 1860 then type 14 could represent a parallel series produced at Milan and Venice mints between 1820 and 1866. As type 15 is so obviously copied from type 14 the possibility is suggested that it was an 'unofficial' issue c. 1870, from perhaps Milan in Italian hands. Type 16 then represents the official Austrian design minted only in Vienna for the next twenty years.

The evidence to support these hypotheses is minimal and they are offered only in the hope that their demolition may generate a more soundly based picture of this interesting series.

I acknowledge with thanks the assistance given by Lt.-Col. D. D. Vigors in permitting three specimens from his collection to be used in the preparation of the plates; by the Bundessammlung von Medaillen Münzen und Geld-zeichen, Vienna, the 's Rijks Munt, Utrecht, and the Cabinet des Médailles,

---

[1] Davenport, *The Dollars of Africa, Asia, and Oceania* 192.

Brussels, in providing casts of coins in their collections; by Messrs. B. A. Seaby Ltd., in providing photographs of a coin of the Kremnitz mint and by many other people who have given me free access to their collections.

I should like to record the help given by the late Professor Holzmair who read and commented on my paper. My thanks are due also to Mr. R. A. G. Carson and Dr. J. P. C. Kent of the British Museum who encouraged the preparation of this paper; and to Mr. E. G. V. Newman of the Royal Mint who, by providing my first specimen, aroused my curiosity and hence generated the research described in this paper.

## APPENDIX

### Description of the Varieties

#### CLASS I

*General description*

Obv.     Legend, commencing near the top of the coin,
M. THERESIA.D.G.—R. IMP.HU.BO.REG.
Bust to right, with a veil falling from the back of the head to the shoulder. A pearled diadem shows above closely curled hair. The frilled top of a low-cut dress is hidden on the shoulder by an ermine stole fastened with a brooch.

Rev.     Legend, commencing near the top of the coin,
ARCHID.AVST.DUX.—BURG.CO.TYR.1780. X
Beneath an Imperial crown a double-headed eagle displayed and diademé. On the breast of the eagle, a shield, crowned dexter with the crown of Hungary and sinister with the crown of Bohemia. The shield is quarterly:

1. HUNGARY: Per pale HUNGARY-ANCIENT: Barry of eight argent and gules. HUNGARY MODERN: Gules, on a mount in base vert, an open crown or, issuant therefrom a patriarchal cross argent.
2. BOHEMIA: Gules, a lion rampant argent, double queué.
3. BURGUNDY-ANCIENT: Bendy of six or and azure within a bordure gules.
4. UPPER AUSTRIA: Per pale or, an eagle displayed sable, gules, two pallets argent.

Over all, on an escutcheon crowned with an archducal crown, AUSTRIA: Gules a fess argent.

Edge     IVSTITIA ET CLEMENTIA, each word being separated by arabesques.
*Obverse varieties* [Pl. 20. 1–5]
There are five obverses.

Obv. 1.     Shoulder brooch oval, almost square and with a central depression. Diadem decorated with five diamond-shaped jewels. Heavy irregular lettering. Upper loops of P and B broken. Similar to Günzburg issues of 1774–7. [Pl. 20. P1]

*Obv.* 2. Shoulder brooch slightly larger than *obv.* 1 and nearer to a true oval. Jewels in diadem less obviously diamond and more circular. Drapery folds altered to give a smoother line to the veil and at the truncation. Features more aristocratic. Lettering more regular and indented at base with small breaks on P and R. Sometimes occurs with a pellet below the bust. Similar to Vienna issues of 1774–9. [Pl. 20. P2]

*Obv.* 3. Similar to *obv.* 2 but shoulder brooch now surrounded with nine pellets or pearls. Diadem plain and prominent. More detail in the drapery, and vertical lining added to the dress top. Nose larger and more pointed. Strands of stole beginning to merge. B below the bust.

*Obv.* 4. Similar to *obv.* 3 but rounder, slightly hooked nose and B omitted. Five pellets on the narrower diadem. Strands of stole almost merged and ermine tails visible.

*Obv.* 5. Similar to *obv.* 4 but drapery changed to give smoother head line and more accentuated folds on shoulder. Ermine tails formalized and stole reshaped. Dress frill more symmetrical but with no binding to edge. Diadem now shows eight pellets or pearls. Nose almost bulbous. Definite break in the line of P, B, and R and a minor break in C and G.

*Reverse varieties* [Pl. 21. A–H]

There are eight reverses.

*Rev.* A. U used instead of V in AUST. Large Burgundian cross with distinct branchlets—a pellet follows. Large pellets in nimbi but usually none between eagle's beaks. Onion-shaped Habsburgh crown.
   S.K.–P.D. under claws at sides of tail.

*Rev.* B. Now AVST. Square or slightly flattened Burgundian cross but with no pellet following. Nimbi now outlined with a double line and some pellets show between eagles' beaks. Dome-shaped Habsburgh crown. Three, four, or five pellets on tapes between crown and eagles' heads.
   T.S.–I.F. under claws.
   Breaks to line of upper loop of R.

*Rev.* C. Similar to *rev.* B but more regular engraving. Three pellets to tapes.

*Rev.* D. Similar to *rev.* C but some varieties with the Burgundian cross tall and thin with smaller branchlets.
   A.H.–G.S. under claws.
   Breaks to R and B.

*Rev.* E. As *rev.* D but A.H.–G.S. smaller.

*Rev.* F. Possibly similar to *rev.* C but EvS.–I.K.

*Rev.* G. Similar to *rev.* C but P.S.–I.K.

*Rev.* H. Similar to *rev.* D but I.C.–F.A.
   Breaks to line of loops of many letters.

*Edge Arabesques* (Fig. 1) [Pl. 22. E1–E3]

| | | | |
|---|---|---|---|
| *a.* | Plume as Vienna 1778 | *f.* | Cinqfoil |
| *b.* | Plume as Günzburg 1771 | *g.* | 8 foil |
| *c.* | Cross as Günzburg 1771 | *h.* | Pellet (presumably the rivets |
| *d.* | Floret as Vienna 1778 | | fastening the collar seg- |
| *e.* | Large floret | | ments). |

*Class I coins*

| No. | Obv. | Rev. | Edge | Notes | Refs.* |
|-----|------|------|------|-------|--------|
| 1 | 1 | B | *b, c, f* | Struck at Vienna mint for use in Günzburg<br>T.S. = Tobias Schöbl<br>I.F. = Josef Faby | H512 |
| 2 | 2 | D | *e,* | Initials of mint officials at Karlsburg<br>A.H. = A. J. Hammerschmidt<br>G.S. = G. Schickmayer | D1146<br>H558 |
| 3 | 2 | E | ? | | D1146<br>H559 |
| 4 | 3 | A | *b, f* | B on *obv.* is mint-mark for Kremnitz<br>S.K. = Sigmund A. Klemmer<br>P.D. = Paschal J. V. Damiani | D1134<br>H607 |
| 5 | 4 | C | *b, c, f* | Initials of mint officials at Günzburg<br>T.S. = Tobias Schöbl<br>I.F. = Josef Faby<br>Specimen in the National Collection. Vienna | D1151D |
| 6 | 5 | F | ? | Initials of mint officials at Prague<br>E.v.S. = Paul Erdmann v. Schwingerschuh<br>I.K. = Ignaz Kendler | D1140A<br>H535 |
| 7 | 5 | G | ? | Initials of mint officials at Prague<br>P.S. = Paul Erdman v. Schwingerschuh<br>I.K. = Ignaz Kendler | D1140B<br>H536 |
| 8 | 5 | H | *a, d, g, h* | Initials of mint officials at Vienna<br>I.C. = Johann Aug. v. Cronberg<br>F.A. = Franz Aicherau | D1117<br>H437 |

\* D = J. S. Davenport, *European Crowns 1700–1800.* H = Ludwig Herinek, *Österreichische Münzprägungen von 1740–1969.*

## CLASS II

*General description*

*Obv.* As Class I.

*Rev.* As Class I except that the fourth quarter shows the arms of the Margrave of Burgau, namely:
BURGAU: Bendy sinister of eight argent and gules, a pale or.

*Edge* As Class I.

*Obverse varieties* [Pl. 26. 6–10]

There are five new obverses.

*Obv.* 6. Similar to *obv.* 1 but with S.F. under bust. Varieties have double stops after D or after S and F. Lettering varies but mostly large and square.

*Obv.* 7. Similar to *obv.* 3 but nose more like *obv.* 4. Shoulder brooch now large and circular. Diadem has seven large pearls. F.S. below bust.

*Obv.* 8. Similar to *obv.* 7 but S.F. below bust. Brooch even larger.

*Obv.* 9. Similar to *obv.* 8 but with a small S and T below the bust and above and to the right of S and F respectively. Coarser engraving and sharper nose.

*Obv.* 10. Similar to *obv.* 5 but with S.F. under bust.

*Reverse varieties* [Pl. 23. J–O]

There are six new reverses.

*Rev.* J. Similar to *rev.* A but with Burgau arms in the fourth quarter and no initials under claws. Dome-shaped Habsburgh crown. Considerable variations apparent with some dies showing fine random pelleting in the nimbi similar to pre-1780 Günzburg issues, and other (and later?) dies with fewer, larger pellets set in rings. Five or more pellets on tapes below crown. Generally no stops on either side of the Burgundian cross which is more like that on *rev.* B.

*Rev.* K. Similar to a late version of *rev.* J but AVST.

*Rev.* L. Similar to *rev.* C but with Burgau arms in the fourth quarter and no initials under claws. Large Burgundian cross with pellets both before and after. Nimbi outlined with a double line and pellets tending towards two concentric rings. Usually five pellets on tapes but sometimes four and five. Two centre tail feathers, the upper one being part of a row of five.

*Rev.* M. Similar to *rev.* L but characteristically narrow digits in the date. Heavy square lettering. Lower edge of the centre shield tending to a point.

*Rev.* N. Similar to *rev.* M but engraving very much coarser. Small date and Burgundian cross, and tail of seven no longer ends in a ball. Six pellets on tapes.

*Rev.* O. Similar to *rev.* H but Burgau arms in the fourth quarter and no letters under claws. Three pellets only to tapes and twelve to sixteen in eagle beaks.

*Edge arabesques*

*j*    Six-foil.

*k*    Quatrefoil (possibly derived from the cross of Burgundy).

*l*    Plume similar to Hall 1774.

*Class II coins*

| No. | Obv. | Rev. | Edge | Notes | Refs. |
|---|---|---|---|---|---|
| 9 | 6 | J | *b, c, f* | Initials of mint officials at Günzburg<br>S = Tobias Schöbl<br>F = Josef Faby | H510 |
| 10 | 6 | J | *b, c, j* | Similar but six-foil fleur instead of five-foil on edge | |
| 11 | 6 | K | *b, c, f* | Now AVST | |
| 12 | 7 | L | *b, c, f* | Initials of mint officials at Günzburg<br>F = Josef Faby<br>S = Fr. Stehr<br>Brooch now surrounded with pearls | D1151c<br>H511 |
| 13 | 8 | L | *b, c, f* | Initials changed back to S.F. | |
| 14 | 8 | M | *b, c, f* | Narrow date | |
| 15 | 9 | N | *f, k, l* | S.T. Unknown. Possibly S.S.–F.T. | D1151b<br>H513 |
| 16 | 10 | O | *a, d, g, h* | Normal restrike type | D1151a<br>H514 |

# Numismatic Research in Russia, the Ukraine, and Byelorussia in the Period 1917–1967*

I. G. SPASSKY

AMONG the so-called auxiliary historical disciplines it is undoubtedly numismatics which has undergone the most substantial changes in the fifty years since the foundation of the Soviet Union. Without in the least losing its 'auxiliary' character with regard to many different historical questions, numismatics has found its main function as a historico-economic discipline. This is particularly true of the study of the numismatic monuments of our own national history, i.e. in Russian numismatics.

The use of money on Russian territory had begun, and had already undergone a long process of development, before the appearance of the first Russian coins, and even in later periods foreign coins were current. It is understandable then that a great deal of research based on Russian finds of coins from various foreign states is concerned with broad questions of the history of monetary circulation in ancient and medieval Russia. A similar trend in numismatic research is developing successfully in many of the republics of the Soviet Union, without in the least diminishing the importance of the study of the national coinage. In the same way the coins of the Russian state remain the chief source for Russian numismatics.

The main reorientation of numismatics has taken place primarily in the area of organization. One of the peculiarities of numismatics which has long set it apart from its allied disciplines is the distinctive character and size of its following, which has consisted mainly of amateur coin-collectors. In pre-Revolutionary Russia amateur interests exerted a constant pressure on scientific research, which was itself to a considerable extent the result of more or less haphazard amateur activity.

* [This is a translation of an article 'Numizmaticheskie issledovaniya (Rossiya, Ukraina, Belorussiya) v 1917–1967' at pp. 91–115 of the second volume of a symposium published by the Historical Section of the Academy of Sciences of the U.S.S.R. at Leningrad in 1969, entitled *Vspomogatel'nye istoricheskie distsipliny* ['Auxiliary historical sciences']. British Standard 2979:1958 (British system) has been used for transliteration, with the omission of diacritics and the simplification of final -i, -ii, -yi, etc. in personal names to -y. Note that the medial -y- appears in the British Museum and Bodleian Library catalogues as -ui- and -î- respectively. Material that does not appear in the original article is enclosed in brackets—as this note. Further bibliographical information communicated by the author to the translator is given in the last footnote. W. F. RYAN.]

The rare publications of museums went almost unnoticed among the publications of numismatic societies or private individuals, while even in the societies of St. Petersburg and Moscow the few specialist scholars were lost among the amateurs for whom the collection of coins and medals, and sometimes even scholarly work, were simply a pleasant hobby. It did of course happen that the occasional amateur in time became a serious recognized, specialist (for example A. A. Il'in). At the same time among the private publications there were not a few writings with pretensions to scholarship which merely flattered the vanity of their authors.

The largest and most active of the societies was the Moscow Numismatic Society with some hundred members in Moscow and the provinces. Its publications were typical of the prevailing level of scholarship and interests of the most qualified section of amateur numismatists. The publishing activities of the Numismatic Section of the Imperial Russian Archaeological Society were of a more academic nature. The appearance of 'Imperial' in its name gave this society and its numismatic section the status of quasi-official institutions. The St. Petersburg Russian Numismatic Society, founded only in 1911, has left only a few thin brochures of its proceedings. It was in fact a restricted circle of select collectors in the capital.

Another important characteristic of numismatics is the extreme complexity of its management, that is, its collections of material, its accessibility, completeness, good order, and, most important of all, the search for, and collection of, new material, in particular coin hoards.

Like archaeology, numismatics is insatiable—true progress can be ensured only by energetic and ever-increasing basic research. However, unlike archaeology, which carries out its own field-work and processes its own finds, numismatics depends entirely on the happy chance which sends it ancient hoards from time to time.

Coin hoards in pre-Revolutionary Russia were the concern of the Imperial Archaeological Commission. Working within the legal limits of the time (the right of private ownership of land and what it contained), the Commission systematically supplied the Hermitage with quantities of coin hoards found all over the country. A vast number of coins supplemented the collections every year, and by the beginning of the twentieth century the numismatic collection of the Hermitage was one of the best in the world, but remained almost completely inaccessible to Russian scholars. What the Hermitage did not need was returned to the landowners, and if the finds were made on state property they were sometimes given to other museums, or, quite often, sent to the mint. Many hoards to which the Commission had a right found their way into the antiques market and thus into private collections, sometimes even going abroad.

Hoards collected in the last two to two and a half centuries, when interest in ancient coins began, make up the fund of coins, estimated at millions, which is now at the disposal of numismatists of the U.S.S.R., but for a long time hoards were considered simply as a source for enriching collections. The independent scientific value of hoards as complete sets, enabling scholars to discover the main characteristics of money circulation in different periods, was realized very slowly.

Unquestionably the few state numismatic collections of pre-Revolutionary Russia and even the Hermitage collection belonging to the Imperial family owed their completeness to the collecting enthusiasm of private individuals whose collections were at various times acquired by museums or donated to them. At the same time there still remained in private collectors hands numismatic treasures inaccessible to scholars which left the best museums, including the Hermitage, far behind. Huge collections lay forgotten for decades in the palaces of the aristocracy after the death of those who had collected them.

After the October Revolution the situation with regard to numismatics described above became impossible and soon disappeared. After two or three years the Moscow society ceased to function—many of its members had emigrated with or without their collections. The same fate overtook the main numismatic organization of Petrograd (St. Petersburg), the Numismatic Section of the Russian Archaeological Society and the Russian Numismatic Society.

In 1917 the Archaeological Commission, which supervised the Hermitage and was situated in the Imperial palace, ceased. The registering, collection, and distribution of archaeological and numismatic 'gifts from the bowels of the earth' in the multinational Soviet state had to be organized on new principles. The Hermitage became a national museum and lost its right to dispose of hoards found anywhere in the country.

The last echo of 'private' numismatics was the publication in 1918 of a book by A. A. Il'in (1858–1942)—a manual for collectors of coins of Peter I.[1] A. A. Il'in in Petrograd and the curator of the collections of the Historical Museum A. V. Oreshnikov (1855–1933) were the greatest specialists on Russian coins after the death in 1916 of Count I. I. Tolstoy. The latter was the author of many fundamental works on the coins of the pre-Muscovite period. His incomparable collection of Russian coins and medals, which was considerably more complete than the Hermitage collection, was, in 1917, when the alarming situation on the front caused the museum collections to be evacuated, presented to the Hermitage by the collector's son, later Academician, I. I. Tolstoy the Younger (1880–1954), on condition that it was evacuated immediately.

In the early years of the Soviet state the reorganization of numismatics could depend on only a very few old cadres—for the most part the curators of

---

[1] A. Il'in, *Russkie monety. Mednaya moneta s 1700–1725 g. Petra I. Prakticheskoe rukovodstvo dlya sobiratelei* ['Russian coins. The copper coin of Peter I, 1700–1725. A practical guide for collectors'] (Pgr., 1918). Litho.

the very few state numismatic collections—in Petrograd, Moscow, and two or three university cities and a few amateurs who had come to work in the museums. These were for the most part elderly people and there was hardly anyone to replace them. Only in Petrograd there were the young N. P. Bauer (1888–1942) and R. R. Fasmer [Vasmer] (1888–1938), working together with the old scholars, and in 1922 they were joined by A. V. Oreshnikov's Moscow pupil, A. N. Zograf (1889–1942).

If in Petrograd the work of the Hermitage numismatists continued, and after the return of the evacuated collections in 1921 increased tremendously in scope, the treasures of many other museums in the country were often threatened by the conditions of the civil war and foreign intervention. The care of the main numismatic collections was placed in the hands of the People's Commissariat of Finance who made their vaults available for storing the country's numismatic treasures. Experience showed how wise this choice had been. While the *émigré* press was asserting that the communists were melting down all the state and private collections, even the most valuable and unique coins, these great numismatic treasures were in fact carefully preserved and, when the time came, returned to the museums. Coin hoards which came into the hands of the Finance Commissariat were also preserved and later also transferred to the museums.

In Petrograd the care of numismatic treasures became the direct responsibility of the Hermitage. For a number of years it was concerned with accessioning and processing the nationalized collections from the palaces of the former imperial family and aristocracy. Then it began to bring together systematically the long untended collections of many teaching institutions, former academic societies, and institutions of the Academy of Sciences. By the mid 1930s the numismatic collection of the Hermitage had increased by almost four times. The Russian collection, which had already incorporated the invaluable collection of I. I. Tolstoy, was particularly enriched by the superb collection of the Academy of Sciences and the collection of S. G. Stroganov (1794–1882).

In 1921 a special decision of the Council of Peoples Commissars instructed the Finance Commissariat to ensure that copies of all Soviet coins struck by the newly restored Petrograd mint should be given to the Hermitage in perpetuity. This decision was amended several times to deal with the appearance of new types of product (medals, orders, emblems) and in the post-war years was extended to several other museums.

The cradle of Soviet scientific numismatics was the Section of Numismatics and Glyptics set up in Petrograd in place of the old Archaeological Commission of the Academy of the History of Material Culture (AIMK, later GAIMK and RAIMK, now the Institute of Archaeology of the Academy of the U.S.S.R.). The section began work in 1919 under the direction of A. A. Il'in and continued until 1929. Its staff was drawn mainly from the numismatists of the Hermitage and after them two Moscow scholars, A. V. Oreshnikov and S. I. Chizhov (1870–1920). After the death in 1920 of A. K. Markov, the curator of the Numismatic Section of the Hermitage, A. A. Il'in was invited to take this post. Thus, under his direction, scientific research and practical museum work were combined.

The AIMK introduced the numismatists into the research world of a large group of archaeologists and historians. Constant contact with this and the great work of the AIMK in the field of methodology soon made itself felt in the Hermitage too. There, in 1927, a numismatic exhibition was opened in which for the first time an attempt was made to illustrate by means of coins the changing forms of society and not simply changes of rulers or dynasties.

The fact that the AIMK had at its disposal the rich archives of the former Archaeological Commission which registered the coin hoard finds of more than fifty years established the main direction of research in the Section—the topography of coin hoard finds of foreign and Russian coins on Russian territory. This research had great significance for Russian numismatics which was still trying to come to grips with its new tasks. By studying the topography and chronology of hoards of Oriental, West European, and Russian coins, the Section was laying the foundations for the study of the complex, changing, and long process of money circulation in ancient Russia and neighbouring territories.

The AIMK continued to receive information about new finds but this gradually began to be restricted to the Russian Federation as the other republics began to develop their own systems of recording and information. The general principles of the state ownership of all coin hoards had been established by law but time was still needed for the creation of a precise system for recording and collecting them.

In the 1920s and early 1930s, mainly in the publications of the AIMK and, after the abolition of the Numismatics Section, abroad, a series of complete topographies of Russian coins, currency bars, and hoards was published, together with descriptions of individual hoards. R. R. Fasmer, who was unable to complete his work on the topography of hoards of Cufic coins, then prepared two surveys of coin hoard finds of recent years.[2] To him also we

---

[2] A. A. Il'in: (1) 'Topografiya kladov drevnikh russkikh monet X—XI vv. i monet udel'nogo perioda' ['Topography of hoards of ancient Russian coins of the tenth–eleventh century and coins of the appanage period'], *TNK GAIMK*, v (1925); (2) 'Topografiya kladov serebryanykh i zolotykh slitkov' ['Topography of hoards of silver and gold bars'], *TNK*, i (1921); N. Bauer: (1) 'Die Silber- und Goldbarren des russischen Mittelalters. Eine archäologische Studie', *NZ*, 62 (1929); 64 (1931); (2) 'Die russische Funde abendländischer Münzen des 11. und 12. Jahrhunderts', *ZfN*, 39 (1929); 40 (1931); (3) 'Nachträge zu den russischen Funden abendländischer Münzen', *ZfN*, 42 (1932); (4) 'Der Fund von Spanko bei St Petersburg', *ZfN*, 36 (1926); (5) 'Der Münzfund von Wichliss', *Deutsche Münzblätter*, 388 (1935); A. A. Sivers, 'Topografiya kladov s prazhskimi groshami' [Topography of hoards containing Prague groschen'], *TNK*, 2 (1922); R. R. Fasmer: (1) 'Spisok monetnykh nakhodok, zaregistrirovannykh Sektsiei numizmatiki i gliptiki AIMK v 1920—1925' ['List of coin

owe many monograph descriptions of the composition of hoards of Cufic coins on which he had carried out research and which represent monuments of ancient Russian currency.[3] He also studied a number of similar hoards in the Baltic area and Finland. In the same period Fasmer's pupil A. A. Bykov published his first description of a hoard and a second description just before the outbreak of war.[4]

One of Fasmer's last articles, setting out the method he had developed for the topographic study of Cufic hoards,[5] is of great importance not only for the study of Oriental numismatics. Fasmer's research showed up the methodological weakness of P. G. Lyubomirov's work which had sought to present a picture of the economic links between ancient Russia and the East by using such literature as was available to him on Oriental coin hoard finds in Russia.[6] The Numismatic Section established possible links at certain points and helped in the preparation of several local surveys of coin hoards.[7]

Among the publications devoted to Russian coins S. I. Chizhov's research into an early Muscovite hoard should be mentioned.[8] Unfortunately his

finds recorded by the Section of Numismatics and Glyptics of the AIMK in 1920–1925'].
*Soobshcheniya GAIMK*, 1 (1926); (2) 'Spisok monetnykh nakhodok II' ['List of coin finds ii'], *Soobshcheniya GAIMK*, 2 (1929).

[3] R. R. Fasmer: (1) 'Vas'kovskii klad kuficheskikh monet' ['The Vas'kovo hoard of Cufic coins'], *Vostok*, 1925, 5; (2) 'Dva klada kuficheskikh monet' ['Two Cufic coin hoards], *TNK GAIMK*, vi (1927); (3) 'Zavalashinskii klad kuficheskikh monet VII—IX vv.' ['The Zavalashino Cufic coin hoard of the seventh–ninth century'], *IGAIMK*, vii, 2 (1931); (4) 'Klad kuficheskikh monet, naidennyi v Novgorode v 1920 g.' ['The Cufic coin hoard found in Novgorod in 1920'], *IRAIMK*, iv (1925); R. Vasmer, 'Ein im Dorfe Staryi Dedin in Weissrussland gemachter Fund kufischer Münzen', *Kungl. Vitterhetts-, Historie- och Antiqvitets-Akademiens Handlingar*, xl, 2 (Stockholm, 1929).

[4] A. A. Bykov: (1) 'Klad serebryanykh kuficheskikh monet, naidennyi v Novgorode v 1903 g.' ['The hoard of Cufic silver coins found in Novgorod in 1903'], *IRAIMK*, iv (1925); (2) 'Novaya nakhodka kuficheskikh monet' ['A new find of Cufic coins'], *KSIIMK*, 8 (1940).

[5] R. R. Fasmer, 'Ob izdanii novoi topografii nakhodok kuficheskikh monet v Vostochnoi Evrope' ['On the publication of a new topography of Cufic coin hoards in eastern Europe'], *Izvestiya Akademii nauk SSSR* (seriya obshchestvennykh nauk), vii, 6–7 (1933).

[6] P. G. Lyubomirov, 'Torgovye svyazi Drevnei Rusi s Vostokom v VII—IIX vv.' ['Trade links of Ancient Russia with the East in the eighth–ninth century'], *Uchenye zapiski Saratovskogo universiteta*, 1 (1923). Reviewed in N. Bauer, *Zeitschrift für slavische Philologie*, III, 1/2 (Leipzig, 1926).

[7] P. V. Kharlampovich: (1) 'Monetnye skarby, znaidzenyya u Belarusi, u zborakh Belaruskaga dzyarzhaunaga muzeyu' ['Coins hoards found in Byelorussia in the Byelorussian state museum'], *Instytut belaruskae kul'tury. Gystarychna-arkheol. zbornik*, i (Minsk, 1927) [Byelor.]; (2) 'Praskie groshi u belaruskikh monetnykh skarbakh' ['Prague groschen in Byelorussian coin hoards'], ibid. [Byelor.]; (3) 'Monetni znakhidki na Pervomaishchini' ['Coin finds in the Pervomaisk region'], *Visnik Odes'koi komisii krajeznavstva*, pts. 4–5 (Odessa, 1930) [Ukr.]; T. A. Gorokhov, 'Monetnye klady Kurskoi gubernii' ['Coin hoards of the Kursk province'], *Izvestiya Kurskogo obshchestva kraevedov*, 1927, 4; A. A. Fedorov, 'Monetnye klady Ryazanskoi gubernii' ['Coin hoards of the Ryazan' province'] *Trudy Spasskogo otdeleniya Obshchestva issledovatelei Ryazanskogo kraya* (Spassk, 1928).

[8] S. I. Chizhov, 'Drozdovskii klad russkikh deneg vremeni vel. kn. Vasiliya Dmitrievicha Moskovskogo' ['The Drozdovo hoard of Russian coins of the time of Grand Prince Vasily Dmitrievich of Moscow'], *TNK GAIMK*, iii (1922).

manuscript *Russkaya numismaticheskaya bibliografiya* ['Russian numismatic bibliography'] on which he had worked for many years, was lost without trace after his death. Several articles on particular problems of Russian numismatics of the fourteenth, sixteenth, and eighteenth centuries were published by A. A. Il'in.[9] An interesting hypothesis about the countermarking of Persian copper by the Russian military administration in Mazanderan during the campaign of 1722–3 was put forward by R. R. Fasmer.[10] His conclusion that the coins he was studying were current in Mazanderan and Persia has recently been substantiated when the Hermitage acquired specimens on which the 'Russian' over-stamp was cancelled by later Persian ones.

R. R. Fasmer and N. P. Bauer were the authors of all the articles on Russian and Oriental coins in Schrötter's numismatic dictionary published in 1930.[11]

In the middle and late 1920s amateur collecting revived. In Leningrad, Moscow, and other cities local societies and clubs were set up and soon had their own printed journals (*Sovetskii kollektsioner* ['The Soviet collector'] and *Sovetskii filatelist* ['The Soviet philatelist']). These were very modest but some of the publications recording ephemeral coinage issues in the first years after the revolution are not without their value.

The hundreds of minutes written by R. R. Fasmer for the Section of Numismatics of GAIMK in the years 1919–29 enable us to trace the difficult but undeviating efforts of the Leningrad numismatists to establish a new outlook on the problems of numismatics, and in particular on the study of our own national coinage. The work undertaken by GAIMK did not cease after the abolition of the Section of Numismatics but was transferred to the Hermitage.

The most widely discussed subject in Russian numismatics in the 1920s and 1930s was that of the early Russian coins bearing the name of Vladimir. N. P. Bauer, relying on the evidence of well-dated foreign coin hoards containing a proportion of early Russian coins, developed the views of I. I. Tolstoy, who had attributed these controversial coins to the tenth and early eleventh centuries.[12] A. V. Oreshnikov[13] had different views. However, the classification which he proposed for early Russian coins was based on the most elementary formal analysis of the variants of the family emblem depicted

---

[9] A. A. Il'in: (1) 'Monety velikogo knyazhestva Chernigovskogo kontsa XIV veka' ['Coins of the Grand Principality of Chernigov at the end of the fourteenth century'], *IRAIMK*, i (1921); (2) 'Dve monety knyazya Andreya' ['Two coins of Prince Andrew'], op. cit.; (3) 'Monetnyi dvor v Yaroslavle' ['The Yaroslavl mint'], op. cit.; (4) 'Pyat' neizdannykh monet Ekateriny II 1796 g.' ['Five unpublished coins of Catherine II of 1796'], *Gosudarstvennyi Ermitazh, sbornik II* (Pgr. 1923).

[10] R. R. Fasmer, 'Persidskie monety s nadchekankami Petra I' ['Persian coins with the over-stamp of Peter I'], *Gosudarstvennyi Ermitazh, sbornik III* (L., 1926).

[11] *Wörterbuch der Münzkunde. Herausgegeben von F. Schrötter* (Berlin, 1930).

[12] N. Bauer, 'Die russische Funde . . .' (n. 2), 1.

[13] See A. V. Oreshnikov, review of N. P. Bauer, 'Drevnerusskii chekan kontsa X i nachala XI v. ['Early Russian coining at the end of the tenth and beginning of the eleventh century'], *IGAIMK*, 5 (1927); *Seminarium Kondakovianum*, ii (Prague, 1928).

on these coins; the 'evolution' which he detected in this was applied to the coins. He refused to take into account the evidence of the composition of the hoards or the principles of dating hoards established by the research of R. R. Fasmer and other scholars.[14]

The classification of A. V. Oreshnikov was published in a more elaborate form only after his death.[15] He had the last word and for some time it seemed that Oreshnikov's proposal to allot the controversial coins to various princes reigning after Yaroslav in Kiev, Vyshgorod, Pereyaslavl, and Chernigov (ending with Vladimir Monomakh) was completely accepted by historians and that there could be no return to the views of Tolstoy.

In Moscow, after the deaths of S. I. Chizhov, A. V. Oreshnikov, and V. K. Trutkovsky (1862–1932), several of whose articles were published in the period 1921–8[16] numismatic research died out completely; in Leningrad attention was focused entirely on cataloguing the Hermitage collections. Research did not cease but after 1929 the possibility of publishing works was severely reduced and there were ever greater obstacles to publishing articles in foreign publications. Up to 1941 there appeared two more articles by N. P. Bauer[17] (on problems of the Russian monetary system and the *kuna* system), a catalogue published by the Hermitage on the occasion of the centenary of the death of A. S. Pushkin,[18] and the first part of a broadly conceived work by A. A. Il'in[19] which has remained unfinished.

The volume of the *Trudy Otdela numizmatiki* ['Works of the Hermitage Department of Numismatics'] which was ready for the press in 1941 and contained articles on Russian numismatics, appeared only in 1945[20] when most

---

[14] A. V. Oreshnikov, 'Klassifikatsii drevneishikh russkikh monet po rodovym znakam' ['Classification of the earliest Russian coins by family emblems'], *Izvestiya Akademii nauk SSSR* (seriya gumanitarnykh nauk), 1930.

[15] *Idem*, 'Denezhnye znaki domongol' skoi Rusi' ['Coin marks in pre-Mongol Russia'], *Trudy GIM*, vi (M., 1936).

[16] V. K. Trutovsky: (1) 'Novye pervoistochniki dlya istorii tsennostei dopetrovskoi Rossii — khudozhestvennye' ['New sources for the history of art treasures in pre-Petrine Russia'], *TOA RANION*, i (1926); (2) 'Veksha, veveritsa i bela' [' "Squirrel skin" monetary units'], *Trudy Etnografo-arkheologicheskogo muzeya*, I (M., MGU, 1926); (3) 'Altyn, ego proiskhozhdenie, istoriya, evolyutsiya. Ekskurs v istoriyu drevnykh russkikh tsennostei' ['The *altyn*, its origin, history, and evolution. An excursion into the history of early Russian currency'], *TSA RANION*, ii (1928).

[17] N. P. Bauer: (1) 'Denezhnyi schet Russkoi Pravdy' ['The money system in the *Russkaya Pravda* (early Russian legal code)], *Vspomogatel' nye istoricheskie distsipliny* (M.–L., 1937); (2) 'Denezhnyi schet v dukhovnoi novgorodtsa Kliments i denezhnoe obrashchenie v severo-zapadnoi Rusi v XIII v.' ['The money system in the will of Kliment of Novgorod and the circulation of money in North-West Russia in the thirteenth century'], *Problemy istochnikovedeniya*, iii (M.–L., 1940).

[18] A. A. Voitov and L. S. Piskunova, *Medali, zhetony i medal'ony v pamyat' A. S. Pushkina* ['Medals, tokens, and medallions in memory of A. S. Pushkin'] (L., 1937).

[19] A. A. Il'in, *Klassifikatsiya russkikh udel' nykh monet* ['The classification of Russian coins of the appanage period'], i (L., 1940).

[20] *Gosudarstvennyi Ermitazh, Trudy Otdela numizmatiki*, i (L., 1945) (V. M. Neklyudov, 'O russkikh denezhnykh slitkakh' ['On Russian money bars']; S. A. Rozanov, 'Zolotye

of the authors were dead. A. A. Il'in and S. A. Rozanov died in the seige of Leningrad and the research student V. M. Neklyudov did not return from the front.

The abolition of the Section of Numismatics of GAIMK in 1929 had meant that there was no longer a centre for the recording and collection of newly discovered coin hoards. Up to 1941 this was little noticed; the administrative organs of the various republics developed their own particular procedures; many coin hoards found their way into museums, although not always by a direct route.

The war did tremendous damage to the numismatic collections of the U.S.S.R. The superb collections of the Hermitage and the Historical Museum did not suffer but the collections of many of the republic and local museums, not to mention private collections, were destroyed or plundered by the enemy. In many cases hasty evacuation either ruined or severely disarranged the scientific systematization of the coins which had been built up by generations of curators. In the Hermitage, for example, it took fifteen years to re-establish the collection systematically! Only a few of the local museums which had preserved their collections were able to call on qualified specialists for even the most elementary reordering of their collections.

After the war the lack of a central organization for the recording and collection of coins hoards was keenly felt. As previously, tens, if not hundreds, of hoards were being found every year, but the law declaring them the undisputable property of the state was not administratively enforced and many hoards were dispersed to private collections. The museums to which finders of hoards usually come do not even have provision in their budgets for the payment of the rewards stipulated by law and have to attempt to buy the hoards as if they were the property of the finder!

In the ever-increasing number of amateur museums, and in particular in school museums, there is frequently a complete absence of any kind of responsibility for the preservation of acquired material, a fact which is exploited by certain 'collectors' of coins.

The law relating to coin hoards is itself in need of more precise formulation; it does not, for example, envisage the finding of hoards of copper coins. Moreover, the museum regulations regarding work with coins are not altogether satisfactory. For inventory purposes they are regarded simply as 'accession units' and even the preservation of the unity of a coin hoard is not provided for; separation according to the metal of the coins leads to the break-up of collections even when they are preserved intact. The inadequate knowledge of numismatics of museum staff and the lack of literature is leading to an increasing disparity in the state of the numismatic holdings between the few central museums and the regional and local museums.

"lobanchiki" ['Gold "lobanchiki" ']; A. A. Voitov, 'Pamyatnaya ural'skaya zolotaya plastina 1803 g.' ['A gold memorial plate of 1803 from the Urals']).

The proposal of the Hermitage and the Historical Museum to create a Numismatic Commission under the Ministry of Culture of the U.S.S.R. which would organize a single register of finds, take charge of instruction and explanatory work, and also make any necessary representations on behalf of the Ministry to other government departments, has not found support.

In contrast to the sad disarray in the organization of numismatics there has been undoubted progress in the field of research work. After the return of the evacuated collections to normal conditions, the Hermitage by the end of the first post-war decade had a new scientific staff. When it had satisfied its own staff requirements it began to train staff for museums in the other republics of the U.S.S.R. also. Remarkable changes took place in the Historical Museum where in pre-war years the numismatics department had been closed under lock and key. The head of the department, A. A. Sivers (1866–1954), in a very short time gathered together and trained a young and energetic staff.

An important factor in this was that the Institute of the History of Material Culture, which had also become a centre of numismatic research and specialist training, included numismatics in the programme of its annual plenary meetings. The annual meeting of numismatists of all the republics assisted them in the co-ordination and planning of their research. There was an unprecedented increase in the number of scientific articles which were readily published by the institute, the Archaeographic Commission, and other bodies. The Hermitage also regularly gave space to numismatic subjects in its publications.

An encouraging circumstance was the growth of interest in numismatics in a number of universities, the introduction of courses in Russian numismatics into the curriculum in Leningrad and Moscow, and the establishment of coin rooms in Odessa and Minsk. (The only university to have preserved its old, pre-revolutionary numismatic collection seems to have been the University of Tomsk.) Young specialists were trained in the Hermitage for Armenia, Byelorussia, Estonia, Uzbekistan, and the Ukraine, and have already made a contribution to Russian numismatics.

The surveys of Soviet numismatic literature published in 1960, 1962, and 1965 include more than 1,500 monographs, serious articles, reviews, etc.[21] More than 250 of these are devoted to Russian numismatics. They demonstrate how numismatic research has been revitalized and broadened since the last years of the war 1944–5.

A number of authors have devoted works to the history of Russian numismatics. New light has been thrown on little-known aspects of coin-collecting,

[21] I. G. Spassky and V. L. Yanin: (1) 'Sovetskaya numizmatika. Bibliograficheskii ukazatel' 1917—1958 gg.' ['Soviet numismatics. A bibliographical index 1917–1958'], NiE, ii (M., 1960); (2) 'Sovetskaya numizmatika. Bibliograficheskii ukazatel' 1959—1960 gg. i dopolneniya k ukazatelyu za 1917–1958' ['Soviet numismatics. A bibliographical index 1959–1960 with addenda to the index for 1917–1958'], NiE, iii (M., 1962); N. Kotliar and M. V. Severova, 'Russia', in A Survey of Numismatic Research 1960–1965, iii, ed. N. L. Rasmussen et al. (Copenhagen: International Numismatic Commission, 1967).

the development of the theoretical side of numismatics (classification) in the eighteenth and early nineteenth century and its main problems in this period, have been examined and for the first time the importance of the work of the librarian of the Kunstkamera [i.e. museum of curiosities], A. I. Bogdanov,[22] in establishing a scientific classification of Russian coins of the fourteenth and fifteenth century has been recognized. L. P. Kharko has studied the Moscow numismatic collections.[23] Much research in the last decade has been concerned with the history of numismatics in Russia. A collective work surveying the history of the Hermitage collection and providing a guide to the collection was written in the Department of Numismatics to celebrate the second centenary of the Hermitage.[24]

There has also been steadily increasing interest in the history of the technology of coin production. In 1949, to mark the 225th anniversary of the Leningrad mint, an outline of its history in the eighteenth century[25] was published, together with a pamphlet about the forgotten inventor I. A. Nevedomsky[26] who worked at the mint; the cranked coin press invented by him is known as the Uhlhorn press. The history of seventeenth-century mints has attracted the attention of A. S. Mel'nikova.[27] An important characteristic of coin production in fifteenth-century Russia—the use of a matrix—has been established by M. P. Sotnikov,[28] thereby opening up new possibilities of a more precise systematization of the coins of the period.

The book *Russkaya monetnaya sistema* ['The Russian monetary system'] is

[22] I. G. Spassky: (1) 'Ocherki po istorji russkoi numizmatiki' ['Essays on the history of Russian numismatics'], *NS* (*Trudy GIM*, xxv) (M., 1955); (2) 'Otdel numizmatiki Ermitazha' ['The Numismatics Department of the Hermitage'], *Soobshcheniya Gosudarstvennogo Ermitazha*, xviii (1960).

[23] L. P. Kharko: 'Myunts-kabinet Moskovskogo universiteta' ['The coin room of Moscow University'], *Trudy GMII* (M., 1960); (2) 'Iz numizmaticheskogo arkhiva' ['From the numismatic archives'], *NS*, pt. 2 (*Trudy GIM*, xxvi) (M., 1957).

[24] V. V. Kropotkin, 'O nekotorykh kladakh rimskikh monet, naidennykh v Rossii (iz istorii russkoi numizmatiki)' ['On certain hoards of Roman coins found in Russia (from the history of Russian numismatics)'], *KSIIMK*, 66 (1956); B. V. Lunin, *Iz istorii russkogo vostokovedeniya i arkheologii v Turkestane. Turkestanskii kruzhok lyubitelei arkheologii (1895—1917)* ['The history of Russian Oriental studies and archaeology in Turkestan. The Turkestan archaeological circle (1895–1917)'] (Tashkent, 1958). See also I. V. Sokolova, 'Drevnebolgarskie monety v muzeyakh SSR' ['Ancient Bulgarian coins in museums of the U.S.S.R.'], *Vizantiiskii vremennik*, xiii (1958); E. S. Shchukina, *Medal'ernoe iskusstvo v Rossii XVIII v.* ['The art of medal making in Russia in the eighteenth century'] (L., 1962).

[25] I. G. Spassky, *Peterburgskii monetnyi dvor ot vozniknoveniya do nachala XIX v.* ['The St. Petersburg mint from its origins to the beginning of the nineteenth century'] (L., 1949).

[26] Idem; (2) *Izobretatel' Nevedomskii* ['The inventor Nevedomsky'] (L., 1949); (2) 'Novye materialy dlya biografii I. A. Nevedomskogo' ['New materials for the biography of I. A. Nevedomsky'], *Trudy Gosudarstvennogo Ermitazha*, iii (1959).

[27] A. S. Mel'nikova: (1) 'Staryi moskovskii denezhnyi dvor vo vremya denezhnoi reformy 1654—1669 gg.' ['The old Moscow mint during the monetary reforms of 1654-1669'], *AE*, 1964 (M., 1965); (2) 'O chekanke monet v Kukenoise v seredine XVII v.' ['On the minting of coins in Kokenhusen in the mid-seventeenth century'], *SA*, 1964, 3.

[28] M. P. Sotnikova, 'K voprosu o tekhnike chekanki russkikh monet v XV v.' ['On the question of Russian coin-minting technology in the fifteenth century'], *KSIIMK*, 66 (1956).

a survey of Russian coinage from the earliest use of money in Russia until our own day. It was published to mark the 250th anniversary of the monetary reforms of Peter the Great and for the first time drew the attention of scholars to the fact that the decimal coinage system, which has long been attributed to the United States of America and France in the revolutionary period, was derived from the early Russian monetary system and was introduced in Russia almost a century before its introduction in the U.S.A. and France.[29] The book devotes a great deal of attention to the problems of technology, the organization of production, and the history of Russian mints in the time of Peter. A number of its sections were preliminary sketches of research published in more elaborate detail later.

Numismatics has reflected the enormous growth of interest in the Soviet Union abroad which has resulted from the great achievements of the Soviet people during the Second World War and in the various branches of science and culture in the post-war period. Russian coins which aroused little interest in the foreign antiquarian market before the war have come to the fore as regards both demand and price. Soviet numismatic literature arouses similar interest. Over the last fifteen to twenty years a number of works have appeared (mostly by American authors) which have been devoted to Russian coins of the eighteenth to twentieth centuries and a few researchers have even ventured into the previously quite unknown field of pre-Petrine numismatics.

Coin hoards have aroused the constant interest of Soviet researchers. The Department of Numismatics of the Historical Museum publishes information about newly discovered coin hoards.[30] The coin hoards of Byelorussia (more than 1,000 finds) was the subject of a research thesis by V. N. Ryabtsevich, a research student at the Hermitage.[31] A similar survey of Ukrainian hoards has been written by N. F. Kotlyar in the Institute of History of the Ukrainian Academy of Sciences. The publication of these two topographical surveys will be an important contribution to Soviet numismatics. Unfortunately local historical work in the field of numismatics and coin hoard registration is proving very slow in re-establishing itself.[32]

[29] I. G. Spassky, *Russkaya monetnaya sistema* ['The Russian monetary system'] (3rd ed., L., 1962). (The first edition was published in 1957 as a textbook for history teachers. An English edition was published in 1967 in Amsterdam—*The Russian Monetary System* (Revised and enlarged edition, Jacques Schulman, Amsterdam, 1967.))

[30] N. D. Mets, 'Klady monet (zaregistrirovannye GIM za 1945—1952 gg.)' ['Coin hoards (recorded by GIM in the period 1945-1952)'], *KSIIMK*, 52 (1953); A. S. Mel'nikova, 'Klady monet . . . 1952—1954 gg.' ['Coin hoards . . . 1952-1954'], *KSIIMK*, 67 (1957); N. D. Mets and A. S. Mel'nikova: (1) 'Klady monet . . . 1955—1958' ['Coin hoards . . . 1955–1958'], *Ezhegodnik GIM* (M., 1960); (2) 'Klady monet . . . 1959 g.' ['Coin hoards . . . 1959'], *Ezhegodnik GIM* (M., 1961).

[31] V. N. Ryabtsevich, *Topografiya monetnykh kladov na territorii Belorussii* ['The topography of coin hoards in Byelorussia'] (Thesis abstract, LOIA AN SSSR, 1965).

[32] I. Polozov, *Klady rasskazyvayut . . . . Topografiya kladov monet, naidennykh na territorii Bryanskoi oblasti v 1948—1960 gg.* ['What the coin hoards tell us . . . . Topography of coin hoards found in the Bryansk region in 1948-1960'] (Bryansk, 1960).

Research and description of Cufic coin hoards as monuments of early Russian currency which was begun so brilliantly by R. R. Fasmer has been continued by A. A. Bykov, S. A. Yanina, and V. N. Ryabtsevich.[33] S. A. Yanina has also continued Fasmer's work in the specialized field of the coins of the Volga Bulgars.[34]

An important event in the research into the currency of Byzantine coins on the territory of ancient Russia has been the publication of a fundamental topography by V. V. Kropotkin.[35] I. V. Sokolova has carried out research into the Byzantine part of an old, little-researched hoard.[36] The superb collection of Byzantine coins in the Hermitage is becoming much better known as a result of the publications of I. V. Sokolova.

Great progress is being made in the research into medieval West-European coins current in the territory of the U.S.S.R., which represent an important stage in medieval Russian coin currency. A number of new hoards have been published, for the most part the work of N. P. Bauer's successor at the Hermitage, A. A. Markova and her pupil and successor V. M. Potin. The latter's thesis contained a topography of these hoards enriched by new material and more detailed analysis of previously known hoards on the basis of the latest systematizing data.[37]

[33] A. A. Bykov: (1) 'Kuficheskie monety ozherel'ya iz Paunkula' ['Cufic coins in the necklace from Paunkul'], Izvestiya Akademii nauk ESSR [Estonia] (seriya obshchestvennykh nauk), x, 2 (1961); (2) 'Vostochnye monety Degtyanskogo klada' ['Oriental coins from the Degtyany hoard'], Trudy Gos. Ermitazha, iv (1961); S. A. Yanina: (1) 'Nerevskii klad kuficheskikh monet X v.' ['The Nerev (Novgorod) Cufic coin hoard of the tenth century'], MIA SSSR, 55 (1956); (2) 'Vtoroi Nerevskii klad kuficheskikh monet X v.' ['The second Nerev Cufic coin hoard of the tenth century'], MIA SSSR, 117 (1963); V. N. Ryabtsevich, 'Dva monetno-veshchevykh klada IX v. iz Vitebskoi oblasti' ['Two coin and object hoards of the ninth century from the Vitebsk region'], NiE, v (M., 1965).

[34] R. R. Fasmer, 'O monetakh volzhskikh bolgar X v.' ['On the coins of the Volga Bulgars in the tenth century'], Izvestiya Obshchestva arkheologii, istorii i etnografii pri Kazanskom universitete imeni V. I. Ulyanova-Lenina, xxxiii, 1 (Kazan', 1926); R. Vasmer, 'Über die Münzen des Wolgabulgarien', NZ, 58 (1925); S. A. Yanina, 'Novye dannye o monetnom chekane Volzhskoi Bolgarii X v.' ['New data on coin minting among the Volga Bulgars in the tenth century'], MIA SSSR, 111 (1962).

[35] V. V. Kropotkin: (1) Klady vizantiiskikh monet na territorii SSSR ['Byzantine coin hoards in the U.S.S.R.'] (M., 1962); (2) 'Novye nakhodki vizantiiskikh monet na territorii SSSR' ['New finds of Byzantine coins in the U.S.S.R.'], Vizantiiskii vremennik, xxvi (1965).

[36] I. V. Sokolova, 'Vizantiiskie monety klada Vella' ['Byzantine coins in the Vella hoard'], Trudy Gos. Ermitazha, iv (1961).

[37] A. M. Maslov, 'L'govskii klad' ['The L'gov coin hoard'], KSIIMK, 23 (1948); A. A. Markova, 'Tretii Lodeinopol'skii klad srednevekovykh zapadno-evropeiskikh monet' ['The third Lodeinoe Pole hoard of medieval west European coins'], NS, 2 (Trudy GIM, xxvi) (1957); V. M. Potin: (1) 'Degtyanskii klad denariev serediny XI v.' ['The Degtyany hoard of denarii of the mid-eleventh century'], Trudy Gos. Ermitazha, iv (1961); (2) 'Topografiya nakhodok zapadnoevropeiskikh monet X—XIII vv. na territorii Drevnei Rusi' ['Topography of finds of west European coins of the tenth–thirteenth centuries in Ancient Russia'], ibid., ix, Numizmatika, 3 (1968); (3) Drevnyaya Rus' i evropeiskie gosudarstva v X-XIII vv. ['Ancient Russia and European states of the tenth–thirteenth centuries'] (L. 1968). See also V. M. Potin: (1) 'Prichiny prekrashcheniya pritoka zapadnoevropeiskikh monet na Rus' v XII v. ['Reasons for the cessation of the flow of west European coins into

The circulation of Oriental, Byzantine, and West-European coins in the territory of ancient Russia make up the background without consideration of which the problem of the first coins of the Russian state cannot be solved. These problems are examined in the section entitled 'Den'gi i denezhnoe obrashchenie' ['Money and its circulation'] of the book *Istoriya kul'tury Drevnei Rusi* ['History of the culture of ancient Russia'].[38] The author of this work defends the view of I. I. Tolstoy and summarizes all that was achieved in this field on the eve of the war. V. L. Yanin goes much further in his monograph[39] which embraces all the problems of money circulation in the pre-Mongol period, beginning with the basic concept of the *kuna* system in the Slavonic world. This research has shed much light on the question of the fundamentally differing characters of the money and weights systems of Kiev and Novgorod; the serious attention paid by the author to the metrological evidence and the profound analysis of the composition of hoards containing *srebreniki* [silver coins of ancient Russia] demonstrates finally and unquestionably the 'return' of the oldest Russian coins into circulation at the end of the tenth and beginning of the eleventh century. The accuracy of I. I. Tolstoy's dating of the coins of the Kievan princes receives new support in a series of sphragistic researches by V. L. Yanin.[40] The noticeable increase in the fund of the earliest Russian coins is reflected in two articles by the late director of the Department of Numismatics of the Historical Museum, N. D. Mets, who died in 1965;[41] one of the recent finds which is particularly interesting in the dating of its archaeological setting has been published by A. A. Medyntseva.[42]

Russia in the twelfth century'], *Mezhdunarodnye svyazi Rossii do XVII v.* ['Russia's international links before the seventeenth century'] (M., 1961); (2) 'K voprosu o sostave i datirovke Skadinskogo klada' ['On the question of the composition and dating of the Skadin hoard'], *Soobshcheniya Gos. Ermitazha*, xvii (1960); (3) 'O serebryanykh monetovidnykh plastinkakh v kladakh X—XII vv.' ['On the silver coin-like discs in hoards of the tenth–twelfth centuries'], *NiE*, ii (M., 1960); (4) 'Osobennosti pritoka zapadnoevropeskikh denariev X—XI vv. i ikh rasprostranenie na territorii Drevnei Rusi' ['Features of the influx of west European denarii of the tenth–eleventh century and their spread in Ancient Russia'], *Zapiski Odesskogo arkheologicheskogo obshchestva*, i (34) (1960); (5) 'Nekotorye voprosy torgovli Drevnei Rusi po numizmaticheskim dannym' ['Some questions of trade in Ancient Russia from numismatic evidence'], *Vestnik istorii mirovoi kul'tury*, 4 (1961); (6) 'Nakhodki zapadnoevropeiskikh monet na territorii Drevnei Rusi i drevnerusskie poseleniy' ['Ancient Russian settlements and the finds of west European coins in Ancient Russia'], *NiE*, iii (M., 1962).

[38] B. A. Romanov, 'Den'gi i denezhnoe obrashchenie' ['Money and its circulation'], *Istoriya kul'tury Drevnei Rusi. Domongol'skii period*, i, (M.–L., 1948). This article is based on unpublished material of N. P. Bauer.

[39] V. L. Yanin, *Denezhno-vesovye sistemy russkogo srednevekov'ya. Domongol'skii period* ['The money and weights system of medieval Russia. Pre-Mongol period'], (M., 1965).

[40] See V. L. Yanin, 'Drevneishaya russkaya pechat' X v.' ['An ancient Russian seal of the tenth century'], *KSIIMK*, 55 (1955).

[41] N. D. Mets; (1) 'Srebreniki iz Mit'kovki' ['Silver coins from Mit'kovka'], *SA*, 1960, i; (2) 'Neizdannye srebreniki Gosudarstvennogo Istoricheskogo muzeya' ['Unpublished silver coins from the Historical Museum'], *NiS*, I (1963).

[42] A. A. Medyntseva, *Srebrenik iz Zarech'ya na Stugne* ['A silver coin from Zarech'e on the Stugna'], *SA*, i (1965).

Research into the technology of the production of southern *srebreniki* shows evidence of a single centre where for a very short period these coins were produced.[43] The Hermitage is now completing its preparation of a union catalogue of the earliest Russian coins. If the number of known *zlatniki* [gold coins of ancient Russia] of Vladimir does not increase, then their previously unknown origin is explained—they all go back to two long-known hoards which previously had been thought to consist only of Byzantine coins. The number of *srebreniki* now known is double that known to I. I. Tolstoy in the 1890s and has now reached 300. M. P. Sotnikova has completed an enormous task in compiling a *curriculum vitae* of literally every one of them.

In two articles K. V. Golenko has expressed his views on the characteristic 'barbarian' imitations of Byzantine coins of the tenth–early eleventh century found almost exclusively on the Taman' peninsula. He discerns in them the first stage of local Russian minting.[44] In one of his articles V. M. Potin attempts to prove that the so-called Scandinavian imitations of the silver coinage of Yaroslav (B. V. Kene at one time thought them to be coins of Oleg) are in fact coins of Yaroslav of an earlier period.[45]

The oldest controversy in the history of money circulation in ancient Russia—that concerning leather money—is still remarkably alive. In 1949 a thesis was defended in Leningrad in which the author, basing his argument on a reference in Karl Marx to Russian leather money, proved that money of this kind was in common use in Russia right up to the fifteenth century.[46] In the *Ocherki po istorii russkoi numiimatiki* referred to above (Note 22) the original source of Jean-Baptiste Say's communication quoted by Marx has been established as a course of political economy compiled by Academician Shtorkh and read by him to the grandchildren of Catherine II at the very end of the eighteenth century.

A further strong argument advanced by the supporters of the theory of leather money—the statements of several medieval Arabic writers concerning the high value among the Russians of certain animal skins from which the

---

[43] I. G. Spassky, 'Nasushchnye voprosy izucheniya russkikh monet X—XI vv.' ['Vital questions in the study of Russian coins of the tenth–eleventh century'], *Soobshcheniya Gos. Ermitazha*, xxi (1961).

[44] K. V. Golenko: (1) 'Podrazhaniya vizantiiskim monetam X—XI vv., naidennye na Tamanskom poluostrove' ['Imitations of Byzantine coins of the tenth–eleventh century on the Taman' peninsula'], *Vizantiiskii vremennik*, viii (1953); (2) 'Novye materialy k izucheniyu tamanskikh podrazhanii vizantiiskim monetam' ['New material for the study of the Taman' imitations of Byzantine coins'], ibid., xviii (1961).

[45] V. M. Potin, 'O tak nazyvaemykh "skandinavskikh" padrazhaniyakh monetam Yaroslava Mudrogo' ['On the so-called "Scandinavian" imitations of the coins of Yaroslav the Wise'], Communication to the second scientific conference on the history, economics, language, and literature of the Scandinavian countries and Finland (M., 1965).

[46] P. G. Zaostrovtsev, *Iz istorii deneg i denezhnogo obrashcheniya v Rossii do XV v.* ['The history of money and its circulation in Russia before the fifteenth century'] (Thesis abstract, Leningrad University, 1949).

hair had been removed—has been examined in a separate article[47] in connection with certain methods of faking of fur-skins by plucking out individual hairs. However, the recent appearance of yet another Arabic source has enabled the adherents of this theory to include in their argument the so-called *drogichinskie plomby*[48]—Russian trade seals [from the village of Drogichin] which have received so far hardly any attention. It is stated that the Russians used knotted threads and bundles of useless leather thongs with lead seals attached as money.

Great progress has been made in the study of currency bars. In a number of publications M. P. Sotnikova has explained on the basis of very extensive material some interesting peculiarities of the method of production of some of the Novgorod bars in which a thin layer of high-quality silver is deposited on baser metal. Study of the many inscriptions found on bars has elucidated many aspects of the organization of production and even certain arithmetical methods used by foundrymen to calculate the loss of metal when melting it down.[49] A new hoard from Gorodets on the Volga has been published by A. F. Medvedev.[50] Two articles by G. B. Fedorov are concerned with the so-called Lithuanian bars.[51]

In his book on Old Russian manuscript illustration A. V. Artsikhovsky has shown how miniatures may be used as sources when conducting research into problems of currency in the 'coinless period'.[52]

The articles of G. A. Fedorov-Davydov are devoted to the topography of finds of coins of the Juchi dynasty, which are important for the dating of the circulation of certain kinds of money-bar, and deal also with Russian

[47] I. G. Spassky, 'Iz istorii drevnerusskogo tovarovedeniy' ['On the history of commodity studies of medieval Russia'], *KSIIMK*, 62 (1956).

[48] A. L. Mongait, 'Abu Khamid al-Garnati i ego puteshestvie v russkie zemli 1150—1153 gg.' ['Abu Khamid al-Garnati and his journey to Russia, 1150–1153'], *Istoriya SSSR*, 1959, 1.

[49] M. P. Sotnikova: (1) 'Iz istorii obrashcheniya russkikh serebryanykh platezhnykh slitkov v XIV—XV vv. (Delo Fedora Zherebtsa 1447 g.)' ['On the history of the circulation of Russian silver currency bars in the fourteenth–fifteenth century. (The case of Fedor Zherebets, 1447).], *SA*, 1957, 3; (2) ' "Petrovi grivni" ' [' "Peter's *grivni*" '], *Soobshcheniya Gos. Ermitazha*, x (1956); (3) 'Ryazanskii klad litovskikh serebryanykh slitkov v sobranii Ermitazha' ['The Ryazan' hoard of Lithuanian silver bars in the Hermitage collection'], ibid., xii (1957); (4) 'Epigrafika serebryanykh platezhnykh slitkov Velikogo Novgoroda XII—XV vv.' ['The epigraphy of silver currency bars from Novgorod of the twelfth–fifteenth centuries'], *Trudy Gos. Ermitazha*, iv (1961); (5) 'Iz istorii drevnerusskoi prakticheskoi arifmetiki XII—XIV vv.' ['On the history of early Russian practical arithmetic in the twelfth–fourteenth centuries'], *Soobshcheniya Gos. Ermitazha*, xxiii (1962).

[50] A. F. Medvedev, 'O novgorodskikh grivnakh serebra' ['On the Novgorod silver *grivni*'], *SA*, 1963, 2.

[51] G. B. Fedorov: (1) 'Klassifikatsiya litovskikh slitkov i monet' ['Classification of Lithuanian currency bars and coins'], *KSIIMK*, 29 (1949); (2) 'Topografiya kladov s litovskimi slitkami i monetami' ['Topography of hoards containing Lithuanian currency bars and coins'], ibid.

[52] A. V. Artsikhovsky, *Drevnerusskie miniatyry kak istoricheskii istochnik* ['Early Russian miniatures as a historical source'] (M., 1944).

territory.[53] The circulation of 'Prague groschen' in west Russia has been examined in the work of N. A. Soboleva and V. N. Ryabtsevich.[54] The coins and money circulation of Chervonaya Rus' [Red Russia] were the subject of N. F. Kotlyar's thesis.[55]

Coins of the period of the appanage principalities are a very old subject in Russian numismatics and work on them has continued ever since they were first investigated in the eighteenth century by A. I. Bogdanov.

Only one new hoard of Russian coins of the fourteenth and fifteenth centuries has been found since the war,[56] but investigation of the coins and money circulation of this period has been very actively pursued. After several articles by G. B. Fedorov[57] some very interesting and promising results for the scientific systematization of coins of the appanage period have been achieved by N. D. Mets, using the extensive material of the Historical Museum and successfully employing a method of research which correlated the dies used at different times in the process of coin production.[58] This scholar's thesis was devoted to the complex subject of the coins of the reign of Vasily Temny [the Dark]. Her publications have led to a change in many of the accepted ideas on the subject of the scientific arrangement of coins of the fourteenth and fifteenth centuries.[59]

[53] G. A. Fedorov-Davydov: (1) 'Klady dzhuchidskikh monet' ['Hoards of the coins of the Juchi dynasty'], *NiE*, i (M., 1960); (2) 'Nakhodki dzhuchidskikh monet' ['Finds of the coins of the Juchi dynasty'], *NiE*, iv (M., 1963).

[54] N. A. Soboleva: (1) 'Prazhskie groshi v muzeyakh Ukrainy' ['Prague groschen in Ukrainian museums'], *NiS*, I (Kiev, 1963); (2) 'Klad prazhskikh groshei iz s. Chaiki Kievskoi obl.' ['A hoard of Prague groschen from the village of Chaika in the Kiev region'], *NiS*, 2 (Kiev, 1965); V. N. Ryabtsevich, 'K voprosu o denezhnom obrashchenii zapadno-russkikh zemel' v XIV—XV vv.' ['On the question of currency circulation in the West Russian lands in the fourteenth and fifteenth centuries'], ibid.

[55] N. F. Kotlyar: (1) 'Denezhnoe khozyaistvo i monetnoe delo Chervonoi Rusi soro-kovykh godov XIV—pervoi chetverti XV vv.' ['Money economy and coining in Red Russia from the 1340s to the 1420s'], (Thesis abstract, LOII AN SSR, 1965); (2) 'K voprosu o pravovom polozhenii L'vovskogo monetnogo dvora v XIV—XV stoletiyakh' ['On the question of the legal position of the Lvov mint in the fourteenth—fifteenth centuries'], *NiS*, 2 (Kiev, 1965); (3) 'Klassifikatsiya chervonorusskikh monet Vladislava knyazya Opol'skogo' ['Classification of the Red Russian coins of Vladislav, Prince of Opole'], *Soobshcheniya Gos. Ermitazha*, xxvi (1965): (4) 'Problemy i osnovnye itogi issledovanii monet Chervonoi Rusi' ['Problems and main conclusions of research on the coins of Red Russia'], *NiS*, 2 (Kiev, 1965).

[56] M. V. Suzin, 'Ozhgibovskii klad XIV veka' ['The Ozhgibovka hoard of the fourteenth century'], *KSIIMK*, 29 (1949).

[57] G. B. Fedorov: (1) 'Proiskhozhdenie moskovskoi monetnoi sistemy' ['Origin of the Moscovite monetary system'], *KSIIMK*, 16 (1947); (2) 'Den'gi Moskovskogo knyazhestva vremeni Dmitriya Donskogo i Vasiliya I' ['The money of the Principality of Moscow in the time of Dmitry Donskoy and Vasily I'], *MIA SSSR*, 12 (1949); (3) 'Moskovskie den'gi vremeni velikikh knyazei Ivana III i Vasiliya III' ['Moscow money in the time of the Grand Princes Ivan III and Vasily III'], *KSIIMK*, xxx (1949).

[58] I. G. Spassky, 'Analiz tekhnicheskikh dannykh v numizmatike' ['The analysis of technical data in numismatics'], *KSIIMK*, 39 (1951).

[59] N. D. Mets: (1) *Monety velikogo knyazhestva Moskovskogo serediny XV v. Vasilii II (1425—1462)* ['Coins of the Grand Principality of Moscow in the mid-fifteenth century.

V. L. and S. A. Yanin have investigated the Ryazan' imitations of coins of the Juchi dynasty and have established that coin minting in Ryazan' began later than in Moscow.[60] V. L. Yanin and the author of this survey have investigated the rise of the *altyn* monetary system in the Russian principalities; V. L. Yanin has also worked out a number of metrological features of Russian coins of the fourteenth to seventeenth century.[61]

Detailed and valuable studies have been devoted to the numismatics of Novgorod and Pskov. The research of A. N. Molvygin[62] has completely cleared up the question of foreign coins current in those cities before the introduction of their own minting. A. V. Artsikhovsky has made a well-argued identification of the design on Novgorod coins as the adoration of St. Sofia,[63] while N. D. Mets, investigating a similar design on one type of Moscovite *denga* [small silver, later copper, coin] has adduced several more arguments in favour of this identification and has suggested that Novgorod borrowed the weight standard from Moscow.[64] A. L. Khoroshkevich has published with his own commentary an interesting foreign account of the Russian monetary situation in the fourteenth and fifteenth centuries[65]—a

Vasily II (1425–1462)'], (Thesis abstract, Institut arkheologii, An SSSR, M., 1956); (2) 'Monety udel'nogo knyazhestva Kashinskogo' ['Coins of the appanage principality of Kashin'], *KSIIMK*, 65 (1956); (3) 'Yaroslavskie knyazya po numizmaticheskim dannym' ['The Yaroslavl' princes from the numismatic evidence'], *SA*, 1960, 3; (4) 'Nekotorye voprosy sistematizatsii monet Suzdal'sko-Nizhegorodskogo knyazhestva' ['Some problems of the systematization of the coins of the Suzdal'-Nizhnii Novgorod principality'], *Istoriko-arkheologicheskii sbornik* (M., 1962); (5) 'Datirovka "deneg moskovskikh" s izobrazheniem rozetki' ['The dating of "Moscow *den'gi*" with a rosette design'], *SA*, 1964, 3.

[60] V. L. Yanin and S. A. Yanina, 'Nachal'nyi period ryazanskoi chekanki' ['The early period of coining in Ryazan''], *NS*, I (*Trudy GIM*, xxv) (M., 1955).

[61] I. G. Spassky, 'Altyn v russkoi denezhnoi sisteme' ['The *altyn* in the Russian monetary system'], *KSIIMK*, 66 (1956); V. L. Yanin: (1) 'Altyn i ego mesto v russkikh denezhnykh sistemakh XIV—XV vv.' ['The *altyn* and its place in the Russian monetary system'], ibid.; (2) 'O metrologicheskikh zakonomernostyakh v razvitii russkikh monetnykh norm XIV—XVII vv.' ['On metrological patterns in the development of Russian norms of coinage in the fourteenth–seventeenth centuries'], *AE*, 1957 (M., 1958).

[62] A. N. Molvygin, 'Nominaly melkikh monet Livonii s serediny XIII do vtoroi poloviny XVI v. i nekotorye voprosy denezhnogo dela Novgoroda i Pskova' ['The nominal values of the small coins of Livonia from the mid-thirteenth century to the second half of the sixteenth century and some problems of the coinage of Novgorod and Pskov'], *Izvestiya Akademii nauk ESSR* [Estonia] (seriya obshchestvennykh nauk), 4 (1963).

[63] A. V. Artsykhovsky, 'Izobrazhenie na novgorodskikh monetakh' ['The design on Novgorod coins'], *Izvestiya AN SSSR* (seriya istorii i filosofii), v, 1 (1948).

[64] N. D. Mets, 'Moskovskaya den'ga novgorodskogo tipa' ['The Moscow *den'ga* of the Novgorod type'], *NS*, i (*Trudy GIM*, xxv) M., 1955).

[65] 'A. L. Khoroshkevich: (1) 'Iz istorii ganzeiskoi torgovli. (Vvoz v Novgorod blagorodnykh metallov v XIV—XV vv.)' ['On the history of the Hansa trade. (The import of precious metals in the fourteenth and fifteenth centuries)'], *Srednie veka*, xx (M., 1961); (2) 'Inostrannoe svidetel'stvo 1399 g. o novgorodskoi denezhnoi sisteme' ['A foreign account of the monetary system of Novgorod in 1399'], *Istoriko-arkheologicheskii sbornik* (M., 1962); (3) 'Nekotorye inostrannye svidetel'stva o russkom denezhnom obrashchenii kontsa XV v.' ['Some foreign accounts of Russian currency circulation at the end of the fifteenth century'], *Voprosy sotsial'no-ekonomicheskoi istorii i istochnikovedeniya perioda feodalizma v Rossii* (Sbornik statei k 70-letiyu A. A. Novosel'skogo) (M., 1961).

record of the Novgorod system of money and weights from the trade accounts of the Teutonic Order.

V. L. Yanin has published an account found in the posthumous papers of A. V. Oreshnikov of a note in a fifteenth-century Menologion which establishes more accurately the date of the beginnings of coin minting in Pskov.[66] A. S. Mel'nikova has applied the analysis of related dies to the vast quantity of known types of coin from fifteenth-century Pskov and has established the sequence of growth of circulation of these extremely similar coins.[67]

Investigation of money circulation in sixteenth- and seventeenth-century Russia has progressed considerably. Until quite recently this period of almost two centuries was a blank in Russian numismatics and its coins of unvarying design with the barest of inscriptions was considered extremely unpromising material for research. Comparative study of the composition of hoards and the application of analysis of related dies to these very common coins has made it possible not only to establish the sequence of issue and the mints involved, but also to distinguish new and hitherto quite unknown groups of coins, for example, Yaroslavl' coins struck for the general mobilization and copecks struck during the Swedish occupation of Novgorod.[68]

G. B. Fedorov has written an article analysing the Chonicle accounts of the monetary reforms of Elena Glinskaya.[69]

Accounts have been published of the coin hoards of two old museums, those of Yaroslavl' and Novgorod.[70] A. S. Mel'nikova has undertaken a systematic analysis of all the copeck coins of the reign of Mikhail Fedorovich and has detected in them the initial period of the temporary Moscow mint.[71] V. L. Yanin had begun to ascribe to 1612–13 yet another group of coins

[66] V. L. Yanin, 'O nachale pskovskoi monetnoi chekanki. (Neopublikovannoe otkrytie A. V. Oreshnikova)' ['On the beginnings of coining in Pskov. (An unpublished discovery of A. V. Oreshnikov)'], NS, 1 (Trudy GIM, xxv) (M., 1955).

[67] A. S. Mel'nikova, 'Pskovskie monety XV v.' ['Pskov coins of the fifteenth century'], NiE, i (M. 1963).

[68] I. G. Spassky: (1) 'Denezhnaya kazna' ['The Treasury'], Istoricheskii pamyatnik russkogo arkticheskogo moreplavaniya XVII v. (L.–M., 1951); (2) 'Iz istorii deneg v Rossii v period pol'sko-shvedskoi interventsii nachala XVII v.' ['On the history of money in the period of the Polish-Swedish intervention at the beginning of the seventeenth century'], Izvestiya Karelo-Finskogo filiala AN SSSR, 2 (Petrozavodsk, 1951); (3) 'Denezhnoe obrashchenie v Moskovskom gosudarstve s 1533 po 1617 g.' ['Money circulation in the Moscovite state from 1533 to 1617'], MIA SSSR, 44 (1955).

[69] G. B. Fedorov, 'Unifikatsiya russkoi monetnoi sistemy i ukaz 1535 g.' ['The unification of the Russian monetary system and the ukase of 1535'], Izvestiya AN SSSR (seriya istorii i filosofii), vii, 6 (1950).

[70] V. L. Yanin, 'Monetnye klady Yaroslavskogo kraevedcheskogo muzeya' ['Coin hoards of the Yaroslavl' Museum of Local History'], Yaroslavskii oblastnoi kraevedcheskii muzei. Kraevedcheskie zapiski, ii (1957); M. G. Meierovich, 'Novye monetnye klady Yaroslavskogo kraevedcheskogo muzeya' ['New coin hoards of the Yaroslavl' Museum of Local History'], ibid.; V. L. Yanin, 'Monetnye klady Novgorodskogo muzeya' ['Coin hoards of the Novgorod museum'], NiE, ii (M., 1960).

[71] A. S. Mel'nikova, 'Sistematizatsiya monet Mikhaila Fedorovicha' ['The systematization of the coins of Mikhail Fedorovich'], AE, 1958 (M., 1960).

which he had distinguished by a number of characteristics,[72] but it soon became clear that they belonged to a complex of coins which had become current in Russia but which had been minted in Copenhagen for the requirements of the Lapland trade.[73]

A. A. Zimin, disputing the opinion of I. G. Spassky, defended the accuracy of the dates given by the Pskov Chronicles for the monetary reforms of Elena Glinskaya in Pskov.[74]

Investigation of related dies has made it possible to elucidate what had seemed completely intractable material—the so-called *mordovki*, that is, imitations of different periods of coins of different periods in pre-Petrine Russia.[75]

Research into the coins of the reign of Aleksey Mikhailovich in the light of the documents of the Moscow mint published in 1935 by K. B. Bazilevich[76] and other sources has made it possible to date exactly the change-over of the circulation of the various types of these coins during the reforms of 1654–63 and establish several previously unknown facts, such as, for example, that in Novgorod copper and silver copecks were minted simultaneously, or to decipher one of the marks found on copecks as the mark of the Kukenois [Kokenhusen, Koknese] mint. The reform of Aleksey Mikhailovich is now seen as the direct result of the annexation of the Ukraine by Russia which required the creation of a unified currency. A union catalogue of large denomination coins of 1654–5—roubles, *poltinniki* [half-roubles] and *efimki* (thalers with Moscow over-stamps)—records a number of coins hoards of the Ukraine and Byelorussia containing *efimki*.[77]

To the studies of the currency of the sixteenth and seventeenth centuries we may add investigation of the *zolotye*, coin-like military medals of pre-Petrine Russia which until recently were described as coins, though they were not. The rich collections of *zolotye* in the Hermitage and Historical Museum when compared with known documents have made it possible to establish a strict system of military awards and the process by which they were awarded; in particular light has been thrown on the award in 1654 to Bogdan

[72] V. L. Yanin, 'Iz istorii russkoi monetnoi chekanki v 1612—1613 gg.' ['On the history of coining in Russia in 1612–1613'], *NiE*, i (M., 1960).

[73] A. S. Mel'nikova, 'Russko-datskie monety XVII v sobranii GIM' ['Russo-Danish coins of the seventeenth century in the GIM collection'], *Ezhegodnik GIM* (M., 1970).

[74] A. A. Zimin, 'O monetnoi reforme Eleny Glinskoi' ['On the monetary reforms of Elena Glinskaya'], *NiE*, iv (M., 1963).

[75] I. G. Spassky, 'Denezhnoe obrashchenie na territorii Povolzh'ya v pervoi polovine XVI v. i tak nazyvaemye mordovki' ['Money circulation in the Volga region in the first half of the sixteenth century and the so-called *mordovki*'], *SA*, xxi (1954).

[76] K. V. Bazilevich, 'Denezhnaya reforma Alekseya Mikhailovicha (1654—1663)' ['The monetary reforms of Aleksey Mikhailovich'], *Izvestiye AN SSSR* (seriya obshchestvennykh nauk), vii, 3 (M., 1935).

[77] I. G. Spassky: (1) 'Denezhnoe khozyaistvo Russkogo gosudarstva v seredine XVII v. i reforma 1654—1663 gg.' ['Money economy of the Russian state in the mid-seventeenth century and the reforms of 1654–1663'], *AE*, 1959 (M., 1960); (2) *Talery v russkom denezhnom obrashchenii 1654—1659 gg.* ['Thalers in Russian money circulation in 1654–1659'] (M., 1960).

Khmel'nitsky and tens of thousands of his cossacks. What were described in the Ukrainian chronicles as payment for service turn out to be service decorations.[78]

In the article devoted to the history of the Russian abacus attention has been drawn to hitherto unnoticed arithmetical functions of a particular kind in the Russian monetary system of the sixteenth and seventeenth centuries. The conventional expression of any fraction in terms of sums of money, for which special reference tables existed, made possible arithmetical calculations in thirds and quarters.[79] The same article explained the regular occurrence in Russian archaeological sites of the sixteenth to eighteenth centuries and in ethnographic monuments of the Volga region and Siberia of Nürnberg reckoning counters (Rechenpfennige) and Russian imitations of them.

We have already noted above the post-war surveys of coin hoards of the Ukraine and Byelorussia and investigations of post-medieval currency (Prague groschen and the coins of Red Russia). The currency circulation of the Ukraine in the seventeenth century received considerable attention in the 1920s. Among the most well-argued and scientifically accurate publications were those of V. A. Shugaevsky,[80] but most were very general and ignored completely numismatic data.[81] The author of works on the history of coins and the monetary system of the Ukraine was also guilty of ignoring elementary numismatic concepts.[82]

[78] Idem, ' "Zolotye" — voinskie nagrady dopetrovskoi Rusi' [' "Zolotye"—the military awards of pre-Petrine Russia'], *Trudy Gos. Ermitazha*, iv (1961).

[79] Idem, 'Proiskhozhdenie i istoriya russkikh schetov' ['The origin and history of the Russian abacus'], *Istoriko-matematicheskie issledovaniya*, 5 (M., 1952).

[80] V. Shugaevsky: (1) *Moneta i denezhnyi schet v Levoberezhnoi Ukraine v XVII v.* ['Coins and the monetary system in left-bank Ukraine in the seventeenth century'] (Chernigov, 1918); (2) 'Do groshovogo obigu Chernigivshchini XVII v.' ['On money circulation in the Chernigov area in the seventeenth century'], *Chernigiv na Pivnichne Livoberezhzhya* (Kiev, 1929) [Ukr.]; (3) 'Do pitaniya pro groshovii obig ta monety na Livoberezhnii Ukraini XVII v. (vidpovid' E. Onats'komu)' ['On the question of money circulation and coins in the left-bank Ukraine in the seventeenth century a rejoinder to E. Onat'sky'], *Nashe minule*, 1919, 1–2. [Ukr.]; (4) 'Do pitaniya pro groshovii obig ta monetu na Livoberezhnii Ukraini XVII v. (Chi bula na Ukraini vlasna moneta?)' ['On the question of money circulation and coins in the left-bank Ukraine in the seventeenth century: what was the native currency in the Ukraine?'], *NZIS*, 1924 (Kiev, 1925) [Ukr.]; (5) 'Chi bula na Ukraini v XVII st. vlasna moneta. Stattya durga. (Vidpovid' na zakidi prof. Slabchenka proti moei statti)' ['What was the native currency in the Ukraine in the seventeenth century. II. (A rejoinder to Professor Slabchenko's objections to my article.)'], *NZIS*, 1926 (Kiev, 1926) [Ukr.].

[81] M. Slabchenko, 'Chi bula v Get'manshchini svoya moneta' ['What was the native currency in the Ukraine of the Hetmans?'], *NZIS*, 1925 (Kiev, 1926) [Ukr.]; M. N. Petrovsky, 'Chi isnuvala na Ukraini vlasna moneta za chasiv Bogdana Khmel'nits'kogo' ['What native currency existed in the Ukraine in the time of Bogdan Khmel'nitsky?'], *NZIS*, 1926 (Kiev, 1926) [Ukr.].

[82] A. Ershov: (1) 'Do istorii groshovoi lichbi i moneti na Livoberezhnii Ukraini v XVIII v.' ['On the history of the monetary system and coins of the left-bank Ukraine in the eighteenth century'], *NZIS*, 1924 (Kiev, 1925) [Ukr.]; (2) 'Do istorii groshovoi lichbi i moneti na Livoberezhnii Ukraini v XVII—XVIII v.' ['On the history of the monetary system and coins of the left-bank Ukraine in the seventeenth–eighteenth century'], *NZIS*, 1929 (Kiev, 1930) [Ukr.].

Since the war both practical organization and theoretical work in the field of numismatics in the Ukraine and Byelorussia has become noticeably more active.[83] Apart from the topography of coin hoards of the Chernigov region and eastern Byelorussia in the seventeenth and early eighteenth century compiled by V. N. Ryabtsevich,[84] a number of other descriptions of coin hoards of the same period has been published in varying degrees of detail and completeness.[85] V. N. Ryabtsevich has published an interesting study of the reasons for the appearance in Byelorussia after the 1640s of one particular type of copper coin from Scotland, linking it with the emigration of Scottish presbyterians to the Commonwealth of Poland and Lithuania.[86]

Numismatic research has been carried out on the appearance of the so-called Virgin of Loretto in Ukrainian iconography. Definite types of Ukrainian coins of the early eighteenth century are to be seen in the necklaces of the Virgin and child.[87]

From 1957 to 1960 E. I. Chernov published a series of studies on the Ukrainian vocabulary based on the historical and modern terminology of the currency.[88]

The thousand years of money in Russia offers a rich choice of interesting and important subjects; it is hardly surprising then that Soviet scholars have paid relatively little attention to later coins of the eighteenth to twentieth century, for in this period coins can hardly compete with written sources. At the same time it is precisely these coins which are more commonly found and easier to identify, which are most studied by a number of American scholars. Harry Severin, who died in 1966, even expressed the opinion in his

[83] N. F. Kotlyar, 'Stan i perspektivi rozvitku ukrains'koi numizmatiki' ['The present state and future prospects of Ukrainian numismatics'], *Ukrains'kii istorichnii zhurnal*, 1963, 11 [Ukr.].

[84] V. N. Ryabtsevich, 'Monetnye klady XVII i pervoi chetverti XVIII v. na territorii Chernigovo-Severskoi zemli i vostochnoi Belorussii' ['Coin hoards of the seventeenth and first quarter of the eighteenth century in the Chernigov-Severskii area and western Byelorussia'], *NIS*, 2 (Kiev, 1963).

[85] A. A. Markova, 'Mogilevskii klad dukatov XVI—XVII vv.' ['The Mogilev hoard of ducats of the sixteenth–seventeenth century'], *Trudy Gos. Ermitazha*, iv (1961); A. G. Zaginailo, 'Mar'yanovskii klad (predv. soobshchenie)' ['The Mar'yanov hoard (preliminary report)'], *Materialy po arkheologii Severnogo Prichernomor'ya*, iv (Odessa, 1962); A. D. Rudenko: (1) 'Bertnikovskii klad zapadnoevropeiskikh i russkikh monet XVII v.' ['The Bertniki hoard of West European and Russian coins of the seventeenth century'], ibid.; (2) 'Kievskii klad zapadnoevropeiskikh monet pervoi poloviny XVII v.' ['The Kiev hoard of West European coins of the first half of the seventeenth century'], *NiS*, 1 (Kiev, 1963); (3) 'Monetno-rechovii klad z s. Pekari' ['The coin and object hoard from the village of Pekari'], *Visnik Kiivs'kogo universiteta*, 8 (seriya istorii ta prava, 1) (Kiev, 1967), [Ukr.].

[86] V. N. Ryabtsevich, 'Shotlandskie monety pervoi poloviny XVII v. v kladakh Belorussii i sosednikh raionov' ['Scottish coins of the first half of the seventeenth century in the coin hoards of Byelorussia and neighbouring areas'], *NiE*, 4 (M., 1963).

[87] I. G. Spassky, 'Neobychnyi numizmaticheskii pamyatnik' ['An unusual numismatic monument'], *NiS*, 2 (Kiev, 1965).

[88] E. I. Chernov. *Istoriya nazvanii deneg i denezhnykh edinits v ukrainskom yazyke* ['The history of the names of coins and monetary units in Ukrainian'] (Thesis abstract, Kiev, 1960).

last book that Soviet numismatists would like to write about coins of the Tsarist period but cannot since they have been declared taboo in the U.S.S.R.![89] In answer to one of Severin's articles N. V. Ivochkina has written an interesting article on the silver bars which were made in the nineteenth century by the St. Petersburg mint for the Russian Orthodox mission in Peking. This article was immediately reprinted in an American numismatic journal.[90]

Articles on the coins of the eighteenth to twentieth century have been published in various numbers of the *Sovetskii kollektsioner* ['Soviet collector'] by P. Kliorin and M. L'vov, V. Koretsky and M. Gornung.[91] O. S. Tal'skaya has published the first broadly based study of interesting material of the eighteenth and nineteenth centuries—the so-called 'coal seals', accounting tokens for the 'assigned' state peasants working in the metallurgical enterprises in the Urals and Siberia.[92]

The author of this article has published a semi-popular book on the extraordinary story of some specimens of the 'Emperor' Constantine's pattern rouble of 1825 and the forged specimens which appeared in Paris in the 1860s.[93] The thesis of R. Z. Burnasheva, prepared in the Hermitage is of considerable interest for the history of money circulation and the financial policy of the Tsarist government in Central Asia.[94]

So far there is very little literature on the coins of the Soviet period; there is only one catalogue, dealing with coins of the period 1921-52.[95]

The research of A. A. Sivers and A. V. Oreshnikov into the identities of Russian medal-makers of the seventeenth and eighteenth centuries[96] has been continued by E. S. Shchukina who has established that the author of the large

[89] H. M. Severin, *The Silver Coinage of Imperial Russia. 1682–1917* (Basle, Amsterdam, London, 1965).

[90] N. V. Ivochkina, 'Po povodu odnoi atributsii', *Soobshcheniya Gos. Ermitazha*, xxvi (1965). Translated as N. Ivochkina, 'Concerning an attribution', *The Numismatic Review*, 1966, 2.

[91] P. Kliorin, 'Feodosiiskii monetnyi dvor '['The Feodosia mint'], *Sovetskii kollektsioner*, 1962, 2.; M. L'vov, V. Koretsky, and M. Gornung, 'Poslednyaya massovaya perechekanka mednoi monety v Rossii' ['The last large-scale over-stamping of copper coin in Russia'], *Sovetskii kollektsioner*, 1965, 3. See also V. Koretsky, 'Annenskii monetnyi dvor' ['The Annenskoe mint'], *Prikam'e* (Perm', 1960).

[92] O. S. Tal'skaya, 'Iz istorii uglezhzheniya na ural'skikh zavodakh' ['On the history of charcoal burning in factories in the Urals'], *Trudy Sverdlovskogo oblastnogo kraevedcheskogo muzeya*, 1 (Sverdlovsk, 1960).

[93] I. G. Spassky, *Po sledam odnoi redkoi monety* ['On the track of a rare coin'] (L., 1964). Translated into Italian in *Italia numismatica*, 1968.

[94] R. Z. Burnasheva, *Denezhnoe obrashchenie i monetnoe delo Bukharskogo khanstva kontsa XVIII — nachala XX v.* ['Money circulation and coining in the Bokhara khanate from the end of the eighteenth to the beginning the twentieth century'] (Thesis abstract, LOIA AN SSSR, 1966).

[95] S. P. Fortinsky, 'Opisanie sovetskikh monet za period s 1921 po 1952' ['Description of Soviet coins from 1921 to 1952'], *NS*, 1 (*Trudy GIM*, xxv) (M., 1955).

[96] A. A. Sivers, 'Medal'er Ben'yamin Skott' ['Benjamin Scott the medallist'], *IGAIMK*, v (1927); A. V. Oreshnikov, 'Fryazhskikh reznykh del master, serebryanik i medal'er kontsa XVII v. ['An engraver, silver-smith and medallist of the end of the seventeenth century'], *Sbornik Oruzheinoi palaty* (M., 1925).

coins of 1654 bearing the equestrian portrait of Tsar Aleksey Mikhailovich was F. Baikov. She has also proved that the author of a number of early medals of the reign of Peter the Great was the Russian engraver F. Alekseev.[97] Her monograph on medal-engraving in Russia in the eighteenth century has made known a number of previously unknown names of Russian medal engravers and also several assayers, mechanics, and other craftsmen who were formerly mistakenly thought to be foreign craftsmen working in Russia. The sections in her book dealing with the organization of the design of medals and historical series are particularly interesting.[98] In particular it has been established that M. V. Lomonosov was the initiator of the large portrait series of Russian princes. Very useful work has been done in separating later retrospective medals and reissues from original medals of Peter's reign.[99] An article by L. S. Piskunova on the Hangö medals throws light on the practice of medal production in the time of Peter.[100]

A catalogue of the commemorative medals of the period 1918–67 was prepared by M. I. Kruchkov with additional material by E. S. Shchukina and published by the Hermitage to mark the fiftieth anniversary of the October Revolution.[101]

The most remote branch of numismatics concerns orders and marks of distinction. A survey of pre-1917 Russian and foreign orders was prepared in connection with the opening of an exhibition in the Hermitage in 1956.[102] It contained completely new sections describing the orders of Shamil [Emir of Dagestan, leader of an anti-Russian uprising, d. 1871] and the Emirate of Bokhara. E. N. Shevelova has published a useful reference catalogue of national orders and insignia, including Soviet awards, in the collection of the Artillery Museum in Leningrad.[103]

In his report to the session of the Historical Sciences Section of the U.S.S.R. Academy of Sciences in 1955 D. B. Shelov reviewed the results of post-war

[97] E. S. Shchukina: (1) 'Rezchiki monetnykh shtempelei vtoroi poloviny XVII v. F. Baikov i Yu. Frobus' ['F. Baikov and Yu. Frobus, coin die engravers of the second half of the seventeenth century'], *NS*, 1 (*Trudy GIM*, xxv) (M., 1955); (2) 'Fedor Alekseev—russkii medal'er i mekhanik nachala XVIII v.' ['Fedor Alekseev, a Russian medallist and mechanic of the beginning of the eighteenth century'], *KSIIMK*, 54 (1958).

[98] E. Shchukina, *Medal'ernoe iskusstvo v Rossii XVIII v.* ['The art of medalling in eighteenth-century Russia'], (L., 1962).

[99] Idem, 'Medali' ['Medals'], *Pamyatniki russkoi kul'tury pervoi chetverti XVIII v.* (L.–M., 1966).

[100] L. S. Piskunova, 'Nagrazhdenie medalyami za Gangutskii boi 27 iyulya 1714 g.' ['The award of medals for the battle of Hangö, 27 July 1714'], *Trudy Gos. Ermitazha*, iv (1961).

[101] *Gosudarstvennyi ordena Lenina Ermitazh. Sovetskie pamyatnye medali 1918—1967* ['The State Order of Lenin Hermitage. Soviet commemorative medals'] (L., 1968).

[102] I. G. Spassky, *Inostrannye i russkie ordena do 1917 g.* ['Foreign and Russian orders before 1917'] (L., 1963).

[103] *Artilleriiskii istoricheskii muzei. Katalog otechestvennykh ordenov, medalei i nagrudnykh znakov* ['Artillery Historical Museum. Catalogue of orders, medals, and decorations'] (L., 1962).

numismatic research. The main line of research of Soviet numismatists, he declared, was 'the investigation of the history of coining, money circulation and the production of merchandise using the evidence of coin discoveries and other numismatic monuments'.[104] This definition concerns particularly Russian numismatics. In the same year V. L. Yanin wrote an article devoted to the most urgent problems of Russian numismatics in which he stated, 'while remaining an auxiliary source in the investigation of problems of political history, the history of art and technology, and palaeography, the coin represents one of the main sources in the study of the circulation of money and commodities'.[105]*

[104] D. B. Shelov, 'Sostoyanie raboty v oblasti numizmatiki i blizhaishie zadachi' ['The state of work in the field of numismatics and the immediate tasks'], *KSIIMK*, 66 (1956), 3.

[105] V. L. Yanin, 'Numizmatika i problemy tovarno-denezhnogo obrashcheniya v Drevnei Russii' ['Numismatics and problems of money and commodity circulation in Ancient Russia'], *Voprosy istorii*, 1955, 8, 136.

* [Since the publication of the original Russian article from which this translation has been prepared the following works have appeared:

N. F. Kotlyar: (1) *Galits'ka Rus' u drugii polovini XIV — pershii chverti XV st.* ['Galician Russia in the second half of the fourteenth and first quarter of the fifteenth century'] (Kiev, 1968) [Ukr.]; (2) *Groshovii obig na territorii Ukraini dobi feodalizmu* ['Currency circulation in the Ukraine in the feudal period'] (Kiev, 1971) (see n. 31) [Ukr.]; (3) 'Russko-litovskie monety XIV v.' ['Russo-Lithuanian coins of the fourteenth century'], *VID*, 3 (1970) (see n. 85); (4) 'Klad monet Vladimira Ol'gerdovicha' ['A hoard of coins of Vladimir Ol'gerdovich'], *NiE*, viii (1970) (see n. 85). (5) 'Monety Vladimira Ol'gerdovicha' ['Coins of Vladimir Ol'gerdovich'], *NiS*, 4 (Kiev, 1971) (see n. 55).
M. L. L'vov, 'O nekotorykh tekhnicheskikh osobennostyakh izgotovleniya monetnykh shtempeley v Velikom Novgorode' ['Some technical peculiarities in the production of coin dies in Velikii Novgorod'], *NiE*, ix (1971) [see nn. 25, 26].
A. S. Mel'nikova: (1) 'Sistematizatsiya monet Alekseya Mikhailovicha' ['The systematization of the coins of Aleksei Mikhailovich'], *VID*, 3 (1970) (see n. 71); (2) 'Pskovskii i Novgorodskii denezhnye dvory v seredine XVII v.' ['The Pskov and Novgorod mints in the mid-seventeenth century'], *NiE*, viii (1970) (see n. 27); (3) 'Novyi ("angliiskii") denezhnyi dvor v Moskve v 1654—1663' ['The new ("English") mint in Moscow in 1654–1663'], *NiE*, ix (1971) [see n. 27].
M. B. Severova, 'Sovetskaya numizmatika. Bibliograficheskii ukazatel'. 1961–5. Dopolneniya k ukazatelyu za 1917—1958 i 1959—1960' ['Soviet numismatics. A bibliographical index. Addenda to the indexes for 1917–1958 and 1959–1960'], *NiE*, ix (1971) [see n. 21].
E. S. Shchukina, 'Nagradnye medali Arkhipelagskoi ekspeditsii 1769—1770 gg.' ['Medals awarded for the Archipelago expedition of 1769–1770'], *Trudy Gos. Ermitazha*, xii (1971) [see nn. 98, 99, 100].
N. A. Soboleva, 'K voprosu o monetakh Vladimira Ol'gerdovicha' ['On the question of the coins of Vladimir Ol'gerdovich'], *NiE*, viii (1970) (see n. 85).]
M. P. Sotnikova: (1) 'Srebreniki Kievskogo klada 1876 g.' ['*Srebreniki* in the Kiev hoard of 1876'], *NiS*, 3 (Kiev, 1968); (2) 'Nerazyskannye ekzemplyary russkikh monet X—XI vv. K korpusy drevneishikh russkikh monet' ['Undiscovered specimens of Russian coins of the tenth–eleventh century. Additions to the corpus of ancient Russian coins', *Trudy Gos. Ermitazha*, XIII (see n. 43); (3) 'Nezhinskii klad srebrenikov 1852 g. Rekonstruktsiya sostava' ['The Nezhin hoard of *srebreniki* of 1852. A reconstruction of its composition'], *NiS*, 4 (Kiev, 1971).
I. G. Spassky: (1) 'Neskol'ko zamechanii po povodu russkoi monetnoi chekanki 1914—1917' ['Some observations on the minting of Russian coins, 1914–1917'], *NiS*, 3 (Kiev,

## ABBREVIATIONS

*AE*           *Arkheografcheskii ezhegodnik.*
AN SSSR        Akademiya nauk SSSR [Academy of Sciences of the U.S.S.R.].
Byelor.        Byelorussian.
GAIMK          Gosudarstvennaya akademiya istorii material'noi kul'tury [State
               Academy of the History of Material Culture].
GIM            Gosudarstvennyi istoricheskii muzei [State Historical Museum].
GMII           Gosudarstvennyi muzei izobrazitel'nykh iskusstv imeni A. S.
               Pushkina [State Pushkin Museum of Fine Arts].
*IGAIMK*       *Izvestiya Gosudarstvennoi akademii istorii material'noi kul'tury.*
*IRAIMK*       *Izvestiya Rossiiskoi akademii istorii material'noi kul'tury.*
*KSIIMK*       *Kratkie soobshcheniya Instituta istorii material'noi kul'tury.*
L.             Leningrad.
LOIA AN SSSR   Leningradskoe otdelenie Instituta arkheologii AN SSSR
               [Leningrad section of the Institute of Archaeology of the AN
               SSSR].
LOII AN SSSR   Leningradskoe otdelenie Instituta istorii AN SSSR [Leningrad
               section of the Institute of History of the AN SSSR].
M.             Moscow.
*MIA SSSR*     *Materialy i issledovaniya po arkheologii SSSR.*
*NiE*          *Numizmatika i epigrafika.*
*NiS*          *Numizmatika i sfragistika.*
*NS*           *Numizmaticheskii sbornik.*
*NZ*           *Numismatische Zeitschrift*, Vienna.
*NZIS VUAN*    *Naukovi zapiski Istorichnoi sektsii Vseukrains'koi akademii nauk.*
Pgr.           Petrograd.
RANION         Rossiiskaya assosiatsiya nauchno-issledovatel'skikh institutov
               obshchestvennykh nauk [The Russian Association of Social
               Science Research Institutes].
*SA*           *Sovetskaya arkheologiya.*
SPb.           St. Petersburg.
*TNK*          *Trudy Numizmaticheskoi komissii.*

1968); *Dukat i dukachi Ukrainy* ['Ducats and their costume-jewellery replicas in the Ukraine'], (Kiev, 1970); (3) *Russkaya monetnaya sistema* ['The Russian monetary system'] (4th edition, enlarged. L., 1970) (see n. 29); (4) 'Sestroretskie rubli (1770, i 1771)' ['The Sestroretsk robles (1770 and 1771)'], *Trudy Gos. Ermitazha* xii (Numizmatika 4) [see n. 91]; (5) 'Katalog efimkov 1655 g.' ['A catalogue of *efimki* of 1655'], *NiS*, 4 (Kiev, 1971). [This catalogue covers 1500 coins—previously only 850 were known, see n. 77]; (6) 'Numizmatika v Ermitazhe. Ocherk istorii Myuntskabineta-Otdela numizmatiki' ['Numismatics in the Hermitage. An outline history of the Coin Cabinet and Department of Numismatics'], *NiE*, viii (1970) [see n. 22]; I. G. Spassky and M. P. Sotnikova, 'Russkie monety. Drevnerusskie pechati' ['Russian coins. Old Russian seals'] in 'Numizmatika v Ermitazhe. Obzor kollektsii' ['Numismatics in the Hermitage. A survey of the collection's], *NiE*, ix (1971).
V. L. Yanin: (1) 'Den'gi i denezhnye sistemy' ['Money and monetary systems'], *Ocherki russkoi kul'tury XIII—XV vv.*, pt. 1 (M., 1970); (2) 'Berestyanye gramoty i problema proiskhozhdeniya novgorodskikh denezhnykh sistem' ['Birch-bark documents and the problem of the origin of the Novgorod monetary systems'], *VID*, 3 (1970).

| | |
|---|---|
| *TOA* | *Trudy Otdela arkheologii Instituta arkheologii i iskusstvovedeniya RANION.* |
| *TSA* | *Trudy Sektsii arkheologii Instituta arkheologii i iskusstvovedeniya RANION.* |
| Ukr. | Ukrainian. |
| *VID* | *Vspomogatel'nye istoricheskie distsipliny.* |
| *ZfN* | *Zeitschrift für Numismatik*, Berlin. |

# Islamic Metrology from Jewish Sources II[1]

## DANIEL SPERBER

### 1. RI MIGASH

MR. YISRAEL TA-SHEMA (Jerusalem) recently called my attention to a responsum of the great Spanish twelfth-century Talmudist Josef b. Meir ha-Levi Ibn Migash (usually called simply Ri Migash), which contains metrological information of interest to students of Islamic numismatics.

Ri Migash was head of the Talmudic academy at Lucena from 1103 until his death in 1141, and this responsum must have been written between these two dates. While he, the responsary, lived in Spain, the question could have been sent to him equally from Spain or North Africa (the Morocco area), since there were very strong ties between these two countries. (Indeed he even visited Fez, according to his own evidence in responsum no. 75.) As we shall see below, though the place from which the question was sent is nowhere mentioned explicitly, the evidence points to its being North Africa. The responsum itself appears in the standard collections of his responsa as no. 195 (ed. princeps Salonica 1791, 2nd edn. Warsaw, 1870. I used the edn. of Jerusalem, 1959). However, it also appears in the *Shita Mekubezet* of Bezalel Ashkenazi (end of sixteenth century) to *Bava Kama* 97b, with slight variants (noted below). The original text of this responsum, as indeed most of his responsa, was in Arabic (as specifically stated in the *Shita Mekubezet*, ibid.). However, all we have is the Hebrew translation.

Below I give a translation of the majority of the text, omitting mainly the quotation of the Talmudic passage cited, with occasional textual notes, etc. There follows a discussion of the metrological aspects of this text.

### Question

Reuben lent Simeon ten weights (or measures) of gold, which in Arabic are called *methakil*, and determined that his (the borrower's) house should serve as collateral. And afterwards, the king added to the weights eight grains (גרעינים) per *mithkal*. And when Reuben came to claim his debt, Simeon wished to pay him with the weights that he had lent him, which are the small weights (i.e. according to the

[1] This continues a series that appeared in: *Sinai* lv (1964), 333–8; lvi (1965), 234–7; lviii (1966), 164–8; and in *NC* 1965, 231–7 (entitled 'Islamic Metrology from Jewish Sources'). This research was supported (in part) by the Research Committee, Bar-Ilan University.

earlier smaller weight standard). Reuben said to him, 'I shall accept from you only in the large weights which are now current.' And a certain authority ruled (הורה המורה) that he should pay him with the large weights now current, since this addition [to the weight standard] did not make an impression on the market (לא עשה רושם בשערים, i.e. did not affect the market prices). But Simeon claimed that you, Our Master, may the Lord make your security constant, have been asked similar questions and have ruled that one should repay only with the weights [initially] lent out . . . Please inform us, Our Master, of the law in this matter, and may his (i.e. your) reward be twofold.

*Answer*

I have gone into this question, and the judges who ruled that Simeon should return [his debt] to Reuben in large weights are untrained and arbitrate in ignorance (מדייני דחצצתא).[1] And there is no doubt . . . that the Talmud (when ruling in a case of change of coin standard that one has to pay in current coin)[2] was talking of a coin which is a *dinar*, a single unit, whole, struck and stamped with the king's die. It was current(ly used) among people, whole, according to its standard (כמו שיוצא טבעו) of that year. One may not detract from it (e.g. clip it); it must have in it no split whatsoever, nor any flaw, nor may it be less than that weight known to be obligatory in every *dinar*. And if it was lacking a little in its weight, behold it is completely cancelled (or withdrawn) from use in dealings (i.e. it is no longer legal tender). It is no longer regarded as coin, for one cannot do dealings with it as such. It is rather considered a bullion, which, in any case, needs to be restruck in the mint (if it is to be used as coin). It was with regard to all such cases that Rava asked whether he who lends his neighbour money according to a certain standard, and it was added to—concerning such cases replied Rav Ḥisda that he repays him [in] coin current at the present time. For the old former *denarii*, of the smaller weight, have already been completely cancelled (or withdrawn) from use, and are not regarded as coin but [only] as bullion—a piece of unstamped gold. But he lent him out something then regarded as coin which was then in current use. Furthermore, he does not have to take into account the addition to it (to the new coin's weight, i.e. he does not have to pay back in new currency but subtract this addition, so as to avoid paying interest and transgressing the law of usury). For he did not lend him a set weight, in which case he would have to calculate what was added to the weight. On the contrary, what he lent him was a certain coin (or denomination), be it (i.e. its weight) what it may.

Consider for yourself [a case where] there was in the *dinar* a little more [weight] than required, he still would not reckon it as more than a *dinar*, since its practical value is no more than a *dinar* (שלא יוצא עליו ביותר מדינר), and he can get no benefit out of that addition (i.e. the purchasing power of the coin is not affected by its additional weight). Neither can he cut it (i.e. clip it of its additional weight). Just as in a case where he lent him out a full-weight *dinar*, and it chanced that the borrower returned an overweight *dinar*—without this addition having been stipulated by the

---

[1] A Talmudic idiom; see *Bavli Bava Bathra* 133b.

[2] *Bavli Bava Kama* 97b. I have omitted the Ri Ibn Migash's citation of this Talmudic passage, which is in itself of interest if only for its significant divergences from our Talmudic text.

king—he (the lender) does not have to take this addition into account, for it is of no practical value, since he cannot use the coin for more than a *dinar*.

Thus, it has become evident that he only lent him out that which was then currently considered a *dinar* and that any additional weight in the coin is of no real consequence. Only a lack of weight [would be of consequence] (since it would cancel the coin, as explained above). And therefore Rav Ḥisda ruled (in the Talmud ibid.) that one need not take into account the additional weight, if that additional weight made no impression on the market (i.e. did not affect the real purchasing power of the coin). However, gold which was given in weight and [is to be] returned in weight, and where each calculates with his neighbour [even] to a single grain, that if it is lacking he make it up, and if there be too much he deduct it, how can we compare this to this (the Talmud's *coin* case), and judge that one who borrow from his neighbour one *mithkal*, and the weight [standard] was then small, and afterwards it was increased, that he should have to repay according to the increased weight [standard]. [Surely this is] as though he had lent him out something *called* a *mithkal* without reference to its weight (מבלי דקדוק משקל), in which case we would obligate him to return that which goes by the same name (read: מה שיוצא),[1] whatever its weight be. [But here] surely he lent him a specific weight. Therefore, according to the law he should return him nothing but the exact same weight, call it what you please, either a *mithkal* as it formerly was, or a *mithkal* less two[2] grains as it now is.

Furthermore, this gold is not [really] one unit. [If it were] we might say that since there has been added to it two[2] grains, the first *mithkal* [standard], lacking as it [now] does a *mithkal*, has already been cancelled from use. Rather, it consists of separate units; each grain is [considered] distinct from its neighbour, and it is possible to deal in single grains out of it (i.e. the total amount) or even less, and most certainly in a *mithkal* less two[2] grains. And since such is the case, by what reasoning can we obligate the borrower to give the lender an amount added to what he lent him? The amount he lent him was not cancelled (or withdrawn) from use in such a manner that it was no longer considered coin. How then could it occur to anyone that one who borrows such a weight should be obliged to return a greater one? Surely this is absolute usury! Such is my opinion.

Now if this addition had been in the beauty of the gold and its fineness, then one could have considered the matter. For example, if this gold had at first been one quarter dross (adulteration), and now it returned to being one eighth dross, one who lent his friend a *mithkal* of the first adulterated gold would be obliged to repay the lender in good gold in current use, since the first [type of] gold is no longer acceptable for dealing in. [In such a case], the lender can say to the borrower: I lent you gold then in current use (read בעת rather than בשת).[3] And he does not have to take account of the difference [in value] between the two kinds of gold, in their beauty . . .

. . . For consider, we have found no way to clarify the amount of interest in an addition of weight except when he wants to make it into bullion; but not in any other way (i.e. one can only calculate the interest in terms of bullion, but coin is not bullion). For since it is only accepted by tale (i.e. sums of money are reckoned in

---

[1] The text reads שיוציא—what he takes out, or uses, which also makes plausible sense.
[2] The parallel rescension in the *Shita Mekubezet* reads *eight* grains here.
[3] The correct reading is found in the parallel rescension in the *Shita Mekubezet*.

multiples of coin-units) and not by weight, the weight neither adds nor detracts from it....[1]

The whole responsum is of considerable significance from a number of points of view; e.g. for its halachic (= Jewish legal) exposition of the theory of a 'money standard', for its relationship to other rulings on this subject, etc.[2] Here, however, we shall interest ourselves solely with the metrological references, i.e. the reform in weight standard alluded to the text.

Firstly we are told that 'the king added to the weights eight grains (גרעינים) per *mithkal*', or in other words, the standard of the *mithkal* was increased. We have, then, to find a change in weight standard in Spain or North Africa between the years 1103 and 1141. Such a change is generally the result of significant political events and/or economic reform, and one would expect it be to reflected in coin weights. We are not told what kind of grains are being spoken of. The Hebrew גרעינים is a generic term (literally: seeds) which could refer to several types. (The Arabic original may have been more explicit.) Indeed, within the responsum itself, the Ri Migash appears to be speaking of two distinct kinds of 'grains'; for further on several times he speaks of 'a *mithkal* less *two* grains', etc., and not the 8 grains of the questioner. (Bezalel Ashkenazi's rescension reads 'eight grains' in all these cases, see p. 277 n. 2 above. However, clearly this is emendation for harmonistic reasons.) It would appear that his grains are worth four of the questioner's grains. We are probably dealing with a carob seed, *kharūba*, which equals 4 grains of barley, *she'ira*.[3] The *mithkal, dinar*, and *dirham* were usually measured in barley grains.[4]

Let us assume for the moment that the *mithkal* (or *dinar*, for they are often used in the same sense) went up in weight 8 grains of barley (= 2 carob seeds). Now the classical *mithkal* = 100 grains of barley (= 20 *kirats*), while the classical *dinar* weighed 72 grains of barley.[5] Since the ancient *dinar* weighed 4·25 gm. of gold, a grain equalled 0·06 gm. gold. An addition of 8 grains would equal approximately 0·48 gm. gold. A survey of the numismatic evidence from Spain between the years 1103 and 1141, the Almoravid period, discloses no such change in weight standard.[6] Neither does the pattern of political and economic development of the period warrant such a reform.

[1] There follows a final extended diatribe against the ignorant judges who ruled otherwise.

[2] See, for example, *Responsa of R. Isaac ben Judah Alfasi*, ed. Wolf Leiter (Pittsburgh, Pa., 1954), 132 no. 243, note; *Responsen der Lehrer des Ostens und Westens*, ed. Joel Müller (Berlin, 1888), no. 13 note; *Alfasi to Bava Kama*, etc. (All these sources are in Hebrew.)

[3] See M. H. Sauvaire, *Matériaux pour servir à l'histoire de la numismatique et de la métrologie musulmanes* (Paris, 1882), 95, 106, etc.

[4] Ibid. 36-7, 54-5, 58-60, 76, 81, etc. See also Tashbaz, *Responsa of R. Simeon b. Zemach Duran*, part 3, response 266, and *Caftor va-Ferah* of Eshtori ha-Farḥi, ed. Grossberg (Jerusalem, 1959), 63a.

[5] Ibid., p. 51. See also Schrötter, *Wörterbuch der Münzkunde* 39-40; see also *Encyclopaedia of Islam*[2] ii, 297.

[6] See, e.g., Juan de Dios de la Rada y Delgado, *Catálogo de monedas arábigas españolas* (Madrid 1892), nos. 493 et seq., where the weight standard of several Spanish towns,

When, however, we look at North Africa (Fez, Meknes, etc.), we find that c. 1130 the recently established Almohad (Muwaḥḥid) dynasty introduces a new *dinar-mithkal* standard of the *doblas*, of c. 469 gm.[1] This is, indeed, an increase of over 0·45 gm. over the previous North African standard of c. 4·22 gm.[2] which itself had been based on the classical weight standard of 4·25 gm. This earlier standard according to the classical equation equalled 72 grains of barley. Thus the new *doblas* (or *dinar-mithkal*) must have been reckoned at about 80 grains of barley. This then is the weight reform alluded to in our responsum.

Our suggestion is, in fact, borne out by another passage in the responsum itself, which may now be better understood; for the Ri Migash argues: 'Furthermore, this gold is not [really] one unit. [If it were] we might say that since there has been added to it two grains (of carob = 8 grains of barley, see above), the first *mithkal* standard, *lacking as it* [*now*] *does a mithkal*, has already been cancelled from use', etc. What he wishes to say is this: If all ten *mithkals* borrowed had been one unit, and the standard was altered by an increase of 8 barley grains per *mithkal*, the total difference in weight would now be *80 barley grains*. And he calls this a *mithkal*! Clearly then, he is reckoning according to the new standard, used at the time the question was raised, of 80 grains per *mithkal*. (This was the questioner's standard, not that of the Ri Migash himself, for c. 1130 at Lucena, the *mithkal* was not of such a weight.)

From the Ri Migash's reply, we see that the Almohad monetary reform was a change in standard from the classical *dinar* of 72 grains to a *doblas* (*dinar-mithkal*) of 80 grains. From the question, we may learn that this monetary reform had little effect upon market prices, i.e. it did not increase the purchasing power of the *dinar*. It remains somewhat unclear whether the *mithkal* referred to in this responsum was coin or weight. For while, on the one hand, a straightforward reading of the text suggest the latter, it is difficult to understand how the 'ignorant judges', who gave the first ruling, made so blatant an error in the understanding of the Talmudic material (which rules as they rule in the case of *coins*). We know, however,[3] that the gold *dinar* used to pass by weight rather than tale (this as opposed to the silver *dirham*). It seems thus probable, that the *mithkals* spoken of are coins; the 'ignorant

Valencia, Granada, Murcia, Seville, Nul Lamta, etc., varies between 3·90 (nos. 521–8) and 4·12 (no. 523). See most recently, Henry W. Hazard, *The Numismatic History of Late Mediaeval North Africa* (Numismatic Studies 8), American Numismatic Society, 1952, 61.

[1] Sauvaire, op. cit. 268; Schrötter, op. cit. 142, cf. 148–9. See Henry Lavoix, *Catalogue des monnaies musulmanes de la Bibliothèque nationale*, ii, 293–5; *BMCO* v, Casto Mª Del Rivero, *La moneda arábigo-española* (Madrid, 1933), 51, 70, and most recently Hazard, op. cit. 66.

[2] e.g. Lavoix, op. cit. 293–5; Hazard, op. cit. 61.

[3] 'In any case the dīnar usually passed by weight rather than tale, except where payments were made in sealed purses (*ṣurra*) of coins of guaranteed weight and fineness'; *Encyclopaedia of Islam*[2] ii, 297, art, 'dīnār' (also *Encyclopaedia of Iaslam*[1] i, 976).

judges' likened them to the Talmudic case, while the Ri Migash, knowing that these particular coins were regarded as weights, treated them halachically as such, so reaching his very different legal ruling.

To summarize: The question was sent from North Africa, sometime shortly after 1130.[1] The Almohad reform referred to must have been the cause of numerous halachic problems of this nature. It is, therefore, by no means surprising that the Ri Migash dealt with this issue on more than one occasion, understood the numismatic situation well, and ruled as he did. The reform itself increased the standard of the *dinar* from 72 to 80 grains, but did not significantly affect its purchasing power.

## 2. ESHTORI HA-FARHI

Below I give a translation and brief notes on a few passages of metro-logical interest taken from a medieval Jewish work entitled *Caftor va-Ferah* by Eshtori ha-Farhi.

Eshtori himself was born c. 1282 at Florenza, Spain, and at an early age his father, Moses, sent him to study under his grandfather, R. Nathan, at Tronquetelle, near Arles, in France. Then when he was nineteen years old he went to Montpellier to study astronomy with Jacob b. Makhir; he also studied Latin, Arabic, and the works of Aristotle, Hippocrates, Ptolemy, and Galen. On the expulsion of the Jews from France in 1306, he went to Perpignan where he remained for the next seven years. In 1312 he decided to go to Palestine, and on his way stopped in at Cairo for a few days. He spent his next seven years exploring the length and breadth of Palestine, and in his *Caftor va-Ferah* he put down the results of his researches into the history, geography, fauna, flora, and antiquities of the Holy Land. He died in Palestine c. 1357.[2]

Thus the passages we bring below belong to the period 1302–9, and were probably put down in writing c. 1310. The information on Palestine is com-pletely up to date, while the information on Europe is most probably up to date, but in any case cannot be more than a decade (and even less) behind the times.

The passages are taken from a long section (chapter sixteen) dealing with biblical and Talmudic weights, measures, and coins. The majority of it is historical metrology, but we have excerpted only that which constitutes con-temporary information.

Little critical work has been done on this, and indeed many other Hebrew metrological texts, with the exception of the pioneer studies of Luncz[3] and

---

[1] Mr. Ta-shema, while approaching the problem from a completely different angle—a comparative legal one—informs me that he reached the same conclusions, namely that the question was from N. Africa, and the responsum from late in the Ri Migash's life.

[2] See *Jewish Encyclopaedia* (hereafter *JE*), v, 343.

[3] e.g. *Luah Eretz Yisrael* (Jerusalem, 1897), 108–30. Also his edition of *Caftor va-Ferah* (Jerusalem, 1897–9).

Zunz in his classic essay 'Münzkunde', which is chapter seven of his *Zur Geschichte und Literatur*.[1] I have used the Grossberg edition of the *Caftor va-Feraḥ* (Jerusalem, 1959), which in turn is based on the Hirsch Edelmann edition of Berlin 1852, but which has numerous additions and corrections to the Berlin edition.

### Caftor va-Feraḥ 63a

In the land of Israel we now use a coin that passes by weight; it is white and its name is *dirham nukra*.[2] It is round and its diameter is roughly half a thumb [breadth]. This coin is also current at the same rate in Amon and Moab, [the land of] Sihon and Og, in Syria and the land of Egypt (i.e. in all the areas bordering of Palestine), and it is the Egyptian *drachmon* (= drachm)[3] that Maimonides[4] of Blessed Memory refers to . . . Its weight never changes: it is sixteen grains of the carob, which grain is called a *ḥabba*[5] or *kirat*[6] . . . Every *kirat* weighs four barley grains.[7] Thus, there are sixty-four barley grains in a *dirham*. So says Avicenna in his great Canon on weights and measures, namely that every *kirat* equals four barley grains; so also are traders and the people in general wont [to reckon].

This *dirham* is subdivided into copper *perutot* (= small coins, a Talmudic term) which are called *flus* (or fulus), and their number is sixty-four, and this is their standard rate. Thus the *kirat* equals four *fulus* and the barley grain one *fulus* (= fals). But sometimes they produce small *perutot* of inferior quality, and they pass only by weight and eighty of them equal a *dirham* . . .

And this *dirham* has ten *kirats*, two and two thirds barley grains of pure silver; for the *dirham* is always two thirds pure silver and one third copper.

### 63b

Here in the land of Canaan (= Palestine) there is a gold coin which in Arabic is called *dinari*; its weight is always one and a half *dirhams*, less half a *kirat*, which equals twenty-three *kirats*.[8] Usually a gold *kirat* equals a *dirham* of silver, and so the *dinar* equals twenty-three *dirham nukra* . . .

After we have given information for those outside [the land of Israel] concerning the coins of the land of Israel, we shall [now] have to give the local people information concerning coins [circulating] abroad. However, we can only give information of the North West [of Europe]. (See introductory note.) Know, then [64a] that in the land of Provence and France there is one kind of coin that passes by tale, and one that passes by weight. The one that passes by weight is called the *zakuk* (= mark)[9] and it weighs eight of their *ukias* (= ounces).[10] And there are two kinds of coin that pass by tale, one of pure silver, except for one twenty-fourth of it which

---

[1] Berlin, 1919. One should also make mention of H. J. Scheftel's *Erekh Milim* (Berdichev, 1907), an Encyclopaedia of Biblical and Talmucic weights, measures, and coins, which contains a wealth of material.

[2] i.e. silver; see Sauvaire 240–3.            [3] See Sauvaire 243.

[4] Leading medieval Jewish Talmudist and Codifier; also a philosopher and physician. Born Cordova 1135, died Cairo 1204. See *JE* ix, 73–86.

[5] Sauvaire 107.                              [6] Ibid. 102 f.

[7] Cf. ibid. 102, 59, 106, etc.              [8] Ibid. 108 f.; Zunz 547.

[9] Zunz, op. cit. 563.

[10] See Schrötter, *Wörterbuch der Münzkunde* 372.

is copper, and it is called a silver *tournois,* or a white *tournois.*[1] Its form is round and its diametre is a thumb [-breath]. The second coin is of mixed silver and copper; it is called a thin *tournois* (= *denier*),[2] and the Arabs call it a *pashit.* The white *tournois* is worth twelve of the thin *tournois,* that is to say twelve *pashits.*[3]

The *zakuk* is worth approximately fifty silver *tournois.*[4] The *tournois* is now to be found [in use] amongst us here in the land of Canaan, and it is exchanged for about two *dirham* with a bit of a squeeze. They also have another coin which they call a *Venetiana,* while the Arabs call it a *banduki.*[5] Here it is exchanged for about a *dirham.* It is of pure silver and weighs eleven *kirats.* They have another coin which they call *esterlin,*[6] and it is of silver and worth four *pashits,* that is to say four thin *tournois.* They have yet another coin which they call an *arginz* (= arienço).[7] If weighs eight *kirats* which is half a *dirham.* The *melgueires,*[8] which is mentioned in the *Ittur*[9] . . . is like the thin *tournois.*

[1] See Zunz 559. Schrötter 242–3. '*Grossus albus*'. or '*Turonensis argent*', etc.

[2] Zunz 558; 'denier tournois', Schrötter 134.

[3] Zunz 558; For the term '*pashit*' (found in the Talmud), compare Spanish *Peseta.* See also R. Payne-Smith, *Thesaurus Syriacus* ii (Oxford, 1901), 3321 s.v.

[4] Cf. Schrötter 372.                                    [5] Zunz 547; Sauvaire 140.

[6] Schrötter 662–3; Zunz 554, 557, 559, etc.

[7] Or 'argent'; Zunz 554–5.                              [8] Zunz 557, 559.

[9] Isaac b. Abba Mari, French codifier; born Provence c. 1122, died 1193 (Marseilles?). See *JE* vi, 618–19.

# More on Sulaimān Mīrzā and his Contemporaries

### N. M. LOWICK

[SEE PLATE 24]

A FEW years ago I discussed in this journal the issues of Sulaimān Mīrzā, an independent scion of the Moghul family who ruled Badakhshān—the area immediately to the north of the Hindu Kush—in the tenth century A.H./ sixteenth century A.D.[1] Coins of Sulaimān are rare; but our perspective of Badakhshān's coinage in this period is broadened somewhat by a small group of gold pieces, of Afghan provenance, lately acquired by the British Museum. Diverse in so far as their attribution is concerned (three dynasties and four rulers are represented), the coins none the less exhibit a uniformity of fabric and design which points to their having been manufactured in the same area and probably at the same mint. Like the already published gold coins of Sulaimān Mīrzā they are of small module and have nothing in common with the opulent gold mohurs of Moghul India. They resemble, rather, certain gold coins of the early Shāhs of Persia struck to a standard of 1·16 gm. (18·0 grs. in Rabino's reckoning),[2] although their weights in fact fall short of this standard, the heaviest being 0·95 gm. and the lightest a mere 0·51 gm. The group comprises one coin of Sulaimān Mīrzā himself, two of his grandson Shāh Rukh, who set himself up as his rival, five of the Moghul Emperor Humāyūn, and one of the Shaibānid Khan of Transoxiana, 'Abdullāh II. The earliest pieces, which include two dated 955/1548, belong to Humāyūn, while the latest is the coin of 'Abdullāh, who expelled the Mīrzās from Badakhshān in 992/1584.

### DESCRIPTION OF THE COINS

Humāyūn (937–63/1530–56)

1. ℕ 0·45 in. 0·77 gm. (12·0 gr.). No mint, year 955. [Pl. 24. 1]

| Obv. Within a circle | Rev. | الله |
|---|---|---|
| لا اله الا الله | | خلد تعالى |
| محمد | | بادشاه غازي |
| رسول الله | | همايون محمد |
| | | ملکه ٩٥٥ |

---

[1] NC 1965, 221–9.

[2] H. L. Rabino, Coins, Medals and Seals of the Shahs of Iran 28, 30; Idem. Album of Coins, Medals and Seals, nos. 1–2, 92–7.

2. N 0·45 in. 0·71 gm. (11·0 gr). No. mint, year 955. [Pl. 24. 2]
As above, but the annulet above شاه is replaced by a pellet.

3. N 0·45 in. 0·83 gm. (12·8 gr.). No mint, year xx5. [Pl. 24. 3]
As no. 1, but ⚜ above شاه. First two digits of date off flan.

4. N 0·45 in. 0·65 gm. (10·1 gr.). No mint or date. [Pl. 24. 4]
As no. 1, but ⌣ above شاه.

5. N 0·4 in. 0·51 gm. (8·0 gr.). No mint or date. [Pl. 24. 5]
Obv. The Kalimah in geometric Kufic characters (reversed) within a square, all
surrounded by a circle; dots in the marginal segments.
Rev. As no. 1, but the horizontal line forming the ى of تعالى has an ornament
ڡ. Double struck.

These coins are of the same type as nos. 8–10a in Lane-Poole's *Coins of the
Moghul Emperors*. Their legends and reverse symbols (particularly the fleur-
de-lis on no. 3) are so similar to those on Sulaimān Mīrzā's coins that I have
no hesitation in assigning them to Badakhshān. They belong to the period
at which Sulaimān, after an unsuccessful bid to cut himself loose from
Moghul vassalage, was assisting Humāyūn against the latter's rebellious
brother Kāmrān. In 955/1548, when nos. 1–2 were issued, the emperor was
himself in Badakhshān, where he inflicted a notable defeat upon Kāmrān.[1]
I conclude that it was either to pay troops or to reward those who had helped
him to victory that these coins were struck.

*Sulaimān Mīrzā (936–92/1529–84)*

6. N 0·45 in. 0·92 gm. (14·2 gr.). No mint or date (c. 987–92). [Pl. 24. 6]
Obv. as no. 1.
Rev.
　　　　· · · · · ·
　　　　سلطان سليمان
　　خاد[م] الحرمين الشريفين

This piece corresponds to nos. 10–11 in my article 'Coins of Sulaimān
Mīrzā'. In describing the latter I commented on the—to me—puzzling words
الحرمين الشريفين beneath the ruler's name. I was unaware at that time that
the title خادم الحرمين الشريفين 'servant of the two noble sanctuaries' (i.e.
Mecca and Medinah) was to be found on certain Mesopotamian issues of
the Ottoman Sulaimān the Magnificant.[2] That the same title was adopted
by his namesake in Badakhshān is proved by the coin described above,
which allows a more complete reading of the legend than the two specimens
hitherto published. It is the use of this unusual title that helps to fix the

---

[1] Abū 'l-Faḍl, *Akbarnāma*, trans. H. Beveridge i, 525–42.
[2] A silver coin of Baghdād dated 932 is described by H. Edhem in the *Catalogue of
Islamic Coins in the Ottoman Museum* vi, 252, no. 857; and an undated gold coin of al-Ḥillah
in *Numizmatika i epigrafika* ix (1971), 129, no. 21.

date of the issue, for we know that in 983/1575, after leaving his kingdom at the mercy of his troublesome grandson, Sulaimān Mīrzā sought and received permission from Akbar to make the pilgrimage to Mecca. This, as it turned out, was merely a pretext for a convenient absence which enabled Sulaimān to assemble troops with which to recover Badakhshān. Abū'l-Faḍl tells us that he went rapidly from the place of pilgrimage to 'Irāq 'Ajam (Persia) in order that he might gain his ends by the help of the Shāh.[1] His assumption of the title 'servant of the two noble sanctuaries' clearly reflects his accomplishment of the pilgrimage. The issue in question must therefore belong to the period between his successful reinvasion of Badakhshān in 987/1579 and his final expulsion by the Uzbegs in 992/1584.

*Muḥammad Shāh Rukh b. Ibrāhīm b. Sulaimān Mīrzā (period of sole rule 983–7/1575–9; in conflict with Sulaimān, 973–83/1566–75, 987–92/1579–84).*

7. N 0·4 in. 0·94 gm. (14·5 gr.). No mint, year 987. [Pl. 24. 7]
*Obv.* As no. 1.
*Rev.*        . . . .

٩ﭪ
[محمد] شاهرخ بادشاه
[الز]مان سلطان
٨٧

8. N 0·45 in. 0·92 gm. (14·2 gr.). No mint, date uncertain. [Pl. 24. 8]
*Obv.* As no. 1.
*Rev.* As no. 7 but محمد visible; date indistinct.

These are the first published coins of Shāh Rukh, the grandson of Sulaimān Mīrzā. His father Ibrāhīm having been killed soon after his birth, he was proclaimed at the age of seven by Badakhshi rebels, during his grandfather's absence in Kābul (971–2/1563–4). He later became an active opponent of Sulaimān, and Badakhshān was rent by their incessant struggles. The root of their disagreement seems to have been Shāh Rukh's refusal to content himself with the fief of Ibrāhīm which formed his lawful inheritance. Eventually he dispossessed Sulaimān and for four years was sole ruler of Badakhshān. After the invasion of the province by 'Abdullāh the Shaibānid in 992/1584 Shāh Rukh came to Akbar's court, where he was raised to a position of honour. He afterwards played a prominent part in Akbar's campaign to conquer Kashmir, but he never succeeded in reconquering Badakhshān. He died in 1016/1607.[2]

No. 7 above belongs to the final year of Shāh Rukh's sole rule. It was probably struck before Sulaimān's reconquest of Badakhshān in the month of Ābān, after which a division of territories was agreed upon.[3]

---

[1] *Akbarnāma* iii., 423. My statement in *NC* 1965, 226, that Suleiman did not make the pilgrimage to Mecca is, therefore, incorrect.
[2] Ibid. (numerous entries).        [3] Ibid. 423–4.

*'Abdullāh II b. Iskandar (991–1006/1583–98)*

9. *N* 0·5 in. 0·95 gm. (14·6 gr.). No mint or date. [Pl. **24. 9**]
*Obv.* As no. 1.
*Rev.* In a scalloped area: الله
عبد
بهادر خان
Portions of marginal legend visible.

Silver coins of this Central Asian ruler are common, but only two specimens in gold have been reported, one by Rodgers[1] and one by Markov.[2] The Rodgers coin, judging from its weight and description, is also a Badakhshān issue. 'Abdullāh gained Badakhshān without a battle in 992/1584 and left his son 'Abd al-Mu'min, the governor of Balkh, to hold the province against the Mīrzās. It remained under Uzbeg domination until 1011/1602, when a supposed son of Shāh Rukh named Badī'al-Zamān gained possession of the province for a short time and coined money in the name of Akbar.[3] The use on no. 9 above of an ornate cartouche to frame the name of the Khan is typical of Shaibānid coins.[4]

By collating the dated Badakhshān issues of the Mīrzās and the Moghuls, we build up a picture of constantly fluctuating allegiances which mirrors the uncertain political status of the area:

| Date[5] | Ruler | Contemporary events |
|---|---|---|
| 939 | Sulaimān | S. sent by Bābur to govern Badakhshān (936). |
| 955 | Humāyūn | S. supports Humāyūn against Kāmrān (953–60); Humāyūn victorious in Badakhshān (955). |
| 971 | Akbar | S. captures Kābul (971); Shāh Rukh proclaimed by Badakhshi rebels (972). |
| 975 | Sulaimān | Civil war between S. and Shāh Rukh (973–83). |
| 979 | ,, | |
| 98x | ,, | |
| 986 | Akbar | Shāh Rukh rules alone in Badakhshān (983–7). |
| 987 | Shāh Rukh | |
| 988 | Akbar | S. and Shāh Rukh in conflict (988–92) |
| ? (987–92) | Sulaimān | |
| ? (992–1006) | 'Abdullāh II | 'Abdullāh conquers Badakhshān (992). |

[1] *Catalogue of the Coins collected by Chas. J. Rodgers and purchased by the Punjab Govt.*, part ii, 150, no. 1.
[2] *Inventory of Musulman Coins in the Hermitage Museum* 694, no. 129.
[3] *Akbarnāma* iii. 652–3, 1221.
[4] See my article 'Shaybānid Silver Coins' in *NC* 1966, 251–330.
[5] With the exception of an unpublished gold coin of Akbar dated 986, in the British Museum, all the issues recorded here will be found in Lane-Poole's *Coins of the Moghul Emperors*, my article 'Coins of Sulaimān Mīrzā of Badakhshān' in *NC* 1965, or in the present article.

We can see from this table that as long as the Mīrzās reigned the shadow of Moghul suzerainty was never far from Badakhshān. Both Sulaimān and Shāh Rukh at various times struck coins in the name of the Moghul emperor. They are, moreover, always treated as vassals by Akbar's biographer, Abū'l-Faḍl. At the same time there is no doubt that had harmony prevailed between them and had they not had to contend with the powerful Shaibānid state to the north, the Mīrzās would not have troubled to pay allegiance to Delhi. Akbar himself took no punitive action against them, as he might understandably have done in view of their frequent usurpation of the privilege of *sikkah* (coining money). The most likely explanation for this is that the state of Badakhshān acted as a convenient buffer against Uzbeg incursions into Moghul territory. Of no vital importance to the emperor in itself, it was of value in ensuring the protection of Kābul, the gateway to Moghul India.

# The Beggars' Badges and the Dutch Revolt

## THE LATE J. D. A. THOMPSON

[SEE PLATES 25–6]

THE badges and medals in this article are the contemporary commemoration of that revolt of the Netherlands against Philip II of Spain which resulted in the foundation of the Dutch Republic. Modern historians like Geyl[1] have shown that the revolt began with the resistance of a group of nobles to the inflexible policies of the government in Brussels, expressing the dictat of Philip II of Spain. Later in the quarrel bitter religious differences and repression, strengthened the opposition to Spanish power. The provinces of the Netherlands regarded themselves as a confederation of semi-independent states owing a double allegiance to the Holy Roman Empire and to the Spanish throne. The provinces also regarded themselves as privileged through their great commercial importance, which derived from the cloth trade of Bruges, Ypres, and other Flemish towns, and from the great maritime activity Antwerp.

The Emperor Charles V had understood and conciliated the aspirations of the provinces, but King Philip II did not. The Netherlands were governed by the king's half-sister, Margaret, Duchess of Parma, advised principally by five councillors who included Charles Count of Berlaymont, Antoine Perrenot, Cardinal Granvelle (Philip's representative at Brussels), and a Dutch lawyer named Viglius. Associated with them were the counts of Egmont and of Hoorn, William 'The Silent', Prince of Orange-Nassau, and his brother Louis. At first Egmont and Hoorn were only loosely identified with the opposition, and William of Orange tried to mediate and remained neutral for as long as possible. The most outspoken critics of Spanish policy were a Dutchman, Henry of Brederode, Lord of Vianen, and Louis of Nassau. All of these figures, with the exception of the last two, were Catholic, and had a genuine loyalty to the Spanish crown.

The trouble began over the reluctance of nobles to support Philip's war against France (1556–9), and in his refusal of their demand for the recall of a Spanish army quartered in the Netherlands. These troops had behaved very badly towards the population and had been the subject of repeated protests.

---

[1] P. Geyl, *The Revolt of the Netherlands, 1553–1609*, 1932.

U

Philip, through Granvelle, tried to bully the nobles into submission, and the Cardinal himself caused bitter resentment by the way in which he created new bishoprics in order to combat the spread of Protestantism and to limit the power of the rich native ecclesiastical authorities. The Cardinal failed in these aims, and had to leave the country in 1564. His departure strengthened the opposition, and Brederode and his friends drew up strong resolutions calling upon the Spanish government to change its policy. The quarrel worsened, and reached a climax in 1566 when Brederode published a 'compromize' proposal which was openly rebellious, especially in religious matters. Philip had already made two concessions, in removing the solidiery and the cardinal, but would go no further. Philip ordered Margaret to execute all of his edicts, including the introduction of the Inquisition, and to refuse any terms for the nobles.

Brederode gathered about 600 of his supporters in Brussels, and on 6 April 1566 he presented Margaret with another petition. This was more conciliatory in its text but the attitude of Brederode and his numerous company was so formidable that the duchess was alarmed and much inclined to give way. She was reassured by Berlaymont, who exclaimed contemptuously, 'What, Madam, is your Highness afraid of these beggars?' (ces gueux). Brederode at once siezed upon this term and turned it into a party slogan; two days later he presided at a banquet attended by 300 of his followers, and declared that all were ready to become beggars in the name of their king and country. The cry of Vivent les Gueux ('Long live the Beggars') was taken up by everyone present, and Brederode displayed a beggar's wallet and drank from a wooden cup which was passed from hand to hand.[1]

Egmont, Hoorn, and the Prince of Orange incautiously visited the meeting in its later stages, and much to their dismay were acclaimed as leaders of the movement. They escaped quickly and gave no immediate support to the Beggars.

As a result of the Brussels meeting a number of oval and round badges, cast in gold, silver, and silver-gilt, were made to be worn by members of the Beggars' party. Most people also had a wooden cup (sometimes bound with silver) made for them as a reminder of their pledge to oppose the Spanish edicts. Many of these badges are seventeenth- and eighteenth-century copies, and originals are rare. An example was first illustrated by Luckius in 1620,[2] and others were described by Van Loon, Bizot and Le Clerc.[3] Since those

---

[1] G. Van Loon, *Histoire métallique des xvii provinces des Pays-Bas*, 5 vols., The Hague, 1732–7, at vol, i, pp. 82–3, illustrates and describes various wooden cups which were souvenirs of the Beggars, and including Brederode's own vessel. Van Loon notes that both the open wooden cup and the stoppered drinking-flask (calebasse), as used by pilgrims, were accepted as symbols by the Beggars.

[2] I. I. Luckius, *Sylloge Numismatum Elegantiorum* (Strasbourg, 1620), 221.

[3] Van Loon, ed. cit. P. Bizot, *Histoire métallique de la République de Hollande*, 3 vols. (Amsterdam, 1688–90), 1 ff. M. Le Clerc, *Histoire des Provinces-Unies des Pays-Bas . . . avec les principales médailles et leur explication* (Amsterdam, 1728), 21, pl. xxix.

publications the badges have been studied only once in detail, by Wigersma in 1906: his material was drawn largely from the Cabinet at Leewarden in his native Friesland.[1]

The name of the original maker of the Beggars' badges is not recorded, for obvious reasons he did not sign his work. The bust of the king is in the style of Jonghelinck, who was later employed by the Spanish crown as Mint-Warden of Antwerp. In 1566 the artist was active as a sculptor in Brussels, and a contemporary reference attributes the badge to him.[2] The majority of the Beggars' badges are the work of a Dutch imitator of the prototype.

There are five versions of the badge, and the rarest has for its obverse type a portrait of Philip II to right or to left, with a reverse of clasped hands through a beggar's wallet, and the legend JUSQVES A PORTER LA BESACE (until beggary) [Pl. 25. 5–7].[3] 'Porter la besace' means 'to beg' or 'to be very poor', so that the inscription possibly quotes the words used by Brederode in his speech at Brussels. The besace was a double bag or wallet, closed at both ends and open in the middle, as in the illustration. This type of leather wallet was carried slung over the shoulder by beggars and by mendicant monks, hence Brederode's gesture in wearing one at the banquet.

The badges occasionally are cast with loops at the edges, from which are suspended models of wallets and of cups [Pl. 25. 3].[4] Some of the badges are dated 1566, but the majority, as would be expected, are undated. There are others, variant in legends and type, and dated 1572, long after the event, but issued during the most catastrophic period of the struggle with Spain.

The second type of the badge has on the obverse the head of Philip, with the same inscription on loyalty, but with a reverse showing two gentlemen wearing wallets and clasping hands. The legend is as before, with the addition of the letters V.L.G. (Vivent les Gueux) below the figures [Pl. 25. 4].[5] The third type of badge has the same obverse type, with a reverse showing a serpent rising from flames and biting a hand extended from the clouds. The legend, SI DEVS NOBISCVM QVIS CONTRA NOS ('if God is with us, who is against us') [Pl. 25. 6],[6] alludes to St. Paul in Malta, when a viper fastened on

---

[1] S. Wigersma, 'De Draggteekens van het jaar 1566', in *De Vrije Fries*, 20 (1906), 1–49.

[2] V. Tourneur, 'Le médailleur Jacques Jongheling et le cardinal Granvelle 1564–1578', *RBN* 69 (1927), 79–93, at 86. 'Le 15 juin 1566, Morillon envoie à Granvelle un plomb de la médaille des Gueux par Jongheling. "Le plomb de la médaille, va auec ceste. Il s'en forge plus de ce métal et d'estaing et de cuyvre que d'or et d'argent, affin peult estre que les gentz demeurent en leur qualité" '. The exhibition catalogues *Médailles des anciens Pays-Bas. Contribution numismatique à l'histoire du protestantisme* (Paris, 1956), no. 51, and L. Wellens-De Donder, *Medailleurs en Numismaten van de Renaissance in de Nederlanden* (Brussels, 1959), no. 119, both illustrate examples of the badge as the work of Jonghelinck.

[3] Van Loon, ed. cit. i, 84, fig. 5. The example illustrated [Pl. 25] is of silver gilt, in the Royal Collection, The Hague. The photograph and notes on these badges were kindly supplied by Miss Gay van der Meer. All of the other illustrations are taken from Van Loon.  [4] Ibid., fig. 3.

[5] Ibid., fig. 4.

[6] Ibid., fig. 6.

to his hand without harming him (Acts 28). The viper is intended to be Philip II, and the hand symbolizes the Beggars. According to Le Clerc and Van Loon, the words also refer to the visit made by Count Egmont to Spain in 1564 for the discussion of religious and other difficulties with Philip. The king's promises deceived no one but Egmont himself, and Philip's orders which arrived in November 1565 made it clear that he would tolerate no opposition. Hoorn went at once to visit his German relations, Egmont remained undecided, and even the Prince of Orange did not attempt to argue. The badge commemorates disappointment, and a belief that better counsels would prevail in the end (did not the Maltese change their hostile attitude to St. Paul after the episode of the viper).

The fourth type of badge bears the busts of Philip and of his second wife Anne of Austria, and the date 1572. The obverse legend is the same, EN TOVT FIDE(les) AV ROY, but the reverse, with the effigy of Anne, has added to her titles the words TIENERON FOY [Pl. 25. 8],[1] meaning that the Beggars would remain faithful to their pledge. The medal has small models of a wallet and a cup attached to the edge, and Van Loon notes that the medal was made for the magistrates of Utrecht to display their loyalty to the Prince of Orange, in the defence of their privileges.

The fifth form of the badge [Pl. 25. 9][2] is the first in which the object of the Beggars' opposition is the 'tenth penny' tax, instituted by Alva to support the royalist forces in the Netherlands. The obverse is composed of a group of symbols arranged around an upright sword, on the point of which is a roundel, and below two rings. On the left there is a flute and a pair of spectacles, on the right are nine further roundels (or coins). Above, flanking the sword, are two human ears. These objects have simple satirical meanings. The flute refers to Alva's success in lulling opponents with fair words or music before pouncing upon them. The ears suggest this deafness to counsel, and perhaps his spy organization. The spectacles are a clear reference to the capture of Brill, near Flushing, by La Marck and his Sea-Beggars in 1572. The Dutch word for spectacles is 'Bril'. The sword and the roundels or coins are an explicit reference to the armed resistance by the Beggars to the 'tenth penny' tax of 1572. The reverse of the badge shows two gentlemen standing upon some roundels or coins scattered on the ground. The type is a variant of one of the earlier Beggars' badges [Pl. 25. 2], and the legends are the standard ones, with the date 1572 on the obverse.

The 'tenth penny' tax produced another medal, in two versions, dated 1572 and 1577 [Pl. 26. 1].[3] The obverse shows a full-length figure of William of Orange in armour, carrying a hammer, and with the Dutch legend P.V.O. DAT. EDEL. BLOET. The reverse has a shield with nine roundels, and the legend HEFT. ONS. VOER. DEN IO. PENNINCK. BEHOT. The whole

---

[1] Van Loon, ed. cit. i, 144.
[2] Ibid., 145–7.                    [3] Ibid., 155–6.

may be translated as 'The Prince of Orange, that noble warrior, will deliver us from the Tenth-Penny'.

The last two of this group of medals on the fortunes of the Beggars, concern the relief of Leyden in 1574. In 1567 King Philip had replaced Cardinal Granvelle by Ferdinand of Toledo, Duke of Alva, as the principal advisor to Margaret of Parma. The duke began to terrorize the Netherlands. He executed Hoorn and Egmont, defeated the German troops raised by William of Orange, established a 'Council of Blood' in order to try the rebels, and the Inquisition to try the heretics. The 'tenth penny' tax was established, and the towns which resisted the tax were mercilessly sacked, until only parts of two provinces, Holland and Zeeland, still defied Philip's authority. The inhabitants were principally seamen, who, realizing that they could not match the Spaniards on land, formed a fleet under the command of the Count of La Marck and of William of Blois, Lord of Treslong, called themselves the 'Sea-Beggars' (Les Gueux de Mer), and held a privateering commission from the Prince of Orange. Their success at Brill in 1572 has already been noted, and reflected in a medal type, and the success renewed the revolt. Holland and Zeeland were joined, one by one, by the other Northern Provinces, Utrecht, Guelderland, Friesland, Overyssel, and Groningen; in 1573 the Dutch fleet gained command of the Zuyder Zee and actually captured the Spanish Admiral, Count Bossu, in his flagship, *The Inquisition*.

Leyden, one of the last outposts in Holland, had to endure a terrible siege in 1574. The city was finally relieved by a fleet of Sea-Beggars under Admiral Boisot, consisting of shallow-draught vessels, galleys, and flat-boats which were rowed or sailed over flooded country. The fleet was partly manned by invalids wounded in previous actions, and everyone wore in their hats or as ear-rings a cresent-shaped silver badge inscribed LI(e)VER TURCX DAN PAVS(ch), and ENDE SPIT DE LA MES(se), meaning 'Sooner Turk than Papist' and 'In spite of the Mass' [**Pl. 26. 2**].[1] The last of the Beggars' medals was made after the relief of Leyden [**Pl. 26. 3**].[2] The medal likens the relief to the delivery of Jerusalem from Sennacherib, when the Assyrian army was routed by an angel. The obverse of the medal shows the Assyrian army attacked by the angel, and the reverse depicts the relief of Leyden, with the Spanish siege-works under attack from the Dutch vessels. The legends point the parallel between the two armies of Assyria and Spain. The saving of Leyden was a turning-point in the fortunes of the provinces in revolt, for the troops of Alva were not paid after their defeat, promptly mutined, and the duke forced to retire to the Southern Netherlands. None of Alva's three successors could improve the Spanish position, and in 1575 there was a short

[1] Van Loon, ed. cit. i, 190–1. The legend 'Liever Turks dan Paaps' is discussed by R. van Lutterveld in *De Gids* (October 1961), 150–63.

[2] Van Loon, ed. cit. i, 192–3. The author notes, and illustrates, one specimen of the medal with chains and a loop for suspension. Such a piece, intended as a presentation medal, was known to Van Loon in one example only.

reconciliation known as the Pacification of Ghent. In 1579, the seven rebellious provinces were linked by the Union of Utrecht, and William of Orange became Stadthoulder of a free Dutch Republic. The revolution against Spain was safely accomplished, although it was not acknowledged by the Catholic world until 1604.

# A Paduan Medal of Queen Artemesia of Caria

## MICHAEL GREENHALGH

[SEE PLATES 27–8]

SIXTEENTH-CENTURY Padua was an important centre for the study and emulation of ancient art. Several of the medallists working there, principally Giovanni Cavino and Valerio Belli, excelled in the production of medals which sought to imitate the antique, and sometimes to copy it exactly. Cavino was the most prolific of all such medallists, and no less than 122 of his dies are preserved in the Cabinet des Médailles of the Bibliothèque Nationale. One of the most interesting, and in previous centuries most popular, of his productions is the medal of Queen Artemesia of Caria, widow of King Mausolus, showing her head on the obverse, and the tomb or 'mausoleum' she constructed in memory of her dead husband on the reverse. This note seeks to show why Cavino should have made such a medal, and to explain why its authority should eventually have come to be discredited.

There is some doubt as to whether or not Cavino and his fellow artists tried to pass off their productions as antique,[1] but it is certain that the real experts from Cavino's time onward have never been deceived by 'Paduans'. The bishop-antiquary Antonio Agustin, for example, admired the medals of Cavino as accomplished productions in the spirit of the antique, and the work of his own friend Pirro Ligorio for the same reason,[2] although his knowledge of genuine antique works of art was sufficient for him to be able to pick out with ease the mistakes in the imitations of his contemporaries. The standards used by Augustin for judging such 'forgeries' were those of elegance and accuracy, and '. . . the more like the genuine article his products were, the greater credit they were to his scholarship. . . .'.[3]

For the ordinary collector or dilettante, however, 'Paduans' represented a serious pitfall. Fabriczy[4] asserts that most purchasers of Cavino's medals

---

[1] R. H. Lawrence, *Medals by Giovanni Cavino, the Paduan* (New York (privately printed), 1883), 5: F. Cessi, *Giovanni da Cavino, medaglista padovano del cinquecento* (Padua, 1969), 22, rightly assert that Cavino was not a commercial faker, he was a skilled reproducer of antique materials. Enea Vico, *Discorsi sopra le medaglie degli antichi* (Venice, 1555), cap. cciii, 67, includes Cavino in a list of artists known for their skill in imitating ancient coins.

[2] Charles Mitchell, 'Archaeology and Romance', in *Italian Renaissance Studies*, ed. E. F. Jacob (1960), 455 ff.

[3] Mitchell, op. cit., 458 and 459 respectively for the two quotations.

[4] C. von Fabriczy, *Italian Medals* (London, 1904), 199–200.

probably thought them genuine, and that Cavino never said anything to disillusion them. Their popularity was great: Vasari, in his 'Life of Belli',[1] writes of how

... The medals of the twelve Caesars, with reverses after the manner of the finest antiques, were prepared by Valerio, as were also many Greek medals, with so large a number of other works in crystal, that the shops of the goldsmiths are full of the impressions taken from the productions of this master, nay, the whole world is supplied with them either in sulphur, gypsum, or other substances, presenting impressions from the heads, figures or other compositions of Valerio Vicentino. ...

Medals were at this time a popular art form, and influenced a whole series of books which showed the likenesses of the great heroes of both ancient and modern times, enclosed in a roundel and made to look like medals. Guillaume Rouillé's *Promptuaire des médailles* (Lyons, 1553),[2] for example, gives the portraits of all famous characters from Adam and Eve onwards, the accompanying text dwelling on the virtues and vices of the characters shown.[3] Artemesia is the prototype of the faithful widow, and the story of how she drank her husband's ashes mixed with wine was well known and popular.[4]

Cavino's medal of Queen Artemesia [Pl. 27. 1] probably filled, in the minds of the sixteenth century, a historical gap, for no antique coins showing the famous mausoleum existed.[5] The difficulties of subject-matter were here

[1] G. Vasari, *Lives* . . ., Bohn's Standard Library edition (London, 1850–2), iii, 477–8.

[2] Editions in Latin, French, and Italian were published at Lyon in 1553, and a Spanish translation appeared in 1561.

[3] Other publications of a similar nature, but without Rouillé's strong didacticism, are as follows: Andrea Fulvio, *Illustrium Imagines. Imperatorum et illustrium Virorum ac Mulierum vultus ex antiquis numismatibus expressi*. . . . (Rome, 1517); Hubert Goltz, *Vitae omnium ferè Imperatorum imagines, à C. J. Caesare usque ad Carolum V. et Ferdinandum ejus fratrem ex antiquis veterum numismatis . . . fideliter adumbratae, necnon eorundem vitae . . . delineatae . . . per H. G.* (Antwerp, 1557); *Onuphrii Panvinii. . . . XXVII pontificum maximorum elogia et imagines* (Rome, 1568); the most famous was probably Fulvio Orsini, *Imagines et elogia virorum illustrium et erudítor. ex antiquis lapidibus et nomismatib. expressa cum annotationib. Ex Bibliotheca F.U.* (Rome, 1570).

[4] *cf. Boccaccio, De Claris Mulieribus*, ed. Guido A. Guarino (London, 1964), 124–5, where a list of his sources is given. Artemesia appears, with her cup of wine and ashes, in the engravings of the mausoleum by Heemskerck, De Vos and Tempesta, and is often mentioned in the text accompanying engravings of the mausoleum in various seventeenth- and eighteenth-century editions of the *Mirabilia Romae*. Often Artemesia appears without the mausoleum, but holding her cup of wine and ashes. For a list of illustrations of the queen, see A. Pigler, *Barockthemen* (1956), ii, 356–7. The parallel was also made between Artemesia and Catherine de' Medicis, another inconsolable widow. (See below, and p. 297, n. 4). The comprehensive nature of the Artemesia legend derives partly from the fusing into one character of two separate women: Artemesia, daughter of Hecatomnus, wife of Mausolus, and her namesake, also Queen of Halicarnassus, who helped Xerxes against the Greeks. Boccaccio combined the two, as did the influential dictionaries of Charles and Robert Stephanus. Houel and Caron, in their poems and tapestry designs celebrating Catherine de' Medicis, made the same mistake.

[5] Lawrence, ed. cit., no. 75. Cessi, ed. cit., no. 115. Guichard and others thought differently (see below, pp. 298–9, 311).

greater than was usually the case with such imitations, when all that was required of the reverse was one or two figures in the antique style—perhaps a sacrifice, a warrior in a chariot, or a prisoner and a pile of trophies. For any representation of the Mausoleum which was to measure up to Agustin's expectations required a certain amount of research into the relevant authorities, but we do not know whether Cavino did this himself.

The mausoleum was one of the Seven Wonders of the Ancient World,[1] and Cavino produced his medal just before[2] engraved sets showing reconstructions of these Wonders were produced: sets were made by Heemskerck (1572), De Vos (1614), and Tempesta (1608).[3] And, in an elaborate series of drawings by Antoine Caron with accompanying verses by Nicolas Houel, the widowed Catherine de' Medicis was compared to Queen Artemesia; these designs were subsequently developed into highly successful tapestries.[4] While Tempesta appears to attempt an 'oriental' style for his reconstruction of the mausoleum, the versions of De Vos and Heemskerck resemble each other, and are derived from the main authority on the subject, Pliny, who writes:

. . . patet ab austro et septentrione sexagenos ternos pedes, brevius a frontibus, toto circumitu pedes CCCCXXXX, attolitur in altitudinem XXV cubitis, cingitur columnis XXXVI. Pteron vocavere circitum . . . super pteron pyramis altitudinem inferiorem aequat, viginti quattuor gradibus in metae cacumen se contrahens; in summo est quadriga marmorea. . . .[5]

Cavino died in 1570, and his medal therefore precedes the three sets of Wonders mentioned above; none of the later artists, however, draw specific inspiration from his version. Heemskerck, De Vos, and Cavino all adopt a pilaster and statue-in-niche motif for the body of the monument, but whereas the first two show a twenty-four step pyramid in accordance with Pliny's description, the medal shows only four steps, possibly because of the medal's restricted size. Apart from this, it is clear that Cavino has followed Pliny's

---

[1] The most usual list is as follows: Pyramids, Hanging Gardens of Babylon, Colossus of Rhodes, Lighthouse of Alexandria, Mausoleum of Halicarnassus, Temple of Diana at Ephesus, and Statue of Zeus by Phidias.

[2] The exact date of the medal is unknown, but Cavino died in 1570 and, since the next forty years saw three popular sets of the Seven Wonders engraved, it is perhaps permissible to assume that the medal was produced not long before his death.

[3] Heemskerck's set (including the Colosseum as an eighth Wonder) was copied, possibly at Haarlem, in 1580, and also in Brussels tapestries in the late sixteenth and seventeenth centuries (see G. Brett in *Art Quarterly* xii (1949), 339 ff.) Guiliemus Blaeu copied them as vignettes for his *Grand Atlas*, 1648–55, as did Pierre Lemoyne in his *Gallerie des Femmes Fortes*, Paris, 1647, then Leiden, 1660, Paris, 1665 and 1667, English translation London, 1652, Spanish translation 1702. The set by De Vos is based mostly on Heemskerck, and accentuates the fame of this latter, whereas Tempesta's archaeologically sensible series appears to have made little impact.

[4] Fénaille, *État général des tapisseries de la Manufacture des Gobelins depuis son origine jusqu'à nos jours, 1600–1900* i, 1923, 109 f.

[5] *Natural History* xxxvi, 30–1.

somewhat confused account; the medal shows a four-storeyed structure, the lowest storey of which has a central door, and Ionic pilasters against a plain wall. The next is similar, but with niches and statues, and no door; above it a shorter storey has a set of bas-reliefs, and above that four decreasing steps on a low base are surmounted by a quadriga. As specified by Pliny, the bottom two storeys do equal in height the upper two plus quadriga, although the 'pteron' is omitted. The motifs Cavino chooses are Roman: the figures with torches, the ox-skull and garland frieze, and the 'emperor' in his chariot being crowned by a Victory. The general arrangement of the structure is that of a Roman funeral pyre, which Cavino would have been able to study on genuine Roman coins.[1]

We can contrast Cavino's conception of the Mausoleum with that shown on another medal, possibly already in existence when he produced his version. There is in the Uffizi a drawing of the mausoleum [Pl. 27. 2], reconstructed according to Pliny's directions, and probably done before the middle of the sixteenth century.[2] The vagueness of Pliny's account allows reconstructors great latitude, and this drawing emphasizes the point, for it shows a simple rectangular temple with Corinthian columns, with a balustrade around the top of the cornice, and a twenty-four step pyramid instead of a pitched roof, on top of which is a manned quadriga prancing forward. The design was exactly copied on to a medal[3] [Pl. 28. 1], and the head of Artemesia given on the reverse, but there is no means of knowing exactly when it was struck. The late sixteenth or early seventeenth century seems the most likely period, because of the general popularity of Wonders sets at that time.

Of the two, Cavino's medal was the more popular, and there seems to have been no hesitation on the part of numismatic experts from the sixteenth century onwards in pronouncing them both modern. But experts were few and far between, and a survey of later opinions of Cavino's medal will demonstrate its popularity, as well as uncovering other supposedly antique medals showing the famous mausoleum.

The first mention of the medal appears to be by the well-known antiquary and engraver Enea Vico who, in his *Discorsi sopra le medaglie degli antichi* (Venice 1555),[4] warns against this clever imitation of an antique coin. It is first illustrated in Claude Guichard's *Funérailles et diverses manières d'ensevelir les Romains, Grecs et autres nations, tant anciennes que modernes* (Lyons, 1581); he states it to be modern, although he does not say who made it. It is obviously, we are told, a reconstruction

---

[1] The motif is a frequent one: see, for example, an aes of Commodus, reproduced in *BMCRE* iv, 101, no. 11. This has garland swags on the lowest storey, then two storeys with statues in niches; from the third storey two torches jut out, and on top of the fourth is a manned quadriga.

[2] Cf. Charles Huelsen in *La Bibliofilia* (1912), 169–70.

[3] Specimen in the Dept. of Coins and Medals, British Museum.

[4] A popular work; editions also Venice, 1558; Paris, 1619; and Padua, 1691.

after Pliny, and he notes that M. de S. Irigny, whose medal it was, thought it antique. But Guichard also gives another medal of the mausoleum, which appears as a seven-step pyramid with a figure on top; this medal he claims to be antique.

The next mention and illustration of the Cavino coin is in André Thevet's *Pourtraits et vies des Hommes illustres Grecz, Latin et Payens . . .* (Paris, 1584, foll. 71 ff.), which proves its great popularity. It is the obverse, not the reverse of the medal which is shown, and this is an extension of the Cavino portrait of Artemesia: the queen is here portrayed half-length, carrying an urn and a goblet. Thevet is convinced that it is antique, and tries to give it a pedigree:

. . . le portrait, tel que je l'ai tiré d'une médaille antique qui est en mon cabinet, peu différente d'une statue en marbre que j'ai vu en la ville de Rhodes . . .

Several of Thevet's portraits, including Artemesia, were added to North's translation of Plutarch's *Lives* (London and Cambridge, 1676).

The exceptionally popular *Dialogos de medallas . . .* by Antonio Agustin (Tarragona, 1587, and many subsequent editions and translations) mentions the Cavino coin in the Eleventh Dialogue; here, he warns against forgeries, specifies a medal showing Artemesia by a certain 'Padovano', and also deals with authors who have been deceived by forgeries such as this. Similarly Sada's *Dialoghi intorno alle medaglie* (Rome, 1592, pp. 291 ff.) issues specific warnings against the Paduans, instancing Cavino's Caesar medal with 'Veni Vidi Vici' and his Augustus medal with 'Festina Lente'. But in spite of both these works, Reineck's *Historia Julia* (Helmstadt, 1594–7),[1] gives a low-quality woodcut of the Cavino coin, which misses out or changes the details of the original. The author expresses no doubts at all about it; '. . . extat de hoc sepulchro . . . nummus Artemesiae aeneus, quem supra dedimus . . .'. He explains, underneath the illustrations itself, that the medal was shown to him by

'. . . Sebastianus Hofemanus Gorlicensis, quo tempore academia Lips. nos ambos cives habuit. Id quod monendum erat, ut in animicum memoris animi studium nostrum, et nummo ipsi quasi fides constaret . . .'

I can find no references to this 'Sebastianus Hofemanus' but, whoever he was,[2] he was not alone in being deceived by the coin: as able a scholar as Guido Pancirolli, who saw it at Padua, declared in 1599 that it was genuine.[3]

---

[1] *Historia Julia, sive Syntagma heroicum, cujus pars prima . . . continet Monarchiam primam, hoc est, Chaldaeorum et Assyriorum imperium . . .* ii, 76.

[2] Is it possible that this could be Abraham Gorlaeus? A numismatist of note, he acquired a reputation for forging coins. Pierre Bayle (*Dictionnaire* 5th edn. (Amsterdam, 1740), ii 577 note E) writes as follows, citing Scaliger: 'Gorlaeus fond des médailles: il m'en a quefois montré, mais j'ai découvert qu'elles n'étoient pas anciennes, il ne m'en a montré depuis que des vraies. . . .'

[3] In his *Rerum Memorabilium iam olim Deperditarum* (Hamburg, 1599), 185.

Most general introductions to numismatics published during the seventeenth and eighteenth centuries contain sections on forgery, and often pick out the Paduans for particular mention,[1] but the next actual illustration of the Cavino coin is in Gijsbert Kuiper's *Disquisitio de nummo Mausoleum Artemesiae exhibente*, a section of his *Apotheosis Homeri* (Amsterdam, 1683, p. 283). He writes that the coin

... qui licet supposititius et malae notae sit, dignus tamen mihi visus est ut post Reinerum Reineccium, qui eum mutilum valde exhibet in Historia Julia, edatur ...'

The nearest the coin ever got to inclusion in a serious architectural work on the Mausoleum was in the second edition of Domenico d'Aulisio's treatise, *Opuscula de Mausolei Architectura*, first published at Naples in 1694, and considered important enough to be reprinted in Sallengre's *Novus Thesaurus Antiquitatum Romanorum* (The Hague, 1710–24, iii, 913 ff.). D'Aulisio's text does not in fact mention the Cavino medal, and Ponarus, in his preface to that second edition, explains why:

Superioribus diebus, cum dissertatiuncula haec de Mausolei Architectura esset jam formis excudenda, accidit, ut Auctori sermo oriretur cum V. Cl. Didaco a Vidania, quem officii causa convenerat, de Nummo qui frequens apud Antiquarios. ... Is statim, ut est eruditissimus, eum a Gisberto Cupero adnotationibus illustratum ostendit, de quo noster Auctor antea inaudierat nihil; quare pro indicio egit viro praestantissimae gratias, quando haec nosse sua vel maxime intererat. De eo nummo quid sentiat, quaeris? Eum quidem cum Cupero fictitium, et malae notae agnoscit: at artificem fuisse ingeniosum, et qui mentem Plinii optime perceperit, ut Cuperus contendit, id vero negat. ...[2]

D'Aulisio, it seems, did not approach his subject with a good general knowledge of its more popular points: he appears to have worked in a void, using only the text of Pliny for his reconstruction, and unaware of other engraved reconstructions. Thus Ponarus, for the sake of completeness, has to give a description of the coin modelled on the Uffizi drawing, also unknown to d'Aulisio, or ignored by him:

Extat et alter Artemesiae Nummus in nobili Museo Francisci Pichetti, adulterinus et ipse, sed inventu rarior, nec Cupero visus, in quo quaedam meliora sunt, quaedam deteriora, nonnulla paria. Scalas exhibet, et quidem expressius. Columnae pariter decem in fronte visuntur, sed saniori consilio extremae duae angulis insident. At vero perperam altitudo inferior una constat. Zona, quam efficiunt Columnae cum trabeatione, quas podium finit. Tum surgit Pyramis multiplicibus distincta gradibus, ubi, quod mireris, latus quodque est per medium, a summo ad imum, profundiori semita intercisum. Unde hoc artifex hausit? sine dubio, ex vano; alioqui commen-

---

[1] The best known is Charles Patin's *Introductio ad Historiam Numismatum* (Amsterdam, 1683), 139 ff., which saw several editions and translations.
[2] The identity of 'Didacus', like that of 'Sebastianus Hofemanus Gorlicensis', is a mystery.

dandus in Quadriga, quae tanquam in cursu est, etsi Agitator attritu obliteratus non appareat. Ita sese Nummi isti invicem refellunt, falsique arguunt. . . .

All of Cavino's coins had in fact been published in 1692, a short time before the first appearance of d'Aulisio's tract, in Claude du Molinet's *Cabinet de la bibliothèque de sainte Geneviève*. Herein, fifty-five of them are illustrated, including that of Artemesia and the Mausoleum. Du Molinet explains in the introduction to the catalogue (pp. 92 ff.) the need for his work:

> Beaucoup de mes amis m'ont engagé à en parler, et m'ont assuré que ce que j'en dirois serait d'une grande utilité aux nouveaux Curieux, et même à quelques-uns qui étant plus versez en la science des Médailles, ne laissent pas d'y être quelquefois trompez. . . . Il aurait été facile d'y surprendre ceux qui n'auraient pas eu la connoissance de ces creux. . . .

But he still maintains that they are easily distinguished from real antique coins, while praising Cavino and Bassiano as follows:

> . . . . il suffit d'avoir tant soit peu de goût pour les Arts, et de jeter les yeux sur quelques-unes des Médailles de ces deux excellens hommes, pour avouer qu'il ne se trouve rien jusqu'à leur temps de plus parfait. . . .

Perhaps Du Molinet's books was of some help to the next man to write about the mausoleum, Johann Christian Avenarius. In his *Dissertatio historico-architectonica de Artemesia et Mausoleo* (Leipzig, 1714), he gives the Cavino medal as his frontispiece, and begins his text by stating his intention of finding out whether or not it is genuine. He manages, in a very few pages, to prove it false, chiefly because he does not think it conforms to Pliny's directions. It is interesting to note that, although he does not mention the coin made from the Uffizi drawing, his own reconstruction of the mausoleum is similar to it.

With Marie Dorothée Loescher's *Réflexions sur une médaille d'Artémise, reine de Carie, et de son mausolée* (Potsdam, 1748), we are confronted with yet another coin supposedly showing the mausoleum and purporting to be antique [**Pl. 28. 2**]. The treatise, a prime example of specious argument,[1] attempts to prove that the coin, given to her by 'un Ami', shows the mausoleum in a half-completed state. I cannot trace any example of her coin but, judging from its illustration in her treatise, it shows a simple temple façade and not the mausoleum.

By the end of the eighteenth century, in spite of Loescher's startling treatise, small-scale reconstructions of the mausoleum had lost their fascination, due

---

[1] For example, she explains away the lack of any sort of pyramid on her coin by noting that Artemesia died before the mausoleum was completed, and '. . . il est évident qu'elle a fait frapper cette Médaille de son vivant, et qu'elle y a fait empreindre le Mausolée, tel qu'il avait été avancé pendant sa vie' (op. cit. 11–12). She surmises that, since Artemesia had the same name as the goddess Diana, and was widowed after the famous destruction of the Temple of Diana at Ephesus, she built the mausoleum in the form of a temple in order to preserve the memory of the Temple of Diana.

not only to the increasing standards of proficiency among coin-collectors, but also to a greater interest in the remains of Greek architecture: Cavino's funeral pyre could not deceive a generation for whom knowledge of the history and progress of architectural styles was, for the first time, of vital interest.[1]

We can never know how many owners of the Cavino medal thought it a genuine antique piece, although we have seen that it did not deceive the experts. More interesting, however, is the fact that this stylistically outrageous reconstruction should be accepted for so long by numismatists as a genuine contribution towards the elucidation of Pliny's text, whilst receiving no attention from other reconstructors such as Heemskerck, Tempesta, and De Vos. In addition, it is puzzling that the coin made from the Uffizi drawing did not achieve greater popularity.[2] One might reasonably have expected to find medallic versions of the mausoleum reproduced in the often highly annotated editions of Pliny popular in the late seventeenth and eighteenth centuries, but they are always ignored. And, as if to underline the point, the Cavino coin and the Uffizi version appear quite gratuitously in Abraham Gronovius's edition of *Pomponius Mela* (Leyden, 1722 and 1748). The text of the *De Situ Orbis* had previously been edited by his father (Leyden, 1685), who had not given any notes on the mausoleum for the excellent reason that Mela does not describe it. His son, adding a section to a note (on other matters) written by his father, indicates in a rather heavy-handed manner that the credibility of these medals was at an end:

... Porro non potui, quin joco tuo, Lector, inserviens ex pluribus, quos variae manus finxerunt, nummis duas aliquas Mausolei formas conferrem; non ut auctoribus elogia ab te contingat, nec enim meruerunt, sed ut falsos cum falsis esse finas, et rideas eos, quibus placuit ad tales nugas edere commentarios . . .[3]

---

[1] John Pinkerton, for example, in his *Essay on Medals* (London, 1784), writes of the sixteenth century as the golden age of forgery, when '. . . the forgeries were very gross; and such as now would not impose even on a novice. . . .' He cites the Artemesia medal by Cavino as an example, and continues: 'Other learned men have been strangely misled, when speaking of coins; for to be learned in one subject excludes not gross ignorance in others. Budaeus, *De Asse*, quotes a denarius of Cicero, M. TULL. Erasmus, in one of his epistles, tells us with great gravity, that the gold coin of Brutus struck in Thrace, ΚΟΣΩΝ, bears the patriarch Noah coming out of the ark, with his two sons; and takes the Roman eagle for the dove with an olive branch . . . Winckelmann, in his Letters, informs us that the small brass piece with Virgil's head, reverse EPO, is undoubtedly ancient Roman; and adds, with amazing prudence and sagacity, that no knowledge of coins can be had out of Rome. Any boy in Iceland, the least versed in the subject, might have told Winckelmann, that these pieces were struck at Mantua, in the sixteenth century, for a jubilee in honour of Virgil; and have pointed out two or three varieties, from the Museum Mazzuchellianum. . . .' It should be added that Pinkerton displays great knowledge of forgery probably because he was himself an able forger.

[2] Hawksmoor's tower of St. George's, Bloomsbury, may owe something to its simplicity, but a more probable source for this is the lantern of the western dome of Wren's Great Model design for St. Paul's.

[3] Quoted from the 1748 edition, pp. 89–90.

Gronovius says that he has selected two medals '. . . ex pluribus . . .', but we do not really know how many forged medals showing the mausoleum existed. We have come across four: the Cavino coin, the Uffizi version, the seven-step pyramid brought forward by Guichard, and the coin illustrated by Loescher. I have found no specimens of the last two coins mentioned. Guichard, indeed, says that he saw some Artemesia coins in Antoine de la Porte's house at Lyon, but he does not say how many; Loescher, in her account, implies that there were several medals showing the mausoleum, all forgeries and recognized as such by connoisseurs but, like Guichard, she gives no further information.

But however many variations existed, it was the Cavino version which stood head and shoulders above the rest—probably, as I have said, because it showed a familiar structure. For a long time it was in tune with conceptions of how the mausoleum must have looked, but the tracts of Avenarius and Loescher displaced it with reconstructions which were both based (or so they thought) on a Greek temple plan. Though still imperfect, such changes show the development of a fuller understanding of the history of architecture.

# NOTES

# An Unpublished Drachm of Antiochus VI

## JOHN A. SEEGER

**FIG. 1.**

THE following drachm of Antiochus VI [Fig. 1] of the mint of Tarsus is said to have been found among a small varied lot of coins purchased in Istanbul.

*Obv.* Diademed head of Antiochus VI r.

*Rev.* Sandan standing on animal, holding double headed axe
   (ΒΑ)ΣΙΛΕΩΣ ΑΝΤΙΟΧΟΥ ΕΠΙΦΑΝΟΥΣ DIONYΣΟY in field l., Ⱥ (?)
   3·9 gm.

This coin was not known to Cox[1] in her survey of the coinage of Tarsus. The city type of Sandan on Seleucid silver first appears on a rare drachm of Alexander Bala,[2] an issue which Cox has suggested was struck at Tarsus in order to pay troops during Alexander Bala's final struggle against Ptolemy Philopator. Shortly after the defeat and death of Bala in 145 B.C., Tryphon proclaimed the young Antiochus king. Much of the Seleucid empire was in the hands of the rightful claimant, Demetrius Soter; but Tryphon and Antiochus gained control in the Orontes valley from Apamea to Antioch. Bevan[3] states that they had some footing in Cilicia, in particular, the city of Coracesium on the coast. The newly found drachm of Antiochus is proof that they also controlled Tarsus, at least for a time.

Acknowledgement is made to Dr. M. Price of the British Museum who informed me of Cox's paper and suggested that the coin be published.

   [1] D. H. Cox, *Excavations at Gözlü Kule, Tarsus*, ed. Hetty Goldman (Princeton, 1950), 38–83.
   [2] Imhoof-Blumer, *Monnaies Grecoues*, 433, 96.
   [3] E. R. Bevan, *The House of Seleucus* ii (London, 1902), 227.

# Moneyers' Mistakes

EMANUELA FABBRICOTTI

GOING through public and private collections of Roman coins, I have been struck by the frequent accidents which occur in ancient methods of coining.

As stated by Hill,[1] a very common fault is the result of a poor impression by the die, so that part of the blank of one or both sides is left empty. This happens mostly with large series struck in a hurry, as with the denarii of L. Calpurnius Piso L. f. Frugi,[2] those of Q. Titius[3] and many others.

FIG. 1.

Coins with the same representations on both sides, one of which is incuse, are rather rare. Double-struck coins, on the other hand, are frequent on Republican as well as on early or late imperial coins. Most of them are nearly perfectly overstruck and only on very close inspection is it possible to notice the 'accident'. Others, however, are really very inaccurate, especially in late Roman bronze coinage, as for example in **Fig. 1**, where on a small bronze of Diocletian (297/8 A.C.)[4] issued in workshop Θ, mint of Rome, we twice have

---

[1] G. F. Hill, 'Ancient methods of coining' in *NC* 1922, 35–36.

[2] *BMCRR* 1859 f.; Syd. *CRR* 650 f.

[3] *BMCRR* 2225–8; Syd. *CRR* 692.          [4] Coh. vi, 476–7, nos. 541–3.

the title IMP (i.e. IMP DIOCLE IMP D); consequently the reverse also has been doublestruck, so that the wreath, instead of being circular, has the appearance of a spiral.

A very interesting double-striking occurs on a republican denarius of C. Censorinus, c. 87 B.C.[1] Both sides have been overstruck, but the artisan forgot to look carefully at the coin before putting it back on the pile-anvil,[2] so that the reverse type was struck on the obverse, and vice versa [**Fig. 2**].

FIG. 2.                                      FIG. 3.

The most unusual of the accidents amongst the coins examined was to a denarius of Antony and Caesar[3] where the reverse is regular [**Fig. 3**] but no type is represented on the obverse, which shows a small ridge along the edge. Evidently two blanks were by mistake put between the dies, so that the obverse was coined on the upper side of the first and the reverse on the lower side of the second, leaving respectively the inner sides of both coins empty. The two blanks were placed together on the anvil; they slipped out of true beneath the pressure, so that the two edges overlapped. The head of Caesar on the reverse is very well preserved, so it is clear that the coin did not circulate very much; but, in my view at least, it should not have been put into circulation at all.

This note is simply to point out that there were no strict laws governing ancient methods of coining in Roman times, and that very probably accuracy depended upon the personal attention of the artisan in charge, who, when checking the coins, would take the decision to have some of them overstruck because the types were not clear, but in other cases took no heed of obvious mistakes such as the denarius of Antony and Caesar.

---

[1] *BMCRR* 2394 f.; Syd. *CRR* 714.
[2] Hill, op. cit. 31, fig. 2.
[3] *BMCRR* ii, 397, 55; Syd. *CRR* 1166.

# The Denarii of Gordian III

K. J. J. ELKS

PRACTICALLY the last issue of denarii containing any real proportion of silver was that made by Gordian III in two issues which have been dated to A.D. 241. One of these issues simply uses types already used on antoniniani and other denominations but the other has only aurei with similar types, and as such has been linked with the marriage of Gordian to Sabinia Tranquillina. This view may now be untenable in the light of recent discoveries.

During this period the Rome mint is believed to have worked in six officinae and Mattingly (*RIC* IV, iii) isolates the six types he associates with the marriage as DIANA LVCIFERA, FELICITAS PVBLICA, PIETAS AVGVSTI, SALVS AVGVSTI, SECVRITAS PVBLICA and VENVS VICTRIX. Unfortunately one of these, FELICITAS PVBLICA, probably does not exist, as the one known and often quoted specimen is false. This leaves a gap, since this reverse is also unknown in the aurei, but there is one denarius type which Mattingly ignored. This coin he appended to a previous issue as a rare supernumerary, but it has the same obverse inscription as the others, IMP GORDIANVS PIVS FEL AVG, and a reverse PM TRP III COS PP showing Gordian on horseback.

The original suggestion that it was this denarius and not FELICITAS PVBLICA that made up the six types was made by Dr. Karl Pink[1] but direct evidence was lacking. Denarii of Gordian III are fairly scarce, and, indeed, were considered to be rare until some recent finds were made which included quite large quantities. The largest of these finds, and practically the only one to be published,[2] contained no less than 255 of Gordian's denarii and of the coins noted all the five remaining 'marriage' issue types were represented by roughly equal numbers. Also, whereas the FELICITAS PVBLICA reverse was completely absent, the one with PM TRP III COS PP was found in almost exactly the same proportion as the others. The other group of denarii, also well represented, but with only half the quantities of the 'marriage' issue, fitted neatly into place as well.

The totals in the hoard were as follows:

(a)

| | | | | |
|---|---|---|---|---|
| PM TRP III COS PP | (*RIC* 81) | 28 | SALVS AVGVSTI | (*RIC* 129A) | 36 |
| DIANA LVCIFERA | (*RIC* 127) | 28 | SECVRITAS PVBLICA (*RIC* 130) | 27 |
| PIETAS AVGVSTI | (*RIC* 129) | 25 | VENVS VICTRIX | (*RIC* 131) | 27 |

[1] 'Der Aufbau der römischen Münzprägung in der Kaizerzeit', *NZ* 1935, 13 ff.

[2] *NC* 1966, 165 ff.

(b)

| | | | | |
|---|---|---|---|---|
| AETERNITATI AVG | (*RIC* 111) | 13 | PM TRP III COS II PP (*RIC* 114) | 10 |
| IOVIS STATOR | (*RIC* 112) | 14 | PM TRP III COS II PP (*RIC* 115) | 12 |
| LAETITIA AVG N | (*RIC* 113) | 19 | VIRTVTI AVGVSTI     (*RIC* 116) | 16 |

Although it is always dangerous to draw conclusions from only one hoard, such evidence as we have, then, seems to support Pink's conclusions. This in turn raises another problem, also discussed in his *Aufbau*. If the 'marriage' issue does include this dated coin then it belongs to the period c. August A.D. 240 to the end of that year, and was followed early in A.D. 241 (note the change from COS to COS II) by the other group of denarii. If the normally accepted date for the marriage is correct then it is impossible for these coins to be associated with it in any way. Our scanty historical sources unfortunately do not shed any light on this point, nor does any other. The nearest one can get to dating the marriage is that the Alexandrian coinage for Tranquillina is all after August A.D. 241. Against this, rare denarii for this empress seem to show a tenuous connection, although it may be the later series from which they stem. On the evidence above, however, it is difficult to escape Pink's conclusion that this coinage was associated with some other event.

# A Gold Coin of Constantius Chlorus

R. A. G. CARSON

FIG. 1. (Scale 3 : 1)

A SMALL gold coin of Constantius Chlorus [**Fig. 1**] is apparently unique and sufficiently unusual to merit recording:

*Obv.* CONSTA-NTIVS C. Head, laureate, r.
*Rev.* VOT·X· in laurel wreath
     1·74 gm. ↑↓

The coin is from the collection of classical coins belonging to the Queen's University, Belfast, on indefinite loan to the Ulster Museum. There is no specific information about the earlier history of the coin, but I am indebted to Mr. W. A. Seaby for his notes on the history of the collection which suggest that it was put together by a local collector in the mid- to late-Victorian period.

In fabric, style, and lettering, the coin cannot be faulted, but it does present some unusual features. The weight, 1·74 gm., is exactly a third of an aureus of the tetrarchie coinage, a most unusual fraction for which no parallel at this period has been found, though at least one quarter-aureus of Galerius is known.[1] The extremely short form of obverse title, though rarely used, does appear on bronze fractions of Constantius,[2] and a similarly shortened form

---

[1] *RIC* vi, Trier 99.        [2] Ibid., Ticinum, 28a, Rome 49a.

is known for Galerius, also on bronze fractions.[1] The mint of the coin mus be Rome.

Cohen 327, citing *ancien catalogue* as source, describes a small gold coin identical in every detail except for the wreath on the reverse which is said to be oak.

[1] *RIC* vi, Ticinum, 28b, Rome 49b.

# REVIEWS

*Athenian Coinage 480–449 B.C.* By CHESTER G. STARR. Pp. 97, 26 plates. Oxford, 1970. £3·25.

RECENT research on the earlier centuries of Athenian coinage has concentrated on the archaic issues. In the words of Professor Starr's opening sentence 'Athenian coinage in the fifth century B.C. is commonly treated as a wasteland'. This is the situation that his study aims at changing, in the conviction that the coinage is not only related to the recorded history of Athens, but, properly understood, can contribute to our understanding of that history.

The only aspect of the archaic coinage which is directly relevant to Starr's subject is its terminal date, and here he opts firmly for 480 rather than 490 (recently championed by the late W. P. Wallace, *NC* 1962, 34 f.). He accepts in general Kraay's sequence for the archaic coinage (*NC* 1956, 43 ff.), and lays emphasis on the Acropolis hoard (Noe 96) as consisting for the most part of recent currency which had passed through the Persian conflagration and then been finally buried in the tidying up of that area in 479/478. The later tetradrachm, which has sometimes been associated with the hoard (though rejected by Seltman, *Athens*, 147 n.), and has thereby provided a straw of hope to those who wished to date the modernization of the designs to 490 rather than to 480 (Wallace *NC* 1962, 34 and n. 4), is now shown to be so much later in date as to have no possible connection either with the hoard or with the 'Perserschutt' (p. 4).

The adoption of 480 rather than 490 as the end of the archaic issues involves the abandonment of another cherished interpretation—that decadrachms and didrachms were minted for the payment of the 10-drachma dole of the middle eighties. In the stylistic analysis of the coinage, which occupies Chapters II and III, Starr demonstrates two things. First, the decadrachms were struck only after a substantial period of stylistic development in the new designs—a development, which, even if those designs had been introduced in 490, could not have been compressed into five years. Second, though the decadrachms represent a single compact issue, the didrachms exhibit far more stylistic variation and were struck over a much longer period, so that decadrachms and didrachms together cannot be associated with any episode as brief as the 10-drachma dole.

The early post-archaic issues of Athens have not previously been the subject of detailed analysis, but a number of never very clearly defined conceptions have combined to create the impression that the undoubtedly copious scale of the archaic coinage was resumed, after only minimal interruption, in the years after the Persian withdrawal. For example, in his Group N Seltman assembled 38 somewhat heterogeneous, but already post-archaic, tetradrachms and attributed them to the decade 490–480. From this it followed that he regarded the heavy output of standard fifth century issues as setting in soon after 478 and continuing throughout the century.

The decadrachm, too, seemed to point in the same direction. For those who remained unconvinced by the proposed association with the 10-drachma dole, the commemorative character of this exceptional denomination seemed self-evident.

And what could be more commemorable than the events of 480/479? Whether the precise event commemorated was Salamis, or Plataea, or victory over the Persians, or the rebirth of Athens, the date could hardly be later than 478/477; and since the decadrachm was clearly not the first of the new issues, this view, too, implied an immediate resumption of coinage on a rather extensive scale, as soon as the Athenians were again in possession of their city. The apparently secure date of the exactly contemporary Syracusan Demareteion seemed to bring welcome confirmation, but this date, too, is now under attack.

Starr's material comprises 235 specimens of denominations down to and including the drachma plus a number of rather rare smaller denominations. Though specimens have doubtless escaped his net, they are unlikely to affect seriously the sequence or the relative size of different issues. His first period of coinage comprises 12 obverse dies for tetradrachms and 2 for drachms, and is distinguished by its stylistic similarity to the latest archaic issues; its individuality lies, of course, in the first appearance of olive leaves on Athena's helmet, and of the lunar crescent on the reverse. Whereas numismatists are perhaps inclined to suppose that the production of coinage was accorded the highest priority in nearly all circumstances, Starr argues plausibly that the primary needs were to rebuild and refortify the city, and that stocks of silver can hardly have become adequate for coining before 477 at the earliest. On the other hand, both the Bowdoin vase painter and the Arcadian coinage show that the newly designed head of Athena was known by c. 470. Starr concludes that Group I lasted for several years spanning the middle seventies.

In Group II the volume of coinage is very much larger for not only are there 21 obverse dies for tetradrachms and 17 for drachms, but also 14 for didrachms and, above all, 11 for decadrachms. This Group is subdivided into three successive stylistic phases; the three lower denominations are represented throughout in more or less constant volume, while the decadrachm is confined to the last phase. Since Group IIA retains some features of the archaic coinage, which have disappeared by Group IIB, these two phases cover the late seventies and early sixties respectively, leaving the heavy output of Group IIC (with the decadrachms) to occupy the middle sixties. On this chronology the increased supplies of bullion implied by the coining of decadrachms fall into place as a reflection of the booty won by Cimon on the Eurymedon c. 467.

By the end of Group II the last features of the archaic coinage had been discarded and the designs had reached the general shape which they were to retain for the rest of the century; henceforth development was to be in detail only. In Group III there are two principal changes on the obverse: the floral tip of the ornamental scroll on the helmet, which had hitherto pointed to the top of the neighbouring leaf, now turns back on itself until it lies parallel with the leaf, and the three leaves, which had hitherto been graded in size, tend to become more or less equal; on the reverse the owl becomes larger. In volume Group III is much smaller than the total of Group IIC, but if allowance is made for the discontinuation of the decadrachm, the output of the remaining denominations is little different from that which had prevailed throughout Group II. Group III may be dated to the later sixties.

Group IV represents the first stage in that intensification of production which was to culminate in the huge issues of the second half of the century, which have provided the overwhelming majority of surviving fifth century Athenian tetradrachms; for tetradrachms, didrachms, and drachms there are respectively 24, 5, and 11 obverse dies. The period of issue appears to have been the early fifties.

Group V is the final, and the largest, series to be treated in detail by Starr. With 51 obverse dies for tetradrachms and only 6 for drachms (the didrachm is now discontinued) it includes a large number of variations in design, but nevertheless exhibits features which distinguish this group from both predecessors and successors. For example, the treatment of the hair on Athena's forehead in shallow parallel curves differs from the waves of previous groups and foreshadows the practice of later issues, while the shape of the owl's tail represents the final phase of an earlier tradition. Starr associates this phase of the coinage with a major change in the economic resources of Athens—'these issues may represent the first efforts of Athens to come to terms with the great mass of silver transported in the Delian treasury to the Acropolis in 454' (p. 63). In the decades following 449 the volume of coinage became much larger still in order to pay for the imperial buildings on the Acropolis and elsewhere in Attica and for the expenses of the Peloponnesian war. This coinage of the second half of the century is dealt with briefly in Chapter IV.

Such is Starr's thesis; it can be summarized by saying that he distributes over three decades (478–449) issues which Seltman in his Groups N and O had attributed to one (490–480). There can be little doubt that a period substantially longer than ten years is required for the volume and variety of coinage described; and Starr's view that the coinage in question began with the withdrawal of the Persians in 479 and ended with the decrees of the early forties which inaugurated massive standardized issues seems entirely plausible. Hoard evidence, such as it is (and there is always hope that more may come to light) does appear to support this chronology, particularly in its final phase.

Where some may part company with Starr is over the implications of the numismatic evidence for the history of Athens after the Persian Wars (pp. 81 ff.). We may agree that after 449 Athens produced 'the greatest masses of coinage ever struck by a Greek city state' (p. 86). But was Athens as poor before 449 as Starr suggests? 'Athens was not a wealthy state in the 470s and 460s' (p. 81). The state's 'resources were initially so meagre as to be strained in meeting the expenses of its part in the war against Persia' (p. 83). Cimon's ruthless policy towards the allies 'reflects . . . the exigencies of the domestic financial position' (p. 83). 'The opulence of the Periclean age . . . must not . . . blind us to the strong possibility that conditions were quite different before 449' (p. 85).

The coinage of the years 478–449 was certainly much less than either the archaic coinage or the later fifth-century coinage, but it was not thereby a small or insignificant coinage. In all his five groups Starr records 117 obverse dies for tetradrachms, but since the 51 obverses of Group V may represent the coining of part of the treasure of the Delian League removed to Athens in 454, these are best subtracted, leaving 66 dies for twenty-five years (478–454)—an average of between 2 and 3 dies per annum for tetradrachms. In addition during the same period of twenty-five years 23 obverses were used for didrachms and 34 for drachms, quite apart from the 11 obverses used to convert the Eurymedon booty into decadrachms.

Moreover, as Starr himself points out (pp. 79 f.), our surviving sample of the coinage may be far from representative. Out of 217 recorded die combinations, only 15 survive in more than one specimen, and links between die combinations are far from numerous; only thirty-nine such links are recorded by Starr for the denominations from the decadrachm to the drachma inclusive.

By contemporary standards anywhere in the Greek world this was a very ample coinage. Only at Syracuse is there evidence for a comparable volume, though comparison is complicated by the current uncertainty over Syracusan chronology. But it is not disputed that between c. 465 (or perhaps a decade earlier) and the end of the century Syracuse consumed about 111 dies for tetradrachms (which was the only major denomination minted in quantity); moveover the constant repetition in successive finds of very varied date of dies already known make it likely that this figure is close to the total number of dies actually consumed. At Athens within a period of only twenty-five years the figures are

| Decadrachms | 11 obverse dies |
| Tetradrachms | 66 „ „ |
| Didrachms | 23 „ „ |
| Drachms | 34 „ „ |

If the tetradrachm is taken as the standard and the other figures are adjusted accordingly (28+66+12+9) the total (115) is very close to that of Syracuse, except that the Athenian figures, unlike the Syracusan, appear to be far from complete. In fact the true Athenian total may be not far from the 142 dies for tetradrachms which, according to the revised chronology, Syracuse used in the fifteen or twenty years following the battle of Himera (cf. Kraay, *Greek Coins and History*, Ch. II).

The really perplexing feature is the following: the pre-Persian War coinage of Athens was enormous and is amply represented in hoards in Sicily and Italy and in the East Mediterranean and beyond; the late fifth century coinage was also vast, and has been found in great numbers in hoards mainly from the Near East; yet in between, from 480–450, there was a coinage shown by the die statistics to have been at least as prolific as the largest known contemporary coinage, yet this is comparatively thinly represented in finds from the Near East and elsewhere. How is this to be explained? Here we enter the realms of speculation, but a possible framework for an answer can be suggested.

In the last decades of the sixth century relations between Athens and other parts of the Mediterranean were close, and Athenian silver flowed in the course of trade both eastwards and westwards; in the East Mediterranean the demand for Greek silver may have been stimulated by the creation of a provincial organization in the Persian Empire with an assessment of tribute in silver. This pattern of relationships was disrupted at about the same time in both the West and East Mediterranean, though different factors operated in each area.

In the West the establishment of tyrannies in Sicily, each with its own vigorous coinage, prohibited the circulation of foreign currency; this is not to say that foreign currency was no longer imported, but only that what was imported was quickly melted down for conversion into local coinage, and so no longer appears in western hoards. In the East Mediterranean on the other hand, the break appears to have been caused by the period of active hostility between Persia and Greece which began with the collapse of the Ionian Revolt in 494, and ended with the withdrawal of the Persians from Greece in 479. Allowing about a decade for Athenian recovery, it might have been supposed that the flow would have been resumed about 470, and thereafter have continued with steadily increasing strength. But in fact the Jordan hoard, reinforced by that from Zagazig, shows that this did not happen. Archaic Athenian coins, subdivided into ever smaller fragments continued to circulate, but there was only the smallest supplement from the considerable issues of the period 478–449. In this area there can have been no melting down to serve the needs of local coinage, for no such coinage yet existed. The only conclusion can be that the issues of 478–449, unlike their predecessors and successors, did not reach the Near East in quantity.

Yet a count of the dies shows that these issues were not inconsiderable. Since there is little trace of them outside Attica, it appears possible that they remained for the most part within the home territory. If this were so, the coinage of Athens would have been behaving like the coinages of most less well-endowed cities. It may be that the devastation of the Persian occupation coupled with the loss of revenues from overseas trade so depleted Athenian resources that it took twenty-five years before the accumulated silver became sufficient for local needs and a surplus became available for export. If the issues of the period 478–454 circulated mainly in Attica, it is possible that in the course of time they were largely withdrawn from circulation to be melted down and recoined into the great issues of the second half of the century.

After 450 conditions changed dramatically. Not only had the Delian Treasure (5000 talents?) been transferred to Athens in 454 and was available to be converted into Athenian coin; but the annual tribute of the Delian League was now also paid to Athens direct, in addition to any silver mined locally. Moreover the discontinuation of military and naval expeditions against Persian territory allowed foreign trade to develop, so that Athenian tetradrachms once again flowed abroad in great numbers to be hoarded as bullion, and so to survive to modern times.

This has been a long review of a modestly sized book, but it has perhaps shown the interest of its contents and their importance for the history of the fifth-century Athens.                                          COLIN M. KRAAY

---

*Greek Coins in the Courtauld Collection.* By GRAHAM POLLARD. Pp. 92, 13 plates. University of Rhodesia, 1970. £3·50.

THIS collection of Greek coins (along with the Roman) was presented to the University College of Rhodesia by Sir Stephen Courtauld. A condition of the gift was that the collection should be published and used as a basis for teaching. The last part of the condition probably accounts for the format of the catalogue. The issues of each state represented are introduced by a general description on the lines of those in Kraay's *Greek Coins* and a bibliography: the coins themselves are closely described and the plates are bound at the back. There are five indices—mints, rulers, types, symbols, and legends; two appendices, one on monograms, the other on the provenances of the Roman coins in the collection (already published by Professor Carney), and a page of maps. Assuredly Sir Stephen would have been well satisfied with this catalogue, and students of the University College are to be considered fortunate in the gift.

There are 116 fine coins with a good spread over the whole field of Greek coinage and particular richness in the period c. 480–c. 400. Among engravers there are represented Euainetos (2), Kimon (2), and Herakleidas: the early Naxos tetradrachm appears, a Syracusan tetradrachm from the Demareteion section, an Amphiktionic stater, and a good selection of Hellenistic portraits. The plates do the coins justice, although there are several illustrations distinctly light in tone.

There are a few minor points. The date of no. 14—is it as early as c. 420–c. 390? No. 16, the Terina stater, lacks a specific reference to Regling's dies: it is 78–83 with reverse ΠΠΠ, but students would have difficulty in finding the signatures of Euainetos on these Terina issues as Mr. Pollard promises, presumably depending on Evans. Is Arethusa's wreath in no. 33 of laurel rather than of olive? On the same point there is confusion on pp. 51 ff: on p. 51 Athena's helmet has leaves of laurel, but on p. 53 they have become leaves of olive. In no. 54 an epsilon appears by mistake in the legend of Demetrios, also in index 5, while in index 2 the letter I is omitted. In no. 76, as this is a teaching catalogue, it might have been pointed out that this stater has a T turtle obverse coupled with the earlier non skew reverse, so that Kraay 336 is hardly a parallel. R. T. WILLIAMS

*The Norman Davis Collection.* By HYLA A. TROXELL. Greek Coins in North American Collections, 1; The American Numismatic Society, New York, 1969. $4.00.

MANY of the coins of the Norman Davis Collection were published by Mr. Davis in his *Greek Coins and Cities* (1967). The present volume contains an illustrated and well-documented record of the whole collection: a total of 345 coins arranged on 28 plates. It is doubly welcome, both in itself, and as the first of a projected series of publications of numismatic material in otherwise unknown or relatively inaccessible collections.

The coins are for the most part of silver, with several gold, and a few bronze, pieces. Regal issues form the core of the collection: the kings of Macedon, the Seleucids, and the Indo-Greek rulers, are all particularly well represented by some fine specimens. But the range of issues is wide both in time and place, and very few areas of the Greek world are not represented by at least one coin. Several individual pieces have helped to clarify points of detail in a series. For example, on no. 202 (Ilium), a previously indistinct magistrate's name is clearly read as AKKOY, and the *rev.* of no. 236 (Phaselis) provides similar clarification of a name. Among the western coinages, no. 34, a tetradrachm of Gela, is overstruck on Catana, and there are six splendid incuse staters from South Italian mints: two from Sybaris (nos. 14 and 15), and one each from Metapontum (no. 11), Poseidonia (no. 13), Caulonia (no. 22), and Croton (no. 23). Among the Campanian issues, I would support the attribution of no. 5 to Neapolis rather than to Nola (and similarly, London, Lloyd Coll. 83, 7·26 gm.): the only other *rev.* found coupled with this *obv.* bears the ethnic of Neapolis (Berlin, Löbbecke Coll., 7·18 gm.). It is true that die-transferences between cities are relatively common among Campanian coins, but there is no evidence that this *obv.* was one of them. N. K. RUTTER

*An Introduction to the Coinage of Parthia.* By DAVID SELLWOOD. Pp. 315, 8
plates. Spink & Son Ltd., London, 1971. £3·00.

No comprehensive revision of the Parthian coinage has been attempted since the
turn of the century, if we omit de Morgan's works, which have never been very
accessible or popular. The fact that both Wroth and von Petrowicz, and even
Gardner's treatise of nearly a century ago, though they disagree radically in their
attributions of the coins, have recently been reprinted is clear evidence for the need
of a standard work. Its absence no doubt reflects the reluctance of numismatists in
this field to tackle the classification of a coinage which is largely unnamed, is concerned with a kingdom for which no adequate list of kings exists, and would now
seem to have been without unified rule during several periods in its history. Nevertheless the coins are intrinsically attractive, and recent times have seen a marked
resurgence of interest in them so that a great deal of new information has come to
light. David Sellwood's studies in particular have argued for considerable revision
in several important areas of the classification, and his new book encompasses for
the first time data on many new coins. It is thus an opportune and important work.
It is also an attractive one both in its price and in the distinctive format, which results
from the use of clear italic script and of facsimile drawings of all the major silver
types. These do in fact, capture the feeling of the designs better than any other form
of reproduction. Many of the coins, too, are shown in the plates, where a pleasant
degree of uniformity has been achieved by photographic reproduction from plaster
casts, though it must be said that more judicious lighting would have softened the
harsh contrasts and considerably improved their clarity.

The book is an introduction to the coinage of a period in Persian history spread
over six centuries. As such, it is basically a description and a classification of the
coin types, and the discussion of their relations, origins, and so on has a limited
treatment. One would like to hear more about the latter since the recent advances
in our general knowledge of these aspects of Parthian numismatics have been very
considerable, but within the scope which he has allotted himself the author's choice
can scarcely be faulted. A succinct treatment of weights, flans, monograms, and the
like in the introductory chapter is accompanied by a brief historical sketch of each
ruler in its proper place, and this will largely satisfy the general reader. There is
a full, up-to-date bibliography, comprehensive as regards modern works except for
some minor hoard descriptions, though perhaps Bellinger's Final Report on the
coins from Dura Europas could well have found a place. The specialist would very
much like to see the sources stated for the many new coins described, especially
among the coppers. It is a pity, too, that the autonomous coins, which for Seleucia
and Susa are an intrinsic part of the series just as are the royal issues, are not included. Again, the author has limited his range mainly to types which he has
personally examined, and the propriety of this procedure is evident in the minor,
but important, corrections which appear for the first time in descriptions of several
of the obscure copper types, but it is a fact that there still exist many Parthian coins
scattered in collections which are as yet unrecorded. This is one of the attractions
of the series, and there is as yet a long way to go before a definitive study of it is
possible.

In this respect, the author's allocation of a specific number to each main coin
type, rather than its firm attribution to a particular ruler, is a realistic one, though

not, perhaps, wholly satisfying to the ordinary collector. It will need amendment if important new types should appear, as they have done in recent times, but no better solution has so far been devised. He has been venturesome indeed in the more speculative matter of re-attributing many of the coins to different rulers. For the difficult period which followed the disappearance of Mithradates II there is—in spite of the evident importance of the Avroman documents—little agreement among the various writers: the critical information is exceedingly slender. Sellwood's re-arrangement here is perhaps the simplest, and it is also the one which involves least change in the position adopted by the old authorities. The wholesale revision of the later Parthian issues after Vonones II's time is more fully backed by his own critical study of the die engravers during this obscure period, and further research along these lines may be the most ready way of advancing Parthian numismatics. However, while it has been shown very clearly that apparently trivial details in portraiture on the later drachm issues are the sole characteristic of particular rulers, one wonders if such features as simply reversed monograms have real significance, and there are a few cases such as the anchor adjuncts on Orodes II's coins where variable details of perhaps greater importance are omitted.

At the moment, the choice in most of these matters is a very open one, and in the field which the book encompasses there is little which can be criticized. One would be glad, indeed, if it had been possible to extend it to treat some of the broader aspects of the Parthian coinage and in particular, the major advances in numismatics —le Rider's demonstration of the organization of the Susa issues and that of MacDowell for Seleucia on the Tigris come immediately to mind. Many points could stimulate comment and discussion. One is the rather tentative reading of the reverse monograms on the drachm and copper issues from the time of Phraates III onwards as mint marks. Newall suggested this more than thirty years ago particularly for the Ecbatana monogram. One would have felt that with our improved know-ledge of the coinage it would now be accepted that the marked uniformity in style, as well as the singular deterioration both in portraiture and in metal which is associated with each monogram throughout its range, could only represent a series of separate mints in Iran.

Another point of importance which has received little consideration since both Wroth and von Petrowicz attributed it to a Seleucid prototype is the origin of the most familiar feature of the Parthian coinage—the characteristic drachm reverse. Sellwood takes the same line, although his own identification of the early Beardless Head types as products of the first Arsacid rulers makes it quite clear that the archer-on-throne type preceded that with the omphalos by seventy years or so. It owes nothing to the common Hellenistic type of Apollo on omphalos, but one is reminded forcefully by it of the Tarsiote state of Datames with the seated satrap reverse. Though it seems extraordinary that such influence should span a gap of more than a century, peculiar features such as the attitude of the seated figure, of his draped cloak, and the perspective of the legs and stool seem to be unmistakably present in both. It will be remembered that the independent mints of Gaizura and Hieropolis continued to reproduce the old coin designs long after Alexander's conquests. In the former, too, copper coins of the early Cappadocian kings have portraits dis-tinctly in the Persian style just as do the first Arsacid issues. There is, in fact, no reason to believe that the coins of the Parthian rulers, who so often bear names with good Achaemenid pedigrees, were other than Persian in their inspiration. The omphalos type appears on the coinage only a century later when, as le Rider has shown, there was a direct passage in Ecbatana from the issues of Alexander Bala to those of the first Mithradates.

David Sellwood's book will certainly encourage interest in this sphere of numismatics. To the specialist it is an authoritative work, to the novice a handsome introduction. It will have served a major purpose if it should stimulate more intensive study in the homeland of the coinage itself where the direct answer to many of these questions may well be found. Some more information on the association of the copper coins—which did not generally travel far—with particular centres would be an invaluable aid to identification of the principal mints. Again, a full listing of the contents of hoards secreted during the troubled times might be expected to establish the succession during such periods as the early first century B.C. After all, much of the history of pre-Sassanian Iran must rely very considerably for its further advancement on the study of its coinages.                                    JAMES C. BRINDLEY

*Les Monnaies gauloises des Parisii* (part of *Histoire générale de Paris, Collection de documents publiée sous les auspices de l'édilité parisienne*). By J.-B. COLBERT DE BEAULIEU. xxxiii+171, 1 plate in colour. Paris, Imprimerie nationale, 1970. Price not stated.

DR. COLBERT DE BEAULIEU is the leading authority in France on Gaulish coins, but his work is not as well known to the general reader as it deserves to be because so much of it is scattered in articles in smaller learned journals of France and other countries. To assemble what he has written involves a major bibliographical exercise. It is, therefore, particularly welcome that he had distilled a large part of his hitherto recorded wisdom and experience, together also with much that is new, into this his first major book on the subject.

*Les Monnaies gauloises des Parisii* describes the long and aesthetically pleasing series of gold coins which has for many years been attributed, with good reason, to the tribe of the Parisii, whose oppidum was at Lutetia or Paris. He has arranged the staters and quarter-staters into seven classes (one known only from a single specimen, now lost) and within each he has assembled what is intended as a Corpus of coins and findspots. He has established the dies and die-links in each class. More importantly, he has taken advantage of the measurement of sample specific gravities (much of it, so it appears, undertaken for the late and much missed Mademoiselle Gabrielle Fabre of the Bibliothèque nationale, to whom full credit is given). From these emerges a rational and wholly convincing demonstration of the sequence already arrived at by arguments based on typology. This is a valuable feature of the book, which deserves commendation and the flattery of imitation. Although another author might have been content to compress the same information into a shorter compass, the exposition in the first half of the book seems to me a wholly satisfying description and presentation of this most important series of coins.

No 'corpus' is ever quite complete, and I have come across several coins or other particulars not mentioned. It is a pity, for instance, that Dr. Colbert de Beaulieu has missed the delightful detail that the coin he reproduces in fig. 21. 15, which is in the British Museum (why not a direct photograph, incidentally?) was found at

Durham and that Durham is located in the canton of the British Parisii. But, in addition, he has omitted one excellent stater of Class IV in the British Museum, one quarter-stater of Class II in the Hunter Collection and another of Class V in the British Museum (f.s. environs de Neufchateau). (A stater of Class VI in the Pitt Rivers Museum, Farnham, would have been more difficult to find.)

The second half of the book, which deals with the relationships of the coinage of the Parisii to contemporary and other coinages, does not seem to me, as an exercise in presentation, to succeed equally well. This is largely because the average reader will not be sufficiently familiar with the context to evaluate the relevance of each separate argument. A book, as opposed to a learned article, should not be addressed too exclusively to a public of specialists. Let me hasten to say, none the less, that, though I would have favoured a less Euclidian presentation, there is very little in the conclusions with which, as a specialist, I would wish to quarrel.

With the dates for the series to which Dr. Colbert de Beaulieu arrives I am in full agreement. He argues that the coinage of the Parisii began soon after (*patrum memoria* according to Caesar) the tribe had split from the Senones, and he places this event in the bracket 103–93 B.C. He also reaches the conclusion that the coinage of the Parisii is in some degree derived from, and hence posterior to, the coinage known in Britain as Gallo-Belgic A, and in France traditionally and quite wrongly as of the Bellovaci. It is not necessary to follow him equally in his more controversial judgements (pp. 103–5) on the chronology of the earlier stages of Gaulish coinage, amongst the Arverni and Ambiani, but this is fortunately incidental and secondary to the argument regarding the Parisii.

Having argued that the coins of the Parisii date from the period after the tribe had separated from the Senones (whose frontiers he does not describe), Dr. Colbert de Beaulieu is left with the difficulty that he cannot with certainty identify any gold coins of the Senones, if such existed, as seems probable. He makes some suggestions on p. 118, n. 339, which perhaps lack conviction, but he also attempts in one Appendix (pp. 135 f.) to find more of them in the gold 'bullets' marked with a cross, which have been found so widely scattered in France that they cannot, it seems to me, be attributed yet to any particular tribe or area. The largest finds come from too far east for an attribution to the Senones to be *prima facie* easy. (Incidentally he has missed B. Roth's important article in *BNJ* iv (1907), 221–8 as a source. He records on p. 139 the findspot of this hoard as Boncourt, while on p. 137 he describes it as from 'entre Reims et Châlons-sur-Marne, sans autre précision'; which is right?) This coinage is of interest in Britain since, in addition to the Kinkurd hoard, which he mentions, a coin of the type has now been found stratified in excavations at Pilsdon Pen, Dorset, a findspot which would have helped to add conviction to the western drift of his map.

A few other interesting Gaulish coinages are dealt with *en passant*, one a common gold series almost entirely of quarter-staters, long attributed to the Parisii. (I do not think he aims here at a Corpus, but he does not mention four in the British Museum, including one found in the Seine at Paris.) Dr. Colbert de Beaulieu concludes, rightly, that this is not part of the main sequence, but it still seems to me that the coinage must be classed with those of the Parisii; its recorded distribution suggests no other home and the typological link is demonstrable. He seems to have omitted another type, which is also linked with the Parisii, of which B. Roth had a specimen, see *BNJ* ix, (1912), pl. v. 135; another with head facing left is recorded in a Sale Catalogue (Münzen und medaillen, Basel, xi 23 January 1953, lot 6).

I have more sympathy with his verdict of non-proven in the case of several silver and bronze coins which have been assigned, on insufficient evidence, to the Parisii. I shall be surprised if, in the long run, the potin coin reproduced from a particularly beautiful example in fig. 59 does not prove to be Parisian. I will not pursue here my reasons for doubting Dr. Colbert de Beaulieu's conviction that all or most potin coins were made after the Conquest, when, as he rightly concludes, the gold coinage in these parts had ceased. That they circulated afterwards there is no doubt, but that is another matter. I would definitely refuse to accept as Parisian the bronze coins of Eccaios, which have a fairly well defined distribution to the north east of the city.

Minor points of comment such as these do not detract from the lasting value of this comprehensive demonstration of the artistic and monetary unity of the gold coinage of so famous a tribe and city. We shall all look forward to the major work on Gaulish coins as a whole and on the methods to be applied to them, which we know Dr. Colbert de Beaulieu has on the stocks.                    D. F. ALLEN

*Las monedas hispánicas del Museo Arqueológico Nacional de Madrid, Vol. ii.* By J. MA. DE NAVASCUÉS. Pp. 59, 37+62 plates. Barcelona, 1971.

IT is a pleasure to welcome this second volume of Professor Navascués' publication of the Iberian coins in the Madrid collection, the first volume of which was noticed in *NC* 1970 pp. 328–31. The same high standards are well maintained in the new volume which, like its predecessor will certainly be a most valuable addition to our literature on the ancient coinage of the Iberian peninsula.

The new volume contains two distinct sections. The first covers the 'Ciclo Andaluz', the southern coinages with Iberian inscriptions. Each of the mints included in this volume is given in its entirety, that is including the issues of Latin coins. The mints are: Castulo; Iliberris (modern Granada); Ilteraca (? = Iliturgi); Obulco; Abra; another uncertain mint closely connected with Obulco and Abra; Cetouian (? = Cetobriga); and Tamusiens. This section of the work comprising some 1019 specimens is illustrated on the first thirty-seven plates.

The wealth of numismatic material here displayed is impressive, and it is certain that this rich material, so meticulously illustrated and recorded, will give a powerful stimulus towards detailed study of the individual coin-series. In the Castulo series, for instance, it is interesting to observe that the heaviest specimens are by no means placed at the beginning, the first stages of the coinage being represented by lighter pieces of varying and unusual styles and other variations such as the leftward reading of the legend. There can be little doubt that Navascués' sequence is the right one, and this is, from the metrological angle, interesting. Then there are numerous overstrikes of Castulo on Obulco which will surely help to define the relationship between these two important southern series. As for Obulco, it seems not unlikely that die-links between the various groups might eventually be discovered which would enable us to reconstruct the exact sequence of the series and so to throw additional light on the precise relationship of the various Latin coinages with those of the Iberian type.

As students of the Iberian coinages are aware, the coins of Obulco are specially rich in epigraphic material, presenting a considerable series of personal names in a southern form of the Iberian script. The transliterations followed in the present work are those of Gomez-Moreno (1962) in *La Escritura Bastulo–Turdetana* (to which a few modifications have been suggested by U/Schmoll in *Zeitschrift für vergleichende Sprachwissenschaft* 80, Göttingen 1966). The same authority is cited for the reading of the Iberian legend of Iliberris—Ilberir, of which legend the third letter is perhaps still something of a crux for Iberian specialists as it closely resembles a letter elsewhere = *du* rather than *Be*, but which has an undeniable attraction as giving a closer equivalence to the Latin name of Iliberris. To Gomez-Moreno is also due the reading *Cetouion* on the coins attributed by e.g. Vives to Salacia, but which Gomez-Moreno suggests may be the Iberian equivalent of Cetobriga (modern Setúbal, Portugal). This is not the place to take up the discussion of such difficult questions, which must remain for the linguistic experts. Suffice it to say that, as in Navascués' first volume, the actual forms and appearance of the legends is given in meticuluous facsimiles drawn by the author's own hand, giving, as nothing else can, the actual appearance of the legends on the coins: moreover the preparation of such drawings, as the reviewer also knows personally from other fields, is an exciting and rewarding experience which, as Professor Navascués truly wrote in vol. i, p. 15, enables one to penetrate directly into the manner of execution of the original lettering.

The second section of the present volume covers several hoards which are preserved either fully or partially in the Madrid collection. Unquestionably the most important of these are the hoards discovered in 1920 at the site of Azaila, near to or identical with the ancient Celsa, on the river Ebro. The Azaila hoards are fully illustrated on some 58 plates, forming a large part of this volume, and a very welcome material for all future studies of the Iberian coinages, enabling us to gauge in detail not only the stylistic variants represented in the hoards but the relative degrees of preservation—both factors of great importance for assessing the significance of the coins. In fact there are two hoards from Azaila, as originally noted by Cabré in his preliminary publication in 1921; the difference in character between the two lots has been discussed again by Romagosa in the new *Acta Numismatica* I (Barcelona 1971). It is to some extent unfortunate that in the intervening period the specimens from the two hoards have become confused, so that it is not possible for Professor Navascués to designate all of them with certainty to their respective hoard, and many have had to be given here the blanket heading of 'Lotes I y II'. This is, however, less of a disadvantage than might otherwise be the case, since, in spite of the fact that the two hoards come from different find-spots within Azaila, it seems clear that both must have been buried at about the same period. The chronology of the hoards is not discussed by Navascués, but there seems good reason to follow Cabré, the excavator, in believing that both deposits were made at the time of the Sertorian war (and not, as Pio Beltran argued in 1945, at a later time).

With the splendid material now provided by Navascués, it seems legitimate, by way of comment, to point out a strong confirmatory argument for this dating, which has not hitherto, so far as I am aware, been noticed. This concerns the coins of Celsa itself, the Iberian town which may be identical with the site of Azaila; the equation would certainly gain support from the fact that the best represented of all the Iberian coins in the finds are precisely those of Celsa. There were 223 of them in hoard II, amounting to nearly half the total; thus all but one specimen of the

Celsa coins here catalogued certainly belong to hoard II (whose more homogeneous and 'local' character has been commented on by Romagosa). These specimens clearly give us a pretty full representation of the Celsa coinage down to the date of the deposition; some of them are markedly fresher and should on that account be the latest issues. But the most important fact is that, as we can see from Navascués, vol. i, there exist a number of further issues of Celsa, of quite distinct styles, which do not occur at all in Azaila finds, and must therefore be subsequent to the date of the burial (e.g. Navascués, vol. i, nos. 1585–634), and to these we may add the bilinguals (ibid. nos. 1642–56), also not represented at Azaila. Now all these latter issues, for which some time must be allowed, have to be accounted for before the foundation of the Roman colony at Celsa by Lepidus in the 40s. B.C. It thus becomes clear that the deposit of Azaila hoard II must be appreciably earlier than Pio Beltran's suggested date c. 49 B.C., and if so it is difficult to find another earlier date except during the Sertorian war. Thus the date of the Azaila finds to that period is confirmed, and as a result we have in the Azaila finds a reliable criterion for the dating of many other Iberian coin-series. All this can be deduced from the material so splendidly expounded by Professor Navascués.

After this somewhat lengthy excursus on Azaila, we must come back to the other hoards also given in Navascués' catalogue, those of Salvacañete and Cerro de la Miranda, in both cases hoards of denarii. The sixty-eight specimens from Salvacañete (Ocsa, Icaloscen, Roman) are preserved in the Madrid Museum, and those which are not are duly indicated in the commentary, among them the unique Secaisa denarius given by Gomez-Moreno, *Miscelaneas*, pl. 46.13; the Roman denarii in this hoard indicate a date c. 95 B.C. and this gives in turn a useful landmark for the dating of other Iberian issues such as the late class of Osca denarii, e.g. Salvacañete 50, a class also present not only in the great Palenzuela hoard but also at Azaila nos. 138–40—perhaps a further confirmation for the dating of those hoards! Finally there is the Cerro de la Miranda hoard, of which the Museo Arqueologico has some 12 specimens, evidently part of the same hoard from which a further 34 specimens (in private possession) are illustrated under the heading of 'Palencia III' in the important recent work by K. Raddatz (*Die Schatzfunde der Iberischen Halbinsel*). This hoard, consisting predominantly of denarii of Segorbriga and Turisso, has a composition typical of a number of other Iberian denarius hoards of the earlier first century B.C.

To conclude, we must say the two volumes on the Madrid collection form an outstanding contribution to our knowledge and understanding of ancient Iberian coinage. As in so many branches of human knowledge, facts are worth more than theories and it is the factual nature of this publication that will act as a lasting stimulus. All students of the subject will be profoundly grateful to Professor Navascués and his collaborators for their patient and careful achievement.

G. K. JENKINS

*A Collection of Sculpture in Classical and Early-Christian Antioch.* By DERICKSEN M. BRINCKERHOFF. Pp. 83, 78 figs. New York University Press, 1971. $15.00.

THE subject of this learned and perceptive monograph is a cache of sculptures, mostly of Proconnesian marble, which was buried, almost at ground-level, below the floor of a room in a late-fourth or early-fifth-century villa just outside the city wall of Antioch. Discovered in 1934, it has only now received the detailed study and discussion that it undoubtedly deserves as a fascinating social and cultural document of the period of transition from the pagan to the Christian Roman world.

The collection contains three imperial portraits (chapter 2) and thirteen fragments of mythological statuary (chapter 3). The marble bust of Pertinax, once governor of Syria, with its spiky beard descending to the chest, resembles that emperor's coin-portraits more closely than does any other of the sculptural busts that have been identified as him. Less certain, but receiving considerable support from the coin-likenesses, is the identification of a second marble head as Gordian III, whose successes against the Persians would readily explain his commemoration at Antioch. Again, it is on coin- and medallion-portraits that is mainly based the equation with Constantius Chlorus of the third imperial piece—a startling porphyry head worked in the characteristically cubistic and 'ugly' style of the First Tetrarchy. What particular connection that emperor had with Antioch remains obscure. In a later chapter (4) these three portraits provide the text for some important observations on the method of dissemination of imperial likenesses throughout the Empire.

The interest of the mythological sculptures lies less in their aesthetic value than in the light that they throw on the antiquarian tastes of the times and on the ways in which third and early-fourth century sculptors adapted and interpreted, in their own techniques, classical Greek and Hellenistic originals. Here, as with the portraits, abundant use is made of other relevant, including numismatic, material: comparisons are drawn between the Antiochene pieces and sculptures from other East-Mediterranean sites, notably in Cyrenaica, Egypt, and Asia Minor; and local sculptural features are defined. An as yet little-studied, late-antique, and largely unified artistic world in the East is brought into sharper focus.

The sculptures were apparently displayed in the villa from some time in the fourth century until the Persian sack of Antioch in 540 or, more probably, until the Arab conquest of 637. For the whole of that period the Empire was, of course, officially Christian. Yet the emperors whose portraits were cherished were all pagans and all the other pieces are of mythological content. This might possibly imply that the owners of the villa had remained obstinately pagan throughout. It is, however, much more likely that, whereas the earlier occupants, who could have amassed the whole collection, may well have been pagans, their successors had embraced Christianity and found it perfectly compatible with their new faith to preserve and venerate these visual records of their classical inheritance. The author cites some apposite examples of similar collections of works of pagan art that existed in unequivocally Christian contexts; and he illustrates some telling instances of individual monuments in various media, dating from the fourth, fifth, and sixth centuries, which are either wholly pagan in content or, when Christian, obviously much indebted inconographically to pagan prototypes. The evidence adduced is drawn not only from the eastern provinces but also from western lands; and the cache from Antioch serves to strengthen one's belief that no real problem is created by, for example, the juxtaposition of pagan and Christian paintings in the new Via Latina catacomb in Rome or by the frankly pagan mythological motifs that accompany the dominant Chi-Rho monogram and dominant monogram with the bust of Christ on the Frampton and Hinton St. Mary mosaic pavements in this country. Such pagan elements would have been either interpreted allegorically or valued for their cultural associations.

A few very minor criticisms may be made. (1) Figs. 34, 35: read 'Dionysus' for 'Apollo' in the caption; (2) p. 38 and fig. 56: the Ulpia Epigone monument in Rome is not a sarcophagus but a mural relief presenting the deceased on her funerary couch and her semi-nudity is a sign of her apotheosis (cf. pls. 79 and 84 in my *Death and Burial in the Roman World*, 1971), not of her being thought of as a sleeping Maenad—no one could look less Maenad-like than she!; (3) p. 54: the great collection of portrait-busts and heads, etc. found at Chiragan (Martres Tolosanes) near Toulouse is much more likely to have come from one of the sumptuous villas in the area (*Rev. Arch.* 1891, ii, p. 73) than from a basilica: it is hard to imagine a place of public business being cluttered up with so large a sculpture gallery.                                                     J. M. C. TOYNBEE

*Roman Coins.* By RICHARD REECE. Pp. 189, 64 plates. Ernest Benn. £3·00

So vast, varied, and complex is the Roman coinage that a record with any pretence to completeness of detail inevitably involves a series of publications running to many volumes. There is—there always has been—an obvious need for something less than such a full-scale treatment. Quite apart from the now innumerable outlines of the series in general handbooks, there have been serious attempts to present a compact but comprehensive account of the Roman coinage. One category, despairing of reducing the multiplicity of detail to manageable form, has been content to establish the framework of the coinage—its systems of denominations, weights, mints, titulatures, types, and so on, for example, Bernhart's *Handbuch zur Münzkunde der römischen Kaiserzeit* or Picozzi's *La monetazione imperiale romana*. Another kind is exemplified by Mattingly's *Roman Coins* which discussed under various topic headings the successive periods of coinage with fuller detail of description, background and interpretation. The present work is a more pragmatic and straightforward description of the coinage in chronological sequence.

The book is one in a series of *Practical Handbooks for Collectors* and indeed the novel element here is a chapter on 'Practical Identification'. This is an attempt to analyse and set down in words the processes of observation, recognition, and elimination by which a precise indentification is arrived at. Mr. Reece is here writing from a vast experience gained from his surveys of coin material in a long list of European collections and from the great quantity of archaeological coinage which he has handled. The processes which he details will be recognized by the experienced as the almost automatic reflexes of their thinking when identifying a coin. The acid test will be the degree of success of a real tyro using Mr. Reece's method.

By and large the book presents a fairly faithful account of the development of Roman coinage and manages to bring in a great deal of description of issues and individual types. It is not clear, however, how practical an instrument of identification it will prove to be for the inexperienced. There is information here in plenty, and the expert can turn it up quite readily, but for others a fuller apparatus of indexes is necessary to guide them to the answer. Because so much information has been packed in, the book proves a little indigestible. It is, however, fair to say, I imagine, that the book was primarily designed to be consulted rather than to be read right through. The account would have benefited by giving greater prominence to some of the more unusual types connected with events and policies. Admittedly such types are not usually the staple issues of the coinage but are often the more interesting and informative.

While in an account of a massive coinage covering some eight centuries some omissions are inevitable, a number of quite important aspects have escaped mention: the very earliest Roman coinage—the *aes signatum*, Nero's experimental series of orichalcum all with marks of value, the appearance of the first officina marks on antoniniani of Philip I, and the chronological significance of the different forms of obverse inscription for Carausius. On some specific points, Mr. Reece's views may be questioned. He still accepts a posthumous coinage of Galba, though Kraay's die-study is against this. Perhaps by unfortunate conflation he appears to date Caracalla's introduction of the antoninanus to A.D. 211 not A.D. 215. The antoniniani of the mid-third century are described as copper coins with silver coating, but recent work has demonstrated that they are in a base alloy to which minting technique has imparted a silver-enriched surface. The amount of illustration is generous but the woeful quality of reproduction makes much of it quite useless. That this book is less than a total success is mainly due to the intractable nature of the material. Despite the criticisms of points of detail this remains a very useable and straightforward modern account of the Roman coinage. R. A. G. CARSON

*Roman Imperial Coins in the Hunter Coin Cabinet, University of Glasgow. II. Trajan to Commodus.* By ANNE S. ROBERTSON. Pp. clxviii+534, 124 plates. Published for the University of Glasgow by Oxford University Press. £12·60.

THE second volume of this catalogue is impressive in its sheer size. Impressive, too, is the richness of the Hunter Cabinet here revealed with a collection of just under three thousand coins for about a century of the Roman Empire. Anyone who has ever catalogued even a few coins in full detail and can assess the amount of time and labour involved in the production of this volume will envy and admire Dr. Robertson's steadfast industry. Admiration does not stop here, but is heightened by a closer survey which shows with what command of the material and with what meticulous attention to detail the catalogue has been constructed.

The richness of the collection is not only one of quantity. The catalogue is studded with pieces of great rarity, notably in the gold series. There are no less than four 'restored' aurei of Trajan as well as an aureus of Trajan with Nerva and Trajan Senior, Trajan with Plotina, Diva Marciana, Matidia, and Matidia with Plotina. There is a fine series of Trajan's buildings on aurei and of Hadrian's 'province' and 'restitutor' coins also in gold. Much of the bronze coinage is, to judge from the plates, in very fine condition. There is again a particularly good series of sestertii in Hadrian's later issues, a charming Commodus sestertius with the Four Seasons reverse and a very fine Commodus/Hercules obverse, to name only some of the more outstanding pieces. In addition to the catalogue proper Dr. Robertson provides us with a conspectus of types whether represented in the Hunter Collection or not. The integration of all metals here goes some way towards meeting a criticism of the continuation of a 'dyarchy' in separating precious metals from bronze in the catalogue. The full apparatus of indexes which we have come to expect makes for ease in using the volume, and the very generous amount of illustration in collotype maintains a high quality of reproduction.

With all its many qualities, in some respects this volume disappoints expectation. We miss here the introductions to reigns with their detailed discussion which was such a valuable feature of Dr. Robertson's first volume, for they provided a most useful series of *état des études*. It is true that the second century coinage has not attracted the same amount of study since the last full treatment of the period in the British Museum Catalogues as was the case with the first-century coinage; but as Strack's work was appearing almost at the same time as the British Museum Catalogues Mattingly was not able to take full account of it, and we should have valued a fuller statement of Dr. Robertson's own views than she gives us in her brief summary.

This volume follows the pattern of presentation set by the first volume. There, it may be argued, there was a case for the separation of the precious metal coinage from the bronze, for there might have been at that time two distinct mint organizations at Rome. From Trajan onwards there is a case for regarding coinages in all metals as the product of a single mint at Rome, and consequently for the presentation in the catalogue of the coinage similarly integrated. Such a presentation requires the sequence of issues to be established first of all, and despite the difficulties arising from the lack of complete parallelism between types in precious metals and in bronze, the excellent conspectus of types which Dr. Robertson has constructed and her comments on officina organization and pattern suggest that such sequences of issues could be established. At any rate it might be possible to break down into more closely dated groups some of the long series in the coinages of Trajan, Hadrian, and the early years of Antoninus Pius. It is appreciated, of course, that, rich though the Hunter Collection is, not every type in every denomination in such series of issues would be represented, and that the resultant *lacunae* would vitiate the full pattern which is being arrived at.

In her introduction Dr. Robertson foresees that two further volumes will be required to complete the catalogue and registers the hope that they will appear in a few years time. We congratulate her on this splendid second volume and wish her all success with the further instalments.                    R. A. G. CARSON

*Le Trésor de Saint-Mard I; Étude sur le monnayage de Victorin et des Tétricus.* By J. LALLEMAND and M. THIRION. Éditions Cultura, Wetteren, Belgium, 1970. Pp. 264, 55 plates.

THIS, the latest in the fine series of studies of the Roman coinage which includes, among others, the work on the bronze coinage of Postumus by Pierre Bastien (reviewed in *NC* 1969) uses the information gleaned from the publication of a third-century hoard of antoniniani as the basis for the first study in depth of the coins of the Gallic emperors Victorinus and Tetricus since Elmer (*Die Münzprägung der gallischen Kaiser*, 1941). The result is a book which, despite one serious fault, deserves to take its place as an essential handbook on the period concerned, especially for all work on similar hoards.

The hoard itself was found in Luxembourg some time in the nineteenth century and was preserved, apparently intact, in the collection of a Dr. Jeanty, from whose family it passed to the museum at Virton in 1952. It consisted of 5,684 coins, including 1,782 barbarous imitations. Some 2,546 coins were of the Gallic emperors; and all but eight of these were either Victorinus or the Tetrici. The hoard, typical of the period, is almost totally lacking in silver coins and covers the reigns from Valerian I to Probus, though coins prior to A.D. 265 are hardly represented and the knowledge that the hoard extends to the reign of Probus comes from one barbarous coin with the letters PRO . . . visible.

After a discussion of the probable site of discovery come brief details of the composition, then an assessment of the sequence of issues for the two Gallic mints, comparing details from a number of hoards, weights and chemical analyses, a rather inconclusive article on the Consecration coinage of Claudius II and finally a study on the barbarous content of the hoard. The book is rounded off with an individual listing of each coin showing details of legend visible and the weight of each, and 53 plates of the coins including photographs of obverse and reverse of all but seven of the 1,782 barbarous coins. Two additional plates in the text show die-links in these imitations, one showing links to coins in other hoards. As someone who has undertaken similar work I could not help but be impressed by such dedicated attention to detail and the clear resolve to extract every vital piece of information from the material on hand.

My first quibble, and I think a major one, is the bland acceptance by the authors of Elmer's attribution of the two Gallic mints to Cologne and Trier. It would have been better if they had examined the evidence since Elmer's time to test this theory, and even if the result were inconclusive, at least they would have shown they were aware of the problematical nature of the attribution. As it is, I was forced to make my own check using the information they had assembled and it became obvious that at least one of these attributions did not stand up to close examination. For example, in the nearest hoard to Cologne, found at Kattenes (Rheinpfalz), the proportion of Trier coins is much higher than might be expected. Only in hoards centred on the area between Paris and the Upper Rhine do the 'Cologne' coins predominate. (Since 'Cologne' has two officinae, a proportion of 2:1 approximately can be expected, a figure confirmed by the average of all hoards. At Kattenes the ratio in only 1·6:1 whereas in the area mentioned 'Cologne' coins outnumber Trier by over 3:1. In the Saint-Mard find the ratio is only 1·24:1, which, in view of the short distance from Trier, at least shows that attribution to be fairly safe.)

Another point not mentioned is the simplest way of distinguishing between the coins of the two mints, at least for Victorinus and Tetricus I. This is that the 'Cologne' coins are always draped, those of Trier always cuirassed, and it is this that enables one to attribute with certainty those coins with a defective obverse inscription, e.g. coins of Tetricus I with 'Trier' obverse inscription IMP TETRICVS PF AVG but reverses proper to 'Cologne' COMES AVG or PAX AVG (RIC 57 and 101 respectively)—cf. NC 1962, 185 ff. in the report on the 1961 Beachy Head Hoard. The doubts are dispersed by the draped obverses showing they are 'Cologne'. It is notable, in this connection, that the armoured busts (facing left) of Victorinus are all from Trier.

In the discussion on the coinage of Victorinus, backed up by statistics from twenty hoards including that of Saint-Mard I, the authors have shown beyond any doubt that the three officinae system which Elmer sought to impose on the 'Cologne' mint is untenable. They argue instead the much more supportable system of two officinae which has gained acceptance in recent years. In doing so they seem to have introduced errors of their own on the rather flimsy assumption that the coinage began with progressively longer periods for each issue building up to the major types of INVICTVS and PAX AVG (Elmer 683 and 682 respectively). By doing this they impose a rather artificial pattern on the early coinage and either they should reverse their issues 2 and 3 or alternatively combine them in an issue where the types are not changed in synchronization. This would give an issue where the reverses of issue 1 are repeated with the new obverse inscription, but whereas one, FIDES MILITVM, is continued for some time before being replaced by INVICTVS ★ | the other, a plain PAX AVG is replaced almost immediately by one with V | ★. Both these later types are used in issue 4.

The same idea of a build-up to a main issue is also responsible for what I consider to be another mistake. Contrary to Elmer they have reversed the order of the final issues at both mints so that at 'Cologne' the brief VICTORIA AVG and VIRTVS AVG (starting left) is followed by the longer SALVS AVG and VIRTVS AVG (starting right) while at Trier the scarcer VICTORIA AVG is superseded by PROVIDENTIA AVG. Since all the previous issues were quite substantial it would have been better to reason that the cause of the abrupt cessation of the shorter issues was the death of Victorinus, so that these issues (5 and 6 at 'Cologne' and 4 and 5 at Trier) should be reversed. This would in no way interfere with the view of M. Giard, followed in essence by the authors, that the coins of Divus Victorinus at Trier were minted early in the reign of Tetricus as there are hybrid types with VICTORIA AVG as well as those with PROVIDENTA AVG to go with the CONSACRATIO reverse proper to the series.

The sequence for the coinage of Tetricus is much more soundly argued and they appear to have resolved the difficulties quite well. Like them I can see no reason why Elmer should have rejected the PIETAS AVGG coins of Tetricus II as barbarous and it was pleasing to see them rehabilitated in the series. I must point out that the coins with the longer reverse inscription which accompany these read, in fact, PIETAS AVGVSTOR and not AVGVSTORVM as given.

One point which they brought out, but which deserved more prominence, was the difficulty of distinguishing between the Trier coins with reverses LAETITIA AVGG and LAETITIA AVG N. In cataloguing hoards various authorities must surely have resorted to guesswork as it is only on specimens where the vital last letter is visible that a true identification can be made. In my experience this represents precious few coins from an average hoard yet the numbers quoted are nearly always positive with few listed as 'either/or'. According to hoard statistics one can find considerable variations. From four such hoards one finds quoted 30, 16, 296, and 152 with AVGG against 161, 302, 118, and 88 for AVG N in the respective hoards. It is therefore ironic to find that the totals from a dozen hoards add up to 1082 of the former against 1016 of the latter. We may safely assume that an average hoard will contain roughly equal totals of both.

It is satisfying to note, in view of my own recently expressed thoughts on the subject which came to a similar, if less well-defined, conclusion, that Mme. Lallemand

and M. Thirion realised that two British hoards, Emneth and Beachy Head 1961, were, among others, deposited before the end of the reign of the Tetrici. In the latter case this accounted for the virtual absence of the two SALVS AVGG types which formed the final issues at both mints, and also for the almost complete lack of barbarous coins noted by the authors of the report.

They also have interesting observations on the degree to which the coins of the two Tetrici are the subject of hybrids, especially the COMES AVG and PAX AVG types which occur in large numbers for Tetricus II and PRINC IVVENT for Tetricus I. No comment, however, is forthcoming on the fact that this hybrid coinage is mainly at the two officinae mint of 'Cologne', perhaps because the smaller Trier mint was more experienced at making the distinction between the two emperors or more closely controlled.

In the discussion of minor types they correctly discern that MARS VICTOR is proper to Tetricus I and NOBILITAS AVGG to his son but fail to realise that they are both 'Cologne' and not Trier as Elmer would have it. This was probably due to the fact that they had no examples in the hoards to enable them to form an opinion.

One extremely important discovery made by examination of the Saint-Mard coins is that the average weight of the antoniniani fell during the last issues of Victorinus from about 2·7 gm. down to *circa* 2·3 gm. They remained at this weight for the reign of Tetricus until in his last issues the weight is restored to 2·7 gm. again. This, I believe, was a response by the Gallic Empire to the currency reforms of Aurelian which were even then taking place in the Central Empire. If this is true, and can be substantiated in other hoards, then they have made a real contribution to our knowledge of the economic history of the times.

Probably of greater importance, but as yet unrecognizable as such, is the work they have put in on the barbarous coins in the hoard. Most authorities now will readily agree to the point, amply made in this book, that barbarous copies of Gallic coins belong almost exclusively to the period after the fall of the Tetrici to the end of the reign of Probus. From maps showing the distribution pattern of finds they demonstrate that the north-east of Gaul was a probable centre for this illegal activity and that its coins gained circulation over a considerable area. With more attention to this in the future even greater advances will undoubtedly be made.

The maps and notes showing die-links between hoards as far removed as La Vineuse in Central France and Mildenhall in East Anglia is a valuable commentary on the spread of such coins and may eventually disprove the theory of their being purely local in character. With the provision of the excellent plates showing practically every example of the barbarous coins in this find the authors have prepared the ground for future discoveries in this neglected facet of the Roman coinage.

K. J. J. ELKS

*Die Fundmünzen der römischen Zeit in Deutschland, Abt I–2 Niederbayern*, By HANS-JORG KELLNER; *IV–3 Trier*, by MARIA R.-ALFÖLDI; *VI–4 Münster*, by BERNARD KORZUS.

THE appearance of new volumes in this invaluable series is always an event of importance to the numismatic and archaeological world. Since its inception in

1960, *FMRD* has given us an unrivalled opportunity to study the currency of Germany under Roman rule; it is the achievement of the editors and authors that one-third of the country has now been covered.

No-one has been more closely associated with the work from its beginning than Dr. Hans-Jorg Kellner, Direktor of the Prähistorische Staatssammlung at Munich. His volume, covering the eastern tip of southern Germany, is the clear and informative account we have come to expect of him. Dr. Kellner has the detailed knowledge of the Roman coinage necessary to express in brief compass the numerous finds which he lists. It is interesting to see how the bulk of the finds clings to the southern bank of the Danube, so long the imperial frontier. We note how the north bank, too, has its share of finds, whereas the hinterland of the province is relatively sparsely represented, and the lands beyond the frontier largely empty. Outstanding sites whose material is here collected include those of Eining and Straubing, where the range and quantity of the coin finds make valuable contributions to our understanding of the currency during the entire period of Roman rule. Of the hoards, I would single out for special mention Kirchmatting, 1169 denarii from M. Antony to Severus Alexander, which include such varieties as a denarius of the latter as Caesar, and one of Clodius Albinus as Augustus; it is unfortunate that inconsistencies in listing make the Severan section a little difficult to disentangle. A small Constantinian hoard from Eining adds usefully to our knowledge of the currency of the later 320s.

Maria Alföldi, in compiling her monumental volume on Trier, had perhaps the hardest task of any of the authors. The city has produced an enormous mass of material. A little surprising is the record of two contorniates among the site finds, and it will be of particular interest in Britain to observe the close correspondence of the latest Roman coins at Trier with the latest pieces found here. It is certain that Trier was in Roman hands and struck silver coins as late as the beginning of the reign of Valentinian III; perhaps we should be cautious in evaluating the comparable evidence of British finds.

Dr. Korzus's volume, covering Münster, is no less useful for its more modest size, for it covers a portion of Germany as yet little dealt with by *FMRD*. His work is dominated by the great series of coins from the fort of Haltern. Hoards and single finds from this site illustrate the first stage of the Roman advance into Germany under Augustus and its calamitous termination, and give much valuable insight into the currency of that period. The hoard from Seppenrade, 66 denarii of the Republic and Augustus, confirms the picture. A characteristic feature of the later Roman currency of this region is the relative abundance of finds of solidi; this is well illustrated by the hoard from Westerkappeln, in which it is surprising to note the presence of solidi of Magnentius, some of the light standard, more than a decade after the usurper's fall.

These three volumes are worthy successors to those which have gone before; they enhance the reputation of their authors, and leave us in no doubt that Maria Alföldi will ably continue the editorial standard set by the late Drs. Gebhart and Kraft.                                        J. P. C. KENT

*The Ancient World seen through its Coinage.* By V. BRABITCH. Leningrad, 1970. Pp. 64, 58 figs.

ONE of the many remarkable features of ancient coinage is that it can serve as a picture gallery illustrating almost all aspects of life in the ancient world. This side of ancient coinage is ably exploited by Mr. Brabitch in this little book, aimed at the general reader. It puts beautifully reproduced, enlarged photographs of ancient coins side by side with striking parallel representations from vase-painting, sculpture etc. The book goes in this way through travel and recreation, famous monuments and aspects of wild life; it is pleasing evidence of the vitality of numismatic studies in Russia.                                               M. H. CRAWFORD

*Byzantine Coins (Archaeological Exploration of Sardis, Monograph no. 1).* By GEORGE E. BATES. Pp. 159, 4 maps, 9 plates. Harvard University Press, 1971. £7·25.

THIS volume, the first of the Monograph Series on the Sardis excavations, augurs well for the future: its limited field is fully covered on pleasantly designed pages from the visual, critical, site-find, and catalogue angles. Overall there are 1,234 identifiable coins dated from 491 to 1282, all found in the period 1958 to 1968. It was no glamorous task that Professor Bates undertook in his spare time. Many coins were unidentifiable or disintegrated in handling; only one tenth of the identifiable coins are illustrated and one wonders what some of the chosen few might have looked like without excellent photography and reproduction. An account of earlier excavation on the site, of which is yet only about 5 per cent. has been touched, included a volume on coins published in 1916: the new volume is able to confirm and sharpen the earlier conclusions especially through the discovery of some later coins of Heraclius.

Some 80 per cent of the 1958/68 coin finds catalogued come from the period up to and including the first decades of the seventh century when the town was sacked, another 7 per cent from a mid-seventh-century encampment and the rest from minor re-settlements. Amongst the early coins are 13 folles of the two types issued by Heruclius in the year 615/16: eleven are of the earlier type, of which the earlier excavation also produced substantial numbers, and two are of the later type, now found for the first time on the site. The destruction of the city can thus be confidently pinpointed to this year, probably 616 when the Persians were following up their advance on Chalcedon which they reached in 615.

The mint of Constantinople provided more than half the earlier group of coins, with Nicomedia, Cyzicus and Thessalonica following in that order. Only two coins are from Carthage, which makes the four (all Justin II year 8, K) from the newly identified mint of Constantine in Numidia, seem unlikely: yet an explanation is needed for these pieces and the Sardis evidence does no more than cast a slight shadow over the new identification.

This volume is also timely in giving full treatment to the copper coinage of Constans II with its 13 types (A–M) even if the original manufacture and present condition of the pieces scarcely appears to deserve it. Now that Dumbarton Oaks Catalogue II has been published the critical points are clear and Bates disagrees with Grierson's attribution of Class D to Heraclonas, on the basis of overstrikes which have been read differently by experts. Each scholar states his case with judicial fairness, but your reviewer has always felt that overstrikes unfortunately went against Grierson's brilliant suggestions which if correct, would solve a number of other problems too. Without specifying his reason Bates splits Grierson's Class 5 into F and G though calling them a 'continuous series': thus Constans II has thirteen classes in Bates's calculations and only eleven in Grierson's.

In dealing with the Anonymous series Professor Bates consciously rejects the distinction between the smaller (John I) and large (Basil II) Class A coins: this seems regrettable as there is here a real difference even if blurred by the condition of the coins and intermediate stages. If necessary a dubious class as is often provided elsewhere (e.g. Justinian I through Heraclius) might have been added. One notable absentee in the Anonymous series at Sardis is the generally common Class D.

Amongst the later coins one must note a strange misdescription of 1227 where the obverse is not a Virgin but St. George complete with his name. Nor need there be much doubt over 1230 as belonging to Michael VIII with a catalogue reference to Wroth 9. It is a credit to the illustrations that such points can be made here, tiny flaws as they are in a volume most useful to the Byzantine numismatist.

P. D. Whitting

*Anglo-Saxon England.* By F. M. Stenton Third edn., Clarendon Press, Oxford, 1970. Pp. 750. £3·50.
*Preparatory to Anglo-Saxon England, being the collected papers of Frank Merry Stenton,* D. M. Stenton (ed.). Clarendon Press, Oxford, 1970. Pp. xiv+425.

Sir Frank Stenton's *Anglo-Saxon England,* published in 1943 and in a corrected second edition in 1947, now appears in a new edition which takes account of additional corrections noted by the author up to his death in 1967 and also provides some editorial comment in footnotes at points where Stenton's text needs to be supplemented in the light of subsequent research. The changes made do not affect the essential narrative, which remains that of 1943, and the reader can continue to admire the book's familiar sweep and balance and the qualities that make it the standard work on the period and peoples involved. Some of the factors that made for its success are patent: the lucidity of Stenton's style, his judicious but always decided handling of controversial topics, his thorough grounding in Domesday and place-name studies, the knowledge and appreciation that he displays of the work of Stubbs and Maitland and others of his predecessors. One further factor is not so obvious to the reader but emerges very clearly from a study of the volume of Stenton's collected papers now also available. The papers make it apparent that Stenton's origins in and affection for the debatable tract of Eastern England north of Bedford and south of the Humber were decisive to his development as a historian as leading him to the study and proper appreciation of the role played by Midland England and the Danelaw in the Anglo-Saxon period and that his Midland roots better equipped him than anyone to counter an earlier school of historiography which had placed undue emphasis on the political and cultural importance of the West Saxon kingdom. This did not mean that he failed to recognize the achievements of the West Saxon kings and it is a striking testimony to his historical gifts that *Anglo-Saxon England* achieved throughout a balance between the pretensions of the various English kingdoms and did so so dispassionately as to obscure the fact that the balance struck was a wholly novel one.

For numismatists Stenton had the special merit that alone among historians of his rank and generation he appreciated the contribution to historical studies that research into coinage could make. There is not much evidence of this in the narrative of *Anglo-Saxon England* itself, for it was not until after he had written it that events brought Stenton as student, collector, and administrator into close contact with numismatic studies, but it is apparent that he had always had the will to use the evidence of coins and was only deterred from using it earlier by the state of confusion in which the Anglo-Saxon coinage then lay. When he did take up the subject he did so wholeheartedly and his opinions carried considerable weight. This facet of his historical interests is best reflected among the papers now collected by a previously unpublished address to the British Numismatic Society in 1958 on 'The Anglo-Saxon Coinage and the Historian', which sets out with great charm and force the case for 'a conscious and continuous alliance between numismatists and historians' and concludes with some important observations on the coinage of King Offa of Mercia (757–96). It is evident that what Stenton says on the coinage of Offa represents his considered opinion on one of the most obscure areas of Anglo-Saxon numismatics and it is worth briefly reviewing the questions at issue and the case he presents.

Stenton's main concern is with the dating of the series. There is a good deal of uncertainty about the date when the earliest issues carrying Offa's name were struck, largely because they were struck in Kent and it is difficult to establish quite when Offa's authority was recognized there. Rival schemes attribute the whole of Offa's Kentish coinage to the last 15–20 years of his reign or some of it to this period and some of it to an earlier period; on the second view the earliest of the coins might date to the early 760s. Stenton plumps unhesitatingly for the second view, pointing *inter alia* to documentary evidence that shows Offa exercising authority in Kent in and after 764 and to the existence of coins parallel to those of Offa in the name of a Kentish king Heaberht who is known to have ruled in 764–5. His prime argument however is of rather a different character. He takes the view that the distinctive features of the coinage of the period, of which the most notable is the appearance for the first time on coins of Southumbrian England of the names of king and moneyer, are likely to stem from a deliberate exercise of will by the ruler, 'emphatically, even flamboyantly exercising his royal dignity'; and that the date of its introduction can be established by considering Offa's possible motives for such exercise of will and the circumstances in which he might have acted. The suggestion Stenton advances in this respect is both bold and original: that in issuing coins carrying the royal name and title Offa 'was deliberately emphasizing his position as a hereditary king in contrast to the position of the new dynasty, noble, but not royal, which had recently come into power among the Franks'. He cities in support of this evidence from a latish date in Offa's reign that Offa was not prepared to give his daughter in marriage to one of Charlemagne's sons without some reciprocal arrangement involving his son and one of Charlemagne's daughters, which he sees as proof that Offa considered his regality at least as being as good as that of Charlemagne; and he cites, perhaps more pertinently, the description of Offa in a Kentish charter dated 764 by the elaborate phrase *Offa rex Merciorum regali prosapia*

*Merciorum oriundus*, which he sees as an assertion of the superlative quality of Offa's royal ancestry. As the charter belongs to the very period where he wishes on other grounds to date the coins he claims both as expressions of Offa's attitudes and policy at the time when he had just established his authority over the Southern English and had for the first time come into contact with the emergent Carolingian dynasty.

It will be evident from this summary that Stenton had decided views on the coinage of Offa which are not reflected in accounts of the coinage of the period produced since 1958 by other hands. It remains to be seen whether they will be approved by scholars now that they are in print. If they are not it will in part be because Stenton places a greater emphasis on the personal factor in the inception of this coinage than numismatists would generally. It is also possible that the evidence adduced might be interpreted differently. One suggestion in this direction must suffice. The phrase about Offa's descent from the royal stock of the Mercians, *regali prosapia Merciorum oriundus*, which Stenton sees as stressing Offa's regality, seems to this reviewer as likely just to be a statement of fact; Offa could not claim as most rulers to be the son, brother or near kinsman of a predecessor and his only hold on the position of hereditary king was that he belonged to a very junior branch of the Mercian royal house, which is more or less what the phrase used conveys.

H. E. PAGAN

*Money in Britain*. By C. R. JOSSET. Illustrations by Gaynor A. Barnes. Pp. 390, 49 plates in half-tone and line. David & Charles, 1971. £4·20.

THE author deals with his subject in considerable detail. Taking full advantage of his broad title, he covers money in most of the forms in which it was used in Britain. This is not, therefore, a book confined entirely to the coinage—a refreshing change. In fact, not a little of the text is set out from the angle of an historic account, taking in the relevant money as it goes along.

The early part of the book deals with the pre-Roman and Roman Occupation periods and then divides up the English hammered series under dynasties. Under each of such sections a short account is given, where appropriate, of Scottish and Irish coinages, again a refreshing change. Tally sticks as a method of reckoning and as a popular auxiliary currency, and paper money and cheques are all covered. Some proofs and patterns are included, while the coinages of the Channel Islands and of the Isle of Man have not been forgotten. Altogether, a very comprehensive text, of value to numismatist and historian alike.

One or two minor points were observed by your reviewer. It is noted that the author still holds to the belief that several millions of 'Pieces of Eight' were brought home from Vigo and turned into money. He is apparently unaware of the article by Kamen on the subject, published in 1968 (Spink's *Numismatic Circular*, p. 186), or, if aware, makes no comment. In dealing with the history of the Maundy ceremony, admittedly difficult to do in a number of sections, reign by reign, the amusing story of the reason why cloth was substituted for clothing is mentioned. The reason why this, too, had to be discontinued might also have been included, if only to round off the account.

While the author has not fallen into the trap of stating that Pistrucci was Chief

338 REVIEWS

Engraver to the Royal Mint, he seems to have misread other facts concerning the artist. While it is true that a waiter at Burnet's Hotel posed as St. George, it is hardly true to say that 'the substitution for St. George for the rider was made and adapted by an Italian employee . . .' which could be read as indicating that the waiter carried out the design. Moreover, it is news to your reviewer that Pistrucci was brought over to England by the Prince Regent in 1814. Since Forrer in his 'Dictionary' says that the artist was born in 1784, he would have been 30 years of age in 1814, not 40.

The author also seems to be at variance with Craig, who twice states that the Government placed a contract with Boulton & Watt for the copper coinage (*The Mint*, p. 264), while Josset holds that they received a Royal Mint warrant after a number of unsuccessful attempts to obtain a Government contract. The comments on the gradual removal of coin striking to Llantrisant now need updating.

In dealing with the designers of the issues of Elizabeth II, the veteran artist, Cecil Thomas, whose initials appear on the Halfcrown, Florin and Sixpence of the 1953 series, receives no mention. The part he played in the coinage of the new reign may one day be published.

All these are but minor points and should not be allowed to detract from the value of a most comprehensive and broad work, which finishes with a select biblio-graphy and useful catalogue-list of coins in the various series. Printed Note Issues in Britain form a part of the appendixes and is a useful brief catalogue in its own right. Finally, there is a list of legend translations.

The choice of line drawings for illustrating the coins was not a happy one, and one is surprised at so progressive a publishing house reverting to the methods of a past age. Most of the drawings of hammered coins are but caricatures: one could shed tears over the beautiful Offa Penny of Canterbury. Once out of the hammered period, the artist is on a little surer ground. Even so, one doubts if Lady Susan Hicks-Beech who, at the time she was modelled for the coinage was a lady of striking charm, would be very happy with the craggy features given to her on Mr. Barnes's Florin.                                                    H. W. A. LINECAR

*Trade Tokens, A Social and Economic History*. By J. R. S. WHITING. Pp. 192, 27 plates. David & Charles, 1971. £2·75.

MR. WHITING's book is an extremely useful addition to the scant literature of trade tokens. It is very refreshing to find a social historian devoting time and energy to a serious study of this subject. Herein lies the chief significance of the book. Although no numismatic problems are solved, considerable light is thrown on the fascinating story underlying the issuing of tokens—in the author's words 'a story of the initiative of local authorities, companies and individuals in the face of state ineptitude'. The most valuable chapter in the book is the first one dealing with the historical background. The author provides a more complete picture than has been painted hitherto of the economic and social factors influencing the evolution and disappearance of token currency in this country, using state papers, and domestic and contemporary local records as his source material.

The second chapter devoted to the seventeenth century, I found a little dis-appointing. Mr. Whiting does not really seem 'at home' in the seventeenth century.

He does not explore the absorbing problem of how the seventeenth-century pieces circulated, although this is perhaps expecting rather too much of a non-numismatist. In the section on minting and design, he should have mentioned David Ramage as the chief designer of the earlier tokens (1648–*circa* 1662) and the means of identifying Ramage's style.

The author's survey of the tokens themselves is sound and well organized. The division into shop tokens, crafts, transport, inns, coffee houses, and town tokens is sensible. He presents his material in an interesting way, although he has relied rather too heavily on secondary sources. This is inevitable, I suppose, in a survey of such a massive series. The background information that Whiting gives on the life and hazards of various seventeenth-century occupations is illuminating. For example he outlines the problem continually faced by carriers of being legally liable to pay for losses through robbery, though if they managed to raise a hue and cry and it failed to do its duty, then the village concerned had to pay for the losses. He points out that carriers used to ride at intervals of a hundred paces so that they could scatter if one of them was attacked.

The section on inns, taverns, and ordinaries is particularly well developed, and contains full and fascinating details of celebrated London inns, which issued tokens, such as the Bear at Bridge Foot, the Mitre in Fenchurch Street, and the Bull in King Street, Westminster, all of which were favourite haunts of Samuel Pepys.

Mr. Whiting's book contains few errors. There is one, however, which should be rectified. He states that the Mermaid Tavern (p. 64) has been variously described as being in Bread Street, Friday Street, and Cheapside, the reason being that it faced all three streets. He concludes that the token (W., London 591) showing the Mermaid at Cheapside and the token (W., London 396) depicting the mermaid in Bread Street were issued at the same inn. Burn in his *Catalogue of London Trade and Tavern Tokens*, produced as long ago as 1853, claimed that the three Mermaids were all the same and that the one tavern had alleys connecting with all three thoroughfares—a view perpetuated by Mr. Whiting. Dr. Kenneth Rogers in his *Mermaid and Mitre Taverns in Old London* (1928) exploded the theory by proving the existence of three separate Mermaids. The mermaid in Bread Street which issued the token (W., London 396) was situated between Bread Street and Friday Street close to Old Fish Street. The mermaid in Cheapside which issued the token (W., London 591) lay close to Saddlers Hall near Foster Lane.

It is a great pity that the illustrations of the seventeenth century series take the form of line drawings. These are not really acceptable to the student. One realizes that seventeenth-century tokens do not photograph as easily as those of the later series, yet it should have been possible to have produced two or three plates of an acceptable standard.

Chapters three and four dealing with the eighteenth- and nineteenth-century tokens respectively are, on the other hand, profusely illustrated with extremely fine photographs which are both a delight to the eye and a boon to the student. Mr. Whiting is much more at home in these two periods; he provides an interesting and colourful background of the actual tokens he describes. His brief survey of the Ironmaster tokens of John Wilkinson, for example, is masterly. His division of the eighteenth-century series is not altogether appropriate, I feel. It would have been helpful to have subdivided Industry into textile, copper, iron, coal mining, leather, and small industries. The section heading 'People and Places' is rather meaningless. I do not see the need for Sections 7 and 8 entitled 'Ships' and 'Soldiers' as the latter refers to devices appearing on certain tokens and not to the purpose of their issue. The author's division of the nineteenth-century series cannot be faulted.

A full bibliography and list of museum collections conclude a work, which will find a worthy place on the bookshelves of all students and collectors of tokens.

GEORGE BERRY

*Coins in History: a survey of coinage from the Reform of Diocletian to the Latin Monetary Union*. By JOHN PORTEOUS. Pp. 251+index, 286 illustrations, frontispiece, 4 plans. Weidenfeld & Nicolson, 1969. £5·25.

THIS book is not only one of the most handsome numismatic works ever produced, but one of the most useful. Certainly the reviewer found it so when faced with the task of preparing panels of medieval coins for exhibition at the National Museum of Wales. Porteous has the happy gift of being able to review an immense and enormously complicated range of currencies and to reduce them to order—a little breathlessly at times, perhaps, and the last chapter flags, but, unquestionably, to order. His approach is throughout that of the economic historian. This is welcome and valuable, for it does permit the reader to follow the general thread of the complex story without becoming bogged down in purely numismatic detail. It may perhaps be characterized as a book which the numismatic specialist will recommend to the historian, but one which he will probably be found dipping into himself from time to time.

The greatest utility of the work lies in the chapters which cover the development of the medieval coinages on the ruins of the Roman system and, at a later period, the gradual evolution of larger denominations in response to the greater needs of trade in the late Middle Ages and, eventually, to the impact of new reserves of bullion oversea. I think no single work has ever put these subjects together. I can find no errors.

The coins illustrated are all photographed from the originals. The black and white pictures are superb, and most of the colour ones also—there are thirty-two of these, mostly taken on very carefully chosen backgrounds, so that the results, whether reproduced at actual size or enlarged, are of great beauty. Despite the requirements of three- or four-block colour-printing, these plates are nearly all sharp, and the rendering of metallic surfaces successful. It might here be noted that the author very largely leaves the coins to speak for themselves as works of art. There are many agreeable discoveries to be made among the plates from the art-historical point of view.

In addition to the coins, the illustrations include a variety of other subjects, some of which are well known, but others (such as the frescoes of the 15th-century moneyers at Kutná Hora, no. 154) can have been little known in Britain previously. In short, throughout the work, although a great many well-known facts are put together (as well as an equal number of others as far as this reviewer is concerned) there is not the least flavour of the *déjà vu* about it. The production is excellent, and Porteous has done the numismatic community a great service.

GEORGE C. BOON

*Historic Gold Coins of the World from Croesus to Elizabeth II.* By BURTON HOBSON.
Pp. 192, 244 plates. Blandford Press. 1971. £8·00.

IN one respect at least the publisher's claims for this book are justified: turning its pages is rather like turning the pages of an album of real gold coins. So good is the technical quality of the reproduction that the yellow gold really appears to be there on the page, with all its physical appeal for the miser that lurks so closely under the skin of many coin collectors; an illusion which is strengthened by the weight of the book, printed as this is on shiny art paper throughout.

The author has cast his net wide. His period is from Croesus to Elizabeth II; his theme the historic; his only limitation the metal, gold.

Anyone who takes history for the theme of a numismatic work must either treat of coins for historians or of history for numismatists. Now the second of these alternatives is not really valid. History for numismatists is no different from history for everyone else, and the numismatist who wants to study it must turn to the works of the professional historians. Numismatics for the historian is another matter. There is something to be done here. It is surprising how often even the most distinguished economic, social, and general historians are seen to be wrong when they come to touch on matters of coinage. However, the author of a book of this sort must write allusively. It is not for him to write history: he must assume that the historical facts are known to the reader and fit the story of coinage to that background.

That, however, is not an idea which is likely to appeal to an American publisher with a mass market in mind—and the book under review is written by an American for, primarily, an American readership. So here we have the facts spelled out every time, not just the history of gold coinage from Croesus to Elizabeth II in a series of what amount to extended captions, but the political and cultural history of the period as well. Thus the Luther centenary ducat of John George of Saxony is accompanied by a paragraph on the Lutheran reformation and the coins of the United Provinces by two paragraphs on the rise of the Dutch Republic. It is typical of the book that these two paragraphs contain no information on the monetary system of the United Provinces, and make no reference to the economic importance of the Dutch.

History, treated in this fashion, proceeds unevenly as a succession of capriciously selected snippets of information. About a quarter of the Byzantine section is taken up by a biographical note on John II Comnenus. This would seem disproportionate, even if the coin actually illustrated were not one which the best authorities ascribe to the Nicaean emperor John III.

Where the author's historical statements are not simplistic ('a certain religious atmosphere prevailed in the Byzantine empire') they are often wrong. For the Crusades he gives us Geoffrey for Godfrey de Bouillon and, in the same sentence, ascribes the foundation of the county of Tripoli to Bertrand instead of Raymond of Toulouse. Charles of Anjou is described as a Norman, his title of king of Jerusalem as inherited by some unspecified process from earlier kings of Sicily, not bought, as it in fact was from Mary of Antioch.

On purely numismatic points, the author is no more reliable. 'The first of the Renaissance popes to use his own likeness on coins was Julius II', he tells us. In fact Sixtus IV struck silver portrait coins and Alexander VI a gold one. A half-noble of

Edward III is captioned as a noble (an example this of the loss of the sense of scale which follows from the indiscriminate use of enlarged photographs). The plural *solidii* appears so frequently and invariably that it can scarcely be just a printer's error. Mr. Hobson falls into the old trap of calling Ferdinand and Isabella's *excelente* a *double excelente*, and thus gets the multiples wrong all the way up the scale. When he deals with the ducat of Venice, the author gives another airing to the theory that the name was derived from the reverse legend, though in this instance, like the allegorical figure of the synagogue in gothic cathedral sculpture, he seems deliberately to have blinded himself to the truth, since he actually mentions the reasons why this etymology must be false.

The author seems scarcely to be able to touch on questions of heraldry without falling into error. He describes the label of difference which appears on the arms of Gaston of Orléans, brother of Louis XIII, as an initial M for Montpensier. He mistakes the arms of Sicily in the shield of the Catholic Kings for those of Navarre, and for some reason he ascribes to the town of Münzenberg the arms of Falkenstein on a coin of Kuno von Falkenstein, archbishop of Trier.

Again and again the author picks up the wrong end of the historical stick. We are given a brief description of the Hapsburgs' inheritance of Mary of Burgundy's possessions in the Netherlands. However, the coin chosen to illustrate this point is a gulden of the 'three cities', Deventer, Kampen and Zwolle, which were not part of the Burgundian inheritance, and which issued coins in Charles V's name because they were free cities of the Empire. Sometimes the author gives the impression of never having looked at the coin he describes. Thus he writes of a coin of Mary of Guelders as showing the figure of the duchess—and there she is with drawn sword, beard and all.

The author is evidently an expert on modern American coins, and he treats these in some detail without filling in with the irrelevant historical detail which is so irritating in the earlier part of the book. It really is interesting to know that Theodore Roosevelt thought it blasphemous to put the name of God on a coin. What a contrast that makes with the coins of Byzantium and Islam in the earlier part of the book and what volumes it speaks of the nature of religious feeling in these different civilizations.

However, such nuggets of information are scarce, and in a book where so much is wrong, one would want to check every fact elsewhere. It must be said that this book is typical of all that is worst in modern 'collectors' numismatics'. If numismatics are in danger of falling into contempt with historians, it is because of the rash of books like this. Beneath a glossy surface it is ill-balanced and ill-informed, confounding the significant with the irrelevant and the trivial. Only its beautiful illustrations may appeal to the miser in us; though even that appeal is limited at eight pounds a copy.

JOHN PORTEOUS

*Numismatic Art in America.* By CORNELIUS C. VERMEULE. Pp. 265, illustrated. The Belknap Press of Harvard University Press, Cambridge, Mass., 1971.

DR. VERMEULE can claim well deserved credit for this splendid effort to rescue American coinage and medallic art from their unfortunate past obscurity. For some decades, it has been fashionable for American collectors and numismatists to belittle native artists and die-cutters. Critics of the United States coinage have too often compared its artistry with that of the classical period—surely an unfair comparison when one considers how greatly the requirements of modern mint production differ from those of the ancients.

The challenge faced—and accepted—by the young American nation in 1793 was the designing of a coinage which, while differing from that of the Old World, at the same time expressed something of the spirit which pervaded the newly independent land. The many problems encountered, enormous as they were, were still further aggravated by an unfriendly Congress which considered the newly established Philadelphia Mint an extravagant and foolish waste of money. Unkind critics labelled the eagle depicted on the first gold and silver coins as 'a sick turkey', and the head of Liberty as 'a wild squaw with the heebie jeebies'. In fact, the Liberty head was a compelling design, executed to express America's newly won freedom from Britain, and was quite possibly inspired by the 'Libertas Americana' medal designed by the French medalist, Augustin Dupré. The reverse eagle, originally chosen as a symbol of strength, was later modified into an heraldic representation symbolizing an aloof but strong nation. From the beginning, the coins carried an inscription, such as 'Liberty', or a motto, such as 'E Pluribus Unum'; later, during the period of the Civil War, the motto 'In God We Trust' was used.

The iconography during the first century of the Republic underwent little change, with the eagle and Liberty remaining the principal devices used. Artists, however, were able to express themselves more freely in the creation of historical commemorative medals, which presented opportunities to exercise talent and craftsmanship entirely free from the limitations imposed by the requirements of a national coinage.

Vermeule compares and evaluates American numismatic design from the beginning down to the present time, drawing upon a wide knowledge of other art forms which are seen to have influenced both the coinage and medallic art. The text, presented in eminently readable style, is complemented by 249 excellent illustrations, and is to be considered a 'must' for collectors who all too frequently—and sadly, it must be said—overly concern themselves with dates and mintmarks to the virtual exclusion of the artistic merits of their country's coins and medals.

Having furnished his readers with a wealth of data pertaining to American designers and engravers, in which their influence on other art forms is clearly shown, the author concludes with the hope that today's artisans will produce works reflecting a creative skill which will assure coins and medals the continuation of their place among the most enduring forms of historical documents.

HENRY GRUNTHAL

*The Coinage of the Arab Amirs of Crete.* By GEORGE C. MILES (American Numismatic Society, Numismatic Notes and Monographs no. 160). Pp. 86, 9 plates. New York, 1970.

IN this short monograph the author consolidates some fifteen years of continued interest and research into a series the existence of which was not suspected until 1953, when John Walker, published a modest article entitled 'The coins of the Amirs of Crete'. If Walker's was the original discovery, to Dr. Miles belongs the credit for enormously enlarging the evidence, partly by recourse to museum collections, partly by the exploration of private sources (chiefly in the Aegean area) and partly by his own work as an archaeologist in Crete. Nearly 300 coins of perhaps eleven rulers are now known, as compared with a mere fifteen pieces recorded by Walker. Their provenances fully confirm the attribution to Crete, while the numerous dated and dateable pieces among them supply a framework for a more complete chronology of the amirs than is feasible from the desultory references of Arab and Byzantine historians. Thus Shu'aib (Greek Saipis), the son of 'Umar the conqueror of Crete, has left coins dated 271/884 to 281/894, an improvement on the chronicles from which we know only that Saipis may still have been living in 875. The amir named Kouroupas who is known to have been captured by Nicephoros Phocas in 961 can be identified with 'Abd al-'Azīz, whose coins show him to have reigned for at least seven years prior to the disaster which ended Arab rule in Crete. But Dr. Miles goes further in his deductions and constructs a complex genealogical tree, involving four branches at its latest stage, in an endeavour to interrelate all the individuals whose names appear on the coins. The task is fraught with difficulties, for a number of these persons are not historically attested and where (as with the majority of specimens) two rulers are named on the same coin there is often no 'ibn' to show the link between them. It is worth noting that of 25 types described, no less than 14 show the name Shu'aib: one is prompted to wonder whether this does not sometimes allude to the ancestor of the dynasty rather than to a ruling amir of this name. The discovery of fresh types may supply answers to many of the questions relating to kinship and succession in the Cretan series. In the meantime Dr. Miles has been wise to stress the speculative nature of his genealogical scheme.

If the introduction exhibits the author's Holmes-like ingenuity in piecing together evidence, the corpus itself testifies to his enthusiastic Wanderlust. It is pleasing to follow him, in the footnotes to the coin-descriptions, through vineyards and up mountain paths in quest of some elusive (and sometimes illusory) remnant of Crete's Islamic past. There is consolation in the knowledge that even the most eminent have their setbacks; as at the Cairo National Library, where 'it was never possible to assemble at one time the three functionaries with different keys required to open the cabinets'. Glosses such as these are a welcome supplement to more essential information concerning find-spots, archaeological contexts, and museum registration, as well as full commentaries on problematic pieces. In this respect the monograph should serve as a model to pioneers in other areas of numismatic study, demonstrating as it does the value of omitting no apparently trifling detail which may shed light on a hitherto uncharted series. N. M. Lowick

*İstanbul Arkeoloji Müzeleri Teşhirdeki İslâmî Sikkeler Kataloğu Cilt I* (Catalogue of Islamic Coins from the Exhibition of the Istanbul Archaeological Museum, Vol. i). By I. and C. Artuk. Pp. 451, 58 plates. Istanbul, 1971.

This is the first catalogue of Islamic coins published by the National Archaeological Museum of Turkey since the important series of volumes which appeared between 1893 and 1916 under the general title of *Meskukat-i Kadime-i Islamiye*. Those familiar with these latter publications will be aware of the richness and variety of the Museum's holdings and will therefore be disposed to extend a particular welcome to Ibrahim and Cevriye Artuk's new catalogue. Itself only the first part of a projected two-volume work, the catalogue describes 2,574 coins and covers a wide geographical and chronological spectrum, ranging from Spain to Turkestan and from the Umayyad period up to the present century. Most Islamic dynasties are represented, the chief omissions being the Ottomans and the Mongol and later dynasties of Iran, which will presumably find a place in the second volume. As its title implies, this is a selective work, only the most notable coins of each series having been singled out. There are arguments both for and against such an approach. On the credit side it can be maintained that much unnecessary duplication has been avoided and the space saved used to advantage in the fuller description and discussion of outstanding pieces. Many specialized catalogues and monographs on particular Islamic series now exist and little would be gained by listing every specimen, however well known, of a series that has already been catalogued *in extenso* elsewhere. At the same time one cannot help regretting that series for which no corpus yet exists (the Būyids, for example, or the various Seljuq dynasties) should not have received more comprehensive treatment. To the few typical or unusual specimens described might well have been appended, without swelling the work to absurd dimensions, a short list of all the mint and date varieties represented in the Museum. As the catalogue stands, one is left with no clear idea of the true size of the collection or of the range of material available for study in each series.

A gratifying feature of the catalogue entries is the inclusion of references to other published examples of the types described, which bear witness to thorough consultation of the standard works. An adequate number of pieces is illustrated, the somewhat blurred quality of the photographic reproduction being partly compensated for by the enlargement of many of the smaller items. Most will regret the sacrifice of even a single plate to such modern non-entities as the 1921 half piastre of Syria. An introduction (in Turkish) comprises a short history of Islamic numismatic studies in Turkey and a survey of the main developments in Islamic coinage, with a number of interesting references to passages in medieval writers. It is a pity that all the indexes had to be relegated to a forthcoming volume.

Collectors in need of a general guide to assist them in identifying Islamic coin types will find this book a serviceable one. Those studying individual series in depth will also derive profit from it, while bearing in mind that it provides but a glimpse of the wealth which the Museum has at its disposal.

N. M. Lowick

*Kushan and Kushano-Sasanian Seals and Kushano-Sasanian Coins: Sasanian Seals in the British Museum* (Corpus Inscriptionum Iranicarum Part III: Pahlavi Inscriptions. Vol. vi: Seals and Coins. Plates. Portfolio I: Plates I–XXX). Introduction by A. D. H. Bivar, Pp. 25. London, 1968.

*Sasanian Seals in the Collection of Mohsen Foroughi* (Corpus Inscr. Iran. Part III. Vol. vi: Portfolio II: Plates XXXI–LIV). Introduction by R. N. Frye. London, 1971.

These are the first in a projected series of five portfolios illustrating seals and coins bearing Pahlavi inscriptions. The Kushan and Kushano-Sasanian material in the first portfolio is drawn from collections throughout the world, including the Hermitage, the Kabul Museum and various private collections. The Sasanian seals shown on Plates XI ff. of Portfolio I and those in Portfolio II, on the other hand, are derived from two sources only, the British Museum and the Foroughi collection in Tehran respectively. The enlarged photographs, reproduced by the collotype process, are exceptionally fine, despite the difficulties inherent in illustrating the many pieces with sharply curved surfaces. In the case of the coins a selective approach has been adopted, only one clear specimen of a type being shown unless several are needed to obtain a complete reading of the legend. The few pages of text accompanying each portfolio contain source details and short descriptions of the coins and seals illustrated. The inscriptions themselves are to be discussed in an eventual series of volumes to follow the publication of the plates.          N. M. LOWICK

*Coins.* By PARMESHWARI LAL GUPTA. India—The Land and People Series. Pp. 241, 34 plates. New Delhi, 1969.

THE coinage of the Indian sub-continent is so vast and comprises series so diverse in design and script that it is not surprising that it has seldom been made the subject of an overall study. C. J. Brown's *The Coins of India*, published in 1922, for long the only general survey, fully merits the recent decision to reprint it. The Indian section of Carson's *Coins* characterizes the main series satisfactorily for the beginner, though it is too compressed to give full coverage to the types. Dr. Gupta's little book, while retaining the format of a beginner's guide, sets out to treat the subject at somewhat greater length than its forerunners. The approach is in essence descriptive, historical background and the discussion of social and economic implications being kept to a minimum except in the case of outstanding issues. An introductory chapter deals with the substitution of an ingot currency for barter with animals in the Vedic period. Certain of the later chapters, those on the Indo-Greeks and Kushanas, for example—parallel closely those in Brown and contain little extra information. The author makes no attempt to present or evaluate the various theories on the crucial question of Kanishka's dating and merely notes that the Kushanas 'built up a great empire which lasted more than a century'. A certain cautiousness is characteristic of the whole book and, commendable in some areas (such as medieval South India), seems in others to mask an unwillingness to take account of recent research. A conspicuous exception is the chapter on early punch-marked pieces, which reflects the author's pioneer work on the attribution and dating of Mauryan and pre-Mauryan issues. The numerous Muslim coinages are well covered, the often strange transliterations of Arabic and Persian legends being supplied with English translations in parentheses.

The plates, though numerous, are a failing of the volume, since apart from the (perhaps inevitably) poor quality of the photographic reproduction the individual coins are enlarged or reduced arbitrarily, giving the impression, for example, that a Hephthalite drachm is no larger than a hemidrachm of the Guptas. The plates are provided with a detailed key but the text itself contains no plate references—an inconvenience which the reader could have been spared at little cost to the author.

Thanks to its breadth of scope the book has certain advantages denied to more specialized works on Indian coins. How helpful, for instance, to find within the space of two pages an account of all the bull-and-horseman coins issued by early medieval dynasties. Information scattered through the learned treatises of Cunningham, Rapson, and others is reproduced here in a concise and readable form which bears witness to Dr. Gupta's far-ranging study and grasp of his subject.

N. M. LOWICK

*British Battles and Medals.* By MAJOR L. L. GORDON. Fourth edition, revised by E. C. JOSLIN. Pp. xiv+440, 41 plates (1 in colour) and 4-fold medal ribbon chart. Spink & Son Ltd., 1971. £10·00.

TEN years ago the third edition of this book appeared, and was enthusiastically welcomed by all serious collectors of British campaign medals, particularly as many of the errors in the earlier editions had been corrected. Major Gordon undoubtedly made an important contribution to medallic literature in that, not only were all British campaign medals fully described, together with details of the actions, but particulars were included of most of the units engaged.

And now, with advancing years, the author has felt that he could not undertake the heavy task of again bringing the book up to date. He has disposed of the entire copyright to Spink & Son Ltd., and Mr. E. C. Joslin, manager of their medal department, has completely revised the work, not only in respect of the additions of the last ten years, but has re-written some of the earlier matter although still retaining much of the original material, in Major Gordon's inimitable style.

A certain amount of superfluous matter has been advantageously omitted and several new features have been introduced, among which collectors will welcome the detailed figures of the strength of each unit at Waterloo, with notes of casualties, similar data for the British South Africa Company's medals, naval awards of the China 1900 and Queen's South Africa medals, and details of Australian units serving in the Boer War. For the first time details of all the Imperial Yeomanry companies, with their relative clasps, have been given, and also a full list of units serving in the Natal Rebellion of 1906, with numbers of medals awarded. The list of British recipients of the French Military Medal and the Sardinian War Medal for the Crimea is also welcome, as are details of the modern make-up of infantry and cavalry regiments.

On the debit side, it is a pity that many of the mistakes on the third edition are still uncorrected. A number of these concern the names of recipients of the Naval General Service Medal, 1793–1840; frequently there is doubt as to their correct spelling, but when the entries relate to officers, whose details can easily be checked in *The Navy List* or in O'Byrne's *Naval Biographical Dictionary*, they should be corrected, especially as many of them were notified to the original author twenty years ago.

The Dutch Cross, 1865, for veterans of the 1813–15 campaign is still mis-described as the Belgian Star, and on several occasions the adjective, *Peninsular*, appears instead of the noun, *Peninsula* (particularly when quoting medal bars). One wonders why the detailed description of the Louisbourg Medal, 1758, still appears under the heading of five unconnected medals, two of which are allocated incorrect dates.

There is some inconsistency in quoting the width of medal ribbons, some being given in fractions and others in decimals, while in several cases the descriptions of the ribbons are still somewhat misleading. We again read that the medal for South Africa, with two bars, 1877–8 and 1879, awarded to Pte. J. Connor, 90th Regt., is the only one known, although it is well known that a similar medal to A/Asst. Commissary J. L. Dalton, V.C., was on view at the Victoria Cross Exhibition in July 1956.

The second footnote on p. 259 is, to say the least, complete nonsense. Referring to the battle of Khartoum, 2 September 1898, it states that 'after the entry into Khartoum a pewter star was distributed to the troops. We have been unable to ascertain who made it or who bore the cost.' There is plenty of evidence, including General Gordon's own letters, well known to collectors, that these stars were issued some fourteen years earlier, in 1884, by General Gordon himself. They were fully described and illustrated in *The Graphic*, 11 April 1885 (p. 354) and also in a booklet, *Gordon and the Mahdi*, published in the same year.

There is an unfortunate error on p. 264, where a Col. Morgan, who founded the Field Force Canteen, is also credited with being 'well known as a medal roll researcher who has supplied much useful information'. This latter description must surely relate to Capt. W. A. Morgan, late 13th London Regt. It is also unfortunate that Queen's South Africa medals to mounted infantry are described as scarce; as a consequence dealers are already raising their prices for these medals, which are, in fact, far from scarce. There were many thousands of mounted infantry, and although not all their medals are impressed M.I., they can usually be identified by having bars different from those won by foot contingents of the same regiment.

Among the medals for 1914–18, we note that the myth is still continued that in the naming of the British War and Victory medals, artillery officers have R.A. after their names. For the Polar Medal, 1904, the naming of the designers as E. G. Gillick and Mrs. Mary Gillick, is only correct as far as the Elizabeth II issues are concerned, while it is inaccurate to say that the naming on the Edward VII, George V, and George VI issues is in *engraved* capitals, as certainly the George V medals with bars, ANTARCTIC 1910–13, and ANTARCTIC 1912–14, were *impressed*.

The bars for the Crimea medal are described (as, indeed, other writers have described them) as of unique design, but this is only true as far as British medals are concerned; the same design was copied by Saxony for the bar, WELTKRIEG 1914–16, when awarded to women with the Carola medal and the Friedrich August medal.

In describing the grades of condition, surely these should follow the usual trade range, and include EF between mint and VF? And we would think that most collectors would prefer the omission of the ugly last sentence in the footnote to p. 429.

The same set of photographs has again been used, but brought up to date with additional items. It would obviously be too expensive to replace them with a new set, but it is such a pity that all the lettering has been touched up with white, as this distorts the shape of the letters on the bars, and thus gives the collector no guide in recognizing genuine bars from false ones. The caption of the Khedive's Star gives the bar for Tokar as Tofrek.

The omission of the page headings—title on the left and subject matter on the right—is not serious, since they are really only a convention, but the page, with its

55 lines of type and the pagination at the bottom, although undoubtedly economical
is rather unpleasing in appearance; and if economy was essential, then nearly 74
half-pages could have been utilized by re-planning the layout of the data on the
Naval General Service Medal, 1793–1840.

In a work of this size and scope, it is inevitable that many minor errors should
occur—and those listed above by no means complete the list of those recorded—yet
one must applaud this most useful volume, with its mass of essential information
not easily obtainable elsewhere. It is certainly one of the most important books for
the medal collector's library.                              ALEC A. PURVES

*Mints, Dies and Currency:* Essays dedicated to the memory of Albert Baldwin.
  Ed. R. A. G. CARSON. Pp. XV+336; 23 half-tone plates. London, 1971.
  £10·50.

THIS reviewer's deeply regretted inability to contribute to this volume by the time
required cannot be compensated by the writing of a review. Nevertheless, there is
now the opportunity of saying how successfully these essays commemorate the
memory of a most remarkable man.

For those nurtured in the Ashmolean, the name of Baldwin has always been
specially respected. J. G. Milne, the approximate contemporary of Roy and Fred
Baldwin, had a firm connection of friendship and numismatic interest even earlier
with A. H. Baldwin, the founder of the firm; and this connection was continued
and deepened in the era of Roy and Fred, whose friendship towards the Heberden
Coin Room was unfailing and often—in spite of their wishes—conspicuous. Nor
was that friendship changed in the era—all too short—of Albert. Mr. Whitting,
in a moving and beautifully written introductory memoir to this volume, has
formed a true estimate of the man: a man, necessarily of business, who was severe
in principle but serene in spirit; a man who preferred to conceal his extraordinarily
wide knowledge under a thick cloak of modesty; a man whose essential gentleness
enabled him to gather a large band of grateful friends.

Albert Baldwin, through close study, a fine eye, and a powerful memory, was at
home in a surprising number of numismatic fields. These essays bring this out,
ranging as they do from the Roman Republic (an important list of addenda to
Sydenham, compiled by C. A. Hersh) down to J. G. Pollard's characteristically well
documented study of a hitherto unknown sixteenth-century Flemish medal. The
title of the volume—*Mints, Dies and Currency*—is a little formidable, and perhaps
unnecessarily so, suggesting the centrality of a main theme. In fact, few numismatic
contributors today can afford to exclude these three methods of study; and, if such
a title is specially appropriate in this case, it should probably be because Albert
Baldwin, with material pouring through his hands for some 35 years, saw sooner
than many, and more clearly than most, that numismatic study, to be successful,
must depend upon the patiently accumulated study of minutiae in ever increasing
degree.

Of the other contributions, Sellwood on Parthia, Hill on Hadrian's COS. 111 *aes*,
Carson on Carausius and Allectus, and Kent on Theodoric, all deal with important
problems of ancient coinage, with which one should include a valuable Celtic note

by D. F. Allen. The main strand in the volume is Albert Baldwin's main strand—medieval and early post-medieval hammered coinage. Here the papers are in depth and detail: their authors—Donald, Whitting, Blunt, Dolley, Lyon, Elmore Jones, Brand, Marion Archibald, Winstanley, W. A. Seaby, Seltman, and Ian Stewart—represent that special band of scholars for whose difficult and laborious fields Albert Baldwin's perception and knowledge provided so much finely comprehended material. Easily the major contribution among these is Stewart's long paper (124 pp.) entitled 'Scottish Mints', which is in a real sense the documentary and analytical appendix to his earlier *The Scottish Coinage*. This is a substantive work of obviously fundamental importance, compiled with great precision.

The volume, launched originally by Mr. Whitting, was finally edited by Mr. Carson, whose care is evident at all points. It is well illustrated. For all numismatic scholars it will be a necessity; and as a memorial to Albert Baldwin it will certainly endure, *aere perennius*.                                                                C. H. V. SUTHERLAND

# Index

'Abd al-Mu'min, 286
'Abdullāh II, 283, 285 f.
Abū'l-Faḍl, 285, 287
Abyssinia, invaded by British, 235 f.; the use of talers, 236
Achaemenid sovereigns of Iran, 29
achesons, 177
Achesoun, Thomas, 177
Acragas, 4, 18
Actium, battle of, 89 ff.; 109
Adrianople, 128
Aedes Neptuni, 51
Aegium, coins of, 40
Aeteriutas type, 99
Aetna tetradrachms, 8 f., 22
Africa, N., 276, 278 f., 280
Agnellus, 134
Agrippa, Marcus, 58, 95
Agrippina, 106
Agustin, Antonio, 295, 299
Ahenobarbus, Cn. Domitius, 100, 106
Aicherau, Franz, 233
Ainesidemos, 18
Aistulf, 194, 200
Akbar, 285 f.
Alekseer, F., 270
Alexander Bala, 305
Alexander Tyrans, 47
Alexandria mint, 117 f., 120
Alferg at Canterbury, 174
ALLEN, D. F., reviews J.-B. Colbert de Beaulieu, *Les Monnaies gauloises des Parisii*, 321 ff.
Almohad dynasty, reforms, 279
Alva, Duke of, 292 f.; 'tenth penny' tax, 292 ff.
Ambianum, 119, 122
Amisus, 30
Anaxilas of Rhegium, 4
Anne of Austria, 292
Annona type, 100, 102
Annulets as ecclesiastical symbols, 172 ff.; on coins of Edward, 174 f.
Anthony, 91, 100
Antioch mint, 111 f., 117 f., 125, 129 f.
Antiochia ad Orontem, mint, 30
Antiochus IV, Epiphanes, 28
Antiochus VI, an unpublished drachm of, 305
Antoninus Pius, 163

Antonius, 31
Antony and Caesar, mistake on denarius of, 308
Antwerp, 289; taler production at, 237
Aorsians, 32
Apollo/Horseman types, 105
Appianus, 32; on Tigranes, 30
Aqua Aemilia Fulvia, 58
Aqua Marcia, on coins, 51, 57 f.
Aquileia, 117 f., 126 f., 129 f., 139, 142 f., 146, 153 f.
Arcadius, 128, 136 ff.
Architectura Numismatica, 45 ff.
Ariarathes, resemblance to Pharnaces II, 27
Aripert II, regal coinage of Lombardy, 195, 204
Aristotle, on Gelon, 9 f.
Arles mint, 117 f., 121 f., 141 f., 146, 151 f., 157
Armenia, 30 f.
Armorican, 61
Arta mint, 190
Artavasdes, 31, 33
Artaxata, mint, 30
Artemesia, Queen of Crete, 295 ff.
Artsikhovsky, A. V., 262, 264
Asander, 32
Asclepieum, 41
Ashkenazai, Bezalel, 276, 278
Ashmolean Museum, Serbian coins in, 188 f.
Asia Minor, invasion of, 31 ff., 32, 34
Athenian coinage 480–449 B.C., research into, 313 ff.
Athens, 39
atkinsons, 177
Augurinus, C., column type, 104
Augustodunum, 122
Augustus, 56 f., 98 f., 101, 106, 108, 160, 162; and Agrippa, 95; coins imitated by Vespasian, 89 ff.
d'Aulisio, Domenico, 300 f.
Aurelian, 111
Austrian Netherlands, 226
Austro–Bavarian Monetary Convention, 233
Autun, temple of Janus, 56; coins in the Museum, 160 f.
Auxerre, coins in Museums, 160 f.
Avallon, coins in the Museum, 160 f.
Avenarius, Johann Christian, 301

a

b

c

d

e

f

1

1

2

3

4

5

6

7

8

9

21  22

23

24  25

26

27  28  29

30  31  32

TRELL : ARCHITECTURA NUMISMATICA (3)

33

34

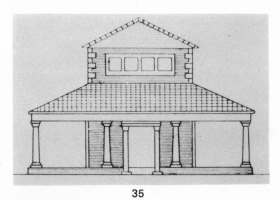

35

36

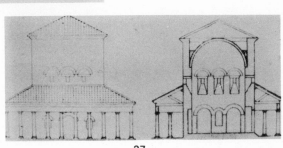

37

69 73 75 81 90

91 97 98 102 104

113 114 115 116 117

119 120 125 128 129

130 132 136 138 139

140 141 142 143 144

146 150 151 152 161

164 166 169 173 174

HERSH : QUINARIUS HOARD (3)

BUTTREY : VESPASIAN AS MONEYER (1)

13    14    15    16

17    18    19    20

21    22    23

BUTTREY : VESPASIAN AS MONEYER (2)

ELKS : TRAJAN DECIUS (1)  (Scale 1½ : 1)

ELKS : TRAJAN DECIUS (2)   (Scale 1½ : 1)

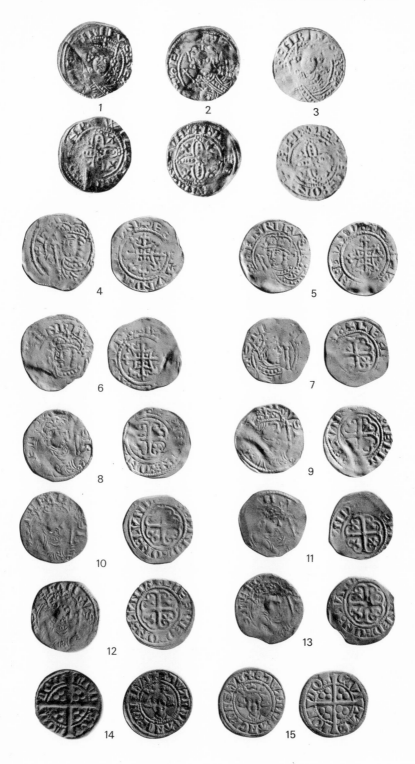

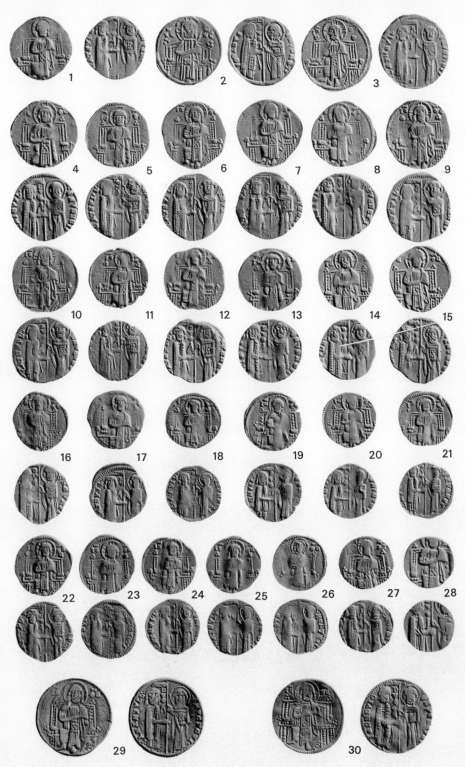

METCALF : IMITATION VENETIAN GROSSI IN THE BALKANS

Class I

291  292  293  295  296  298

299  300  301  302  305

Class II

307  309  311  312  313

Class III

315  317  318  319  322  330

ODDY : LOMBARDIC TREMISSES (1)

Class III cont.

332    335    336    337    338    340

Class IV

342    343    345    346    347    349    350

353    354    356    357    359    362    364

Class V

365    366    367    369    370    371

Class VI

372    373    375    377    378    379

CLASS I OBVERSES

BROOME : MARIA THERESIA RESTRIKE THALERS (1)

CLASS I REVERSES

A

1779 Vienna

B

C

D

H

CLASS II OBVERSES

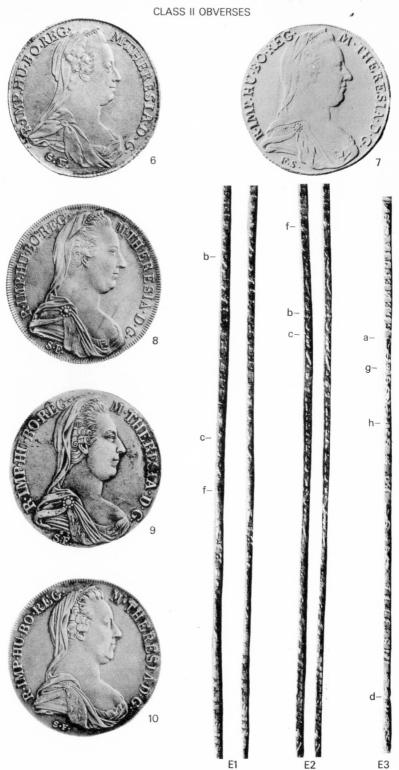

BROOME : MARIA THERESIA RESTRIKE THALERS (3)

CLASS II REVERSES

1775 Günzburg

5

K

L

M

N

O

O

London

3–feathers–2

BROOME : MARIA THERESIA RESTRIKE THALERS (4)

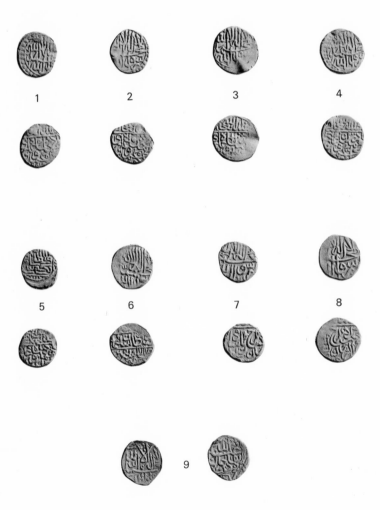

LOWICK : SULAIMÄN MIRZÄ

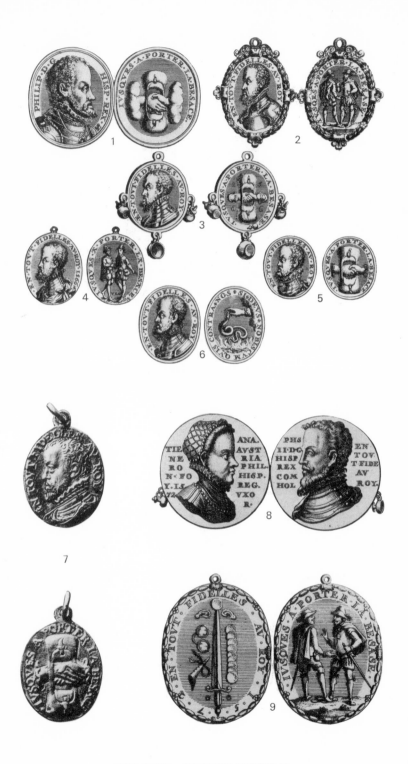

THOMPSON : BEGGARS' BADGES (2)

1

2

GREENHALGH : QUEEN ARTEMESIA MEDAL (1)

1

2

GREENHALGH : QUEEN ARTEMESIA MEDAL (2)

# THE PRESIDENT'S ADDRESS
## SESSION 1971-72

*Delivered 20 June 1971*

*President*: DR. COLIN M. KRAAY, M.A., D.Phil., F.S.A.

### REVIEW OF THE YEAR

THE Secretary has given you the Society's vital statistics. It now rests with me to say something of personalities, achievements, and aspirations.

Among those whom we have lost through death I mention first our Honorary Fellow, Professor Dr. Eduard Holzmair (d. December 1971), for many years Director of the great Vienna Coin Cabinet, and an authority on Austrian coins and medals. Mrs. C. H. Biddulph (d. April 1972) used to attend our meetings regularly in the company of her husband until his death in 1966; she had been a Fellow in her own right since 1957. Richard Du Cane (d. January 1972) gave pleasure to many more than knew him personally, for he was a skilful numismatic photographer, and many of the colour transparencies which have illustrated our lectures in recent years will have been his work; his monument is the long series of duplicates of all his transparencies of British Museum coins which he deposited in the Department of Coins and Medals. Enrico Leuthold (d. 9 July 1971) was not seen among us in person, but numismatists visiting Milan were sure of a hospitable welcome from him. He built up a fabulous Byzantine collection, which was his principal interest, but he also owned impressive series of Greek and Roman coins; his interests were shared by his son, who is also one of our Fellows.

On reading the list of New Year's Honours in January we were all delighted to learn that our Patron, Her Majesty the Queen, had conferred a knighthood on our Honorary Vice-President, Stanley Robinson, for services to numismatics and the Ashmolean Museum. His expert generosity to both the British Museum and the Ashmolean are well known, and of the continuation of his scholarly activity there has recently been welcome evidence in the sumptuous first volume of the catalogue of the Gulbenkian collection of Greek coins.

In the Birthday Honours list an O.B.E. was awarded to Mr. L. V. Grinsell whom the University of Bristol has also honoured with an honorary M.A.

At our meeting in May Robert Carson was presented with the medal of the Cabinet des Médailles, Luxembourg; this will be followed by the presentation of our own medal this evening. We congratulate Michael Dolley on his appointment in March as senior Vice-President of the Royal Irish Academy, and W. A. Seaby on an honorary degree from the Queen's University, Belfast.

We have also noted with pleasure the appointment of our last President, Derek Allen, as a Trustee of the British Museum. It must be unusual—and perhaps also salutary—for a former member of the staff to return to the museum in this high capacity. And lastly, a year ago the Society added the name of Philip Whitting to the roll of its Honorary Fellows.

This year there are also several numismatic appointments to record. At Birmingham Michael Hendy has been appointed as the first holder of a new lecturership in the Department of Fine Art, where he will be in charge of the Whitting and Haines collections in the Barber Institute, and responsible for numismatic teaching in the university. To the post in the Fitzwilliam Museum, Cambridge, vacated by M. Hendy, our Fellow, T. R. Volk, has been appointed. Finally, I should note that the post in the Ashmolean, vacant since the death of J. D. A. Thompson in September 1970, has been filled by N. Mayhew since last August.

I turn to the affairs of our Society. This year for the first time the *Numismatic Chronicle* has appeared in an enlarged format, which provides more space for both print and illustration. *The Inventory of British Coin Hoards after 1500* by Mr. Brown and Mr. Dolley, published in conjunction with Messrs. Spink, has now appeared, and R. T. Williams, *The Silver Coinage of the Phokians* is on the point of appearing, and a pre-publication offer has been circulated. Finally, the *Proceedings of the Symposium on Methods of Coin Analysis* is scheduled for publication on 29 September. Thus by the autumn our present programme of Special Publications will be complete. Our financial advisers appear confident that it can be paid for but there is not much margin, especially in an inflationary period like the present. It will be some time before our reserves are re-established from sales, so that we can again contemplate a volume of publication greater than that of the annual *Chronicle*.

In such a period of financial stringency it is particularly welcome to be able to record the receipt of a bequest to the Society of around £800 from Miss D. Stockwell. Council has not yet decided to what use this bequest should be put. It occurs to me that in about 130 years of its existence the Society has succeeded in attracting surprisingly few benefactions which could be used to support numismatic research or publication. It would, I think, be a fine thing if we were able to found an annual scholarship which would enable a numismatist from abroad to spend, say, two months in London or Oxford or Cambridge in the close company of groups of scholars working in the same field. For many who are isolated in their museums or universities this would be a valuable opportunity to share ideas and to be in contact with the most recent research.

For some months past your officers have been involved in examining the resources of the Society in relation to present price trends and future publishing policy. The current subscription has remained at 4 guineas since 1959, that is thirteen years, and increasing costs have hitherto been offset by the steady rise in the number of Fellows; it seems unlikely that this can save us much longer. One alternative would be to raise subscriptions to, say £6 or £6·50; in a Society in which much of the administrative work is performed by unpaid officers, frequent changes in the rate of subscriptions must be avoided. Another alternative which has been suggested, but which some Fellows find objectionable, is to make the subscription not £6 payable by a Fellow, but £6 receivable by the Society. This would enable a Fellow who was prepared to sign a seven-year covenant to pay approximately the present subscription, the difference being made up by recoverable tax. Indeed, this matter of covenants lies at the root of the problem. If we could overcome the reluctance of Fellows to sign covenants our problems would disappear at least for the time being. In fact, out of about 350 Fellows resident in the British Isles, only about seventy have been persuaded to sign covenants, an act which costs *them* nothing, but provides the Society with substantial extra income.

I realize of course that Fellows who, like myself, can claim their subscriptions as professional expenses against income tax, would be asked to pay more, but this is going to happen to them whatever change is made, but part of their increase will in any case continue to be set against their tax liability. Needless to say I myself, or any officer of the Society, will welcome the views of any Fellows before next October, when a firm proposal for increasing the Society's income from January 1973 will have to be formulated.

Another matter which is currently under discussion is a proposal formulated by Dr. Price that the Society should sponsor a new periodical to be devoted to hoards and to recording year by year supplements to the standard bibliographies. It is arguable that the technical apparatus of our subject is not yet up to the standard normally expected by epigraphists, for example, and that here is an opportunity to make a further useful contribution to the study of coinage. The principal difficulty is financial, and Dr. Price is exploring the possibility of co-operation with another society. There are also problems of demarcation, as, for example, with *Numismatic Literature*, since it is important to avoid duplication. But we hope that these difficulties can be circumvented, and that some viable scheme will be produced.

This is also the occasion to record on your behalf thanks to your executive officers—the Treasurer, the Secretaries, the Librarian, and the Editor. They are the people who do all the real work, and without their efforts our Society would have no effective existence.

Finally I come to our annual sherry party to be held once again after this meeting for the third successive year. Hitherto the Fellow who has made it possible has asked to remain anonymous, but this year I am permitted to reveal his name—it is Mr. Norman Davis of Seattle. He has, however, imposed one not very onerous condition, that we should drink his health in the phrase 'To Norman Davis, wherever he may be'. When originally formulated, this phrase was intended to refer to the uncertain prospects of

Mr. Davis after his ultimate decease, but as he is still very much alive and frequently on the move the phrase seems appropriate today as well. Once again I will end by thanking Miss Archibald and her helpers for arranging this party.

ADDRESS

THE HEBERDEN COIN ROOM IN THE ASHMOLEAN MUSEUM, OXFORD

It will have escaped no one in this room that we are this year celebrating the fiftieth anniversary of what is perhaps the greatest archaeological discovery of all time, that of the unplundered tomb of Tutankhamen, of which the first step was laid bare on 4 November 1922. Some ten days earlier, on 24 October, about one hundred persons, headed by the Vice-Chancellor of the University, had assembled in Oxford at the Ashmolean Museum; in the company were a number of numismatists, whose names are still remembered today—Arthur Evans, G. F. Hill, Ernst Babelon, Théodore Reinach, and George Macdonald. The occasion was the public opening of the university's newly constituted Coin Room. For Evans it was a moment of personal triumph, for the unification under a single roof of Oxford's numismatic and archaeological resources was something for which he had striven for nearly forty years. In his address on that day he said 'it would not be human—it would not certainly be honest— if I did not confess to a special personal satisfaction . . . at the opening of the Coin Room in the Ashmolean Museum. It is in fact the realization of a pro- ject for which I have contended from the very beginning of my actual Keeper- ship in 1884, and was embodied in my Report in 1885 to the Visitors (1884– 1922). Why had it all taken so long?

I cannot this evening attempt to unfold the history of the Oxford collection; I must restrict myself to the circumstances of the foundation of the Coin Room in the Ashmolean in 1922, but in order to do this something must be said of the state of the numismatic collections of the university before Evans's appointment as Keeper in 1884. At that time the Ashmolean was not the building we know by that name today; it was still the old Ashmolean building in Broad Street, erected to receive Ashmole's original gift in 1683, but by the 1880s the collections had been partly dispersed and in particular the coins and medals had been sent in 1858 to join the main university collection in the Bodleian Library. This collection was large and varied, but was by no means easy to consult. The material was classified not by the series to which it belonged but according to the donor, and for reasons of security, as Evans said, 'The Bodleian statutes regarding the Coin room have . . . been rendered so stringent that they have made it practically inaccessible to students' (Evans, 1885, p. 10). One rather obscure and inhibiting rule reads '4. No person except the librarian and sub-librarians may handle one of the coins or medals when comparing it with a specimen not belonging to the University'

(Draft statute 18 March 1886). Apart from the main university collection in the Bodleian, further collections, some of considerable size, were to be found in a number of the colleges. Archaeological material was similarly dispersed throughout the university.

Soon after his appointment Evans prepared a comprehensive scheme for rationalizing the university's collections: the Ashmolean would surrender various anthropological collections and would receive in return archaeological material which had ended up elsewhere probably 'by the simple process of mis-direction'. It was an essential part of his scheme that the coins and medals should be transferred from the Bodleian to the Ashmolean: 'the juxta-position of the Numismatic Collections with our other antiquities is of vital importance for the sound study of Archaeology in the University' (1885, p. 9). So far as the archaeological collections were concerned Evans was wholly successful. Since the cramped site of the Old Ashmolean building could not provide the additional accommodation required, new rooms were built on to the existing university galleries, and in 1894 the Ashmolean Museum was transferred to the new site, where it has remained ever since. But over the coins Evans met with strong opposition; Bodley's Librarian (E. W. B. Nicholson) and the Curators refused to surrender their charge, though they did eventually offer to restore to the Ashmolean its own collection, which had been transferred to the Bodleian in 1858; but 'it did not require the wisdom of Solomon to persuade the Visitors to reject the proposed vivisection', as Evans tartly remarks (Opening Address 1922). When Evans resigned the Keepership of the Ashmolean at the end of 1908, to be succeeded by D. G. Hogarth, the coins were still in the Bodleian.

The climate of opinion, however, was changing and the Ashmolean was beginning to be seen as the right home for numismatic material; in 1907 New College had deposited there its large collection on loan and H. de la Garde Grisell had bequeathed to the Ashmolean his fine series of papal coins; and by 1912 the Curators of the Bodleian were believed to look favourably upon the idea of transferring the university collection.

In October 1912 the Visitors appointed a subcommittee to examine the whole problem of creating a coin room equipped to receive the Bodleian collection; it consisted of Evans, Macan, Master of University College, Gardner, Professor of Classical Archaeology, Madan, Bodley's Librarian, and Hogarth, the Keeper of the Ashmolean. The problem was that the strong room of the Ashmolean was thought to be too small to accommodate the Bodleian cabinets, and a new coin room would therefore have to be constructed; this would, of course, cost money. The committee wasted no time, for by the end of 1912 their plans and estimates had been prepared:

> for building coin room and consequential alterations    £1,300
> exhibition cases and books                              600
> curator                                                 200–300 p.a.

It is interesting to note that it was already envisaged that 'ultimately the Curator of Coins might well give instruction in some branches of numismatics'; the idea that the Coin Room should be a teaching department thus has a very respectable antiquity. But of course the *sine qua non* was the £1,300 for the construction of the room itself.

On the basis of the subcommittee's report Hogarth next approached the Curators of the Bodleian, who in January 1913 resolved that they 'would be prepared to transfer the coins, medals and similar objects now in the Bodleian, to the Ashmolean Museum as a loan' providing certain reasonable conditions about security and responsibility were fulfilled. The Hebdomadal Council proved sympathetic, but the Curators of the University Chest declared that they had no money available. On 4 March 1913 Bodley's Librarian wrote to Hogarth 'Now what is to be done? Sir Arthur Evans? Oxford University Endowment Fund? Will any College contribute a Fellowship for the Lecturer in Numismatics? Can the capital sum be borrowed as a loan? Anything's better than nothing!'

In October 1913 the Visitors again applied to the university for funds, but received the same reply; they tried again early in 1914 with the same result. In March Hogarth felt that if he could raise part of this sum from college contributions, the university might be forced or shamed into providing the rest; he wrote to the President of Magdalen, 'the matter is an absolute *impasse* ... and this great collection, which ought to be one of the assets of the University, remains practically useless'. The President's reply is not on the file, but since Hogarth was a Fellow of the college it was probably given verbally.

The outbreak of war in 1914 inevitably blocked all schemes involving fresh expenditure but even during the war years Evans remained optimistic. In 1916 when sending to the Ashmolean some contemporary war medals, including that for the 'Jutland Bank Victory', he hoped that some progress could soon be reported, and wrote 'this is a matter of permanent importance to historic studies and should not be affected by temporary conditions due to the war'.

Immediately after the war the question of the transference of the Bodleian coins was revived with vigour. In order to circumvent the financial impasse Hogarth was now able to discover 'by careful measurements' that the Bodleian collection could in fact just be accommodated in the existing strong room of the Ashmolean and was therefore prepared to accept custody of it at once. To win support in the university for the transfer the Professor of Classical Archaeology (Percy Gardner) circulated a resounding memorandum on the value of coins as a source of history: 'unlike the writings of historians, they cannot misinform us; they constitute a very bedrock of fact. Historic statements which they contradict cannot stand; historic statements which they confirm are placed in an unassailable position.' Thus armed, Hogarth tried to elicit from the Curators of the Bodleian approval for an immediate transfer.

Bodley's Librarian (now A. Cowley) expected to secure the necessary approval without difficulty, but there was opposition from an unexpected quarter—a numismatist! Charles Oman, without apparently fully understanding the prevailing conditions, argued that whereas there was always someone available in the Bodleian to show coins to accredited students, the same would not be true in the Ashmolean. On these grounds he persuaded the Curators to reiterate their conditions of 1913, which, strictly interpreted, implied that the transfer could not be approved until both a secure room *and* a specialist curator had been provided in the Ashmolean.

Cowley thought that he had been let down by his Curators and expressed his feelings in a letter to Hogarth (1 December 1919): 'it's hopeless to try to get anything done in this place—tho' one only wants what is best for one's institution'. Evans's reaction was more forceful, for he wrote to Hogarth on 9 December 1919 a long letter which was intended to produce results: not only are there several typescript copies of his not very easily legible autograph letter still on the file, but he also ended with a postscript saying 'I do not mind your showing any part of this letter to any discreet persons concerned with these matters'. After expressing his irritation over a project which had dragged on for more than twenty years, he delivered an open threat in his last paragraph, and declared in a phrase which has since become classic that his patience was at an end:

> 'Personally, I am sick of these delays. You know that I am in a position to further the development of the Coin Collections in a very considerable degree, but, for over twenty years, I have been thwarted by a state of opinion on these matters existing among those who control University affairs, which is impervious to the place which Numismatics should occupy in Historical research. This indeed is not surprising in an University which has no Ancient History School and leaves to side tracks of its curriculum some of the most important ages of history, such as those of Alexander and Constantine. But my own personal patience is at an end, and I have taken sure measures that further delays on the part of the University in properly housing its Coin Collections and in putting the Numismatic science on its proper footing shall result in the diversion of anything that I have to contribute to quarters where it will be of greater usefulness.'

After this events moved relatively fast. Hogarth again wrote to the Hebdomadal Council on 9 December 1919 pressing the case for the transfer of the coins: 'the comparison of the equipment of the University of Cambridge in Numismatics is at present, and must remain till the Bodleian Coin question is settled, very unfavourable to Oxford'. Council after considering his letter on 19 January 1920 set up a committee to examine the question once again. Early in March the committee invited three representatives of the Visitors (Evans, Gardner, and Hogarth) to join their deliberations, and finally on

8 June 1920 a Decree in Congregation was passed authorizing the transfer to the Ashmolean. The decree was quickly acted on, and in October the Keeper of the Ashmolean could report to the Visitors that the university collection, to the number of about 65,300 pieces, was now 'stacked' in the Ashmolean strong room. The important word here was 'stacked', which as Hogarth explained did not imply convenient access: 'accredited students can only see coins on giving long notice to the Keeper, who must extract from the cabinets specimens, particularly designated, and bring them to his private office. The Honorary Curator . . . will have to work upon single trays carried to and from a distant room' (Hogarth to Vice Chancellor, 22 January 1921).

The provision of a secure coin room was now urgent, and on 21 October 1920 the Visitors passed a resolution urging upon the Hebdomadal Council 'the necessity of the provision of a properly protected Coin Room', and asking them to take steps to procure the necessary funds; at the same time they reminded Council that as long ago as 1917 it had agreed to raise such funds after the war. At the same meeting Dr. F. P. Barnard was invited to act as Honorary Deputy Curator of Coins—'honorary' because the post was unpaid, and 'deputy' because responsibility for custody remained with the Keeper of the Ashmolean. In transmitting this invitation to Barnard Hogarth was able to mention 'a distinct hope of funds being found'.

The above meeting of the Visitors was the first to be chaired by the new Vice-Chancellor, L. R. Farnell, Rector of Exeter College, to whose beneficent interest the eventual realization of the Coin Room was largely due; of him Evans was to say at the opening ceremony two years later, 'no man has a clearer conception of the intimate bearing of numismatic science on our central studies, and of the light they throw on ancient art and religion, as well as on general history and economics'. Early in the new year (on 22 January) Farnell obtained from Hogarth a statement of his requirements in which he estimated that some £1,500 would suffice for the basic work: this statement was then forwarded by the Visitors to the Council for onward transmission to the Oxford University Endowment Fund.

It was not until 2 May that the trustees of the fund were able to inform Hogarth that they had decided 'to make a grant of £1,500 for the provision of Cabinets for the Ashmolean Collection of Coins'. Hogarth acknowledged their grant 'with great joy and much appreciation', but he did not fail to point out that, since he had cabinets in plenty, what he wanted was a *room* to put them in. Though this little difficulty was easily overcome by the adoption of the equivocal phrase 'the provision of new accommodation for the coins', further inquiry elicited that the trustees did not have the whole sum immediately available, that its full payment would be 'a case of years rather than months'. Nevertheless, on the strength of the trustees' assurance, Hogarth was able to negotiate a loan of £1,500 from the University Chest repayable over ten years.

Satisfaction at this grant of £1,500 was not unanimous. Evans argued strongly before the Visitors (5 May 1921) that in 1919 a committee had found that £4,000 was the minimum required for the establishment of a coin room (including structural alterations, exhibiting cases, and library), and that the whole operation was 'one and indivisible'. Hogarth, on the other hand, felt that it was expedient to take what was offered and proceed with the construction of the room, in the hope that provision for equipment would follow. In the upshot, as will appear, his faith was justified, but Evans remained convinced that it was a tactical mistake to accept part instead of the whole. The next day he wrote furiously to Hogarth, 'the truth is that the idea that numismatics forms an integral part of historical research, so strongly felt by mere Germans, like Mommsen, is foreign to our lecturers here. It is almost unimaginable, but it is true!'

Nothing further of importance happened until Hogarth received a letter from the Vice-Chancellor dated 1 July; it is short and deserves to be quoted in full.

'My dear Hogarth,

As a sum of £1000, free of legacy duty, has been left by the late Dr. Heberden to the Vice-Chancellor of the time being, to devote to any University purpose that he thinks fit, I hereby inform you that I have finally decided to devote the sum to the further equipment of the new Coin-Room in the Ashmolean Museum; and you can act on this assurance.

Yours very sincerely,
L. R. Farnell
Vice-Chancellor'

Charles Buller Heberden was a classical scholar who had been Principal of Brasenose since 1889, and who had recently died on 30 May 1921. It is worth noticing at this point the close connection which has existed between B.N.C. and the Ashmolean. Ashmole himself was a Brasenose man, and the college has long maintained a benevolent interest both in the museum named after Ashmole and in the Coin Room which bears the name of one of its Principals. Since 1931 this interest has taken the very practical form of an annual grant to the Coin Room from trust funds at the disposal of the college.

Hogarth now had at least the promise of the funds he needed—£1,500 for structural alterations and £1,000 for exhibition cases and other furnishings—and the work could now be put in hand; the alterations were in fact completed well before the end of 1921. At this point Hogarth applied to the Chest for the promised loan of £1,500; the Chest in reply agreed to pay over the money before the end of the year, but cunningly said they would pay only £1,350, that is £1,500 less £150, as the first instalment of the repayment. But Hogarth protested that the figure was £1,500, and £1,500 he must have, no repayment being due until a year hence. In the face of this show of strength the Chest climbed down.

By 24 October 1922, when the Coin Room was formally opened, the coin collections were installed in their new premises, the foundation of a numismatic library had been laid, valuably supplemented by the loan of a number of books and periodicals from the Bodleian, and fifteen out of the eighteen show-cases, provided from the Heberden bequest, had been filled. The range of the display and the number of people involved in its preparation is of some interest:

English coins (including Ancient British): 3 cases;

Greek coins: 2 cases, selected by Professor Gardner 'from our somewhat meagre collections of Ancient Greek coins'. That adjective could no longer today be used of the Ashmolean's Greek collection.

Greek Imperial of Asia Minor: 1 case, nearly all 'a gift from Mr. J. G. Milne to whom the University is already indebted for numerous benefactions'; this beneficence was to be maintained until his death twenty-nine years later, and is indeed still active today through the terms of his will.

Roman: 3 cases, selected by the Revd. E. A. Sydenham.

Chinese: 1 case, selected by the Assistant Keeper, E. T. Leeds, who had spent his youth in the Chinese customs service at Shanghai, and who later devoted the years of his retirement to arranging Oxford's vast collection of Chinese coins.

Italian Medals: 1 case, for which the Keeper of Fine Art, C. F. Bell, had helped to select the exhibits.

Special Medals: 1 case, which included those presented to Elias Ashmole, and two splendid Naval Medals of 1653, one of which had been presented to Admiral Blake; these last had been deposited on loan by Wadham College and are still in the museum.

Three cases remained unfilled, one destined for Indian coins, and two for European.

Looking back over this saga, it is clear that though the original policy of uniting the university's coin collections with the other archaeological material was due to Evans, its ultimate realization was achieved by Hogarth through the powerful support of the Vice-Chancellor, Farnell. The chief delaying factors had been first the opposition of Bodley's Librarian, and then the restriction on all developments necessarily imposed by the war of 1914–18.

# PROCEEDINGS OF THE
# ROYAL NUMISMATIC SOCIETY
## SESSION 1971-72

### SPECIAL GENERAL MEETING

#### 19 October 1971

DR. COLIN M. KRAAY, President, in the Chair.

In the Treasurer's absence, the President presented the audited accounts for the year ended 31 December 1970. The accounts were approved, *nem. con.*

### ORDINARY MEETING

#### 19 October 1971

DR. COLIN M. KRAAY, President, in the Chair.

The minutes of the May meeting were approved and signed.

The names of the following were read for the first time: Mr. R. H. J. Ashton, Mr. W. L. S. Barrett, Mr. R. J. Box, Mr. B. B. Braun, Mr. G. Brosi, Mr. A. Campana, Mr. E. K. Coleman, Mr. R. Dalton, Mr. P. D. Done, Mr. S. Glasby-Baldwin, Mr. P. J. Isaac, Mr. D. G. Kilgore, Jr., Mr. F. L. Kovacs, Dr. E. Leuthold, Dr. P. M. Lewis, Mrs. G. D. R. McQuade, Mr. E. H. Mair, Mr. J. C. St. A. Malcolm, Mr. C. Martin, Mr. R. L. Mitchels, Mr. W. A. Oddy, Mr. C. D. Rivett, Mr. T. R. G. Sear, Mr. C. C. Sirr, Mr. R. B. Smith, Mr. P. R. Thompson, Mr. W. A. R. Tonkin, Mr. I. Vecchi, Mr. C. M. Webdale, Mr. J. L. Welborn III.

The following were elected into the Society: Mr. B. Altman, Barber Institute of Fine Arts, Mr. C. Narbeth, Mr. C. B. Theodotou.

Mr. D. L. F. Sealy exhibited on behalf of Mr. William George an Edward III half-noble of the Treaty Period (transitional series). The coin, which weighs 3·83 gm. (59·1 gr.), was an isolated find made in February 1971 on the beach at Wrabness, Stour Estuary, Essex.

The President, in presenting the Society's medal to Dr. H. A. Cahn, said:

'Our usual custom is to present the Society's medal at our Annual General Meeting in June, but when this year Dr. Cahn was unable to be present on that date I declined to perform the usual charade of presenting the medal by proxy in the hope that he could soon be among us in person. That hope is fulfilled today. But before I present the medal, I should like to state the grounds upon which Council decided to award it to Dr. Cahn this year.

First was the long series of published works culminating, but not, we hope, terminating, in his great study of the coinage of Cnidus in which he has skilfully woven the numismatic strands into the artistic pattern of the period as a whole. Second is the help he has always so readily provided to any serious student of numismatics, whether young or old. And third is his activity in spreading the understanding of our science through his courses in the University of Heidelberg; these courses are already yielding valuable results through theses devoted to topics of central importance in Greek numismatics.

Dr. Cahn, it gives me very special pleasure to be able to present the first medal of my presidency to one whose friendship over many years has survived a whole series of major numismatic disagreements.'

Dr. Cahn replied:

'I am happy that it has proved possible to receive the medal in person and express to you, to the Secretary and to the Fellows the deep gratitude I feel towards the Society. The letter from Mr. Carson announcing that I was chosen as Medallist of this year came as a great surprise. To belong to the circle of those students honoured by receiving the medal of the Royal Numismatic Society is certainly a challenge, both to continue work and to duplicate efforts.

It was Leonard Forrer senior—he himself medallist in 1944, and the second Swiss since Imhoof-Blumer (1888)—who suggested to me in 1935 to apply for Fellowship. I owed him much fatherly advice as scholar and as coin dealer; he also was a close friend to those who first introduced me to the world of coins: my mother, Johanna Cahn, my uncle, Dr. Julius Cahn, his wife Emmy—whom you all knew at Seaby's—and Heinrich Hirsch, the senior director of Otto Helbing Nachfolger in Munich. The leading spirits of your society in those days were scholars considered as giants in the whole numismatic realm, such as Arthur Evans, G. F. Hill, George MacDonald, Harold Mattingly, Stanley Robinson, and Charles Seltman.

Looking now at the List of Fellows of 1970, I realize that I already belong to the old guard: of 754 fellows, according to the state on December 31st 1969, 24 only, including myself, were elected before 1940!

However, I still feel I am "nel mezzo del cammin" and hope to continue to contribute to numismatics, as coin dealer, as teacher, and as student, my main goal being the study of ancient coins as works of art and their integration into the pattern of art history.

I take the opportunity to express my thanks to those three English numismatic institutions who in an outstanding and exemplary way open their doors to all serious students seeking advice, help, and collaboration. I mean, of course, the British Museum, the Ashmolean, and the Fitzwilliam. Innumerable services have been and are provided by these institutions to all numismatists in the world. Let me add to these thanks, again, my heartfelt gratitude for the honour conferred upon me.'

Mr. W. A. Seaby gave a talk entitled 'A comparison of the Irish Long-cross elements in the Brussels and Colchester hoards'.

This was illustrated with tables and histograms showing the differences of the two moneyers, Davi and Ricard, by percentages in the numbers of coins of each, the comparative weights of early and late groups, the pattern of combinations, and other data. There were also slides showing both authentic coins and contemporary counterfeits from the two hoards. The most remarkable feature of the comparison was the closeness in all major groupings from each deposit—often less than 1 per cent and rarely more than 5 per cent. Only in the proportions of early and late coins of Davi at Colchester, in contrast to Brussels, was there a difference of more than 10 per cent; and several reasons were put forward for this disparity, which showed a higher percentage of specimens and on average a somewhat heavier weight per coin in the early group than the late group at the East Anglian town.

Since the main bulk of the Colchester hoard had been laid down not later than early autumn 1256, average weight-loss per coin, attributable to general wear, was almost exactly what might be expected if the coins had been struck as 22·5 gr., so that culling and clipping could be regarded as negligible. The Brussels coins exhibited an average weight-loss assignable to a further four or five years of general circulation before incarceration; and it was suggested that most of the pieces in the hoard had probably found their way to the Continent and to this particular region as part of the largesse which Richard of Cornwall bestowed on church potentates and princelings in support of his claim to the Holy Roman Empire during his earlier campaigns. The speaker demonstrated how the much higher percentage of counterfeits at Brussels (5·5 per cent of all 'Irish' coins as against 1 per cent at Colchester) was due to the manufacture of some quantities on the Continent, mostly, it was thought, in the Brabant region itself.

ORDINARY MEETING

*16 November 1971*

Dr. Colin M. Kraay, President, in the Chair.

The minutes of the October meeting were approved and signed.

The name of the following institution was read for the first time: The London Numismatic Club.

The following were elected into the Society: Mr. R. H. J. Ashton, Mr. W. L. S. Barrett, Mr. R. J. Box, Mr. B. B. Braun, Mr. G. Brosi, Mr. A. Campana, Mr. E. K. Coleman, Mr. R. Dalton, Mr. P. C. Done, Mr. S. Glasby-Baldwin, Mr. P. J. Isaac, Mr. D. G. Kilgore, Jr., Mr. F. L. Kovacs, Mr. E. Leuthold, Dr. P. M. Lewis, Mrs. G. D. R. McQuade, Mr. E. H. Mair, Mr. J. D. St. A. Malcolm, Mr. C. Martin, Mr. R. L. Mitchels, Mr. W. A. Oddy, Mr. C. D. Rivett, Mr. T. R. G. Sear, Mr. C. C. Sirr, Mr. R. B. Smith, Mr. P. R. Thompson, Mr. W. A. R. Tonkin, Mr. I. Vecchi, Mr. C. M. Webdale, Mr. John L. Welborn III.

Dr. A. D. H. Bivar read a paper on 'The Heads of Ishtar: some problems, real and imaginary, in the currency of ancient Mesopotamia'.

Certain of the early Assyriologists had drawn attention to the occurrence of phrases in cuneiform tablets which seemed to imply the existence of forms of currency of accurately regulated weight and bearing an official stamp, in particular passages cited by Johns describing payments in 'Heads of Ishtar'.

These interpretations had not been confirmed by material finds, and it seemed more likely that 'Heads of Ishtar' was an abstract term relating to capital funds.

There was, however, considerable evidence for the existence of a currency of silver ingots, and the terms 'cake-ingots', 'slab-ingots', 'bar-ingots', 'cut-silver', and and 'ring-money' were appropriate to different varieties. The first clearly attested find of 'bar-ingots' was provided by the British Institute of Persian Studies' excavations at Nush-I Jan, near Malayir in Iran, and included several large pieces marginally over 100 gm. in weight.

The lecturer suggested that these pre-Achaemenid 'bar-ingots' may have been ancestral to some of the Indian 'bent-bar' currency. He illustrated groups of straight and bent-bars in the Mir Zakah residue of the Kabul museum, one weighing exactly 8·34 gm., the standard of the Achaemenid (Babylonian) shekel. If some of the cut silver were adjusted to exact weights, studies by means of the frequency table would help to elucidate the standard.

ORDINARY MEETING

*21 December 1971*

DR. COLIN M. KRAAY, President, in the Chair.

The minutes of the November meeting were approved and signed.

The following names were read for the first time: Professor K. Enoki, Mr. H. J. M. Good, Mr. R. C. Grossman, Mr. Gene Hessler, State Museum, Lucknow, Mr. J. D. Parry, Mr. D. F. Payne.

The following institution was elected into the Society: The London Numismatic Club.

Dr. J. R. Melville Jones read a paper on 'Ancient coins in the Delian Inscriptions'. More than eighty inscriptions from Delos, of the fourth to the second centuries B.C., contain references to coins deposited in the island's temples, as votive offerings or deposits of capital. These holdings were carefully recorded (except for bronze, which was usually treated only as metal by weight) and described with precision and economy. There are a few problems of identification: 'Cretan staters' will refer to the pseudo-Aeginetan issues, and 'Arbulic Obols' were probably coins of Argos, while Ptolemaic *tettigia* may have been *tetarta*, gold quarter-staters. The various coins with names ending in -phoros need to be considered as a group, and their is room for conjecture about some of the denominations listed, which are not those which we usually consider to have been in use.

ORDINARY MEETING

*18 January 1972*

MR. C. E. BLUNT, Vice-President, in the Chair.

The minutes of the December meeting were approved and signed.

The following name was read for the first time: The Revd. G. Watkins Grubb.

The following were elected into the Society: Professor K. Enoki, Mr. H. M. Good, Mr. R. C. Grossman, Mr. G. Hessler, Lucknow State Museum, Mr. J. D. Parry, Mr. D. F. Payne.

The Vice-President announced that a knighthood had been awarded to the Society's Hon. Vice-President, Dr. E. S. G. Robinson. The Society's congratulations would be sent to Sir Edward by the President.

The death of the Society's Hon. Fellow, Professor Dr. Eduard Holzmair, formerly Director of the Vienna Cabinet, was announced.

Mr. H. Gordon Slade exhibited an unworn dupondius of Nero found in the mortar of a wall at Wroxeter which has generally been accepted as Hadrianic in date.

Miss D. E. Shackleton and Mr. J. D. Brand were appointed to act as Hon. Auditors of the Society's accounts for the year ended 31 December 1971.

Dr. M. J. Price read a paper on 'The Survival of wall paintings and reliefs on Greek coins of the Roman period'. He inspected the criteria which have led scholars to suggest that some coin types owe inspiration to monumental paintings and reliefs. There is a definite closeness of technique between the three media; and with many coin types well suited to monumental treatment, the idea may be considered seriously. However, no individual example can be proved without a painting, relief, or detailed literary description for comparison.

ORDINARY MEETING

*15 February 1972*

DR. COLIN M. KRAAY, President, in the Chair.

The minutes of the January meeting were approved and signed.

The following names were read for the first time: Mr. C. G. E. Alterskye, Dr. J. F. G. Bynon, Mr. P. Degraaf, Mr. P. E. Flanagan, Mr. D. J. M. Ford, Mr. S. A. Hargovinddas, Mr. J. F. Pritchard, Mr. Stewart Taylor.

The following was elected into the Society: The Revd. G. Watkins Grubb.

Mr. R. A. G. Carson read a paper on 'The campaigns of Septimius Severus in Britain, A.D. 208–211'. He related the coinage issues of these years to the evidence of contemporary historians and archaeology to demonstrate what a close and detailed commentary on the campaigns of these years is provided by the coinage.

ORDINARY MEETING

*21 March 1972*

DR. COLIN M. KRAAY, President, in the Chair.

The minutes of the February meeting were approved and signed.

The following names were read for the first time: Mrs. L. B. Beer, Mr. T. V. Buttrey, Mr. R. D. Coon, Dr. A. S. De Shazo, Mr. N. Fairhead, Mr. W. A. D. Freeman, Mr. P. J. Goddard, Mr. M. A. Guilding, Mr. C. A. Kirkpatrick, Mr. F. L. Morgan.

The following were elected into the Society: Mr. C. G. E. Alterskye, Dr. J. F. G. Bynon, Mr. P. Degraaf, Mr. P. E. Flanagan, Mr. D. J. M. Ford, Mr. J. F. Pritchard, Mr. A. H. Sanghvi, Mr. F. S. Taylor.

The appointment of Miss D. E. Shackleton and Mr. J. D. Brand as auditors of the Society's accounts for the year ended 31 December 1971 was confirmed.

Mr. G. C. Boon read a paper on 'Some facts and thoughts on local coining in Roman Britain', concentrating on the Claudian, Severan, 'radiate', and 'falling horseman' epidemics with reference to continental material. The decline in size and weight was due to progressive use of counterfeits as prototypes, and barbarity was not a chronological factor and did not affect acceptability. Diminution was relatively similar in all the epidemics, a parallel thread in which, no doubt, was scarcity of orthodox small-change, whether brought on by inadequacy of official mintage, inflation, or demonetization. Only the Carausian series seemed distinct, and judging by its high proportion of overstrikes (which did not add to the volume of coin in circulation), may have been officially inspired; if so, centrally, thus accounting for die-links in widely distant hoards. In the radiate series it was suggested that since orthodox Gallic and Reform antoniniani were cut into quarters to make minims in one Somerset group, the originals were (*a*) of the same worth and (*b*) not worth more than 4 minims. Several suggestions for further research were made, e.g. in correlating follis moulds with variations in the value of the coin adduced by the Aphrodisias edict and metallurgical studies.

ORDINARY MEETING

*18 April 1972*

Dr. Colin M. Kraay, President, in the Chair.

The minutes of the March meeting were approved and signed.

The following names were read for the first time: Mr. D. P. Chandaria, Mr. D. P. Hogan, Centro Internazionale di Studi Numismatici, Naples.

The following were elected into the Society: Mrs. L. B. Beer, Mr. T. V. Buttrey, Mr. R. D. Coon, Dr. A. S. De Shazo, Mr. N. Fairhead, Mr. W. A. D. Freeman, Mr. P. J. Goddard, Mr. M. A. Guilding, Mr. C. A. Kirkpatrick, Mr. F. L. Morgan.

Mr. D. F. Allen exhibited the sketch book of Thomas Simon, which he had published in the Journal of the Walpole Society, vol. xxvii (1938–9) together with a copy of George Vertue's book on Thomas Simon, into which had been bound the original warrants authorizing him to make various seals and coins. These documents were published in the *British Numismatic Journal*, vol. xxiii (1938–42), and are the property of the Raymond-Barker family, who have kindly made them available for exhibition.

Miss G. van der Meer read a paper on 'Medallic relations between England and the Netherlands'. She had selected a number of medals relating to British history, made by Dutch artists, ranging from the beginning of the sixteenth to the nineteenth century. With the help of these medals she illustrated the development of the various medal genres which flourished in the Netherlands during that period. Special attention was given to recently published and unpublished material. She discussed Renaissance portrait medals, 'triumphal' medals, repoussé work and engraved medals. The work of Jan Smeltzing was treated in some detail and it was suggested that too many unsigned satirical medals have been attributed to him. Finally, the work of the Holtzheys, father and son, was discussed, and the share which his assistant Küchler had in the engraving of the dies signed by the latter.

ORDINARY MEETING

*16 May 1972*

Mr. C. E. Blunt, Vice-President, in the Chair.

The minutes of the April Meeting were approved and signed.

The following names were read for the first time: Mr. J. E. Balchin, Dr. C. Boehringer, Mr. B. Warren Enzler, Mr. W. B. Ferguson, Mr. L. Ilisch, Mr. A. M. Neu, Dr. G. van der Meer, Mr. S. H. Sana, Mrs. J. Vecchi, Mr. P. Vecchi.

The following were elected into the Society: Mr. D. P. Chandaria, Mr. D. P. Hogan, Centro Internazionale di Studi Numismatici, Naples.

Mr. F. L. Kovacs was admitted into the Society.

The Vice-President announced that the Society's medal for 1972 would be awarded to Mr. R. A. G. Carson.

Mr. R. J. M. A. Weiller presented the medal of the Cabinet des Médailles, Luxembourg to Mr. R. A. G. Carson. Mr. Carson expressed his thanks for the honour paid to him.

Mr. R. J. M. A. Weiller read a paper on 'Roman coin circulation in Luxembourg'. During the first half of the first century B.C. Republican coins were not numerous, but the common Celtic coins were replaced by Roman issues after Caesar's Gallic war, i.e. after 51 B.C. Hoards concealed in the first to the mid third century are rare, but twenty hoards may be associated with the invasion of 275–6, which is marked by a destruction level in many local Roman sites including Trier. Of particular interest are two hoards of barbarous radiates. The first, from the Tetelberg, contains many die duplicates suggesting that the mint was nearby. The second, from a cave near Berdorf, included blanks and the remains of the bronze rod from which the blanks had been cut. In the fourth century the bronze issues of Trier predominate in the early period but are overtaken by those of Lyons and Arles under the house of Valentinian. The Trier siliquae, well known from British hoards, are surprisingly uncommon in Luxembourg. Theodosian issues are common, again predominantly of the Trier mint; the latest are datable to A.D. 402. Finds of gold coins are infrequent, but have included the Moselle hoard of 1958 which contained about 100 solidi and multiples of the Valentinian period.

## ANNUAL GENERAL MEETING

### 20 June 1972

DR. COLIN M. KRAAY, President, in the Chair.

The minutes of the Annual General Meeting on 15 June 1971 were read and signed.

Dr. J. P. C. Kent and Dr. M. J. Price were appointed scrutineers of the ballot.

The names of the following were read for the first time: Mr. S. Album, Mr. A. Jarvis, Mr. C. J. Martin, Mr. R. H. Owen.

The following were elected into the Society: Mr. J. E. Balchin, Dr. C. Boehringer, Mr. B. Warren Enzler, Mr. W. B. Ferguson, Mr. L. Ilisch, Dr. G. van der Meer, Mr. A. M. Neu, Mr. S. H. Sana, Mrs. J. Vecchi, Mr. P. Vecchi.

The following report of Council was laid before the Society:

Council regrets to report the death of one Honorary Fellow, Professor Dr. Eduard Holzmair, and ten Ordinary Fellows:

| | |
|---|---|
| Dr. Tommaso Bertele | Signor Enrico Leuthold |
| Count Alexis Bobrinskoy | Signor Pietro Quaroni |
| Prof. Erich Boehringer | Dr. Walter Tauss |
| Mr. S. Brumby | Mr. Samuel Whetmore |
| Mr. Archibald Knowles | Mr. K. J. Wyness-Mitchell. |

Two Fellows have resigned:

The Revd. A. R. Bowers
Mr. D. Mangakis.

Thirty Fellows have been removed under by-law 15.

Council, however, is pleased to report the election of one Honorary Fellow and 71 Ordinary Fellows:

*Honorary Fellow*

Philip D. Whitting.

*Ordinary Fellows*

B. Altman
R. H. J. Ashton
W. L. S. Barrett
R. J. Box
B. B. Braun
G. Brosi
T. C. Cabot
A. Campana
B. J. Castenholz
J. H. Cohen
E. K. Coleman
R. Dalton
P. D. Done
C. M. Eyre
S. Glasby-Baldwin
E. A. Griffin
R. W. Higginbottom
W. A. Honour
R. Hudson
P. J. Isaac
J. D. Kean
D. G. Kilgore, Jr.
F. L. Kovacs
I. Lee
G. Y. Leng
E. Leuthold
A. S. Lewis
R. M. Lewis
R. Lobel
Mrs. G. D. R. McQuade
E. H. Mair
J. C. St. A. Malcolm
P. Marchetti
C. Martin
J. M. Mata
R. L. Mitchels

Mme C. Morrisson
K. Mulcahy
C. Narbeth
W. A. Oddy
E. Osband
A. J. Parker
R. J. Pesant
E. Pochitonov
G. S. Raivid
C. D. Rivett
K. H. Rosenberg
T. R. G. Sear
R. Senior
E. E. Sim
C. C. Sirr
R. H. Smith
M. Smookler
E. Szauer
W. Tauss
J. Taylor
C. B. Theodotou
D. R. Thompson
W. A. R. Tonkin
I. Vecchi
K. J. Veryard
Mrs. C. C. Vick
M. J. Walport
W. B. Warden, Jr.
C. M. Webdale
J. L. Welborn III
J. A. Williams
M. M. S. Zigler
Barber Institute of Fine Arts
London Numismatic Club
Quebec, Bishop's University
  Library

The state of the Society as at 31 December 1971 compared with 31 December 1970 is:

|  | Ordinary | | Honorary | | Total | |
|---|---|---|---|---|---|---|
| December 1970 | 785 | | 19 | | 804 | |
| Elected | 71 | 856 | 1 | 20 | 72 | 876 |
| Deceased | 10 | | 1 | | 11 | |
| Resigned | 2 | | | | 2 | |
| Removed | 30 | | | | 30 | |
| Transferred from | | | | | | |
| Ordinary to Honorary | 1 | 43 | — | 1 | 1 | 44 |
| | | 813 | | 19 | | 832 |

In the absence of Dr. MacDowall, Mr. Jenkins presented the Treasurer's report and the accounts for the year 1971 were approved (see below, pp. xxi–xxv).

The President in presenting the Society's medal to Mr. R. A. G. Carson said:

'For two years past our medal has been awarded to scholars from outside these islands. In surveying the home field it did not take Council long to light upon the name of Robert Carson. This evening I will not shirk my duties by taking refuge behind the well-worn formula that "he needs no introduction", for I think this is an occasion for repeating even what is well known.

'Robert Carson is a worthy successor of his former colleague and teacher, Harold Mattingly, and he has forwarded projects which Mattingly himself began: the *Roman Imperial Catalogue* of the British Museum, and *Roman Imperial Coinage* of which he has been an editor since 1949. With the growing size and complexity of each volume published this has been no sinecure. He has contributed, sometimes jointly with colleagues in the British Museum, enormously to our understanding of fourth-century Roman coinage, as, for example, in a long article of which the initial letters of the title—no doubt an involved joke in the devious minds of its authors—form the word CHAOS (Constantinian Hoards and Other Studies), though its effect is just the opposite. In his name alone there are to date at least forty articles, many of them publishing hoards or finds of high importance. He has also edited and contributed to volumes in honour of Harold Mattingly and Albert Baldwin. Finally he has produced a work of which the title is both brief and comprehensive—*Coins*, and which by an ingenious process of ternary fission has recently multiplied itself into three separate titles to feed the paperback market.

'In addition, Robert Carson as Secretary conducted our affairs for many years with meticulous efficiency, and still as Chief Editor produces the *Numismatic Chronicle* with a regularity which is disturbed barely perceptibly by power-cuts, postal strikes, printing disputes, and railway go-slows.

'This year we offer him our medal not as a silver hand-shake, but as a sign of our admiration and as an encouragement to achieve still more. He has already been honoured by the French Numismatic Society and by the Cabinet des Médailles of Luxembourg. If our recognition appears by comparison a trifle tardy, this will at least have the advantage for him that he must now have elaborated a formula for acceptance. I will end by hoping that he will have many occasions to use such a formula in the future.

'Robert Carson, I have much pleasure in presenting to you the medal of the Royal Numismatic Society.'

In accepting the medal Mr. Carson said:

'Mr. President and Fellows, this is indeed for me *dies lapide candidiore notanda* —a day to be marked with a white stone. I thank you, Mr. President, for the kind words you have addressed to me and I thank Council of the Society for according me the honour of the Society's medal.

'In the course of a good many years' association with the Society's affairs I have listened to, and in a good many cases subsequently edited, the words of those who have stood in this place on previous occasions. I find that I share the sentiment expressed by them all, a sense of being honoured above one's deserts; for, as our Society's medal was instituted in 1883, the roll of recipients represents a kind of history of numismatic endeavour and achievement. To be deemed worthy to be included in the company of men whose names have become household words in our study is a signal honour, especially for me as the list includes my two great predecessors in Roman numismatics in the British Museum, Harold Mattingly and Herbert Grueber.

'If I have been able to make some contribution to our subject, this is due to the good fortune that placed me in the Coin Room of the British Museum, with its solid tradition of Roman numismatic studies, its superlative collection and resources and, not least, the encouragement of and the stimulating if sometimes deflating discussion with colleagues both past and present.

'The Society has done me great honour. I trust that with such encouragement I shall in the years to come more amply merit this distinction.'

The President gave his review of the year and in his annual address he described the course of events which led up to the formal opening of the Heberden Coin Room in the Ashmolean Museum on 24 October 1922 (see above, pp. i–x).

The result of the ballot for officers and members of Council for the session 1972–3 was announced as follows:

*President*: COLIN M. KRAAY, M.A., D.PHIL., F.S.A.

*Hon. Vice-President*: SIR EDWARD ROBINSON, C.B.E., M.A., D.LITT., F.B.A., F.S.A.

*Vice-Presidents*:
C. H. V. SUTHERLAND, C.B.E., M.A., D.LITT., F.B.A., F.S.A.
C. E. BLUNT, O.B.E., F.B.A., F.S.A.

*Treasurer*: D. W. MACDOWALL, M.A., D.PHIL., F.S.A., F.R.A.S.

*Secretaries*:
MISS M. M. ARCHIBALD, M.A.
F. K. JENKINS, B.A.

*Foreign Secretary*: D. SELLWOOD, B.SC.(ENG.), C.ENG., M.I.MECH.E.

*Librarian*: N. M. LOWICK, B.A.

*Members of Council*:
G. C. BOON, B.A., F.S.A.
M. R. BROOME, B.SC.(ENG.), C.E.
R. A. G. CARSON, M.A., F.S.A.
P. A. CLAYTON, F.L.A., F.S.A.
J. G. POLLARD, B.A.
JOHN PORTEOUS, M.A.
M. J. PRICE, M.A., PH.D.
RICHARD REECE, B.SC., F.S.A.
W. M. STANCOMB
DAVID D. YONGE, M.C., M.A.

As there was no other business the President closed the meeting and the Society adjourned until the beginning of the new session on 17 October.

# THE ROYAL NUMISMATIC SOCIETY

## BALANCE SHEET

### *As at 31 December 1971*

| 31.12.70 £ | | £ | £ |
|---|---|---|---|
| | CAPITAL ACCOUNT | | |
| 12,915 | Balance at 31.12.1970 | 12,552 | |
| 387 | Excess of income over expenditure | 27 | |
| | | | |
| 13,302 | | 12,579 | |
| 750 | *Less* transfer to Life Membership Fund | — | |
| | | | |
| 12,552 | Balance at 31.12.1971 | | 12,579 |
| 434 | ENDOWMENT FUND | | 434 |
| 1,281 | LIFE MEMBERSHIP FUND | | 1,474 |
| — | STOCKWELL BEQUEST FUND | | 500 |
| | | | |
| £14,267 | | | £14,987 |

| | ASSETS | | |
|---|---|---|---|
| 1 | Library, furniture, etc. at nominal value | | 1 |
| | Investments at cost | | |
| 11,112 | General Fund | 11,012 | |
| 434 | Endowment Fund | 434 | |
| 1,099 | Life Membership Fund | 1,099 | |
| | | | 12,545 |
| 1,372 | Debtors and unexpired expenditure | | 2,566 |
| | Cash at bank | | |
| 3,715 | Deposit accounts | 4,015 | |
| 2,350 | Current account | 3,613 | |
| | | | 7,628 |
| | | | |
| 20,083 | | | 22,740 |
| | *Less* LIABILITIES | | |
| 3,500 | Reserve for printing current year's *N.C.* | 4,350 | |
| 227 | Subscriptions paid in advance | 286 | |
| 1,706 | Balances with Special Funds | 2,792 | |
| 383 | Sundry creditors | 325 | |
| | | | 7,753 |
| | | | |
| £14,267 | | | £14,987 |

# INCOME AND EXPENDITURE ACCOUNT
## Year ended 31 December 1971

| 31.12.70 £ | | £ | £ |
|---|---|---|---|
| | INCOME | | |
| 54 | Entrance Fees | 59 | |
| 2,800 | Subscriptions | 3,526 | |
| 236 | Income tax on subscriptions paid under covenant | 226 | |
| | | | 3,811 |
| 941 | Sales of Society's publications (less costs) | | 1,068 |
| — | Bequest received | | 500 |
| 702 | Income from investments | 774 | |
| 195 | Interest on deposit accounts | 135 | |
| | | | 909 |
| £4,928 | | | £6,288 |

| 31.12.70 £ | | £ | £ |
|---|---|---|---|
| | EXPENDITURE | | |
| 2,708 | *Numismatic Chronicle* 1970 | 3,979 | |
| 174 | *Less* receipts for advertisements and offprints | 420 | |
| 2,534 | | 3,559 | |
| 750 | *Add* increase in reserve for *N.C.* 1971 | 850 | |
| 3,284 | | 4,409 | |
| 94 | Postages, printing, and stationery | 121 | |
| 60 | Hire of Room | 80 | |
| 380 | Library expenses | 337 | |
| 23 | Subscriptions | 23 | |
| 43 | Insurance | 43 | |
| 102 | Secretarial assistance | 164 | |
| 7 | Lantern slides | 15 | |
| 48 | General expenses | 69 | |
| 500 | Special Publications Fund | 500 | |
| — | Stockwell Bequest Fund | 500 | |
| 4,541 | | | 6,261 |
| £387 | EXCESS of income over expenditure | | £27 |

# LHOTKA PRIZE FUND

|  |  | £ | £ |
|---|---|---|---|
|  | CAPITAL ACCOUNT |  |  |
| 428 | Balance at 31.12.1970 | 470 |  |
| 21 | Income from investment | 21 |  |
| 41 | Donation from Dr. Lhotka | — |  |
| 490 |  |  | 491 |
| 20 | *Less* award for year |  | 20 |
| £470 |  |  | £471 |
|  | ASSETS |  |  |
| 399 | Investment | 399 |  |
| 71 | Balance with Society | 72 |  |
| £470 |  |  | £471 |

# F. PARKES WEBER PRIZE FUND

|  |  | £ | £ |
|---|---|---|---|
|  | CAPITAL ACCOUNT |  |  |
| 218 | Balance at 31.12.1970 | 223 |  |
| 16 | Income from investment | 17 |  |
| 234 |  |  | 240 |
| 11 | *Less* award for year |  | 10 |
| £223 |  |  | £230 |
|  | ASSETS |  |  |
| 206 | Investment | 206 |  |
| 17 | Balance with Society | 24 |  |
| £223 |  |  | £230 |

# W. S. MARSHALL MEMORIAL FUND

|  |  | £ | £ |
|---|---|---|---|
|  | CAPITAL ACCOUNT |  |  |
| 1,196 | Balance at 31.12.1970 | 1,004 |  |
| 38 | Income from investment | 38 |  |
| 1,234 |  |  | 1,042 |
| 230 | *Less* cost of books for presentation |  | — |
| £1,004 |  |  | £1,042 |
|  | ASSETS |  |  |
| 1,042 | Investment | 1,042 |  |
| 38 | *Less* balance with Society | — |  |
| £1,004 |  |  | £1,042 |

# CAMARINA PUBLICATION TRUST FUND

| 31.12.70 £ | | £ | £ |
|---|---|---|---|
| | CAPITAL ACCOUNT | | |
| 1,807 | Balance at 3.12.1970 | 1,915 | |
| 108 | Income from investment | 108 | |
| £1,915 | | | £2,023 |
| | | | |
| | ASSETS | | |
| 1,701 | Investment | 1,701 | |
| 214 | Balance with Society | 322 | |
| £1,915 | | | £2,023 |

# SPECIAL PUBLICATIONS FUND

| | CAPITAL ACCOUNT | | |
|---|---|---|---|
| 5,979 | Balance at 31.12.1970 | 6,555 | |
| 53 | Income from investment | 70 | |
| 23 | Interest on deposit account | 19 | |
| 500 | Grant from General Funds | 500 | |
| £6,555 | | | £7,144 |
| | | | |
| | ASSETS | | |
| 1,000 | Investment | 1,000 | |
| 276 | Debtor | — | |
| 450 | Cash on deposit account | 650 | |
| 1,441 | Balance with Society | 2,374 | |
| 3,167 | | 4,024 | |
| — | *Less* Creditor | 789 | |
| 468 | Sums received for future publications | 617 | |
| 2,699 | | | 2,618 |
| | VOLUMES PRINTED at cost less amounts | | |
| 4,165 | received to 31.12.1970 | 3,856 | |
| — | Expenditure on Nos. 5 and 6 | 3,174 | |
| 4,165 | | 7,030 | |
| — | *Less* Grants received for Nos. 5 and 6 | 1,480 | |
| 309 | Sales (less expenses) for year | 1,024 | |
| 3,856 | Expenditure not recouped at 31.12.1971 | | 4,526 |
| £6,555 | | | £7,144 |

## NOTES

1. The stock of *Numismatic Chronicle*s in hand and the subscriptions in arrear have both been valued at nil.

2. The mid-market value of the investments of the Society and of the Special Funds at 31 December 1971 was £21,376 (1970—£16,210).

3. The Camarina Publication Trust Fund includes an interest-free loan of £1,607 made to the Royal Numismatic Society by the executors of the late Professor Eunice Work in order to enable it to publish her monograph on the coinage of Camarina.

4. Printing of special publications, estimated to cost £6,250, was in progress at 31 December 1971 and has not been provided for in these accounts. Grants and advance subscriptions amounting to £617 had been received in respect of those publications, and a further £1,750 in respect of grants had been promised.

DAVID W. MACDOWALL
*Hon. Treasurer*

We have examined the above Balance Sheet together with the annexed Income and Expenditure Account, the Accounts of the Special Funds, and Notes thereon. In our opinion they have been properly prepared and give a true and fair view of the state of affairs as at 31 December 1971 and of the income and expenditure for the year ended on that date.

J. D. BRAND, F.C.A.
D. E. SHACKLETON
*Honorary Auditors*

# LIBRARY ACCESSIONS, 1971

ARTUK, I., and C., İstanbul Arkeoloji Müzeleri Teşhirdeki Islâmî Sikkeler Kataloğu, Cilt I. Istanbul, 1971.

BASTIEN, P., and VASSELLE, F., Les Trésors monétaires de Fresnoy-les-Roye (Somme). Amiens, 1971.

BATES, G. E., Archaeological Explorations of Sardis: Byzantine Coins. Harvard, 1971.

BERGHAUS, P., and KORN, H. E., Münzen, Wappen und Siegel der Stadt Arnsberg. Arnsberg, 1971.

BIAUDET, J. C. (ed.), Monnaies au pays de Vaud. Berne, 1964.

BRINKERHOFF, D., A Collection of Sculpture in Classical and Early Christian Antioch. New York, 1970.

COMBE, C., Nummorum veterum populorum et urbium, qui in Museo Gulielmi Hunter asservantur, descriptio figuris illustrata. London, 1782.

DANSON, E. W., The Anglo-Saxon and Norman Mint of Tamworth, Staffordshire. South Staffordshire Archaeological and Historical Society, 1969–70.

DAVIS, N. M., The Complete Book of United States Coin Collecting. New York, 1971.

DE MEY, J., Les Monnaies de Bretagne. Bruxelles, 1970.

—— and POINDESSAULT, B. Répertoire de la numismatique française contemporaine, 1793–1968. Bruxelles, 1969.

GEIGER, H. U., Der Beginn der Gold und Dick-Münzenprägung in Bern. Bern, 1968.

GÖBL, R., Sasanian Numismatics (trans. P. Severin). Braunschweig, 1971.

—— Regalianus und Dryantilla. Wien, 1970.

GORDON, Major L. L., British Battles and Medals (4th edn., revised by Edw. C. Joslin). London, 1971.

HOBSON, B., Historic Gold Coins of the World. London, 1971.

JONES, J. R., A Numismatic Index to the Journal of Hellenic Studies, 1880–1969. Cambridge, 1971.

—— A Numismatic Index to the Journal of Roman Studies, 1911–1968. Cambridge, 1971.

JOSSET, C. R., Money in Britain (2nd edn.). Newton Abbot, 1971.

KAIM, R., Russische Münzstatten, Münzzeichen, und Münzmeisterzeichen. Braunschweig, 1971.

KRAAY, C. M., Greek Coins and History: some Current Problems. London, 1969.

KUBIAK, S., Monety Pierwszych Jagiellonow (1386–1444). Warsaw, 1970.

LALLEMAND, J., and THIRION, M., Le Trésor de Saint-Mard I (Étude sur le monnayage de Victorin et des Tétricus). Wetteren, 1970.

MANSŪR IBN BAʿRA AL-DHAHABI AL-KĀMILI, Kitāb kashf al-asrār al-ʿilmiyyah bi-dār al-ḍarb al-miṣriyyah (Discovery of scientific secrets of the Egyptian mint). Cairo, 1966.

MEDCALF, G., and FONG, R., Hawaiian Money and Medals. Hawaii, 1967.

MUKHERJEE, B. N., An Agrippan Source—a Study in Indo-Parthian History. Calcutta, 1969.

NARBETH, C., How to Collect Paper Money. London, 1971.

NAVASCUÉS, J. MA. DE, Las monedas hispánicas del museo arqueológico nacional de Madrid, II (Ia y 2a partes): ciclo andaluz, grupo bastulo-turdetano: tesoros de Azaila, Salvacañete y Cerro de la Miranda. Barcelona, 1971.

PATALAS, W., *Chinesische Münzen*. Brunswick, 1965.

PAUWELS, G., *Les Monnaies de Gaule belgique*. 1971.

PESANT, R., *Collected Notes: Coins of the Crusader Princes of Antioch*. (MS. donated by the author). 1971.

POLIVKA, E., *Mince Ferdinande V (1835–1848)*. Praha, 1971.

PORTEOUS, J., *Coins in History*. London, 1969.

REECE, R., *Roman Coins*. London, 1970.

REMICK, J., and JAMES, S., *Guide Book and Catalogue of British Commonwealth Coins, 1798–1967*. Winnipeg, 1967.

RETHY, L., and PROBSZT, G., *Corpus Nummorum Hungariae* (Graz reprint). 1958.

RODE, V. P., *Catalogue of Coins in the Central Museum, Nagpur: Coins of the Mughal Emperors, Part I*. Bombay, 1969.

SEABY, P., *Coins and Tokens of Ireland*. London, 1970.

—— ed., *Standard Catalogue of British Coins*. London, 1971.

—— H. A., *Roman Silver Coins, Vol. IV. Gordian III—Postumus*. London, 1971.

SELLWOOD, D., *An Introduction to the Coinage of Parthia*. London, 1971.

SIRCAR, D. C., *Studies in Indian Coins*. Delhi, 1968.

STENTON, F. M., *Anglo-Saxon England* (3rd edn.). Oxford, 1971.

*Sylloge Nummorum Graecorum. The Royal Collection of Coins and Medals, Danish National Museum, 42. North Africa: Syrtica-Mauretania*. Copenhagen, 1969.

TERLECKI, W., *Mennica Warszawska 1765–1965*. Warsaw, 1970.

VERMEULE, C., *Numismatic Art in America*. Harvard, 1971.

WHITING, J. R. S., *Trade Tokens. A Social and Economic History*. Newton Abbot, 1971.

WROTH, W., *Catalogue of the Imperial Byzantine Coins in the British Museum* (Argonaut reprint). 1966.

MEETINGS are held in the rooms of the Society of Antiquaries, Burlington House, London, W. 1, from October to June on the third Tuesday in each month at 5.30 p.m.

THE SOCIETY'S LIBRARY is housed at the Warburg Institute, Woburn Square, London, W.C.1. Books can be sent to fellows by post on request either to the Society's Librarian, Mr. N. M. Lowick, at the British Museum, or to Mr. J. Trapp at the Warburg Institute.

THE *Numismatic Chronicle* and Journal of the Society is published at the end of each year. Each volume, containing upward of 250 pages of articles, notes on hoards and finds, reviews and notices of selected new publications, is sent free to all Fellows whose subscriptions are not in arrears. Fellows may purchase copies of back numbers of the Chronicle still in stock, *NC* 1961 to date, at £4 ($12) per volume, and should send the appropriate remittance with their order to the Hon. Secretary, Miss M. M. Archibald, at the British Museum. Non-fellows may purchase volumes of the *Numismatic Chronicle* at £5 from Bernard Quaritch, 5–8 Lower John St., Golden Square, London, W1V 6AB. Articles and other communications on coins or medals of all periods are invited by the Editor, Mr. R. A. G. Carson. They should be submitted to him at the British Museum after careful reference to the 'Guidance for Contributors' printed below, and should be accompanied by an abstract (not normally exceeding 50 words in length) suitable for inclusion in *Numismatic Literature*, the bibliography of numismatic works published by the American Numismatic Society.

SPECIAL PUBLICATIONS are issued from time to time—approximately every two years. Fellows are entitled to subscribe at favourable pre-publication rates, and may purchase copies of earlier publications still available direct from the Society at reduced prices:

| | Price to Fellows | Price to Non-fellows |
|---|---|---|
| 1. J. D. A. Thompson, *Inventory of British Coin Hoards* | £3·00 or $9.00 | £4·00 or $12.00 |
| 2. G. K. Jenkins and R. B. Lewis, *Carthagian Gold and Electrum Coins* | £4·50 or $13.00 | £6·00 or $17.00 |
| 3. J. M. F. May, *The Coinage of Abdera* | £4·50 or $13.00 | £6·00 or $17.00 |
| 4. M. H. Crawford, *Roman Republican Coin Hoards* | £3·00 or $9.00 | £4·00 or $12.00 |
| 5. C. H. V. Sutherland, *The Cistophori of Augustus* | £4·50 or $13.00 | £6·00 or $17.00 |
| 6. I. D. Brown and Michael Dolley, *Coin Hoards of Great Britain and Ireland, 1500–1907* | £3·00 or $9.00 | £4·00 or $12.00 |
| 7. Roderick T. Williams, *The Silver Coinage of the Phokians* | £3·75 or $11.00 | £5·00 or $14.00 |

Fellows who wish to purchase copies should send their order together with the appropriate remittance to the Hon. Secretary, Miss M. M. Archibald, at the British Museum. Non-fellows may obtain copies from Spink & Sons Ltd., 5–7 King Street, St. James's, London, S.W.1.

SUBSCRIPTIONS. The annual subscription, currently £4·20 or $12.00, is under review, and is likely to be increased in 1973. Details may be obtained from the Hon. Secretary.

## PRIZES

### The Dr. F. Parkes Weber Prize

1. Through the generosity of the late F. Parkes Weber, Esq., M.D., F.S.A., the author of many studies concerning coins and medals, an annual prize was instituted in 1954 under the administration of the Council of the Society.

2. The value of the prize will be £10·50. The prize-winner will also receive, inscribed with his or her name, a small bronze replica of Dr. Parkes Weber's portrait medal by Frank Bowcher.

3. Competitors for the prize must be under the age of twenty-one on the final day of entry, 31 August. Competitors may be of any nationality.

4. The prize will be awarded for an original essay of not more than 5,000 words on any subject relating to coins, medals, medallions, or tokens. Competitors should choose their own subject, but may seek guidance if they wish.

5. The essay should be clearly written or typed in English on one side of the paper only and should be sent, with a stamped addressed envelope for return, to Mr. D. G. Sellwood, 44 Richmond Road, London, S.W.20, the Hon. Secretary of the Parkes Weber Prize Committee.

6. The award will be announced in December of the same year.

7. The Council of The Royal Numismatic Society reserves the right to advise that no award be made in any given year, if entries are not of a sufficiently high standard.

8. The award shall not be made to any candidate who has won it previously.

### The Lhotka Memorial Prize

In June 1961 Professor J. F. Lhotka, M.D., Ph.D., of the University of Oklahoma, endowed a prize under this name in memory of his father, Dr. J. F. Lhotka, and entrusted the administration of the awards to the Royal Numismatic Society, which with his consent has made the following Regulations.

1. Subject to paragraph 3 below, the prize will be awarded annually in December to the author adjudged to have published in the previous two calendar years the book or article in English most helpful to the elementary student of numismatics.

2. Submissions, accompanied by a copy of the work submitted, which will be returned if requested, may be made by any person before 30 September in each year to the Honorary Secretary of the Royal Numismatic Society, c/o Department of Coins and Medals, British Museum, London, W.C.1.

3. Works submitted will be examined by the Publications Committee of the Society, who will report to the Council. The adjudication will be made by members of the Council present at the ordinary December Meeting, or such other Meeting as the Council may decide. In the event of even voting the Chairman of the Meeting shall have an additional casting vote. No award shall be made in any year when the majority of those present at the Council Meeting are of the opinion that no work submitted is of adequate quality.

4. The prize will be of the approximate value of £20, and will be accompanied by an official certificate of The Royal Numismatic Society recording the award.

5. The above Regulations may be varied from time to time by the Council, provided that no part of the capital or income of the Trust Fund shall be expended for purposes other than those of the advancement of education in numismatics.

# THE ROYAL NUMISMATIC SOCIETY

*Patron*: HER MAJESTY THE QUEEN

# LIST OF FELLOWS

June 1972

*The sign * indicates that the Fellow has compounded for his annual contribution.*
*The sign † indicates that the Fellow has subsequently died.*

ELECTED

1967 AARON, ROBERT, B.A., LL.B., 171 Glen Cedar Road, Toronto 10, Ontario, Canada.

1962 ABECASSIS, RAUL, Rua de S. Nicolau 123, Lisbon, Portugal.

1962 ABGARIANS, MESROB T., D.D.S., 6 Kutchehyi Tamadon, Khiyabani Ferdowsi, Teheran, Iran.

1966 ABLESON, MALCOLM, 59 Sandhill Oval, Leeds 17, Yorks.

1967 ABRAHAMS, SETH G., 917 Innes Chambers, 84 Pritchard Street, Johannesburg, South Africa.

1947 ABSALOM, HAROLD W. D., Delaval, 71 Darnton Road, Ashton-under-Lyne, Lancs.

1970 ACOSTA Y LARA, R. S., Rio Branco 1226, Montevideo, Uruguay.

1970 ADAMS, F. E., 162 Upton Court Road, Langley, Slough, Bucks.

1967 ADAMS, N. W. J., St. Andrews, 148 Northwich Road, Weaverham, Cheshire.

1961 AIRD, GEORGE S., 57 John Street, Sunderland, Co. Durham.

1970 ALDRED, DEREK J., 30 Wolstenbury Road, Rustington, Sussex.

1953 ALDRIDGE, E. F., 9 Cherry Hill, St. Albans, Herts.

1935 ALLEN, DEREK F., C.B., M.A., F.B.A., F.S.A., Grenna House, Chilson, near Charlbury, Oxon.

1963*ALLEN, HAROLD DON, B.Sc., M.S.T.M., F.C.C.T., c/o K. Hill, 368 Merton, St. Lanbert, Montreal 23, Quebec, Canada.

1965 ALLEN, PETER GERALD, 9 Dorset Square, London, N.W.1.

1969 ALLISON, B. E., 'Tobruk', Beaumont Drive, Ballintemple, Cork, Eire.

1965 ALMIRALL BARRIL, JUAN, Avenida General Goded 13 e 15/7°, Barcelona 6, Spain.

1972 ALTERSKYE, C. G. E., B.Sc. (Econ.), Dip. Ed., F.R.S.A., 10 Wheatlands Drive, Molescroft, Beverley, Yorks., HU17 7HR.

1971*ALTMAN, BRIAN, M.D., 155 Retreat Avenue, Hartford, Conn. 06115, U.S.A.

1961 ANDERSON, M. J., M.A., 51 Patching Hall Lane, Chelmsford, Essex.

1969 APPLETON, 4312 Windsor Parkway, Dallas, Texas 75205, U.S.A.

1962 ARCHIBALD, MISS M. M., M.A., Dept. of Coins & Medals, British Museum, London, W.C.1; *Hon. Secretary*.

1953 ARNOLD, G. R., 'Arnridge', Barns Lane, Burford, Oxon.

1948 ARTUK, BAY IBRAHIM, Arkeoloji Müzesi Numizmati, Istanbul, Turkey.

ELECTED

1971 ASHTON, R. H. J., 20 Cwrt-y-vil Road, Penarth, Glamorgan.

1955 ATKINSON, PROFESSOR K. M. T., M.A., F.S.A., Dept. of Ancient History, The Queen's University, Belfast, N. Ireland.

1957 ATLAN, DR. SABAHAT, Edebiyat Fakültesi Üniversite, Istanbul, Turkey.

1952 AULOCK, H. VON, Set Sokak 12, Arnavutköy, Istanbul, Turkey.

1967 AZAMI, CHERAGH ALI, Darou Pakhsh Welfare Organisation, Tehran, Iran.

1970 BACHARACH, JERE L., Dept. of History, University of Washington, Seattle, Washington 98105, U.S.A.

1965 BADIAN, PROFESSOR E., Dept. of History, Harvard University, Cambridge, Massachusetts 02138, U.S.A.

1963 BAGNALL, A. G., M.A., 2 Kennet House, Harrow Park, Harrow-on-the-Hill, Middlesex.

1969 AL-BAKRI, MRS. MUHAB DARWISH, Coinage Division, Directorate-General of Antiquities, Baghdad, Iraq.

1972 BALCHIN, J. E., 162 Buriton Road, Winchester, Hants.

1969 BALDWIN, A. H. E., 11 Adelphi Terrace, London, WC2N 3BJ.

1964 BALMUTH, MRS. MIRIAM, 170 Mt. Vernon Street, Winchester, Massachusetts 02161, U.S.A.

1951 BALOG, PROFESSOR PAUL, Via Marostica 29, Rome, Italy.

1969 BARDONI, EUGENIO, Foro Buonaparte 52, Milan, Italy.

1959 BAREFORD, HAROLD S., 6 East 45th Street, New York, New York 17, U.S.A.

1968 BARKER, R., 1 Hazel End, Swanley, Kent, BR8 8NU.

1962 BARNES, C. V., P.O. Box 3546, Little Rock, Arkansas 72203, U.S.A.

1971 BARRETT, WILLIAM L. S., Box 1747, Station B, Montreal 110, P.Q. Canada.

1960 BARREY, T. F. H., A.R.I.C., 'Kandaw', 19 Oakleigh Park South, Whetstone, London, N.20.

1958 BARRON, J. P., M.A., D.Phil., 35 Rochester Road, London, N.W.1.

1967 BARTHOLD, ROLAND, 65 Avenue de l'Argent Sarre, Colombe (Seine), France.

1957 BASTIEN, DR. PIERRE, 48 Boulevard Alexandre III, Dunkerque, France.

1947 BATTY, WILLIAM RAYNER, c/o Mrs. Hobson, 24 Coudray Road, Southport, PR9 9NL.

1969 BAVAIRD, H. G., P.O. Box 6127, Bay Osos, California 93401, U.S.A.

1963 BEDOUKIAN, PAUL, Ch.E., Ph.D., 40 Ashley Road, Hastings-on-Hudson, New York, U.S.A.

1959 BEECHAM, MISS IRENE D., 46 Dundee Road, London, E.13.

1972 BEER, MRS. L. B., 20 Broom Water West, Teddington, Middlesex.

1970 BEHRENS, DERICK, B.A., B.Sc., Cherry Hill, Wood Road, Hindhead, Surrey.

1961 BENDALL, SIMON, c/o A. H. Baldwin & Sons, 11 Adelphi Terrace, London, WC2N 6BJ.

1967 BENNETT, GEORGE, 505 So. Lafayette Park Road, Apt. 307, Los Angeles, California 90057, U.S.A.

1967 BEREND, MME DENYSE, 43 Boulevard d'Auteuil, 5 Villa Persane, Boulogne-sur-Seine, France.

1953 BERG, R. M., M.D., Box 1818, Bismarck, North Dakota, U.S.A.

ELECTED

1954 BERGHAUS, PROFESSOR DR. PETER, Domplatz 10, Münster 21a, Westfalen, Germany.

1969 BERNAREGGI, PROFESSOR DR. E., Corso Garibaldi 104, 20121 Milan, Italy.

1963 BERNSTEIN, B. L., Anglovaal House, 56 Main Street, Johannesburg, South Africa.

1964 BERRY, GEORGE, M.A., 70 Heath Road, Holtspur, Beaconsfield, Bucks.

1964 BETTON, JAMES L., Jr., P.O. Box 533, Santa Monica, California 90405, U.S.A.

1968 BHATIA, DR. P., 28/17 Shakti Nagar, Delhi 7, India.

1951 BIAGGI DE BLASYS, DR. LEO, Villa dei Pini, Bogliasco, Genoa, Italy.

1953 BIRLEY, PROFESSOR ERIC, M.B.E., M.A., F.S.A., Observatory House, Durham City, Co. Durham.

1948 BIVAR, A. D. H., M.A., D.Phil., School of Oriental and African Studies, University of London, London, W.C.1.

1944 BLAKE-HILL, P. V., B.A., Ph.D., 99 Lower Richmond Road, East Sheen, London, SW14 7HU.

1960 BLANCO, DON FELIX FERNANDEZ, Don Quixote 1, Madrid 20, Spain.

1970 BLOCH, LEONARD M., 90 Rodney Court, London, W. 9.

1965 BLUCK, JOHN L., 1601 West Avenue, Monroe, Louisiana 71204, U.S.A.

1966 BLUMHOFF, ROMAN JAN, 7 Fisher Avenue, Belmont, Geelong, Victoria, Australia.

1961 BLUNDEN, R. H., 2045 East Broadway Street, Vancouver 12, B.C., Canada.

1923 BLUNT, CHRISTOPHER E., O.B.E., F.B.A., F.S.A., Ramsbury Hill, Ramsbury, near Marlborough, Wilts.; *Vice-President*.

1970 BOATSWAIN, T. J., The Barber Institute of Fine Arts, The University, Birmingham.

1972 BOEHRINGER, DR. CHRISTOF, Archäologisches Institut der Universität Göttingen, 3400 Göttingen, Nikolausberger Weg 15, Germany.

1966 BOOMERSHINE, DONALD, Box 92, Gratis, Ohio 45330, U.S.A.

1954 BOON, GEORGE C., B.A., F.S.A., National Museum of Wales, Cardiff.

1965 BORDELL, GERALD, 5 Abbotswood Gardens, Clayhall, Ilford, Essex.

1969 BORGOLTE, MRS. PEGGY E., P.O. Box 2377, Sepulveda, California 91343, U.S.A.

1969 BOTH, H. J. J., Oud Bussumerweg 24, Huizen-NH, Holland.

1959 BOUNDY, WYNDHAM S., 2 Springfield Terrace, Westward Ho, Bideford, Devon.

1955 BOURGEY, ÉMILE, 7 rue Drouot, Paris XIᵉ, France.

1962 BOUX, G. J., Box 87, St. Norbert, Manitoba, Canada.

1968 BOWER, MERVYN, Tasmanian Museum, 5 Argyle Street, Hobart, Tasmania, Australia.

1963 BOWERS, Q. DAVID, Bowers and Ruddy Galleries Inc., 6922 Hollywood Blvd., Suite 810, Hollywood, California 90028, U.S.A.

1948 BOWMAN, FREDERICK, 210 53rd Avenue, Lachine, Quebec, Canada.

1971 BOX, R. J., Cold Comfort Farm, Dowdeswell, nr. Cheltenham, Glos.

1956 BRACE, BRUCE R., 654 Hiawatha Boulevard, Ancaster, Ontario, Canada.

1963 BRAND, J. D., F.C.A., 5 Ridley Road, Rochester, Kent.

1971 BRAUN, B. B., P.O. Box 2728, Amherst Station, Buffalo, N.Y. 14226, U.S.A.

ELECTED

1948 BRAZENOR, H. F., The Museum, Brighton, Sussex.

1958 BREAULT, EARL, 4213 Oak Drive Lane, Hopkins, Minnesota, U.S.A.

1963 BRESSETT, K. E., Whitman Publishing Co., 1220 Mound Avenue, Racine, Wisconsin, U.S.A.

1964 BRETTELL, R. P. V., Ropewind Lynch, Shalbourne, near Marlborough, Wilts.

1961 BRIDGE, R. N., Greensleeves, 11 Sutton Lane, Banstead, Surrey.

1970 BRIGGS, JAMES R., 865 West Marshall Blvd., San Bernardino, California 92405, U.S.A.

1932 *BRIGGS, L. CABOT, M.A., Hancock, New Hampshire, U.S.A.

1963 BRINDLEY, PROFESSOR JAMES C., Dept. of Geology, University College, Science Buildings, Upper Merrion Street, Dublin, Eire.

1946 BROMWICH, J. I'A., T.D., M.A., 153 Huntingdon Road, Cambridge.

1970 BROOK, JULIAN A., M.P.S., 813 Mount Eden Road, Auckland 4, New Zealand.

1948 BROOKS, E. H., c/o Sheppards & Chase, Clements House, Gresham Street, London, E.C.2.

1969 BROOME, M. R., B.Sc.(Eng.), C.Eng., 30 Warren Road, Woodley, Berks.

1971 BROSI, GEORGE, Schlachthofstrasse 55, CH–4000 Basel, Switzerland.

1959 BROWN, MRS. HELEN W., M.A., M.R.A.S., Heberden Coin Room, Ashmolean Museum, Oxford.

1955 BROWN, L. A., 'Imladris', Heath Ridge Green, Cobham, Surrey.

1967 BRUHN, DR. MARCUS C., Dept. of Economics, Central Michigan University, Mt. Pleasant, Michigan 48858, U.S.A.

1951 BRUUN, DR. PATRICK MAGNUS, Furuvaegen 32 B 2, 20540 Turku, Finland.

1966 BURNELL, E. A. W., The Devon and Dorset Regiment, 19th Cadet Training Team, Basil Hill Barracks, Corsham, Wilts.

1969 BUSSELL, MRS. M. E., 69 Oakleigh Park Drive, Leigh-on-Sea, Essex.

1972 *BUTTREY, T. V., 1256 Ferdon Road, Ann Arbor, Michigan, U.S.A.

1972 BYNON, DR. J. F. G., School of Oriental and African Studies, University of London, London, W.C.1.

1962 *BYRNE, R. A., 701 North Negley Avenue, Pittsburgh 6, Pennsylvania, U.S.A.

1968 CABARROT, J. JEAN, 12 rue Jean Paul-Alaux, Bordeaux-Bastide, Gironde, France.

1971 CABOT, THOMAS C., Finca el Capricho, Casa del Monte, Marbella, Spain.

1935 CAHN, DR. HERBERT A., Malzgasse 25, 4002 Basel, Switzerland.

1944 *CALEY, PROFESSOR EARLE R., Department of Chemistry, The Ohio State University, Columbus, Ohio, U.S.A.

1969 CALHOUN, PAUL J., 3454 Fenton Avenue, Apt. 20, Bronx, N.Y. 10469, U.S.A.

1947 CALICO, DON XAVIER, Plaza del Ángel 2, Barcelona, Spain.

1964 CAME, MELVIN E., 4 Hillcrest Drive, Dover, N.H., U.S.A.

1971 CAMPANA, ALBERTO, via L. Ungarelli 23, 00162 Roma, Italy.

1950 CAMPBELL, DR. CHARLES S., Physicians Building, 1234 Commercial Street, S.E., Salem, Oregon, U.S.A.

1967 CAMPO FERNANDEZ, PEDRO, Pasaje Senillosa 7, Barcelona 17, Spain.

1967 Cancio, L., 2800 Arizona Terrace N.W., Washington, D.C. 20016, U.S.A.

1969 Capozzolo, J., P.O. Box 73, Solvay, New York 13209, U.S.A.

1959 Cargill Thompson, Mrs. J. A. W., c/o Dr. W. D. J. Cargill Thompson, Dept. of Ecclesiastical History, King's College, Strand, London, W.C.2.

1961 Carney, Professor T. F., Dept. of Classics, University of Manitoba, Winnipeg, Manitoba, Canada.

1960 Carroll, Michael, Dairy Cottage, Goring Hall School, Goring-by-Sea, Worthing, Sussex.

1959 Carroll, Major S. S., Curator of the Numismatic Collection, Bank of Canada, Ottawa 4, Ontario, Canada.

1947 Carson, R. A. G., M.A., F.S.A., Deputy Keeper of Coins and Medals, British Museum, London, W.C.1.

1957 Carter, Brian L., Silver Trees, Slad Road, Stroud, Glos.

1955 Carter, G. E. L., M.A., Pine Hollow, Budleigh Salterton, Devon.

1968 Casey, John, 23 Anselm House, Cottington Street, London, S.E.11.

1971 Castenholz, B. J., 1055 Hartzell Street, Pacific Palisades, California 90272, U.S.A.

1962 Chalmers, Dr. T., M.B., Hazelwell, 174 Derwen Fawr Road, Sketty, Swansea, Glamorgan.

1956 Chambers, W. J., 18 Debden Road, Saffron Walden, Essex.

1972 Chandaria, D. P., 9 Hyde Park Street, London, W2 2JW.

1961 Chapman, Mrs. Audrey, Flat 4, 74 Montpelier Road, Brighton 1, Sussex.

1929 *Chapman, G. E., 7 Oaklands Way, Sturry, near Canterbury, Kent.

1958 Charlton, J. E., Charlton Coin and Stamp Co. Ltd., 92 Jarvis Street, Toronto 1, Ontario, Canada.

1966 Cheeseman, Anthony John, 43 Beverley Gardens, Bangor, Co. Down, N. Ireland.

1963 Cherry, A. F., 7 West Towers, Pinner, Middlesex.

1967 Chilton, C. W., M.A., Ph.D., Dept. of Classics, The University, Hull.

1950 Clain-Stefanelli, Dr. Vladimir, 2608 North Nelson Street, Arlington, Virginia 22207, U.S.A.

1957 Clain-Stefanelli, Mrs. V., 2608 North Nelson Street, Arlington, Virginia 22207, U.S.A.

1969 Clapp, J. F., Jr., 20 Bellevue Avenue, Cambridge, Massachusetts, U.S.A.

1969 Clay, Curtis L., Christ Church, Oxford.

1962 Clayton, P. A., F.L.A., F.S.A., 6 Handside Close, Welwyn Garden City, Herts.

1971 Cohen, James H., 319 Royal Street, New Orleans, Louisiana 70130, U.S.A.

1960 Colbert, Charles, Box No. 263, Yellow Springs, Ohio, U.S.A.

1965 Coleiro, The Most Revd. Mons. Professor E., O.B.E., B.A., D.D., Ph.D., J.C.B., 181 Britannia Street, Valetta, Malta G.C.

1971 Coleman, E. K., 70 Rockville Crescent, Newtown-park Avenue, Blackrock, Dublin, Ireland.

ELECTED

1966 COLLINS, DANIEL W., 621 Chester Avenue, Moorestown, New Jersey 08057, U.S.A.

1970 COLLINS, ROGER J. H., The Queen's College, Oxford.

1963 COMSTOCK, MISS M. B., 54 Dudley Street, Brookline 46, Massachusetts, U.S.A.

1955 CONGAS, CONSTANTINE, 113 Appleton Street, Boston, Massachusetts, U.S.A.

1972 COON, R. D., 915, N. Buena Vista St., Burbank, California 91505, U.S.A.

1955 COPE, L. H., F.I.M., A.M.Inst.W., 27 Twiss Green Lane, Culcheth, Warrington, Lancs.

1956 COPINGER, THE REVD. H. S. A., S.S.F., B.A., The Friary, Hilfield, Dorchester, Dorset.

1953 CORBITT, J. H., A.I.C.S., 73 Western Way, Darras Hall, Ponteland, Northumberland.

1953 CORMACK, PROFESSOR J. M. R., Dept. of Greek, King's College, Old Aberdeen.

1965 COUGOUL, DOCTEUR JACQUES, 271 Avenue de Lattre de Tassigny, 33 Bordeaux-Cauderan, Gironde, France.

1957 CRAIG-JEFFREYS, CMDR. A. L., K.M., O.St.J., R.N. (retd.), 84 Queen Edith's Way, Cambridge.

1946 *CRAUFORD, W. G., 47 Blacketts Wood Drive, Chorley Wood, Herts.

1964 CRAWFORD, M. H., M.A., Christ's College, Cambridge.

1969 CRESSWELL, JOHN C. M., Pacific Commemorative Society, Auckland 7, New Zealand.

1969 CRIBB, P. S., 355 Hounslow Road, Hanworth, Feltham, Middlesex.

1951 CROWTHER, D. J., 8 Upperton Road, Sidcup, Kent.

1953 CURIEL, RAOUL, 10 bis rue du Pré aux Clercs, Paris VIIᵉ, France.

1969 CURRY, M. R., 269 Avondale Avenue, Ottawa 3, Ontario, Canada.

1965 CURTAIN, BRIAN P., 42 Beach Street, Bellerive, Tasmania, Australia.

1967 CURTIS, BEVERLEY, c/o 76 New Bond Street, London, W1Y 0HN.

1951 CURTIS, COL. JAMES W., 2117 Noble Avenue, Springfield, Illinois, U.S.A.

1968 d'ALTON, IAN, 'South Winds', Maryboro', Douglas, Co. Cork, Eire.

1971 DALTON, ROGER, 58 Walham Grove, London, S.W.6.

1958 DAVENPORT, PROFESSOR J. S., Ph.D., Knox College, Galesburg, Illinois 61401, U.S.A.

1953 DAVIDSON, COL. H. D., U.S.A.F., 804 Castlewood Lane, Deerfield, Illinois, U.S.A.

1970 DAVIDSON, DR. JAMES, Linton Muir, West Linton, Peeblesshire.

1964 DAVIS, ALBERT, F.R.C.S., 93 Harley Street, London, W.1.

1963 DAVIS, J. S. S., C.Eng., F.I.E.E., F.I.R.S.E., 51 Woodland Drive, Watford, Herts.

1964 DAVIS, NORMAN, 6052 Upland Terrace So., Seattle 18, Washington, U.S.A.

1958 DE FALCO, GIUSEPPE, 24 Corso Umberto I, Naples, Italy.

1972 DEGRAAF, PETER, 26 Carlyle Avenue, Ottawa 1, Ontario, Canada.

1960 DE GUADAN Y LASCARIS (COMNENO), DR. ANTONIO MANUEL, Don Quijote, 1, Sexto, Madrid 20, Spain.

1960 DE LACY-SPENCER, R., Forge Cottage, Belloo, Enniskillen, Co. Fermanagh, N. Ireland.

ELECTED

1956 DENARO, V. F., 88 Old Mint Street, Valetta, Malta G.C.

1961 DENBY, E. E., 1206 Yonge Street, Toronto 7, Ontario, Canada.

1963 DENHAM, D. J., Berwick, 69 Seabrook Road, Hythe, Kent.

1972 DE SHAZO, DR. A. S., P.O. Box No. 7132, Metairie, Louisiana 70002, U.S.A.

1963 DICKIE, G. J., 3374 Ontario Street, Vancouver 10, British Columbia, Canada.

1967 DIETZ, ALEXANDER, 1133 Temperance Street, Saskatoon, Saskatchewan, Canada.

1964 DIVO, JEAN-PAUL, c/o Bank Leu & Co., 32 Bahnhofstrasse, Numismatic Department, Zürich, Switzerland.

1951 DODSON, REAR-ADMIRAL OSCAR H., U.S.N. (retd.), Director, The Classical and European Culture Museum, University of Illinois, 484 Lincoln Hall, Urbana, Illinois, U.S.A.

1951 DOLLEY, MICHAEL, B.A., M.R.I.A., F.S.A., Reader in Modern History, Queen's University, Belfast 7, Northern Ireland.

1955 DONALD, P. J., 9 Wentworth Road, Manor Park, London, E.12.

1971 DONE, P. D., 4 Mossfield Road, Kings Heath, Birmingham 14.

1968 DONEGAN, DANIEL A., 677 Akoakoa Street, Kailua, Hawaii 96734.

1949 DOUBLEDAY, G. V., Goat Lodge Farm, Great Totham, Maldon, Essex.

1959 DOUGLAS, R. W., Hillside, 24 Warden Hill, Cheltenham, Glos.

1967 DRUMMOND, R. H., 8408, Des Rapides, La Salle, Province of Quebec, Canada.

1965 DU QUESNE BIRD, NICHOLAS, 148 Fishponds Road, Bristol, BS5 6PT.

1970 DUSENBURY, MRS. ELSPETH, Institute of Fine Arts, New York University, 1 East 78th Street, New York, U.S.A.

1966 DUTT, DR. CHINMOY P., 795A Lake Town, Patipukur, Calcutta 28, India.

1959 DUVEEN, SIR GEOFFREY, Grosvenor House, London, W.1.

1958 DYKES, D. W., M.A., F.R.Hist.Soc., 64 Windsor Avenue, Radyn, Cardiff, S. Wales.


1967 EDMUNDS, D. R. D., M.A., Ancient House, Fenn Street, Nayland, Colchester, C06 4HT.

1964 EDMUNDSON, LT.-COL. J., M.C., Blue Hills, Beacon Drive, St. Agnes, Cornwall.

1955 EGAN, HAROLD, B.Sc., Ph.D., 49 Medway Gardens, Wembley, Middlesex.

1970 EISENHAUER, HARRY, P.O. Box 84, Oromocto, New Brunswick, Canada.

1967 ELKS, K. J. J., Kyrenia, Kingston, Canterbury, Kent.

1969 ELTON, HAROLD, Elton Lodge, Rathgar Close, Finchley, London, N.3.

1969 EMMANS, LESLIE ROBERT, 9 Woodend Road, Heacham, King's Lynn, Norfolk.

1972 ENOKI, PROFESSOR K., c/o The Toyo Bunko, Honkomagome 2–28–21 Bunkyo kw, Tokyo, Japan.

1972 ENZLER, B. WARREN, 15 Lotus Street, Cedarhurst, L.I., N.Y. 11516, U.S.A.

1960 ERIM, PROFESSOR KENAN T., M.A., Ph.D., Dept. of Classics, New York University, Washington Square, New York 3, New York, U.S.A.

1969 ESNER, D. R., 71 Sheen Lane, London, S.W.14.

1971 EYRE, CLIVE M., 99 Dove Park, Hatch End, Middlesex.

ELECTED

1969 FABBRICOTTI, DR. M. E., 29 Via B. Tortolini, 00197 Rome, Italy.

1968 FAGERLIE, DR. JOAN M., American Numismatic Society, Broadway at 156th Street, New York, New York 10032, U.S.A.

1968 FAGLEMAN, B. M., 23 Prestwick Gardens, Newcastle upon Tyne 3, NE3 3DN.

1970 FAIRBAIRN, STUART WILLIAM, 123 Seventh Avenue, Maylands, Perth, 6051, W. Australia.

1972 FAIRHEAD, NIALL, 19 Helenslea Avenue, London, N.W.11.

1958 FALKINER, R., 15 Yarrell Mansions, Queens Club Gardens, London, W.14.

1970 FALLANI, LA DITTA, via del Babuino 58 A, 00187 Roma, Italy.

1964 FAULKNER, CHRISTOPHER, 4 Monaco Drive, Northenden, Manchester 22.

1968 FEARON, DANIEL, 98 Archway Street, Barnes, London, S.W.13.

1970 FELLOWS, MAURICE JAMES, High Trees, Bromwich Lane, Pedmore, Stourbridge, Worcs.

1945 *FERGUSON, J. DOUGLAS, Rock Island, Quebec, Canada.

1972 FERGUSON, W. B., 37 Buckstone Crescent, Edinburgh, EH10 6PP.

1964 FERRARI, DR. J. N., Libertad 1550, Buenos Aires, Argentina.

1969 FINDLAY, R. P., Box 28, King City, Ontario, Canada.

1968 FINN, P., 25 Cunningham Avenue, Boxgrove Park, Guildford, Surrey.

1972 FLANAGAN, PHILIP E., 900–9th Street, S.W. Canton, Ohio 44707, U.S.A.

1958 FLESCH, DR. MAX, 24 Dubnow Street, P.O. Box 1446, Tel Aviv, Israel.

1969 FLETCHER, LESLIE H., 4 Morris Close, Henlow, Beds.

1958 FLYNN, V. J. A., 12 Ginahgulla Road, Bellevue Hill, New South Wales, Australia.

1961 FORBES, K. B., 894 Eglinton Avenue East, Apt. 215, Toronto 17, Ontario, Canada.

1972 *FORD, DAVID J. M., 7 Silhill Hall Road, Solihull, Warwickshire.

1952 FORD, JOHN J., 176 Hendrickson Avenue, Rockville Center, New York, U.S.A.

1951 FORRER, RUDOLPH, 18B Highview Road, Sidcup, Kent.

1970 FÖRSCHNER-WRUCK, DR. G., 6 Frankfurt-am-Main, Untermainkai 14–15, Rothschild Palais, Historisches Museum, Münzkabinett, Germany.

1960 FORSTER, B., P.O. Box 9059, Hamilton North, New Zealand.

1969 FOSTER, DEREK, 15 Nash Place, North Ryde, N.S.W. 2113, Australia.

1972 FREEMAN, W. A. D., 5 Grosvenor Court, Claremont Road, Seaford, Sussex.

1956 FREEMAN-GRENVILLE, G. S. P., D.Phil., F.S.A., North View House, Sheriff Hutton, Yorks.

1954 FRENCH, WILLIAM C., 7 Blenheim Street, New Bond Street, London, W.1.

1969 FREUND, DR. JOHN E., 7035 North 69th Pl., Scottsdale, Arizona 85251, U.S.A.

1960 FULD, PROFESSOR G. J., P.O. Box 5745, Baltimore, Maryland 21208, U.S.A.

1964 GANCE, L. H., 24 Hatton Garden, E.C.1.

1955 GARDNER, T. H., Smear Lane, Reydown, Southwold, Suffolk.

1953 GARTNER, JOHN, The Hawthorn Press, 15 Guildford Lane, Melbourne, Victoria, Australia.

1966 GASE, HELMUT, St. Fillans, 33 Micawber Terrace, Hillingdon, Uxbridge, Middlesex.

ELECTED

1963 GAVER, MRS. E. L., 23 Rue de Bretagne, Préville, Quebec Province, Canada.

1969 GAYTAN, C., Pilares 116, Mexico 12, D.F., Mexico.

1969 GEE, DAVID, P.O. Box 334, Surfer's Paradise, Gold Coast, Queensland 4217, Australia.

1969 GIARD, J.-B., 94 rue Broca, Paris 13e, France.

1962 GIBER, DR. P. B., 24 South State Street, Girard, Ohio, U.S.A.

1967 GILBERT, E. H. R., 27 Wyburn Road, Thundersley, Benfleet, Essex.

1964 GILBERT, HAROLD, Kiloran, 18 Perrymead, Prestwich, Manchester.

1944 GILSON, B., Flat 2, 6 Grand Parade, Westbourne, Bournemouth, Hants.

1962 GINGRAS, L., P.O. Box 15, Richmond, British Columbia, Canada.

1971 GLASBY-BALDWIN, S., 53 Cornwall Road, Newport, Mon., NPT 7SS.

1972 GODDARD, PHILIP J., 22 Jews Walk, London, S.E.26.

1947 GODEFROY, J. V. L., M.A., Rhinefield, Brockenhurst, Hants.

1964 GOLDMAN, JEROME L., P.O. Box 5397, Daytona Beach, Florida, U.S.A.

1966 GOLDSMITH, JOHN CHARLES, Havenfield Hall, Alkham Valley, near Folkestone, Kent.

1972 GOOD, HAROLD J. M., 7 Wood Road, Ashurst, nr. Southampton.

1970 GORDUS, PROFESSOR ADON A., Dept. of Chemistry, University of Michigan, Ann Arbor, Michigan 48104, U.S.A.

1968 GORINI, DR. G., Museo Civico, Padova, Italy.

1947 GOUGH, MICHAEL R. E., M.A., F.S.A., 51 Quebec Avenue, Toronto 165, Ontario, Canada.

1962 GOULD, MAURICE M., Box 1500, Tustin, California 92680, U.S.A.

1969 GRAHAM, DAVID F., COL. (retd.), 22 Knight Road, Framingham Center, Massachusetts 01701, U.S.A.

1936 GRANT, MICHAEL, C.B.E., M.A., Litt.D., F.S.A., Le Pitturacce, Gattaiola, Lucca, Italy.

1960 GRANT, P. McG., c/o National and Grindlays Bank Ltd., 54 Parliament Street, London, S.W.1.

1963 GRANTIER, B. J., 7 Tiverton Drive, Ottawa, Ontario, Canada.

1953 GRAY, SURG.-CMDR. P. H. KER, R.N., Frankfield, Farnham Lane, Haslemere, Surrey.

1970 GREEN, MRS. TAMARA M., Hunter College, New York University, 609 West 114th Street, New York, New York 10028, U.S.A.

1966 GREENALL, P. D., 20 Gardner Mansions, Church Row, Hampstead, London, N.W.3.

1957 GREENE, VINCENT G., 77 Victoria Street, Toronto, Ontario, Canada.

1968 GREENWOOD, D., 39 Newchurch-on-Pendle, Burnley, Lancs.

1961 GRICOURT, M. JEAN, 91 Avenue Pottier, Lambersart (Nord), France.

1945 GRIERSON, PHILIP, M.A., F.B.A., F.S.A., Gonville and Caius College, Cambridge, Honorary Keeper of Coins in the Fitzwilliam Museum.

1956 GRIFFIN, A. C., 27 Westmoreland Street, Bath, Somerset.

1971 GRIFFIN, EUGENE A., Town House 3, Great Neck, New York 11020, U.S.A.

1968 GRIFFIN, H., 25 Schoolhouse Lane, Teddington, Middlesex.

1959 GRINSELL, L. V., O.B.E., M.A., F.S.A., 32 Queen's Court, Clifton, Bristol 8.

1972 GROSSMAN, ROBERT C., Suite 1900, 75 East Walker Drive, Chicago, Ill. 60601, U.S.A.

1947 GROVER, BRIAN, 23 Beauchamp Road, East Molesey, Surrey.

1972 GRUBB, THE REVD. G. WATKINS, Wheatridge Lodge, Torquay.

1960 GRUNTHAL, HENRY, American Numismatic Society, Broadway at 156th Street, New York, New York 10032, U.S.A.

1965 GUEST, DR. R. G., 1648 Victoria Park Avenue, Toronto 16, Ontario, Canada.

1972 GUILDING, MICHAEL A., 211 Gilesgate, Durham, Co. Durham.

1962 GUPTA, DR. P. LAL, Patna Museum, Patna 1, Bihar, India.


1961 HACKENS, TONY, Promenade 9, Hergenrath, Belgium.

1969 HADDAD, SELIM S., Phoenicia Hotel, P.O. Box 2615, Beirut, Lebanon.

1970 HADZIOTIS, COSTAS C., P.O. Box 1369, Athens, Greece.

1948 HAGLEY, SYDNEY V., 20 Garden Avenue, Burnside 5066, South Australia.

1968 HAIGH, CAPT. JOHN, 15 Granville Square, London, W.C.1.

1916 *HAINES, GEOFFREY COLTON, O.B.E., F.C.A., F.S.A., 31 Larpent Avenue, Putney, London, S.W.15.

1968 HALE, C., B.Sc., Montes Escandinavos 210, Mexico 10, D.F., Mexico.

1965 VON HALLE, WALTER F. E., 25 Carlyle Square, London, S.W. 3.

1969 HALLIWELL, DR. E. O., 233 Hallgate, Cottingham, Yorks.

1951 HAMILTON, DUDLEY C., c/o National & Grindlays Bank Ltd., 13 St. James's Square, London, S.W.1.

1960 HAMMOND, J. F. D., Reeves, Mill Lane, Great Steeping, Spilsby, Lincs.

1964 HANCOCK, VIRGIL, 4901 Bellaire Boulevard, Bellaire 101, Texas, U.S.A.

1966 HARDAKER, T. R., B.A., 'Willcott', 79 Millwood End, Long Hanborough, Oxford, OX7 2BP.

1963 HART, G. D., M.D., F.R.C.P.(C), 7 Hatherton Crescent, Don Mills, Ontario, Canada.

1951 HART, THE REVD. H. ST. JOHN, M.A., Queens' College, Cambridge.

1958 HARTMANN, J., 5 Avenue Arnold Delvaux, Brussels 18, Belgium.

1950 HEALY, J. F., M.A., Ph.D., Royal Holloway College, Englefield Green, Surrey.

1951 HECHT, R. E., A.B., Via di Villa Pepoli 5, Rome, Italy.

1943 HELLER, PROFESSOR H. S., M.D., Ph.D., M.R.C.P., University of Bristol, Bristol.

1962 HENDY, M. F., M.A., Lecturer in Numismatics, The Barber Institute of Fine Arts, The University, Birmingham 15.

1967 HENSON, C. T., 57 St. Martin's Street, Peterborough, Northants. PE1 3BB.

1949 HERSH, C. A., M.A., 190 First Street (Apt. 3–D), P.O. Box 268, Mineola, New York 11501, U.S.A.

1972 HESSLER, GENE, Chase Manhattan Bank Money Museum, 1254 Avenue of the Americas, New York, N.Y. 10020, U.S.A.

1953 HEWITT, THE REVD. K. V., St. Augustine's Vicarage, 117 Queen's Gate, London, S.W.7.

ELECTED

1971 HIGGINBOTTOM, R. W., The Crossways, Bruntingthorpe, Nr. Rugby, Warwickshire.

1965 HIGH, CLAYTON E., P.O. 386, Eau Claire, Wisconsin, U.S.A.

1967 HIGNETT, E. J., B.A., Dip.Ed., 2 St. Anne's Grove, Aigburth, Liverpool 17.

1944 HILL, SIR FRANCIS, C.B.E., M.A., LL.M., Litt.D., F.S.A., The Priory, Lincoln.

1959 HILL, LESLIE C., P.O. Box 662, New Westminster, British Columbia, Canada.

1969 HILLEL, M., 27 Kingsley Way, London, N.2.

1970 HILLGARTH, TRISTAN, Illannanagh House, Ballinderry, via Nenagh, Co. Tipperary, Eire.

1970 HIND, J. G. F., M.A. Cantab., Dept. of Classics, University of Otago, New Zealand.

1966 HIPÓLITO, DR. MARIO DE CASTRO, R. Arantes e Oliverra 31A-6-DIR, Coimbra, Portugal.

1943 HIRD, HORACE, M.A., F.S.A., 30 Haworth Road, Bradford 9, Yorks.

1962 HODGKIN, LUKE, 108 Cannon Park Road, Coventry, Warwickshire.

1950 HODGKIN, T. L., 94 Woodstock Road, Oxford.

1952 HOFFMANN, DR. E., 8 München 81, Pienzenauerstrasse 103, Germany.

1972 HOGAN, PATRICK D., 614 So. Johnson St., Iowa City, Iowa 52240, U.S.A.

1967 HOLLIS, A. S., M.A., D.Phil., Keble College, Oxford.

1961 HOLMES, DR. URBAN T., Kenan Professor of Romance Philology, University of North Carolina, 102 Pine Lane, Chapel Hill, North Carolina, U.S.A.

1971 HONOUR, W. ARTHUR, 1033 E. 12 Avenue, Vancouver 10, B.C., Canada.

1949 HOPPER, R. J., B.A., Ph.D., F.S.A., Dept. of Ancient History, The University, Sheffield 10.

1968 HOULTON, C. M., M.A., 275 Stockingstone Road, Luton, Beds.

1969 HUBBARD, C., Avenida de las Fuentes 664, Mexico 20, D.F., Mexico.

1971 HUDSON, RODNEY, 5 Graham Bell Close, Newport, Mon., NPT 6PD.

1963 HUMPHRIES, L. C., 4 Ascot Avenue, Dulwich, South Australia.

1970 HUMPHRIS, MRS. J., 4 Pembroke Walk, London, W.8.

1955 HUNTER, T. F., 69 Dene View Crescent, Hylton, Sunderland, Co. Durham.

1967 HURTER, MRS. SYLVIA, Klosbachstrasse 111, Zurich 8032, Switzerland.

1957 HUSTWAYTE, R. L., 33 St. James Avenue, Marden Ash, Ongar, Essex.


1972 ILISCH, LUTZ, 4425 Billerbeck, Bahnhofstrasse 7, Germany.

1960 INGHOLT, PROFESSOR HARALD, Newton Road, Woodbridge, Connecticut 06525, U.S.A.

1957 INGRAMS, S., 'Patina', Whitsburg Road, Tinkers Cross, Fordingbridge, Hants.

1966 IRVINE, A. K., M.A., D.Phil., School of Oriental and African Studies, University of London, W.C.1.

1971 ISAAC, PHILIP J., Rose Cottage, Chapel Lane, Willesley, Wotton-under-edge, Glos.

1969 ISHERWOOD, G. H., 52 Brown Lane, Heald Green, Cheadle, Cheshire.


1953 JACKMAN, F. A., B.Sc., Crendon, Church Lane, Pinner, Middlesex.

ELECTED

1965 JACKSON, MRS. A. E., B.A., 46 Fairholme Road, Withington, Manchester, M20 9SB.

1946 *JACOB, KENNETH ALLEN, Lynstone, 32 Gilbert Road, Cambridge, CB4 3PE.

1969 JAMESON, MISS S., M.A., D.Phil., Ph.D., Girton College, Cambridge.

1962 JANOVSKY, KONSTANTIN, Avenue Sevom Esfand, Teheran, Iran.

1962 JARVIS, MAJOR CALE B., Suite 1109, 62 Richmond St. West, Toronto 1, Ontario, Canada.

1962 JARVIS, CECIL A., 100 Wellesley Street E., Suite 2512, Toronto 5, Ontario, Canada.

1946 JEFFERY, F. J., 20 Warwick Crescent, Melksham, Wilts.

1947 JENKINS, G. K., B.A., Keeper of Coins and Medals, British Museum, London, W.C.1; *Hon. Secretary.*

1961 JEWELL, RAY, 107 Addison Street, Elwood, S. 3, Victoria, Australia.

1962 JEWETT, F. C., 26 Davean Drive, Bayview Hills, Willowdale, Ontario, Canada.

1959 JOHNSON, CAPT. ARTHUR F., U.S.N., 6501 Blue Bill Lane, Alexandria, Virginia 22307, U.S.A.

1967 JOHNSON, DONALD J., 164 Cheshire Drive, Penllyn, Pa. 19458, U.S.A.

1962 JOHNSON, D. WAYNE, Medallic Art Company, 325 E. 45th Street, New York, U.S.A.

1968 JOHNSON, G. D., 50 Bayswater Road, Moonah, Tasmania, Australia.

1970 JONES, DAVID J., 38 Milford Road, Wolverhampton, Staffs.

1948 JONES, DORAN A., North Haverhill, New Hampshire 03774, U.S.A.

1953 JONES, F. ELMORE, 133 Moorgate, London, E.C.2.

1946 *JUDD, DR. F. HEWITT, 234 The Doctor's Buildings, Omaha, Nebraska 68131, U.S.A.

1968 JUNGE, EWALD, 29 Warwick Crescent, Arthur Road, Edgbaston, Birmingham, BI5 2LH.

1970 KALDOR, ROBERT G., 1 Ellerslie Place, Toorak 3142, Melbourne, Victoria, Australia.

1970 KAMMERER, DR. RICHARD C., P.O. Box 25146, Los Angeles, California 90025, U.S.A.

1958 KAPAMADJI, MME N., 17 rue de la Banque, Paris IIe, France.

1966 KAPLAN, DR. S. M., P.O. Box 132, Germiston, South Africa.

1967 KASZEWSKI, MRS. P., 78 Cornwall Street, Plymouth, Devon.

1948 KATEN, FRANK J., P.O. Box 4047, Colesville, Silver Spring, Maryland 20904, U.S.A.

1969 AL-KAZZAZ, MRS. WIDAD ALI, Coinage Division, Directorate General of Antiquities, Baghdad, Iraq.

1971 KEAN, JOHN D., 17 Midland Avenue, Hicksville, N.Y., 11801, U.S.A.

1949 KELLEY, ROBERT F., The Westchester, Apt. 443 B, 400 Cathedral Avenue, N.W., Washington, D.C. 20016, U.S.A.

1948 KENT, J. P. C., Ph.D., F.S.A., Dept. of Coins and Medals, British Museum, London, W.C.1.

ELECTED

1965 KETTLE, LT.-COL. ALAN FREDERICK (retd.), A.A.I.B., F.R.S.A., F.R.G.S., Sutton Manor, Sutton Scarsdale, Derby.

1970 KEYES, MICHAEL, 8512 N. Jefferson Drive, Spokane, Washington 99208, U.S.A.

1968 KIENAST, G. W., 7330 Grant Boulevard, Cleveland, Ohio 44130, U.S.A.

1971 KILGORE, DONALD G. Jr., M.D., 129 Rockingham Road, Greenville, South Carolina 29607, U.S.A.

1962 KINDLER, DR. ARIE, Director of the Kadman Numismatic Museum, 4 Kahanstam Street, Tel Aviv, Israel.

1954 KING, H. H., M.A., Undershaw Hotel, Hindhead, Surrey.

1972 KIRKPATRICK, CLIFFORD A., 14 Westways, Stoneleigh, Surrey.

1962 KLAWANS, ZANDER H., 1204 Sylvan Road, Monterey, California, U.S.A.

1970 KLEINER, FRED S., 5011 17th Avenue, Brooklyn, New York 11204, U.S.A.

1963 KLIMOWSKY, DR. ERNST W., 10 Pinsker Street, Tel Aviv, Israel.

1945 KNOBLOCH, FREDERICK S., P.O. Box 15725, Pine Hills, Orlando, Florida 32808, U.S.A.

1970 KOORLANDER, BERNARD, 7 Allhalland Street, Bideford, Devon.

1946 KOSOFF, A., P.O. Box 456, Encino, California, U.S.A.

1971 KOVACS, FRANK L., P.O. Box 10071, Oakland, California 94610, U.S.A.

1948 KRAAY, COLIN M., M.A., D.Phil., F.S.A., The Ashmolean Museum, Oxford; *President*.

1960 KREISBERG, ABNER, 228 N. Beverly Drive, Beverly Hills, California, U.S.A.

1968 KREMERSKOTHEN, T. P., 44 Warragul Street, Launceston 7250, Tasmania, Australia.

1951 KROLIK, P. D., 45 Eaton Square, London, S.W.1.

1959 KRUPP, ERNEST, 139–45 87th Road, Jamaica, Long Island, New York, U.S.A.

1959 KRUPP, FRANK, 139–45 87th Road, Jamaica, Long Island, New York, U.S.A.

1968 KUYAS, T., Haus Semadenipromenade, P.O. Box 88, CH-7270, Davos Platz, Switzerland.


1959 LAGERQVIST, MUSEILEKTOR LARS OLOF, Ymervägen 20, S–182 63 Djursholm, Sweden.

1965 LAHIRI, DR. A. N., M.A., D.Litt., Block 9, Flat 8, Govt. Housing Estate, Regent Park, Calcutta 40, India.

1955 LAINCHBURY, A. W., Trigmoor, Kingham, Oxon.

1967 LAING, LLOYD R., M.A., F.S.A. (Scot.), Department of Archaeology, 14 Abercromby Square, P.O. Box 147, Liverpool, L69 3BX.

1961 LANE, C. H., Stanfield, Spital Lane, Chesterfield, Derby.

1970 LANE, DENNIS, 105–2120 West 44th Avenue, Vancouver 13, B.C., Canada.

1968 LANE, PETER, 23 Price Avenue, Lower Mitcham, South Australia.

1970 LANE, ROGER DE WARDT, 4107 Fillmore Street, Hollywood, Florida 33020, U.S.A.

1964 LANE, STUART NASSAU, B.A., Bridestream House, Kilcock, Co. Kildare, Eire.

ELECTED

1953 LANG, PROFESSOR D. M., M.A., Ph.D., D.Litt., Litt.D., Professor of Caucasian Studies, School of Oriental and African Studies, University of London, London, W.C.1.

1970 LANGLEY, JOHN, Barton, 1 Winifred Road, Pound Lane, Poole, Dorset.

1970 LANNON, DONALD B., 1464 N. Chestnut Avenue, Rialto, California 92376, U.S.A.

1964 LA PIERRE, LORENZO, 901 So. Idaho St. Apt. 39, La Habra, California 90631, U.S.A.

1955 LARSEN, L. V., 1136 Kenilworth Avenue, Coshocton, Ohio, U.S.A.

1970 LAURITSEN, FREDERICK M., Eastern Washington State College, Division of History and Social Science, Cheney, Washington 99004, U.S.A.

1967 LAWRENCE, J. N., P.O. Box 8113, Johannesburg, South Africa.

1967 LAX, E. R., Hotel Bristowe, Grange Road, Southbourne, Bournemouth, Hants.

1969 LAYNE, I. P., 54 Rayens Cross Road, Long Ashton, Bristol, BS18 9DY.

1967 LEADER, M. E. B., 119 Warwick Way, London, S.W.1.

1971 LEE, IAN, 7 Adderley Court, Alexandra Road, Parkstone, Poole, Dorset, BH14 9ER.

1966 LEFFLER, W. S., 3 Holly Cottages, Handcross Road, Staplefield, Sussex.

1971 LENG, G. Y., F.R.H.S., F.R.Com.S., 90 Jalan Dua, Eng Ann Estate, Klang, Selangor, Malaysia.

1955 LE RIDER, GEORGES, 3 rue Eugénie Gérard, 94 Vincennes, France.

1968 LESSEN, M., 164 Homestead Avenue, Albany, New York 12203, U.S.A.

1971 LEUTHOLD, DR. ING. ENRICO, Piazza Repubblica 25, Milan 20124, Italy.

1967 LEVANTE, E., P.O. Box 37, Iskenderun, Turkey.

1970 LEVICK, MISS BARBARA, St. Hilda's College, Oxford, OX4 1DY.

1971 LEWIS, A. S., 8A Newlyn Place, Preston, Lancs., PR2 3ZA.

1966 LEWIS, D. A., 6 Mount View Road, Kingsbury, London, N.W.9.

1958 LEWIS, G. D., M.A., F.S.A., F.M.A., 78 Freshfield Road, Freshfield, Formby, Lancs., L37 7BD.

1971 LEWIS, DR. PAUL M., Flat 1, 65 Compayne Gardens, London, NW6 3DB.

1950 *LEWIS, R. B., M.A., F.S.A., Flat 2, 46 Green Street, London, W. 1.

1953 *LHOTKA, PROFESSOR JOHN F., M.D., Ph.D., University of Oklahoma, 800 Northeast Thirteenth Street, Oklahoma City 4, Oklahoma, U.S.A.

1948 LIDDELL, D. G., 17 Ryecroft Street, London, S.W.6.

1964 LINDAMOOD, W. W., P.O. Box 428, Guelph, Ontario, Canada.

1965 LINDGREN, HENRY C., Ph.D., Professor of Psychology, San Francisco State College, California, 94132, U.S.A.

1946 LINDSAY, CARMEN C., 46 Briscoe Street East, London, Ontario, Canada.

1969 LINECAR, H. W. A., 5–7 King Street, St. James's, London, S.W.1.

1971 LOBEL, RICHARD, Morley House, 320 Regent Street, London, W1R 6QJ.

1963 LOWICK, N. M., B.A., Dept. of Coins and Medals, British Museum, London, W.C.1; *Hon. Librarian*.

1960 LOWTHER, A. W. G., F.S.A., A.R.I.B.A., The Old Quarry, Warrens Estate, Ashtead, Surrey.

1970 LUND, WILLIAM R., Gulf Building, Pittsburgh, Pennsylvania 15230, U.S.A.

ELECTED

1955 Lyon, C. S. S., B.A., F.I.A., F.S.A., Cuerdale, White Lane, Guildford, Surrey.

1970 Lyons, R. S., 17 Lansdowne Avenue, Codsall, near Wolverhampton.

1970 McClung, Ed, P.O. Box 7229, Burbank, California 91505, U.S.A.

1969 MacDonald, D. J., 1004 Howard St. Apt. A, Normal, Illinois, U.S.A.

1952 MacDowall, D. W., M.A., D.Phil., F.S.A., F.R.A.S., Admont, Gravel Path, Berkhamsted, Herts.; *Hon. Treasurer.*

1969 McDowell, R. S., 885 Camino Encantado, Los Alamos, New Mexico 87544, U.S.A.

1962 MacHugh, Jay, 1515 West 8th Street, Little Rock, Arkansas, U.S.A.

1955 Mack, Cmdr. R. P., M.V.O., R.N. (retd.), West House, Droxford, Hants.

1969 McKay-Clements, J. L. C., 610 Lake Shore Road, Haileybury, Ontario, Canada.

1954 MacKechnie, Mrs. Margaret, 4 Watch Bell Street, Rye, Sussex.

1958 Macnaghton, R. D., M.A., 2 Common Lane, Eton College, Windsor.

1965 McNeice, Roger V., 8 Orana Place, Taroona, 7006, Tasmania, Australia.

1971 McQuade, Mrs. G. D. Ruth, 183 Island Park Drive, Ottawa, Ontario, K1Y OA3, Canada.

1956 Madden, Ian B., Rosslea, 16 Belvedere Street, Epsom, Auckland, S.E.3, New Zealand.

1968 Magnay, D. E., 11 Westfield Close, Laverstock, Salisbury, Wilts.

1971 Mair, Errol H., 111 Hastings Parade, North Bendi, Sydney, N.S.W. 2026, Australia.

1971 Malcolm, J. C. St. Alban, Denver Hall, Denver, nr. Downham Market, Suffolk.

1923 Mallinson, The Revd. Arnold, St. Frideswide's Vicarage, Oxford.

1969 Malloy, Alex. G., P.O. Box 38, South Salem, New York 10590, U.S.A.

1970 Malter, Joel L., P.O. Box 777, Encino, California, U.S.A.

1967 Manganaro, Dr. G., via Androne 55, Catania, Italy.

1963 Manville, H. E., U.S. Consulate General, 1558 McGregor Avenue, Montreal 109, P.Q. Canada.

1970 Manville, Ray, P.O. Box 275, Springfield, Pennsylvania 19064, U.S.A.

1971 Marchetti, P., Van Monsstraat 115, 3000 Louvain, Belgium.

1964 Margrave, Robert N., Ph.D., 3612 Macomb Street, N.W., Washington 16, D.C. 20016, U.S.A.

1959 Martel, Russell, 10 Lake Crescent, Toronto 14, Ontario, Canada.

1965 Martin, A. B., 40 Prey Heath Close, Mayford, Woking, Surrey.

1971 Martin, Colin, 1 rue Pépinet, CH-1000 Lausanne, Switzerland.

1955 Martin, Mrs. J. S., Dept. of Coins and Medals, British Museum, London, W.C.1.

1958 Massimo, Prince Vittorio, Palazzo Massimo, Rome, Italy.

1971 Mata, José M., Isabel II 16–3°A, San Sebastian, Spain.

1951 Mateu y Llopis, Dr. Felipe, Director, Biblioteca Central, Barcelona, Spain.

1956 Mattingly, Harold B., B.A., School of History, The University, Leeds.

1943 May, Harry, 58 Rosslyn Hill, Hampstead, London, N.W.3.

ELECTED

1963 MELVILLE-JONES, J. R., M.A., Ph.D., Dept. of Classics and Ancient History, The University of Western Australia, Nedlands, W. Australia.

1957 MERKIN, LESTER, 65 E. 56th Street, New York, New York 10022, U.S.A.

1962 MERRITT, L. G., Jr., Attorney at Law, 3319 Pine Belt Road, Columbia, South Carolina, 29204, U.S.A.

1969 MESHORER, Y., M.A., Hebrew University, Jerusalem, Israel.

1957 METCALF, D. M., M.A., D.Phil., 55 Bainton Road, Oxford.

1960 MEYSHAN, DR. JOSEF, 39 Balfour Street, Tel Aviv, Israel.

1965 MICHAELIDES, PHILIPPOS TH., 19 Joannis Polemis, P.O. Box 1184, Limassol, Cyprus.

1929 MILBANK, S. R., 20 Exchange Place, New York, New York 10005, U.S.A.

1953 MILDENBERG, DR. LEO, c/o Leu and Co.'s Bank, Bahnhofstrasse 32, Zurich, Switzerland.

1969 MILES, A. A., 33 Knoll Road, Bexley, Kent.

1968 MILLER, D. M., 11 Etna Road, St. Albans, Herts.

1970 MILLER, ERIC J., P.O. Box 211 Station R, Toronto, Ontario, Canada.

1970 MILLIGAN, JAMES C., M.A., B.Sc., Ph.D., M.Ed., F.S.A. (Scot.), 25 Hilton Street, Aberdeen.

1964 MILLWARD, M. S., 64 Great Portland Street, London, W.1.

1932 MITCHELL, D. D., 19 Lime Grove, Twickenham, Middlesex.

1967 MITCHELL, P. D., Thainston, Hill View Road, Claygate, Esher, Surrey.

1966 MITCHELL, R. E., University of Illinois, Champaign, Illinois, U.S.A.

1971 MITCHELS, R. L., 131 Briarhurst Drive, Tonawanda, New York 14150, U.S.A.

1967 MITCHINER, DR. M. B., 'Ravenhill', Recton Park, Sanderstead, S. Croydon, Surrey, CR2 9JR.

1970 MONINS, I. R., P.O. Box 122, Jersey, C.I.

1959 MORCOM, CHRISTOPHER, 1 Essex Court, Temple, London, E.C.4.

1959 MORCOM, JOHN, 24 Lawn Crescent, Kew, Richmond, Surrey.

1972 MORGAN, F. L., F.S.A. (Scot.), 42 Claremont Road, Morecambe, Lancs.

1968 MORRIS, R. W., 3503 Lakeland Drive, Austin, Texas 78731, U.S.A.

1971 MORRISSON, MME CÉCILE, 10 rue Jeanne D'Arc, 92 Sèvres, France.

1961 MOSSOP, HENRY R., Greenleaves, Marshchapel, Grimsby, Lincs.

1958 MOSSOP, J. C., M.A., c/o Mossop and Bowser, Holbeach, Lincs.

1971 MULCAHY, KIERAN, 1 Maryville, Ballintemple, Cork, Eire.

1953 MULLER, GEORGE E., c/o Messrs. Spink and Sons Ltd., 5–7 King Street, St. James's, London, S.W.1.

1965 MUÑOZ, MIGUEL L., Apartado 897, Mexico 1, D.F.

1967 MURRAY, LT.-COL. J. K. R., 13 Homecroft Drive, Uckington, Cheltenham, Glos.

1967 *MYERS, ROBERT J., Box 442, Lenox Hill, New York, New York 10021, U.S.A.

1953 *NARAIN, A. K., M.A., Ph.D., Dept. of History, University of Wisconsin, 435 North Park St., Madison, Wisconsin, 53706, U.S.A.

1971 NARBETH, COLIN, 103 Kirby Road, Walton-on-Naze, Essex.

ELECTED

1967 NASCIA, SIGNOR G., 1 Piazza S. Maria Beltrade, Milan, Italy.

1965 NASSAR, EDWARD, 32 Chemin de Craivavers, Lausanne, Switzerland.

1969 NASTER, PROFESSOR P. M. F., Bogaardenstraat 66D, Leuven, Belgium.

1954 NAVASCUÉS, PROFESSOR J. Mª. DE, Ministro Ibanez Martin 3, Madrid 15, Spain.

1966 NEDELTCHEV, DR. KIRIL, Benkovski 45, Sofia, Bulgaria.

1972 NEU, A. M., 120 Vermilyea Avenue, New York, N.Y. 10034, U.S.A.

1965 NEVIN, T. R., T.D., LL.B., J.P., Rawdon Hall, Rawdon, near Leeds, Yorks.

1966 NICKLE, CARL O., Anglo-American Bldg., 330–9th Avenue S.W., Calgary, Alberta, Canada.

1967 NISBET, J. D. F., c/o Barclays Bank, 2 Worcester Road, Great Malvern, Worcs.

1954 NORWEB, MRS. R. HENRY, 9511 Lake Shore Boulevard, Cleveland 8, Ohio, U.S.A.

1936 NOTMAN, JOHN W., Boswall House, Boswall Road, Edinburgh EH5 3RR.

1969 NUSSBAUM, H. J., 1420 K Street, N.W., Washington, D.C. 20005, U.S.A.


1955 O'BRIEN, HON. W. E., RFD No. 1, Glendalough, Plymouth, New Hampshire, U.S.A.

1970 O'CONNOR, J. S., 68 St. Elmo Parade, Kingsgrove, N.S.W., Australia, 2208.

1971 ODDY, W. A., Research Laboratory, British Museum, London, W.C.1.

1965 OECONOMIDES, MRS. MANDO CARAMESSINI, Heyden 30, Athens 104.

1967 O'HARA, M. D., 11 Angel Road, Harrow-on-the-Hill, Middlesex.

1964 OLSON, LIEUT. JOHN G., U.S.N.R., H.Q. Eighth Naval District, Bldg. 11, New Orleans, Louisiana 70140, U.S.A.

1925 OMAN, CHARLES CHICHELE, M.A., 13 Woodborough Road, London, S.W.15.

1960 ORTON, COLIN H., B.A., 607–8 Avenue, S.W., Calgary, Alberta, Canada. *Curator of Numismatics, University of Calgary; Curator, Nickle Foundation in the Alberta Govt. Glenbow Museum.*

1971 OSBAND, E., Sproughton, Courtenay Avenue, Kenwood, London, N.6.

1953 OSBORNE, B. R., M.P.S., Central Pharmacy, Clare, Sudbury, Suffolk.

1967 O'SHEA, P. P., G.P.O. Box 2021, Wellington, New Zealand.

1961 OSI, HAROLD, 2 Harding Way, Cambridge.

1945 OVERTON, E. MAURICE, Weston Manor, Honiton, Devon.

1962 OXMANTOWN, LORD, Birr Castle, Co. Offaly, Eire.


1960 PAGLIARI, RENZO, Rua Suecia 212, São Paulo, Brazil.

1963 PALMER, WAYNE N., Utica College, Utica, New York 13502, U.S.A.

1961 PANVINI ROSATI, DR. F., Medagliere, Museo Nazionale Romano, Rome 1, Italy.

1947 PARKE, PROFESSOR H. W., Litt.D., 9 Trinity College, Dublin, Eire.

1963 PARKER, NICK, 17 Parkside, Knightsbridge, London, S.W.1.

1955 PARRISH, JAMES, M.D., 251 Riverside Drive, Portsmouth, Virginia, U.S.A.

1972 PARRY, J. D., 7 Cantilupe Road, Ross-on-Wye, Hereford.

1957 PARSONS, OWEN F., Boundary Cottage, Churchdown Lane, Hucclecote, Glos.

ELECTED

1954 PATEL, P. R., 3 Pavlova, 10 Little Gibbs Road, Bombay 6, India.

1960 PAVAL, PHILIP, 2244 Stanley Hills Drive, Hollywood 46, California, U.S.A.

1972 PAYNE, D. F., 8 St. Andrew's Close, North Baddesley, Southampton, SO5 9GJ.

1966 PEARCE, LT.-COL. G. T., M.B.E., R.C.T., H.Q., B.A.O.R. (Q LE.Man.), B.F.P.O. 40.

1968 PECK, PHILIP, 446 West 50th Street, New York, New York 10019, U.S.A.

1962 PEDDIE, J. ALBERT, 593 St. Clair Avenue West, Apt. 6, Toronto 10, Ontario, Canada.

1962 PEGAN, EFREM, Prazahova 8, Ljubljana, Yugoslavia.

1954 PEGG, H., 8 Devonshire Avenue, Beeston, Notts.

1967 PENTLAND, D. H., 575 Wardlaw Avenue, Winnipeg, Manitoba 13, Canada.

1966 PERE, NURI, Yapi ve Kredi Bankasi, Beyoglu, Istanbul, Turkey.

1971 PESANT, ROBERTO J., 215 East 80th Street, New York, N.Y. 10021, U.S.A.

1966 PETERSON, RICHARD E., 300 Hoodridge Dr., Mt. Lebanon, Pa. 15234, U.S.A.

1961 PETRIE, A. E. H., 60 Stanley Avenue, Apt. 18, Ottawa, Canada.

1969 PHILIPSON, FREDERICK, 5 Windermere Road, Beeston, Nottingham, NG9 3AS.

1957 PHILLIPS, JOHN R., 5 Albion Place, Northampton.

1967 PHILLIPS, WAYNE C., P.O. Box 544, Santa Susana, California 93063, U.S.A.

1969 PINCHES, JOHN (MEDALLISTS) LTD., 1 St. Luke's Avenue, London, S.W.4.

1959 PINKUS, MAX, 34 Nassau Street, Toronto 2-B, Ontario, Canada.

1957 PIRIE, MISS E. J. E., M.A., F.S.A. (Scot.), City Museum, Park Row, Leeds 1.

1967 PITCHFORK, C. E., M.A., B.Sc., 11 Florida Avenue, Ermington, Sydney, N.S.W., Australia.

1953 PITCHFORK, W. H., Dovercourt, 9 Woodlands View, Scunthorpe, Lincs.

1968 PITSILLIDES, A. G., 10 Pythonos Street, Nicosia (101), Cyprus.

1961 PITTMAN, JOHN J., 4 Acton Street, Rochester 15, New York, U.S.A.

1971 POCHITONOV, EUGEN, Prague 2, Jugoslavska 11, Czechoslovakia.

1956 POLLARD, J. G., B.A., Keeper, Department of Coins and Medals, Fitzwilliam Museum, Cambridge.

1964 PORTEOUS, JOHN, M.A., 52 Elgin Crescent, London, W.11.

1967 PORTER, W/CMDR. G. H., R.A.F. (retd.), 98A Church Road, Bexleyheath, Kent.

1967 PRATLEY, L. J., 36 Elstree Road, Bushey Heath, Herts.

1956 PRAWDZIC-GOLEMBERSKI, E. J., 93 Whitemoor Road, Basford, Nottingham.

1964 PRICE, MARTIN J., M.A., Dept. of Coins and Medals, British Museum, London, W.C.1.

1972 PRITCHARD, J. F., Grove House, 59 Staunton Road, Coleford, Glos.

1967 PURVES, A. A., 'Four Trees', Laurel Drive, Brundall, Norwich, Norfolk.

1955 PURVEY, FRANK, c/o B. A. Seaby Ltd., Audley House, 11 Margaret Street, Oxford Circus, London, W.1.

1954 PYKETT, R. H. A., B.Com., F.C.I.S., 'Ivanhoe', 10 Marlborough Road, Woodthorpe, Nottingham.

1961 RAINCOCK, J. L., B.A., A.C.P., The Queen's School, Wisbech, Cambs.

ELECTED

1971 RAIVID, G. S., M.P.S., M.I.Pharm.M., 42 Foscote Road, London, N.W.4.

1968 RAJAKARUNA, W. E., 448 Great West Road, Hounslow, Middlesex.

1962 RANDERIA, P. K., M.B., B.S., c/o Lloyds Bank, 39 Piccadilly, London, W.1.

1963 RAO, RAMESH, The Concord of India Insurance Co. Ltd., 'Finance House', Patullo Road, P.O. Box 2725, Madras 2, India.

1963 RATHBONE, M. J. S., 2 Brierley, Chelmsford Road, Durban, Natal, South Africa.

1937 RAVEN, E. J. P., B.A., 12 Beaconsfield Place, Aberdeen.

1956 RAYMOND, DR. DORIS, Panormon, Doridos, Greece.

1969 REDFERN, E. H., 'Perry Dene', Pear Tree Lane, Shorne, Gravesend, Kent.

1963 REECE, RICHARD, B.Sc., F.S.A., Institute of Archaeology, Gordon Square, London, W.C.1.

1969 REID, J. M., Apt. G-10, 2531 Lake Shore Boulevard West, Toronto 14 Ontario, Canada.

1969 REMICK, JEROME H., P.O. Box 9183, Quebec 10, P.Q. Canada.

1968 RHODES, N. G., 28 Holland Park Avenue, London, W.11.

1970 RICARD, C. J., P.O. 321, Northbrook, Illinois 60062, U.S.A.

1966 RICHARD, JEAN-CLAUDE, 9 Rue de Chèvrefeuille, 34 Montpelier, France.

1970 RIDGE, LARRY OLIN, P.O. Box 291, 219 E. Walnut Street, Ripley, Mississippi 38663, U.S.A.

1952 RIGOLD, S. E., M.A., F.S.A., Ministry of Public Buildings and Works, Sanctuary Buildings, Great Smith Street, London, S.W.1.

1962 RIVA, DR. RENZO, Via Borghi 2, Gallarate, Italy.

1971 RIVETT, C. D., 8 Eastwood Road, South Woodford, London, E18 1BW.

1937 ROBERTSON, MISS ANNE S., M.A., D.Litt., F.S.A., F.S.A.(Scot.), Hunterian Museum, The University, Glasgow.

1911 *ROBINSON, SIR EDWARD, C.B.E., M.A., Hon. D.Litt., F.B.A., F.S.A., Stepleton, Iwerne Stepleton, Blandford Forum, Dorset; *Hon. Vice-President*.

1966 ROBINSON, G. W., Royal Mint, Perth, Western Australia.

1967 RODEWALD, C. A., M.A., Dept. of History, The University, Manchester 13.

1969 ROEPE, HAROLD, 2003 Grand Boulevard, Cedar Falls, Iowa, U.S.A.

1970 ROMAGOSA, JUAN, Ganduxer 15, 4 C4, Barcelona 6, Spain.

1959 ROPER, I. T., c/o Merebonn Ltd., 1 Philpot Lane, London, E.C.3.

1950 ROSE, MRS. ANNE L., M.A., Horsepools House, The Edge, near Stroud, Glos.

1967 ROSEN, DR. J., Arnold Böcklinstrasse 17, CH-4000, Basel, Switzerland.

1971 ROSENBERG, KARL H., 2517 N.W. 77th Street, Miami, Florida 33147, U.S.A.

1955 ROWLANDS, THE REVD. J. F., 7 Brewer Avenue, Durban, Natal, South Africa.

1970 ROY, P. C., M.A., Ph.D., 272 Anugrahapuri, Gaya, Bihar, India.

1958 RUEHRMUND, CMDR. JAMES C., U.S.N., 712 Westover Road, Richmond, Virginia 23220, U.S.A.

1963 RULAU, RUSSELL, 520 North Ohio, Sidney, Ohio, U.S.A.

1955 RUNDLE, P. W., M.A., Woodline Cottage, Burcombe, Salisbury, Wilts.

1969 RUTTER, N. K., Dept. of Greek, The David Hume Tower, George Square, Edinburgh, EH8 9JX.

ELECTED

1946 *STACK, MORTON B., 123 West 57th Street, New York, New York 19, U.S.A.

1969 STALBOW, B. D., 123 Sudbury Court Drive, Harrow, Middlesex.

1959 STANCOMB, W. M., Hill House, Manuden, Bishop's Stortford, Herts.

1970 STARR, PROFESSOR CHESTER G., Dept. of History, University of Michigan, Ann Arbor, Michigan, U.S.A.

1963 STATHATOS, MME M. C., 11 Neophitou Douca, Athens, Greece.

1970 STEIN, JACOB, 7125 Elbrook Drive, Cincinnati, Ohio 45237, U.S.A.

1958 STERN, DR. SAMUEL, 160 East 89th Street, New York, U.S.A.

1957 STERN, DR. S. M., All Souls College, Oxford.

1948 STEVENS, C. E., M.A., B.Litt., F.S.A., Magdalen College, Oxford.

1956 STEWART, B. H. I. H., M.A., F.S.A., F.S.A. (Scot.), 121 St. George's Road, London, S.E.1.

1969 STOPP, FREDERICK JOHN, Gonville and Caius College, Cambridge.

1961 STRAUSS, PIERRE, Schöllenenstrasse 2, CH-4054, Basel, Switzerland.

1969 SULLIVAN, P. L., P.O. Box 2353, Station D, Ottawa 4, Ontario, Canada.

1945 *SUMNER, DR. LAURA B., Mary Washington College, Fredericksburg, Virginia, U.S.A.

1936 SUTHERLAND, C. H. V., C.B.E., M.A., D.Litt., F.B.A., F.S.A., Westfield House, Cumnor, Oxford, Keeper of the Heberden Coin Room, Ashmolean Museum, Oxford; *Vice-President*.

1969 SWEETEN, MRS. MARGARET, 34334 Fraser Street, Abbotsford, B.C., Canada.

1954 SYME, PROFESSOR SIR RONALD, M.A., F.B.A., Brasenose College, Oxford.

1971 SZAUER, EMIL, 69 Grace Park Terrace, Drumcondra, Dublin 9, Eire.


1970 TALKINGTON, FRED M., 4216 Venado, Austin, Texas 78731, U.S.A.

1963 TAMIYA, ELECHI, 178 Teramaecho, Kanazawa-Ku, Yokohama, Japan.

1957 TANER, MRS. SAADET, Arkeoloji Müzesi Assistan, Ankara, Turkey.

1972 TAYLOR, F. STEWART, Canadian Imperial Bank of Commerce, 25 King Street West, Toronto 1, Ontario, Canada.

1957 TAYLOR, G. F., American University of Beirut, Lebanon.

1971 TAYLOR, J., 31 Swansea Street, Victoria Park 6100, West Australia.

1959 TAYLOR, R., Hon. Keeper of Coins, Black Gate Museum, Newcastle upon Tyne, Northumberland.

1964 TAYLOR, STANLEY NORTON, 'Southgate', Deganwy, Wales.

1970 TAYLOR, TIMOTHY L., Grove Place, Goudhurst, Cranbrook, Kent.

1958 TEASDILL, GRAHAM, 99 Carberry Avenue, Southbourne, Bournemouth, Hants.

1954 TERRY, W. N., 22 Christchurch Road, Northampton.

1966 TESORIERO, THOMAS, 125 96th Street, Brooklyn, New York 11209, U.S.A.

1962 TESTAFERRATA, THE MARQUIS, 29 Villegaignon Street, Mdina, Malta G.C.

1971 THEODOTOU, CHRIS B., M.D., 156 Parsons Avenue, Bryson Bldg., Columbus 15, Ohio, U.S.A.

1953 THOMPSON, PROFESSOR F. C., D.Met., M.Sc., F.I.M., 'Appledore', 45 Moss Lane, Bramhall, near Stockport, Cheshire; Hon. Curator of Coins, Manchester Museum.

ELECTED

1971 WALPORT, MARK J., 3 Mandeville Road, Northolt, Middlesex.

1969 WALTERS, B. K., 'Pen-y-Bryn', 38 Westminster Road, Ashwood Park, Wordsley, Stourbridge, Worcs.

1968 WARD, T. H. G., Godleys, North Chailey, Lewes, Sussex.

1971 WARDEN, WILLIAM B., Jr., P.O. Box 356, New Hope, Pa. 18938, U.S.A.

1971 WEBDALE, C. M., 24 Salcombe Close, Devon Park Estate, Bedford.

1967 WEDGE, T. A., 102–11 Catford Road, Downsview, Ontario, Canada.

1970 WEEKES, NIGEL, The Common Room, Bloxham School, Banbury, Oxon.

1956 WEIBEL, JOHN, 85 Clare Court, Judd Street, London, W.C.1.

1967 WEILLER, R. J. M. A., 6 Avenue de la Fayencerie, Luxembourg-Limperstberg.

1971 WELBORN, JOHN L. III, 10029 San Lorenzo Drive, Dallas, Texas 75228, U.S.A.

1969 WELCH, C. K., 'Banyandah', 15 Nepeon Avenue, Penrith 2750, N.S.W., Australia.

1946 *WERNER, LOUIS S., 1270 Broadway, New York, New York 10001, U.S.A.

1957 WHITE, P. G., 18 Frenches Road, Dunstable, Beds.

1955 WHITTINGHAM, R. D., 1 Down Lane, Carisbrooke, Isle of Wight.

1965 WILKINSON, JOHN, 18 Coopers Lane, London, S.E.12.

1960 WILLEY, ROBERT C., P.O. Box 726, Española, Ontario, Canada.

1971 WILLIAMS, JOHN A., 37 Trelawney Road, Camborne, Cornwall.

1969 WILLIAMS, R. D., 12 Merton Street, Box Hill, Victoria 3128, Australia.

1965 WILLIAMS, R. P., Spanish Point, Pembroke West, Bermuda.

1958 WILLIAMS, RODERICK T., M.C., M.A., Lecturer in Classics, The University, Durham.

1969 WILSDON, KENNETH FRANK, M.A., B.Ch.(Oxon.), F.R.C.S.(Edin.), 22 Parkside, Cambridge.

1965 WILSON, R. E., 9 Lower Camden Place, Camden, Bath, Somerset.

1934 WILTSHIRE, R. G., Meiringen, Copley Way, Tadworth, Surrey.

1957 WINFIELD, DAVID, B.A., c/o Matthew Farrar, 66 Lincoln Inn Fields, London, W.C.2.

1949 WIRGIN, WOLF, P.O. Box 97, Bronxville, New York, U.S.A.

1969 WISSLEAD, WILLIAM O., 2053 Cypress Avenue, Santa Ana, California 92707, U.S.A.

1970 WITSCHONKE, R. B., 11228 Chestnut Grove Sq., Apt. 230, Reston, Virginia 22070, U.S.A.

1967 WOLFE, C. H., 608 East Fourth Street, Lakeside, Ohio 43440, U.S.A.

1968 WOLOCH, M., M.A., Ph.D., Dept. of Classics, McGill University, Montreal 2, Canada.

1970 WONG, DAN, P.O. Box 1232, Yuma, Arizona 85364, U.S.A.

1960 WOODARD, P. E., B.A., Ph.D., 46 Hickory Cliff Road, Newton Upper Falls, Massachusetts, U.S.A.

1964 WOODBERRY, D. H., 104 Risca Road, Rogerstone, Monmouthshire.

1962 WOODHEAD, PETER, 65 Aldsworth Avenue, Goring-by-Sea, Worthing, Sussex.

ELECTED

1965 WOODHOUSE, CDR. JAMES EVERETT, District Officer for NAVRESSECGRU, 12th Naval District, Bldg. 450 Room 120, Treasure Island, San Francisco, California 94130, U.S.A.

1961 WOODIWISS, A., 33 Grosvenor Road, London, W.4.

1941 WOODWARD, ARTHUR M., M.A., F.S.A., Spa Hotel, Tunbridge Wells, Kent.

1943 WOOKEY, E. E., M.C., 19 Wimpole Street, London, W.1.

1970 WRIGHT, NOEL H., 15 Ferguson Avenue, Punchbowl, N.S.W., Australia 2196.

1968 WYNN, G. D., 14 Wistley Road, Charlton Kings, Cheltenham, Glos.

1966 XILAS, MICHAEL, 48 Berkeley Court, Baker Street, London, N.W.1.

1962 YAS, MAX, P.O. Box 7123, Fort Lauderdale, Florida 33304, U.S.A.

1958 YEOMAN, R. S., 115 Indiana Avenue, Racine, Wisconsin, U.S.A.

1965 YONGE, DAVID D., M.C., M.A., 'Dutch Cottage', Compton, Winchester, Hants.

1962 YOULTON, RONALD R. J., 'Capri', Bossiney, Tintagel, Cornwall.

1965 YVON, JACQUES, Bibliothèque Municipale, 3 Rue Malby, Bordeaux, France.

1957 ZACOS, GEORGES, Engelgasse 28, CH–4052 Basel, Switzerland.

1956 ZARA, LOUIS, 35 East 35th Street, New York, New York 10036, U.S.A.

1970 ZEIGLER, HAROLD W., 1821 Coventry, Oklahoma City, Oklahoma 73104, U.S.A.

1971 ZIGLER, MICHAEL M. S., 74 Chelmsford Avenue, Willowdale 450, Ontario, Canada.

1956 ZYGMAN, EDMUND, 160 W. 73rd Street, New York, New York 32, U.S.A.

## INSTITUTIONS

1959 AARHUS, DENMARK, Institut for Oldtids-og Middelalder-Forskning, c/o Statsbiblioteket, The University, 8000 Aarhus C.

1968 AARHUS, DENMARK, Statsbiblioteket Tidsskriftafdelingen, 8000 Aarhus C.

1946 BAGHDAD, IRAQ, The Director General of Antiquities.

1946 BANKERS, INSTITUTE OF, The Librarian, 10 Lombard Street, London, E.C.3.

1971 BARBER INSTITUTE OF FINE ARTS, The University, Birmingham 15.

1968 BARI, ITALY, Istituto di Archeologia, Università degli Studi.

1959 BERLIN-DAHLEN, GERMANY, Deutsches Archäologisches Institut, Peter-Lenne-Strasse 28–30.

1970 BERLIN, GERMANY, Universitätsbibliothek der Technischen Universität, Strasse des 19 Juni 135, 1 Berlin 12 (Charlottenburg).

1954 BIRMINGHAM, The Keeper, Dept. of Archaeology and Local History, City Museum and Art Gallery.

1895 BRIGHTON, SUSSEX, The Curator, Public Library, Town Hall, Brighton.

1906 BRISTOL, CENTRAL LIBRARY, The Librarian.

1908 CAMBRIDGE, The Director, Fitzwilliam Museum.

1923 CARDIFF, The National Museum of Wales.

1954 CHESTER, The Curator, Grosvenor Museum.

1906 CHICAGO, U.S.A., The Librarian, Newberry Library.

1950 COLCHESTER AND ESSEX MUSEUM, Curator, The Castle, Colchester.

1932 COPENHAGEN, DENMARK, Den Kongelige Mønt- og Medaillesamling, National-museet.

1968 CORK NUMISMATIC SOCIETY, 'South Winds', Maryboro, Douglas, Co. Cork, Eire.

1970 DUBLIN, EIRE, University College Library, Dublin.

1967 DUMBARTON OAKS, U.S.A., Trustees for Harvard University, 1703 Thirty-Second Street, Washington, D.C. 20007.

1970 FRANKFURT AM MAIN, GERMANY, Römisch-Germanische Kommission des Deutschen Archäologischen Instituts, 6 Frankfurt am Main, Palmengarten-strasse 10–12.

1960 FRANKFURT AM MAIN, GERMANY, Seminar für Hilfswissenschaften der Altertumskunde, The University.

1956 GENEVA, SWITZERLAND, Cabinet Numismatique, Musée d'Art et d'Histoire.

1910 GLASGOW, The Librarian, The Mitchell Library.

1968 GÖTEBORG, SWEDEN, Universitetsbibliotek, Göteborg, 5.

1968 GULBENKIAN FOUNDATION, PORTUGAL, Biblioteca Geral, Av. de Berna, Lisbon1.

1969 LECCE, ITALY, Istituto di Archeologia e Storia Antica, Università degli Studi.

1955 LEEDS 2, The Librarian, The University.

1959 LEICESTER, MUSEUM AND ART GALLERY, New Walk, Leicester.

1954 LJUBLJANA, YUGOSLAVIA, Narodni Musej, Numizmatični Kabinet, Presernova Cesta 20.

1954 LONDON, E.C.2, Guildhall Library.

1904 LONDON, S.E.17, The Principal Reference Librarian, Newington District Library, Walworth Road.

1971 LONDON NUMISMATIC CLUB, Hon. Sec. R. Seaman, Taylor's, Takeley, nr. Bishop's Stortford, Herts.

1968 LONDON, W.C.1, University College Library, Gower Street.

1949 LONDON, W.C.1, University, Institute of Archaeology, Gordon Square.

1941 LONDON, ROYAL MINT, The Deputy Master of the, London, E.C.3.

1954 LOUVAIN, BELGIUM, The Librarian, University, Mgr. Ladeuze plein, B 3000.

1972 LUCKNOW STATE MUSEUM, Banarsibagh, Uttar Pradesh, India.

1966 LUXEMBOURG, MUSÉE D'HISTOIRE, Marché-aux-Poissons, Luxembourg.

1953 MADRID, SPAIN, Instituto Antonio Augstín de Numismática, Museo Arqeo-lógico Nacional, Serrano 13.

1954 MADRID, SPAIN, Seminario de Numismática, Facultad de Filosofía y Lettras de la Universidad.

1970 MADRID, SPAIN, Museo Arqueológico Nacional, Serrano 13.

1954 NAPLES, ITALY, Il Medagliere del Museo Nazionale.

1972 NAPLES, ITALY, Centro Internazionale di Studi Numismatici, Villa Livia, Parco Grifeo 13, Secretary: Dott. Enrica Paolini Pozzi.

1959 NEW BRUNSWICK, CANADA, Dept. of Classics, The University, Fredericton.

1929 ONTARIO, CANADA, Royal Ontario Museum, 100 Queen's Park, Toronto 5, Ontario.

ELECTED

1932 OSLO, NORWAY, Universitetets Myntkabinet.

1968 OXFORD, The Librarian, Ashmolean Museum.

1968 OXFORD, The Librarian, Christ Church.

1961 PALERMO, ITALY, Fondazione Ignazio Mormino, Via Generale Magliocco 1.

1952 PARIS, FRANCE, Le Cabinet des Médailles, Bibliothèque Nationale, Paris II⁰.

1962 PRETORIA, SOUTH AFRICA, The Deputy Governor, South African Reserve Bank, P.O. Box 427.

1971 QUEBEC, BISHOP'S UNIVERSITY LIBRARY, Lennoxville, Quebec, Canada.

1947 READING, The Librarian, The University.

1965 ROTTERDAM, NETHERLANDS, MUSEUM VOOR LAND- EN VOLKENKUNDE, Willemskade, 25.

1969 STOCKHOLM, SWEDEN, Kungelige Myntkabinettet, Statems Historiska Museum, Storgatan 41, Box 5405, S 11484, Stockholm, Sweden.

1963 SWANSEA, WALES, The Librarian, University College, Singleton Park.

1966 SWISS CREDIT BANK, Zürich, Switzerland.

1910 SYDNEY, N.S.W., AUSTRALIA, Fisher Library, The University.

1929 TORONTO, ONTARIO, CANADA, The Chief Librarian, The University of Toronto.

1960 VATICAN, ITALY, Biblioteca Apostolica, Città del Vaticano.

1969 VIENNA, AUSTRIA, Institut für Antike Numismatik, Universität Wien, Wien A 1090, Rotenhausgasse 6/11.

# HONORARY FELLOWS

# PRESIDENTS

## OF THE ROYAL NUMISMATIC SOCIETY

| | |
|---|---|
| 1836–39 | JOHN LEE |
| 1839–41 | EDWARD HAWKINS |
| 1841–43 | H. H. WILSON |
| 1843–45 | LORD ALBERT CONYNGHAM |
| 1845–47 | H. H. WILSON |
| 1847–49 | W. D. HAGGARD |
| 1849–51 | EDWARD HAWKINS |
| 1851–55 | THE LORD LONDESBOROUGH* |
| 1855–74 | W. S. W. VAUX |
| 1874–1908 | SIR JOHN EVANS |
| 1908–14 | SIR HENRY H. HOWORTH |
| 1914–19 | SIR ARTHUR EVANS |
| 1919–30 | SIR CHARLES OMAN |
| 1930–35 | PERCY WEBB |
| 1935–36 | SIR GEORGE MACDONALD |
| 1936–37 | PERCY WEBB |
| 1937–42 | E. A. SYDENHAM |
| 1942–48 | HAROLD MATTINGLY |
| 1948–53 | C. H. V. SUTHERLAND |
| 1953–56 | MICHAEL GRANT |
| 1956–61 | C. E. BLUNT |
| 1961–66 | PHILIP GRIERSON |
| 1966–70 | D. F. ALLEN |
| 1970– | COLIN M. KRAAY |

* Formerly Lord Albert Conyngham, President 1843–45.

# MEDALLISTS
## OF THE ROYAL NUMISMATIC SOCIETY

1883 CHARLES ROACH SMITH, F.S.A.
1884 AQUILLA SMITH, M.D., M.R.I.A.
1885 EDWARD THOMAS, F.R.S.
1886 MAJOR-GENERAL ALEXANDER CUNNINGHAM, C.S.I., C.I.E.
1887 JOHN EVANS, D.C.L., LL.D., P.S.A.
1888 DR. F. IMHOOF-BLUMER, Winterthur.
1889 PROFESSOR PERCY GARDNER, Litt.D., F.S.A.
1890 J. P. SIX, Amsterdam.
1891 DR. C. LUDWIG MÜLLER, Copenhagen.
1892 PROFESSOR R. STUART POOLE, LL.D.
1893 W. H. WADDINGTON, Sénateur, Membre de l'Institut, Paris.
1894 CHARLES FRANCIS KEARY, M.A., F.S.A.
1895 PROFESSOR DR. THEODOR MOMMSEN, Berlin.
1896 FREDERIC W. MADDEN, M.R.A.S.
1897 DR. ALFRED VON SALLET, Berlin.
1898 CANON W. GREENWELL, M.A., F.R.S., F.S.A.
1899 ERNEST BABELON, Membre de l'Institut, Paris.
1900 PROFESSOR STANLEY LANE-POOLE, M.A., Litt.D.
1901 S. E. BARON WLADIMIR VON TIESENHAUSEN, St. Petersburg.
1902 ARTHUR J. EVANS, M.A., F.R.S., F.S.A.
1903 GUSTAVE SCHLUMBERGER, Membre de l'Institut, Paris.
1904 HIS MAJESTY VICTOR EMMANUEL III, KING OF ITALY.
1905 SIR HERMANN WEBER, M.D.
1906 COMM. FRANCESCO GNECCHI, Milan.
1907 BARCLAY V. HEAD, D.Litt., D.C.L., Ph.D., Corr. de l'Inst.
1908 PROFESSOR DR. HEINRICH DRESSEL, Berlin.
1909 HERBERT A. GRUEBER, F.S.A.
1910 DR. FRIEDRICH EDLER VON KENNER, Vienna.
1911 OLIVER CODRINGTON, M.D., M.R.A.S., F.S.A.
1912 GENERAL-LEUTNANT MAX VON BAHRFELDT, Hildesheim.
1913 GEORGE MACDONALD, M.A., LL.D.
1914 JEAN N. SVORONOS, Athens.
1915 GEORGE FRANCIS HILL, M.A.
1916 THÉODORE REINACH, Membre de l'Institut, Paris.
1917 L. A. LAWRENCE, F.S.A.
1918 Not awarded.
1919 M. ADRIEN BLANCHET, Membre de l'Institut, Paris.
1920 H. B. EARLE-FOX and J. S. SHIRLEY-FOX.
1921 PERCY H. WEBB.
1922 FREDERICK A. WALTERS, F.S.A.
1923 PROFESSOR J. W. KUBITSCHEK, Vienna.
1924 HENRY SYMONDS, F.S.A.
1925 EDWARD T. NEWELL, New York.
1926 R. W. MACLACHLAN, Montreal.

1927 ADOLPHE DIEUDONNÉ, Paris.
1928 SIR CHARLES OMAN, K.B.E., M.P., D.C.L., F.B.A.
1929 JULES MAURICE, Paris.
1930 THE REVD. EDWARD A. SYDENHAM, M.A.
1931 MISS HELEN FARQUHAR.
1932 H. NELSON WRIGHT, I.C.S. (retd.).
1933 DIREKTOR PROFESSOR KURT REGLING, Berlin.
1934 GEORGE CYRIL BROOKE (posthumously).
1935 PROFESSOR DR. BEHRENDT PICK, Gotha.
1936 JOHN ALLAN, M.A., F.S.A.
1937 PROFESSOR VICTOR TOURNEUR, Brussels.
1938 J. GRAFTON MILNE, M.A., D.Litt.
1939 J. W. E. PEARCE, M.A., F.S.A.
1940 R. B. WHITEHEAD, M.A., Litt.D., F.A.S.B., I.C.S. (retd.).
1941 HAROLD MATTINGLY, M.A.
1942 E. STANLEY G. ROBINSON, M.A., F.B.A., F.S.A.
1943 MRS. AGNES BALDWIN BRETT, New York.
1944 LEONARD FORRER.
1945 CHARLES SELTMAN, M.A.
1946 ØVERINSPEKTOR GEORG GALSTER, Copenhagen.
1947 EDUARD VON ZAMBAUR, Graz.
1948 MISS JOCELYN M. C. TOYNBEE, M.A., D.Phil., F.B.A., F.S.A.
1949 SYDNEY P. NOE, New York.
1950 DR. KARL PINK, Vienna.
1951 H. L. RABINO, C.M.G. (posthumously).
1952 LODOVICO LAFFRANCHI, Milan.
1953 PROFESSOR A. ALFÖLDI, Basel.
1954 C. H. V. SUTHERLAND, C.B.E., M.A., D.Litt., F.S.A.
1955 PROFESSOR A. R. BELLINGER, Yale.
1956 JOHN WALKER, C.B.E., M.A., D.Litt., F.B.A., F.S.A.
1957 DR. GEORGE C. MILES, New York.
1958 PHILIP GRIERSON, M.A., F.B.A., F.S.A.
1959 BARONE OSCAR ULRICH-BANSA, Besano Brianza.
1960 C. WILSON PECK.
1961 PROFESSOR HENRI SEYRIG, Beyrouth.
1962 MICHAEL GRANT, C.B.E., M.A., D.Litt., F.S.A.
1963 DR. WILLY SCHWABACHER, Stockholm.
1964 MISS ANNE S. ROBERTSON, M.A., D.Litt., F.S.A., F.S.A.(Scot.).
1965 JEAN LAFAURIE, Paris.
1966 D. F. ALLEN, C.B., B.A., F.B.A., F.S.A.
1967 MISS MARGARET THOMPSON, New York.
1968 PROFESSOR DR. PAUL BALOG, Rome.
1969 C. E. BLUNT, O.B.E., F.B.A., F.S.A.
1970 DR. PIERRE BASTIEN, Dunkerque.
1971 DR. HERBERT A. CAHN, Basel.
1972 R. A. G. CARSON, M.A., F.S.A.

# NUMISMATIC CHRONICLE
## Guidance for Contributors

CONTRIBUTORS are asked to follow these instructions in preparing their manuscripts. In this way the Editors will be spared unnecessary mechanical work, and the cost of printing will be reduced.

### GENERAL

1. Papers cannot be regarded as having been accepted for publication until they have been submitted to and approved by the Editors in their final form.

2. The Editors are responsible for the Society's publications, and authors are requested in all cases to correspond with them and not with the printers.

3. Manuscripts of papers for the *Numismatic Chronicle* will be regarded as first proofs. They should therefore include all corrections and insertions which authors may wish to make; substantial alterations in page proof cannot be permitted. For the conventional signs used by printers, and for related topics, H. Hart's *Rules for Compositors and Readers at the University Press, Oxford* (37th edn., 1967) may be recommended. Where there are alternative spellings for a word the practice of the *Oxford English Dictionary*, as modified by H. W. Fowler's *Dictionary of Modern English Usage*, should be followed.

4. All manuscripts should be clearly written or typed on one side of the sheet with a left-hand margin of about 1½ inches. If they are typewritten it is very important that they should be double-spaced.

5. Footnotes in the published volume are printed at the bottom of each page and numbered separately for each page, but it is convenient if in the typescript or manuscript they are grouped together at the end and numbered consecutively through the article.

6. Illustration plates made up of either plaster casts or photographs must be mounted on transparent sheets which can be obtained from the editor. Mounted photographs must be trimmed so that no white margins are left.

7. Authors will receive 25 offprints gratis. Further copies may be obtained at cost price on application to the Secretary. Application for these should be made as early as possible before publication.

### TYPE, ETC.

8. *Italics* (which should be indicated in the manuscript or typescript by plain underlining) should be employed as follows:

(*a*) For the titles of books, periodicals, and all substantive publications.

(*b*) For technical terms or phrases in languages other than English (but *not* for quotations or complete sentences, or for the names of coin-denominations).

(*c*) For the following abbreviations: *Obv., Rev.*

9. Roman should be used for the body of the text and notes, and as follows:

(*a*) For titles of articles in periodicals (within single inverted commas).

(*b*) For quotations and short extracts from books, articles, and manuscripts, whether in English or in a foreign language.

(*c*) For the following abbreviations: ad loc., c. (circa), cf., col. (cols.), ed., edn., e.g., f. (ff.), gm., gr., ibid., id., i.e., loc. cit., op. cit., trans. (The abbreviation 'f., ff.' should be used in preference to 'sq., sqq.'.)

10. The need for the use of heavy type should be indicated by wavy underlining. The need for inscriptional type (i.e. for the specially detailed reproduction of coin-legends and mint-marks) should be indicated by an encircling line drawn round the words or letters in question.

11. Authors requiring special signs, scripts, monograms, etc. must submit these in the form of finished drawings, at twice natural size.

12. Quotations which will run to over four lines in the body of the text will be printed in small roman as inserts, without quotation marks. They should be indicated by single spacing in the typescript, and should in any case be marked with a vertical line in the margin.

13. Abbreviations should be used as little as possible in the text, which is intended to be read as continuous English prose.

14. Capitals should be used sparingly. They should be employed for titles and dignities of individuals only when these are followed by the person's name (thus 'Duke William of Normandy', but 'William, duke of Normandy', or 'the duke').

15. Single inverted commas should be used for quotations, and for English words or phrases used in a technical or special sense. Double inverted commas should be used to indicate a quotation within a quotation.

16. A full stop should be used after the following abbreviations: Dr., Mr., Mrs., St., and after the abbreviated forms of the names of counties of the United Kingdom. No stop should be used after Mme and Mlle.

17. Dates should be given in the form: 13 October 1066. The era (B.C., A.D., A.H., etc.), where it is required, should be printed in small capitals, and, except in the case of 'B.C.', should precede the figures: 39 B.C., but A.D. 117.

## TRANSLITERATION

18. Contributors are free to use any modern accepted system of transliteration. For editorial purposes, however, including indexing, where some standardization is necessary, the following system will be used as a basis for transliterating Arabic and related languages:

| | | | | | | | |
|---|---|---|---|---|---|---|---|
| ع (medial and final) | ' | د | d | ط | ṭ | ل | l |
| ب | b | ذ | dh | ظ | z | م | m |
| ت | t | ر | r | ع | ʿ | ن | n |
| ث | th | ز | z | غ | gh | ه | h |
| ج | j | س | s | ف | f | و | w or u |
| ح | h | ش | sh | ق | q | ى | y or i |
| خ | kh | ص | ṣ | ك | k | | |
| | | ض | ḍ | | | | |

19. A list is appended giving abbreviations which may be used (in the exact form printed) to refer to the names of certain standard books and periodicals. An author desiring to use any others should specify them in an introductory note to his article.

20. Reference to substantive works in general, whether to an abbreviated title or not, should take the following form: (i) author's name followed by comma, (ii) title in italics, with volume number (if necessary) in small roman numerals, followed by comma, (iii) page-number. Details of the edition, and of the date and place of publication, should be added only when ambiguity or other difficulty might otherwise arise.

21. The page-number should not normally be prefixed by 'p.' or 'pp.' unless ambiguity would result from its absence. Thus in

*HN*²20
*NC* 1936, 20
*NC* 1936, 20, no. 10

it should be clear that '20' in each case refers to the page, while 'no. 10' refers to a coin on that page. On the other hand, *SNG* iii, 500 will be easily understood as referring to coin no. 500 in vol. iii of the Greek *Sylloge*. Reference to a sequence of pages can be made either in the form '20–21' (or '20 f.'), or '20–30' (or '20 ff.').

22. Reference to a periodical should, whenever possible, be made primarily according to the date it bears on the title-page: its volume number should be added (in brackets) only when ambiguity might otherwise arise.

23. Citation from ancient and medieval authors should follow the form: (i) author's name (which may be appropriately abbreviated), (ii) title of work (in italics) where necessary, (iii) book number in roman numerals, (iv) section or paragraph in arabic numerals: thus, 'Horace, *Odes* i. 4'. Where either the author's name or the title is abbreviated the form should be as follows: 'Cic. *Phil.* i. 1', i.e. with full stops after the abbreviations.


## ABBREVIATIONS

| | |
|---|---|
| *AA* | *Archäologischer Anzeiger* |
| *AJA* | *American Journal of Archaeology* |
| *AJN* | *American Journal of Numismatics* |
| *AM* | *Athenische Mitteilungen* |
| *AMNG* | *Die antike Münzen Nordgriechenlands* (viz. the so-called Berlin Corpus) |
| *ANS* | *American Numismatic Society* |
| *ASFN* | *Annuaire de la société française de numismatique* |
| Bab. *Traité* | E. Babelon, *Traité des monnaies grecques et romaines* |
| *BCH* | *Bulletin de correspondance hellénique* |
| *BMC* with suffix | The appropriate volumes of the *British Museum Catalogue* as follows: *BMCA-S* (Anglo-Saxon), *BMC Byz.* (Byzantine), *BMCH*² (Henry II), *BMCI* (Indian), *BMC Italy*, etc. (the appropriate volume of the *Catalogue of Greek Coins*), *BMCNK* (Norman |

Kings), *BMCO* (Oriental), *BMCRE* (Roman Empire), *BMCRR* (Roman Republic), *BMC Van.* (Vandals, etc.)

| | |
|---|---|
| *BMzB* | *Berliner Münzblätter* |
| *BNJ* | *British Numismatic Journal* |
| *BNZ* | *Berliner Numismatische Zeitschrift* |
| Brooke, *EC³* | G. C. Brooke, *English Coins* (3rd edn., revised, London, 1950) |
| *BSA* | *Annual of the British School at Athens* |
| *BSFN* | *Bulletin de la société française de numismatique* |
| *BSR* | *Papers of the British School at Rome* |
| Coh. | H. Cohen, *Description historique des médailles frappées sous l'empire romain²* (Paris, 1880–92) |
| *CIL* | *Corpus Inscriptionum Latinarum* |
| *CNI* | *Corpus Nummorum Italicorum* |
| *CNP* | *Corpus Nummorum Palaestinensium* |
| *CPANS* | *Centennial Publication of the American Numismatic Society* |
| Syd. *CRR* | E. A. Sydenham, *Coinage of the Roman Republic* (London, 1952) |
| *DOC* | *Dumbarton Oaks Catalogue* |
| *DOP* | *Dumbarton Oaks Papers* |
| *DOS* | *Dumbarton Oaks Studies* |
| E. and S. | A. Engel and R. Serrure, *Traité de numismatique du moyen âge* |
| *HBN* | *Hamburger Beiträge zur Numismatik* |
| Head, *HN²* | B. V. Head, *Historia Numorum* (2nd edn., Oxford, 1911) |
| *IG* | *Inscriptiones Graecae* |
| *ILS* | H. Dessau, *Inscriptiones Latinae Selectae* |
| *IMC* | *Indian Museum Catalogue* |
| *JDI* | *Jahrbuch des Deutschen Archäologischen Instituts* |
| *JHS* | *Journal of Hellenic Studies* |
| *JIAN* | *Journal international d'archéologie numismatique* |
| *JNG* | *Jahrbuch für Numismatik und Geldgeschichte* |
| *JNSI* | *Journal of the Numismatic Society of India* |
| *JRAS* | *Journal of the Royal Asiatic Society* |
| *JRS* | *Journal of Roman Studies* |
| *MN* | *Museum Notes* (ANS) |
| *NC* | *Numismatic Chronicle* |
| *NL* | *Numismatic Literature* |
| *NNÅ* | *Nordisk Numismatisk Årsskrift* (Stockholm) |
| *NNM* | *Numismatic Notes and Monographs* (ANS) |
| *NNUM* | *Nordisk Numismatisk Unions Medlemsblad* (Copenhagen) |
| *NSc* | *Notizie degli scavi* |
| *NZ* | *Numismatische Zeitschrift* (Vienna) |
| *RBN* | *Revue belge de numismatique* |
| *RE* | Pauly–Wissowa–Kroll, *Real–encyclopädie* |
| *RIC* | Mattingly, Sydenham, and others, *Roman Imperial Coinage* |
| *RIN* | *Rivista italiana di numismatica* |
| *RM* | *Römische Mitteilungen* |
| *RN* | *Revue numismatique* |
| *SCBI* | *Sylloge of the Coins of the British Isles* |
| *SMzB* | *Schweizer Münzblätter* |
| *SNG* | *Sylloge Nummorum Graecorum* (Gt. Britain) |
| *SNG* (Cop.) | *Sylloge Nummorum Graecorum* (Copenhagen) |
| *SNG* (von A.) | *Sylloge Nummorum Graecorum* (von Aulock) |
| *SNR* | *Schweizer Numismatische Rundschau* |

| | |
|---|---|
| *TINC* | *Transactions of the International Numismatic Congress 1936* (London, 1938) |
| *VDI* | *Vestnik Drevnei Istorii* |
| *ZDMG* | *Zeitschrift der Deutschen morgenländischen Gesellschaft* |
| *ZfN* | *Zeitschrift für Numismatik* (Berlin) |

# THE LEO KADMAN PRIZE

A FUND has been established for the award of a prize to commemorate the late Leo Kadman. This will be given in every second year for scholarly work in the field of 'numismatics of the land of Israel' (including seals, jewels, weights, and measures, etc., where relevant). Those who wish to compete should apply for further details either to The Kadman Numismatic Museum (Museum Ha'aretz), P.O.B. 17068, Tel Aviv, Israel, or to the Secretary, Royal Numismatic Society.

# INTERNATIONAL NUMISMATIC CONGRESS, NEW YORK, WASHINGTON 1973

In co-operation with the American Numismatic Society and the Smithsonian Institution, the International Numismatic Commission is now preparing its next Congress, which will be held in New York and Washington from 10 to 17 September 1973.

Persons wishing to participate are kindly requested to send as soon as possible a preliminary and tentative application to the Secretariat of the Congress, c/o The American Numismatic Society, Broadway at 156th Street, New York, N.Y. 10032. A circular with full details on arrangements will be sent directly to all applicants.

Suggestions for lectures to be delivered at the Congress should be submitted as soon as possible. There will be a maximum allowance of twenty minutes for each lecture and this time limit must be strictly observed. As the number of communications may have to be restricted, the organizing committee reserves for itself the right to make a selection from the various offers.

Every effort will be made to provide subsidies for younger scholars and for those from countries with strict currency regulations, who would not be able to participate without financial assistance. A screening committee, consisting of members of the Bureau of the International Commission, will advise the organizing committee on the allocation of travel grants. Applicants who will need assistance to defray their expenses, in full or in part, are requested to indicate the approximate amount required when they submit applications for participation.

# ROYAL NUMISMATIC SOCIETY

## Special Publications

1. *Inventory of British Coin Hoards, A.D. 600–1500*
   by J. D. A. THOMPSON, pp. 214, plates 5, 1956.
   £4·00 (£3·00)

2. *Carthaginian Gold and Electrum Coins*
   by G. K. JENKINS and R. B. LEWIS, pp. 140, plates 38, 1963.
   £6·00 (£4·50)

3. *The Coinage of Abdera, 540–350 B.C.*
   by J. M. F. MAY, edited by C. M. KRAAY and G. K. JENKINS, pp. 300, plates 24, 1966.
   £6·00 (£4·50)

4. *Roman Republican Coin Hoards*
   by M. H. CRAWFORD, pp. 180, plates 3, 1968.
   £4·00 (£3·00)

5. *The Cistophoroi of Augustus*
   by C. H. V. SUTHERLAND, pp. 134, plates 36, 1970
   £6·00 (£4·50)

6. *Coin Hoards of Great Britain and Ireland, 1500–1967*
   by I. O. BROWN and MICHAEL DOLLEY, pp. 88, 1971
   £4·00 (£3·00)

7. *The Silver Coinage of the Phokians*
   by RODERICK T. WILLIAMS, pp. 138, plates 16, 1972
   £5·00 (£3·75)

### In preparation

8. *Methods of Chemical and Metallurgical Investigation of Ancient Coinage*
   Edited by E. T. HALL and D. M. METCALF

Bracketed price for Fellows only

# SYLLOGE OF COINS
## OF THE
# BRITISH ISLES

Published by The British Academy except No. 8 which is published by the Trustees of the British Museum and No. 16 by Spink and Son Ltd.

All quarto, cloth bound

### *In preparation*

R. P. Mack Collection. Anglo-Saxon and Norman Coins.

Coins of Bristol and Glos. Mints in the Bristol and Gloucester Museums.

Ashmolean Museum, Oxford. Part III. Coins of Henry VII.

Yorkshire and Leeds Museums and Leeds University. Anglo-Saxon and Norman Pennies.

# CHRISTIE'S

## Fine Art Auctioneers since 1766

A gold medallion pendant which realised £12,075 on October 19th 1970, together with three others similar which sold for a total of £47,775.

The medallion is a double solidus of Constantine the Great, A.D. 321.

Coin auctions are held regularly, and our coin experts, are always pleased to give advice, whether for sale or valuation. Our commission rate for selling coins is 12½%

## 8 KING STREET, ST. JAMES'S, LONDON, S.W. 1

*Telephone*: 01–839 9060   *Telegrams*: Christiart, London, S.W. 1

# MONNAIES

## ET

# MÉDAILLES

**Collections, trouvailles et ouvrages numismatiques**

*ACHAT, VENTE ET EXPERTISE*

# B. FRANCESCHI

**10 rue Croix de Fer, 1000 Bruxelles—Tel. 179395**